Tom Simpson
P9-DMT-996

man among men

man among men

An Introduction to Sociology

EUGENE AND FANCHON MEAD

City College of San Francisco

PRENTICE-HALL, INC., ENGLEWOOD CLIFFS, N. J.

With gratitude and affection
to our teachers and our students

Current printing (last digit):
11 10 9 8 7 6 5

Prentice-Hall Sociology Series
HERBERT BLUMER, *Editor*

PRENTICE-HALL INTERNATIONAL, INC., *London*
PRENTICE-HALL OF AUSTRALIA, PTY., LTD., *Sydney*
PRENTICE-HALL OF CANADA, LTD., *Toronto*
PRENTICE-HALL OF INDIA (PRIVATE) LTD., *New Delhi*
PRENTICE-HALL OF JAPAN, INC., *Tokyo*

Library of Congress Catalog Card No.: 65-13458

Printed in the United States of America
54820-C

Preface

Man Among Men: An Introduction to Sociology exposes the essential subject matter of sociology—*man, culture,* and *society*—against the background of contemporary change. Our major theme is the disruptive disparity between rates of *technological* and *societary* change and the consequent urgency for cultivating and applying the sciences concerned with human behavior.

The unorthodox first chapter is a means of alerting the reader to the need for scientific knowledge of society *before* leading him to an awareness of differences between scientific and nonscientific thinking and an understanding of the development and content of sociology as a scientific discipline.

We offer *Man Among Men* with the hope that it will not only introduce the reader to sociological facts and concepts but awaken in him a sociological perspective. Our intent is to excite his interest in sociology, give him insight into his immediate personal milieu, and involve him intellectually in the larger society of which he is a part.

EUGENE AND FANCHON MEAD

Contents

Know then thyself, presume not God to scan;
The proper study of mankind is man.

ALEXANDER POPE (1688-1744)

i

Science and Change

Human history becomes more and more
a race between education and catastrophe.

H. G. WELLS (1866-1946)

1

Man—
The Next Frontier

ROCKET POWER has lifted us out of earth's atmosphere. We peer into the blackness of outer space and probe the unknown with the sensitive instruments of science. Our aspirations, like our universe, are boundless; but while we seek to conquer other worlds, we are, in many ways, losing control of our own.

> This generation has the responsibility of deciding whether the human race is to prosper or decline, whether our conduct will lead to a beginning or an end. . . . It is the crisis of the human race. (Sir Sarvepalli Radharkrishnan, Vice-President, Republic of India.)

> Mankind today faces the gravest crisis since Noah and the Flood—but we have no ark. (Lord Bertrand Russell, British Philosopher.)

> The unleashed power of the atom has changed everything except our ways of thinking. Thus we are drifting toward a catastrophe beyond comparison. We shall require a substantially new manner of thinking if mankind is to survive. (Albert Einstein, Mathematician.)

> The power of man has grown in every sphere except over himself. . . . The fearful question confronts us: Have our problems got beyond our control? (Sir Winston Churchill, British Prime Minister.)

> We happen to live in the most dangerous time in the history of the human race. (John F. Kennedy, 35th President of the United States.)

OTTO HAGEL

Outer space is a dramatic new frontier, but it is not the last frontier. The next frontier is man himself. Quietly, without fanfare, other explorations have begun in the personal and social spheres created by man among men. Here, too, are intensely exciting discoveries to be made, for the inner mind is less well charted than the solar system, and the ways of men are less well known than the ways of the planets.

To chart the mind and learn the ways of man is the task to which behavioral scientists,* including sociologists, address themselves. These scientists are systematically collecting and analyzing data in an attempt to describe, understand, predict and eventually help direct human behavior. Theirs is a formidable undertaking. Human behavior is complex, variously conditioned by experience and circumstance, and difficult to perceive dispassionately. Although man has long been a concern of philosophy, religion, history, and the humanities, he has only within the last hundred years become a subject of science.

The science of sociology grew out of the conviction that man, through knowledge of society and of himself as a member of society, could shape his society and his culture and thereby help direct his own destiny. Sociologists are committed to making this crucial knowledge available. Much of what we, as laymen, now think we know about ourselves in relation to each other is not verified knowledge but unverified opinions and beliefs. Even what behavioral scientists know—or think they know—about man is relatively little compared to what the physical and biological scientists know about their subject matter. The less intimate the subject matter, the easier it is to study objectively. Man studied the distant stars before he studied himself, and the impersonal physical and biological sciences have all outpaced the behavioral sciences.

The impersonal sciences have underwritten revolutionary techniques for making war and for controlling our physical environment. The behavioral sciences have not yet brought equally revolutionary techniques for making peace, nor for controlling ourselves and our social environment. This disparity has precipitated a condition unique in human history. Man in this twentieth century is the greatest menace to the survival of his own species.

Man has been fruitful and multiplied. He has replenished the earth—with his own kind—and subdued it. He has gained dominion over the fish of the sea, and over the fowl of the air, and over every living thing that moveth upon the earth—over every living thing *except himself*. That is now his urgent command.

---

* Sociology is classified as both a social and a behavioral science. The social sciences generally include six disciplines: anthropology, economics, history, political science, psychology, and sociology. The behavioral sciences include three of the social sciences: anthropology, psychology and sociology, *minus* specialized sectors of these sciences such as physiological psychology and physical anthropology, *plus* social geography, some psychiatry, and the behavioral aspects of economics, political science, and law.[1]

CHANCE AND CATASTROPHE

The human race has survived floods, famines, pestilence, "crime, wrong, oppression and the axe's edge. . . ." [2] Out of fifteen or more major cultures which have come into existence in the last 6,000 years, only Western Christendom, Orthodox Christendom, Islam, Hindu, and the Far Eastern still persist.[3] Today, however, the problem is the survival, not of one culture, but of all human society. The world of the past was small; the perils provincial. Our world is large; our perils encompass the globe.

Already in this century man has suffered, through ignorance, needless poverty, wars, mass murders, enslavements and other degradations. "Man can hardly even recognize the devils of his own creation." [4] Now we are close to other potentially devastating catastrophies: *CBN* (chemical, bacteriological, and nuclear war), *Contamination,* and *Overpopulation.* We discuss these threatening possibilities with the belief that if they are to be averted, it will be by cultivating and applying the sciences of man as intently and effectively as we have cultivated and applied the physical and biological sciences.

CBN Warfare

War itself is no new terror. History records it as a popular sport and a glorified profession.* In the romanticized version, flags wave, bands play, and crowds cheer as Johnny goes marching by. God is on the right side, and superior strength is the final arbiter. Traditional weapons—sticks and stones, arrows and swords, cannon balls and bullets—can break bones and draw blood, but modern chemical-biological-radiological weapons can reach the bloodstream of the future, corrupting genes and polluting the earth's life-sustaining surface. We are toying with destructive forces which cannot be contained within the boundaries of space or time.

Nuclear Warfare †

The loss of life and property in a nuclear world war would be beyond calculation. *Wir können mehr herstellen, als wir uns verstellen können.* (We can produce more than we can conceive.) [5] One twenty-megaton H-bomb is the explosive equivalent of twenty million tons of TNT or one thousand

* We might be misled into assuming that *to war is human,* if there were not isolated cultures with no word for war in their language.

† A-bombs and H-bombs are both nuclear weapons. Blast, heat and release of radioactive materials result from both the *fission* (splitting) of atoms of heavy elements such as uranium or plutonium in the A-bomb, and the *fusion* (combining) of atoms of light elements such as hydrogen in the H-bomb. Fission and fusion are similar in that both convert mass into energy in the amount determined by Einstein's equation: $E = MC^2$ (Energy equals mass times the velocity of light squared.)

old-fashioned twenty-kiloton A-bombs. The initial blast—ten miles in radius—could destroy a central city; the accompanying fire storm * could incinerate an entire metropolitan area. The toll would be millions of people immediately dead, countless others slowly and painfully dying. In 1960, the United States, Russia, and Great Britain all possessed twenty-megaton H-bombs.† By 1961, Russia had tested sixty-megaton H-bombs; and claimed to have 100-megaton bombs. A 100-megaton H-bomb exploded seven miles or more above ground, under average conditions of weather and terrain, would ignite everything within an area larger than the state of Vermont—roughly 11,000 square miles.[6] Bombs of 1,000 megatons or more are theoretically possible.

Never has it been possible to dispose of life so economically. The cost in World War II for the estimated 20,000,000 to 40,000,000 killed ‡ was approximately $50,000 per person. This was the high point in a steady rise from $0.75 in Caesar's wars, $3,000 in the Napoleonic Wars, $5,000 in the Civil War, and $21,000 in World War I.[7] Nuclear weapons reversed the trend. On August 6, 1945, one twenty-kiloton atom bomb leveled Hiroshima and killed 75,000; three days later a second bomb killed 39,000 in the smaller city of Nagasaki—a total of 109,000 people at $2.50 each.§ Now H-bombs offer the biggest bargain in death—only 25 cents per head.

Chemical and Biological Warfare

Chemical and biological weapons are less publicized and less spectacular than radiological weapons but equally as fatal. Even though they are shrouded in official secrecy, they are considered by the military as "normal usable means of war." [8]

Chemical weapons now stockpiled in the United States and other countries include lethal nerve gases, non-lethal tear and vomit gases, and such incapacitating psychochemicals as lysergic acid (LSD), mescaline, and psilocybine, which can produce "temporary insanity . . . anesthesia, narcosis, paralysis, or blindness." [9] The lethal nerve gases dominate the chemical arsenal and are the focus of government readiness-planning; however, some military authorities feel that "the future lies in the psychochemicals." [10] The Army Chemical Center tests hundreds of pharmaceutical compounds each month for possible exploitation of their medically undesirable side effects.

> We are attempting to completely separate these psychochemical agents from the lethal agents . . . since these do not maim or kill. As a result we hope

---

* The fireball of an H-bomb has a temperature exceeding that of the surface of the sun.

† Twenty megatons is approximately twice the power of the grand total of all explosives used in all wars in history.

‡ Numbers in the abstract are relatively meaningless, but assume 30,000,000 people were killed. The bodies, piled on top of one another like bricks, would tower 5,000 miles high. The ghosts, four abreast, would glide past twenty-four hours a day for three months.

§ These figures are based on the estimated cost of the bombs exclusive of research and development.

> to have a weapon which will give the commander much freer reign in its use as compared to toxic agents. It is my hope that through the use of incapacitating agents the free world will have a relatively cheap and rapid means of both fighting and deterring limited war. . . .[11]

We have long been preyed upon by viruses and bacteria, and it is not surprising that such "natural" enemies would be drafted as weapons of war. The biological arsenal reads like a dictionary of pathology. A list of "Human Diseases and Infective Agents for BW" includes bacterial infections and intoxications such as cholera, dysentery, diphtheria, meningitis, pneumonic plague, leptospirosis, tuberculosis, streptococcis, and typhoid; viral and rickettsial diseases such as infectious hepatitis, influenza, mumps, rabies, poliomyelitis, yellow fever, smallpox, and typhus; plus malaria and other protozoal and fungus infections.[12] For these historical diseases, specific protection is not always known or available, and now Army scientists have succeeded in producing bacteria with new hereditary characteristics—strategically superior mutant bacteria which could theoretically wipe out a population before the nature of the disease could even be determined. Animals and plants are also marked as military targets for an army of pests and diseases.

Although the role of chemical and biological warfare has not been publicized, the implications alone are frightening enough to the layman who receives only hints of such top secrets. The United States Defense Department has soothingly suggested that "many forms of chemical and allied warfare are more 'humane' than existing weapons,"[13] but a vulnerable population can't really be expected to think of temporary mass insanity, brainwashing, or plague as humane.

Chemical and biological agents are both strategic and/or tactical weapons. They can produce widespread disaster through morbidity, mortality, or economic disruption, or they can be restricted to limited areas. In either case, there is real economic advantage to the aggressor in being able to dispose of life without disturbing the property he hopes to inherit.

The Dilemma

No sane person wants war, but many sane people are implicated in the preparations for war, or, as we insist, for defense.

> Unfortunately, the law of fear still reigns among peoples, and it forces them to spend fabulous sums for armaments; not for aggression, they affirm—and there is no reason for not believing them—but to dissuade others from aggression.[14]

However, a dilemma grows out of the technological fact that the destructiveness of offensive weapons has outstripped the effectiveness of defensive weapons. Consequently, as military power has increased, national security has decreased.[15] In the United States, particularly, the dilemma is complicated by the massive involvement of both government and business in military affairs. From 1954 until 1962, military contracts increased steadily each year from $11,900,000,000 to $27,500,000,000.[16] The direct federal expenditures in 1960 for major national security functions, including research, development, testing, evaluation, and procurement of aircraft, missiles, ships and other military equipment, totaled $46,627,000,000 or 59.6 per cent of the total federal budget.[17] Veterans' services and benefits, foreign aid for reconstruction, and interest on the national debt bring the total direct and indirect cost of past wars and preparation for "defense" in the event of future wars to more than 80 per cent of the "peacetime" budget. Industries in all 50 states, in Puerto Rico, and in other areas outside the United States get a share of the prime military contracts, and, in turn, let out multitudes of substantial subcontracts. In his valedictory address in January 1961, retiring President Dwight D. Eisenhower warned:

> In the councils of government we must guard against the acquisition of unwarranted influence, whether sought or unsought, by the military-industrial complex. The potential for the disastrous rise of misplaced power exists and will persist. We must never let the weight of this combination endanger our liberties or democratic processes. We should take nothing for granted. Only an alert and knowledgeable citizenry can compel the proper meshing of the huge industrial and military machinery of defense with our peaceful methods and goals, so that security and liberty may prosper together.

A few weeks later in a message to Congress on the defense budget, President John F. Kennedy said, "Neither our strategy nor our psychology as a nation—and certainly not our economy—must become dependent upon our permanent maintenance of a large military establishment."

In 1964, "economic conversion" became a live issue when President Lyndon Johnson ordered a cutback in the production of defense-related materials. "We must not operate a WPA nuclear project," he said, "just to provide employment when our needs have been met." Senator Barry Goldwater, campaigning for the Republican Presidential nomination, called Johnson's action an economic threat, and a spokesman for a major aerospace company said he knew no civilian field which could make use of the specialized resources and skills such firms as his offered.

Altogether, in 1964 the vast military-industrial complex provided more than seven million jobs and spent more money each year than the total net income of all major corporations in the country.[18]

> The production of armaments has become more than a dominant industry —it has become a *way of life* for the entire country . . . the American people . . . have created a Juggernaut—the Warfare State—that is moving inexorably toward that very holocaust it was designed to avoid.[19]

The resolution of the dilemma will come, not through further advance in technology, but through change in political and economic institutions. To understand the forces which motivate and direct institutional change is one of the critical research problems in contemporary sociology.

Contamination

While we live in mortal danger from each other because we have not yet rejected war as a means of resolving issues between states, we are letting loose in our environment other agents of destruction which draw no political boundary lines in dealing death. To maintain industrialized twentieth-century societies, we have begun to alter the environment in which life over millions of years has slowly evolved.

> Along with the possibility of extinction of mankind by war, a central problem of our age is the contamination of man's total environment with substances of incredible potential for harm—substances that accumulate in the tissues of plants and animals, and even penetrate the germ cells, to shatter or alter the very material of heredity upon which the shape of the future depends.[20]

We have brought up from their safe burial grounds in the depths of the earth microbial wastes—particularly carbon, sulfur, nitrogen, and phosphorus. In their natural form and in poisonous alterations of them as antiseptics, pesticides, herbicides, and by-products of combustion and other industrial processes, they are powerful and extensive contaminants, disturbing vital processes at every level of the biotic pyramid.*

> A high degree of cooperation through evolution and adaptation characterizes nature's management of environment. But when man manages environment, competition stands out—with frequent examples of contamination. As managers, we are biased toward aims and benefits for man alone. We have concerned ourselves little with how, in modifying the environment for ourselves, we may be disrupting it for all the other populations of the biotic pyramid—microbes, plants, animals, and man—all supported by the one creative foundation, the soil.[21]

Fallout from nuclear explosions, radioactive and other factory wastes, exhausts from fuel-burning motors, domestic sewage, "pest" control poisons †—these and other contaminants increasingly threaten life.

CONTAMINANTS IN ACTION

1954 Atomic debris carried by an unexpected shift of wind irradiated the Pacific island of Rongelap. Five years later coconut crabs there were still unsafe to eat.

---

* The biotic pyramid is divided into three trophic (nutritional) levels: the *decomposers* or microbes, the *producers* or plants, and the *predators*—insects, birds, herbivores, omnivores, carnivores, and man.

† In 1963 the United States used some 350,000,000 pounds of pesticides. Federal machinery for controlling pesticides was inadequate and the fact that "decisions on safety" were not as well based as those on "efficacy" [22] reveal the dangerous gap between economic expediency and long-term values.

1957 Strontium 90 in the bones of American children increased 100 per cent between 1955 and 1957.

1958 Strontium 90 content in some Minnesota wheat crop samples was 600 per cent above the "safe" level. The average was 150 per cent above.

1959 Exposure to low-level radiation at a critical period in prenatal development can cause sterility in a female foetus.

1960 Insecticides can alter the metabolic activity of soil and adversely affect its productivity. Continued contamination could render it completely sterile.

1962 Runoff from fields in Alabama killed all the fish in fifteen streams tributary to the Tennessee River. Two of the tributaries were part of the municipal water supply system.

1962 Since 1932 the arsenic content of cigarettes made from American-grown tobacco increased more than 300 per cent.

1962 Six million pounds of the deadly organic phosphate, parathion, are applied annually by hand sprayers, motorized blowers and dusters, and airplanes to fields, orchards, and vineyards in the United States. The amount used on California's farms alone, if given directly, would provide lethal doses for five to ten times the world population.

1963 Pesticide residues and measurable amounts of widely used chemicals are found in every type of warm-blooded animal in the United States and in fish far distant in the northern seas.

1963 When California sugar beet farmers opened their fields to irrigation, Endrin, a chemical pesticide, washed into the Sacramento river. As the polluted water flowed along its course, thousands upon thousands of fish exploded and died with an audible "pop"!

1964 The United States Department of Interior released a report listing 35 species of birds, 16 species of mammals, 6 species of fish, and 3 species of reptiles as being in danger of extinction. The report noted that "complex forces of civilization are upsetting delicate life patterns." These forces include "pollution of the natural environment" with "pesticides, atomic energy, and industrial wastes."

Hostile elements in the environment are not new. There is a natural background of radiation from rocks, from cosmic rays, and even from the sun's own ultraviolet. There are deadly viruses, poisonous plants, disease-bearing insects, venomous animals. Neither are adverse geographical phenomena new. Life has adjusted to changes in rainfall and temperature as well as to earthquakes, volcanic eruptions, floods, and erosions. The unique new hazard is in the rapidity and extent of adverse changes which profoundly affect biochemical processes—processes which evolved slowly over billions of years and which cannot be modified in what is left of this uncertain century.

With contamination, as with CBN, expediency leads us into a dilemma of contradictory values. For undeniable immediate advantages—development of nuclear power, industrial use of radioactive substances, national security, efficient mass production of food and other commodities—we are risking yet immeasurable disadvantages of somatic damage to individuals and adverse genetic effects on the species. Immediate benefits seem obvious, harm impersonal and comfortably far away. *But are we now writing in invisible ink the last will and testament of the race?* Scientists question; the insects quietly wait.*

Overpopulation

Although annihilation, quickly by war or slowly by contamination, could cut short the life span of the human race, the life expectancy of the individual is now the highest in history. In the course of evolution, *Homo sapiens* has acquired a high survival rate.† In the course of civilization, he is gradually freeing himself of "natural" limitations. Modern sanitation and improved personal hygiene help the weak as well as the fit survive. The contagious diseases —which in the past have devastated whole societies and changed the course of history—are largely under control. Medical science has techniques for postponing death at every age level; children suffering from almost every congenital or hereditary defect can be kept alive; so, too, can the senile bed patient in the charity home. Neither Neanderthal man nor any of his predecessors up to the Christian era had an average life expectancy of much more than twenty-five years. By the beginning of the modern era (1650 to 1700), life expectancy in Western Europe and North America reached thirty to thirty-five years; by 1900 it was about forty-five to fifty years. Now in North America and some European countries, the average life expectancy is more than seventy years.

Live-saving and life-extending techniques which temporarily outwit death are intrinsically good; but unless they are counterbalanced by techniques which outwit fertility,‡ modern medicine may prove to be very bitter medicine. We could decrease the quality of life by increasing the quantity, and we could intensify international rivalries through competition for the actual necessities of life.

---

* The *rhodinus,* or kissing bug, is innately immune to radioactive poisons. Other insects have developed immunity to the poisons used against them. This, however, leads to no optimistic analogy with the human situation. Insect resistance becomes a species characteristic only after generations of exposure. Insect generations are counted in days or weeks, not decades, and it would take thousands of years for *Homo sapiens* to develop such a serviceable trait. We do not have that much time.

† In general, lower birth rate and higher survival rate correlate positively with evolutionary development. The survival rate of a codfish, for example, is approximately one in 1,800,000; that of the amphibious newt, one in 250; that of the mouse—a small mammal—one in 80; and that of the chimpanzee—a primate—one in eight. Among sub-human forms, survival is still the exception. Among humans, living under modern sanitary conditions, failure to survive is the exception.

‡ Although fertility and fecundity were originally synonymous and are often still used as such, demographers (population specialists) and sociologists customarily distinguish between *fecundity,* the physiological ability to reproduce, and *fertility,* the realization of this potential as measured by the number of offspring.

Who Are All Those Others?

It used to take a long time for a small population to double in size; now it takes a short time for a large population to double. Assuming that *Homo sapiens* began at zero at least one million years ago, it took until the birth of Christ to amass a human population estimated at a quarter of a billion. It took sixteen more centuries to reach half a billion. By 1830, the population doubled again and reached approximately one billion. Then in one more century, it reached two billion. Thirty-two years later, in 1962, it reached three billion.* The growth period from three to four billion is estimated to be only fifteen years; that from four to five billion, only ten years. By the year 2000, the population is expected to be well over six billion. In the course of man's inhabitation of this globe his rate of population growth has increased from about two per cent per millennium to two per cent per year, a thousandfold increase in growth rate.[23]

By 1960 population density had reached more than 42.5 persons per square mile. In the past, each population boom seems to have been followed by a period of relative equilibrium between fertility and restraints on fertility—both natural and cultural. The present population explosion expresses a breakthrough of old restraints by the scientific-industrial revolution. In 1962 when the population passed the three-billion mark, the birth rate was triple that of the normal pulse rate (67-72 pulsations per minute), producing a net increase of more than 100 persons per minute. If this rate should continue until the year 2600, each inhabitant would have only one square yard of living space on the earth's surface; and by the year 3500, the weight of the total population would equal that of the earth mass—an estimated 6,600,000,000,000,-000,000,000—or six sextillion, 600 quintillion tons! Any such paper and pencil calculation is obviously unrealistic; it serves only to dramatize the population problem and to demonstrate that the present growth rate cannot continue. Long before there is "standing room only," the life impetus must somehow be checked.† Population growth does not continue indefinitely. At some level, depending on the species and the environment, forces act against that growth. One of the demographic problems in sociology is to identify the many variables which accelerate, inhibit, or stabilize human population.

---

* In 1964 the fastest growing population in the world was in the South American tropical areas of Bolivia, Brazil, Colombia, Ecuador, Peru, Venezuela and the Guianas where the growth rate was 3.2 per cent annually (compared to a world average of 1.7 per cent). At this rate the largely illiterate population—almost half of which was under fifteen years of age—would double within 25 years.

† Natural law imposes restraints on the population of every species. Without restraints, for example, an invisible single-celled soil bacteria would produce a mass larger than the earth within six days. The eggs of a pair of sea lampreys would fill the ocean in a decade; and rats, multiplying twenty-five times in an average generation time of thirty-one weeks would soon overrun the earth.

To What Purpose Is This Waste?

The twentieth-century population explosion has spread with the diffusion of Western culture. Scientific and industrial advance has both decreased threats to individual life and increased the efficiency with which we produce necessities to support life.

> Expectation of a long life is the most tangible end product of western European civilization. . . . Beside this gift the material things of our civilization seem insignificant. Who would exchange thirty years of life for all the automobiles, radios, television sets, telephones, or even all the bathtubs in the United States? [24]

This gift of greater life expectancy ignited the population bomb. Fewer babies die at birth,* fewer children succumb to disease, more adolescents reach adulthood, reproduce, and live to be grandparents and great grandparents. In the underdeveloped countries, particularly Southwest Asia, Africa, and Central and South America, where a relatively high birth rate has counterbalanced high infant mortality and low life expectancy, the humane use of western pharmaceutical products and advanced medical techniques has not brought uniformly humane results. The Biblical injunction, "Be fruitful and multiply," once a form of group insurance, has become a threat to the group's existence. Both human life and the earth's resources are being squandered.

Efforts made to improve the lot of the common man are being frustrated by a population growth which outpaces economic growth. An unchecked tide of human births is overwhelming limited resources and depressing already low living standards. In spite of world-wide efforts to combat illiteracy, the number of illiterates is greater than before. In spite of world-wide efforts to combat hunger, more than half of the world's three billion people live in perpetual hunger; every day of the week some 10,000 people die of malnutrition or starvation.[25]

> Nine hundred years ago the great physician of Islam, Al Asuli, writing in distant Bokhara divided his pharmacopoeia into two parts: "Diseases of the Rich" and "Diseases of the Poor." If Al Asuli were alive today and could write about the afflictions of mankind I am sure he would again plan to divide his pharmacopoeia into the same two parts. Half his treatise would speak of the one affliction of rich humanity—the psychosis of nuclear annihilation. The other half would be concerned with the one affliction of the poor—their hunger and near starvation. He might perhaps add that the two afflictions spring from a common cause—the excess of science in one case and the lack of science in the other. . . . I have always been puzzled by how few people among the richer nations are really aware of the intensity of world poverty. Contrasting the two

* At the beginning of this century in the United States, 162 babies out of 1,000 died in infancy. By 1960, the fatalities were reduced to 27.7.

> ills of Al Asuli, nuclear death and starvation, it is no doubt true that from Moscow or New York the possibility of ultimate nuclear annihilation appears grimly near. But in Khartoum or Karachi the living death of daily hunger is nearer still. Fifty per cent of the people in my country of Pakistan earn and live on eight cents a day. Seventy-five per cent live on less than fourteen cents. This fourteen cents includes the two daily meals, clothing, shelter, and any education. To us, the unresolved conflicts of the East and the West appear as distant wearying conflicts, inevitable luxuries of a state of physical well-being. For us, the nuclear problem is tragic only in that it leads to a criminal waste of the earth's resources.[26]

The starving people in Khartoum or Karachi are only hours away from those of us who enjoy three good meals a day plus snacks in between. "If we were suddenly to join the less fortunate, our next meal . . . would be a small bowl of rice and perhaps a piece of fish an inch square the day after tomorrow." [27]

In comparison to most of Asia, South America and Africa, the countries of Europe and America are rich and literate. However, even in technologically advanced countries, abundance is not for all. Throughout the world, in prosperous countries as well as in those in which hunger and hardship are a way of life, the growing population presses against the finite resources of the environment; and deprivation—physical and psychological—threatens to undermine the structure of society.

EXTRINSIC RESTRAINTS. Restraints which limit the population of any living thing are of two kinds: *extrinsic* restraints imposed by the environment, and *intrinsic* restraints imposed by the nature of the species. The obvious extrinsic restraints include the limited amount of living space, food, mineral deposits, and the other resources needed to support life. Included also are disease, predatory enemies, accidents, and other threats to life. The scientific-industrial revolution, by creating an environment which protects the individual from the "natural" consequences of disease, has eliminated some extrinsic restraints; the short-run result has been explosive population growth. The long-run effect will be to impose other extrinsic restraints.

The world's total land area is 56,222,511 square miles, or approximately thirty-six billion acres. Half of this is too hot, too cold, too dry, too wet, or too mountainous for cultivation. The most generous estimates classify only half the remainder—twenty-five per cent of the total—as arable. The *average* acreage under cultivation in 1950, when the world population neared 2,350,000,000, was 1.77 per person, or approximately 4,200,000,000 acres. By 1985, when the population is expected to reach 5,000,000,000, the average cultivated acreage per person would be only .885. The amount needed to adequately feed and clothe one person, as of 1953, was approximately 2.5 acres. Production techniques, of course, can be improved; the yield per acre can be increased; unused land in Africa, Latin America, and tropical islands can be developed; arid and semi-arid regions can become productive when inexpensive processes are available for converting sea water to fresh, and the sea itself can be farmed. However, in 1950 two-thirds of the people in the world were undernourished;[28] during the decade from 1950 to 1960 production lagged far behind reproduction; and there is no evidence that even high efficiency production can keep pace with the present rate of population increase. Without a crash program to increase food production and decrease the rate of human reproduction, some experts predict that a massive famine involving hundreds of millions of people will sweep through China, India, and Pakistan in the early 1970's, engulf Indonesia, Iran, Turkey, and Egypt several years later and reach other countries of Asia, Africa, and South America by 1980.

Immediate production is determined by the amount of arable land* relative to the efficiency of farming and manufacturing techniques, but ultimate production is determined by raw materials, which are limited in amount, and, for the most part, irreplaceable. Topsoil is prerequisite to life, but mineral deposits in the deeper strata of the earth are the *sine qua non* of industrialized societies, and industrial development has coincided with and depended upon their exploitation. Since the beginning of this century, more mineral resources have been dug and consumed than in all previous history.[30] Nations rich in minerals are today the powerful nations of the world, but the faster they build their industrial and military power, the faster they exhaust the basis of that power.

INTRINSIC RESTRAINTS. Animal societies do not outgrow the food supply available in their habitat under normal conditions. Innate behavior patterns and biological mechanisms both act as automatic regulators of population density.[31] Staking out nesting and feeding territory, competition for membership in the breeding colony, emigration—even cannibalism and infanticide—are social conventions occurring widely among mammals and birds. Fetal reabsorption, suppression of ovulation and spermatogenesis, lowered resistance to bacterial and viral infections and fatal disorders of the endocrine, nervous, circulatory, and digestive systems are all biological reactions triggered by the stress of overcrowding. Such automatic regulators of population have been experimentally demonstrated. Among laboratory rats kept in high-density cages, females fail to build nests, nurse their litters carelessly or even desert them. Males develop a wide range of symptoms including homosexuality, pathological withdrawal, and cannibalism.[32]

Man lacks the built-in checks on reproduction which tend to keep many animal societies stable century after century. Reproduction at the human level is characteristically a conscious, individual act rather than a subconscious socially or biologically regulated reaction. However, fertility does show an inverse relationship—not to population density as such nor even to starvation

*With the aid of bacteria, plants, and climatic forces, it takes 300 to 1,000 years or more to build one inch of topsoil. In the United States alone, an estimated 5,400,000,000 tons is lost annually. Of this total 3,000,000,000 tons are from farmlands which are being both eroded away and worked out.[29]

or threat of starvation—but to urbanization. In the United States, for example, the difference between urban and rural fertility has been marked and persistent. In 1800 the average fertility ratio * was 845 for urban areas and 1,319 for rural areas. In 1950 the differential was still marked: 479 for urban areas and 673 for rural. Furthermore, the larger the urban or rural area, the lower the fertility. In 1950, urbanized areas of 3,000,000 population or more had a fertility ratio of 433, compared to 510 for those under 250,000. Rural areas with a population of 25,000 or more had a fertility ratio of 522, compared to that of 629 for unincorporated communities of 1,000 or less and 766 for farm areas.[33]

Urbanization seems to act as a sub-rational contraceptive. Perhaps, as in rodents, stress engendered by coping with "all those others" suppresses ovulation and spermatogenesis. Perhaps, theatres, concerts, museums, libraries, clubs, lectures, night baseball, and other characteristic urban activities tend to sublimate the sex drive. However, most of the countries of the world are still predominantly rural, and whatever subtle intrinsic restraints the urban environment might engender cannot be counted on to help in those countries where help is most urgently needed. And, although the changes science and industry are making in the chemical environment may again put the law of "survival of the fittest" into force and give biological advantage to a limited number of individuals who can survive contamination, we cannot count on the slow somatic and genetic processes either to substantially lower the birth rate or to increase the death rate in this critical twentieth century. Neither can we count on voluntary individual effort—abstinence or contraceptive devices. The first isn't popular enough; the second, in addition to being controversial, isn't yet simple nor sure enough. Mass migration is a possibility, but other planets which might be habitable are not yet accessible. Even if they should become so, their hypothetical native inhabitants might view with alarm such an interplanetary *drang nach osten,* and justly censure the environmental and ecological bungling of the wandering aliens.

Overpopulation and the poverty of mind and body which result are threats as potentially catastrophic as CBN or contamination. The earth, even now, is being gutted and ravaged by an increasingly desperate population. The two apparently reasonable palliatives—increased production or decreased reproduction—are so complicated by political, economic, religious, and educational problems that there seems to be little hope of success. Only literate and prosperous people voluntarily plan their families, and most of the people of the world are still illiterate and poor. Some authorities argue that we cannot rationally control the population explosion until universal disarmament under world law makes it possible to use money now spent on weaponry to raise living standards in the have-not nations.[34] We know the number of people on this planet will somehow be adjusted to the resources available for supporting them. The question is, *by what means?*

* Number of children under five years of age per 1,000 women aged 20 to 44.

The crisis of CBN, contamination, and overpopulation grow out of changes wrought through science—changes which affect so profoundly the geographical, biological, and technological conditions under which human society exists that the price of survival is reciprocal changes in man's ways.*

CONTROL AND CHANGE

We are living in the midst of a scientific revolution which has transformed the bases of human existence and disrupted the traditional social order. The culture we have created, like Frankenstein's monster, has begun to bully us. "We are trapped by patterns of behavior and thought which worked fairly well for millennia, but suddenly have become lethal." [36] Assuming our imperative loyalty is to life, *how do we cope?*

History illustrates how ill-prepared man has been, either to prevent crises or to deal constructively with them when they do occur. "If I might attempt a sweeping generalization about the general course of human history I would describe it as a series of flounderings, violent, ill-directed mass movements, slack drifting here, and convulsive action there." [37] Certainly if an impartial extra-planetary intelligence were to assess the social I.Q. of *Homo sapiens* on the basis of even recent efforts to resolve issues which arise out of human group life, the average score would be embarrassingly low. Consider, as examples, the Treaty of Versailles, the Great Depression, and Civil Defense.

The Treaty of Versailles. The end of World War I left Europe exhausted and the United States bewildered and fearful of foreign entanglements. The Fourteen Points which President Woodrow Wilson felt were essential to a lasting peace were branded by his opponents as "thoroughly mischievous," and the Senate refused to ratify a treaty which committed the United States to participation in the League of Nations.

> It was like hearing the squeak of a timid field mouse after the thunder of battle had rolled away. Faced by the responsibilities of a moral leadership in the world such as had never before come to any nation, America backed out of the room frightened and stammering.[38]

The United States brought to an end the war with the Imperial German Government by a simple declaration of fact, while the "peacemakers" at Versailles (by imposing harsh terms on Germany, depriving Italy of the spoils of victory originally promised, and giving Britain and France the lion's share of Germany's colonial goods) set the stage for the rise of Hitler and Mussolini and the disaster of World War II.

The Great Depression. From 1929 to 1939—the beginning of World War

---

* It is no surprise that the most ancient forms of life to survive are in the ocean, less affected by change than the land, and where the web of life is so tightly knit that no organism can easily produce change unfavorable to its own survival.[35]

II—leaders in the United States were helplessly bewildered by an economic collapse which left some 36,000,000 people without visible means of support.

"Experts" got involved in the theory of economic cycles and found themselves, in effect, "lecturing on navigation while the ship was going down." * "Practical men" spoke in redundancies. "When large numbers of men are unable to find work, mass unemployment results." [39] President Franklin D. Roosevelt turned from one promising advisor to another. He experimented. He attempted this and that. "He did not pretend to be a divinity. He was a politician—of exceptional good-will. . . . He showed himself extremely open and receptive for the organized information and guidance—*that wasn't there.*" [40]

Like a complex computer that gets stalled and then starts performing again when an irate clerk kicks it, our economic system—in spite of our ignorance of the principles which sustained it—creaked along until resuscitated by the economic needs of World War II. However, we still have unemployment, and "unemployment in a wealthy economy faced with . . . a vast accumulation of public needs . . . can only be classified as economic idiocy." [41]

Civil Defense. In anticipation of World War III or some other catastrophe, the Office of Civil Defense has adopted both a run-for-the-hills and a duck-for-cover approach to civilian survival.

RUN-FOR-THE-HILLS. After the first H-bomb test in 1953, selected streets and highways throughout the United States were labeled "evacuation routes." As late as 1964, the classroom bulletin boards in a San Francisco college carried notices of the local "Air Raid Dispersal Plan." *If the College is notified by defense authorities that an air raid is imminent, a dispersal alarm will be given over the public address system. All persons on the campus will be advised to go immediately to the parking lots, where all available automobiles will be loaded to capacity. Drivers will proceed to the Herbert Hoover Junior High School, Park and Nagler Avenues, San Jose. . . .* The notice makes three unwarranted assumptions: first, that the target would be San Francisco and not the fast-growing industrial city of San Jose; second, that San Jose, fifty miles southwest of San Francisco, is a safe distance from blast and fire; and third, that it would be possible to get to San Jose—when a flat tire or an accident during normal rush hours stalls traffic for miles along the one available freeway.

DUCK-FOR-COVER. In cities across the nation, Civil Defense signs point to public shelter space in buildings, tunnels, and subways. These existing facilities are supplemented by private family shelters and by federally subsidized shelters in public and private nonprofit institutions devoted to health, education, or welfare. Hydrogen-bomb tests have conclusively demonstrated that millions of persons would be killed by the initial blast and fire. Shelters could protect only against fallout, which, however, spreads thousands of miles beyond the blast.

---

* W. H. Auden, English poet in the United States, 1907-.

Civil Defense is rationalized as "minimal insurance" against the "unlikely event of a nuclear war,"[42] but defense measures tend to destroy public confidence in world leadership and to diffuse anxiety.

Knowledge in the physical and biological sciences—accumulating at an ever accelerating rate for centuries—has erupted in a series of technological breakthroughs. In one generation we have made a transition from electric to atomic power, from natural to synthetic materials, from mechanical to electronic systems, from terrestrial to cosmic explorations. "Some three hundred nuclear explosions have popularized the sense of Einstein's Special Theory of Relativity. Several dozen earth satellites have provided the classical mechanics of Newton with its grandest demonstrations."[43] The behavioral sciences have made no comparable breakthroughs, and great disparity exists between technological and societary * accomplishments. Change has gotten out of control. As a consequence, the social structures through which individuals and groups interact, the processes which characterize such interaction, the cultural norms and goals towards which action orients are in discordant relationship to each other and environmental conditions. In the "underdeveloped" societies, the "traditional order of human relationships has been fatally undermined or even destroyed by Western penetration."[44] Such societies face the inroads of urban-industrialism without preparation. In the already industrialized societies, "leaders and movements whose power and ways of thinking have originated in a different age, continue to control national policies."[45] Until we fully grasp the realities of the new era in which we live and clearly perceive the ways in which we must change ourselves and society in order to survive in it, we play a dangerous game with chance.

We cannot turn back the technological clock, nor would we call a moratorium on physical and biological research. We can, however, "bring into the framing of private and public policy the scientific understanding and scientific attitude that have so profoundly transformed man's relationship to nature,"[46] and we can move ahead in the behavioral sciences with the hope of building a social order commensurate with the technological one.

CBN, contamination, overpopulation and the many lesser issues which now confront us—including automation, urbanization, and anomie †—are symptoms of underlying social disorder—of confusion and disharmony generated by the furiously accelerated advance of physical and biological science. All call for a rational problem-solving approach, the prerequisite for which is more knowledge of man. Sociology is one of the major behavioral sciences intent on gaining such knowledge.

---

* *Technological* refers to non-symbolic material culture and the knowledge and techniques logically associated with it. *Societary* refers to social structures and processes, cultural norms and goals.

† Breakdown of norms—characteristic of mass society.

Notes

1. Bernard Berelson and Gary A. Steiner, *Human Behavior* (New York: Harcourt, Brace & World, Inc.), p. 11.
2. T. S. Eliot, *Murder in the Cathedral,* Fourth Edition (New York: Harcourt, Brace & World, Inc., 1938), p. 45.
3. Arnold J. Toynbee, *Civilization on Trial* (New York: Oxford University Press, 1948), pp. 155-156.
4. Albert Schweitzer, quoted in Rachel Carson, *Silent Spring* (Boston: Houghton Mifflin Company, 1962), p. 6.
5. Gunther Anders, quoted in Max Born, "Physics and Politics," *Bulletin of the Atomic Scientists,* June, 1960, p. 197.
6. "The Fallout Shelter," *Consumer Reports,* January, 1962, p. 9.
7. J. H. S. Bossard, "War and the Family," *American Sociological Review,* June, 1941, p. 339.
8. J. H. Rothchild, former commanding general of the chemical corps research and development command, quoted in E. James Lieberman, "Psychochemicals as Weapons," *Bulletin of the Atomic Scientists,* January, 1962, p. 11.
9. E. James Lieberman, *Bulletin of the Atomic Scientists,* January, 1962, p. 11, quoting General William M. Creasy, former chief chemical officer, U.S. Army.
10. *Ibid.*, p. 11. Quoting *Hearings* before Committee on Science and Astronautics, U.S. House of Representatives, June, 1959 (No. 22).
11. *Ibid.*, p. 11. Quoting General Stubbs before above *Hearings.*
12. Martin M. Kaplan, "Communicable Diseases and Epidemics," *Bulletin of the Atomic Scientists,* June, 1960, p. 237.
13. Lieberman, *Bulletin of the Atomic Scientists,* January, 1962, p. 11.
14. Pope John XXIII, "Pacem In Terris," encyclical, April 11, 1963.
15. Jerome B. Wiesner and Herbert F. York, "National Security and the Nuclear-Test Ban," *Scientific American,* October, 1964, p. 35.
16. U.S. Department of Defense, quoted in *U.S. News and World Report,* October 23, 1961, p. 102.
17. U.S. Bureau of the Census, *Statistical Abstract of the United States* (Washington, D.C., 1961), p. 235.
18. Richard H. Rovere, "Letter from Washington," *The New Yorker,* May 12, 1962, p. 168.
19. Fred J. Cook, "Juggernaut: The Warfare State," *The Nation,* October 28, 1961, pp. 302-303.
20. Rachel Carson, *Silent Spring,* p. 8.
21. William A. Albrecht, "Wastebasket of the Earth," *Bulletin of the Atomic Scientists,* October, 1961, p. 336. © Educational Foundation for Nuclear Science, Inc., 935 E. 60th St., Chicago, Illinois 60637.
22. Report of President Kennedy's Science Advisory Committee, *Scientific American,* July, 1963, p. 64.
23. Philip M. Hauser, "Man and More Men: The Population Prospects," *Bulletin of the Atomic Scientists,* June, 1964, p. 4.
24. Frederick Osborn, *Preface to Eugenics* (New York: Harper & Row, Publishers, 1951), p. xi.
25. "Hunger Round the World," *Newsweek,* June 17, 1963, p. 43.
26. Abdus Salam, "Diseases of the Rich and Diseases of the Poor," *Bulletin of the Atomic Scientists,* April, 1963, p. 3. © Educational Foundation for Nuclear Science, Inc., 935 E. 60th St., Chicago, Illinois 60637.
27. Harlan Cleveland, Assistant Secretary of State, quoted in *Newsweek,* June 17, 1963, p. 43.

28. Julian Huxley, "World Population," *Scientific American,* March, 1956, pp. 64-67.
29. Fairfield Osborn, *Our Plundered Planet* (Boston: Little, Brown & Co., 1948), pp. 186-187.
30. Alan M. Bateman, "Minerals: Supply and Demand," *Bulletin of the Atomic Scientists,* October, 1961, p. 331.
31. V. C. Wynne-Edwards, "Population Control in Animals," *Scientific American,* August, 1964, pp. 68-74.
32. John B. Calhoun, "Population Density and Social Pathology," *Scientific American,* February, 1962, pp. 139-148.
33. William Peterson, *Population* (New York: The Macmillan Company, 1961), pp. 191-217.
34. Hudson Hoagland, "Cybernetics of Population Control," *Bulletin of the Atomic Scientists,* February, 1964, p. 6.
35. Paul B. Sears, "Man and Nature's Balance," in *An Outline of Men's Knowledge of the Modern World,* Lyman Bryson, ed. (Garden City, New York: Doubleday & Company, Inc., 1960), p. 181.
36. Dr. Jerome D. Frank, in Carolyn Anspacher, "Our Behavior 'Skips Point of Atom Age,'" *San Francisco Chronicle,* April 28, 1959, p. 10.
37. H. G. Wells, "The Idea of a World Encyclopedia," *Harper's Magazine,* April, 1937, p. 473.
38. James Truslow Adams, *The Epic of America* (Boston: Little, Brown and Company, 1933), p. 393.
39. Statement attributed to President Calvin Coolidge (1872-1933).
40. Wells, *op. cit.,* p. 473.
41. United States Senate Subcommittee on Manpower, "Towards Full Employment," in *Sane World,* June 1, 1964.
42. Arthur I. Waskow, "The Shelter Centered Society," *Scientific American,* May, 1962, p. 46.
43. Gerard Piel, *Science in the Cause of Man* (New York: Alfred A. Knopf, Inc., 1962), p. viii.
44. Theodore H. von Laue, "Modern Science and the Old Adam," *Bulletin of the Atomic Scientists,* January, 1963, p. 5.
45. Eugene Rabinowitch, "Man Must Prevail," *Bulletin of the Atomic Scientists,* December, 1962, p. 4.
46. Piel, *Science in the Cause of Man,* p. ix.

Cease to be ruled by dogmas
and authorities; look at the world.

ROGER BACON (1214[?]-1294)

2

Sociology and Science

IF HUMAN HISTORY seems an erratic succession of events—a series of climaxes, anticlimaxes, crises, triumphs, and disasters rather than the consequence of antecedents or concurrent conditions—it seems so, in part, because we cannot yet identify the important variables * in human affairs nor state the laws † underlying their interaction. Events are not dictated by caprice or extra-natural interference. They don't just happen. Events are related to each other, and it is the purpose of science to determine relationships. A scientist wants to know how things work, how they act, and implicit in his inquiry is the faith that "things 'work' or 'act' with a regularity sufficient to permit this 'working' to be described." [1]

The essence of scientific method is more than experimentation or mathematics or any specific technique. It is an attitude—an approach to experience as applicable to the behavior of *Homo sapiens* as it is to any other natural phenomenon.

* Related factors of measurable degree under scientific investigation.

† A scientific "law" is not a decree to which nature or man is obedient. It is a description of the predictable behavior of selected variables expressed as a verbal or mathematical formula.

OTTO HAGEL

TOWARDS KNOWLEDGE OF MAN

Knowledge obtained through sociology, psychology, anthropology and the other behavioral sciences will eventually replace superstition and misinformation, and we can expect that with enough knowledge of the "laws" of human interaction, a humane social order can be built—just as with enough understanding of the "laws" of physics, a thermonuclear bomb was built. The development of the behavioral sciences, however, is slowed down for many reasons including the theoretical gulf separating scientific and non-scientific thinking. Few laymen are familiar with scientific method; fewer still *use* scientific method. They do not ordinarily cope with "private troubles" or "public issues" * in a spirit of honest inquiry unfettered by hate or fear or even love. Laymen—and even scientists are laymen outside their field of specialty—characteristically rely to a greater or lesser degree on five means of gaining information on which to base action: *authority, intuition, common sense, observation,* and *informal logic.*

Authority

Much of what we "know" we have accepted on authority. This is a practical necessity. A society, through its culture, transmits information which no individual has time or skill to gather firsthand for himself. We learn from others, and we tend to accept as valid the information we get from "reliable" sources.

Although appeal to authority is a fast and often satisfactory way of gaining information, those who represent authority may rigidly limit information by stifling free inquiry. During the Middle Ages and the Early Renaissance, for example, the Church was the authority in spiritual matters, Aristotle was the authority in "scientific" ones; and those who then upheld authority perceived as impertinent and dangerous the intellectual probings of Renaissance man. Galileo Galilei (1564-1642) championed the irreverent theory of Copernicus † that the earth moves around the sun and performed some of the earliest observations with the telescope. Galileo discovered mountains on the moon, sun spots, and four of the moons of Jupiter, but neither churchmen nor scholars would even look through his telescope.

> As I wished to show the satellites of Jupiter to the professors in Florence, they would see neither them nor the telescope. These people believe there is no truth to seek in nature, but only in the comparison of the texts.[3]

---

* *Troubles* are personal, private matters. *Issues* transcend the personal and concern the "larger structure of social and historical life." [2]

† Nicolaus Copernicus (1473-1543), founder of modern astronomy.

Those who uphold authority typically resent those who question or defy authority, and under threat of torture and death, Galileo was forced to recant. He renounced his teaching that the earth moves and other "errors and heresies" repugnant to the Holy Scriptures and lived out his life as semi-prisoner of the Inquisition.

> I, Galileo, son of the late Vincenzo Galilei, Florentine, aged seventy years, arraigned personally before this tribunal and kneeling before you, Most Eminent and Reverend Lord Cardinals and Inquisitors-General, . . . swear that I have always believed, do believe, and by God's hope will in the future believe all that is held, preached, and taught by the Holy Catholic and Apostolic Church. But whereas—after an injunction had been judicially intimated to me by this Holy Office to the effect that I must altogether abandon the false opinion that the Sun is the center of the world and is immovable and that the Earth is not the center of the world and moves . . . I wrote and printed a book in which I discuss this new doctrine already condemned and adduce arguments of great cogency in its favor. . . . Therefore, desiring to remove from the minds of your Eminences, and all faithful Christians, this vehement suspicion justly conceived against me, with sincere heart and unfeigned faith I abjure, curse, and detest the aforesaid errors and heresies. . . .[4]

In everyday experience, we tend to accept as most reliable those authorities whose position best fits our personal preconceptions. "It appears that the more consistent a particular hypothesis is with one's interests, the fewer cues are necessary for its confirmation." [5] The inherent weakness in any appeal to authority is that the appeal may be to authority as such on the basis of precedent or predeliction, even when that authority supports only unverified opinion or belief.

Intuition

Intuition, which women and dogs are supposed to possess, is the power of knowing without direct recourse to references or reasoning. It is akin to "hunches," "insights," and other discriminations without awareness. They are all manifestations of unconscious mental processes which psychologists have not yet satisfactorily explained. However, the philosophical position of *Intuitionism* assumes that self-evident truths, intuitively known, form the basis of human knowledge. Aristotle (384-322 B.C.), in trying to explain why things happened, began with "self-evident" principles.

> It is, for example, a self-evident principle that everything in the universe has its proper place, hence one can deduce that objects fall to the ground because that's where they belong, and smoke goes up because that's where it belongs.[6]

Thomas Jefferson, some 2,000 years later, assumed such principles when he wrote in the Declaration of Independence, "We hold these truths to be self-evident, that all men are created equal, that they are endowed by their Creator with certain unalienable rights, that among these are Life, Liberty and the pursuit of Happiness."

When intuition is stated, not as self-evident truth but as hypothesis, it can lead to valid information. Democritus (460-370 B.C.) believed matter to be made of atomic particles.* Copernicus believed the earth moved around the sun. Galileo believed that objects of different weights did not necessarily fall with different velocities. Darwin believed in the continuity of life rather than in the separate creation of discrete forms of life. Hypotheses are made prior to adequate factual evidence but are open to proof. The inherent weakness in intuition, as such, is that it relies only on the "sense" of knowing, independent of fact or reason. "The facts of life do not penetrate to the sphere in which our beliefs are cherished. . . ." [7] Intuition may defy reality rather than test it.

Common Sense

The earth appears to be stationary, and for ordinary purposes, it is good common sense to behave as if it were.

> But to the astrophysicist, the earth, far from being at rest, is whirling through space in a giddy and highly complicated fashion. In addition to its daily rotation about its axis at the rate of 1,000 miles an hour, and its annual revolution about the sun at twenty miles a second, the earth is also involved in a number of other less familiar gyrations. Contrary to popular belief the moon does not revolve around the earth; they revolve around each other—or more precisely, around a common center of gravity. The entire solar system, moreover, is moving within the local star system at the rate of thirteen miles a second; the local star system is moving within the Milky Way at the rate of 200 miles a second; and the Milky Way is drifting with respect to the remote external galaxies at the rate of 100 miles a second—and all in different directions! [8]

"A pint's a pound the world around," and three feet make a yard. In everyday practice, common sense demands that we assume the stability of measurements. But mass is not just another word for weight. It is defined by physicists as a change of motion, and mass increases with increase in velocity, so that the closer a pint of anything might come to the velocity of light, the more it would weigh. And a yardstick "moving with ninety per cent the velocity of light would shrink to about half its length . . . and if the stick could attain the velocity of light, it would shrink away to nothing at all." [9]

Common sense assumptions, like intuitively known "truths," seem self-evident, but "common sense is actually nothing more than a deposit of prejudices laid down in the mind prior to the age of eighteen." [10] This "deposit

* Democritus's position was philosophical, not scientific. The scientific theory of the atomic structure of matter was not advanced until the nineteenth century nor tested until the twentieth.

of prejudices" accrues to human as well as physical phenomena. "Men are, by nature, competitive." "Women are intellectually inferior to men." "Sparing the rod spoils the child." The practical experience from which common sense assumptions are distilled is often limited experience, and we find the common sense enshrined in folk-sayings full of contradictory overgeneralizations. *"Out of sight, out of mind,"* and *"Absence makes the heart grow fonder." "Clothes make the man,"* and *"You can't make a silk purse out of a sow's ear." "Repeat a lie often enough and people believe it,"* and *"The truth will prevail." "East is East and West is West and never the twain shall meet,"* and *"We are all brothers under the skin."* The inherent weakness in common sense—when based on inadequate evidence and accepted uncritically—is that while it may serve practical expedience, it also perpetuates inaccuracies and inconsistencies. Any new ideas must then struggle for recognition in an intellectual climate made uncongenial by preconception.

Observation

A stick protruding above the surface of a clear pool of water looks broken. A porous piece of steel looks solid. The wavy edge of a sharp razor looks straight. Two plumb lines look parallel. Observation cannot be trusted. It is too dependent on sense perception which not only is limited, but in some instances, false. "Seeing may be believing," but the wise man knows "All is not gold that glitters." Man has, in fact, a faulty input system. Our perceptions tend to serve our personal purposes rather than reality.* We observe what our particular needs, experience, and expectation prepare us to observe. A dozen witnesses to an event—especially an emotionally charged one such as a crime or an accident—will have not one but a dozen different descriptions of what happened. "One can learn a lot by just watching," remarked one nine-year old boy; and he was right. However, the inherent weakness in observation as a means of information is that the untrained layman is not clearly aware of the distorting filter of opinions, attitudes, and beliefs through which sensory stimuli pass before coming into awareness. Furthermore, the layman tends to confuse *observation* and *interpretation.* He may say he observed a man asleep, when all he actually observed was a man in a reclining position with his eyes closed. Observation is the starting point of science, but the observer must be trained to observe facts objectively and to avoid going beyond the facts in his description of them.

Informal Logic

The information we glean from authority, intuition, common sense, and observation we extend through informal logic or reasoning. We "put two and two together," but because our information may be inadequate or inaccurate and our logic faulty, we do not always get the right answer.

---

* Chapter 6.

When events are experienced in relationship to each other, the mental processes uncritically record an association between the two. A hungry pigeon given a few grains of food every fifteen seconds with no reference to his behavior will tend to associate whatever he is doing at the time with the appearance of food. Because he is hungry, he tends to repeat that particular bit of behavior. Whenever the appearance of food again coincides with the behavior, it further reinforces the association. One pigeon learned clockwise turns; another learned to thrust his head in an upper corner of the cage. Two others learned to swing their bodies back and forth like a pendulum.[11] The relationship between the food and the pigeons' behavior was fortuitous, but the pigeon behaved as if it were causal. People do the same sort of thing.

Everyday living presents us with a succession of illogical fortuitous coincidences. Superstitions arise out of the attempt to explain such coincidences by imposing a logical or causal relationship on them.

Rural people in eastern counties of England and parts of Europe, for example, still believe in a magical connection between a wound and the agent of the wound. In Suffolk, a man came to a doctor with a festered hand, wounded on a thorn. He complained, "That didn't ought to, for I greased the bush well after I pulled it out."[12] In Cambridgeshire, a veterinarian went to a farm to care for a horse which had ripped open its side on a gatepost hinge. The owner had done nothing for the horse. He was busily prying out the hinge so he could grease it and put it away. That was the local remedy. We draw inferences from experience in an attempt to reach a valid conclusion, but if experience is limited or distorted by emotion or other factors, any inferences we make from such experience may be invalid. Even when given factual information, we cannot always perceive logical relationships and arrive at valid conclusions. Informal logic or reasoning, insofar as it is simply a matter of connecting facts or events and drawing inferences from them, is a commonplace tool of thought. The inherent weakness in ordinary reasoning, however, is that we tend to assume that the information with which we begin and the conclusions we draw are valid, whereas, in fact, either or both may be fallacious.

Science

The information available through science is presented, not as truth, but as the closest approximation to truth currently available. Scientists use ordinary sources of information: authority, intuition, common sense, observation, and logic; but the methods of science encourage not belief, but doubt. Science is organized uncertainty, and truth * is an ideal being sought, not a goal achieved. André Gide, French novelist and critic, might have spoken for

* Sense perception, the scientific tools which extend the senses, and the cognitive capacities of the human brain are the only means we have of observing, describing, and understanding objects and events. Whatever model of "truth" or "reality" we construct is limited by the perceiving instrument—man himself.

science when he cautioned, "Believe in those who seek the truth; doubt those who have found it."

Science has grown out of the common means we all use to obtain information. The essential difference is that the scientist is trained in objectivity and that science itself is an *authority*—not of person or position or precedent—but of method. When a scientist refers to authority, he refers to a *professionally qualified* authority and accepts even that authority tentatively. He does not assume that any authority has access to "the truth, the whole truth, and nothing but the truth." And he does not hesitate to question authority. By rejecting the authority of Aristotle, which had been upheld for 2,000 years, Galileo helped establish modern science.

When a scientist has a *hunch,* he tests it scientifically. Einstein expressed a hunch when he said, "I cannot believe that God plays dice with the world."[13] He then spent a quarter of a century trying to demonstrate, through mathematics, the pervading order and harmony of the universe. His Unified Field Theory was an effort to state "in one series of mutually consistent equations the physical laws governing the two fundamental forces of the universe, gravitation and electromagnetism."[14]

When a scientist uses *common sense,* he understands it as a body of fact and opinion based on nothing more than common human experience, and he knows that scientific knowledge often contradicts common sense.

> . . . because of Einstein's unwillingness to ever accept any unproven principle as self-evident . . . he was able to penetrate closer to the underlying realities of nature than any scientist before him. Why, he asked, is it any more strange to assume that moving clocks slow down and moving rods contract, than to assume that they don't?[15]

When a scientist *observes* under natural conditions, he is aware of the limitations of his own sense perceptions and of the necessity to distinguish fact from interpretation. Such "naturalistic" observations contribute to scientific information, but more characteristic are the systematic observations made under the controlled conditions of planned experiments.* Once the experiment is under way, the scientist collects the data objectively—regardless of whether they support either his scientific hypothesis or his personal preferences. "Biased procedures in collecting data have no place in science, nor has biased perception of the results."[16]

Carefully designed and controlled experiments test the validity and reliability of information obtained by other means. "The aim of science is not to open a door to infinite wisdom, but to set a limit to infinite error."[17]

When a scientist uses *logic,* he checks and rechecks each step in the process—always on the lookout for new and contradictory facts and theories,

---

* An *experiment* includes two elements: manipulation or control of some variable by the investigator, and systematic observation or measurement of the result. It involves "active intervention on the phenomena of interest to see what, if any, effects are produced by the intervention."[18]

testing the validity of premises and the soundness of conclusions. The spectacular success of science since Galileo has been the success of a method—the inductive method of formal logical reasoning. Inductive logic has become synonymous with scientific method. It became so when Francis Bacon (1561-1626) pointed out that induction was the one way of determining *cause.* Work backward, he advised, from effects to tentatively defined *cause.* Then use controlled experiments to learn whether or not the assumed cause always produces the same effect. Systematic induction, in retrospect, seems an obvious procedure but it was a startling innovation at the time. Inquiry had been dominated by the deductive logic of Aristotle. Reasoning had proceeded from general premises to specific cases without any device for checking the validity of the original premises. Inductive logic provided that device. Deductive logic remained the method of philosophers and mathematicians and the basis for prediction. Inductive logic became the method of modern research science. Today, however, instead of speaking of cause and effect, which implies precedence of one over the other, scientists identify *variables* and seek to determine relationships between them.

> Science is not a lot of book-learning; it is an active enterprise. It is what scientists do and how they do it. They do not wave magic wands, neither do they proceed by a series of rigid logical steps to sure conclusions. Instead, they keep their eyes open for discrepancies between actual phenomena and the current explanations for them, and they try to improve them in order better to understand, control and predict. They devise instruments for observation and measurement. They use imagination to set up hypotheses, which they test by carefully designed and controlled experiments. Results found to occur so uniformly as to have high probability of recurrence are formulated as "laws," although it is understood that, unlike statute laws, they do not control. These laws are explained, where possible, by theories and models. Mathematics often plays an important role, but its limitation must be kept in mind.
>
> A science develops beyond the initial stages of observing, naming and classifying, by aid of unifying ideas or concepts. . . .[19]

More than any other institution, science is prepared to combat intellectual rigidity; skepticism remains its fundamental attitude. The layman, more typically, craves certainty and tends to become emotionally defensive when his beliefs and behavior are challenged. This difference in attitude is one of the many problems involved in applying scientific methods to human affairs.

OBSTACLES TO KNOWLEDGE

Paradoxically, the common means of getting knowledge can also act as obstacles to knowledge. Authority, intuition, common sense, observation, and informal logic are not self-correcting. They can perpetuate error indefinitely. Insofar as we accept and defend the information we get through such means—

be it valid or invalid—we build "sets" or readiness to respond to certain ideas or events in certain ways. Sets can inhibit the kind of thinking which leads to new knowledge—the critical thinking involved in forming judgments and the creative thinking involved in achieving new solutions to problems and discovering or establishing new relationships. Sets are habits of thought and behavior with a built-in resistance to change,* and the more personal the subject matter to which sets relate, the more resistant we tend to be to knowledge which might change those sets.

> It would appear that the more intimate (to man) the subject matter, the younger the science. Astronomy before geography, physical science before biology, medicine before psychology—even though in each case the availability of data was in the reverse order.[20]

Science, since the days of Galileo, has had its detractors, but we have gradually learned to accept and make practical use of new knowledge available through the physical and biological sciences:

A 200,000-power microscope magnifies a molecule for the geneticist that he might decipher the language of heredity . . . microwave technology helps the astronomer map the Milky Way . . . a laser (light amplification by stimulated emission of radiation) lights the moon in reconnaisance for those who plan lunar explorations . . . transistors operate Telestar satellites and signals from across the seas light the TV screen . . . MAC, a Magnetic Accounting Computer, goes to work for a bank, processing thousands of checks in record time . . . a cardiac pacemaker maintains the normal beat of an impaired heart so that a man may live . . . a synthetic adhesive laminates timbers for a 215-foot open-span building. . . .

In contrast, we are less willing to accept and make practical use of new knowledge in the behavioral sciences. Try challenging with indisputably sound facts and inferences the platform of a politician, the profit motive of a business man, the rituals of a church leader, the grading system of a teacher, the child-rearing practices of a parent. . . . In such areas we generally resist new knowledge by appealing to prior knowledge—knowledge firmly entrenched in habits of thought and behavior and reinforced by emotionally charged opinions, attitudes, and beliefs (OAB's).† Authority, intuition, common sense, observation, and logic can serve either dogma or doubt. Man—insofar as he is a "closed" system, defensive of the information he has acquired and of the habits he has built—is, himself, the greatest of all obstacles to the acquisition and application of knowledge of man.

We all tend to protect the repertoire of more or less serviceable habits of thought and action we have acquired and to regard as suspect the scientists who would expose our behavior to critical analysis and disrupt the arrange-

---

* Chapter 12.

† Chapter 6.

ments we have made with ourselves and our world. Furthermore, man once imagined he had a unique and favored position in the scheme of life. Although we can now perceive ourselves as the species *Homo sapiens* inhabiting one small planet orbitting one star in a universe of a hundred thousand million billion stars, we find it disconcerting to be observed as dispassionately as a colony of ants or a constellation of particles in a molecule.

In spite of public resistance and other formidable obstacles—including shortage of money and personnel plus research difficulties inherent in subject matter—behavioral scientists have proceeded with their work. They systematically *observe* and describe—even record on film and tape—baboons in their forest habitat, workers in factories, street corner gangs, tribal dances, children's play, religious rituals. . . . In such natural situations, however, scientists have little or no control over their subjects. In planned *experiments* they have more control and can isolate and manipulate at least some variables, but experiments are at best artificial and the behavior of subjects (usually animals and college students) is not necessarily typical. With *survey analyses* they try to assay the attitudes, opinions, abilities, and other traits of supposedly sample populations; through *case studies* they seek insights and clues for further study. What ever the approach—*observation, experimentation, survey analysis, case study,* or any variation of these basic research methods—knowledge of the complex, variable and obscurely motivated behavior of man is difficult to obtain and validate. Scientific method has a long history of spectacular successes in the physical and biological sciences, a short history of relatively minor gains in the behavioral sciences.

SOCIOLOGY—A SCIENCE OF MAN

Science has historical roots in two traditions—the technological and the philosophical. Practical skills and information coupled with theoretical concepts make up the body of any science; but physical and biological sciences are closest to the technological tradition; behavioral and social sciences are closest to the philosophical tradition. Only within this century have sociology, anthropology and psychology been accorded the status of science; and although these disciplines have already yielded information indispensable to the understanding and direction of human affairs, some "findings" have no basis in scientific method and would still be considered social hypotheses.

Science, as method and attitude, began more than 400 years ago. The behavioral sciences are an achievement of this century. Men who helped define the fields of study—Plato, Niccolo Machiavelli, David Ricardo, John Locke, Auguste Comte, Herbert Spencer, Robert Owen, Tom Paine, Thomas Malthus, John Stuart Mill, Oswald Spengler, Adam Smith, Karl Marx, Friedrich Engels and others—were all social or political philosophers, not scientists. Sociology was first conceived by the French philosopher, Auguste Comte

(1798-1857), as a grandiose scheme for reorganizing and improving human relationships.*

Origins of Sociology

The chaotic aftermath of the Napoleonic Wars had divided the French intellectual world between the conservatives who wanted to turn back the clock and revive the power of the Old Regime and the social reformers, who, in the name of "reason and humanity" sought a new social order free from the domination of nobles and clergy. Comte, whose studies at the *École Polytechnique* had kindled an enthusiasm for rationalism, began to ask questions. *Why do we suffer social chaos? How can we establish social order?* His attempts to answer his own questions led him to call for a "science of society," which, through observation, experiment, and comparison, could discover the universal laws underlying the historical development of society. Although Comte aligned himself with the reformers, he was from a royalist family, and his basic conservatism showed through in his treatise on *Positive Philosophy*.† He sought intellectual foundations for a society which would have the order and stability of the old feudal regime. He wanted a stability compatible with "progress," a stability such as one finds in a biological organism, which can tolerate change without being disrupted by it. Comte perceived society as a *gestalt*—an organic whole greater and different than the sum of its parts—an entity whose historical progress could be accelerated by man's purposeful and rational intervention. With his philosophical perspective, he made sociology the keystone science which would correlate data from other sciences and offer a synthesis of social facts and theory as a basis for the re-establishment and maintenance of social order.

Other philosophers before Comte, including Plato, Niccolo Machiavelli, and John Locke, had thought in terms which we would now identify as sociological, but Comte was the first to conceive of a comprehensive model for a "science of society" and to coin the term "sociology." Although Comte is generally accorded the status of "father of sociology," another philosopher, the Englishman Herbert Spencer (1820-1903), was equally influential in bringing society into the sphere of scientific inquiry.‡ Spencer was profoundly

* Sociology was first of the behavioral sciences in the sense of a defined area of study but last in the sense of an established repertoire of experimental techniques. Anthropology was founded by James Prichard (1786-1857) and Sir James Edward Burnett Tyler (1832-1917). Psychology dates from the establishment of the first psychological laboratory in Leipzig, 1879, by Wilhelm Wundt (1832-1920).

† Comte's *Positive Philosophy* was originally published in six volumes, the first in 1830, the last in 1842. In the early volumes Comte traced the history and method of the natural sciences and criticized them for worship of the past and relative lack of scientific observation. The last volume Comte devoted to "social physics" or sociology. *Positivism* derives its name from Comte's contention that the only useful knowledge is the *positive* knowledge derived through science.

‡ Spencer's three volume work, *Principles of Sociology*, was published over a twenty-year period, 1876-1896.

impressed by Charles Darwin's *Origin of Species,* published in 1859. He described the principle of evolution as "survival of the fittest," and applied the principle to individuals and species, to ideas and customs and social institutions—even to the solar system. He conceived everything in the universe as completing an infinite number of evolutionary cycles, from origin and development to decay, extinction, and renewal. He assumed the direction of social evolution to progress along a line of least resistance from an unspecialized, unorganized state towards organization and specialization.

Spencer made an analogy between society and a biological organism, as did Comte, but Spencer compared society in structure, not to a plant whose parts are mutually interdependent, but to a polyp—any part of which severed from the whole would take on the shape of the whole. He insisted that society was only an aggregate, neither more than nor different from the sum of its parts. The individual, he emphasized, does not exist for society; rather, society exists for the individual. Comte would have built a system of belief dedicated to social progress and then, through rational intervention accelerate or modify the natural course of that progress. Spencer, a *laissez-faire* individualist,* would let social evolution take its own course. He militantly opposed interference of any kind and let his dissention with Comte be known.

> The disciples of M. Comte think I am much indebted to him; and so I am but in a way widely unlike that which they mean. Save in the adoption of his word "sociology" because there was no other available word . . . the only indebtedness which I recognize is the indebtedness of antagonism. My pronounced opposition to his views led me to develop some of my own views.[21]

Spencer optimistically perceived the course of individual evolution to be from egotism to altruism and the course of social evolution to be from a militant social structure to a pacifistic industrial one. Unfettered competition would insure survival of the fittest and ultimately eliminate the unfit. The automatic result would be social pacifism, individual altruism, and universal peace.

Sociology, being a science of society, draws much of its intellectual content from the particular society in which it develops. Because societies differ, sociology also differs both in assumptions and interests. Spencer, the Englishman, found Comte's theories intolerable, but Comte's successor in Europe, Émile Durkheim (1858-1911) another French social philosopher, accepted Comte's perception of society as a *gestalt* and elaborated on it. Durkheim felt that a social group was definitely different from the sum of its parts—that social facts were not the same as individual facts. He introduced the concepts of *collective conscience* (a participation by the individual in the thoughts and feelings of the group), of *anomie* (absence of group norms), and of *group psychology* as distinguished from individual psychology. He was

* Spencer's excessive distrust of the State extended to even such agencies as the post office, and instead of mailing his manuscripts he delivered them in person to his publisher.

particularly concerned with social integration and the forces in society contributing to or destructive of that integration. He studied religion as a cohesive force in society, analyzed types of social solidarity, and, in an investigation of the causes of suicide, first used statistical methods in social research. Comte philosophically conceived the science of society, but Durkheim was the first to practice it,* and, in this sense, Durkheim is actually the founder of sociology.

Sociology in the United States

Sociology, as it first developed in the United States, is indebted to Comte as well as to Spencer. Comte and Spencer, despite their differences, were both positivists. They understood that method, not subject matter, defined science, and were convinced that scientific method applied to society would yield positive knowledge useful in coping with social maladjustments. Positivism was a welcome idea to men of conscience in a young society which emerged from a civil war to find itself subjected to the rampant forces of industrialism and urbanization. The majority of pioneer sociologists in the United States, though not necessarily religious in the conventional sense, were concerned with the ethical issues of their era, particularly the social pathologies born of immigrant slums and the increasing contrasts between affluence and poverty.

The entrepreneurs of business and industry, although they vehemently labelled Darwin's doctrine as blasphemous and denied man's kinship with apes, eagerly welcomed Spencer's suggestion that "survival of the fittest" was a principle applicable to society. Spencer's interpretation helped rationalize *laissez-faire* industrialism and bolstered faith in the automatic virtues of unfettered competition.

> As late as 1870 Herbert Spencer could affirm that the starvation of the idle, the exploitation of the weak by the strong, "are the decrees of a large, far-seeing benevolence. . . . Under the natural order of things, society is constantly excreting its unhealthy, imbecile, slow, vacillating, faithless members. . . ."[22]

Entrepreneurs embraced the social theories of Herbert Spencer more wholeheartedly than did the sociologists. The sociologists had reservations. As citizens in "the land of the free" they found Spencer's individualism more congenial than Comte's social *gestalt,* but they rejected Spencer's extreme *laissez-faire* doctrine in favor of Comte's belief in the usefulness of melioristic

---

* Durkheim's work includes: *The Elementary Forms of the Religious Life,* trans. Joseph W. Swain (New York: Free Press of Glencoe, Inc., 1947); *The Division of Labor in Society,* trans. George Simpson (New York: Free Press of Glencoe, Inc., 1949); *The Rules of Sociological Method,* trans. Sarah A. Soloway and John H. Mueller, ed. George E. G. Catlin (New York: Free Press of Glencoe, Inc., 1950); *Suicide,* trans. and ed. John A. Spaulding and George Simpson (New York: Free Press of Glencoe, Inc., 1951).

intervention. By this commitment alone did nineteenth century reformist sociologists initially arouse the suspicions of the men devoted to building the economy.

Sociology, however unwelcome some of its tenets might be, had come to stay. The University of Chicago, in the heart of the industrial midwest, established a Department of Sociology in 1893, and other universities added courses under the name of sociology later in the 1890's. Publication of the *American Journal of Sociology* began in 1896, and the American Sociological Society was organized in December, 1905.

From its genesis, sociological development in the United States has gone through three major phases, phases coinciding with historical events which profoundly affected society and the assumptions and methods of sociology. The first formative period ended with World War I; the intermediate period spanned the time between World War I and the Depression; and the recent period, beginning after the Depression, extends through World War II to the present.*

Formative Period (1893-1918)

Industrialization and urbanization were the significant social facts of the period, and the ethically oriented sociologists concerned themselves with the scientific study and amelioration of social problems. The stronghold of sociology was (and still is) in the universities.† The University of Chicago and Columbia University, both strategically located in urban-industrial areas, then dominated the field of sociology. In both universities, courses in sociological history, theory, and method were far outweighed by those concerned with crime, juvenile delinquency, gangs, ghettos, slums, suicide, family disorganization, and other pathologies of the deviant and the depressed. At Columbia, graduate students in a Family Organization course did what amounted to social service work with underprivileged families. Teaching and research in these formative years rested on four basic philosophical assumptions gleaned originally from Comte and Spencer: (1) Society goes through progressive stages of evolution towards a higher order, and social change is synonymous with progress towards that order. (2) Rational intervention based on positive knowledge can modify and accelerate the progress of society. (3) Society is an aggregate of individuals whose thoughts, feelings, and willed actions, though limited by environment, are the ultimate source of all that society is or does. (4) Laws of human behavior comparable to the laws governing physical and biological phenomena can be found through scientific method.

* Discussion of the development of sociology in the United States is adapted freely from Roscoe C. Hinckle, Jr. and Gisela J. Hinckle, *The Development of Modern Sociology* (Garden City, New York: Doubleday and Company, Inc., 1954).

† Today every major university in the United States recognizes sociology as one of the major disciplines, and in 1960 approximately 86 per cent of all Ph.D. sociologists worked in colleges and universities.

Middle Period (1918-1935)

World War I shocked the early sociologists into a realization that some of their assumptions were based on philosophical faith, not scientific fact. The violence and irrationality of war belonged, in theory, to an earlier period of social evolution, but now modern man had behaved in ways as primitive as his prehistoric ancestors. He had wrought misery and destruction, and sociologists could no longer assume that change as such was synonymous with progress toward a higher social order.

Disillusionment forced a shift in rationale. In their distrust of grand a priori assumptions, sociologists became increasingly concerned with making sociology more scientific. They reconsidered their methods, which had been subtly deductive, and began, as the natural scientists had done three centuries before, to slowly build new knowledge inductively. They turned away from reformism as such. They sought empirical data through case studies of individuals and groups, institutions and communities.* They gathered quantitative information and analyzed it statistically. They taught themselves to be objective and to guard against the predispositions of their own culture. And, finally, they realized that the complexity of human behavior indicated a multiplicity of causes—causes which they began to seek outside the limits of man's inherent nature.

During this intermediate period the mainstream of sociological theory was enriched, not only by Comte's successor in France, Émile Durkheim, but by the Austrian psychiatrist, Sigmund Freud (1856-1934); the German historian, political economist, and sociologist, Max Weber (1864-1920); and the Italian economist, Vilfredo Pareto (1848-1923).† Pareto contributed the concept of society as a system in equilibrium, and, with Freud, emphasized the nonrational aspects of human behavior. The super-ego defined by Freud was a built-in conscience—the *collective conscience* of Durkheim internalized or integrated into the structure of developing personality. Furthermore, Freud, through his discovery of unconscious motivation, helped explain some of man's irrational behavior. Weber analyzed all forms of group behavior in terms of individual *action* oriented towards the expectations of others, and

* In *The Polish Peasant in Europe and America* (Boston: Tochard G. Badger, 1918), William I. Thomas and Florian Znaniecki, with the use of letters, autobiographies, and case records, introduced the case study method to sociologists.

† The dominant influence has been Weber's, possibly because his theories are particularly congenial to American individualism. Most of Weber's writings have been translated and useful summaries appear in Talcott Parson, *The Structure of Social Action* (New York: Free Press of Glencoe, Inc., 1948), Chapters XIV through XVII. Pareto's *Mind and Society* appeared in a four-volume translation in 1935. A discussion of his work appears also in Parson's *The Structure of Social Action*, Chapters V, VI, and VII. For selections from the work of Freud, see A. A. Brill, *The Basic Writings of Sigmund Freud* (New York: Modern Library, Inc., 1938). For a summary of the relationship of sociology to psychoanalysis, see George Simpson, *Man in Society* (New York: Doubleday & Company, Inc., 1954), pp. 39-44.

developed the methodological principle of *ideal types,* useful in analyzing unique historical persons or events and in isolating common or recurrent variables present in social situations or historical events. (Modern capitalism as an ideal type, for example, is characterized by the religious ethic of Protestantism.) Weber also argued for greater precision in the social sciences through the mathematical methods used in natural science.

The work of Pareto, Freud, and Weber widened the perspective of American sociologists and contributed to the development of specialized fields.* Awareness of the irrational and subconscious forces in human nature led to a search through social psychology for the variables involved in the development of individual personality and in the adjustment or maladjustment of the individual to society. Knowledge that personality is shaped more by environment than by heredity, and that internal and external forces impinging on the individual are variables determining human action, now placed crime, delinquency, and other deviant behavior in the context of community sociology.† And, finally, as urbanization and industrialization continued to transform the environment and make established norms of behavior obsolete, change itself, as well as the *stresses* in society and in the individual produced by it, became sociological subject matter. A fast accumulating technological-material culture had outpaced the slowly adapting nonmaterial culture expressed through government, family, education, religion, and philosophy. This differential rate of change or *culture lag* ‡ sociologists perceived as a possible explanation of some problems of personal and social disintegration.

Recent Period (1935–Present)

In the intermediate period, sociology achieved scientific respectability and a widened base. Now as one of the family of behavioral sciences, sociology is in a secure enough position to cooperate with other sciences in multi-discipline projects, to reconsider its professional relationship to social problems and social policy, and to return to theory-making as a guide for the interpretation and systematization of a growing body of facts.§

* Through the work of Robert Ezra Park in sociology of the community, of William F. Ogburn in social and cultural change, and of John Dewey, George Herbert Mead, and William I. Thomas in social psychology, the Department of Sociology at the University of Chicago won unrivaled prominence in these three specialized fields.

† *Gestalt* psychology, founded by Max Wertheimer (1880-1943), and its further development as Field Theory by the social psychologist Kurt Lewin (1890-1947), contributed to the sociologist's growing awareness that the structure of the psychological field influenced behavior. *Middletown: A Study in American Culture* (1929), by Robert S. and Helen M. Lynd, was the first sociological research to approach the various facets of life in a total community as parts of a functioning social complex and to try to do so as objectively as an anthropologist would a primitive village.

‡ The concept of *culture lag* was first formulated by William F. Ogburn in *Social Change,* 1922.

§ Contemporary sociology has a central core of theoretical concepts which orients the various sociological specialties to the basic science. The propositions and implications of the various theoretical positions in sociology are a topic of both academic and practical im-

> The systematic study of human behavior, at present, is in some respects much like mathematics before Euclid. There was certainly considerable mathematical knowledge at that time, as is revealed in the astonishing feats of Egyptian engineers in building the pyramids. But geometry consisted of a collection of isolated facts, useful empirical rules for surveying and construction. By introducing precision into definitions, relating the terms into propositions, and deducing propositions from one another, Euclid transformed this existing information into a systematic body of knowledge. Similarly, there is today much accumulated knowledge about human behavior, but it has not yet been adequately systematized.[23]

Sociology is admittedly a young discipline, necessarily intent on continuing its own development as a pure science. But even now, sociologists trained in the objective observation of human behavior and in the theoretical concepts which help make that behavior comprehensible, are in a position to cooperate with other behavioral scientists in both basic research and professional practice. At Harvard University a new department of social relations, founded in 1946 under the chairmanship of Talcott Parsons, united sociology with anthropology and clinical psychology.* In *Towards a General Theory of Action,*† scientists in these fields worked together to set up basic principles on which they could agree. "It was an attempt to find a common ground among the three sciences, to thrash out a series of working concepts and a teminology based on the proposition 'action is the basic unit with which social science deals.' "[24]

At the Center for Advanced Study in the Behavioral Sciences in Palo Alto, California, fifty scholars representing history, anthropology, psychology, psychiatry, mathematics, economics, law, political science, zoology, philosophy, and sociology seek to apply scientific methods to an understanding of what men do and how and why they do it. Sociologists there are collaborating in such studies as the *Historical Absence of Anti-Semitism in Sweden,* the *Regulation of Social Conflict,* and the *Pattern of Social Change in Modern Civilizations.*

In nonacademic practice, sociologists, acting on the basis of the best knowledge now available, collaborate with other professional practitioners in behavioral science. The Great Depression of the 1930's and World War II made thoughtful men keenly aware of the urgent need for the knowledge sought by behavioral scientists.

"Today," said President Franklin D. Roosevelt, "we are faced with the pre-eminent fact that if civilization is to survive, we must cultivate the science

---

portance. For an analysis of the work of seven prominent American theorists, see Charles P. and Zona K. Loomis, *Modern Social Theories* (Princeton, New Jersey: D. Van Nostrand Company, Inc., 1961).

* The trend towards integration of social sciences began at Yale in 1929 with the establishment of the Yale Institute of Human Relations.

† Talcott Parsons and Edward A. Shils, eds., *Towards a General Theory of Action* (Cambridge: Harvard University Press, 1951).

of human relationships." Implicit in his statement was the assumption that the knowledge gained would be used. Sociologists were forcibly turned from their preoccupation with building the scientific core of their discipline to an involvement in the affairs of society.

> During the years of the two great crises sociologists were frequently employed by the Federal government. Throughout the depression years sociologists joined the staff of the Works Progress Administration, the Department of Agriculture, the TVA, the National Resources Committee, and other federal, state, and local agencies concerned with practical problems of social welfare. With the war, sociologists accepted commissions in the armed forces, participated in training programs for servicemen, became consultants or regular personnel for OSS, OPA, the Department of State, and other federal agencies.[25]

Sociology emerged from the war years with the added status accorded a "useful" science, and some sociologists have either abandoned basic research and teaching or combined it with professional practice.*

> An important and rapidly expanding bridge between nonacademic and academic employment is the consultant role in various nonacademic organizations. This ranges from a relatively individualized service to particular clients to a considerable amount of "conferring" where groups of professionals, often interdisciplinary in composition, are called on to help clarify a practical problem area.[26]

Sociologists have established themselves with the Federal Bureau of the Census, the Department of Agriculture, and the National Institutes of Health. They collaborate with psychiatrists, psychologists, anthropologists, and social workers in State and local social service and health agencies. They are active workers and consultants in business and public administration, industrial relations, marketing, and opinion and attitude surveys. More recently, because of the rapid expansion and improvement of education (inspired in the United States by the scientific successes of the Soviet Union) and the problems of law—particularly international law in a world society—sociologists as associated specialists are now entering these two fields.

"A 'sociological era' has begun to emerge, following an 'economic' and, more recently, a 'psychological' era." [27] The term *sociology* is known. Laymen are identifying sociologists as "experts" to be consulted on public issues; and sociologists themselves, in recognition of their status and the practical implications of their research, are deeply concerned not only with basic research but with the relationship of sociology as a science to a whole range of applied professions.

> . . . it seems likely that the problems facing our profession in the coming years will center on the temptations and complications which set in with relative though incomplete success. Sociology is becoming "important." Let us hope

* A 1952 survey showed some 30 per cent of sociologists with Master's degrees and 14 per cent of those with Ph.D. degrees in nonacademic work.

that this accomplishment will not divert us from the main task (development of its discipline and the training of its successors) and at the same time that we take due account of the responsibilities and opportunities presented by our growing involvement in the larger social setting. Primary concentration on the science itself is not incompatible with good citizenship in the scientific community and in the general society. The great challenge is to maintain the proper balances.[28]

Sociology, in slightly more than a century, has established itself as not only an important science, but also, because it impinges on the lives and thoughts of people, a controversial one. Although the lines between it and other behavioral sciences (particularly psychology and anthropology) are not yet sharply drawn, current multi-discipline research and practice is providing conditions under which the nature of each participating science can be more clearly defined. What may eventually evolve is a many-sided but unified *science of man*—better able than any single discipline to contribute to the social order in the making.

Sociological Perspective

Sociology, strictly defined, is the science of society—the study of the structure and hierarchy of groups through which men interact, and of the social processes such as competition and cooperation which characterize interaction. Out of society emerges culture, the material and nonmaterial product of interaction. Out of both society and culture emerges man, the *human social* being, as distinguished from *Homo sapiens*, the *biological* being. Sociology, broadly perceived, is concerned with *man, culture,* and *society* in interaction, and with the variations of social order or disorder generated by the interaction.

Through knowledge of *man*—of his common characteristics as a biological being and his unique development through learning into a human, social being—we can understand him as a creature of culture. As man interacts in society with other men, he develops systems of communication, tools, techniques, norms of behavior, and other ways and means of maintaining, enhancing, and perpetuating himself and his social group. We understand *culture* to be the creature, or creation, of man. Through identifying the social processes which come to characterize interaction and analyzing the structure of the groups in and through which man interacts, we understand *society* to be an agent of man. Provided with an understanding of man, culture, and society, we can move in the direction of a lifetime goal: *sociological perspective.**

Sociological perspective grows out of sociological facts and the spectrum

* We use this term in the sense C. Wright Mills uses the term *sociological imagination*. C. Wright Mills, *The Sociological Imagination* (New York: Oxford University Press, Inc., 1959).

of their relationships, but it is essentially an orientation—a philosophical orientation—which enables an individual to locate himself in place and time and to grasp what goes on within himself, within his personal social milieu, and within world society.

> By its use men whose mentalities have swept only a series of limited orbits often come to feel as if suddenly awakened in a house with which they had only supposed themselves to be familiar. Correctly or incorrectly, they often come to feel that they can now provide themselves with adequate summations, cohesive assessments, comprehensive orientations. Older decisions that once appeared sound now seem to them products of a mind unaccountably dense. Their capacity for astonishment is made lively again. They acquire a new way of thinking; they experience a transvaluation of values: in a word, by their reflection and by their sensibility, they realize the cultural meaning of the social sciences.[29]

Sociological perspective is a way of relating personal biography to the moving stream of history and becoming aware of the many individual actions which influence larger social issues. It is towards the growth of such perspective that we direct this sociological appraisal of *Man Among Men.*

Notes

1. Frederick J. Teggart, *Theory and Processes of History* (Berkeley: University of California Press, 1941), p. 160.
2. C. Wright Mills, *The Sociological Imagination* (New York: Oxford University Press, Inc., 1959), p. 8.
3. John H. Randall, Jr., *The Making of the Modern Mind* (Boston: Houghton Mifflin Company, 1926), p. 233.
4. From the text of Galileo's recantation, in Giorgio de Santillana, *The Crime of Galileo* (Chicago: University of Chicago Press, 1955), p. 312.
5. Tamotsu Shibutani, *Society and Personality* (Englewood Cliffs, N.J.: Prentice-Hall, Inc., 1961), p. 116.
6. Lincoln Barnett, *The Universe and Dr. Einstein* (New York: The New American Library, 1952), p. 17.
7. Marcel Proust, *Remembrance of Things Past,* in Bernard Berelson and Gary A. Steiner, *Human Behavior* (New York: Harcourt, Brace & World, Inc., 1964), p. 556.
8. Barnett, *The Universe and Dr. Einstein,* pp. 43-44.
9. Barnett, *op. cit.,* p. 62.
10. Barnett, *op. cit.,* p. 63.
11. B. F. Skinner, "'Superstition' in the Pigeon," *Journal of Experimental Psychology,* Vol. 38, 1948, pp. 168-172.
12. Sir James G. Frazer, *The Golden Bough,* abridged edition (New York: The Macmillan Company, 1939), pp. 13 and 42.
13. Barnett, *op. cit.,* p. 39.
14. Barnett, *op. cit.,* p. 14.
15. Barnett, *op. cit.,* p. 63.
16. Bernard Berelson and Gary A. Steiner, *Human Behavior* (New York: Harcourt, Brace & World, Inc., 1964), p. 17.
17. Bertold Brecht, *Galileo,* scene 8. Actor's Workshop Production, San Francisco, 1963, Herbert Blau, Director.
18. Berelson and Steiner, *Human Behavior,* p. 19.
19. Joel H. Hildebrand, "How Scientists Work and Think," Office of Naval Research, *Research and Reviews,* 1956, p. 34.
20. Berelson and Steiner, *Human Behavior,* p. 11.
21. Herbert Spencer, quoted in H. R. Hays, *From Ape to Angel* (New York: Alfred A. Knopf, Inc., 1958), p. 296.
22. Stuart Chase, *The Proper Study of Mankind* (New York: Harper & Row, Publishers, 1948), p. 54.
23. Tamotsu Shibutani, *Society and Personality,* p. 10.
24. H. R. Hays, *From Ape to Angel,* p. 398.
25. Roscoe C. Hinckle, Jr., and Gisela J. Hinckle, *The Development of Modern Sociology* (Garden City, New York: Doubleday and Company, Inc., 1954), p. 44.
26. Talcott Parsons, "Some Problems Confronting Sociology as a Profession," in *Sociology, The Progress of a Decade,* Seymour Martin Lipset and Neil J. Smelser, eds. (Englewood Cliffs, N.J.: Prentice-Hall, Inc., 1961), p. 24.
27. Parsons, *op. cit.,* p. 22.
28. Parsons, *op. cit.,* p. 30.
29. C. Wright Mills, *The Sociological Imagination,* p. 7.

Custom, then, is the great guide of human life.

DAVID HUME (1711-1776)

ii

Culture—Creature of Man

We first make our habits,

and then our habits make us.

JOHN DRYDEN (1631-1700)

3

Heritage of Habits

CULTURE, says Emily Post, is correctly pronounced "culcha." You can have more of it or less of it. If you have more of it, you know about Arnold Toynbee, Christopher Fry, Li Po, James Joyce, Franz Kafka, Béla Bartók, Morris Graves, C. P. Snow, and other "important people" in the arts and humanities. You have "good taste" and "good manners." You move skillfully within the labyrinths of polite and learned society. You know when to come and go, when to stand or sit, which fork to use, and how to say convincingly that it's been a perfect party. Books of etiquette are written for the person striving to be cultured, and you can "improve yourself" or "get culture" by studying art, literature, music, or philosophy.

"Culcha" is a British pronunciation—a legacy from the early settlers who were predominantly British and whose descendents established themselves in the new country and gained authority through seniority. "*Culcha*" and *culture,* however, are not the same thing. "*Culcha*" is a distinguishing mark of class position or pretension or refinement. Culture is a product of group history, a social heritage, as compelling as is biological heritage. Culture makes and modifies our physical and psychological environment, and thereby defines "reality" as we perceive it. Subtly, the culture of our group molds our feelings, our thoughts, our actions. We identify with it so completely that we cannot imagine what we would be without it. We are as sustained and engulfed by culture as fish are by the

WERNER BISCHOFF

sea. To be aware of the water which sustains him, a fish has to encounter the contrasting medium of air. Comparably, to be aware of culture, a man first has to encounter the contrasting culture of other societies.

CULTURE DISCOVERED

Men have been crossing cultural boundaries for centuries, but what early travelers perceived was different people, not different cultures.

The Babylonians under the reign of Hammurabi (circa 1955-1913 B.C.) were interested enough in the Summerians to collect their artifacts. Herodotus (fifth-century B.C. Greek explorer and historian) described alien Mediterranean people to the folks back home. (The barbaric Egyptians, he noted, retired into the privacy of their homes to perform toilet functions instead of using the streets as did civilized Greeks.) Chinese scholars of the Han dynasty (206 B.C. to 220 A.D.) studied a neighboring light-eyed tribe. Tacitus (Roman historian, circa 55-117 A.D.) wrote a treatise on the Germans. Fifteenth-century explorers were interested in comparing strange lands and strange people with their own familiar world.

In the following centuries, as Europeans went farther and farther afield to trade, to conquer, to colonize, and to convert, they brought back more information and misinformation. Too often missionaries were merely shocked at natives whose deities differed from their own, and others only chose to tell what would make a good story for a credulous home-town audience.

Louis, Comte de Bougainville (1729-1811), in his attempts to found colonies for France, encountered the Patagonians. He coached them to shout "*Vive le roi,*" and noted that men refused wine and accepted tobacco and that women plucked their eyebrows and permitted the friendly French sailors to fondle their breasts. He sailed on to Tahiti where he and his men "were greatly affected by the splendid proportions of the women." [1] James Cook (1728-1779), a less sanguine British navigator and explorer who followed the French to the South Seas, was not so impressed with the Tahitians. The women, he reported with an indignation appropriate to an Englishman's sense of the sacredness of private property, had a propensity to steal. Furthermore, "neither the music nor the dancing was calculated to please a European." [2] In the same century white men came to America. Here they encountered a rich indigenous culture, but the typical pioneer and prospector recognized no virtues in the Indian way of life. When they could not enslave the Indian and put him to work in the mines and on the plantations, they "classed him as a nuisance in the same general category as the panther and the grizzly." [3] Not until he was no longer a threat to expansion and industrialization did the white man romanticize the Indian and pair him with the cowboy in stories of the West.

The concept of *culture* as a significant variable in determining human behavior came as an important intellectual discovery in the nineteenth century. Scientists and philosophers in the two preceding centuries had prepared the way. In the seventeenth century Galileo demonstrated the ultility and validity of inductive logic and emphasized the importance of looking objectively at the world. In the eighteenth century, rationalists—particularly Voltaire (1694-1778)—anti-rationalists—particularly Jean Jacques Rousseau (1712-1778), and skeptics—particularly David Hume (1711-1776)—helped dispel the superstitions and illogical assumptions which still clouded the Western world and gave the perspective needed by man to perceive himself and his society more objectively. The emerging behavioral sciences were part of a new *Age of Enlightenment* * and drew strength from its philosophical assumptions: (1) Reason is the only infallible guide to wisdom. (2) Universal laws govern the order of nature. (3) Man is not marred by original sin; he and his society would be perfect were he free to follow reason and instinct. (4) The simplest and most natural social structure, that of the "noble savage," is preferable to that of civilized societies with their outworn conventions.[4] With such ideas pervading the intellectual environment, someone, sooner or later, was certain to discover *culture*.

Today, as a consequence of the discovery of *culture* and its significance we have a healthy respect for other cultures, and for other people. When a treasure of ancient Indian cave paintings was found in a remote Lower California canyon in 1962, the leader in charge of the expedition told his men:

> These people may be poor according to our standards but they are actually rich. They have everything they want within reason. They live a peaceful existence.
>
> They don't have to inhale smog and they aren't bothered by confiscatory taxes. They have good health without the aid of biotics, capsules or vitamins. They are free of nerve strain and they have a tolerant regard for each other and an infinite capacity for friendship.
>
> Treating these people with courtesy will do a great deal to help the expedition. Trying to order them around to take advantage of their generosity or to patronize them can be fatal.[5]

Early sociologists were primarily concerned with society—its structure and processes. It was a pioneer anthropologist, Edward Burnett Tyler (1832-1917), who first used the English word *culture* in the sense of the material and nonmaterial achievements of man, and contributed the still widely cited definition: *Culture is that complex whole which includes knowledge, belief, art, morals, law, custom, and any other capabilities and habits acquired by man as a member of society*. Anthropologists were as aware as the sociologists of the problem of scientific objectivity and recognized that "the value we attribute to our own civilization is due to the fact that we participate in this civilization and that it has been controlling all our actions from the time of our birth." [6]

---

* The Age of Enlightenment began in England in the late seventeenth century and spread to other countries, including the United States.

Culture as a concept and as an area of study is now claimed by both sociology and anthropology. Although sociology is theoretically still the study of society, and anthropology the study of culture, sociologists recognize the significance of *culture* for their discipline, just as anthropologists, especially social anthropologists, recognize the significance of *society* for theirs.

> Ever since man left his inarticulate animal ancestry behind him, he has been living in groups varying in size from the family to the village or tribe, to the nation or federation of states. These groups, at every level, have developed shared beliefs and customs. Out of such communal heritage, civilizations and cultures have emerged.[7]

Society is made up of individuals—of individuals acting in relationship to each other in positions defined by the structure of the group and through processes characteristic of the group. Groups interact with other groups and with individuals in the larger total society. Culture distinguishes the modes of living of one group from those of another. A society can exist without a culture, but a culture cannot exist without a society. One colony of ants, one herd of cows, one troupe of baboons is essentially like another. They have no culture, but they are societies. Culture develops out of human society, and, in turn, modifies that society; it modifies both the conditions under which social interaction takes place and the action itself.

COMPONENTS OF CULTURE

Once culture was discovered and defined, the next step in understanding the confusing and seemingly endless cultural diversity was to abstract common cultural components as foci for comparative studies. The components identified and now commonly used by anthropologists and sociologists provide at least a working basis. The *material means* and the *nonmaterial* ways * by which a society maintains, perpetuates, and enhances itself include individual *culture traits, culture complexes* (relationships of interdependent traits), *behavior patterns* (folkways, mores, taboos, and laws), and the *primary institutions* which provide a structure in and through which culture complexes and behavior patterns function.

Culture Traits

Any single aspect of a culture, material or nonmaterial, is a culture *trait.* Umbrellas, voodoo dolls, frozen spinach, cyclotrons, ready-mix cake flour, belt buckles, tranquilizing pills, juke boxes, bongo drums, feather pillows, ball-

* The distinction between material and nonmaterial culture is originally an anthropological one. Some sociologists limit the meaning of culture to "a series of integrated patterns for behavior developed from mass habits." [8] This definition excludes material means.

point pens, boomerangs . . . shoes and ships and sealing wax . . . are all material traits. Every physical object in the environment made or modified by man and commonly used by a society is a cultural *object* and part of material culture.

A word, a wolf whistle, a wink, a kiss, a thumb of the nose, a raspberry, a curtsey, a handshake, a driver's signal, a prayer, an algebraic formula, the right to vote, a traffic law – any *fact, technique, idea, expressive symbol, value* or other emotional or cognitive communication common to the society is part of nonmaterial culture. Culture modifies society insofar as the reciprocal and interdependent actions of individuals and groups within a society are shaped and colored by the traits available to and sanctioned by those individuals and groups. *Society is made up of individuals; culture is made up of traits.* Out of context, however, individual traits are either ambiguous or relatively meaningless. Culture traits are understood in the context of culture complexes, behavior patterns, and institutions.

Culture Complexes

Culture traits have specific meaning and significance for the society only in relationship to each other.

> A culture consists of elements or single traits, but the significance of a culture is less in its inventory of traits than the manner of integration of the traits. It is theoretically possible for two societies to possess identical inventories of culture elements, and yet so to arrange the relationships of these elements to each other that the complexes within the two cultures and the total forms of the two cultures will be quite unlike.[9]

Various traits can serve the same purpose; if one must write on a wall, it can be done with a pen, pencil, crayon, lipstick, or piece of charcoal. And the same trait can serve various purposes: chalk, in relationship to a teacher, an eraser, a blackboard, and a written language serves one purpose. It serves quite different purposes in relationship to a small boy and a sling shot or to a pregnant woman with a calcium deficiency. The use or meaning of any object or act depends upon its relationship to other objects and acts.

A meaningful, functioning relationship of interdependent traits is a *culture complex.* What is the significance of the following culture traits: a 12-volt battery . . . an inner tube . . . a rear-view mirror . . . a traffic law . . . a driver's license . . . a gas pump . . . a boulevard stop sign . . . a key . . . a drive-in movie? These individual traits take on specific meaning only when they are perceived as part of a culture complex. In this instance, the automobile *complex* includes not just the automobile, but the production and service industries such as steel, oil, and rubber without which automobiles could not be produced or used. It includes the highway systems, much of the police force, and all of the drive-in services: restaurants, theatres, banks, post offices, motels, marriage bureaus in Nevada, and palmistry stands in California. Even courtship practices are a part of the complex. Some babies are conceived in a mobile bedroom. In fact, "the auto has become the family's jewel, escutcheon, conveyor, entertainer, protector, potential destroyer, and sometimes, it seems, its most important member." [10] In 1958 a total of 10,314,073 people, one sixth of all the workers in the United States, were employed in highway transport industries and owed their jobs to the automobile.

Behavior Patterns

A culture tends to "grow like Topsy"; it is not consciously planned. Man is both an inventor and a borrower. One culture borrows and modifies what another has invented. Various traits come to serve the same purpose; and various purposes may be served by the same trait. Especially in complex cultures inconsistencies and contradictions abound. Yet out of continued social interaction and the confusion of many ways and means, a consensus of what is "right" or expected gradually emerged. The natural environment, the material culture, and historical circumstances combine to set the stage for social action, and out of social action develop *norms* or patterns * of behavior.

Most behavior patterns had a functional origin in psychological or physical necessity: certain ways were more expedient, more efficient, more satisfying to the individual, the group, or the gods. However, even as conditions change, behavior patterns once established tend to persist, their form fixed and made inflexible by habit. The patterns remain though their functions may change. *Some patterns persist as mere ritual.* There is no longer danger from runaway horses on Broadway, but it is still the impulse of "courteous" men when escorting a woman to walk on the curb side of the pavement. *Some patterns are useful in the sense that recipes are useful.* They provide easy, ready-made answers, expedient social formulas to spare one time and effort. Does an invitation to a wedding reception call for a gift to the bride? Look in Emily Post. *Some patterns safeguard the individual.* Traffic can be regulated and lives protected if *all* cars drive on the left side of the road *or* on the right side. The only prerequisite is knowing the pattern and acting accordingly. (An acquaintance of ours, brought up in New York, was buried in London, because he looked first to his left as he stepped off the curb into the street. His action, appropriate to crossing any street in the United States, was fatal in England where cars drive on the "wrong" side of the road.) *Some patterns unite the group.* Refuse to stand at an American Legion meeting when the Star Spangled Banner is played. You could get anything from a hard nudge to a beating.

* *Pattern* sometimes refers to the dominant character which pervades a culture, and it is so used by the anthropologist Ruth Benedict in *Patterns of Culture,* 1934. More commonly, however, pattern means the regularities and agreements within a culture which form a consensus of behavior or belief.

In every culture, patterned behavior, as it originates and persists, has varying powers of persuasion and coercion depending on the function it serves. In a discussion of American Neighborhood Customs, Emily Post writes: "Aside from the fixed rules for speech and manner and deportment, which are the same for all well-bred persons, people living in this neighborhood or that follow the customs of the locality in which they live. In other words to *do exactly as your neighbors do* is the only sensible rule." [11] To this admonition, one might or might not turn a deaf ear. The pressures to which any particular individual responds depends on the nature of the group exerting pressure, how closely the individual identifies with the group, and how vital the behavior pattern is to the survival of the group. Behavior patterns to which a majority of individuals accede have ascending importance as the *folkways, mores, taboos* and *laws* of nonmaterial culture.

Folkways

"Folkways" * are the accepted or expected ways of performing the nearly infinite number of minor rituals of normal social living. They emerge gradually out of the collective action of generations of anonymous people without the benefit of deliberate rational thought. Although folkways evolve unwittingly and can rarely be logically defended or explained, they exert enough pressure to give us a comfortable sense of "belonging" if we conform to them and an uncomfortable sense of awkwardness if we don't. We would be embarrassed, for example, to be caught eating peas with a spoon, even though a spoon is obviously a more efficient scoop than a fork. We habitually attack a beef steak with a zig-zagging exchange of knife and fork from left to right hands and feel that the more direct European system of keeping the fork in the left hand and cutting and pushing with the knife is a bit uncouth. However, penalty for violation of folkways is mild, and the worst that happens is that the offender is shunned or ridiculed or held in mild contempt.

FOLKWAYS ARE NOT UNIFORM. The amount of pressure exerted by any particular folkway varies within a society according to sex, region, class, national background, and religious affiliation. In the United States, for example, *women are permitted a greater degree of public demonstrations of affection for members of their own sex than are males.* Men limit physical contact to shaking hands and slapping each other on the back. Even the best of friends will not kiss each other, and holding hand is unthinkable. In Russia, however, men do embrace and kiss full on the mouth, with no implications beyond that of friendship, and they do walk down the street holding hands. *Formality of dress and manners vary geographically.* People in Boston tend to be formal; people in

* Term coined by William Graham Summer (1840-1910), American sociologist and educator.

Los Angeles tend to be informal; men are more likely to wear sport shirts on Wilshire Boulevard than on Beacon Street. And *the greater the psychological distance between an individual and a cultural group the less he feels compelled to conform to its patterns.* A lower-class person who identifies with his own sub-culture may ignore or actively resist conforming to the speech or manners or dress of the dominant middle class. An individual belonging to a minority group which maintains its own ethnic identity—such as the Chinese, Japanese, or Mexicans in California—tends to conform to the folkways of his own culture and to be *relatively* immune to outside pressures. A member of the strict Amish sect of Pennsylvania * is most removed of all from the dominant patterns of our culture. He even refuses to own an automobile. Only as an individual renounces loyalty to groups with variant norms and seeks to identify with the larger community does he become significantly responsive to the behavior patterns of that community.

FOLKWAYS ARE NOT FIXED. They respond to changes in the total culture. In the nineteenth century, for example, to use first names in public was bad form. A well-bred wife called her husband "Mister" and spoke of him to others as Mister. In the twentieth century such formality would seem absurd. Gentlemen once unquestionably gave their seats to ladies on public conveyances. Today, either the number of gentlemen and ladies has declined, or the folkway is disappearing; for the courtesy is observed with increasing rarity.†

> I was on the A train, riding up to 168th Street. . . . There were no seats to be had, but I had a good grip on the pole at the end of one of the seats. . . . All of a sudden I felt a tap on my arm . . . and there was a man beginning to stand up. . . . "Would you like to sit down?" he said. Well, I said the first thing that came into my head, I was so surprised and pleased to be offered a seat in the subway. "Oh, thank you very much," I said, "But I am getting out at the next station." He sat back and that was that, but I felt all set up and thought what a nice man he must be . . . and then all of a sudden I realized that I wasn't getting out at the next station at all but the one *after* that, and I felt perfectly terrible. I decided to get out at the next station anyway, but then I thought, if I get out at the next station and wait round for the next train I'll miss my bus, and they only go every hour, and that will be perfectly silly. So I decided to brazen it out as best I could, and when the train was slowing up at the next station I stared at the man until I caught his eye, and then I said, "I just remembered this isn't my station after all." Then I thought he would think I was asking him to stand up and give his seat, so I said, "But I *still* don't want to sit down because I'm getting off at the *next* station" . . . but just as the train was shutting its doors I peered out and there it was 168th Street. "Oh dear!" I said, "That *was* my station and now I *have* missed the bus!" . . . I felt chagrined beyond belief and extremely foolish, and I looked down, and the man who had offered me his seat was partly looking at me . . . I hesitate

---

* Chapter 4.

† George Bernard Shaw once observed that women should "stand up" for their rights.

to think how he must have regretted offering me his seat. Sometimes it is very hard to know the right thing to do.[12]

Mores

Mores,* like folkways, evolve gradually without plan or foresight or quasi-legislative action, but they rank higher than folkways in that they define beliefs and behavior more crucial to the identity and survival of the group. They give vigor and support to sanctioned patterns. Mores protect and perpetuate the group, and their violation is interpreted by the group—or representatives of the group—as dangerous. Some mores, such as patriotism, filial piety, marital fidelity, and respect for life and property, are tenacious and abiding. Only great social upheavals can change them, and even then only at the cost of tearing the heart and meaning out of the lives of those who love the old ways.

> Daizo Nanigashi survived World War II. He was a brilliant, rebellious student, eager to do graduate work in Western philosophy at Cambridge, willing to break with pre-war tradition and make Japan a modern country. His parents survived the war, too, but afterwards they killed themselves, and in killing themselves, they killed all that Daizo was or hoped to be. Before they died they wrote a bitter letter to him and mailed copies to the priest at the family shrine, to their relatives, and to their friends. In the letter they said not that they were old and tired and heartbroken, not that they had sold, one by one, all the family treasures left from the bombing-fire which destroyed their Tokyo home, not that they who had been proud and rich were now destitute and hungry. No, they told him they had killed themselves because he, Daizo, was ungrateful, because he hadn't accepted as a wife any of the girls they had chosen for him, because he wanted to go to that English university, because he didn't care what happened to the family name. Now he would owe nothing to anyone in the world, he would be free to go and be a foreigner. But Daizo couldn't go. His parents shamed him into a complete moral collapse by evoking the mores of the culture he had once lightheartedly mocked.
>
> Daizo could not live in a new culture nor could he believe in the old. He went to Naniwara where the Nanigashi family had an ancient home, a once splendid sixteenth- or early seventeenth-century house with a garden which had been famous for its all-white blossoms of azalea, iris, camelias, wild cherry, and magnolias. Now the garden was overrun with dwarf bamboo and the house was miserably shabby. Here, with no one but an old maid servant to wait on him, Daizo secluded himself, a broken man amid the decaying remnants of his family and his culture.[13]

Other less fundamental mores may change without tragedy but not without pain. Consider the dismay of the nineteenth-century Southern matron whose daughter dared violate the mores of her social group by going to the theatre in Mobile, Alabama.

---

* *Mores* is the Latin word for custom. From it we derive the word *moral.*

Woodland Falls, Ala.
February 22, 1866

My dearest Margaret:

It distresses me to think you have committed the great and double sin, of deserting the house of God, and going to the house of the Devil, that school of vulgarity, profanity, and immodesty, the theatre. What a return for God's mercy to you in sparing your father, and both your brothers. After four years of desolating war we were permitted *all to meet, under circumstances of mercy, beneath our own roof.* How different it might have been! Had I died last winter, worthless as I am, home would not have seemed like home to any of you. Had your father been killed at Selma, or either, or both the boys, fallen in battle, or all three perished, how desolate you would have felt! This agony you have been spared. Not a limb did one of them lose. What thank offering have you made to God for these great and countless lesser blessings?

With all the madness of a maniac you have rushed after the phantom pleasure, until you have pursued it into the very gate of Hell. You have deliberately absented yourself from the house of God, saying by your acts that He to whom you owe your whole heart, with the perfect consecration of all your faculties to His service, shall not even have the benefit of your example in turning away your feet from the theatre; that you will give it to the Devil; and use your influence over your young cousins to carry them along with you in the broad road to perdition.

It is no light thing you have done, and I tremble to think what may be the consequences. May God, in mercy, lead you to repentance, and grant you that forgiveness, which you refuse to your *enemies.* When ever tempted to speak against the Yankees, just stop, and ask yourself, if you have not acted as meanly, as perfidiously to God the Infinitely Great, and Good? Could I have had any idea you would have done so, I would not have permitted you to have gone to Mobile one step. I hope and pray, if you ever marry, your husband will have the good sense, the Christian firmness, to hold you back from doing so wickedly. Apart from the inconsistency of a professing Christian going to such a place, common decency ought to keep a modest woman from the theatre. If you have *any respect* for my feelings, while living or my memory when dead, *never* again enter that school of iniquity.

Keep this letter, and read it over whenever you go where there is a theatre. May God control you by a *higher motive,* still never forget your mother's expressed wish, and teach it to your children, should you have any. Were I a Christian man, I would not marry a woman who frequented the theatre. May God keep all my sons from the curse of having such a wife.[14]

Outraged response to action which does not conform to group expectations—this is the substance and the strength of mores. Mores change only in the face of anxiety-ridden resistance. New imperatives may invalidate and erode old mores, but the ultimate collapse takes time. Those who dare defy ruling mores risk grave penalties: shame, assault, banishment, death. *Mores, not might, make right.*

> It is difficult for the modern man to realize that, in the earlier period, individuality did not exist; that the unit was not the single life, but the group; and that this was the embodiment of a relatively fixed system, from which escape was normally impossible. So completely was the individual subordinated to the community that art was just the repetition of tribal designs, literature the repetition of tribal songs, and religion the repetition of tribal rites.[15]

As a member of society, man is not free. Even today, culture precedes the individual and one has available only the choices his culture provides. We tend to conform to the dominant mores without seriously considering any other course of action. We marry one spouse—at least, one at a time. We nurture our children, protect them, and send them to school. We attain and maintain our property, earn an honest living, respect the rights and property of others, and remain loyal citizens. Mores are social injunctions to which people in good conscience respond. However, if we study folkways and mores objectively, we are made aware that "the social animal is capable of the most fantastic beliefs, the most shocking and cruel activities, and subscribes to the most insane prohibitions, all of which, in one part of the world or another, are solemnly justified by tradition and ritual." [16]

Taboos

Mores define "right" and "rights"; taboos define "wrong" and "wrongs." In primitive cultures, taboos are a form of negative magic. The anthropological scholar, Sir James Frazer, in *The Golden Bough* (an encyclopedic survey of primitive life) lists forty-five separate index entries under *taboos,* including those "on parents of twins . . . on intercourse with strangers, on eating and drinking, on showing the face, on quitting the house, . . . on blood, on hair, on spittle, on knots and rings, on words. . . ." [17] One does not, for example, tell the name of the king lest knowledge of it enable someone to do him harm. Nor does one name the gods for fear other gods or men try to use or usurp the power. (We, too, deny the casual use of sacred names. Small boys who violated the taboo have had their mouths washed out with soap, as if sacred words resting lightly on the tongue would foul it.) In "advanced" cultures none but trivial taboos such as walking under a ladder or breaking a mirror are associated with magic. The important taboos are traditional prohibitions which single out particularly offensive or dangerous violations of the mores for special emphasis. The most significant taboos of all are in the areas of sex and food.

Incest, for example is an almost universal taboo. In the United States, the greatest insult one male can hurl at another is to accuse him of having sex relations with his mother. The force of this taboo in Western culture is historic; it is the crime around which the Greek dramatist Sophocles (525–456 B.C.) centered the tragedy of *Oedipus Rex.* Most contemporary cultures, including the United States, prohibit marriage within the immediate family. However, incest is *culturally* defined. The Veddas of Ceylon accept a brother's marriage to a younger sister but consider his marriage to an older sister or aunt incestuous. Among the ancient Incas and the ancient Egyptians brother-sister marriages were common. In fact, Cleopatra (69–30 B.C.) came from a long line of brother-sister marriages; and she, in turn, married her brother and had children by him. In the royal families of Siam, Burma, and Polynesia, brother-sister marriages have been an expedient device for keeping the throne in the family.

Sex taboos are of special interest in Western culture where, traditionally, sex is limited or, at least, strictly controlled. In most cultures of the world sex is more abundant than food; and in cultures where food is the dominant concern, food taboos supersede sex taboos. However, no culture is completely rational in that it sanctions whatever food is available and nutritious.

SOME FOOD TABOOS RELATE TO RELIGION. In 1500 B.C. Jewish patriarchs forbade the eating of pork, and the ancient Jews neither ate nor killed swine. The taboo is generally thought of as relating to the uncleanliness of the pig, but there is some evidence that, at least originally, the taboo was in deference to the pig's sanctity. Down to the time of Isaiah, Jews gathered in secret religious rites to eat the flesh of mice and pigs.[18]

The gentle cow with ample udder has a long history of reverent acclaim. Ancient Egyptians and peoples of other early civilizations paired her with woman as a symbol of the power of nature, of fruitfulness, and of life. Today in India, the cow is still sacred. *Wasn't Krishna reared at Co-hula (cow-station)? Isn't he called Govinda (cow-finder, recoverer of the earth)? And isn't his heavenly abode in go-lucka (cow world)?* Thousands of people die every day in India from malnutrition, but for a Hindu to kill a cow would be a crime as heinous as murder.

SOME FOOD TABOOS RELATE TO WHETHER FOOD IS DEAD OR ALIVE, RAW OR COOKED, FRESH OR STALE. A snake swallows a live mouse whole; a bird gulps down a worm; a wolf tears the rabbit limb from limb; but people eat relatively few things raw and only mute things alive—fruits and vegetables and invertebrates, such as sea urchins and oysters. Indians of Vancouver Island pick up sea urchins on the beach and suck them out of their shells. And oysters, contend the gourmets who serve them with sherry, should show a strong muscular twitch when the acid lemon juice stings their flesh. Some of us may enjoy beef tartar; but only a few of us eat raw brain or raw liver. And who but Eskimos relish decayed fish heads and munch deer droppings?

The whole question of food leads from aesthetic into moral problems. For moral reasons we don't eat pets. Pets have personality, and personality is a protection in this devouring world. We don't eat our pet canary, our cat, our dog, or our horse. However, in some cultures, dogs, "man's best friend," are raised as food, and they are said to be very tasty. The dog taboo is typical of European cultures; the horse taboo is comparable, but not quite as strict. In the United States during World War II when meat was rationed, the

Harvard Faculty Club served horse steaks as did some public restaurants. Some people object to killing any animals for food and, in protest, become vegetarians. But are uncooked plants "alive" or merely "raw"? Samuel Butler * (1835–1902) pointed out in *Erewhon,* that even plants have rights; and the Erewhonians, following a moral decision to its logical conclusion, could eat only cabbages which had died a natural death.

We don't eat pets, and we don't eat people. Although people are expendible for other than basic biological purposes, cannibalism in most cultures is the ultimate food taboo. But, as with all taboos, there are exceptions. Cannibals do exist; and, according to one cannibal connoisseur, the white man well roasted tastes like a ripe banana.

> You whites will not eat crocodiles or apes, although they taste well. If you did not have so many pigs and crabs you would eat crocodiles and apes, for hunger hurts. It is all a matter of habit. When I have killed an enemy it is better to eat him than to let him go to waste. . . . The bad thing is not being eaten, but death, whether our tribal enemy eats me or not. I know of no game which tastes better than men. You whites are really too dainty. . . .[19]

Culture can so condition an individual that he has strong gastronomical as well as moral and aesthetic reactions to food. In Mexico, Central, and South America, the great tropical iguana lizards are a delicacy; not so in Europe. A gentle French madame at a dinner party in Honduras was thoroughly enjoying a well-seasoned chicken-like meat until she understood she was eating the flesh of an iguana. "*Mon dieu! Iguana! C'était un lézard!*" She left the table violently nauseated.

Taboos relating to the condition of the food, to sentiment, or to religion seem reasonable, but other food taboos defy rationalization. Some may relate to the place of creatures in the evolutionary scale of life. Some may be a function of the availability of protein in the environment. (People living in an area where protein is abundant can afford to be particular.) Some may be only generalizations of individual taste or distaste. But all are culturally determined.

Folkways, mores, and taboos are the characteristic controls in a small or primitive society. Larger societies need the formal control of laws established by legislative action and enforced by judicial and police action.

Laws

In a small social group where everyone knows nearly everyone else, what "they" think matters. Group pressures tend to keep individual behavior within the established norms; few people can tolerate the continued displeasure of close associates. However, as a society becomes larger and more impersonal,

* Samuel Butler (1835-1902), English novelist and satirist. Note that *Erewhon* spells *Nowhere* backwards.

informal controls become less effective. Neighborhood gossip, a means of broadcasting violations of folkways and mores, is something to be reckoned with in a small village; but it can be ignored by the relatively anonymous private citizen in a big city. In the course of history, as societies have grown more complex, decreasing control through folkways, mores, and taboos has been compensated for by increasing control through laws.

Some laws give official support to patterns of behavior first established through folkways, mores, and taboos; some laws are written by legislative or quasi-legislative bodies in a deliberate attempt to meet specific needs; but all laws have certain unique characteristics in common. They are formally defined. They are rationally designed. They spell out the penalty for infringement and they are enforced mainly by law enforcement agencies. Hammurabi (circa 1955–1913 B.C.), King of Babylon, developed the first known system of *civil* laws defining personal rights and property rights. Emperor Justinian (A.D. 527–565) summed up one thousand years of Roman law in a systematized body of statutes, a "Civil Code," which ever since has served certain Western nations as a model. During the Middle Ages the people of Europe were governed by *canon laws* developed by the church, but with the "discovery" of the pre-Christian world and the growth of political states, the power of the church waned and *civil law,* based on Justinian's book of laws, gradually replaced canon laws. After Napoleon Bonaparte (1769–1821) codified civil law as it had developed in France, the system of *civil law* came to dominate Europe, Central and South America, Quebec, Louisiana, and other areas of the world settled by the French, Spanish, Portuguese, and Dutch. However, another system of law, *common law,* developed concurrently in England and extended to the United States (except Louisiana which was first occupied by the French), to Canada (exclusive of French Quebec), to Australia, New Zealand, and other areas settled by the English. In contrast to civil law based on the Roman and Napoleonic codes, common law is based on local customs —on folkways, mores, and taboos. When a judge in a country where common law prevails is required to make a decision in a situation not covered by custom or previous judicial action, he appeals to the people—to their reason and their conscience. That decision then becomes a precedent on which subsequent decisions are based. Common law is distinguished from both civil law and *statute law* enacted by such legislative bodies as the English Parliament and the United States Congress. In addition to common and statute laws, we recognize *military law* which governs the action of army, navy, and air force personnel on home or foreign territory and *international law* which governs the interaction of nations. International law, we should note, differs at this time in history from all other law in two significant ways: it does not yet cover the field, and no established means of enforcement exists. International law could not prevent World War II nor could it prevent violations of international law during the war. International law today, primarily through the United Nations, is still in the making.

The United States has been called the most law-making and the most law-breaking nation on earth. Since 1900 state legislators have passed more than 500,000 state laws. In a large state such as California or New York, each legislative session considers as many as 5,000 bills, and usually passes somewhat less than half of them. We have gone further than most nations in codifying mores and taboos, regulating by law what many others still regulate by informal social pressure. Our faith in law has roots in historical circumstances. The United States began in an act of law, the framing and adoption of the Constitution; our Puritan heritage gave us a tradition of imposing strict standards of behavior on ourselves *and* others; and finally, ours is a culture of many cultures, derived from so many sources that no single set of mores could possibly apply. Some unifying force had to be found for different and potentially conflicting ways of life.

Contradicting the optimistic and sometimes self-righteous haste with which we tend to make laws is the casual disrespect with which we often break them. This disrespect for law, like our faith in it, has historical roots. The Constitution protects individual rights; we traditionally emphasize and respect individualism.* During the long period of Western expansion, frontier tradition was "beyond the law." We will often feel "there ought to be a law," to control, not ourselves, but all those others.

We are not alone in our disrespect for impersonal authority. To a C.B.S. correspondent in Paris who protested to his taxicab driver for going through a red light, the Frenchman replied:

> "What did I do? Went through a red light. Well, did you ever stop to consider what a red light is, what it means. . . . It is only an automatic stop signal and it does not mean that there is cross traffic. Did you see any cross traffic during our trip? Of course not. I slowed down at the light, looked carefully to the right and to the left. Not another car on the streets at this hour. Well, then! What would you have me do? Should I stop like a dumb animal because an automatic, brainless machine turns red every forty seconds? No, monsieur," he thundered, hitting the door jamb with a huge fist. "I am a man, not a machine. I have eyes and a brain and judgment, given me by God. It would be a sin against nature to surrender them to the dictates of a machine." [21]

Some laws we live by; some we ignore. Others we eventually laugh into oblivion. One once risked arrest if he cooled his feet in Massachusetts by hanging them out a window, whistled under water in Vermont, or held a kiss for more than five minutes in Iowa! Even now in New York City it is illegal for a man to keep or yard cattle, swine, sheep, or goats without a permit.

---

* We should note, however, that "Western peoples, for all their professional devotion to individualism, show considerable ambivalence in this area, as demonstrated in the periodic hounding of political, economic, artistic, philosophical, and other heretics." [20]

Primary Institutions

In popular speech, *institution* refers to organizations serving a public need: prisons, hospitals, insane asylums, schools. This is in agreement with sociological usage as applied to *secondary institutions;* but sociologists distinguish between such deliberately created organizations and the *primary institutions* which arise spontaneously out of personal and social needs, specifically: family, religion, education, economics, and government. Perceived as part of society, the primary institutions are *social structures,* made up of formally organized as well as less formally defined groups. Perceived as part of culture, the primary institutions are *norm complexes*—groupings of behavior patterns around central social needs. Together, institutions and their relationships integrate culture with society and make up the total social order.

An institution is a *social structure* insofar as each individual and group within an institution has a *position* * with an actual or implied power differential relative to that of the other individuals and groups. Position is strictly a social phenomenon, a basic unit of social structure characteristic of both human and animal societies.

The social structure of an institution, in turn, embodies *norm complexes.* Any action of an individual filling a particular position in a group or a group filling a particular position in an institution is partially predetermined by the role-image † associated with that position. In government, for example, an individual in the position of judge acts as a judge, not as a prosecuting attorney

* The Linton-Parsons concept of *status-role* commonly replaces *position* in sociological usage. However, we use *position* as a structural unit in society and *status* as a cultural qualifier—a measure of the worth accorded to a position, an incumbent, or the performance of the incumbent. For example, the position of teacher in the Soviet Union has a higher status than the position of teacher in the United States. The position of doctor in the Soviet Union has a lower status than the position of doctor in the United States. In either society, the qualifications or the performance of the particular teacher or doctor could raise or lower his status without affecting the status of the position itself.

The status-role concept derives originally from the anthropologist Ralph Linton who used the terms *status, position,* and *role* in describing society as a pattern of reciprocal behavior between individuals and groups (*The Study of Man,* 1936). Linton defined *status* as a *position* in a particular pattern and as a collection of rights and duties. He defined *role* as the performance of the rights and duties of a status. Role represents "the dynamic aspect of a status" and is inseparable from it; hence the term *status-role.*

The sociologist Kingsley Davis makes a distinction between *status*—a position growing out of folkways and mores, and *office*—a deliberately created position in a formally organized group (*Human Society,* 1949). Davis also uses status in the sense to which we confine it—that of a value associated with a position or an incumbent.

† In sociology *role* is both a descriptive term (referring to how a person acts) and a prescriptive term (referring to how others expect him to act). We use *role* in the descriptive sense to mean the way an individual carries out the requirements of his position—his actual behavior as distinct from his expected behavior. We use *role-image* in the prescriptive sense to mean expected behavior—the behavior patterns or norms associated with a position. See Chapter 6 for a further discussion of role and role-image.

or a defendant. And a law-making body engages, not in judicial or executive action, but in legislative action. Role-images reside in the culture; roles are performed through society.

In a social relationship role-images make reciprocal action based on common understanding possible. They define the *qualities, performances,* and *possessions* * expected of ideal incumbents and clarify mutual rights and responsibilities. *Positions* are the *structural* units in institutions and groups. *Role-images* are the cultural units. Together they determine the form and function of a total institution as well as the form and function of the groups and individuals within it.

The family, for example, as a primary institution is both a social structure and a norm complex; it is a composite of a variety of interdependent positions and correspondingly interdependent role-images. In the United States, the family structure is characteristically monogamous and nuclear with a limited number of positions: one husband, one wife, and one or more children. When the first child is born, the husband becomes a father; the wife becomes a mother, and both have new roles to play. Each additional child further changes the family structure, and each in turn, according to sex and order of birth, has changing positions and changing roles.

In the family institution a constellation of folkways, mores, taboos, and laws actively directs the pre-marital and post-marital behavior of all parties involved. If the lover on bended knee presents his love with an engagement ring, if friends "shower" the bride-to-be with presents, if guests at the wedding lie in wait at the church door and pelt the bride and groom with rice for fertility, if at a reception the couple hand on hand make the first cut in a white three-tiered cake, if they drive away for a honeymoon in a car trailing tin cans and old shoes, if, when they come back to their new home, the husband carries his wife over the threshold—then *folkways* have pointed the way. All such colorful, lighthearted rituals are a traditionally romantic but quite unnecessary part of marriage.

Marriage *mores* and *taboos* are sterner stuff. Woe to the partner who, instead of "I do," dares to say, "No! I do not!" or who refuses to consummate the marriage, or who prefers another sex partner. And shame to the husband who does not or cannot support his wife and children, and shame to the wife who willfully neglects her husband and her children. Such gross failures to live up to the role-images can lead to despair and the break-up of the marriage.

Minimum age requirements and blood tests, the marriage contract and legal obligations for financial support, definitions of incest, and the adultery, divorce and other laws relating to marriage and the care of children proclaim the responsibility society as a whole feels for the protection and perpetuation of the family.

* Chapter 9.

Culture develops out of human society. Institutions develop out of both. As societies become complex and culture accumulates, institutions gradually formulate themselves around the central social needs of family, religion, education, economics, and government. All the institutions are responsive to the particular society and the particular culture of which they are a part, but, especially in modern urban-industrial societies, the independent careers and values of these institutions are not always compatible. As entities, institutions may cooperate, but they also compete and occasionally conflict with each other.

We tend to take our institutions for granted, just as we take our total society and our total culture for granted. We are made aware of institutions mainly when the norms they embody no longer direct us into appropriate social action. This happens in crises situations when changing circumstances demand new positions and new role-images. We can up-date institutions, but all the stress and confusion associated with change in folkways, mores, taboos, and laws is compounded once those patterns have been institutionalized. Institutions are thus extremely resistant to change. They not only embody constellations of behavior patterns as norm complexes; they sustain and implement those patterns by providing established interdependent positions and role-images.

Real and Ideal Patterns

The folkways, mores, taboos, and laws embodied in institutions are norms or patterns of behavior defining the expected social actions of individuals and groups in interdependent positions within a social structure. Implicit in the concept of behavior norms is both *ideal* behavior and *real* behavior. *Ideal* behavior is the rarely achieved goal. *Real* or actual behavior is largely either *acceptable* in that it approaches the ideal, or *unacceptable* in that it defies or falls far short of the ideal.

"Father," said little George Washington, "I cannot tell a lie." Whatever little George, or any boy with an ax, actually would say, were he caught chopping down a cherry tree, is *real* behavior. What we are told little George said represents *ideal* behavior. Society sets up model folkways, mores, and taboos—*ideal patterns* for its members to follow. They are an expression of social conscience, Durkheim's *collective conscience,* and an appeal to the individual for the acceptance (within reasonable limits) of the priority of social over personal interests. Just as an individual conscience has power to change individual behavior, so the collective conscience working through individuals and groups of individuals has power to change group behavior. The equality of men and their right to equal opportunity for "life, liberty, and the pursuit of happiness" is an *ideal* pattern—an ideal which has acted and is still acting as a lever to shift the *real* patterns of discrimination and unequal rights in the United States toward the *ideal.* Every society has its cultural ideals, and "progress" is broadly perceived as any change which tends to lessen the breach between real and ideal patterns.

ACCUMULATION OF CULTURE

Traits, complexes, folkways, mores, taboos, laws, institutions—the real and ideal patterns they represent—all happen here. They are the common nonmaterial habitual ways of living. We accept them together with all the material means of living our culture provides, as our rightful heritage willed to us by centuries of time and generations of men. This heritage had a beginning.

THE MISSTEP

Keepers at a London zoo have taught an orangutan to clean its own cage, say the National Geographic Society.—The Times.

This is the way it starts, you know:
A first misstep in the long ago,
An Early She in the foul cave's gloom
Fumbles with twigs, and behold—a broom!
At first, the dimmest sort of revulsion;
Centuries later, a washing compulsion.
From jungle dark with fern and creeper
Up to the light of a Bissell's sweeper;
A fateful moment—Woman Emergent,
Sowing the seeds of a pink detergent.

E. B. White

Nearly a million and a half years before the first known man appeared on earth, an ingenious ape had made the beginnings of a material culture; * he had tools and weapons. Among his fossil remains in the Olduvai Gorge in Tanganyika are stones with cutting edges plus traces of the frogs, rodents, pigs, and antelopes he hunted. From this ancient cousin † of the contemporary

* The date for man-apes of the Olduvai varies, but the latest potassium-argon measurements place them at nearly two million years ago.

† Chimpanzees are distinguished from other apes by their tool-making and tool-using capacity. To catch termites (a favorite food) a chimpanzee gathers stems and trims them neatly to a nearly uniform length. With stems in hand he steps up to a termite hill, pushes a stem into a hole, and leaves it there a few seconds. When he pulls out the stem, it is covered with clinging termites which he then triumphantly licks off.[22]

chimpanzee man apparently evolved. To this ancestral creature's innate capacity for inventing and learning, man owes his unique development and his unique achievement—a culture which he can pass on through the ages from generation to generation.

Exactly when and where man and culture began is not crucial information for the sociologist. The important sociological facts are that man does have a culture, and that, since its origin, it has shown a tendency to accumulate. Despite setbacks and lost traits, culture has accumulated at an ever accelerating rate. Late in the nineteenth century, the director of the United States Patent Office naïvely recommended to Congress that the Patent Office be closed on the grounds that all the inventions which could possibly be made had been made. Inventions, however, for the most part, represent a rearrangement of existing culture traits. The more traits that exist, the greater the number of possible arrangements, and the greater the number of possible inventions.

Knowledge in the natural sciences, doubling now every eight years or less, continues to widen the culture base, and the next twenty-five years include a potential for making as many inventions as have been made in all the 50,000 years of *Homo sapiens'* history.

> Tools, hunting, fire, complex social life, speech, the human way, and the brain evolved together to produce ancient man of the genus *Homo* about half a million years ago. Then the brain evolved under the pressures of more complex social life until the species *Homo sapiens* appeared perhaps as recently as 50,000 years ago.
>
> With the advent of *Homo sapiens* the tempo of technical-social evolution quickened. Some of the early types of tools had lasted for hundreds of thousands of years and were essentially the same throughout vast areas of the African and Eurasian land masses. Now the tool forms multiplied and became regionally diversified. Man invented the bow, boats, clothing; conquered the Arctic; invaded the New World; domesticated plants and animals; discovered metal, writing, and civilization.[23]

Contemporary man, the proud primate, lives in the midst of his latest tool-making revolution, a revolution made possible by the knowledge and techniques of modern physical and biological science.

Man's technological development, his material culture and the knowledge and techniques logically associated with it, has changed from *unplanned* discovery to *planned* invention. His earliest achievements were elaborations of the accidental. Seeds sprouting from garbage heaps could have suggested agriculture. A rolling stone could have suggested the wheel. A plant with an "eye" on fruit or blossom applied to an ailing eye sometimes caused blindness but sometimes it cured or at least coincided with a cure. Man took centuries to arrive at the scientific way of stating a technical problem and then systematically going about finding a solution.

Societary development, particularly primary institutions and the norm complexes they embody, has been, in one sense, comparable to technological development. It has tended to change from *unplanned* adaptation to *planned* intervention; from folkways, mores, and taboos to laws; from small, simple biologically based social structures to large, complex nationally defined states.

Social organization has proceeded from the biological adaptation which is the family, to environmental adaptations which have given rise to clans or tribes and eventually to still larger more deliberately planned societies.

> Man had to make inventions in social organization and in distribution of goods and in the political field before large organized states were possible. As man made more and more of these inventions, he was able to live in larger communities and to achieve law and order over larger and larger areas.[24]

Man has not yet arrived at a scientific way of stating societary problems and then systematically going ahead, as he does with technical problems, to find a solution, but the historical direction of societary change projected into the future indicates an eventual world organization with social structures and processes and norm complexes serving not sovereign states, but the entire society of man.[25]

In the meantime the great discrepancy in advanced industrial societies between the rapid rate of technological change and the slow rate of societary change threatens us with a suffocating surfeit of material means.

We take vacations—trips to the mountains, to tropical islands, to deserts; periodically we try to escape from too much culture. If physical escape isn't possible, there are "happy pills," and "don't-give-a-damn pills." In 1956 one out of every seven persons in the United States took some form of tranquilizer; in 1957 druggists filled 36,000,000 prescriptions—1,125,000,000 pills—a total of about 300 tons.[26]

> The poor earnest American spends his day importuned to keep to the right, to curb his dog, move to the rear, watch where he is going, dim his lights, throw trash here, not smoke there, fasten his seat belt, face the front, not stand in this place or park in that; he is asked to remember Pearl Harbor; he is tempted with fattening foods and warned to watch his weight; he is urged to think this and told not to think that; he is solicitously invited to go into debt to pay for a car, a TV set, or a vacation—and urged to be thrifty; he is asked to consider the Jews, reminded of Arab refugees, and cautioned to be kind to minorities; and he is asked why he also doesn't relax.[27]

A jet zooms and shakes the earth with a sonic boom . . . horns honk and brakes squeal while a child dodges through traffic after a silently soaring blue balloon . . . a juke box blares and a man takes an elevator to the forty-second floor and jumps . . . the rat-tat-tats rivet girders for a building big enough to house the population of a decent country town . . . and sociologists wonder with the doctor and the philosopher: *How much of our culture is blessing? How much is blight?* The questions have more than academic interest. Only by understanding our increasingly complex culture can our necessary adaptation to it become intelligently directed instead of being haphazard and unguided.*

---

* Chapter 14.

Notes

1. H. R. Hays, *From Ape to Angel* (New York: Alfred A. Knopf, Inc., 1958), p. xi.
2. *Ibid.*, p. xii.
3. *Ibid.*, p. 15.
4. Edward McNall Burns, *Western Civilizations,* 5th edition (New York: W. W. Norton & Company, Inc., 1958), p. 522.
5. Erle Stanley Gardner in *San Francisco Chronicle,* March 4, 1963, p. 23.
6. Franz Boas in H. R. Hays, *From Ape to Angel,* p. 268.
7. Hays, *From Ape to Angel,* p. vii.
8. E. A. Hoebel, "The Nature of Culture," in Harry L. Shapiro, ed., *Man, Culture and Society* (New York: Oxford University Press, 1956), p. 171.
9. *Ibid.*, p. 177.
10. Tom Armstrong, "Views and Reviews," *The Reporter,* April 4, 1957, p. 131.
11. Emily Post, *Etiquette* (New York: Funk & Wagnalls Co., 1950), p. 410.
12. *The New Yorker,* February 15, 1958, p. 23.
13. Anthony West, "The Stranger," *The New Yorker,* May 16, 1959, pp. 103-121.
14. Letter from the family records of Eugene Mead.
15. Frederick J. Teggart, *Theory and Processes of History* (Berkeley: University of California Press, 1941), p. 272.
16. Hays, *From Ape to Angel,* p. vii.
17. Sir James George Frazer, *The Golden Bough,* abridged edition (New York: The Macmillan Company, 1960), p. 859.
18. *Ibid.*, p. 547.
19. William Graham Sumner, *Folkways* (Boston: Ginn & Company, 1907), pp. 331-332.
20. Joseph Church, *Language and the Discovery of Reality* (New York: Random House, 1961), p. 138.
21. David Schoenbrun, "Manners and Morals of the French," *Harper's Magazine,* March, 1957, p. 50.
22. John E. Pfeiffer, "The Apish Origins of Human Tension," *Harper's Magazine,* July, 1963, p. 57.
23. Sherwood L. Washburn, "Tools and Human Evolution," *Scientific American,* September, 1960, p. 63-65.
24. Ruth Benedict, "The Growth of Culture," in *Man, Culture and Society,* Harry L. Shapiro, ed. (New York: Oxford University Press, 1960), p. 194.
25. *Ibid.*, p. 195.
26. Thomas Whiteside, "Getting There First with Tranquility," *The New Yorker,* May 3, 1958, p. 90.
27. Thomas Griffith, *The Waist-high Culture* (New York: Harper & Row, Publishers, 1959), p. 159.

I have made a ceaseless effort not to ridicule,

not to bewail, not to scorn human actions,

but to understand them.

BENEDICT SPINOZA (1632-1677)

4

Family and Religion— Declining Institutions

IN THE PAST 500,000 YEARS, at least 14,000,000,000 members of the genus *Homo* have lived on earth. Today, more than 3,000,000,000 *Homo sapiens,* the only surviving species of the genus, have inherited the accumulated culture of the ages. Like our ancestors before us, we live in societies where, as individuals and members of families, clans, tribes, larger organizations and collectivities, we act and interact with each other and our environment, modifying through our actions the institutions of society and the cultural complexes they embody.

Any particular society develops a way of life which is meaningful and viable, relative to the geographical, biological and historical conditions under which it exists. Because conditions differ, societies and their cultures differ. To the scientist, intent on understanding *man among men,* the pertinent question regarding any society, including even such controversial culture traits as polygamy, infanticide, cannibalism, and communism, is not, "Is this behavior or belief good or bad, right or wrong," but "Does it serve the survival needs of the group?" Diversity is not perversity. It is rather testimony to the ingenuity of man in response to what he perceives as practical necessities or desirable goals.

African Bushmen live in deserts, Negritos in the equatorial rain forest, Fuegians on the cold rainy tip of South America, but they all have a similar *patrilineal* social organization. Why? One explana-

ESTER BUBLEY

tion is that they have the same subsistence problem: they depend on non-migratory game which is best hunted by small bands of men who know their territory. Grandfathers, fathers, and sons make a convenient hunting coalition.

The Athabaskans and Algonkians of Canada, in contrast, live in *multi-family* or *multilineage* groups. Why? The caribou on which their life depends exists in large herds and is best hunted cooperatively by large groups of men. It is expedient to include uncles, cousins, and friends. The Eskimos, however, with comparable technical equipment and a similar subsistence problem, live in small family groups. Limited fish and sea mammals as well as the sparse Eskimo population make cooperative hunting unrewarding.

Even before contact with modern Europe, the people of the Baganda kingdom in Uganda concentrated in relatively permanent settlements, and had enough surplus time and energy to develop complicated rituals, manufacture goods, maintain markets, and build a network of roads. Why? Bananas! Bananas were a main source of food, and, once established, plants sent up new shoots and continued to produce abundant, easily harvested fruit for twenty-five to thirty years.

The relationship between the structure of a society, its culture and the geographical, biological and historical conditions under which it exists seem deceptively direct in pre-industrial societies, but even then it is not a simple matter of cause and effect. The variables are many, and even though opportunity as well as necessity can be pointed to as a mother of invention, neither the same necessity nor the same opportunity necessarily leads to the same invention. Furthermore, profound change in any aspect of society, culture, or the environment can upset any "mutuality" which might originally exist. We are often surprised by differences where we expect to find similarities, and *vice versa!*

PREDICTABLE INSTITUTIONS—UNPREDICTABLE PATTERNS

Diverse as the ways of man are, man is still the common denominator; all men everywhere try to provide for the same human needs. Patterns of culture first develop around the biological facts of man's structure and functioning: sex differences, birth, growth, aging, and death; the helplessness of human infants; drives generated by hunger, thirst, and sex; the need, in some environments, for clothing and shelter. Although the concept of instinct is now confined to such *specific, unlearned,* patterned behavior within a species as web-spinning in spiders and nest-building in birds, and no longer applies to the behavior of man, in the broad *non-specific* categories, man's behavior *is* species predictable. We cannot predict, for example, what games or music a society might have; but we can predict that any human society, ancient or modern, primitive or advanced, will have games and music. The Human Relations Area Files,* a storehouse of information for social scientists at Yale University, list the following common traits in every known culture:

> . . . athletic sports, bodily ornament, calendar, cleanliness training, community organization, cooking, cooperative labor, cosmology, courtship, dancing, decorative art, divination, division of labor, dream interpretation, education, eschatology, ethics, ethnobotany, etiquette, faith healing, family, feasting, fire making, folklore, food taboos, funeral rites, games, gestures, gift giving, government, greetings, hair styles, hospitality, housing, hygiene, incest taboos, inheritance rules, joking, kin-groups, kinship nomenclature, language, law, luck, superstitions, magic, marriage, mealtimes, medicine, modesty concerning natural functions, mourning, music mythology, numerals, obstetrics, penal sanctions, personal names, population policy, postnatal care, pregnancy usages, property rights, propitiation of supernatural beings, puberty customs, religious ritual, residence rules, sexual restrictions, soul concepts, status differentiation, surgery, tool making, visiting, weaning, and weather control.[1]

In every society, the children born are cared for and educated into the ways of that society. Death is as inevitable, as necessary, and as mysterious as birth; and men everywhere attempt to rationalize and explain it and other phenomena of nature. In every society, work is done and compensated for. In every society, mutual rights and responsibilities of individuals and groups need clarification and regulation. Out of these common social needs arise the common primary institutions. The family institution protects and socializes children. Religious institutions establish relationship with the natural and the supernatural. Economic institutions regulate work and compensation for work. Political institutions distribute power and maintain social order. Educational institutions teach the skills and provide the understanding needed to maintain and perpetuate the society.

Two sociological phenomena are thematic in our discussion of these primary institutions: first, the variability in structure and norms of the same institution in different societies, and, second, the effect of contemporary conditions on these institutions, particularly in the United States. Although the primary institutions † are common to all societies, they differ not only in their structure and in the norm complexes they embody, but also in relative importance. *Family* and *Religion,* which have dominated pre-industrial societies, are declining in industrially advanced societies, while *Economics, Government,*

* Originally set up as the Cross-Cultural Survey in 1937 by George P. Murdock.

† Some discussions of primary institutions include both the military and recreation. These are primary in the sociological sense of developing spontaneously rather than being deliberately preconceived; but they are not core institutions. The military, traditionally, is subordinate to or a part of the political institution; and recreation is an institution independent of religion, education, and family only in those societies where technology gives an excess of leisure. We limit our discussion to those institutions which are both crescive in nature and central to the history of most cultures.

and *Education,* originally a part of Family and Religion, are expanding institutions.

FAMILY

The family is the heart of society. It is the oldest and most important of all groups. The race could not have evolved; the infant *Homo sapiens* could not have survived without the protection and nurturance of others. Traditionally, those "others" have been a family. As an institution, the famliy has declined in scope and status, but it is still the fundamental group, even in modern multi-group society. The family is the first point of exchange in the relay of culture from one generation to the next. It initiates the long process of socialization. We are born into a family as demanding, self-centered individuals. We emerge from the family as group members. Within the family we participate in the basic social processes. We assimilate attitudes and behavior. We conflict and compete. We cooperate and accommodate. If we live in a family which functions harmoniously and constructively, we are prepared for harmonious and constructive relationships within other groups. We know from intimate experience that sibling rivalry can turn into brother love.

The first essential family group was mother and infant; then, with luck, the male was brought in on a more or less permanent basis. From this nucleus the family in some cultures extended to include brothers, sisters, cousins, aunts, uncles, grandparents and great-grandparents; and its socially defined functions encompassed religion, economics, government and education. However, over the centuries, as societies have grown larger and more complex, the family has grown smaller, and its functions have been reduced to physiological and psychological essentials.

> To the individual member [of a primitive society], the family's property is the source of livelihood, its ancestors are his gods, its elders his government, and its young men his defense and his support in old age. In simpler cultures (e.g., the Australian Aborigines) family and society are actually coterminous. . . . We, in contrast, are primarily citizens, not kinsmen. The family is organized anew with each marriage. It must share our allegiance with the many competing claims of our society: the loyalties we owe to the institutions that employ us, to our professional organizations, to political parties, to community and nation.[2]

Whatever the size of the family or its place in society, as an institution it invariably embodies norm complexes regulating sex behavior and the care of children. It is in the ways the family meets these original and persistent imperatives that we find the most significant variations.

Is Love Necessary?

Sexual differentiation, viviparous propagation, and helpless infancy—these are biological facts which make parents and children a natural unit. However, our invariant biological nature is expressed in variant family structures in keeping with social needs and cultural mores and taboos. The *monogamous, nuclear* family we know—mother, father, and children—is a living pattern, not a biological necessity. *Extended* families including three or more generations, *consanguine* families involving all who claim a common ancestor, even *polygamous* families having more than one husband or wife in the household, serve family purposes in some societies. Most families demand marriage outside the kinship or social group (*exogamy*); others encourage or demand inbreeding (*endogamy*). Some families, regardless of structure, are male-dominated (*patriarchal*), some female-dominated (*matriarchal*), some democratic. Some are child-centered, some adult-centered. All may or may not be either founded on or sustained by the emotional attitude we call "love."

Boy Meets Girl

In the United States, sex mores are concerned mainly with pre-marital chastity and the exclusive possession of a spouse. As a prelude to marriage and a family, we expect romantic love and sanction physical contact if it is restrained enough to avoid violating virginity. The socially approved sequence is this: Boy meets girl. They fall in love, become engaged, and, after a decent interval, marry. If parents happen to object, the weight of society is with the lovers, and parents are under pressure to welcome the son- or daughter-in-law with as much good grace as they can muster.

Reverence for romance is a relatively recent phenomenon.

> . . . The concept of romantic love did not appear in Europe until the time of the thirteenth-century troubadours, and these experts ruled at first that it was impossible to married people. Even as late as the eighteenth century it played a very small part in European marriage. All societies recognize that there are occasional violent emotional attachments between persons of opposite sex, but our present American culture is practically the only one which has attempted to capitalize these and make them the basis for marriage. Most groups regard them as unfortunate and point out the victims of such attachments as horrible examples. Their rarity in most societies suggests that they are psychological abnormalities to which our own culture has attached an extraordinary value just as other cultures have attached extreme values to other abnormalities. The hero of the modern American movie is always a romantic lover just as the hero of the old Arab epic is always an epileptic. A cynic might suspect that in any ordinary population the percentage of individuals with a capacity for romantic love of the Hollywood type was about as large as that of persons able to throw genuine epileptic fits. However, given a

> little social encouragement, either one can be adequately imitated without the performer admitting even to himself that the performance is not genuine.
>
> Most societies are less keen on romance than on congeniality. They train their young people to believe that any well-bred boy and girl, once married, will be able to live together contentedly and will in time develop a real fondness for each other. In most cases this seems to be correct. The percentage of happy arranged marriage is probably as high as that of happy romantic marriages, and they are likely to be much more satisfactory to the families involved.[3]

Some of the difficulties inherent in our sex mores and taboos are avoided by societies in which marriage has little to do with either love or satisfaction of the sex drive. Instead of deifying romantic love, some cultures contrive to prevent it. Instead of restricting pre-marital sexual contact, some cultures encourage or require unrestricted contact; others manage to avoid contact of any kind.

The ancient Greek city-state of Sparta was totalitarian; and, for survival of the system, the individual had to be subordinate to the state. The state required undivided devotion. Any other love was competitive and distracting, yet the race had to be continued. Sparta needed soldiers. The dilemma was solved by marrying men and women in a lottery-like love game. Prospective brides with shaven heads were herded into a pitch-dark room furnished with straw mats. Into this room went an equal number of men who groped around in the dark, found a bristly-headed female, and consummated the relationship then and there. For several nights, the only contact between "man and wife" was in this room. Records do not disclose if the same partners met every night; but finally, couples were taken out of the room, allowed to see each other for the first time, and established in a house as husband and wife.[4] Here the wife dominated the home, but the state dominated the family. The husband's first loyalty was not to his wife and children, but to Sparta. The Nazi love camps in Germany were a cultural descendant of the Spartan system.

In a society such as ancient Sparta, where loyalty to the state was accepted as the supreme virtue, it didn't matter whom an individual married as long as the relationship was productive. In other societies, the particular choice of a life partner is an important personal decision and young people are expected to shop around. The Dobu youth of New Guinea marries only after his future mother-in-law has blocked with her own person the door of her house, within which the boy and her daughter are sleeping.

> . . . since the time of puberty, the boy has slept each night in the houses of unmarried girls. By custom his own house is closed to him. He avoids entanglements for several years by spreading his favours widely and leaving the house well before daylight. When he is trapped at last, it is usually because he has tired of his roaming and has settled upon a more constant companion.[5]

If family genealogy is more important in marriage than personal preference or welfare of the state, then selecting a mate is a family affair. In the classical Chinese culture, which prevailed unchallenged until the 1912 revolution led by Sun Yat-sen, parents or marriage brokers arranged marriages sometimes even before the partners were born. Custom discouraged pre-marital contact of any kind, and often the engaged couple did not meet until their wedding day. The Chinese ideal was to marry, *then* fall in love. A Chinese sage once said, "American marriage is like putting a pot of boiling water on a cold stove; Chinese marriage is like putting a pot of cold water on a hot stove."

The system in pre-war Japan was similar. After a century of exposure to Western literature and almost half a century of imported "kiss-kiss" movies, public opinion still supported the old order in parts of Japan as late as 1958. The relationship between parent and child took priority over that between husband and wife, and steady, tranquil friendship and affection were more highly prized than the turbulence of "love." In the local theatres of Japan, boy met girl night after night on the screen, but in real life, Japanese boys and girls were making the marriages their parents had arranged for them.[6] Arranged marriages had been a rigid custom for more than 2,500 years, and romantic love was generally thought both undignified and improper. Not until 1959 did a Crown Prince of Japan dare break with tradition and marry a commoner of his own choice.

As the ways of the West continue to invade the East, more and more young people demand the right to choose their own mates. But with this right comes insecurity. If parents are responsible for arranging marriages, a young woman can relax and be herself. She knows she will be married. If she must compete on the open market for a mate, she does not relax. Clues to her doubts and anxieties appear in Western culture.

Note the topics discussed by our newspaper columnists:

> Certainly it is now acceptable to wear falsies, and if you are a smart and proper woman, he'll never know your treasure chest is half empty until you get him licensed. By then his love for you should be above such little things.[7]

And consider the suggestive names of perfumes: *Love potion . . . Intoxication . . . Menace . . . Temptation . . . Taboo . . . Passion . . . Possession . . . My Sin . . . Surrender.* Just in case the name is too subtle, the message is spelled out in the advertising copy: "the frankly flirtatious perfume," "a whispered invitation for a man to be masterful," "not too innocent," "with conquest aforethought."

When love is necessary, the boy-girl game is highly competitive, time-consuming, and sometimes heart-breaking. Many young men and women, for a variety of reasons, get beyond the point where they can successfully compete before they are fully aware of their plight. *Are romance and free choice worth the risk?*

Exogamy and Endogamy

However it happens—through choice or chance or decree—the universal norm is that eventually a boy meets and gets a girl; but mores, taboos, and some laws govern which boys get which girls. The field is not wide open. Some restrictions are exogamous; some restrictions are endogamous. Most cultures include both exogamy and endogamy; but in different cultures different groups have different restrictions.

Most civilized as well as most primitive family groups are exogamous in keeping with the general taboo against incest; but sometimes the restriction goes beyond the immediate family. Chinese, traditionally, have not allowed persons to marry who have the same surname; a Wong may not marry another Wong—they might be related. Throughout Australia, the natives are divided into great "families," and a man will not marry a woman with his own family name, even if her home is half a continent away. Exogamy may also apply to tribes, clans, or other social or political groups. The Ostiaks of India and the Yakuts of Siberia consider marriage within the clan a crime. In British Columbia, the Tsimsheean Indian tribes are subdivided by totems—crests of the Whale, Porpoise, Eagle, Coon, Wolf, and Frog. These crests are common to all tribes, and relationship between persons of the same crest is considered closer than that between members of the same tribe. Members of the same tribe may marry; those of the same crest may not. A "Whale" may marry a "Frog," but not another "Whale"!

Although most family groups are exogamous, there are endogamous families in Alaska, Central America, India, Java, New Zealand, Great Britain, and Europe. A Kalang of Java must prove his common descent before he can marry into a family. A Bedouin male has the exclusive right to his female cousin. In some fishing villages in Great Britain, in-breeding has given most inhabitants the names of Stephenson, Stanton or Stewart.

Family in-breeding, however, is relatively rare in contemporary cultures, and endogamous restrictions more often apply to age, and to educational, social, religious, and racial groups. Even in the United States, mores, taboos, and laws exert confining pressures. "For a young man to marry a young woman is of the Lord; for an old man to marry a young woman is of man; but for a young man to marry an old woman is of the devil!" * If a young woman marries a man old enough to be her father or grandfather, self-appointed keepers-of-the-mores insinuate that she just wants to cash in on his will. "They that marry old people merely in the expectation of burying them, hang themselves in the hope that someone will come and cut the halter." † If a young man marries an old woman, it is a rare enough event to make newspaper headlines.

IT MUST BE LOVE

Louisa, Kentucky

Grandma and Shorty are still together though ages apart. Grandma is now 94 and Shorty is 34, and after 17 years of marriage they live happily on in the hills of northeastern Kentucky. . . .[8]

---

* Thomas Fuller, 1608-1661.

† Jeremy Taylor, 1613-1667.

Co-education in the United States furthers educational endogamy. "You were my queen in calico; I was your bashful, barefoot beau; I wrote on your slate, 'I love you so' . . ." sang the swain generations ago. Boy still meets girl in the classroom, and extended education for both sexes and a trend towards earlier marriages make the chance of choosing a schoolmate for a life mate greater than ever before. In 1920 only 17.8 per cent of eighteen- and nineteen-year-olds were enrolled in school, compared to 28.9 per cent in 1940 and 42.4 in 1960. For the twenty- to twenty-four-year age group the 1920 figures are not available, but in 1940 the percentage was 6.6 compared to 14.6 in 1960. As the number of years spent in school has increased, the average age of marriage has decreased. (The two phenomena are not necessarily causally related.) The average age of marriage is now 22.3 for males, 20.2 for females compared to 26 and 22 years, respectively, circa 1890.

Opportunity favors social endogamy. Schools, occupations, and social groups tend to be segregated by class. Rarely do upper-uppers have the opportunity to meet or marry lower-lowers or even lower-middles. When it does happen, however, our log-cabin-to-White-House tradition brings public sentiment to the defense of the lovers. Didn't a Rockefeller marry Bobo, daughter of a coal miner? And didn't a Rockefeller son marry a Danish maid? We are more liberal in this area than the British, whose culture we share. King Edward VIII had to give up the British throne to marry a divorced commoner, and Princess Margaret, bowing to family and social pressure, renounced her love for a British Air Force officer.

Religious groups in the United States, particularly Catholics and Jews, favor endogamy; but should a Catholic or a Jew marry outside the faith, both the family and the religious community try to convert the mate and claim the children.

We speak of the United States as a melting pot, but, racially, the pot is hot enough to melt only Caucasian ingredients easily. Mexico, South America, Europe, Pacific Islands, and Asia assimilate genetically more races than the United States. Many states in the United States forbid interracial marriages by law, and in no part of the country are they generally approved.

Negro-Caucasoid marriages are particularly difficult. A man and a woman have to have unusual courage and conviction to cross that racial boundary. The few congratulations they might receive for pioneering in the amalgamation of mankind would be far outweighed by expressions of dismay, disgust, and disbelief, mainly on the part of Caucasians. Said a father whose daughter married a Negro classmate, "some friends, even years after the marriage, continued to greet us as though we had a death in the family." [9]

Mongoloid-Caucasoid marriages, particularly when they are intercultural as well as interracial, are also exceedingly difficult. After the G. I. invasion of the Orient during and following World War II, some veterans did bring home foreign brides, but rarely were the couples wholeheartedly welcomed.

Illegitimate children of mixed parentage are victims of racial endogamy. Both sides of the family tend to reject them, and social agencies generally classify them as unadoptable. However, we know of one Irish-Japanese girl adopted by a childless couple in spite of vehement protests from close relatives. "*How could you do such a thing!*" "*You don't think about us!*" "*Imagine my children having her for a cousin!*" And we know another blond, blue-eyed boy with a Negro grandfather. His foster parents avoid dissension among their unsympathetic relatives by just "not telling."

In no society are individuals completely free and equal—especially in marriage.

Supply and Demand

"And of every living thing of all flesh, two of every sort shalt thou bring into the ark, to keep them alive with thee; they shall be male and female." * One male and one female—this is monogamy, a practical system for us, considering the nearly equal distribution of the sexes in the United States at puberty. Monogamy is our way, and the way of the vast majority of *people* in the world; but polygamy is accepted by the majority of *societies* in the world. Polygamy, meaning plurality of spouse, has three variations: polygny, polyandry, and group marriage. One male may have two or more females. This is criminal in our culture, respectable polygyny in another. One female may have two or more husbands. This isn't disguised prostitution; it is polyandry. A number of men and women may even share sexual privileges with each other; this is group marriage.

MONOGAMY—TWO BY TWO. "One alone to be my own, I alone to know your caresses. Mine to be, eternally, the one my worshipping soul possesses. . . ." So sings the monogamous lover. We accept the sentiment at face value. If either partner fails to live up to monogamous mores, the consequences may be disastrous. The wife may suffer a nervous breakdown; the husband may get ulcers; either may sue the other for divorce on the basis of mental cruelty or adultery. In our culture, monogamy is synonymous with morality; but we still do not take it as seriously as some cultures. In India, prior to British control, a wife proved her devotion by throwing herself on the funeral pyre of her dead husband. *Suttee* was widely practiced, but sometimes it functioned as a symbol rather than an actuality. The wife was expected to *try* to die with her husband, but friends were permitted to try to dissuade her, and, not too surprisingly, they were frequently successful.

Loyalty in our culture is expected only during marriage and for a decent interval of mourning after death of either partner. However, no interval is expected after divorce. We are increasingly tolerant of plural matings, as long as they are not simultaneous. Our rising divorce rate suggests a trend toward *sequential polygamy*. In a few instances, this rapid marital turnover has been carried to the point of caricature. A picture sent out to the

* Genesis 6:19.

nation's press in 1957 by United Press Telephoto showed a happy bride with two males flanking her. The caption read in part: "A millionaire showed just what kind of a sport he is yesterday. His ex-wife, his ninth ex-wife, has just remarried . . . and he showed up to kind of give her away." Later that year he married his tenth wife.

POLYGAMY—HAREMS AND HOMESTEADS. Although the Old Testament implies monogamy, polygyny was permitted among the ancient Jews. Although the New Testament nowhere forbids the people polygyny, monogamy has been the common rule. Within the United States there has been only one strong dissenting group, the Mormons, led by Brigham Young, who, when he died in 1877, was survived by twenty-four wives and more than forty children. Today, however, legal polygyny is found only outside the United States.

Sometimes polygyny exists as idealized in an adolescent male's daydream—a classical harem, where each lovely lady, set up in a private apartment within a luxurious household, holds perpetual open-house. A few Mohammedans approximate this dream. The Koran permits four wives; etiquette allows a sultan seven, but 95 per cent of the Mohammedan population maintains only one wife and a few female servants. The first wife is usually a love match. Additional wives are symbols of status. A man acquires them as he can afford them, but once married, his love life is no longer his own. The other woman has to be approved by his first wife. A third wife has to be approved by the first two. The more wives he has, the more difficult it is for him to get unanimous approval for another. The household is rather like a sorority, where any fully initiated member can blackball a pledge.

Sometimes polygny exists as in the sailor's dream—a girl in every port. Among some Indian castes, professional husbands travel a regular circuit from one village to another, spending a few days en route with as many as 100 wives. (The shortage of males in these castes is severe!) In Liberia, no man of standing has fewer than three wives—each paid for at the standard price of $40.00. Wives are a good investment: they produce valuable children and care for a man's house and land without expecting to be paid. If a wife is unfaithful, the husband can get $10.00 damages against each man, or, if he gives up his wife, he can sue for return of his original $40.00.

> The local chief had a hundred wives—each one decently housed in a separate hut in his compound. Unfortunately, the tendency was for a man's wives to increase in number as he himself advanced in years, and . . . , well . . . , the women sometimes found themselves with a fair amount of time on their hands. This meant that they were inclined to get into hot water, and although most possessors of large harems took a pretty civilized view of the subsidiary friendships that wives might form, there were a few narrow-minded and litigious husbands who went to court—usually to sue for the return of the forty dollars after a wife had run off with some other man.[10]

Polygyny was common in Madagascar before the French domination, but even a rich man rarely had more than three wives. Each wife had to have not only a separate house but an equal amount of land for rice cultivation and an equal share of her husband's time. He systematically and conscientiously spent a day and a night in succession with each wife—no days off. If he neglected one wife for another, she could sue for divorce, claiming adultery, and get an economic settlement equivalent to her share of the total family property. If, however, he neglected one wife for a woman outside his household, then the other wives just teased the offended one. The offense was not taken seriously and the husband could get off the hook by appearing on schedule the next time with a gift. However, if he persisted in chasing another woman, the wives would gang up on him, force him to marry her. She then had to take her place in line and help with the baby-sitting and housework.

The male is usually not as blissfully happy in polygamous societies as cartoon stereotypes suggest. Either the wives get along too well together, in which case they can form a solid block against the husband and protect each other even in their adulterous adventures, or they don't get along at all, and the husband is in the line of fire trying to mediate their fights. It is a rare male who can handle more than one wife without being hopelessly henpecked.

Polyandry. Polygyny is often a measure of wealth. Polyandry is nearly always a measure of poverty so severe that it requires the labor of more than one man to support a wife and children. Under conditions of such deprivation, it is vital to keep down the population. The simplest and most obvious technique in a primitive society is female infanticide. Killing off potential producers of population preserves the group, but it throws the adult sex ratio seriously out of balance. The relatively small number of females who survive to maturity must be shared among the males. In Tibet, polyandry exists in all possible variations. Several brothers may share a wife to keep their own family heritage intact. A woman who happens to own property can choose husbands who may or may not be related. If a mother dies, the widower may share a son's wife, or he may remarry and invite his sons to share his new wife. Tibetans have so few resources they can't afford to keep dividing them. Our monogamous system, in which younger sons leave the family and take private wives, seems to Tibetans not only expensive and difficult but morally inferior to polyandry. Monogamy, Tibetans point out, stresses the individual; polyandry unselfishly puts the family above the individual.[11]

Group Marriage. Group marriages—simultaneous polyandry and polygyny—are the rarest of family forms. In Tibet, a polyandrous family is not necessarily restricted to one wife. Several daughters may inherit the family possessions and take several husbands among them. The Todas of India, who practiced polyandry and infanticide, were persuaded by the British to stop infanticide. This restored the biological balance of males and females; but it did not improve the economic situation. The Todas were as poor as or poorer than before, and monogamy was not practical. With an increased supply of women, the men, who traditionally had never expected to have exclusive right to one woman, still grouped together and took two or more wives among them, rather than just one.[12] Their limited fortunes were preserved and shared within the larger family combine.

Monogamy, polygyny, polyandry, and group marriage—these are the four main forms of the family institution; but they still do not encompass all the variations in male-female behavior. There are other variations which occur either as aberrations or temporary, socially accepted variations. Among the Eskimos, for example, "murder results quite regularly in the murderer taking over the widow and children of the victim. In many instances the desire to acquire the woman is the cause of the murder, but where this is not the motive, a social principle requiring provision for the bereaved family places the responsibility upon the murderer." [13] This is conceivably a more fitting consequence of his crime than hanging!

Sex, however regulated, is prerequisite to children. When children are born, their nurturance is the second traditional function of the family.

Whose Child Is This?

We assume a child belongs to his parents and that his parents are responsible for his care. This is not universally so. A child may belong not to his parents but to other relatives, to the clan, or to the community. Designating the one to whom the child belongs and the intensity of that belonging are correlatives of family structure. The structure sets the stage not only for the interaction of adult males and females, but for the interaction of children with each other and with the adult world.

In the monogamous nuclear families of Western culture, children are typically emotionally dependent on parents; and the smaller the number of children, the more intense the affectional involvement tends to be. Sibling rivalry and the Oedipal problem * both grow out of this intensity. Monogamy however, is the world's dominant family structure, and it helps insure its own continuity by instilling in the child's developing personality a capacity and a need for an intense love relationship. Extended, consanguine, and polygamous families, in contrast, increase the number of members in a household, diffuse nurturance, and thereby distribute and lessen the intensity of affectional attachments.

In some societies, a child may live not with his parents, but with other relatives. Among the Baganda of Africa, for example, only children of tribal nobility live with their parents. Other children are distributed at the discretion of the son of their father's oldest brother, but he traditionally assigns a girl to one of her married brothers, and a boy to a brother of his father.[14] The child knows and expects nothing more.

"It is a wise father that knows his own son." † The problem of biological paternity—a difficult enough one on occasion in a monogamous society, is beyond solution in a polyandrous one. The Todas of India, for example, don't even try to solve it. Instead, sometimes during the later months of a child's prenatal life, they assign a "social" father. Usually the father chosen for the

* Chapter 7.

† William Shakespeare (1564-1616), "Merchant of Venice," Act II, Scene 2.

first-born is the oldest of the pregnant woman's husbands. He goes together with his wife into the woods, makes a ceremonial bow and arrow from sticks and grass, and then ceremoniously "gives the bow" to his wife in front of relatives. Thus he signifies his social paternity. This same father accepts paternity for the next child or two, and then passes the honor on to another husband.[15]

Sometimes a child is not accepted automatically into a family or any other social group. Acceptance may be conditioned by "practical" consideration as among the Ammassalik of Greenland, where no sickly or motherless child is allowed to live.[16] Or acceptance may be determined by superstition or ritual. The Baganda strangle infants born feet first. *Would they not grow up to be thieves and murderers?* And they withhold acceptance of other infants until their legitimacy can be ceremoniously tested.

> An event of transcending importance in the child's early life is the naming ceremony, inasmuch as it is not until this ceremony is completed that the child's legitimacy is once and forever established. In a gathering at the clan chief's house children of both sexes are brought by the mothers carrying a piece of each child's umbilical cord—carefully kept from the day of birth. The paternal grandmothers drop these into a can containing beer, milk, and water. If they float, the clan chief accepts the children as legitimate; but if any cord sinks, the child to whom it belongs is considered born in adultery and disowned by the clan.[17]

Contemporary Western societies do not ceremoniously disown an illegitimate child, but the mores brand him. A child without a family is a child without status.

In April, 1948, the Social Commission of the United Nations called for a study of homeless children—illegitimate children and children orphaned or otherwise separated from their families and in need of foster home or institutional care. The study, confined to homeless children in their native countries—particularly Great Britain, France, The Netherlands, Sweden, Canada, and the United States—revealed that in general the unadopted illegitimate child is both a personally and culturally deprived child. He does not belong even to the community.

In the communal *kibbutzim* of Israel, in contrast, parents turn the child over at birth to the community. He is nursed by the mother, but he is cared for by the professional staff of the Infants' House. At one year of age, children transfer from the Infants' House to a Toddlers' House, and at five years of age, the toddlers in one House join those of another to form a *kevutza*. Until they reach high school age, children of a *kevutza* eat, sleep, play, and attend school together. A child's status comes from his membership in the community, but he still identifies emotionally with his family.

> For most couples the hours spent playing with their children are frankly considered the most gratifying in their day-to-day *kibbutz* life. An index of the strength of this feeling is seen in the inclination of the *kibbutz* members to start work almost at sunrise in order to have more afternoon time to spend with the children. Thus, while the nurses are responsible for supplying most of the child's needs, parents, the mothers especially, do have several hours a day to spend in sustained contact with their offspring. It bears repeating that the interaction of parents and child will almost completely be given over to expressions of affection, but will not involve disciplining or attempts to train or socialize him. At the age of six months, the child may be brought to the home of the parents to visit for an hour. Henceforth for the rest of his youth the child will regard the visit to the parents' room as an important, perhaps the important, event of the day.[18]

The philosophical basis of the *kibbutz* combines the socio-economic theories of Karl Marx with the psychological theories of Sigmund Freud. Not only is property held in common ownership, and production and consumption communally organized, but the care of children is a community responsibility to a degree unknown in any other Western society.*

Psychologically, a child of the *kibbutz* "belongs" in part to the peer group with whom he lives, in part to his parents who love and play with him, and in part to his nurses and teachers who feed, bathe, and clothe him, nurse him when he is sick, and give him knowledge of his culture and his world.

Whose child is this? Perhaps it matters less than we think, as long as society somehow provides three conditions which seem imperative for healthy personality development: first, a continuing relationship with one or more adults who nurture and educate the child with understanding and love; second, membership in a community of peers with whom the child can interact on a relatively independent and equal basis; and third, a congenial physical environment in which the child can exercise his developing physical and mental capacities.

Who Wears the Pants?

The regulation of sex and the care of children are traditional family functions carried on regardless of the personal inter-relationships within the family. However, within most families, as within most societies, men have priority, and women rank below them.

---

* Communist China also reduces family function to its biological and psychological essentials. In 1960, eighty per cent of the Chinese were living in communes where mothers and fathers worked while nurses and teachers cared for the children. Parents and children came together during leisure hours of the day in an atmosphere of happy relaxation. A discussion of the Chinese Communes by the Canadian psychiatrist, Dr. Lazure, was published under the title of "The Cheerful Children of the Chinese Communes," *Maclean's Magazine,* March 11, 1961.

> And the Lord God said, It is not good that the man should be alone; I will make him a help meet for him. . . . And the Lord God caused a deep sleep to fall upon Adam, and he slept; and he took one of his ribs, and closed up the flesh instead thereof; and the rib, which the Lord God had taken from man, made he a woman, and brought her unto man. And Adam said, This is now bone of my bones, and flesh of my flesh; she shall be called Woman, because she was taken out of Man.*

A Hindu myth is as clear as Genesis about the relative status of man versus woman.

> In the beginning, when Twashtri came to the creation of woman, he found that he had exhausted his materials in the making of man, and that no solid elements were left. In this dilemma, after profound meditation, he did as follows. He took the rotundity of the moon, and the curves of creepers, and the clinging of tendrils, and the trembling of grass, and the slenderness of the reed, and the bloom of flowers, and the lightness of leaves, and the tapering of the elephant's trunk, and the glances of deer, and the clustering of rows of bees, and the joyous gaiety of sunbeams, and the weeping of clouds, and the fickleness of the winds, and the timidity of the hare, and the vanity of the peacock, and the softness of the parrot's bosom, and the hardness of adamant, and the sweetness of honey, and the cruelty of the tiger, and the warm glow of fire, and the coldness of snow, and the chattering of jays, and the cooing of the *kokila,* and the hypocrisy of the crane, and the fidelity of the *chakrawaka,* and compounding all these together, he made woman and gave her to man. But after one week, man came to him and said: Lord, this creature that you have given me makes my life miserable. She chatters incessantly and teases me beyond endurance, never leaving me alone; and she requires incessant attention, and takes all my time up, and cries about nothing, and is always idle; and so I have come to give her back again, as I cannot live with her. So Twashtri said: Very well; and he took her back. Then after another week, man came again to him and said: Lord, I find my life is very lonely, since I gave you back that creature. I remember how she used to dance and sing to me, and look at me out of the corner of her eye, and play with me, and cling to me; and her laughter was music, and she was beautiful to look at, and soft to touch; so give her back to me again. So Twashtri said: Very well, and gave her back again. Then after only three days, man came back to him again and said: Lord, I know not how it is; but after all I have come to the conclusion that she is more of a trouble than a pleasure to me; so please take her back again. But Twashtri said, Out on you! Be off! I will have no more of this. You must manage how you can. Then man said: But I cannot live with her. And Twashtri replied: Neither could you live without her. And he turned his back on man, and went on with his work. Then man said: What is to be done? For I cannot live either with her or without her.[19]

Male dominance is deeply entrenched in most societies, but women are beginning to defy it. Women in China have unbound their feet. Women in many Moslem countries have lifted the purdah. Women in Western societies

---

* Genesis 2:18, 21-23.

have loosened their corset. . . . Everywhere women are emerging as individuals in their own right. They are no longer a mere possession of man; and patriarchal authority, particularly within the family, is giving way to a democratic coalition which includes both women and children.

The shifting balance of power within the family is nowhere clearer than in the United States. Early immigrants to this country were mainly males, who wanted freedom and fortune and needed females. Females, however, were few and far between; and the law of supply and demand gave those few a competitive advantage. A wife had to be wooed to be won and then handled with care. With the first Women's Rights Convention at Seneca Falls, New York, 1848, women asked for equal rights and equal responsibilities—including equal education, equal work opportunities and a single standard of morality. Elizabeth Cady (who had insisted that the word "obey" be omitted from the ceremony when she married Henry Brewster Stanton in 1840) also dared ask for women's suffrage, even though her friend Lucretia Mott protested, "Why, Lizzie, thee will make us ridiculous!" But the feminists were determined to prove women's capacities and improve their status. In 1890, only eighteen per cent of women (aged fourteen or more) were gainfully employed. During World War I, many women entered the labor force for the first time. After the war, in 1920, they won the legal right to vote. During World War II, still more women entered the labor force. By 1960, thirty-four per cent of women worked, and 60.7 per cent of these were married women. Their median yearly income was only $1,029, compared to $4,103 for men, but women in increasing numbers were entering higher paid and traditionally masculine professions such as law and medicine. And in 1964, Margaret Chase Smith, Senator from Maine, made a serious bid for the Republican presidential nomination!

Husband, home and children no longer fully occupy nor fully satisfy educated women; and as their earning power and independence increase, the "double standard" becomes less tenable. Men still sow their wild oats, but women, more openly and freely, help reap them. There are fewer professional prostitutes and fewer pre-marital virgins; and when a woman does marry, she marries not a lord and master, but a partner. She promises to love, honor, and cherish her husband, but not to obey.

In the United States, the status of children has risen with the status of women. In 1732 Susan Wesley wrote to her son John, founder of Methodism, "In order to form the minds of children, the first thing to be done is to conquer their will and bring them to an obedient temper." [20] Mrs. Wesley spoke for mothers in the stately homes of England. In our rapidly expanding and mobile society, however, parents needed children longer than children needed parents. Pioneer life encouraged independence and broke the ties of the old extended family. Parents who wanted their children to stay home and work for them had to make the terms attractive. From 1700 to the middle nineteenth century, critics made increasing attacks on corporal punishment and de-emphasized the importance of breaking the child's will. As early as 1832, travelers from Europe commented on the "looseness" of American discipline.[21] Since the middle nineteenth century, corporal punishment and arbitrary authority have incurred increasing disfavor.

Some contemporary parents still adhere to the staunch child-rearing principles of earlier times, but current literature on the subject has a new theme: sympathetic nurturance to insure basic trust.

> . . . if a child is handled in a friendly way, he wants to do the right thing, the grown-up thing, most of the time. When he occasionally goes wrong in his early years, he is best straightened out by such methods as distracting, guiding, or even removing him bodily. As he grows older, his parents at times have to explain firmly why he must do this, not do that. If they are sure in their own minds how they expect him to behave, and tell him reasonably, not too irritably, they will have all the control over him that they need. It's not that he'll *always* obey perfectly, but that's not necessary.[22]

This changing attitude towards child rearing was born, not only of new psychological knowledge and insights, but of bureaucratization. Middle-class child-rearing practices in the eighteenth, nineteenth, and early twentieth centuries tended to favor the development of personality traits serviceable in a highly competitive entrepreneural society. Today children do not need to "make their own way" as much as they need to "belong." The new middle-class families are, for the most part, the families of "organization" men (and women) who tend to favor those child-rearing practices which engender in children affection for authority-figures and a capacity for getting along with others.

And so the heavy hand of patriarchal authority has lifted. Woman's place in the world is not yet equal to man's, but woman's place in the Western family is certainly, in every sense of the word, beside man; and children, with acknowledged identity, gleefully make themselves both seen and heard. After all, perhaps democracy, as well as charity, begins at home.

Will the Family Survive? *

When we say, "Honor thy father and thy mother," we repeat the ancient Hebrew's fifth commandment. When we make a virtue of monogamy, we follow a Roman code. If we value the family as a kinship group, accept male dominance within it, and, through discipline, try to maintain strict control of children, we find precedent in Hebrew, Roman, and Anglo-Saxon tradition. Any guilt we may feel about sex is a shadow cast by early Christians who proclaimed a virgin birth and called sex vile. Our romantic love songs are an echo of chivalry from Medieval England. And when church and state question each other's right to sanction marriage and grant divorce, it is a conflict born of the Reformation.

The monogamous, patriarchal, extended family pattern came to our East-

* This is more than a rhetorical question. A symposium presented by the University of California School of Medicine and Health Sciences, January, 1964, brought educators, historians, sociologists, psychologists, psychiatrists, and anthropologists together to discuss "The Family's Search for Survival."

ern seaboard with the British colonists—a legacy traced from England and Europe back to early Christian times. We know the history of the Western family, but we cannot clearly predict its future. The family as we know it today is still monogamous, but the patriarch is nearly extinct; and when we say *family*, we generally mean mother, father, and an average 2.5 children. Change in family structure, from patriarchal and extended to nuclear and more democratic, has been concurrent with change in family function.

Declining Functions

In Colonial settlements, the family was supplemented by the village and could draw on its limited resources—schools, churches, laws, and the skills and knowledge of neighbors. Rural and pioneer families had to be more self-sufficient. They were, in effect, isolated from each other even when they lived only a few miles apart. Each family, of necessity, functioned as a society in miniature, encompassing all the primary institutional areas: *religion, economics, government,* and *education.* In contrast today, religion, economics, government, education, and even recreation are now prime concerns of larger groups in the community, the state, and the nation. In these well-institutionalized areas, the urban family now plays a relatively minor role.

RELIGION. "The family that prays together stays together . . ." but, in 1942, only thirty per cent of Protestant urban families and thirty-eight per cent of rural families said grace before dinner.[23] The percentages would be even less today. And in 1942, no more than ten per cent of Protestant urban families and twenty-two per cent of rural families gathered to hear father read the Bible. Today, family Bible reading is almost unheard of. If religion were a strong element in family life, it would be a major source of marital tension. However, even when the husband is Catholic and the wife Protestant—the most difficult religious combination—only eleven per cent of the families feel that their religious differences seriously handicapped their adjustment.[24]

EDUCATION. Public school teachers in the United States number more than 1,500,000 strong, and parents tend to keep hands off formal education. They hesitate to teach Johnny to read for fear of starting him "wrong," and they are generally intimidated by the "new math." Educators encourage this attitude.

> The school feels a serious obligation to teach children effective work habits and to motivate them to improve their academic skills. This often results in their carrying research and practice work from the classroom into the home after school hours. . . . The parents' basic responsibility in this matter of helping a child to gain independence in his work is to see that the place and time are provided and let the teacher deal with the results.[25]

Schools also give instruction in hygiene, democratic living, personal adjustment, vocational adjustment, driving, ballroom dancing, cooking, sewing, home management and other nonacademic areas which used to be the responsibility of the family. Some parents have even abdicated in the area of sex education. School hygiene and biology classes include sex information; sex talks for children are recorded on LP records, and paperback books on "What to Tell Your Child About Sex" the child himself can buy at the corner drug store. Junior may already have more actual facts than his parents!

When a child enters kindergarten, the contemporary family tends to relinquish all major educational responsibilities, sometimes with an audible sigh of relief. Even before kindergarten, private nursery schools, cooperative nursery schools staffed in part by public school teachers, and state-supported child-care centers are increasingly involved in educational processes. In California in 1964, 234 child-care centers taught and tended more than 25,000 children of working mothers.

The relatively few children who now attend nursery schools are mainly those of either working mothers or educationally sophisticated ones. Thousands of other children could benefit by being taken out of inadequate home environments and put into well-equipped nursery schools.* Many culturally deprived children, both urban and rural, enter grade school so inadequately equipped for academic work that they never catch up. Some have had so little exposure to language as used in sustained conversation or in written narrative that they cannot follow the meaning of an average-length sentence from one end to the other. Some have lived in the midst of such domestic chaos that they cannot screen out distracting stimuli and concentrate on a learning task. The pre-school years are a critical period in the acquisition of both verbal and social skills. *In a society which demands a high level of both, how much responsibility should educational institutions assume for the nurturance of pre-school children?*

ECONOMICS. The family has a history of economic self-sufficiency. It was once the family—not the farmer, rancher, butcher, baker, canner, weaver, lumberman, carpenter—which raised wheat and oats, beans and barley, fruit and vegetables; kept cattle, sheep, pigs, and poultry; butchered meat, salted pork, and smoked bacon; baked bread; canned food; wove cloth and tanned hides; cut trees and sawed wood to build houses and wagons. The need for labor gave status to everyone in the family who could work. The special skills of women supplemented those of men, and children were taught early to help with the essential business of living. If there had been such a thing as radios and television, with soap operas for mother and cartoons for the kiddies, no one would have had time to look or listen. The old spinning wheel in a window of the antique shop is a symbol of a lost past. Today, a woman would feel abused if, unaided, she had to do the cooking, cleaning, and sewing for her family. She relies on the supermarket, the shopping center, the downtown stores to provide goods; the laundries, cleaners, cobblers, and an array of

* In California, under the McAteer Act of 1963, a compensatory educational program for three- to five-year-olds is demonstrating the effectiveness of nursery schools for children from families of low educational and socio-economic status. In New York City, a pilot nursery school program is giving at least some slum children a fighting chance.[26]

mechanical house servants to provide services. Though "a woman's work is never done," urbanization and mechanization have decreased her traditional homework. And if there isn't enough work in the home to keep a woman busy full time, what is there for children to do beyond token tasks and maintenance of their own rooms and possessions? The urban family is still an economic unit, but it is primarily a dependent unit of consumption, rather than a self-sustaining productive unit.

GOVERNMENT. Lawmaking, law enforcing, and other protective activities of government have been the areas most readily relinquished by the family to the larger community. The lawless, gun-slinging rough-rider of the plains is a romantic figure in Westerns, but an ephemeral figure in fact. His days were limited. Across the plains on the long migration west, law and order followed close on the heels of settlers. Today, law and order surround us, and the chief weapon of the urban dweller is his telephone. He calls for help against fire, theft, noisy neighbors and invasion of ants. His home is still his castle, but the troops that defend it are beyond its walls. For minor matters, there are some homemade rules. *Wash hands before eating. Brush teeth after eating. Homework before TV. Dates only on Friday and Saturday nights.* Under normal circumstances, the governmental functions of the family are limited to such minor personal matters.

RECREATION. Although recreation is not a primary institution, it is, in urban societies, an emerging institution competing with the family for the time and loyalty of its members. From the standpoint of family togetherness, two somewhat contradictory trends exist in recreation. *First, peer-group pleasures tend to take precedence over family fun.* Family picnics are rare events. The automobile and TV were each, in turn, heralded as cultural developments which could reinstate family-centered recreation. And the whole family did once crowd into the new car for a "Sunday drive," and, a generation later, around the television set to watch a "family program." However, such togetherness was transitory. Programs for adults and programs for children come at the same time on different channels; and the family, as soon as possible, buys an extra TV for the children. Sunday drivers still clog the highways, but the children in the car are the dependent younger ones, and it isn't unusual to find that each child has brought along his own special friend. The independent teen-ager won't get caught with the family if he can help it. The second significant trend: *active recreation has increased as compared to passive amusements.* Some of these activities—skiing, boating, swimming, hiking, skating, bowling, for example—can be family activities. The more skillful can help the less skillful. Everyone can laugh at mistakes and applaud successes. In skills that are fun to acquire and fun to practice, the family may yet find a key to enduring *togetherness.* The family that plays together may be the one that stays together.

ENDURING FUNCTIONS. You can get a meal in a restaurant, sleep on a park bench, use the facilities of a gas station, and have sex in a car; but home is better. It is familiar, more comfortable, and, in some cases, less expensive.

Furthermore, "Home is the place, where, when you have to go there, they have to take you in." * It is where you feel you belong. It is where, beginning with the intense mother-child relationship, you first took root, psychologically. Home, and the people in it you love, first administered to your subtle emotional needs and nourished your emerging ego. Although the contemporary family is no longer held together by strong religious, educational, economic, governmental, or recreational functions, it *is* held together by urgent physiological and psychological functions.

The family institution exists in every known human society. It is part of social structure and, by providing the members born into it with at least an initial status in the larger social hierarchy, it supports and perpetuates that structure. A more extensive study of the family in other places and other times would reveal more variations than we have noted, but the essential similarities would persist. Every society has its own code of family morality—its own mores and taboos—which gives a framework within which the essential physiological and psychological needs of its members can be met. The various codes function more or less satisfactorily to channel sexual behavior, legitimatize and nurture children, and provide continuing emotional support for the mature and maturing family members.

Within the United States the family is functioning somewhat less satisfactorily than we might wish. Witness the high divorce rate † and the number of illegitimate, neglected and delinquent children. Change and turmoil have shaken the framework of family morality. War, over-population and even such pragmatic considerations as the efficacy of birth-control techniques and medical gains over venereal disease have an impact on mores and taboos—or at least on the ways in which mores and taboos are presented and defended. The extended family of the nineteenth century was a God-fearing family held together by the legal reins of patriarchal authoritarianism and by a multitude of religious, economic, educational, and recreational functions. The isolated nuclear family of modern urban-industrial society is a relatively voluntary coalition of more or less autonomous individuals, held together by a little more than mutual physiological and psychological needs. Husband and wife have equal rights and equal authority under the law, and even children are legally considered as persons in their own right, rather than the property of either parent. The family is no longer the domineering or dominant social unit it once was, but it is still the main primary institution—the only institution responsible for providing those continuing personal relationships basic to the healthy growth of the child and the healthy functioning of the adult.

---

* Robert Frost (1875-1963), from "Death of the Hired Man."

† Increase in divorce rate does not necessarily mean increase in marital problems. Shortly after the Civil War, when women were financially dependent on men and *divorce* was equated with *scandal,* only one out of thirty-six marriages ended in divorce; but desertion, bigamy, prostitution, and maintenance of a mistress were more common than now. In this half of the twentieth century, an average of one out of four marriages ends in divorce; in California the rate is one out of two! Two-thirds of all divorces occur in the first nine years of marriage.

Although the family of the future may not be the same as that we now know and cherish, whatever the variation in form and function, it can be no better or no worse than the kinsmen who comprise it. *No family system has a monopoly on morality.*

RELIGION

Darkness and strange far lights, great glowing eye appearing and disappearing, blinding streaks, rumbles and crashes . . . pelting water and menacing skyborn shapes . . . unseen forces wrestling the trees . . . burning ball and scorching heat . . . an old woman fallen, a man crazed, a child lost, a birth cry. Dangers magnified by mystery. "In the beginning there was fear; and fear was in the heart of man; and fear controlled man. At every turn it whelmed over him, leaving him no moment of ease. . . . All the days of man were gray with fear, because all his universe seemed charged with danger." [27] With what groping words and signs could man understand and ease this encompassing fear? Throughout his history, he has tried. One hundred thousand years ago he buried, with his silent dead, treasured bits from this life for comfort in the next. Out of his emerging intelligence, he began spinning webs of belief.

Because we cannot accept evidence for some men's beliefs, we call them pagan superstitions; but the sociologist does not make this value judgment. Define religion as belief charged with attitudes of awe or devotion about universal forces man does not understand, then religion is common to all men.

Components of Religion

Through the centuries, religion has meant many things to many men. It began in the childhood of the species as emotion and belief. It endures in contemporary urban societies as emotion and belief institutionalized and sustained by ritual and organization.

Emotion

Deep are the emotions of men when they glimpse the power and plan of the unknown, which some call God. The astronaut in a space capsule swinging in orbit around the earth sphere . . . the college student alone on the barren granite slopes of a mountain peak . . . the sailor becalmed at sea under the star-studded net of night . . . a native watching a smoking volcano rise out of the sea . . . a woman seeing her first-born . . . a scientist discovering in a microscopic cell a "law" of nature. . . . Religion channels and communicates feelings which can overpower mortal man.

"He that loveth not knoweth not God; for God is love." I John 4: 8.

"Serve Jehovah with fear and rejoice with trembling. Kiss the son, lest He be angry and ye perish in the way, for His wrath will soon be kindled." Psalms 2: 11-12.

"And God shall wipe away all tears from their eyes; and there shall be no more death, neither sorrow, nor crying, . . . Revelation 21:4.

"My God, my God, why hast thou forsaken me? Why art thou so far from helping me, and from the words of my groaning? O my God, I cry in the day-time, but thou answereth not . . ." Psalms 22: 1-2.

Each religion has its own words for making memorable the profound emotions of men. Sanctioned rituals for focusing emotion are one of the greatest services of religion. Holy images for evoking emotion are one of its greatest strengths.

Belief

Out of emotions come beliefs—meanings which men impose on their experiences. The great variation in religious beliefs gives evidence of man's intense need to explain the unexplainable—to contain the infinite in some concept of finite mind.

Existence is the ultimate mystery; explanation of this mystery, a universal human effort.

The Babylonian heaven and earth were created when their God, Manduk, fought and killed Tiamut, the great dragon, the watery chaos. Half of the monster became heaven, half became earth.

The Samoan God, Tangaloa, created earth when he cast a rock into the boundless sea to be a home for his bird child. When the bird complained that the earth had no shade, the God sent a vine which grew and gave shadow. Later, in anger, Tangaloa sent worms which fed upon and killed the vines. From the worms man was made.

The Navajo earth always existed as one of six worlds, with a sky world above and four other worlds below. One of the lower worlds was inhabited by ants, one by swallows, one by grasshoppers, and the fourth by the Yei or gods, who created man. Water monsters in each world, angered by adultery, witchcraft, and quarreling, caused floods which drove the inhabitants into the next higher world. When floods came on the fourth world, man escaped to earth through hollow reeds which grew up into the sky. The first men on earth then created the mountains, stars, moon, and sun.

We sympathize with primitive beliefs because they stir our own childhood imagination.

There is power in everything—power we do not understand. Call it mana. It is a useful Melanesian word. Mana is a force. It can exist in the living, the dead, the inanimate, in the way of doing. Indians of the Northwest thought of mana as "pervading the world, like an electric current or a cosmic ray. It might show itself in anything from the cackle of a bluejay to the flash of the Thunderbird's eye which is the lightning." [28]

Everything in the Eskimo world has a spirit; the bear and the iceberg, the drift of snow, the pool of water, the sled and hunting knife. Some of the spirits possess mana. The shell in the bottom of the pond will guard the child from drowning; worn around the neck, it will protect from other harm. Eskimo animism allows for higher gods, too, who uphold the moral order. Violate the mores and risk not only personal punishment but retribution brought down on all the tribe by an offended deity. What is defined as good is what supports and strengthens group life; what is bad weakens it. *How great are the pressures to conformity when gods are the gestapo!*

The world of the African Bagandas is a lively place peopled with the spirits of tribal ancestors. Remember Aunt Nagawonyi, who knew how to cast spells? She is not just one of the ordinary spirits; she is one of the *lubale* now, along with those others who in life had mana. There is a lubale for each clan and occupation, and for each lubale there is a shrine with relics of his material existence—Kibuka's navel cord—a stone once sacred to Mukasa.

In primitive societies, one religion tends to involve the total society in a collective experience. In more advanced societies, many religions involve many sub-groups in both collective and individuated experience. Because religious beliefs are sanctioned and incoporated into the mores and taboos of the institution, religious beliefs are both a powerful force for the integration of any one particular religious community and a potential source of conflict among themselves and secular groups.

Primitive religions have only relatively limited influence. Many ancient religions died with their cultures; but nine vigorous living religions affect and are affected by the societies which support them. *Hinduism* has one of the richest literatures and longest histories; *Buddhism* originated in India but draws most followers from China and Japan; *Confucianism* and *Taoism* are both native to China; *Shintoism*, originally the primitive religion of Japan, has been modified by later teachers; *Zoroastrianism* stems from the teachings of Zarathustra, prophet of Iran; *Islam*, the religion of Muslims, claims almost as many followers as Roman Catholicism; *Judaism* is the oldest of the monotheistic religions; and *Christianity*, based on the teachings of Jesus Christ, claims, in all its forms, approximately one-third of the world population.*

In general, the more complex the society, the more varied and more individuated the religious beliefs and experiences become. In the United States, for example, the range of Christian beliefs alone is extreme.

Some Christian beliefs are of broad philosophical nature, and concern the ultimate nature of God or the universe or the ultimate meaning of life. Christians traditionally believe that God is a Trinity—the Father, the Son, and

---

* In spite of zealous missionary work, Christianity has converted only a fraction of the non-Christian world and has had little or no impact on its main competitors. Considering that the population increase is greatest in Asia, Christianity eventually may lose its present lead.

the Holy Ghost—that He created the universe and formed man in His own image, and that the ultimate meaning of life is a preparation for salvation. Beliefs of lesser scope concern such practical matters as how to achieve salvation. *Is salvation to be gained by faith, by good works, or is a man's fate predestined?* Other beliefs lack philosophical content and have the quality of myth.

The heritage of nearly all religions includes essential counsels and truths as well as nonessential myths and propositions. It is among the central themes that we find the most consensus. Typically, the influential living religions proclaim belief in a power or powers beyond man and hold man's right conduct in daily matters—especially in relationship to other men—to be a way of pleasing the gods or God and of insuring a better life here or in some distant heaven.

Ritual

What protection can men devise against the omnipresent spirits and gods? It isn't comfortable to be so at their mercy. Perhaps we can insure their friendship by sacrifice. Would the raw heart of a girl please? Perhaps, if we are clever enough, we can influence the gods, making their power ours. Primitive ways are various.

> Malayan, if you would be rid of your enemy, make his image a footstep long. Mutilate it. The gods will understand and know what to do. Pierce the image eye; cut the stomach. The eye will no longer see; the stomach will sicken. Transfix the head with a palm twig, enshroud the image, pray over it as if you were praying over the dead and bury it. Your enemy will not be long in dying.
>
> The beasts thirst and the fields are dry. Gather, Dieri of Australia, for rain-making. Dig a hole; build a hut over it. Bleed two old men with a cut inside the arm—just below the elbow. Throw handfuls of duck down in the air. Put two stones in the middle of the hut and call the women to see them there. Pound gypsum and throw it into a water hole. Now, men, butt against the hut with your heads and knock it down. If no rain comes, the Mura-Mura must be angry.

And the civilized ways grow out of the primitive to manifest emotion and belief. Performed generation after generation, the rituals of the higher religions symbolize the sacred and acquire the aura of the sacred.

> Moslem, wash all the body's orifices before you pray to Allah . . . Jew, light the nine candles of the Menorah at Hanukkah . . . Catholic, count your beads and make the sign of the Cross . . . Baptism, Confirmation, Extreme Unction, Ordination, and Matrimony are ritual "rites of passage," marking an individual's change of status. Even family grace before dinner and a private, "Now I lay me down to sleep," are ritual behavior.

Each religion and each church has its repertoire of ritual. Rituals are the patterned ways of worship, of appeal, and of recognition. They formalize devotional action; they symbolize and sanction, investing word and gesture with dignity and drama. And when men together join in ritual ceremony, the ritual itself is a force uniting them one to the other and to their common religion.

Organization

A religion needs an abiding structure which can serve, generation after generation, to define and sustain emotion, belief, and ritual. All the influential living religions have perpetuated themselves through establishing institutional structures which embody clearly defined roles for the priesthood, ministry, and other functionaries.

Christian organizations are of four types: churches (sometimes called ecclesia), sects, denominations, and cults. The term *church* in this context means a religious body believing itself to be the sole means of essential grace dispensed through an ordained priesthood. Most members are "born" into a church, but some churches make aggressive missionary efforts to recruit converts. (The Medieval Roman Catholic Church, for example, not only claimed control over nearly all sacred life of the times, but through the Inquisition forcefully extended its control over the secular life of the populace.) Membership in *sects,* by contrast, is voluntary and characterized by a strong sense of fellowship. The sect as a whole tends to withdraw from secular life and requires no special clergy to intercede for salvation. The Salvation Army, Jehovah's Witnesses, and the Amish are representative Christian sects. *Denominations* are sects which "made good." Typically, denominations are more worldly and better integrated into the middle- and upper-class structure of society. As in sects, the members of Christian denominations (the major branches of Protestantism) do not seek Grace through the clergy. Grace comes, if at all, through predestination, faith, or good works. A *cult* centers around a powerful leader who gives effective expression to some dominant idea and who is often believed by his followers to be divine. (The *Father Divine* cult and the *I Am* are typical.) Cults find followers particularly in large urban centers where lonely and alienated members of the mass society are eager for the security they might gain by identifying with one they believe to be a divine leader.

Emotion and belief fixed in ritual and sustained through organization make up a total religious heritage of amazing variability. Embedded in this heritage are truths and counsels of enduring validity.

Secularization of Religion

For Europeans in the Middle Ages, religion was a central institution, inseparable from life; for many early Americans, religion gave direction to a significant part of community and personal life. The church had authority over education, recreation, public welfare, and such legal concerns as death and divorce, which could be interpreted as involving man's relationship to God. Today, in our urban-industrialized society, religion is on the periphery of life. Secular agencies predominate in performing many functions formerly the main or exclusive responsibility of the church. Instead of the sacred pervading the secular institutions, secular ways are pervading the churches. Religion as an institution in the service of God has lost power, not only over other social institutions, but over individuals.

Religion seems to be a declining institution in spite of the fact that the percentage increase in church membership has outpaced the population increase. In the United States in 1790, approximately ten per cent of the population were church members; in 1860 it was sixteen per cent; by 1962, the Yearbook of American Churches reported a total of two hundred and fifty-six religious bodies with 114,449,217 members—slightly more than sixty-three per cent of the population. Some people cite increased church membership as evidence of a religious revival. Others, including church leaders, recognize that church membership may indicate only social conformity, not religious conviction.

> The religious organizations conspire to maintain the hypocrisy that the religious enterprise is significant, and yet professionals know better than anyone else how little the religious meanings are penetrating the American consciousness. Every serious study indicated unequivocally that the detachment of Americans from the fundamental meanings of the Christian message is almost total despite the repetition of pious phrases.[29]

In the deep steel and concrete forests of our cities, we are separated from intimate contact with the strong forces of nature which once stirred men of the mountains and forests and plains to humility before powers beyond their control.

> Certainly urbanized society has built shields between itself and the primal experiences of life. Biblical man, lifting up his eyes to the hills, thought of the mystery of creation and providence. Metropolitan man, lifting his eyes through the smog to the skyscrapers, is impressed with human accomplishments. Frustrated as he often is by the problems of the megalopolis, he may feel himself victim rather than master, but he is reminded more of the power of engineering and economics than of God.[30]

Like all other institutions, religion is responsive to the cultural environment which envelops it. When the symbolic spire of the New England church reached high towards heaven and clearly dominated the physical structure of the community, the church itself dominated the life of the community. Today, when the church building is dwarfed by skyscrapers, religion itself, in competing with secular institutions, is losing its sacred identity. The church offers, in addition to spiritual guidance, personal counseling and social gratifications. Seminaries train divinity students in psychology and other social sciences to prepare them for the mundane problems they will meet. The pragmatic values of action-oriented industrial society permeate religious organizations. The social utility of a church may seem more important than its specific theology.

Increasingly, the urban church is sanctioning secular ways and secular means.

Churches have social activities. A church in California announced a fund-raising drive "to build *first* a social hall, then a rectory, and finally a chapel." Churches characteristically have their "socials"—picnics, dances, tournaments, sings. In one suburban church, the congregation was repeatedly urged to linger after the service, "*Remember our coffee hour. We hope you will join us.*"

Churches have economic activities. They have to support themselves.

> The peculiar American pattern of religious institutions, in which each church has to fend financially for itself, has put a strong emphasis upon economic activities. The pastor who is a good businessman, gets contributions, pays the debts, and maintains a large assemblage of buildings, is the man who receives wide approval. The United States is probably the only country in which a biography of Christ depicting him as a successful businessman could be a best seller. The parable of the talents is often interpreted to mean that a man is morally obligated to use his abilities for economic and material advancement.[31]

Churches advertise. They advertise as does any secular organization via radio and television . . . on billboards . . . in newspapers. "*Go to church this Sunday, the church of your choice, but go!*" The United Presbyterian Church, after testing a series of 900 radio spots in St. Louis and Detroit, decided to start a saturation-spot campaign in 15 of the Nation's biggest urban centers. The spots were devised by Stan Freberg, comedian and ad man. They started off with a brief dialogue and concluded with a singing jingle. Some churchmen thought the lines too secular, but, said one Presbyterian official, ". . . After all, this country has seen jazz masses and night clubs taken over by church groups. We must think of the greater good." [32]

And churches use modern means of mass communication. Churches broadcast and televise their services and otherwise make worship convenient. A Boston church advertised ingenious mechanical devices in the church itself.

> Worship God in an air-conditioned sanctuary. Visitors to Davis Chapel at the . . . Church will be able to select from 150 hymns, sermonettes, organ and choir selections, and readings, by compressing buttons on a keyboard installed in a wooden, simulated lectern. A set of speakers . . . will be placed in the organ loft. In this way the air of authenticity is retained, for organ selections will emanate from there. . . . Here's an electronic system that shows how progress in scientific research becomes a means to an end which is unmatched . . . personal worship.[33]

Urban society is a mass society—impersonal and mechanized. In it religious experience may be less a collective experience than an individual one. The church welcomes saint and sinner alike; and today, with the wonders of technology at its service, the individual in need of comfort and reassurance need only pick up the telephone and "Dial a Prayer." This is the "Dial a Prayer" message given the day of this writing.

> Each day think of this—God loves me and needs me. I am a part of God's perfect plan. God loves me and needs me. The greatness of the Father is seek-

ing expression through me, and I love letting it come forth that all people may recognize it to be doing so. God loves me and needs me. God bless you.

The rise in the percentage of church members could be interpreted not as a revival of religion in the pious theological sense nor as an increase in the importance of religion as a sacred institution, but rather as evidence of the extensive personal and social services the church in the name of religion now offers *The Lonely Crowd.**

> The central fact of modern history in the West—by which we mean the long period from the end of the Middle Ages to the present—is unquestionably the decline of religion. No doubt, the churches are still very powerful organizations; there are millions of churchgoers all over the world; and even the purely intellectual possibilities of religious belief look better to churchmen now than in the bleak days of self-confident nineteenth-century materialism. A few years ago there was even considerable talk about a "religious revival," and some popular and patriotic periodicals such as *Life* magazine gave a great deal of space to it; but the talk has by now pretty much died down; the movement, if any, subsided, and the American public buys more automobiles and television sets than ever before. When *Life* magazine promotes a revival of religion, one is only too painfully aware . . . that religion is considered as being in the national interest; one could scarcely have a clearer indication of the broader historical fact that in the modern world the nation-state, a thoroughly secular institution, outranks any church.
>
> The decline of religion in modern times means simply that religion is no longer the uncontested center and ruler of man's life, and that the church is no longer the final and unquestioned home and asylum of his being.[34]

Although religion no longer holds the powerful position it did when church and state were one, or when church and state were competing equals, religion as an institution still has a role to play in modern society. That role seems to be one which will give more attention to ethical issues in the secular world than to the rituals and theology of the sacred one. Religious articles in popular magazines on topics such as religious dogma, the after-life, atonement, baptism, the devil, and church work decreased two-thirds between 1905 and 1940 but articles on the relationship of religion to politics, economics, and science increased.[35]

When Pope Paul VI reconvened the Ecumenical Council in 1963, he defined as one aim of the Council a closer contact between the church and the contemporary world. To help achieve this aim, he appealed for a union of all faiths of Christendom into a single, universal church.

Varieties of Religious Expression in the United States

In the United States, separation of church and state and the advance of urban-industrialism have led to an unparalleled proliferation of religions. Al-

* David Riesman (*The Lonely Crowd,* 1950) suggests that the individual feels alienated from the mass society of which he is a part.

though Christianity, in one form or another, dominates, other religious emotions, beliefs, and rituals also find expression. George Bernard Shaw understated when he remarked, "There is only one religion, though there are a hundred versions of it." There are a thousand and more versions, and many of them find followers here.

The range is from the primitive to the sophisticated and sedate—from small groups of recent origin to large institutions centuries old—from beliefs in the magical to doctrines of highest ethical character. The ministry includes ignorant bigots and men of outstanding educational and moral qualifications.

We support religious cults, camp meetings, and more than two hundred and fifty specific religious groups ranging, alphabetically, from the *Advent Christian Church* to the *Volunteers of America.* The Baptist denomination alone has twenty-seven divisions, including *Duck River (and Kindred) Associations of Baptists, General Conference of Evangelical Baptist Churches, General Baptists, General Six Principle Baptists, Independent Baptist Church of America, National Baptists, Evangelical Life and Soul Saving Assembly of the United States of America, Primitive Baptists, Regular Baptists, United Baptists, United Free Will Baptists.* In one city of approximately 750,000 population, the telephone directory impartially listed more than four hundred churches.

Even the pathological disguises itself in the raiment of religion.

> The girls and women soon began to sway. They chanted; they moaned; they "spoke in tongues" and cried aloud while the prophet seemed to gain in stature and his normally calm eyes sank deep into his head, where they glowed like two pits of fire. The swaying and the chanting went on.
>
> Suddenly, like a thunderbolt, the prophet's voice boomed out: "Vile clothes, begone!" The whiskered fellow then disrobed and, without urging on his part, many of the women present did likewise. There was nothing coy about it, no sense of shame. They threw off their peekaboo waists, their skirts, and the multitude of petticoats; they tore wildly at their whalebone corsets, meanwhile moaning like all get-out.
>
> "Roll, ye sinners, roll!" thundered Joshua; and roll they did, some in chemises, some without, all over the bare floor, with Joshua and Brother Brooks rolling happily among them.
>
> Either at this or at a subsequent meeting Joshua began to expound the canons of his sect. He had already announced that he and his followers were members of the Church of the Bride of Christ. Now he let it be known that the Lord had commanded him to select from among his followers she who was to become the Mother of a Second Christ.
>
> It soon became apparent to the faithful that Joshua was going about his quest for a second Mother in a thorough and searching manner, which manner was obviously of the empirical school.[36]

We pride ourselves on our religious tolerance, but we draw the line at sexual license. Joshua was shot by the irate brother of a seventeen-year-old parishioner designated by Joshua as Mother of Christ for His second coming. The girl, in turn, frustrated by being deprived of such a divine mission, shot her brother. She was sent to the state mental asylum.

The United States is 91.9 per cent Christian (66.2 per cent Protestant, 25.7 per cent Roman Catholic), 3.2 per cent Jewish, 1.3 per cent other religions, and 1 per cent non-committed.[37] Christianity is the norm, and although freedom of worship is our ideal, in practice we are more tolerant of diversity in Christian belief than we are of either disbelief or non-Christian beliefs.

> Our failure to go to temple or to send our children to any sort of religious school is not a *failure*. It is not a negative thing that happens out of carelessness or laziness. It is a positive thing, arising out of a deep and serious conviction, and it is as important to us as any religion could be to a religious person.
>
> We teach our children to love, to try to be honest and truthful, to try to help others without self-aggrandizement, to try never to hurt another, to feel a sense of responsibility to society, and to respect other peoples' concepts and ideas, not only about religion, but about ways of life. . . .
>
> But I will not teach them anything I cannot believe, and I will not teach them any ritual which seems to me as senseless as knocking on wood when you say you haven't had a cold for a long time. . . . My children are pressured from every side to do something contrary to our beliefs. . . . The television programs tell them to go to church on Sunday, ("and take Dad and Mom, too"). . . . My children played occasionally with a child whose father is a minister. They don't go there any more because every time they did, he told them they should believe in God and go to church. . . . In our public school a teacher reads to the class from the Bible in the morning.[38]

Nor is it easy for non-Christian parents to raise their children without having them feel discriminated against.

> Karen, a sixteen-year old high school girl living in Berkley, Michigan, went to the movies one night and couldn't believe the plot. The movie was "Gentlemen's Agreement," the story of a writer . . . who adopts a Jewish name for a bit to see if it will make any difference in the way he is treated. The high-school lass thought it "very far-fetched" that nothing more than a Jewish sounding name would subject a nice friendly American to snideries and humiliation.
>
> "Things like that just don't happen any more," said Karen.
>
> The next day, some friends happened to ask Karen about some of the charms on her bracelet, and she remarked, "They're Jewish symbols." That's all she said. In the days that followed, her friends began to avoid our girl, and soon she even found it hard to get friends to walk home with her. Karen's sister's popularity began to suffer most peculiarly, too.
>
> After six weeks, Karen went to her teacher and told him her troubles . . . and a school assembly was called. At this assembly, Karen, in the brave and untutored accents of the young, announced: "It happens that I'm not Jewish. I am of Scotch and French descent. I attend Berkley Community Church. But for six weeks, I have lived in a different world. . . . What made you all act this way? Now I understand that prejudice is more than a word in the dictionary" [39]

Religious prejudice and intolerance do exist in the United States, but relative to most societies, we have an unusual degree of religious freedom and tolerance. A minister canvassing a mass-produced suburb for church members encountered one man who said he was an atheist. Without batting an eye, the minister responded, "Well, you should have a club. I'll see if I can find some others and get you all together." [40]

Science and Religion

Early in the history of sociology and psychology, religion was brought into scientific focus. Notable were the lectures of psychologist William James (1842-1910) on "The Varieties of Religious Experience" and the theoretical works of the sociologists Émile Durkheim (1858-1911) and Max Weber (1864-1920). However, the psychology and sociology of religion failed to develop as an area of scientific research. Religion is an intimate, value-laden realm, full of potential conflict for both researchers and subjects. Twentieth-century sociologists and psychologists, anxious to get their disciplines on firm scientific footing, by tacit agreement classified religion as a taboo topic. We have statistics about religious organizations, religious rituals, and religious beliefs. But we know little about the depth or vitality of religious beliefs in any given society, about the relationship between religious beliefs and secular beliefs, about the effect of religious beliefs on general behavior. However, after World War II gave new professional status to the behavioral sciences and brought mankind face to face with the problems of world salvation, it seemed not only reasonable but urgent that behavioral scientists extend their concern beyond the gathering of facts to the discernment of meanings.

> . . . questions of meaning-value-commitment, of faith relationship to a Supreme Being in trusting dependence and ethical obedience . . . are or can be among the major determinants of an individual's life style, major ingredients in the "mix" of the psychic process. Social science cannot claim adequacy if it disregards religion.[41]

Societies for the scientific study of religion, new journals for the publication of scientific treatises on religion,* courses in the psychology and sociology of religion in both theological and secular educational institutions, and books by scientists on religion all give evidence of the re-establishment of religion as a respectable field for scientific research.

Devout champions of Christianity in the United States today do not necessarily welcome scientific probings. Although they point to the limitations of reason and the uncertainties of empirical knowledge, they often feel the faith they have built on intuition, authority, and other ways of "knowing," to be threatened by science. Many persons perceive science as an adversary rather than as a possible ally of religion. But science—even the biological and physical sciences—in no way invalidates religious *emotion*, religious *ritual*, or

* Journals include the *Journal for the Scientific Study of Religion* and *Review of Religious Research.* Societies include the *Religious Education Association,* the *Society for the Scientific Study of Religion,* the *Academy of Religion and Mental Health,* and the *Religious Research Association.*

religious *organization.* Furthermore, science champions the right and even the need of each individual to his own beliefs in such areas of admitted uncertainty as the means to personal salvation or the ultimate nature of God and the Universe. If any inherent conflict exists between religion and science, it is only in the area of myths—of those beliefs which are subject to proof or disproof. But myths, even when mortally wounded by indisputable fact, die hard.

The myths each culture, including the Christian culture, invented to explain existence and the profound experiences of man have necessarily reflected the level of knowledge and the morality of the culture at the time of invention. The origin of a myth may be historical or fictional, but once accepted and institutionalized in religion, it shows all the resistance to change typical of other institutional components. Although time might bring new knowledge and new moral insights, to doubt the myths has been to doubt the "Word of God."

From an objective sociological view, we can understand why the Biblical story of Creation, historically a part of our mores and religious institutions, has been so resistant to change. Biblical chronology was given specific form in 1650 when Archbishop Usher of England established the date of Creation as 4004 B.C. Other equally serious scholars soon determined the moment of man's origin as being Friday, October 23, 4004 B.C. at 9:00 a.m. After Darwin's *Origin of Species* was published in 1859, intellectual discussions of evolution were commonly condemned as atheistic attacks on the fundamentals of religion itself rather than considered as another attempt to understand the universal mystery. The *authority* of the Bible was challenged! *Mores* and *institutions* dependent on that authority were threatened. People were troubled and uneasy.

Gradually, as *knowledge through science* increased, some myths lost some of their ancient power of persuasion. Our last official skirmish in the battle of "science" versus "religion" was in 1925 when the American Civil Liberties Union tested a Tennessee law forbidding the teaching of evolution in public schools. The "monkey trial," as the newspapers labeled it, brought literal interpretation of the Bible into direct conflict with evolution. *Biblical authority* was challenged by *scientific authority*. The accused high school biology teacher was given only a token fine and later was legally cleared of this first "conviction." The publicity accompanying the trial sharpened the issue for many people and advanced the cause of evolution. Today, even though isolated resistance remains, evolution is taught in public schools, and is accepted as fact by most Christian denominations.

If we accept man's origin as evolutionary, we are led to seek more scientific answers to questions about the age of the earth and the time when the first creature identifiable as human appeared.

According to Archbishop Usher's calculations, the earth, in 1960, would be 5,964 years old. According to geologists' calculations, the earth is approximately 5,000,000,000 years old. Geologists substantiate their calculations with some impressive evidence. They work within a basic principle of science—the orderliness of nature's processes: those processes observable today are characteristic of all times. This assumption is essential in studying what is spatially or historically beyond our perception. When geologists apply this principle of *Uniformitarianism* to the science of earth, they find that 5,964 years could not possibly account in natural terms for the earth's physical form and substance. Hundreds of millions of years were needed for the geological formations of the Grand Canyon. It would take at least a billion years for the observable processes of erosion and evaporation to contribute the percentage of salt found in the oceans. Approximately five billion years are minimum to produce mineral deposits known to be the end product of radioactive elements which lose radioactivity at a rate determined through nuclear physics.

The authority of science is convincing; and, for some, it is a satisfying psychological equivalent to the authority of myth. Einstein, often called an atheist by the conventionally religious, declared:

> The cosmic religious experience is the strongest and noblest mainspring of scientific research. . . . My religion consists of a humble admiration of the illimitable superior spirit who reveals himself in the slight details we are able to perceive with our frail and feeble minds. That deeply emotional conviction of the presence of a superior reasoning power, which is revealed in the incomprehensible universe, forms my idea of God.[42]

Many men of good will and serious intent are unable to accept the dogmas of Christianity or any other institutional religion, but the awe and humility and reverence they feel for the order perceived in life and matter may be as deeply religious as that of any prophet.

Is Religion Necessary?

Religion orients the individual ideologically to both God and man. For many seeking spiritual comfort and guidance, religion does more than science can to justify God's ways to man. Science may explain *how* things happen, but when an individual is confronted with overwhelming sorrow—with the premature death of one beloved—his anguished question is not "*How?*" but "*Why?*" *Why did this happen? Why? He loved life. He had good work to do. Why take him now?* Such *why* questions can't be answered by explaining the laws of physics involved in a fatal accident or the chemistry of a puff adder's poison without seeming irrelevant and even irreverent. To survive deprivation and personal tragedy, even to steer a clear course through the vagaries of everyday existence, the individual seeks a life-orienting framework of personal meaning and value. This religion offers.

Religion offers, too, an approach to the society of men. Religion may justify that society; it may denounce that society; or it may actively seek to cope with that society, believing that "here on earth, God's work must surely be our own."[43]

Religion may justify every detail of the secular society, admonishing those discontented with the *status quo* not to question the "will of God." The Judaeo-

Christian religion in its time has fiercely opposed free speech and free action; it has even opposed democratic government. And today some theologians defend segregation and subordination of Negroes on the grounds that Negroes, being sons of Ham, are divinely ordained to be the drawers of water and hewers of wood.

Religion may oppose society as the work of Satan, and reject the secular world as sinful and beyond redemption. Believers withdraw and cooperate with the "outside" world as little as possible; effort must be directed to personal salvation rather than wasted on a wicked and doomed world. A number of small sects in the United States take this stand. Jehovah's Witnesses, for example, refuse to serve in the Armed Forces, to salute the flag, to enter politics, or otherwise accept the social mores. The Amish of Pennsylvania resist all temptations held out by a seductive secular culture: they will not use tractors, automobiles, or electricity. They increase their social distance by their severe, colorless dress and by their own Pennsylvania Dutch dialect.*

And, finally, religion may accept the basic tenets of the secular order, but continually try to bring the real patterns of culture into conformity with the ideal patterns. This is the position taken by liberal theologians of different faiths. They bring to their work a knowledge of history, an awareness of social issues, a consciousness of religious ambiguities, and an admission of uncertainty.[44]

> One could pose the opposition between the atavistic forms of Christianity in the United States and the emerging Christendom in terms such as these: *Pietism,* cast in a setting suitable to an era of geographical frontiers, versus *Servanthood,* manifest in the struggle for a humanized world. Pietism reflects a preoccupation with individual sentiments and private salvation. These themes merely reinforce irresponsibility among religious people. Servanthood, on the other hand, reflects the new role of Christianity in a world come of age—an apostolate of laymen who strive to discern the ultimate meanings and claims that are being disclosed in the historical struggles of our time.
>
> Whereas pietism, whether of the Graham type or of the more common type experienced in suburbanized Christianity, summons the laity away from involvement in historical struggles to preoccupation with "religious" activities, servanthood evokes their responsibility to God for the world he creates with them. Pietism defines the "religious" as individualism and sentimentality. Servanthood defines the "religious" as involvements, commitments, meanings, and responsibilities for the world to be created.[45]

The immediate effect of the liberal movement among theologians in the United States is, in many instances, creating a breach between themselves and

---

* The Amish patois includes unique words and novel grammatical structures. They might say *furhuddled* for mixed up, *all* for finished, or *stroobly* for sloppy. If the doorbell is out of order (a mechanical, not an electric one), they might put out a warning sign, "Bump, the bell don't make." And a caboose might be described by saying, "When the little red one comes, the train's all, ain't?"

congregations unready for adventurous unorthodox thought. Of young men recently graduated from a leading theological seminary, eighty-eight per cent left the ministry before completing three years of service. The young ministers were concerned with the philosophical, scientific, and social implications of their work. They found themselves impatient with the narrow literal interpretation the typical congregation had of the ministerial role, and dissatisfied with the vague generalities in which they were expected to speak. However, in spite of the complacence of many congregations, leaders of the major denominations in the United States today are increasingly liberal. Protestants are praising the "Social Gospel"; Jews and Catholics are stressing personal and national ethics. White ministers, priests, and rabbis have joined Negro protest demonstrations demanding equality for all God's children. Pope John XXIII spoke with charity as the conscience of the world in his memorable encyclical, *Pacem in Terris.*

> The fact that one is a citizen of a particular state does not detract in any way from his membership of the human family as a whole, nor from his citizenship of the world community. . . . We must remember that, of its very nature, civil authority exists, not to confine its people within the boundaries of their nation, but rather to protect, above all else, the common good of that particular civil society, which certainly cannot be divorced from the common good of the entire human family. . . . This entails not only that civil societies should pursue their particular interests without hurting others, but also that they should join forces and plans whenever the efforts of an individual government cannot achieve its desired goals. But in the execution of such common efforts, great care must be taken lest what helps some nations should injure others.

The moral force of Pope John's words diffused beyond Catholicism, beyond Christianity, to reverberate through all the world. His widened world conscience epitomizes the emerging concept of religious function—a concept which casts religion into the vital role of ethical and moral arbiter in a troubled world.

Relative to the increasing power of the national state, to the growth of an urban-industrial economy, and the expansion of education to meet the demands of a mobile and striving population, religion is a declining institution. However, it retains its vital personal function of orienting man to his God and his society, and it has assumed a social conscience which makes it a potential partner with science in defining the means and goals of the emerging social order. Religion is a diminished but not an invalidated institution. Its actual specific power is less, but its influence remains. Said Voltaire: "If God did not exist, it would be necessary to invent Him."

Differences in religious emotion, belief, ritual and organization are but variations on a common theme. Men need to believe something. If we do not have truth, we must have faith. Whatever form conviction or questioning takes, it expresses the common human search for an explanation of the miracle that is life. *No religion has a monopoly on God.*

Notes

1. George P. Murdock, "The Common Denominator of Culture," in *The Science of Man in the World Crisis,* ed. Ralph Linton (New York: Columbia University Press, 1945), p. 124.
2. Meyer Fortes, "Primitive Kinship," *Scientific American,* June, 1959, p. 147.
3. Ralph Linton, *The Study of Man* (New York: Appleton-Century-Crofts, Inc., 1936), p. 175.
4. Arthur Weigal, *Sappho of Lesbos: Her Life and Times* (New York: Frederick A. Stokes Company, 1932), pp. 100-101.
5. Ruth Benedict, *Patterns of Culture* (New York: Pelican Books, Inc., 1946), pp. 123-124.
6. Anthony West, "Kyoto Days," *The New Yorker,* April 26, 1958, pp. 120-134.
7. Count Marco, "Beauty and the Beast," *San Francisco Chronicle,* July 27, 1959, p. 19.
8. *San Francisco Chronicle,* August 19, 1963, p. 1.
9. Anonymous, "My Daughter Married a Negro," *Harper's Magazine,* July, 1951, p. 40.
10. Norman Lewis, "Tubman Bids Us Toil," *The New Yorker,* January 11, 1958, pp. 81-82.
11. H.R.H. Prince Peter of Greece (anthropologist specializing in polyandry), cited in *The New Yorker,* September 18, 1954, pp. 56-57.
12. Stuart A. Queen, Robert W. Habenstein, and John B. Adams, *The Family in Various Cultures* (New York: J. B. Lippincott Company, 1961), p. 23.
13. E. Adamson Hoebel, "Social Controls," in *Societies Around the World,* Howard Becker, ed. (New York: The Dryden Press, 1956), p. 106.
14. Queen, Habenstein, and Adams, *The Family in Various Cultures,* p. 77
15. *Ibid.,* p. 22.
16. Jeanette Mirsky, "The Eskimo of Greenland," in Margaret Mead, ed., *Cooperation and Competition Among Primitive Peoples* (New York: McGraw-Hill Book Company, 1937), pp. 71-86.
17. Queen, Habenstein, and Adams, *The Family in Various Cultures,* p. 76-77.
18. *Ibid.,* pp. 125-126.
19. F. W. Baid, *A Digit of the Moon* (New York: G. P. Putnam's Sons, 1905), pp. 32-34.
20. Daniel R. Miller and Guy E. Swanson, *The Changing American Parent* (New York: John Wiley & Sons, Inc., 1958), p. 11.
21. Frances Trollope, *Domestic Manners of the Americans* (New York: Alfred A. Knopf, Inc., 1949), p. 213.
22. Benjamin Spock, *The Common Sense Book of Baby and Child Care* (New York: Duell, Sloan, and Pearce, 1946), p. 270.
23. *White House Conference on Children in a Democracy,* Final Report (Washington: Children's Bureau Publication No. 272, 1942), pp. 185-186.
24. Judson T. Landis, "Marriages of Mixed and Non-Mixed Religious Faith," *American Sociological Review,* 14 (1949), 405.
25. Marin Country Day School, Corte Madera, California, *Bulletin of Information for Parents,* 1961-1962, p. 3.
26. Charles E. Silberman, "Give Slum Children a Chance: A Radical Proposal," *Harper's Magazine,* May, 1964, pp. 37-42.
27. Lewis Browne, *This Believing World* (New York: The Macmillan Company, 1926), p. 27.
28. Ruth Underhill, *Indians of the Pacific Northwest* (Washington, D.C., Bureau of Indian Affairs, 1944), p. 184.

29. Gibson Winter, "The New Christendom in the Metropolis," *Christianity and Crisis,* November 26, 1962, pp. 210-211.
30. Roger L. Shinn, "Protestant Reconstruction in Urbanized Culture," *Christianity and Crisis,* November 26, 1962.
31. Joseph Fichter, *Sociology* (Chicago: The University of Chicago Press, 1957), p. 257.
32. *San Francisco Chronicle,* April 20, 1964, p. 6.
33. The Worcester, Massachusetts, *Evening Gazette,* November 6, 1958, reprinted in *Harper's Magazine,* February, 1959.
34. William Barrett, *Irrational Man: A Study in Existential Philosophy* (Garden City, N.Y.: Doubleday & Company, Inc., 1958), p. 24.
35. Murray Gendell and Hans L. Zetterberg, eds., *A Sociological Almanac for the United States* (New York: Charles Scribner's Sons, 1964), p. 23.
36. Stewart H. Holbrook, "Oregon's Secret Love Cult," in *Grand Deception,* ed. Alexander Klein (New York: J. B. Lippincott Co., 1955), pp. 16-23.
37. Gendell and Zetterberg, *op. cit.,* p. 24.
38. Elinor Goulding Smith, "Won't Someone Tolerate Me?", *Harper's Magazine,* August, 1956, pp. 34-38.
39. Leo Rosten, "The Easy Chair," *Harper's Magazine,* October, 1957, p. 18.
40. Harry Henderson, "Rugged American Collectivism–The Mass-Produced Suburbs," Part 2, *Harper's Magazine,* December, 1953, p. 81.
41. William Douglas, "Religion," in *Taboo Topics,* Norman L. Farberow, ed. (New York: Atherton Press, 1963), p. 93.
42. Lincoln Barnett, *The Universe and Dr. Einstein* (New York: A Mentor Book, 1952), pp. 117-118.
43. John Fitzgerald Kennedy, Inaugural Address, 1961.
44. Herbert J. Muller, "Second Thoughts on the Religious Revival," *Harper's Magazine,* February, 1963, p. 93.
45. Gibson Winter, "The New Christendom in the Metropolis," *Christianity and Crisis,* November 26, 1962, p. 207.

Difference from me is not the measure of absurdity.

TERENCE (190-159 B.C.)

5

Economics, Government, and Education—Expanding Institutions

FAMILY AND RELIGION in technologically advanced societies have declined. Family structure has been reduced to the nuclear core; family function is mainly confined to biological and psychological essentials; and family mores and taboos are less clearly and strictly defined. Religion has differentiated into a great variety of separate organizations of extreme variability in belief and ritual. The various churches, sects, denominations, and cults are increasingly secularized, and their norms have shifted accordingly. Neither *Family* nor *Religion* has its previous scope and authority. However, the same forces * which have contributed to the diminishing influence of these two institutions have supported the expansion of three others: *Economics, Government,* and *Education.*

Wherever and whenever scientific technology has activated industrial development, the unfamiliar demands of routinized factory work, specialization, and urbanization have combined to disturb traditions and supporting social institutions. In the early nineteenth century, one small island with no more than two per cent of the world's population produced more than half the world's industrial output. As the century advanced, industrialism spread from England to other nations of northwestern Europe, to the United

* These include the geographical discoveries of the fifteenth and sixteenth centuries, the ideological discoveries of the Renaissance and the Reformation, and the scientific discoveries of the eighteenth and nineteenth centuries.

States, Canada, Australia, and New Zealand. So far this century, the Soviet Union and one non-European nation—Japan—have developed industrially and become, by world standards, "rich." These "rich" nations have approximately one-third of the world population, but they consume more than two-thirds of the world's goods. Technologically advanced societies are complex societies. They incorporate not only their original agrarian base, but a superstructure of productive and service industries, including maintenance, manufacturing, commerce, transportation, finance, recreation, communication, research, and development—a network of legislative, executive, and judicial offices, plus a system of education committed to the formidable task of integrating maturing individuals into a rapidly changing social matrix. Whereas a simple agrarian society can maintain and perpetuate itself through a relatively undifferentiated social structure, an urban-industrial society needs a differentiated structure commensurate with its functional complexities. The direction of change in technological advancing societies is thus from undifferentiated to differentiated structures, and from generalized to specialized functions.

In technologically developed societies, differentiation and specialization have eliminated from *Family* and *Religion* most of the economic, governmental, and educational functions these institutions once incorporated, and have expanded *Economics, Government,* and *Education* into independent and often competing institutions—each with its own bureaucratic structure, its own norms, and its own goals.

ECONOMICS

All social institutions necessarily interrelate. Even though there are orphans, agnostics, truants, anarchists, and derelicts, most people have families, accept a religion, become educated, make a living, and participate in government. When we study *man among men,* we never isolate any one institution without remaining aware that our subject—*man*—has other institutional commitments. Economic activities, however, are basic; unless man "makes a living," he will not live. His economic efficiency determines where he can live and how well he can live.

Primitive Economies

Primitive life is relatively undifferentiated, and work is unspecialized. Primitives, ordinarily, do not "make a living"—they live. The economy is just one more facet in an integrated system of survival, inseparable from family, religious, educational, and governmental necessities.

> In many primitive societies the large amount of time and human energy spent in ritual, magic, and other religious practices seems to be wasted in the eyes of the agricultural expert. But to the native, they give him faith in his work,

saving him from the anxieties which so often attend the work of the cultivator; and where agriculture is a total pattern of life rather than a means of earning a living, this means only that the areas of religion and agriculture are not compartmentalized. Instead of putting all his religion into Friday, Saturday, or Sunday, he practices it as a part of his daily activities.[1]

Agricultural activity is often conceived as an interrelationship with the cherishing earth. In India the Baiga refused to use an iron plough, since this would repay with harshness the generosity of the land, tearing her breasts and breaking her belly; they found the wooden hoe more gentle. The Hopi Indians do not think of themselves as wrestling a living from the arid land, but rather conceive of the relationship as one of aid to the land, which wants to grow the valued corn of the Hopi, but cannot do so without their help.[2]

Primitive economy, though cloaked in religion and sentiment, is often as resourceful as that of the most "hard-headed" industrialist. Consider, for example, the Eskimos and Pygmies.

Eskimos

Along the American Arctic coastlands, Eskimos survive in an uncongenial white world of endless cold, midnight days, and meager vegetation. Their economy derives from the ample animal population of land and water.

> Knowing nothing of glass he fashions his window out of ice, or from the translucent intestinal membrane of a sea mammal, the gullet of the white whale or of birds, or the pericardium of the caribou. For thread he uses sinew, generally procured chiefly from the back and hind legs of the caribou but also from the white whale, and from the gullet, tail, back, and flippers of the seal. Whalebone serves as cord for lashing implements; and the thin fiber stripped from the surface of bird quills is used for finer lashings. . . .
>
> In natural resources, particularly in wood, the Eskimos of the central and northernmost regions are most poorly supplied. Their own resourcefulness is correspondingly conspicuous as under these circumstances they make their sledges of bone or ivory. In Baffin Island if wood is scarce the natives make a strange shovel-shaped sledge by stitching together sheets of whalebone. The height of ingenuity is displayed in the building of a sledge of frozen hide. Pieces of walrus skin or musk-ox skin are soaked in water, folded into the desired forms, and allowed to freeze solid . . . the Eskimo fights the inexorable North with its own weapons.[3]

Thus does environment define and limit economy. If the Eskimo is ever to probe the frozen earth for wealth, other technical economies will have to supply the means.

Pygmies

The economy of African Pygmies in their lush equatorial lands, like that of the Arctic Eskimos, is based on hunting rather than agriculture. These smallest of humans eat little things: white ants, bee grubs, and beetle larvae; but they also hunt the largest of land animals—the elephant—for meat and ivory.

> Elephant hunters work in groups of four or five. They use elephant dung to disguise their body odor, marijuana to increase their courage, and knives and spears to make the kill. When they find a herd and pick their victim, two men sneak up, and simultaneously slash the tendons of the elephant's rear legs. As they then scurry for safety, the other hunters shout and howl. Sometimes the elephants, enraged by the noise, trample and gore the hunters; but, with luck, the herd stampedes and the wounded elephant can be speared to death. Decomposition is rapid in the tropics, and by the time the rest of the tribe gathers for the cutting-up ceremony, the elephant is bloated like an over-inflated blimp by internal gases. The chief hunter plunges in his spear, releases a seven- to eight-foot geyser of stomach juices, and the hunters all push their faces into the putrid liquid and gulp. This is part of their magic. Elephant juices consumed equals elephant strength gained. The drenched hunters then cut a doorway into the stomach, walk inside, cut off bits of entrails, and emerge with them between their teeth. They offer bites, teeth to teeth, as a victory symbol. Then all the men join in cutting up the elephant. They throw pieces to their waiting wives; and when the animal is stripped and every family has a share, they have their celebration feast.[4]

This is primitive economics exemplified. Though the hunting is the work of specialists, the rest is a tribal function, tied closely to community structure, family, and religion. It is not economic activity in our sense, it is life itself.

Industrial Economies

Civilized life is differentiated and work is specialized. "Making a living" is an extensive institution invading all other institutions, a network of specific activities, paid for in the coin of the realm. The Dictionary of Occupational Titles, compiled by the United States Employment Service, lists more than 21,000 gainful occupations. The average person "works" a specific number of hours a day. He goes *to* work. He has vacations *from* work. In effect, he actually rents or leases himself to another. He has muscles or mind worth a few cents to a thousand or more dollars a day.*

Economic institutions have expanded most rapidly since the Industrial Revolution, commonly dated as beginning in eighteenth-century England with the invention of the Spinning Jenny. Within the expanding economies of countries undergoing industrialization, free citizens have had a varying degree of freedom. Men, women, and, until recently, children have worked as virtual

---

* In Bombay, a businessman analyzed the costs of bottling natural water. He discovered that the labor cost per bottle was less than the cost of the water. In the United States, a thirty-two-year-old head of an advertising research firm was available for consultation at $1,000 a day, or $125.00 an hour.

slaves to relentless demands, not only of machines, but of fields and farms and shops. In England, in 1833, the first labor laws limited children under eleven to not more than nine hours' work in one day, or forty-eight in one week; those from eleven to eighteen years old, to no more than twelve hours' work in one day, or sixty-nine in one week. In 1844, another law limited adult women to twelve hours' work a day. One of the earliest labor laws in the United States, passed by the Massachusetts Legislature in 1842, set the limit for children under twelve at ten hours' work a day, presumably six days a week. President Van Buren, in 1840, had already proclaimed the ten-hour day standard for government offices. Today, a professional, executive, or self-employed individual may work that long or longer, but the average working day is eight hours—in some cases, seven hours—five days a week, or six hours, six days a week. Two-week paid vacations were once a rare luxury. Now, even three-week vacations are occasionally outmoded by union contracts allowing four- and five-week vacations, and some union leaders anticipate standard three-month vacations in another forty years. Economists predict a continued long-range trend towards more leisure for more people. As mechanization and automation increase, the amount of work left for men and women to do will decrease. This shifting ratio will eventually change both economic practice and economic theory.

> . . . Until now men always faced the distasteful difficulty of dividing up too few goods among too many needy people. Now we have an economy running at 75 per cent or 80 per cent of capacity producing more goods than we can consume, and we are told that automation can quickly increase our capacity while employing even fewer workers. Instead of rejoicing that our problem is no longer scarcity, we try to think up ways to pretend that everyone is back at work. We cannot meet the problem of plenty head-on. Our old ideas about the evils of idleness and the injustice of getting something for nothing . . . force us to worry about full employment, when we ought to be worrying about the humane activities of human beings about to be liberated at last from what the ancients knew was a curse—routine, mechanical, drudging work.[5]

Since the beginning of industrialism, the amount of control (measured in time) which an employer has over an employee has steadily decreased. But this is only one crucial variable in the economic system. Another is the amount of control which the government has over all economic activities. The world-splitting struggle between the Western democracies and the People's democracies, which we tend to think of as political, is also economic: American-style Capitalism vs. Russian-style Socialism. Capitalism is integral to the United States; socialism, to the Soviet Union. Variations between the two reflect larger variations in their respective societies. The economy, like other primary institutions, affects and is affected by the total culture and by the specific geographical, biological, and technological conditions under which a society maintains itself. Because these conditions change, institutions, in spite of built-in resistance, eventually change. Neither capitalism nor socialism is a static system; their definition is not the same today as it was half a century ago.* Both have responded and will continue to respond to changing world conditions and to internal innovations—particularly technological ones. *Technology is shaping ideology;* it is a reality which makes common demands upon all modern societies irrespective of their original theories or practice. Technological advance in Russia and the United States has tempered the ideologies of both. The main variation today between capitalism and socialism is the amount of government control over the economy. Propagandists of both sides, referring to their ideal patterns, would have us believe that the differences are absolute. In the real pattern, striking differences co-exist with surprising similarities.

Capitalism

Economic success is our most widely advertised achievement. Through capitalism (private ownership of land and production means) plus a favorable combination of geographic and historical circumstances, we established unprecedented productivity. As recently as 1948, the United States, with about six per cent of the world's population, produced over fifty per cent of the world's manufactured goods. We consumed most of these goods ourselves, and our standard of living was without parallel. But now we are in a race with the Soviet Union. "The beep of the Soviet Satellite is an intercontinental outer-space raspberry to a decade of American pretensions that the American way of life was a gilt-edged guarantee of our material superiority." [6]

Capitalism is not an American invention. Private ownership of land and means of production are as old as culture; and the assertion of personal values important for the success of capitalism are traced to the Protestant sect founded by John Calvin, sixteenth-century French theologian. Calvin asserted that the fate of each one of us is predestined: we are either condemned to hell or chosen for the House of the Lord. We know neither our own fate nor that of our family or friends. To relieve anxiety about our eternal status in the next world, we can try for security in this one. And, perhaps, there is a connection. Success may be a sign of God's grace; the successful may be God's elect. Not that one could buy his way into Heaven as some bought their way into the royal court, but hard work, initiative, and self-discipline are practical ways to pray; and they often bring the devout economic gain. *But what can one who has renounced worldly pleasures do with economic gain?* Put it back into the business; build up capital; expand the good work! Never mind the competitor—the competitor may be predestined for hell. Each man alone is responsible before God. Failure, too, may be a sign! [7]

Puritans accepted this Protestant ethic. Hard work, self-discipline, personal initiative, perseverance, honesty, obedience served the early New England settlers well. Through the first decades of deprivation and danger, such

* In 1965 the Soviet government shifted regulation of production in 400 consumer goods factories from central planning to a supply and demand system.

values contributed to personal as well as group welfare. They provided a secure, moral foundation on which the economy of a young country could build.

LAISSEZ FAIRE VS. COUNTERVAILING POWER. John Calvin gave Capitalism a moral foundation. Adam Smith gave it an intellectual rationalization; in 1776 he wrote *The Wealth of Nations.* Smith accepted Calvin's view that economic behavior is motivated by self-interest, but he further asserted that there is a natural law by which individual self-interest tends to operate in the long run for the social good.

> The individual . . . neither intends to promote the public interest, nor knows how much he is promoting it. . . . He intends only his own gain, and he is in this, as in many other cases, led by an invisible hand to promote an end which was no part of his intention. Nor is it always the worse for the society that it was not part of it. By pursuing his own interest he frequently promotes that of the society more effectually than when he really intends to promote it. I have never known much good done by those who affected to trade for the public good . . . every individual, it is evident, can, in his local situation, judge much better than any statesman or lawgiver can do for him.[8]

In the *laissez-faire* arena, competition would adequately regulate economic activity, adjusting production and price to demand, insuring quality products, and creating wealth which would be distributed throughout society by an "invisible hand."

These thoughts were heartily welcomed by God-fearing men who had come to a new country seeking personal freedom and fortune. Growing industries and business wanted self-determination. No interference from government, please. *Laissez faire*—translated, "let to do"—was the ideal. Said Thomas Jefferson: "That government is best which governs least."

How fares *laissez faire* today? If we look for the answer within the United States, we find that the ideal still exists but that the reality is gone.

> Perhaps a quarter of all the money the federal government collects in taxes from businesses goes back to business enterprises (including farms) in the form of subsidies. One study estimates the rise in direct federal subsidies from 1.9 billion in 1951 to 7.5 billions in 1960. Business mail is subsidized to the tune of half a billion dollars, and so is the transportation industry, particularly airlines and maritime companies. The largest recipient of federal subsidies is agriculture, which received 0.9 billion in 1951 and 3.6 billions in 1960.[9]

No economic group consistently desires noninterference by government; each wants government support of its own interests and control of the other fellow. Industries want tariffs for protection against foreign competition and control of labor unions by federal law. Labor wants support by federal law of its right to organize and control management. Farmers, who traditionally are portrayed as the soul of independence, have powerful lobbies in Congress to guarantee high farm prices. In complex urban industrial societies, an institution does not operate as a single homogeneous entity. Typically internal competition and conflict manifest themselves in the form of various power blocs, each striving to achieve various and often contradictory goals. The economic institution is no exception.

Capitalism in the United States today can be understood, not in terms of competing individuals, but in terms of competing power blocs.[10] Big business, big labor unions, farm blocs (theoretically representing private interests) and government (theoretically representing public interest) are countervailing forces vying with each other for both economic and political control. Within the arena of competitive action there is constant parrying for position between vested and emerging interest groups. One function of a government by, for, and of the people has been to restrain the power of private vested interests and encourage that of emerging groups. Organized labor, for example, was favored by New Deal legislation, and the number of union members increased from 3,500,000 in 1935 to 14,000,000 in 1944; the once forgotten farmers, encouraged by New Deal legislation, have developed a powerful Farm Bloc and secured a variety of government supports. In the Soil Bank program, the government pays the farmer for *not* producing. The Government further guarantees parity prices for much of what is produced, even though this policy brings surplus production, with costly storage and disposal problems.

Even in theory, capitalism is no longer a *laissez-faire* arena of economic action dominated by business. Capitalism is sustained as a counter-balanced interplay of four main organized groups: business, labor, agriculture, and government.

COMPETITION VS. PRIVATE SOCIALISM. Competition has been thought of as the economic equivalent of Darwin's Law of Natural Selection, eliminating the weak and insuring survival of the fittest. In past generations, individuals who were the most aggressive within the limits of law and morality did fight their way to the top. Capitalism's strong men were rugged individualists: John D. Rockefeller, Cornelius Vanderbilt, Daniel Drew, Jay Gould, Jim Fisk, Andrew Carnegie, Leland Stanford, J. P. Morgan. Such men have been called "Robber Barons," and they have been called "Makers of America." However we evaluate their achievements, they are at least makers of economic history—fathers of Big Business. In this generation, Big Business is anonymous: General Petroleum, General Motors, U. S. Steel, American Telephone and Telegraph, General Electric, General Dynamics. Such anonymous corporations, though fathered by individuals, have in turn given birth to a new breed of *Homo Americanus*, "the organization man." The organization man does advance himself through competition, but his strength is measured not in terms of independent initiative but in terms of subordination: how well can he adjust his personal interests, attitudes, and desires to the requirements of his job?

We have a traditional ideal of "personal freedom" and regard the controls placed upon individuals by socialist governments as intolerable;

> Yet few societies exert the selective and molding force of the corporation; however unconscious of it they may be, executives in the same company tend to think, talk, and act alike—and to hire and promote people who similarly "fit in." And if a "misfit" does manage to stay on, it's quite probable that he will either be boxed off as a sort of iconoclast, or remold himself to the pattern and take up a hobby.[11]

The key roles in the corporate structure are clearly defined. Organization man must know his cues and play his part. Should one man fail or move on, an understudy is ready to take his place. If no man is indispensable, the corporate structure remains intact. Rugged individualists are not interchangeable; organization men are. Now the corporation is extending control beyond the factory or office.

> "We control a man's environment in business and we lose it entirely when he crosses the threshold of his home," one executive says mournfully. "Management, therefore, has a challenge and an obligation to deliberately plan and create a favorable, constructive attitude on the part of the wife that will liberate her husband's total energies for the job." [12] "Successes here," says one official, "are guys who eat and sleep the company. If a man's first interest is his wife and family, more power to him—but we don't want him." [13]
>
> Increasingly, corporations are interviewing the wife before hiring an executive, and some are not uninterested in fiancées . . . roughly half of the companies on which we have data have made wife-screening regular practice and many of the others seem about ready to do so. And the look-see is not academic. Roughly 20 per cent of its otherwise acceptable trainee applicants, one large company estimates, are turned down because of their wives.[14]

The organization man, his life, his loves are subordinate, not to the State but to the Corporation; and it is corporations, not individuals, which are the units of operation and competition.

> In the production of motor vehicles, agricultural machinery, rubber tires, cigarettes, aluminum, liquor, meat products, copper, tin containers, and office machinery, the largest three firms (in each of these areas) in 1947 did two-thirds or more of all business.[15]

Consider the following estimates of the capital needed for each of eight factories in 1951.[16] Add at least 30 per cent to equate for inflation since that date. How many individuals could possibly compete?

Flour milling	\$ 700,000–\$ 3,500,000
Shoe manufacturing	\$ 500,000–\$ 2,000,000
Petroleum refining	\$193,000,000
Steel	\$265,000,000–\$665,000,000
Cigarettes	\$125,000,000–\$150,000,000
Automobiles	\$250,000,000–\$500,000,000
Tractors	\$125,000,000
Fountain pens	\$ 6,000,000

Even in retail business, individuals find it difficult to compete. The neighborhood grocery, drug store, variety store, in fact, all small, independent merchants have an insecure existence in the shadow of chain stores.

Whatever our ideals or pretensions, individual competition no longer exists in big business, and monopoly—*by government or business*—has replaced it. Within capitalist society, Big Business operates not as free enterprise but as *private socialism.*

Contrasting Ways

"Capitalism" is a word. What it meant in 1776 is not the same as what it means today. But as we adjust the meaning of the word to the realities of contemporary economic practice, we find that a basic assumption of capitalism persists: the right and desire of an individual to make a profit from his own labor or through ownership of land or means of production.

> When the sale of Thrale's brewery was going forward, Johnson (who was an executor), on being asked what he really considered to be the value of the property, answered: "We are not here to sell a parcel of boilers and vats, but the potentiality of growing rich, beyond the dreams of avarice." *

As obviously desirable as growing rich may seem to those of us with champagne appetites and beer incomes, it is an error to generalize. Profit is not necessarily a primary social incentive; it may be considered relatively unimportant, or it may even be considered immoral when it accrues to one through the work of others.

WHERE PROFIT IS UNIMPORTANT. In native markets throughout the world, every article has three prices: the price the merchant asks, the price he expects, and the actual selling price determined by bargaining. If a tourist fails to bargain, the merchant is usually disappointed. The pleasure of bargaining may be greater than the bargain. A native Madagascar merchant sold one piece of raffia cloth for 25 per cent higher than his usual price, but refused to sell his total supply. He was not going to forfeit a day of bargaining for a profit! A Mexican craftsman made and sold one chair at a good profit. With mass production he could effect economies, but he would not make duplicate chairs for the same price and certainly not, as the customer hoped, at a reduced price. He lost the sale by insisting on a higher price for duplicates—compensation for the boredom of doing the same thing over and over again.

Even within a capitalist society, there are many individuals—artists, craftsmen, educators, research scientists, for example—who prefer congenial work with less pay to less congenial work with more pay. Within a capitalist society, there are also ethnic groups, such as the Spanish Americans of New Mexico, who do not respond with enthusiasm to the lure of profit. Sub-group culture shapes individual motives and values.

---

* James Boswell, *Life of Samuel Johnson.*

> The idea of higher pay does not immediately interest the Spanish American (of New Mexico). There has been a shift from an agricultural to a money economy as a practical adjustment to changing times, but this does not mean that monetary incentives have been accepted. Spanish Americans seldom, if ever, express the desire to make a lot of money and become rich. There is an attitude of acceptance toward the hierarchy combined with a fear of ostracism for standing out from the group, that operates to keep Spanish Americans out of competitive work situations. His status in his own community may be lowered rather than raised by achievement—and he has no other community. It is much more important to be than to do: to be a good son, or a good Catholic, or a good member of the village. . . . There is no moral corruption in being idle, or in staying away from one's job. A worker may stay away from wage-work, but may spend the day repairing a neighbor's door or helping build a hen house for nothing. This is needed work and within the framework of community cooperation. . . . Working for oneself, and not for an employer, is thought of as desirable, because then one is free to work at one's own tempo.[17]

WHERE PROFIT IS IMMORAL. During the Middle Ages, the Catholic Church specifically forbade lending money for interest (usury). Paying money for the use of money was considered immoral. Today collectivist economies repudiate profit as an essential social incentive and refuse to accept the capitalist rationalization that self-interest operates in the long run for the public good. Instead, both Communists and Socialists frankly reject the primacy of the individual and assert the primacy of the group: land and the means of production should be owned, not by individuals, but by society, and used for the good of all.

Socialism and Communism. Socialism and Communism are often confused, and with good reason. The Union of Soviet *Socialist* Republics is controlled by the Communist party. What goes on? Who is what?

Economically, the distinction is easily made. Socialism means the social ownership of productive means; Communism means this plus the common ownership of some or all forms of consumers' goods.*

Politically, the distinction becomes more complex. The difficulty comes in part from differing concepts of Socialism. Fabian Socialism—as represented by the British Labor Party—accepts constitutional democracy and advocates reform of the economic system within the framework of democracy. Scientific Socialism—as represented by Marxism—does not accept constitutional democracy and advocates reform of the economic system through revolution.

Fabian Socialism is thus compatible with democracy as we define it, and a staunch defender of civil liberties as we define them. Except in the nightmares of extreme conservatives, Fabian Socialists cannot rightfully be accused of being less devoted to the principles of democracy than Republicans

* The Hutterite Brethren in the James River Valley of South Dakota are true religious, social, and economic (but not political) communists. Hutterism originated in Austria in the sixteenth century—300 years before Marxism. Ideological support for Hutterism comes from the Old Testament, which, according to the Hutterites, proclaims that all men should live in communal societies.

or Democrats. Spokesmen for vested interest groups who enjoy advantages from private ownership of capital (producer's goods), however, may argue that any degree of government ownership is drifting down the "Road to Serfdom." * Any challenge to existing economic relationships is commonly branded as "un-American," any criticism of the workings of the "free enterprise" system as a sign of disloyalty. For example, the California State Senate established a committee to investigate public school books. Books were labeled "subversive" by this committee because they stated that grazing cattle and sheep could cause soil erosion or because they contained pictures of slums and dust storms.[18]

According to available historical evidence, such fears for our democracy —if they are fears and not mere rationalizations of privilege—are misplaced if Fabian Socialism is the bogy man. The British Labor Party—frankly socialist in philosophy—has been *voted into power by democratic means,* and, more significantly, has been *voted out of power.*

All Socialism, however, is not Fabian. Scientific Socialism is another matter. It is based on the work of Karl Marx (1818-1883) and is called "scientific," because Marx and his followers believed he had discovered the natural laws of social evolution—"tendencies working with iron necessity towards inevitable results." [19] Marx took the Industrial Revolution in England as a classic model and forecast both economic growth and social conflict. For Marx, "the evolution of the economic formation of society is viewed as a process of natural history." [20] History is a ceaseless class struggle, in which the dominant class has always utilized the machinery of the state to effect its supremacy. As the working classes become more numerous through industrialization, they will inevitably come into conflict with the capitalists, who, according to Marx, will become fewer and fewer in number through the growth of monopoly. The working class has the historic mission of ultimately overthrowing the political structure used by the capitalist. *Now we find out what a Communist is,* for the Communist Party is to provide the leadership in provoking and carrying the "inevitable" social revolution to success.

> Capitalism "has exhausted its social role; the revolutionary forces, under the leadership of the Communist International, are gathering to sweep it away and to build in its place a social system based upon the common ownership of the means of production and the carrying on of production for social use." [21]

After the Revolution envisioned by Marx a "dictatorship of the proletariat," which cannot be voted out of power, would be established. The political machinery of the state would smash all opposition, and ultimately create a classless society. The state, then no longer needed as a means of class domination, would "wither away."

Soviet Socialism. From the time of Ancient Greece, the motto of socialist philosophies has been, "From each according to his capacity, to each according to his needs." This extension of the family ideal to the state was modified in

* For an expression of this view, see *Road to Serfdom,* by Friedrich A. Hayek, The University of Chicago Press, 1944.

the nineteenth century to a motto of potential equality: "From each according to his capacity, to each according to his merit." This is more nearly the theory of Soviet Socialism today. The state owns and operates all means of production, transportation, and land. (Land is leased to collective farms.) Individuals may build, buy, or sell private residences, but they do not own the land on which they are built—just as we build, buy, or sell houses in some national forests, but never own the land. In the Soviet Union there can be no legal accumulation of wealth through buying cheap and selling dear, but individuals can sell their own farm products or crafts on the open market. No one is permitted to employ labor except the state; but from our point of view, many people working for the state are "exploited." People earn salaries of varying size and pass on accumulated wealth to children. Class differences are real.

Private enterprise, as we know it, exists in present-day socialist societies, but the government controls imposed would give the Statue of Liberty ulcers. Consider what one woman had to go through to open a dressmaking establishment in Warsaw, Poland (1958).

> Before my friend could set herself up in business, she had to prove to the government that she had worked three years as a dressmaker's helper and another three years as an apprentice. She also had to pass two examinations. In the first of these, she was given a few yards of calico and a picture of a dress, and told that she must make a dress like it in three days. The dress she submitted was declared satisfactory by a jury of dressmakers and bureaucrats, whereupon she was given the second test—an oral one, in which she was questioned about her knowledge of trade laws, wage regulations, fabrics, and economic and social conditions in Poland. She passed that, too, and spent the next two weeks in a tangle of red tape before she was granted a "work card," entitling her to open her store. But the government's interest in her enterprise did not end there; its agents will dictate the prices she may charge for her dresses. The state will keep her guessing as to what her tax rate is going to be, but will considerably compensate for this by relieving her of the trouble of filling out tax forms and simply telling her at the end of the year how much she owes. Only then will she know whether she has made money (and possibly become rich) or has lost money (and possibly gone bankrupt). The whole matter of the price she may charge and the taxes she must pay rests on the outcome of a visit by a team of government inspectors, who, shortly after she started business, came around to make an appraisal of the shop's worth, adding in not only the value of the inventory and furnishings but their estimate of her ability to run the place. On the basis of their findings, her shop will be classified in one of three categories. She has yet to hear how she fared at the hands of these visitors, but hopes that they will not give her a first-category rating; because, while this would mean that she could charge somewhat higher prices, she would also have to pay much higher taxes.[22]

A compensatory feature of a socialist economy is that income tax can be low or nonexistent. In the 1950's, the Russian income tax rate ranged from 5 to 13 per cent. In the early 1960's there was talk of eliminating it completely. The United States income tax rate ranges from 20 to 77 per cent and supplies slightly more than half the total revenue. *How can the Soviet Union get enough money to support the government?* The money comes mainly from profit made by government-owned industry and business. When the Russian citizen buys consumer goods, he supports the government rather than other individuals or groups.

PRODUCTION FOR PRODUCTION VS. PRODUCTION FOR CONSUMPTION. The average citizen of the United States looks at the average citizen of the Soviet Union and thinks, "not only holier and more democratic, but better dressed, better fed, better housed than thou," and with this satisfies himself that capitalism is therefore superior to socialism. *But is the present material inferiority of the Russians inherent in their economic system, or is it due to other historical circumstances?* Obviously, Russians claim the latter, and they have good reasons for their contention. In 1917 their industrial potential was miserably low; they contributed only 1.7 per cent of the total world industrial production. In 1955 they contributed 19 per cent of the total, and the percentage is still rising. (They produced 4,200,000 tons of steel in 1913—51,000,000 tons in 1957; 29,100,000 tons of coal in 1913—462,000,000 in 1957.) Between 1928, the beginning of the first Five Year Plan, and 1957, the Russians increased their gross industrial output twenty times, or 2,000 per cent.[23]

The Russians are still producing mainly for production. Consumer goods are sacrified for capital goods. More than 50 per cent of their total production is put back into industry to further increase their productive capacity. In a socialist society, individual desires are subordinated to group goals.

In the United States we already have high productive capacity. (In 1956 we produced 115,000,000 tons of steel compared to Russia's 49,000,000.) The emphasis in our economy is production for consumption. Pressure is put on the consumer to buy as much as possible. "Keep the wheels of industry rolling." We produce quantity fast and inexpensively.

> A visiting Frenchman who has his feet on the ground—financially, at least—tells us that he found himself short of handkerchiefs and, after looking the situation over with some care, bought himself a dozen at one of the Woolworth stores for seven cents apiece. This seemed to him a delightfully reasonable price. His hotel laundry, however, charged twelve cents apiece to wash and iron them. This seemed to him a hideously unreasonable price. "What are you doing about it?" we asked him. "But naturally," he said, waving his arms, "like all sensible Americans, I buy more at Woolworth's when I need them, and then I throw them away." [24]

Our advertising is designed to increase rather than defer consumption. Many industries deliberately create artificial obsolescence through style changes in order to cause dissatisfaction with the old and demand for the new. Major consumer industries have a yearly estrus cycle, and when the latest models emerge from the assembly lines, consumers are ready and waiting with open arms and pocketbooks.

In Russia, forced obsolescence is inconceivable. Consumer goods must last as long as possible. There is little effort to push sales through advertising, little effort to *create demand;* but price is used to *direct demand* into officially approved channels. A suit of clothes, for example, costs as much as the average worker makes in a month—about $140.00, but a good quality LP record costs only about 50 cents.

The Russians consume less than 50 per cent of their production; we consume nearly 75 per cent; and since, at this point in history, our production is greater to begin with, our standard of living is inevitably higher. However, the Russians claim they will overtake us in production before 1980.

> When I visited Russia . . . earlier this year, we were invited to take a look at a chicken farm near the remote city of Alma-Ata. On the wall of one of the chicken coops we saw a graph comparing the egg-laying accomplishments of Russian chickens with the production of U. S. chickens. Underneath this graph was a slogan in Russian: "Catch up with the United States!"
>
> The United States is on every Russian's mind. You can't travel anywhere in the Soviet Union without seeing graphs like this, as well as slogans, charts, posters, and other reminders that the Russians are determined to pull ahead of us in production.[25]

If relative growth rates for production continue as they now are, the Russians *will* get ahead of us.

Red China is another rapidly expanding economy linked to a political institution different from our own.

> The greatest social transformation of our time is now taking place in China.
>
> A giant of a nation is emerging as a full-fledged member of the mechanical and nuclear age. . . .
>
> Communism, now an established and vibrant fact in China, will next sweep through South and Southeast Asia, in particular, India, unless economic standards are raised to the point where it offers no attraction. . .
>
> Communist party members in Peiping told me confidently, "We will beat you simply because you work on a profit motive." [26]

The profit motive, however, has served us well. It has offered incentives to the individual and contributed to the vitality of urban-industrial development. Under the free-enterprise system we have achieved a rich society; and for the first time in history, production equals or exceeds need.

The techniques of production are mastered; but those of distribution are not. In the shadow of plenty there is deprivation. Ours is an economy of contradictions. We live amidst incredible affluence and sickening squalor. In 1964, at the start of the "war on poverty," the Johnson Administration counted one-fifth of the nation—35 million people—as poor. Of these, eight million were receiving public aid, and the number of needy was increasing twice as fast as the population. Mechanization had already replaced muscle power; automation was replacing brain power. Experts estimated that two per cent of the population would some day be able to produce all the goods needed to maintain the total society. Our problems are not those of an impoverished society but of an uncoordinated one.

Free enterprise in the United States in the latter half of this twentieth century is not the same as it was in the nineteenth century. The system now demands, not *laissez faire,* but government aids and controls. Its structure and processes, its norms and goals evolved under conditions of scarcity in a rapidly growing new nation. Utilizing scientific technology, free enterprise helped transform the economy from one of scarcity to one of unparalleled abundance. Today this affluence is giving rise to further ideological issues. *Does the Protestant ethic have limited validity? Is work really "a life purpose willed by God?"* [27] *In a technological society, how much need one work to earn the right to the good life?*

> Economic development is a process . . . that extends in range from new nations of Africa only slightly removed from their tribal structure to the elaborate economic and social apparatus of Western nations. At each stage along this continuum there is an appropriate policy for further advance. What is appropriate at one stage is wrong at another.[28]

How will free enterprise in the United States be defined by the end of this century?

Scientific technology is not contained by national boundaries nor constrained by national politics. It flourishes alike under free enterprise and under all manner of government controls. It has already transformed Russia into a formidable power, and the newly developing Cinderella nations of Asia, Africa, and South America covet its golden coach. The United States may not always lead the world in production. *No economic system has a monopoly on technology.*

GOVERNMENT

Men are not created equal in the eyes of other men, nor do they ever achieve equality. By reason of intellectual, physical, economic, social or political advantage, or even chance, some individuals have superior positions in society. Some lead; others follow. Some exert influence which cannot be effectively reciprocated. In the political arena some have power to represent and uphold the social order. The distribution and use of such power is *Government.*

In many primitive societies political power is synonymous with public opinion and informal councils rather than with formally constituted authority. In urban-industrial societies, however, government has become a complex institution with its own bureaucratic structure and processes, its own norms, and its own goals. Like all other institutions, it has a built-in resistance to change, but resistance to change is not the same as immunity to change. No government is so immovably monolithic or autocratic that it is not responsive to pressures arising from changing conditions. In the United

States, as in other developed and developing nations, government is an expanding institution. It coexists with technology, and with technological advance, government extends its scope and broadens its services. Variations in government as an institution are most evident in the complexity and stability of the institutional structure, in the functional roles of government, and in the manner and amount of mutual restraint between subjects and sovereignty.

What Price Fraternity?

PROHIBITED ON BEACH: SITTING ON PAPER, LITTERING, BALL PLAYING, PEDDLING, GYMNASTICS, FIRES, DOGS. DO NOT SIT ON STEPS.

We read the sign and thought, "This is one for the book!" And as we stood there preparing to photograph the sign, a bystander said helpfully, "Better move on. A man just got arrested for standing right there." We took the photo, then obediently moved on. "In the land of mules, there are no rules." [29] But this was Coney Island, famed for concentration of human population. Webster was right when he defined society as "the social order, especially as a state or system *restricting the individual.*" Association with others is bought with personal freedom; the more people, the less freedom. Individualism helped build our urban-industrial society, but today that society restrains rather than exalts individuality. Freedom in a complex society can be had only within an elaborate legislative framework.

A system of ordered relationships is a primary condition of group life at every level. Government is not necessarily limited to political institutions. *In small, primitive societies, controls are mainly personal, informal, uncentralized, and expressed through folkways, mores, and taboos.* Where all members of a group know each other, peer pressure is a mighty and usually sufficient restriction on individual freedom. Chiefs, tribal councils, wise men and elders have influence and authority in day-to-day interactions. There is little need to institutionalize controls in a separate system. *In complex societies, controls are impersonal, formal, centralized and expressed through laws.* In complex societies, there is very definite need for institutionalized controls. If an individual's inner controls—his own moral and ethical convictions—are not clear and strong enough to direct him, is he going to respond to anonymous censure unless that censure carries with it the power of legal authority? The universal role of government as a power structure is to keep individual and group action consistent with the unity and order of the larger social system. A populace organized under one government and occupying a defined territory is recognized as a political state.* The structure of government within a state is the "flow-line" of power, determining who does what to whom.

* The state is a *political* entity, a power structure, not to be confused with the nation, an *historical* entity which can and does persist through changes in the form of the state. When, for example, Soviet leaders during World War II appealed to the people to support "Mother Russia," they were calling on those patriotic sentiments which the image of a nation—not a state—tends to evoke.

What Price Liberty?

Government is not the only institution having formal controls, but it does have the most effective ones. The Ford Motor Company can and does impose rules upon workers in Ford plants; the United Automobile Workers impose other, sometimes conflicting, rules. A church can excommunicate (exclude an individual by authoritative sentence from the communion of the church) for breaking church rules. Such controls, however, are essentially only high-powered advice. An individual can renounce his faith or quit his job, or stop paying union dues, but "Government is not mere advice; it is authority, with power to enforce its laws." * Government alone has the ultimate authority to *command* obedience. It can force you to pay taxes to support projects you despise; it can force you to violate your religious beliefs by limiting yourself to one spouse; it can force you to fight and die in a war you consider highly immoral. It may be true that all men "are endowed by their Creator with certain inalienable Rights, that among these are Life, Liberty and the pursuit of Happiness," † but these rights can be realized only if the government so permits. Governments possess a sufficient monopoly of force to restrict or deny any citizen his rights.

> The creation of constitutional government is a most significant mark of the distrust of human beings in human nature. It signalizes a profound conviction, born of experience, that human beings vested with authority must be restrained by something more potent than their own discretion.[30]

"The price of liberty is eternal vigilance," and the price of fraternity is restricted liberty. The manner and amount of mutual restraint between subjects and sovereignty is a major source of controversy, particularly between the peoples' democracies led by the Soviet Union, and the Western democracies, led by the United States.

Government maintains and furthers the norms and goals of other institutions, and, in turn, develops its own unique institutional character. Government is an expression, not only of political theory but of historical experience. Many national differences are products of circumstantial pressure as well as ideological preference. For example, the friendly, open receptiveness ascribed to us as a national trait may be born, not of innate tolerance and trust, but of favorable experience. Foreigners have come to our shores only as visitors of more or less good will, or as aspiring citizens not as merciless invaders and conquerors. Governments and the norms characteristic of them can only be fully understood in their historical context.

---

* George Washington, 1732-1799.
† Thomas Jefferson, 1743-1826.

More Democratic Than Thou

Democracy has become a synonym for government among leading modern states. Fascism, a form of monarchy and frankly anti-democratic in theory and practice, was defeated in World War II. Since then, only a few die-hard or backward political leaders fail to label themselves and their governments "democratic." Both Communism and Fascism are now being sold, like many pocket books, under an eye-catching cover. Said Francisco Franco in 1961, "Spain has become an organic democracy, without the blight of elections."

Democracy means many things to many people. What is one man's democracy may be another man's tyranny. When the Cold War began in 1946, the world divided into two hostile camps of "democratic" nations, each berating the other as tyrannical. However, the word *democracy* literally means only *rule by the people*. It is a "protest movement against the uneven distribution of power. . . . Ideally, it means that everyone has equal power. In practice, it means that everyone exerts some influence on the governmental process, by voting and by expressing opinions publicly." [31] In both the Communist and the Western democracies the people theoretically rule; in both they vote in elections for their official representatives.

Majority Rule

If the measure of democracy were the number of eligible voters who participate in elections, the Soviet Union would be more democratic than the United States. In 1946, 99.7 per cent of the Russian electorate voted for the Supreme Soviet (Parliament). The per cent of eligible voters in the United States voting in presidential elections is consistently less: 62 per cent in 1940, 64 per cent in 1952, 60 per cent in 1956, 64 per cent in 1960, 62 per cent in 1964.

"But," you might say, "the Russians merely vote for or against the block of communists and nonparty members presented on the ballot. They have no choice." Soviet philosopher Aleksandrov would answer, "You do not judge democracy by counting parties or contending groups. The democratic or anti-democratic nature of . . . a government's policy is determined . . . by whether this or that policy is carried out in the interests of its people, in the interests of its overwhelming majority, or in the interests of its minority." [32] The Communist Party includes less than two per cent of the people, but it is theoretically committed to decisions favoring the welfare of all. In the United States the platforms of contending political parties may or may not be for the good of *the people*. However, we measure democracy not only by voter participation and representation, but by voter power. We can vote incumbents out of office or force them to change their policy. This Russian voters cannot do.

Civil Liberties

If you should ask about some of the traditional freedoms of Western democracy—freedom of speech, of religion, of the press—and how they fare in Russia, a Russian could point out that civil liberty is a relative matter.

FREE SPEECH. Soviet citizens have more freedom of speech than you might realize—though far less than we enjoy. Furthermore, we have less freedom of speech than we commonly assume. During the Cold War, fear of Communist subversion has led to suppressions inconsistent with our tradition. The "Loyalty Security" program went far beyond the needs of national security. For several years, teachers in Los Angeles were forbidden by the Board of Education to discuss UNESCO (United Nations Educational, Scientific, and Cultural Organization). Since 1947 many politically "liberal" teachers have been fired for fear they might speak indiscreetly in the classroom and, furthermore, the use of public auditoriums has been denied "controversial" persons. A study of American Communism between 1919 and 1957 indicates that United States citizens who joined the Party did not necessarily surrender intellectual freedom, nor did they consciously participate in any unlawful conspiracies.* Yet how many employers, even today, will hire a person who speaks in favor of Communism? A national opinion poll taken in 1955 included these questions: *If a person wanted to make a speech in your community favoring government ownership of all the railroads and big industry, should he be allowed to speak, or not?* Of the national cross-sectional sample (rural and urban), 31 per cent said "No," 11 per cent were undecided, and 58 per cent said "Yes." *Suppose an admitted Communist wants to make a speech in your community. Should he be allowed to speak, or not?* Of the national sample, 68 per cent said "No," 5 per cent were undecided, and only 27 per cent said "Yes." Community leaders were more willing than the average citizen to grant the nonconformist free speech. Eighty-four per cent of selected community leaders would let a person speak in favor of government ownership; 51 per cent would let a Communist speak.[33] In general, the higher a person's socio-economic and educational status, the more he values and defends civil liberties.†

RELIGIOUS FREEDOM. "Congress shall make no law respecting an establishment of religion, or prohibiting the free exercise thereof . . ." reads the first part of Amendment I to the Constitution of the United States, spelling out boldly our cherished freedom of religion. "What," you may ask, "can the

* Irving Howe and Lewis Coser. *The American Communist Party: A Critical History* (1919-1957) (Boston: Beacon Press, 1958).

† A survey on attitudes towards free speech among Iowa farmers in the fall of 1963 showed an increase in tolerance over a comparable survey six years earlier. To the question as to whether a Communist should be allowed to speak at a public meeting, 34 per cent in 1963 agreed that "anyone, regardless of his views, has the right to speak," compared to 14 per cent in 1957.[35]

Russians claim?" Article 124 of the Soviet constitution, guarantees "freedom of religious worship," *and* "freedom of anti-religious propaganda." There is toleration of religion by the Soviet government, but hardly encouragement. In Moscow there were 400 churches before the Revolution; in the mid-1950's there were 30. [34] Parents may give religious instruction in the home, but teachers in schools and other institutions may not, unless the students are more than 18 years of age. Religion there has a status comparable to atheism here; it is permitted, but frowned upon. It would no doubt be as damaging to an aspiring political candidate in the Soviet Union to be known as religious as it would to his counterpart in the United States to be known as an atheist. Religious freedom for the Russians does not include very much toleration of religion. Religious freedom for us does not include very much toleration of irreligion. To the question, *"If a person wanted to make a speech in your community against churches and religion, should he be allowed to speak?"* 60 per cent of a national cross-sectional sample said, "No!" [36]

FREE PRESS. "Our liberty depends on the freedom of the press, and that cannot be limited without being lost," wrote Thomas Jefferson in 1786. Since then we have traditionally assumed this freedom. But just as "democracy" has different meanings, so has "freedom of the press." Article 125 of the Soviet Constitution announces freedom of the press and other civil liberties:

> These civil rights are ensured by placing at the disposal of the working people and their organizations printing presses, stocks of paper, public buildings, the streets, communications facilities, and other material requisite for the exercise of these rights.

But freedom of the press is not unlimited. Soviet authorities claim that the people are not permitted to use the press to preach race hatred and national enmity or to call for war against other countries. As philosopher Aleksandrov puts it, the purpose of the press is to defend "the democratic rights of the people. . . . Our press is wholly at the disposal of the entire people, at the disposal of a state standing guard over the interests of the people." [37] "Freedom of the press" in the Soviet Union means that the press is an agency of the government and expresses the official government view.

> The periodical *Kommunist*, organ of the Central Committee of the party and a towering ideological fountainhead, carried a choice little item lately. It was to the effect that American workmen are "permitted" to have automobiles only because this saved them from the strain of having to go to work by subway or train! In consequence they were less fatigued while on the job, and so made more money for their employers. The fact that TV is universal in the United States was explained by similar reasoning. The capitalist class has wickedly managed to get TV installations into the workers' homes, so they will not waste time drinking or going to parties at night, and consequently will be fresher for the next day's work, to earn more money for the capitalists.[38]

Shocking distortions? Yes, but does freedom of the press, American style, guarantee truth? Jefferson had a second thought on the subject by the time he was serving a second term as President. The experiment of a free press had been in effect for about 20 years, and Jefferson's original enthusiasm was tempered. In 1807 he wrote:

> It is a melancholy truth, that a suppression of the press could not more completely deprive the nation of its benefits, than is done by its abandoned prostitution to falsehood. Nothing can now be believed which is seen in a newspaper. Truth itself becomes suspicious by being put into that polluted vehicle. The real extent of this state of misinformation is known only to those who are in situations to confront facts within their knowledge with the lies of the day. I really look with commiseration over the great body of my fellow citizens, who, reading newspapers, live and die in the belief that they have known something of what has been passing in the world in their time.[39]

Private ownership of the press *as such* does not mean the owners are committed to truth or are necessarily capable of presenting it to the reading public. Truth can be distorted by the press in three basic ways: through bias, through speed to beat the competitor to the date line, and through "non-interpretive" reporting.

Bias we can easily understand. Selectivity is a common device for editing news to fit bias. News can be headlined on the front page, buried on the back, or omitted altogether.

Distortion through speed is exaggerated in the old newspaper cliché: "Don't get it right, get it written." Obviously, this is not the motto of any contemporary newspaper or news service; but the pressure to get a "scoop"—to be first with the latest—does make it difficult for a reporter to check on his facts.

Distortion through non-interpretive reporting is a defect which has grown out of a virtue: the effort to be objective and avoid bias.

> The good newspaper, the good news broadcaster, must walk a tightrope between two great gulfs—on one side the false objectivity that takes everything at face value and lets the public be imposed on by the charlatan with the most brazen front; on the other, the "interpretive" reporting which fails to draw the line between objective and subjective, between a reasonably well-established fact and what the reporter or editor wishes were the fact. To say that is easy; to do it is hard. No wonder that too many fall back on the incontrovertible objective fact that the Honorable John P. Hoozis said, colon quote—and never mind whether he was lying or not.[40]

We have freedom of the press, but do we have the truth, the whole truth, and nothing but the truth?

Liberty, Equality, Fraternity! Democracies of all varieties have paid lip service to this rallying cry of the French Revolution, but none have given Liberty, Equality, and Fraternity equal value. We have emphasized Liberty—freedom of the individual from governmental control. Thomas Paine expressed the sentiment in his revolutionary pamphlet, *Common Sense:* "Government, even in its best state, is but a necessary evil; in its worst state, an intolerable one." We are still suspicious of concentrated political power, but we also have learned that Liberty unrestrained can negate both Equality and Fraternity which we also value. When Capitalism temporarily collapsed during the Great Depression (1929-1933) government, mainly through work projects, meliorated gross inequalities in wealth and power. When years of separate education for Negro and white proved to be years of unequal education, government, via Supreme Court decision, declared such inequality unconstitutional. When unequal access to public accommodations, jobs, and the voting booth were challenged by civil rights groups, Congress passed Civil Rights legislation. In an urban-industrial society complete Equality and Fraternity are unrealistic goals, but government can restrict the liberty of some to gain a measure of "liberty and justice for all."

We label the Soviet Union "authoritarian," or "totalitarian" because of what seems to us extreme infringements by government on individual liberty. Soviet democracy, however, stresses Equality and Fraternity rather than Liberty. Aleksandrov claims that Soviet democracy has eliminated the exploitation and oppression of workers and "really abolished inequalities among peoples." In spite of anti-Semitic outbursts, particularly under Stalin, all persons of all races and creeds are theoretically equal. Discrimination against minorities is illegal. Furthermore, Aleksandrov asserts, "boundless loyalty on the part of citizens of socialist society to their country, their state, and their people; undisputed and conscious, sincere preference for the public interests, the state's interests and the interests of the group, as opposed to private interests" [41] demonstrate Fraternity.*

A number of political careers in the United States have risen to heights on the blast of "the Communist menace." As real as this danger has been—and the FBI has evidence that cannot be discredited—there is disturbing indication that our form of democracy is also threatened from within by equally subversive enemies: ignorance and indifference.

> More than half of our teenagers believe that censorship of books, magazines, newspapers, radio, and television is all right. More than half believe that the Federal Bureau of Investigation and local police should be allowed to use wiretapping at will, that the police should be permitted to use the "third degree," that people who refuse to testify against themselves should be forced to do so. About half of our teenagers assert that most people aren't capable of

* That Russians are human and do not always prefer public interests to private ones the behavior of Aleksandrov himself demonstrated. After the death of Stalin in 1953, Aleksandrov, a respected historian and philosopher, was put in charge of a new Ministry of Culture.

He was supposed to have given wild parties in his office, where ballerinas and other pretty girls were brilliantly—even scandalously—entertained. Once in a brawl over a movie star in Leningrad, Aleksandrov was actually arrested. He lost his job as minister, and was shipped out to Siberia forthwith, to be, of all things, Rector of Tomsk University. But the students there, having got wind of his fondness for high jinks, refused to have him and went on strike.[42]

> deciding what's best for themselves; fully 75 per cent declare that obedience and respect for authority are the most important habits for children to learn. On practically all questions of social policy, the youngsters lean strongly to stereotyped views.
>
> Such answers may represent either unthinking responses or convinced and deliberate acceptance of an authoritarian point of view. In either case the picture is equally unhappy. The road to totalitarianism is the same length whether we walk down it consciously or merely drift down it. Unthinking conformity provides a setting which makes it possible for a demagogue to lead a nation into slavery.[43]

More than 2,000 years ago, Solon (640-559 B.C.) set the course of democracy by drafting a constitution for Athens and writing a set of laws which included a definition of the citizen's role. Of these laws Plutarch wrote:

> Among Solon's other laws, most peculiar and surprising is the one which ordains him disfranchised who in time of civil strife takes neither side.
>
> He means apparently to keep the citizen from remaining apathetic and insensible to the common good, setting his own affairs in order, the while priding himself that he neither suffers nor sympathizes with the nation.
>
> Of his own, the citizen must ally himself with the better and more just cause, take part in the risk and in the rescue, and not securely wait it out until the more powerful prevail.

Unless we have an enlightened and responsible citizenry in the making, we can lose our democracy without the action of a single Communist agent.

Our Brother's Keeper

Government is the institution which, through legislation, administration, and enforcement of laws, protects and maintains a society. This universal role of government, however, is expanding. In the United States, as in other developed and developing nations, government is taking increasing responsibility for the planning and promotion of economic development. Furthermore, government is responding to the demands of citizens for equalized educational opportunities, for old-age pensions, unemployment insurance, family allowances, health insurance, and other social services associated with a welfare state. *Is the criteria for good government changing? Is that government best which governs least or which gives the most?*

We have a proud tradition of individual responsibility and self-sufficiency. In the past, perhaps idleness and poverty in an able-bodied man did betray some character defect, but *is this implication still valid?* Today millions of people in the United States live in deprivation because they happen to be born in Appalachia or some other economically obsolete area. Others are barred from full and effective participation in the economic life of the nation by reason of race or insufficient education. Others are disabled physically, mentally, or emotionally. These latter are the "case study" poor; their suffering is personal, but they, too, are mainly products of environmental impoverishment. Perceiving this new dimension of poverty in the United States, we are beginning to ask: *How responsible is the government for the well-being of its citizens?*

Our government can win the "war on poverty" if the people so sanction. Means are at our disposal: conservation and development of natural resources, subsidies for new industries, urban renewal and slum abatement, guaranteed civil rights, retraining and relocation of workers, special programs for deprived youth, medical care and psychological counseling for all who need it, and, above all, federal aid to equalize educational opportunities in all states for all children.* These are among the practical tactics, but they involve government functions which are relatively new and often difficult to institute and to administer. However, displacement of workers by mechanization and automation, increased life expectancy after retirement, and decreased economic opportunities for those of limited education add urgency to the problem of clearly defining the role of government in our technologically advanced society. *Should the group accept responsibility for the well-being of the individual? Are we our brother's keeper?*

Government is an expanding institution; it has taken on new functions and it has extended old functions to serve a growing population. Furthermore, over the centuries, city-states have merged into states, states into nations, and now nations are joining together in international alliances. Citizens of any single political unit are being called upon for ever-widening loyalties—loyalties which may eventually include a world state.

For those who may fear conflicting loyalties or believe our own national democracy endangered by incorporation into larger political units, we note that the stability of a government by the people is endangered not by constructive commitments to other nations, but by destructive conditions endured within its own borders. Excessive disparities in standards of living and cultural norms and goals, individuals immobilized within class boundaries and barred from leadership roles, large sections of the lower social strata—the "undesirables" and the dispossessed—poorly integrated into the total society, such conditions—insulting to human dignity and crippling to human potential—are adversive to democratic government. The reverse conditions—diversity without gross discontinuities, mobility, and a network of organizations which integrate the individual into the larger society and promote and protect his interests—these all contribute to the stability and effectiveness of democratic institutions.

As conditions favorable to democracy become clearly defined and understood, then we have a rationale for the expanding role of government. *Should not democracy accept responsibility for securing and maintaining conditions conducive to its own survival?*

---

* For a fuller discussion of practical approaches to poverty in the United States, see John Kenneth Galbraith, "Let Us Begin: An Invitation to Action on Poverty," *Harper's Magazine*, March, 1964, pp. 16-26.

Patriotism

As a nation we are loyal to democracy as we know it and confident of the superiority of our way. However, loyalty to a nation or even a political state is not an emotion unique with us. All people in all periods have made voluntary sacrifices for their country. During World War II, the *kamikaze* attacks by Japanese pilots were a common and devastating tactic. The people of Germany and Japan, living under tyrannical "enemy" states—endured without moral collapse bomb devastation as great as or greater than that of the free people of England. And Russia, under the "tyrannical" rule of Stalin, suffered more than thirty times our casualties. We should not be surprised that loyalty, like other emotional commitments, is learned. We identify with the state into which we are born; we tend to accept the ways of the culture to which we are exposed. Although ours is the great promised land, immigrants are not without pangs of homesickness for all they left behind in "the old country." In fact, a United States news correspondent, long-time resident of Russia and husband of a Russian woman, remarked that Russians suffer such nostalgia away from home that they make the "world's worst immigrants." [44]

Our national policy is conducted on the assumption that our way is right and best and will prevail. Russian national policy is conducted on the assumption that communism will win the world. Who has misplaced confidence? Or will the twain meet? *Are established communist countries becoming more "democratic" and Western democracies more socialistic?* It may be too soon to tell, but of this we can be sure: *No government has a monopoly on patriotism.*

EDUCATION

When the British went into India in the 18th and 19th centuries, they used technology to change desert and scrub lands into gardens. In the Punjab region, they constructed dams across rivers and diverted water into great irrigation canals, and they built what was probably the best railway system east of Suez. In this technological sense, the nation of Pakistan began. But the technology was only skin deep, and the prosperity it engendered was short-lived. The British had built thirty-one liberal arts colleges where they taught British history, the metaphysics of Aristotle, principles of jurisprudence, and the laws of equity. But no one had thought of using the educational institutions to integrate Western technology into the economy. For a population of fifty million people, Pakistan had only one engineering and one agricultural college. In 1947 when Pakistan separated from India and gained independence from Britain, native technology was no less primitive than it had been a century before, and the per capita income was fifteen cents a day! [45] Today, newly developing countries are sending vast numbers of students to the United States and Russia and other industrial nations to study agricultural and industrial techniques, but each nation in turn will build its own educational institutions to meet its own needs. For without means of perpetuating essential technological knowledge and skills, a society cannot enter the mainstream of history.

In a simple folk society, education need not and usually does not involve separate institutional structures. Education in such societies is effective and meaningful only insofar as it is integrated with everyday experience and expectation. The desire for the formal skills of reading, writing, arithmetic and ideological adventuring comes after acquiring the basic practical skills necessary for survival.

Education helps provide individuals with the skills and insights needed to play satisfactory roles within the particular society. Education also provides society with the kind of workers needed to maintain and perpetuate itself. In folk societies, work and life are inseparable. In a pre-industrial agrarian society, the bulk of essential work can be done by illiterate laborers. In the early stages of industrialism, factory workers need only simple skills and a minimum of formal education. As a society becomes further industrialized and urbanized, it needs better educated technicians and managers, and other skilled personnel, particularly in research and development, in service industries, government service, and education.

Education in Folk Societies

At least fifty per cent of the people in the world are illiterate. They live in folk societies—in intellectually isolated communities where lessons need be only in provincial folkways and mores. "These 'little people' of the world fill the teeming villages of the Orient, they form the bulk of the population in southern and eastern Europe, and they pass on from one generation to another the colorful costumes and customs of the Latin Americas." [46] What education they get is relatively unorganized and informal. The "schooling" of the Ammassalik Eskimo of Greenland is typical.

> The child is brought up in the midst of the household. It goes from the small summer tent to a larger winter house, but wherever it goes it is an intimate part of the family; it sees its mother at work, it awaits its father's return with food, it watches as the father makes his tools and implements, it listens to the adult conversation, it hears the songs that are sung and the tales that are told on long winter nights, it goes with the mother when she goes berrying or visiting or to a drum match, it sleeps under the same cover as its parents. Small boys make hunting implements and show an extraordinary skill in making the models with which they practice shooting and harpooning. A boy usually gets his own kayak, made for him by his father, when he is about twelve. One boy who had received a kayak when he was ten had within three years caught thirty seals. Little girls are given dolls to play with and to dress. . . . By the time a

> boy is thirteen to fifteen he has become quite adept at making tools and implements and has learned the technique of hunting. From that time on it is a matter of constant practice. The transition from play to adult occupations is made early and follows a consistent training. The same is true of girls, and by the time they are this age they are able to do excellent sewing.
>
> . . . Neither boy nor girl needs any further preparation for marriage. Each can carry on the work that is required of him; they have liberal sex knowledge, for there is no privacy achieved or desired in sex; they have no social structure to learn, nor formalized ritual. They are as they are, and that is the way society takes them.[47]

In the undifferentiated Eskimo society, an individual does not suffer from educational discontinuities. The same mores and taboos and values prevail in all areas of life. A complex society with separate institutions has, in contrast, inherent ambiguities and contradictions. Each institution has its own structures, processes, norms and goals; values learned in school may conflict with those upheld by other institutions. "Book learning" may be economically impractical or contradict religious dogma or expose patriotic myths. In folk societies, such contradictory learning is inconceivable; life is a unity of experience.

In dealing with folk societies, religious missionaries and government agents in the past have tended to impose an educational program as unrelated to the life needs of the people as that of the British program in Pakistan and as unmindful of the values of the indigenous culture as our own treatment of the American Indian.

> During most of the half century that we have been trying to educate the Navajo both the Indian Service and missionaries have started with the assumption that to educate an Indian you had first to strip him of every vestige of Indian culture. The Navajo language was forbidden, the home life was considered an evil influence, and Indian ceremonies of any kind, tools of the devil. The result has been that after four or five years the child is sent back to his family, hopelessly split between the white man's world and his Indian culture. He is not "Americanized," for a new culture is not assumed so easily. He has been told that everything his beloved parents did was wrong, but he has not been given any better tools to take the place of Navajo ways. He has neither learned to make a better way of life on the reservation nor to find a new home for himself elsewhere.[48]

Children were taught as if they were white children and would always live in white society, even though 95 per cent of them remained on the reservation and led a life for which their education had in no way prepared them.

With a point of view corrected by past trials and errors and strengthened by knowledge and insights gained from behavioral sciences, the United States, in 1961, established the Peace Corps and made available teachers, technicians, and other personnel to the newly developing countries of Africa, Asia, and Latin America. More than half of the Peace Corps volunteers are teachers, and more than 80 per cent of these teachers work in rural areas or small villages.

They teach soil conservation, land reclamation, irrigation, forestry, animal husbandry, and other practical skills. Peace Corps technicians help build roads, bridges, schools, and hospitals. Others help set up public services, or implement democratic processes through community projects.

> "Community action," said a Peace Corps volunteer, "builds the muscle of the community by banding together the members of the area in a common project. It acquaints one with his neighbor and his neighbor's problems. It gives a neighborhood a taste of self-rule and self-guidance and independence. It provides the means for unity and the idea that in many there is strength." [49]

Each Peace Corps volunteer takes a training program tailored for the specific country and project to which he is assigned. This program includes the language of the host country, its history, geography, economy, traditions and customs, a review of American history, culture, and institutions, and specialized training in each volunteer's skill area. Once simple folk societies are now emerging nations. Our common humanity as well as economic and poltical interdependence makes education of these societies in the ways of the twentieth-century world an essential undertaking. But we must learn in order to teach, and who can say who will benefit most from the reciprocal education?

Education in Industrial Societies

Education as an institution tends to keep pace with the society it serves. The United States in the late seventeenth century, for example, was a preindustrial agrarian society, and schools could largely content themselves with teaching children minimum skills in reading, writing and arithmetic. As the country developed industrially and immigrants continued to pour in, educational goals had to be extended. We needed more than semi-literate workers, and we had to have some way of melting foreign ingredients into a national product. The logical means seemed to be free compulsory public schools which would teach not only the Three R's, but the American Way. Massachusetts established a State Board of Education in 1836, and by 1850 the principle of free education was accepted in all the northern states. The principle has been applied to ever higher levels of education, and, in a number of states, essentially free education is now provided through university graduate school. By 1964 we carried at public expense a larger percentage of our population farther through school than any other contemporary society.

During these years of expansion, the red schoolhouse in rural districts has given way to district schools. In urban centers, too, schools have become increasingly larger. Many metropolitan high schools have 3,000 or more students. In the country schoolhouse, the teacher was often both his own janitor and his own boss, but size and complexity have made necessary specialized administration. The chain of command typically extends from the Board of Education and city or district supervisor, down through the school principal and vice-principals and department chairmen, to the individual teacher, who, in turn, must cope with administrative red tape. In 1955 elementary school teachers were spending between 21 and 69 per cent of their time at school on clerical and housekeeping jobs having little to do with teaching.[50] And some of the remaining time was spent not teaching, but trying to keep order among too many children with too many different capacities and interests.

Other changes in education reflect more than the growth of a new nation. We have been a people on the move—from east to west, from south to north, from rural to urban, from urban to suburban. A rare child spends his whole school career in one district. Sometimes he goes to many public schools in a variety of states. This creates problems. Different states, even different cities and different schools, have different educational standards.

Education in Lynchburg, Tennessee, is not the same as education in Wellesley, Massachusetts. Education in Koochiching, Minnesota, is not the same as education in Berkeley, California. Education in the slums of New York is not the same as education in Westchester County. There are differences and deficiencies in opportunity, in curricula, in teaching theory and techniques. Furthermore, schoolteachers were once mainly men; now, below the high school level, they are mainly women. Teaching has been one of the few occupations traditionally open to women, and with the changing status of women following the First World War, more and more women made teaching their professional goal. It was respectable work nice girls could do. Our traditional wage discrimination against women helped keep the general level of teacher salaries at the low level of other feminine occupations, such as nursing. However, following World War II came a baby boom, and a potential teacher shortage. Following the Russian launching of Sputnik I came a sense of educational urgency. In response to both, men have been re-entering the field, and salaries are rising. Those actively involved in education in the United States, however (teachers, students, and administrators), have yet to achieve the status many feel due them. A comparison of education in the United States and Russia at the time of Sputnik I gives perspective on the issue. In October, 1957, the Russians put Sputnik I into orbit. We were baffled, disturbed, even frightened. How could they do it when we hadn't? There was a partial answer. The Russians were spending two per cent of their gross national product on higher education; we were spending seven-tenths of one per cent! *

Education in the Soviet Union, Circa 1957

In 1957 at the time Russia launched its first satellite, a Soviet student would have been going to school six days a week—a total of 213 days a year. Counting homework, he would have spent ten to twelve hours a day on his

* In 1957, the United States spent $44,321,000,000 on military defense; $12,000,000,000 on public education. In 1965 President Johnson did ask Congress for $4,100,000,000 to finance Federal aid to education.

studies. With this concentration of effort, he could have gone from the first grade through high school in ten years, and he would have had behind him ten years of arithmetic and mathematics, six of biology, five of physics, four of chemistry, and five of foreign language. A reformed plan introduced by Soviet educators in 1958 included an eight-year school to replace the ten-year school, and three- to four-years' training and work in industry and agriculture, or specialized study in mathematics, science, or humanities.

If the student qualified for the university, he would work five more years for his degree. If his parents could not afford to finance his education, he would be paid by the government $75 a month for the first year, increasing up to $125 by the fifth year, with extra bonuses for good grades. And, as a student, he would have special considerations. For example, in his dormitory room, he would have a telephone, still a rare luxury for the general population. He would find the library open twenty-four hours a day, and conveniently adjacent to the library, a snack bar. After graduation, he would have earning power that reflected his years of education. If he were one of the sixty-five per cent aiming for a degree in science, he could look forward to a job in industry beginning at $500 a month. If he qualified for a teaching job at a university, his salary would begin at $825 a month and increase to $1,375 in ten years—approximately three times as much as any skilled but relatively unschooled laborer.[51]

Intelligence is distributed on the normal curve in the Soviet Union, just as it is in the rest of the world. The Russians, realistically, are not trying to educate everyone to the same level. Schools, in effect, are a series of hurdles. Those who are tripped by the high standards are not given crutches and allowed to limp on. They are redirected to fields and factories. Russian universities are for the academically fit, the politically "reliable," the intellectually elite of both sexes, and the enrollment is biologically balanced, half male, half female. Those young men and women who have the highest academic qualifications have opportunity to win the highest economic and social rewards.

Education in the United States, Circa 1957

The experience of a student in the United States at the same time was considerably different. He went to school five days a week. Counting out holidays and summer vacations, this was a total of 180 days a year instead of 213, as in the Soviet Union. In some lower grades there was a no-homework policy. Few exceptional students consistently spent even eight hours a day, five days a week, in school and study. Only about ten per cent of the high schools had any physics courses; only fourteen per cent had chemistry. The ten-year Russian program gave the Russian student more science than most of our college graduates and more than five times the amount of mathematics stipulated for entrance into even such a specialized school as the Massachusetts

Institute of Technology.[52] Only 15,000 of our students were learning Russian. In contrast, 10,000,000 Russians were learning English under the tutelage of some 41,000 teachers.

To meet the cost of college in the United States, a student used one of several techniques: worked his way through (which sometimes meant that he spent more time on the job than on studies); depended upon parents, spouse, or a rich uncle; or tried for a scholarship. But then, as now, full scholarships covering room, board, and tuition were rare. Nine months after Sputnik I, President Dwight Eisenhower suggested a cut in the number of federal scholarships in the aid-to-education bill approved by the House Education Committee. The bill stipulated 18,000 to 23,000 scholarships a year. The administration originally proposed 10,000. A minority report by members of the House Education Committee stated, "We find ample evidence that able young people who wish to go to college find ways to go to college." One member gave a speech before the House entitled, "Federal Scholarships? What For?" [53]

But the previous year (1957), lack of money kept at least 150,000 qualified youth from attending college, and in 1958, fewer than half the upper ten per cent of high school graduates went on to college. The total college enrollment was approximately 3,000,000–2,000,000 men and 1,000,000 women. Even 23,000 scholarships would have helped only 0.0076 per cent of these students. The Soviet Union, which guaranteed an education to those who qualified, in 1956, in the field of engineering alone, graduated 70,000 compared to our 30,000. "We have either to learn physics and mathematics—or else Russian." [54]

A student in the United States who did spend four years getting a Bachelor's Degree and three more getting a Ph.D. might, if he were lucky, find a university teaching job. The median salary in 1958 was $5,000 a year. (Only one college professor in eight earned more than $7,500.) In comparison, if the student were strong enough to lift a 140-pound sack of sand, he could get a civil service job as a laborer at $5,560 a year. As a bricklayer, plumber, or garage mechanic he could earn even more. One retired Columbia University professor went to work for a circus as a lion trainer. "It is a deplorable truth," he said, "but teaching human beings—and the results there are the future generation—is worth only one-fifth as much money as teaching animals, which results in but a few minutes of entertainment." [55] And as the space age began, learning in the United States brought highest economic rewards as entertainment on television quiz shows!

Eggheads There and Here

In the Soviet Union, an intellectual is "envied, not scorned, and has an honored place in the community from the moment he gets out of college." [56] In the United States, we have had a curious indifference, even a scorn, toward learning. In some of the mass-produced suburbs which surround metropolitan centers, as many as fifty per cent of the men and twenty-five per cent of the women are college graduates, yet "there is a pronounced prejudice against 'braininess' or 'thinking too much.' Any aloofness is apt to be interpreted as 'being too smart' or 'too good for the rest of us.' . . . A writer found himself attacked by a woman at a neighborhood party for 'reading too many books.' . . . One man remarked, 'If you have any brains, you keep them in your back pocket around here.'" [57] The norm seems to be amiable, thoughtless conformity. Said one wife, "It's a very worthwhile bunch we have here. Edith S———, down on Follansbee Road, is sort of the intellectual type, but most of the gang are real people." [58] Popular distrust of intellectuals reached a national peak when the political party campaigning with an avowed contempt for "eggheads" won the 1952 presidential election.

The adult attitude had its counterpart among teen-agers. A survey made of public high-school students in the period just prior to Sputnik I revealed a prevalent anti-intellectualism.

> Almost three-quarters of the high-school students believe that the most important thing they can learn in school is "how to get along with people." Only fourteen per cent place academic learning first. In a recent poll of a representative sample of college students we found that the same attitude prevails at the university level: sixty per cent would rather be popular than brilliant; fifty-one per cent believe that students with low grades are more likely to be popular than those who get good marks; seventy-two per cent believe that development of a well-rounded personality is the main purpose of education; seventy-one per cent feel that personality counts more than grades when it comes to looking for a job.
>
> The disdain for learning shows up most sharply and most dismayingly in the attitude of teen-agers toward science and scientists. Forty per cent of the high school students think that the earth is the center of the universe, and sixty-three per cent believe the earth's circumference is 125,000 miles! More than a third find scientific work boring; twenty-five per cent think scientists as a group are "more than a little bit odd"; about thirty per cent believe that a scientist cannot enjoy life or raise a normal family. In a poll in October, 1957—the month of Sputnik I—sixty-eight per cent of the teen-agers said they would not like to be scientists. A majority asserted that scientists are likely to be radical, that they take no thought of the consequences of their work, that science should be restricted to physics and chemistry, that it is impossible to formulate scientific laws of human behavior.[59]

Our common indifference and distrust of intellectual values has roots in our historical past. Although a number of founding fathers were themselves intellectuals, the basic need of a growing nation was for men of action. The conquest of the frontier, the building of railroads, the development of economic and industrial complexes were not the successes of men who dealt with ideas. They were tangible achievements of practical men who knew what they wanted and risked and worked to get it. Such men had little regard for men of letters who concerned themselves with ideas. Russia's Sputnik jarred us into a realization that ideas and the educational system which nourished them had more practical value than we had traditionally recognized.

Since Sputnik

In 1959, state and local boards of education, aided by federal funds, launched a four-year testing program to discover and encourage high-school students with brain power—particularly those with brain power in science, engineering, and mathematics. Colleges have raised requirements and stiffened standards. They are encouraging high schools to do the same.

> As a minimum academic quota for all high-school students four years of English, three or four years of history and social studies, and a year each of mathematics and science. For the more able youngsters (the top fifteen per cent) . . . add a "tough program" including three years of a foreign language, three years of mathematics, and two of science, plus either another year of mathematics and a tough physics course, or three years of a second language.[60]

In 1963 Congress passed the most extensive program of federal aid to education in our history, and increasingly, at state and local levels, gifted students are being encouraged more than ever before to continue their education beyond high school. In the schools themselves standards are being upgraded and teaching methods evaluated and revised. Television is now not only utilized as a partial compensation for teacher and classroom shortages, but as an established teaching technique in its own right. In 1963, approximately six million school children were getting some formal education via TV. Other mechanical aids—movies, tapes, and teaching machines—are adding to the effectiveness and efficiency of teaching.

Educational Goals

Formal education was once the monopoly of a privileged minority. Today, in modern societies, it is every child's birthright. This is not an unmixed blessing. Universal education was first hailed as "a triumph of justice and enlightenment which might be expected to usher in a new era of happiness and well-being for mankind." [61] These hopeful expectations have been thwarted by unforeseen factors.

> One stumbling-block has been the inevitable impoverishment in the results of education when the process is made available for "the masses" at the cost of being divorced from its traditional cultural background. . . . Our mass-produced intellectual pabulum lacks savour and vitamins. As we look at the the tremendous humanitarian and scientific problems of the twentieth century, one of the questions we most urgently need to answer is, "How is it possible to provide education for the masses without sacrificing optimum standards for the most gifted minority?"

> A second stumbling-block has been the utilitarian spirit in which the fruits of education are apt to be turned to account when they are brought within everybody's reach.[62]

No one would deny the practical benefits of education to individuals or to nations. It is only when utility displaces other values that education is being prostituted. In one study, sixty-six per cent of all parents having sons in college wanted them there primarily to get preparation for a job with high earning power. Twenty-five hundred years ago, Aristotle said:

> All people do not agree in those things they would have a child taught, both with respect to improvement in virtue and a happy life; nor is it clear whether the object of it should be to improve the reason or rectify the morals. From the present mode of education we cannot determine with certainty to which men incline, whether to instruct a child in what will be useful to him in life, or what leads to virtue, or what is excellent; for all these things have their separate defenders.

Our historic preference for practical values has made it particularly difficult for us to agree on "those things we would have a child taught." In 1955 a citizens' committee, meeting in Stamford, Connecticut, submitted the following list of goals. The evident failure to distinguish clearly between the intrinsic values of education and its tangible benefits is typical.

> To prepare young people for a career.
> To teach a man how to think.
> To make it possible for people to get along with one another.
> To enable a person to look up important information when he needs it.
> To develop good taste in the things a person does outside his job.
> To develop the kind of interests and enthusiasm that will enable a person to put his leisure time to good use.
> To teach a person how to use the English language proficiently.
> To teach a man how to listen.
> To enable people to know how to run a home intelligently.
> To teach a man how to keep up with the news, how to read a newspaper or a magazine, how to appraise the news, and how to tell which columnists or commentators are reliable.
> To prepare young people for travel.
> To be a success.
> To acquaint a man with ways in which people climb the ladder of success.
> To prepare young people for bringing up children of their own, and for assuming family responsibility.
> To develop spiritual and moral values.
> To know something about human experience and the course of history.
> To be able to make moral judgments.
> To give a child a strong mind and body.
> To develop to the fullest whatever possibilities or potentialities a human being may have.[63]

Defining educational goals has always been difficult, but it is especially so today when the conditions of life are changing so rapidly. Can a school teach *what* to think or only *how* to think? *Can education offer answers or only techniques for finding answers?*

In a time of accelerating change educational institutions have a particularly crucial role. Only through education can the realities which the scientists are discovering be recognized and understood by publics and policy makers. Only through education can all men gain perspective on the particular realities of their time. And "in the conditions of modern life, the rule is absolute: the race which does not value trained intelligence is doomed." *

Education is dealer in the game, but the trump card is held not by the schools, but by society. Society, as powerfully represented by popular communications—television, radio, newspapers, magazines—by business and industry, by family, church, and state, must respect, reward, and use intellectual skills. Plato expressed this incisively when he said: "What is honored in a country will be cultivated there." Not until the mores of society are unmistakably on the side of education can the educated best serve society.

It is the task of education to train intelligence, and this is a universal task. *No race or nation has a monopoly on intelligence.*

BUREAUCRACY

In the expanding institutions of economics, government, and education, *bureaucracy* is on the increase. Of the five basic primary institutions, only the family lacks formal bureaucratic structure. Religion, although a declining institution, has its own traditional hierarchy of positions which have tended to remain essentially intact. Economics, government, and education, in keeping with their increasing size and complexity in urban-industrial societies, have become increasingly formal in structure and impersonal in function. Although the word *bureaucracy* is most commonly used in connection with government, it applies equally to large-scale religious, economic, and educational organizations.† The characteristic features of any bureaucracy are essentially as follows:

1. Each official has his own bailiwick—a sphere within which his conduct is limited by rules or laws.
   a. Each person is assigned official duties, certain fixed jobs.
   b. Authority to issue orders is lodged in specific offices and officials operating under specific rules.
2. Each office is supervised "from above" by a higher authority. Levels of authority are arranged in pyramid-fashion.
3. Management depends on written records for its authority; the individual is custodian of, not a substitute for, the written records.

---

* Alfred North Whitehead (1861-1947).

† Some sociologists now use *organization* and *bureaucracy* synonymously.

4. Office management is highly specialized and trained.
5. Official duties have first call on the official's working time.
6. Conduct of the office is regulated by general rules. These rules are:
   a. Stable; they do not normally change over night or over a period of time.
   b. All-embracing; they try to anticipate every type of situation that may arise.
   c. Learnable; they can be readily understood and mastered through study by officials.[64]

In bureaucracies, individuals come and individuals go, but the organization goes on indefinitely. No man is indispensable. He is, rather, interchangeable—like a part in a precision-made machine. His importance and value come not as much from his unique personal qualities as from the position he holds and the efficiency with which he functions in that position. His behavior on (and sometimes off) the job is governed by the goals, policies, procedures, rules, and regulations of the organization. This is a safeguard against favoritism and dishonesty within the organization. It makes, the behavior of bureaucrats predictable, rigid, and exasperating to others, particularly when the issue at stake is not covered by "the rules." Consider the case of Bernt Balchen, who piloted Admiral Byrd's South Pole flight.

> According to a ruling of the Department of Labor, Bernt Balchen . . . cannot receive his citizenship papers. Balchen, a native of Norway, declared his intention in 1927. It is held that he has failed to meet the condition of five years' continuous residence in the United States. The Byrd Antarctic voyage took him out of the country, although he was on a ship carrying the American flag, was an invaluable member of the Antarctic expedition, and in a region to which there is an American claim because of the exploration and occupation of it by Americans, this region being Little America.
>
> The Bureau of Naturalization explains that it cannot proceed on the assumption Little America is American soil. That would be *trespassing on international questions* where it has no sanction. So far as the Bureau is concerned, Balchen was out of the country and technically has not complied with the law of naturalization.[65]

To readers of Franz Kafka's *The Castle,* this has a familiar ring. No one in the Bureau of Naturalization saw Bernt Balchen. The disposition of his case was a matter of paper work. Bureaucrats, in fact, have been stereotyped as "paper shufflers," and the amount of paper used in a bureaucracy is a measure of its size.

In 1798, Winthrop Sargent, preparing to set up his office as Governor of the newly designated Mississippi Territory, requested a shipment of supplies from Secretary of State Timothy Pickering. His requisition included: [66]

Folio writing paper of the ordinary size	6 reams
Quills	500
Penknives	6
Black lead pencils	2 dozen
Tape—red—for tying papers	20 pieces

In 1955, a United States federal bureau *Task Force Report on Paperwork Management, Part I,* included this information.

> Every year the Federal Government uses 25 billion pieces of writing paper. Wastepaper is the single largest export of Washington, D.C. From each Army division, 126,000 reports are required annually. Federal filing cabinets are valued at one hundred million dollars. Selective Service considers "permanent" nearly nine out of every ten documents in its files. Federal agencies on the average, classify one out of every four documents. As a result, nine billion documents are added to permanent federal files each year.[67]

Government itself is one vast and total bureaucracy. Religion, economics, and education are a complex of relatively independent and more or less bureaucratic organizations. In general, increasing size, complexity and heterogeneity in a society are accompanied by increasing bureaucratization. *What church, business firm, industrial organization, labor union, school, or government agency in the United States could function now for even a day with only twenty pieces of red tape?*

Notes

1. Margaret Mead, ed., *Cultural Patterns and Technical Change* (Reprint of UNESCO Manual) (New York: Mentor Books, 1955), p. 188.
2. *Ibid.*, p. 181.
3. Edward M. Weyer, Jr., "How the Eskimo Uses His Environment," in *Societies Around the World*, Howard Becker, ed. (New York: The Dryden Press, 1956), p. 409.
4. Lewis Cotlow, *Zanzabuku* (New York: Holt, Rinehart & Winston, Inc., 1956), pp. 119-126.
5. Hallock Hoffman (of the Center for the Study of Democratic Institutions), "The Understanding Gap," KPFK Commentary, October 13, 1963.
6. Clare Boothe Luce, in John Gunther, *Inside Russia Today* (New York: Harper & Row, Publishers, 1958), p. 283.
7. Max Weber, *The Protestant Ethic and the Spirit of Capitalism*, translated from the German by Talcott Parsons (New York: Charles Scribner's Sons, 1930), Vol. I, Chapter 1.
8. Adam Smith, *An Inquiry Into the Nature and Causes of the Wealth of Nations* (first published in 1776; modern edition, New York: Random House, 1937), p. 423.
9. Gendell and Zetterberg, *A Sociological Almanac for the United States* (New York: Charles Scribner's Sons, 1964), p. 14.
10. John K. Galbraith, *American Capitalism, the Concept of Countervailing Power* (Boston: Houghton Mifflin Company, 1952), pp. 108-153.
11. William H. Whyte, *Is Anybody Listening?* (New York: Simon and Schuster, Inc., 1952), pp. 123-124.
12. *Ibid.*, p. 146.
13. *Ibid.*, p. 191.
14. *Ibid.*, p. 180.
15. Galbraith, *American Capitalism: The Concept of Countervailing Power*, p. 42.
16. Meyer Weinberg and Oscar E. Shabat, *Society and Man* (Englewood Cliffs, N.J.: Prentice-Hall, Inc., 1956), p. 470.
17. Margaret Mead, ed., *Cultural Patterns and Technical Change*, p. 175.
18. Zechariah Chaffee, *Blessings of Liberty* (Philadelphia: J. B. Lippincott Company, 1956), p. 86.
19. Karl Marx, *Capital* (first published in German in 1867; American edition, Charles H. Kerr & Company, 1906), p. 13.
20. *Ibid.*, p. 15.
21. William Z. Foster, *Toward Soviet America* (New York: Coward-McCann, Inc., 1932), pp. 2-3.
22. Joseph Wechsberg, "Letter from Warsaw," *The New Yorker*, July 12, 1958, p. 42.
23. John Gunther, *Inside Russia Today* (New York: Harper & Row, Publishers, 1958), pp. 354-355.
24. *The New Yorker*, June 21, 1958, p. 22.
25. John Fell Stevenson, "The Russians' Big Obsession: You!," *This Week Magazine*, December 7, 1958, p. 7.
26. Gerald Clark, "*Red China Can't Be Ignored—the Case for Recognition*," *San Francisco Chronicle*, December 7, 1958, Section III, p. 6.
27. Max Weber, *The Protestant Ethic and the Spirit of Capitalism*, trans. Talcott Parsons (New York: Charles Scribner's Sons, 1958), p. 177.
28. Galbraith, in "Technology and Economic Development," Asa Briggs, *Scientific American*, September, 1963, p. 60.
29. Ogden Nash, *The Private Dining Room* (Boston: Little, Brown & Company, 1952), p. 60.

30. Raymond Moley, in *The New Dictionary of Thoughts,* Tyron Edwards, ed. (Standard Book Company, 1957), p. 242.
31. Gendell and Zetterberg, *A Sociological Almanac for the United States,* p. 10.
32. Weinberg and Shabat, *Society and Man* (Englewood Cliffs, N.J.: Prentice-Hall, Inc., 1956), p. 213.
33. Samuel A. Stouffer, *Communism, Conformity, and Civil Liberties: A Cross Section of the Nation Speaks Its Mind.* (Garden City, New York: Doubleday & Company, Inc., 1955), pp. 29 and 41.
34. Gunther, *Inside Russia Today,* p. 336.
35. *Civil Liberties,* February, 1964, No. 213, p. 4.
36. Stouffer, *op. cit.,* p. 33.
37. Weinberg and Shabat, *Society and Man,* p. 214.
38. Gunther, *op. cit.,* p. 74.
39. Saul K. Padover, ed., *Thomas Jefferson on Democracy* (New York: Penguin Books, Inc., 1946), p. 97.
40. Elmer Davis, *But We Were Born Free* (New York: Bobbs-Merrill Company, Inc., 1954), pp. 175-176.
41. Weinberg and Shabat, *op. cit.,* pp. 210-211.
42. Gunther, *op. cit.,* pp. 136-137.
43. H. H. Remmers and D. H. Radler, "Teenage Attitudes," *Scientific American,* June, 1958, p. 26.
44. Eddy Gilmore, "*Is Russia Leaning Toward a New Capitalism?*" College of Marin, Kentfield, California, February 28, 1964.
45. Abdus Salam, "Pakistan: The Case for Technological Development," *Bulletin of the Atomic Scientists,* March, 1964, p. 3.
46. Irwin T. Sanders, "Characteristics of Peasant Societies," in *Societies Around the World,* p. 409.
47. Jeanette Mirsky, "The Ammasalik Eskimo of Greenland," Margaret Mead, ed., in *Cooperation and Competition Among Primitive Peoples* (New York: McGraw-Hill Book Company, 1937), pp. 51-86.
48. Mary and John Collier, Jr., "Navajo Farmer," in *Societies Around the World,* p. 168.
49. *College Education Plus: Liberal Arts Students and the Peace Corps,* Washington, D.C., Office of Public Affairs, n.d., p. 7.
50. L. Joseph Stone and Joseph Church, *Childhood and Adolescence* (New York: Random House, 1957), p. 253.
51. Gunther, *Inside Russia Today,* pp. 257-262.
52. *Ibid.,* pp. 257-258.
53. *San Francisco Chronicle,* July 21, 1958, p. 26.
54. Gunther, *op. cit.,* p. 264.
55. George Keller, "This World," *San Francisco Chronicle,* August 19, 1959, p. 2.
56. Gunther, *op. cit.,* p. 262.
57. Harry Henderson, "Rugged American Collectivism—The Mass-Produced Suburbs, Part 2, *Harper's Magazine,* December, 1953, pp. 80-81.
58. Whyte, *Is Anybody Listening?,* p. 154.
59. H. H. Remmers and D. H. Radler, "Teenage Attitudes," *Scientific American,* June, 1958, pp. 27-28.
60. "Science and the Citizen," *Scientific American,* June, 1958, p. 44.
61. Arnold J. Toynbee, *A Study of History,* Abridgment of Volumes I-VI by D. C. Somervell (New York and London: Oxford University Press, 1946), p. 292.
62. *Ibid.,* p. 292.
63. Fred M. Hechinger, *An Adventure in Education: Connecticut Points the Way* (New York: The Macmillan Company, 1956), pp. 10-11.
64. Summarized in Weinberg and Shabat, *Society and Man,* pp. 610-611.
65. *Chicago Tribune,* June 24, 1931. Quoted in Paul B. Horton and Chester L. Hunt, *Sociology* (New York: McGraw-Hill Book Company, 1964), p. 225.
66. Leonard D. White, *The Federalists* (New York: The Macmillan Company, 1948), p. 498. Quoted in Weinberg and Shabat, *op. cit.,* p. 609.
67. Weinberg and Shabat, *op. cit.,* p. 608.

Man is the highest product
of his own history.

THEODORE PARKER (1810-1860)

iii

Man—Creature of Culture

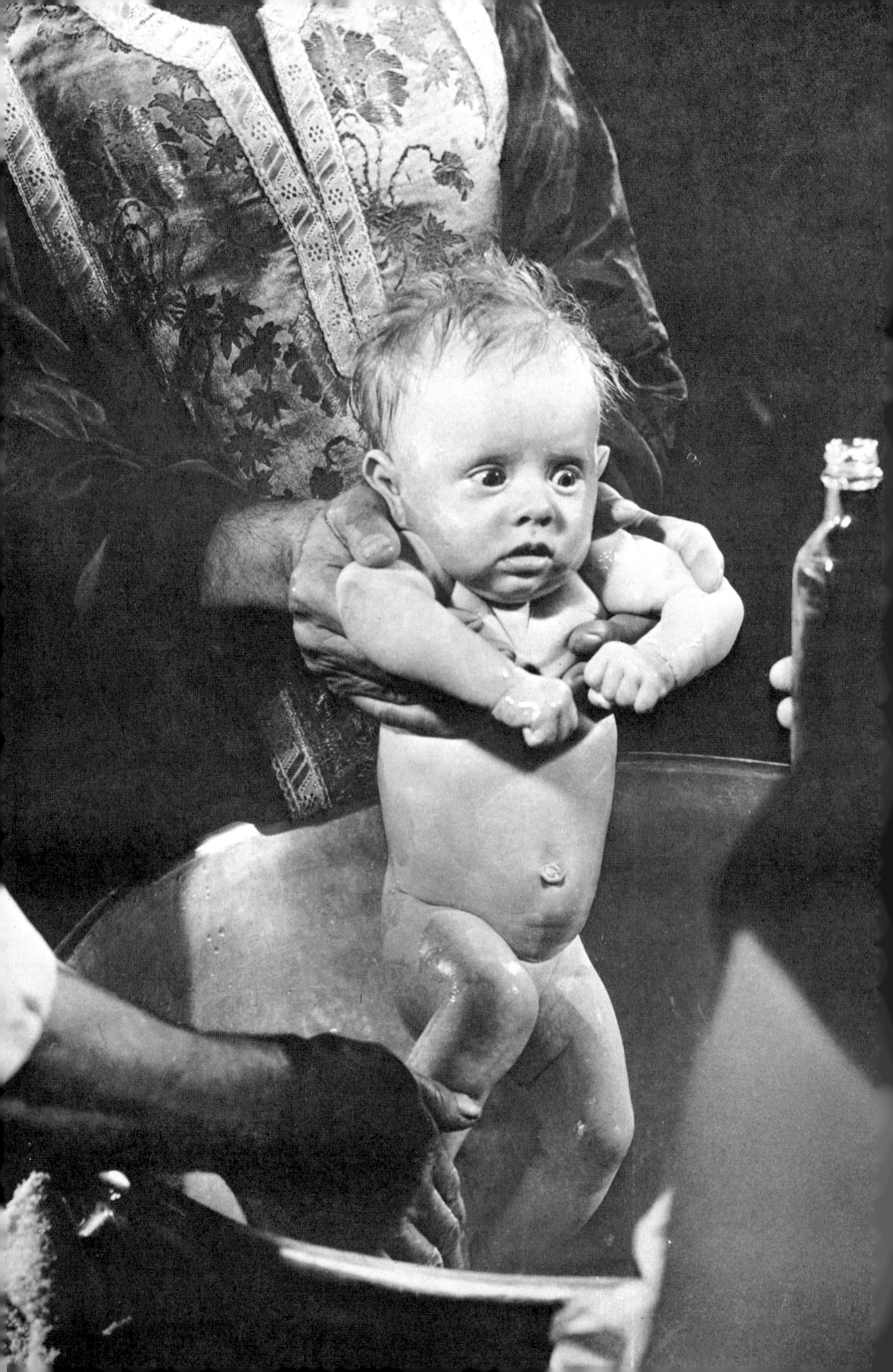

A human being is not, in any proper sense,

a human being until he is educated.

HORACE MANN (1796-1859)

6

Learning to Be Human

HOW MUCH OF WHAT we are would be the same if, as infants, we had been separated from our parents and our culture and been raised among Australian Bushmen, Tibetans, or head hunters of Ecuador? How much of what we are is inherited—dependent on the maturation of potentials contained in our chomosomes since conception? How much is acquired in interaction with our particular environment?

Physiological traits in general are more dependent on heredity; psychological ones are more dependent on environment. But even physiological traits are inherited only as potentials dependent on the environment for their full development, and qualities which make us uniquely human are almost entirely learned. We become human gradually as we respond to others. We learn to be human, and we learn to be the particular human beings we are through *socialization.* Socialization is the process by which an Eskimo becomes an Eskimo, a Bushman becomes a Bushman—the process by which the infant *Homo sapiens* becomes a participating, responsible member of his society. Any one of us could just as easily have learned to be a member of a different society.

> . . . the culture itself, the whole complex patterned way of life through which people relate to one another, to their environment, and to the universe, is so constructed that it can be learned by all who are born within it, except the very deviant. Difficult as it is for individuals who have learned one single language to form the sounds of other languages when they try to learn them as adults, the human

> infant learns Bushman clicks, Polynesian glottal stops, the liquid sounds of a Romance language, or the harsh consonants of the Germanic languages with equal facility. To a young child no one language is more difficult than another. . . . So a whole human culture—the way of life of any people which has lasted through more than one generation and permitted them to marry, rear their children and hand on in turn that way of life to their children—is a system which has been so learned that it can be learned again, without too much variation, by the next generation.[1]

Culture precedes the individual and lays down the patterns available to him. The individual, potentially capable of reacting in a variety of ways, reacts only to the environment he experiences. This environment his society and its culture provide.

In simple societies where the personality type best adapted to the culture is clearly defined, the effects of social conditioning are most obvious. "Human nature is almost unbelievably malleable," [2] and children in different cultures —children essentially the same in average capacities and needs—gradually become different as they take on the ways of the group into which they were born. Consider, for example, three New Guinea tribes: the Arapesh, the Mundugumor, and the Tchambuli.

The Arapesh of New Guinea perpetuate a cooperative society by deliberately creating a prejudice in favor of friendliness and trust. Children are gently nurtured from conception. In the womb the child has the physiological environment created by a calm woman. After birth he is never far from the comforting arms of his elders. He is usually nursed until he is three or four, and while he is being nursed, the mother is relaxed and strokes him so that he experiences the pleasure and satisfaction of eating in combination with bodily contact and caresses. "The dog or the little tame pig that thrusts an inquisitive nose under the mother's arm is held there, the child's skin and the dog's rubbed together, the mother gently rocking them both, and murmuring, 'Good dog, good child, good dog, good, good, good.' " [3] The child's relatives, the parent's friends, even strangers are also commended to the child. "This is your other mother . . . other mother. See your other mother. She is good. She brings you food. She smiles. She is good." Boys and girls alike tend to grow up friendly, accepting, and cooperative.

The Mundugumor share many economic and social traits with the Arapesh and live only about a hundred miles from them, but they perpetuate a contrasting competitive culture. They live in mutual distrust of one another, and protect their high fertile land from impoverished neighbors by their strength and ferocity. Children are harshly nurtured from conception. The Mundugumor male abuses his wife for having become pregnant. He fears a male child who will become his hostile rival. His wife dreads a daughter who, according to custom, will belong, not to her, but to her husband. After the unwelcome baby is born, it is kept in a stiff, opaque basket. When it cries, someone will try to distract it by scratching on the outside of the basket. If it continues crying, it is eventually suckled, but the mother stands in a strained position, and the baby must suck rapidly and vigorously, for the moment it stops it is put back into his basket. The child is weaned by blows and cross words. Under this rigorous treatment, only the strongest children survive, and those boys and girls who do grow up tend to be violent, competitive, and aggressive.

The Arapesh, both men and women, are gently nurturing in a way we consider most appropriate to women. The Mundugumor behave with the fierce aggressiveness we associate with the male temperament.

The Tchambuli, a third tribe living within a hundred miles of the other two, reverse the traditional sex role. The unadorned women are energetic and managerial. The men, complete with ornaments and delicate coiffures, are sensitive, artistic, and charming. Tchambuli women hold the purse strings. They do the major work: they catch the fish and make the mosquito bags. Men take the fish and bags to market, but the proceeds, the strings of conus rings, the talibun and kinas, belong to the women; and no man may spend them without permission. Men get money and property from women in return for "languishing looks and soft words." The sex role, too, is the reverse of ours. In courtship women initiate and choose; men wait to be chosen. "Are women passive, sexless creatures who can be expected to wait upon the dilly-dallying of formal considerations of bride price? Men, not so urgently sexed, may be expected to submit themselves to the discipline of a due order and precedence." [4]

The Arapesh, the Mundugumor, and the Tchambuli, as groups, are basically different; but there are unknown human variables—genetic, psychological, and physiological—which account for deviants in all three societies. There are a few hostile Arapesh, a few gentle Mundugumors, and some "masculine" males and "feminine" females in Tchambuli. However, consistent social conditioning has a high degree of success; it "takes" on the bulk of the population.

The intangibles of a culture—the folkways, mores, taboos, and goals—all extrinsic to the newborn are, through socialization, gradually incorporated into the developing personality structure as emotional and cognitive responses. These learned responses come to seem as "natural" as the physiological processes. Culture even pervades the subconscious.

The *Oedipus* complex (a subconscious hostile sex rivalry with the father for the affection of the mother) was identified by the Viennese psychoanalyst Sigmund Freud (1856-1939) as a sub-conscious factor in the neuroticism of his male patients. Freud assumed the complex was universal. However, in the Trobrian Islands, where the maternal uncle is the disciplining authority, and in New Guinea, where the father is a tender, indulgent guardian, males show no such rivalry. The *Oedipus* complex seems to be a manifestation, not of human nature, but of nurture in a patriarchal and authoritarian society.

The social and cultural environment provides or deprives; individuals respond and are thereby shaped.

CHANNELS OF CULTURE

Every society is a population of infants, children, young adults, mature adults, aging adults . . . and the identity and continuity of any one society depends on channeling essential culture traits to and through its members. Culture is a social achievement and its perpetuation is a social responsibility. When an infant is born into a society, all the forces of that society combine to "humanize" him—theoretically in ways consistent with social needs and values. Culture accumulated over the centuries is channeled through the institutional structures of society to the individual and incorporated more or less fully by the individual into the structure of his developing personality.

Parents begin the socialization process. Other individuals representing other institutions continue it: teachers, preachers, policemen, advertisers, employers.

> A human being can be a human being only because other people have taught him, directly and indirectly, explicitly and implicitly, how to be human and what the important characteristics of the world, human and nonhuman, are that he is going to have to live with.[5]

In simple societies where the social structures are stable and the norms and goals of the culture consistent, it is not difficult to teach a child the "important characteristics of the world" in which he will live. The child acquires consciously and subconsciously normative opinions, attitudes, beliefs, skills, understandings, and social behavior. He accepts without conflict the "reality" defined by his culture. In complex urban-industrial societies, however, where social relationships are shifting and where norms and goals are inconsistent, the "important characteristics of the world" are not easily agreed upon. Socialization is child rearing in the broadest sense, and involves the deliberate efforts as well as the incidental actions of persons representing all the institutions with which the child has contact: family, religion, economics, government, and education. The less support these institutions give each other, the slower, more difficult and uncertain the process of socialization.

Social Structures

Social institutions incorporate a variety of social structures ranging in size and intimacy from the family and friendship groups to larger, more impersonal organizations and bureaucracies. The structure of a social group, except in the most casual and transitory associations, tends to be a phenomenon apart from its membership. The structure tends to endure; the members, to come and go. The structure of a group is defined by *positions* of various rank within that group. The facts of physiology, for example, establish positions of father, mother and child within the family. Purpose, size, and other practical needs determine the various positions characteristic of other groups and organizations: president, third vice-president, clerk; principal, teacher, student; *Maitre d'hôtel*, waiter, cashier. Each position in a social structure has a culturally conceived *role-image* associated with it—an image gradually built up by the requirements of circumstance, and the expectations of others.

As in chess, a position defines the expected and accepted behavior of each piece. Queens may move any distance in any direction; kings, in any direction but only one space at a time; bishops move only diagonally; castles move only horizontally or vertically; knights jump two horizontally or vertically, and one to either side; pawns move forward but capture diagonally. Prescribed behavior for each position makes the game possible. In social structures, prescribed behavior for various positions facilitates interaction, but it does not guarantee a game!

Positions and Role-Images

When an infant is born into a society, he has family position—son or daughter, brother or sister. Socialization prepares him to fill a variety of other positions in other groups during the course of his lifetime. "All the world's a stage, and all the men and women merely players: They have their exits and their entrances; and one man in his time plays many parts. . . ." * An individual may have numerous *concurrent* positions: son, student, friend, lover; and pass through other *consecutive* ones: child, adolescent, husband, parent, grandparent. Each position carries with it the behavioral expectations we call role-images. A role-image is essentially an embodiment of norms or sanctioned behavior patterns associated with a particular position. A *role-image* is a conceptual consensus of *expected* behavior associated with a position. A *role* is the *actual* behavior of the individual occupying the position.

Some roles are learned through experience. A daughter learns the role of mother by being mothered. One friend told us, "I was a good mother until my child was three years old. After that I was at a loss to know what to do. She seemed just a little guest in the house. My own mother died when I was three."

Other roles are learned by hearsay. Name a common position and one tends to conjure up the role-image associated with it. Try, as example, the position *National Park Ranger.* What are the connotations? Outdoor type, young male adult, clean-cut, rugged, fearless, gentle with lost fawns, firm with bears, friendly with hikers. . . .

> One summer I worked as a *Seasonal Ranger* in Olympic National Park. But I was *unseasoned,* and the only instruction I got before I started off alone to man an isolated station was, "Get some experience climbing glaciers. A favorite

* Shakespeare, *As You Like It,* Act II, Scene vii.

one is ten miles from your place and you'll probably have to lead a rescue party. Somebody always falls in a crevasse." How do I get experience? "Just tag along with the first mountaineeers who come through. They like having a Ranger in the party."

Within two weeks a group of seventeen did come through en route to the glacier. This was my cue, and I joined them. The first day we got ourselves and equipment to the foot of the glacier. The second day after breakfast all eighteen of us started out, hoping to get over the glacier and beyond to the top of a prominent peak. We made good progress until, near the top, a crevasse about ten feet wide blocked our path. Thirteen of the mountaineers took one look and sat down to enjoy the scenery. But I was *The Ranger*. I went into the blue-black depths with the intrepid four, roped behind their leader. Fifteen feet down, the crevasse was only four feet wide. The leader let go of the holds he had chopped in the sheer ice face, jumped backwards, turned in the air, and landed on a small ledge on the other side. It was my turn next. I jumped and found myself, not on the ledge, but several feet farther down the crevasse dangling head first. I couldn't right myself. I, *The Ranger,* had to be inched back up by the rope in that undignified position. My self-image suffered a slight revision, but I rationalized: this was the first time I had ever even seen a glacier. The other mountaineers all made the leap; and we went on until, at the end of the glacier, we were confronted by precipitous rocks which led to the peak. Two mountaineers sat down there to enjoy the scenery. The other two eyed the peak and kept going. I was *The Ranger*. I went with them. We were no longer roped together, and somehow in the confusion of climbing, I got in the lead. I crawled straight to a spot with a perpendicular drop of at least 400 feet down and what seemed unclimbable rocks above. I couldn't go back as I had come, because the rocks I had worked my way up on were decomposed. They had crumbled away under my weight, and now every tentative move I tried showered rubble down the mountainside. I looked 1,000 feet down to the two brave men who had courageously admitted they were afraid to come. I managed to grin at my two sympathetic but perplexed companions. They had no easy answer. I clung to the spot and to my fading role-image, sweated and cursed. The only way to go was up—15 feet at about an 80-degree angle—and I would have to do it faster than the rocks I clutched could give way. I, *The Ranger,* took a deep breath and scrambled.[6]

How any individual plays any particular role is determined by both his aptitude for the role and his interpretation of the role.

When an individual changes positions, he tends to also change perspective and behavior. The strict judge may be the indulgent father. The docile son may be the aggressive ballplayer. The demure daughter may be the flirtatious belle.

When Ko-Ko in Gilbert and Sullivan's *Mikado* * is appointed Lord High Executioner of Titipu, all other officers of the state, too proud to serve under a

* W. S. Gilbert and Arthur Sullivan, first produced at the Savoy Theater, London, March 14, 1885.

"cheap taylor," resign. Ko-Ko appoints Pooh-Bah to these vacated positions, and Poo-Bah, to "mortify his pride," and collect the various salaries, accepts. Ko-Ko, about to be married, asks the advice of Pooh-Bah and gets a variety of answers.

KO. Pooh-Bah, it seems that the festivities in connection with my approaching marriage must last a week. I should like to do it handsomely, and I want to consult you as to the amount I ought to spend upon them.

POOH. Certainly. In which of my capacities? As First Lord of the Treasury, Lord Chamberlain, Attorney-General, Chancellor of the Exchequer, Privy Purse, or Private Secretary?

KO. Suppose we say as Private Secretary.

POOH. Speaking as your Private Secretary, I should say that, as the city will have to pay for it, don't stint yourself, do it well.

KO. Exactly—as the city will have to pay for it. That is your advice.

POOH. As Private Secretary. Of course you will understand that, as Chancellor of the Exchequer, I am bound to see that due economy is observed.

KO. Oh! But you said just now "Don't stint yourself, do it well."

POOH. As Private Secretary.

KO. And now you say that due economy must be observed.

POOH. As Chancellor of the Exchequer.

KO. I see. Come over here, where the Chancellor can't hear us. . . . Now, as my Solicitor, how do you advise me to deal with this difficulty?

POOH. Oh, as your Solicitor, I should have no hesitation in saying "Chance it—."

KO. Thank you . . . I will.

POOH. If it were not that, as Lord Chief Justice, I am bound to see that the law isn't violated.

KO. I see. Come over here where the Chief Justice can't hear us. . . . Now, then, as First Lord of the Treasury?

POOH. Of course, as First Lord of the Treasury, I could propose a special vote that would cover all expenses, if it were not that, as Leader of the Opposition, it would be my duty to resist it, tooth and nail. Or, as Paymaster-General, I could so cook the accounts that, as Lord High Auditor, I should never discover the fraud. But then, as Archbishop of Titipu, it would be my duty to denounce my dishonesty and give myself into my own custody as First Commissioner of Police.

No two professional actors speak the same lines on stage with the same effect. Neither do two individuals ever play social roles in quite the same way. A role-image defines only the central core of expectations; positions have room for individual interpretation and some freedom of expression. However, an individual acting in a position—especially a prominent one—will find that circumstance and position both guide and coerce him. *Do great men make history, or does history, in fact, make great men?*

Costumes and Props

Every position in a social structure has a corresponding role-image and many such images the culture sustains with costumes and props. One should not only act the part; he should look the part. The Ranger has his badge and hat; the judge, his robe and gavel; the banker, his business suit. And around the universal and inescapable facts of sex, each society builds its own images and provides its own costumes and props. From birth on, behavior is guided by role-images and appearance is modified by culture. In our own society, boys are traditionally dressed in blue, girls in pink. Boys get a haircuit at least by eighteen months of age; girls do not. Girls get dolls for Christmas; boys get toy trucks and airplanes. How happily and successfully a male or female plays his sex and social roles depends, in large measure, on how closely his appearance fits the role-image of "maleness" or "femaleness."

In the 1920's, the female image was "boyish." Any natural assets a woman had she strapped down as tightly as possible. Today the image has shifted, and a woman without natural assets may use artificial substitutes.

> For that Forward Look: "Radiant" bra with famous "push-up" half-pads. The invisible foam rubber half-pads in each wired undercup subtly raise the smallest bosom to the full, rounded lines demanded by fashion today.
>
> Some women wearing pneumatic "normalizers" in airplanes have discovered the inverse relationship between volume and pressure. When the air pressure has decreased, increased hypermammalianism has, on occasion, been followed by minor explosions.
>
> Late in 1957, a meeting of 500 plastic surgeons in San Francisco heard a report recommending "inside falsies" of polyvinyl sponge to give women the large bosoms demanded by fashion. Psychiatrists commented on remarkable personality improvements in 31 out of 32 cases. One plastic surgeon opposed inserting a foreign substance and putting falsies inside, on the grounds that, "Fashions change. My waiting room used to be full of women wanting smaller breasts. Now, doubtless because of people in the public eye, without mentioning any names, it's the opposite." Other surgeons objected to sponges inside the breasts for aesthetic reasons: with time the sponge hardens, and the breasts become—as one surgeon put—"hard as baseballs." [7]

Men are no less susceptible than women to the dictates of role-images. They, too, are sold props to "normalize," and, as in women's fashions, one era's norm is another's abomination.

The heavy shoulder padding in men's coats, giving that "virile, broad-shouldered look" becomes grotesque next to the "natural shoulder" so "slimming and flattering." Today a man with a sagging middle may wear a girdle to retain that "flat, youthful look." In Elizabethan times, the normal flat stomach of a healthy young man was padded out into a monstrous "pot belly" by a whalebone or wooden foundation filled with old rags, bran, or sawdust.

> A gallant needed six pounds of bombast at least to make up his peascod-belly, and the slightest shower of rain was disastrous. So was the accidental catching of his garment on a nail, such as happened to one unfortunate courtier just as he was advancing to make his reverence to the Queen, the chaff with which he was so proudly stuffed escaping in a twinkling, leaving him completely deflated.[8]

In the Middle Ages, men wore "tights," a costume evolved from two separate stockings which were made longer until they joined and extended to the waist. They were so tight that a fold had to be put in the front, but the fold proved to be too revealing. The Church, in 1461, ordered that the fold be covered by a pouch, or cod-piece. However, instead of serving the intended purpose of modest concealment, the cod-piece was for more than one hundred years a focus of fashion.

Costumes and props help create an illusion consistent with a current role-image. To play a part, one ordinarily dresses the part.

> Musicians gave a spirited rendition of "Here Comes the Bride" while Sissie ———, daughter of the owner of a Florida nudist camp, walked through Bermuda grass to the altar. She carried a bouquet but wore nothing except "a simple white veil." Three nude bridesmaids accompanied her. The groom, Charles ———, was a former sailor. He wore neither his old school tie nor his white sailor hat. The bride's graying father and the best man—with no pocket in which to keep the ring—stood by Charles. Two hundred invited guests and newsmen—all nude—congratulated the young couple. Only the Miami lawyer who performed the ceremony and a few special guests were dressed.[9]

This scene does not coincide with role-images. In a large wedding a bride traditionally has a bouquet, veil—and gown! A groom has a dress suit; the minister, a robe. Clothes make the social man. Underneath is the biological one.

Personality Structure

Positions and role-images exist as abstractions—separate from the flesh-and-blood people who happen to be playing the parts. This social context influences individual behavior, but whether or not a particular individual is capable of playing a part and how closely he conforms to social expectations is determined by the particular personality structure he has developed. Heredity, maturation, learned habits, and understandings—these and other interacting variables build the personality.

With the passage of time in a normally stimulating environment, the infant *Homo sapiens* matures; inherent characteristics unfold in accordance with the dictates of his particular heredity. His learnings come in a favorable environment with maturation readiness: when his skeletal-muscular system is mature enough, he learns to walk; when his central nervous system is mature enough, he learns to talk. With increasing physical maturation he learns the increasingly complex *habits and understandings* required by his society. To get along well in our society, for example, we need to read and write and do arithmetic. We cope with zippers, dial telephone numbers, operate push-button elevators and dishwashers, drive cars, balance bank accounts. We amass factual knowledge and develop concepts and understandings. The more complex the society, the greater the number of skills and understandings needed by its individual members. And as the individual matures and learns, he also builds a concept of the world and a concept of himself as an entity in relationship to that world.

Whatever an individual experiences he relates to his repertoire of concepts. No one perceives raw sensory data as such. If you look at a rock, for example, you see at least a solid shape with a colored and textured surface. You may also see an object which could be enjoyed aesthetically, analyzed chemically, used to build a wall, crushed into little pieces, or thrown through a window. We organize and impose meaning on stimuli coming to us through our senses and act in any particular situation according to such meaning. Perception guides action, and action reveals personality. The total personality structure is a complex configuration of action potentials, circumscribed by an individual's perception of himself and of his environment.

Perception of Self

How positive or negative is your self-image? To what extent do you perceive yourself as a person of integrity with trust in yourself and others—capable of self-direction, initiative, industry, intimacy, parenthood, and productive work? To what extent do you perceive yourself with despair as a person burdened with doubts, dependent, anxious, inferior, isolated, and without pride in what you do? * The entire configuration of personal characteristics consciously perceived comprises the self-image.

No one is born with a self-image. The neonate (newborn) has no clear awareness of self apart from environment. He reacts to bodily states—to hunger, satiation, sleepiness. He reacts to external physical stimuli—a loud noise, a touch on the cheek. And he reacts to others—becoming tense when handled by an abrupt, impatient adult, or relaxed when comforted by a tender, confident adult. But he cannot recognize people or objects, and he is relatively uninvolved in what goes on around him. Day by day as he becomes increasingly aware of the external world, he becomes increasingly aware of himself. He begins to identify his "self" in relationship to those aspects of the world most important to him. He is to a greater or lesser degree loved and therefore worth loving. He is accepted or rejected, encouraged or constrained, guided or coerced. Others evaluate his person and his behavior, and eventually he evaluates himself.

* For a discussion of the socialization process as a cumulative development of personality through eight psychosocial crises, see Erik H. Erikson, *Childhood and Society*, 2nd ed. (New York: W. W. Norton & Company, Inc., 1964), Chapter 7.

Listen to parents: "Mary has always been rather frail. . . ." "That's my fine, strong boy. . . ." "Ellen is shy. She wouldn't be happy there with all those strange children. Would you, dear? . . ." "Can't I trust you to do anything right? . . ." "You bad, naughty boy. . . ." And to peers and playmates: "Sissy, sissy, boy." "Come on, stupid. . . ." "Let's not invite her. She isn't any fun. . . ." "Look, there goes old Anna. . . ." And to teachers: "I guess I'll have to call on Sue. She always knows the answer. . . ." "You have a good mind. If you just weren't so lazy. . . ." The interaction is endless, and it is impossible to know how much of the self is fact, how much is fiction. "It is thus with most of us: we are what other people say we are. We know ourselves chiefly by hearsay."[10] The self-image is in large measure a "looking-glass self"[11]—dominated by the reflection of what others see, and, as the self-image develops it becomes an ever more powerful dictator. The school child ignored by his peers may become a nonentity even to himself. The rejected lover may leap. "Faith in ourselves, like every other faith, needs a chorus of consent."[12]

The self-image can coerce.

An innocent man was convicted of murder and condemned to die. His attorney had won a stay of execution by presenting evidence implicating a man we'll identify as Farris. Farris did not fight the charges. He came forward and freely confessed. Why? Farris said a statement in the Bible, "Blessed are those who are persecuted for righteousness' sake" (Matthew 5:10) had stirred his conscience. He perceived himself as "blessed" if he confessed, and once he had thus identified himself, he *had* to confess.

We tend to obey the dictates of conscience.* Conscience is tension generated by a felt dissonance between behavior and self-image. It implies an incorporation into the self-image of the cultural norms. If one has a "guilty conscience," it is because he has let his "self" down. As long as the self-image remains the same, the guilt can be relieved only by amending or changing behavior.

And the self-image can constrain.

In the mid-1950's, domestic help in Rome could be had for as little as $16.00 a month. My husband and I, school teachers on sabbatical leave for a year, decided that even we could afford the luxury. Our Tia was an exceptionally bright, attractive young woman in her late twenties, with clear olive skin, green eyes, lustrous dark hair, and volatile emotions. She had a flair for clothes and kept her "day-off" outfit in perfect condition. When she left the house on Sunday morning in her blue suit, white gloves and high-heeled pumps, she could hold her own with anybody. She had watched several of her friends leave the arid, stoney farmlands of her native Sardinia as G.I. wives, and after her family forbade her to marry a G.I., she had run away to the city. As might be expected, she was avidly interested in everything American. She assiduously studied

* Conscience is a product of culture, and we can find a word for the concept in most languages. In German it is *gewissen;* in Italian, *coscienza;* in Swedish, *samvete;* in Yiddish, *gevisn.* The old English phrase *Ageyn bit of inwit* means, "against the bite of conscience." And we still use the Middle English "*pricke*" of conscience.

English from a book we had given her and listened carefully to even our end of telephone conversations. One day she heard me arrange to meet a friend for coffee at Doney's on the Vita Veneto. At that time, Doney's was *the* place in Rome—famous for the panorama of personalities which passed before its crowded tables. "How much," asked Tia, "*is* coffee at Doney's?" "Oh," I said, about 150 lire." * She was astonished. That was only twice what it cost at any ordinary café. "Why," she said, "*I* could afford that." I assured her she could and encouraged her to arrange to meet her friend Elena there that very Sunday. "I'll do it, Signora," she said. "I'll wear my blue suit. . . ." Then she stopped. "No, it's all foolishness." "Not at all. You look lovely in that suit." "No, no, it's not that. I know the suit is pretty and the shoes fit well, but . . . I could never sit down at Doney's on the Via Veneto with all those elegant people." "For Heaven's sake, why not?" "Because . . . because I'm a maid!" [13]

The self-image has its beginnings in infancy; it normally reaches a stable identity by adulthood, but it is still not a finished product. As the adult continues to learn, as he takes on new social roles or abandons old ones, the more peripheral aspects of the self-image shift: ". . . a person is a fluid process, not a fixed and static entity . . . a continually changing constellation of potentialities, not a fixed quantity of traits." [14] Although the rate of socialization decelerates with increasing age, as long as an individual remains open to experience he continues to be modified by experience.

Out of the complex interplay of personal experiences we each gradually achieve a central, relatively stable self-image which we adapt, more or less successfully, to the requirements of the social positions in which we find ourselves. Our greatest successes are in positions having role-images compatible with our self-image. A maid can be a good maid and a happy maid as long as she does not perceive herself a mistress.

In a well-integrated and stable folk society, tradition shapes the self-image to fit fixed positions in the social structure.

> . . . the child is from infancy continuously conditioned to responsible social participation, while at the same time the tasks that are expected of it are adapted to its capacity. The contrast with our society is very great. . . . The gravity of a Cheyenne Indian family ceremoniously making a feast out of the little boy's first snowbird is at the furthest remove from our own behavior. At birth the little boy was presented with a toy bow, and from the time he could run about, serviceable bows suited to his stature were specially made for him by the man of the family. Animals and birds were taught him in a graded series beginning with those most easily taken, and as he brought in his first of each species his family duly made a feast of it, accepting his contribution as gravely as the buffalo his father brought. When he finally killed a buffalo, it was only the final step of his childhood conditioning, not a new adult role with which his childhood experience had been at variance.[15]

In a society as complex and mobile as ours, the self-image rarely develops in response to clearly understood and fixed social positions. The individual must

---

* At that time, 150 lire was the equivalent of twenty-four cents.

fit himself into a vast and intricate social framework which, instead of being sustained by tradition, is being assaulted by change. Positions and the role-images associated with them vary from group to group and from sub-culture to sub-culture. They are constantly being realigned and modified by unpredictable conditions. The role-images of even so certain a position as *mother* vary with ethnic groups, with social class, with income, with family size, with rural or urban settings. The individual in a heterogeneous culture is confronted with a confusing array of alternatives to action, among which he is often ill-prepared to choose.

Continuity of experience and consistency in values would facilitate socialization, yet our society provides neither. Consider the discontinuities between the dependent, nonresponsible roles most urban children play in the family and the responsible adult roles expected of them after an unsettled and poorly defined period of adolescence.* Psychiatrists report, for example, on the immature, dependent husband who, perceiving his wife as half-mother, cannot share her affection with a baby nor accept the responsibilities of fatherhood.

> It would be well for the obstetrician and the family doctor to ascertain what meaning fatherhood may have for the husband of his pregnant patient. Certain serious reactions may be averted by giving the potential father support in becoming established in his new role.[16]

And note the inconsistency between sacred and secular values represented by mass communication in just one Sunday morning hour of TV.

Time	*Channel*	
9:00 A.M.	2	Services from Boston's Holy Cross Cathedral
	4	Last Hours
	5	Power of the Resurrection
	7	Western Feature
	8	The Master's Hand
	10	This is the Life
	11	Feature Film: "Getting Gertie's Garter" [17]

The common technological conditions we share make assimilation of the nonsymbolic, material aspects of our culture relatively easy. The shifts from a broom to a vacuum cleaner, from silent black and white movies to color and sound, from DC 4's to jets—these pose no serious problems of decision for the individual. In the value-laden societary areas of goals and norms, however, lack of consensus does pose serious problems. Peers, parents, teachers, business leaders, church leaders, political leaders and other lesser agents of socialization give inconsistent advice and direction. Our minister may urge, "Listen to *Power of Resurrection,* Channel 5." Our friend may say, "Don't miss *Getting Gertie's Garter,* Channel 11." The choices an individual does make day after day, week after week, year after year, all contribute to the building of his

* For a discussion of cultural discontinuities see "Discontinuities in Cultural Conditioning," in James A. Dyal, *Readings in Psychology* (New York: McGraw-Hill Book Company, 1962), pp. 62-71.

self-image. What culture he does assimilate becomes part of his psychological self, and as he, in turn, becomes a socializing agent, he acts as a channel for that culture. A baby exposed to TV Westerns by his older brother spoke his first word, "BANG!"

If a society would have its members serve as effective channels of culture, then society must minimize discontinuities and inconsistencies and seek consensus on the norms and goals it would perpetuate. If, for example, we value democracy, we must practice democracy in all the institutions of society. Democracy must be made one of the continuities of our culture—introduced first to the child through his family and then through peer groups in schools and churches, and finally through business groups and government agencies in the larger community. Without having been a part of the democratic process at immediate personal levels during the formative years, the individual reaches adulthood without the sense of worth and responsibility which commits him intellectually and emotionally to the democratic ideal. The self-image of a citizen in a democracy needs to be that of a responsible actor, not of an observer being acted upon.

Perception of Environment

Perception of self and perception of environment are inseparable aspects of personality. Stimuli from the external world reach consciousness only through the filter of self. We perceive, not objective reality, but an organization of meaningful stimuli. "We see things not as they are but as we are." *

> Men attempt to cope with their environment through perception. Although it is generally assumed that what is experienced is a mirror-like reflection of what is "out there," in reality, all perception is selective. . . . It is not so much a reaction to stimuli but a serial process in which men note and respond to cues to which they are already sensitized. . . .[18]

Meanings, once they have been formed, tend to be self-sustaining. *Habitual* use of an object makes its *novel* use more difficult. The use of a paper clip as a hook, for example, one can perceive more readily if he has not habitually used paper clips to hold papers together. *Understanding* relationships among events or entities makes it difficult to perceive such events or entities in isolation. A music lover who understands a sonata as a temporal structure, for example, cannot perceive it as a mere succession of auditory stimuli. And who can see one big cat with five little kittens without assuming that the big cat is the mother?

Immediate needs and expectations, as well as basic habits and understandings, impose meaning on stimuli. If a man *needs* food, he first perceives a trout swimming in a mountain stream, not as an aesthetic object, but as food. And if

* Immanuel Kant, 1724-1804.

a man is waiting for a friend, he may perceive a stranger in the distance walking towards him as his *expected* friend. The meanings we impose on present experience are a product of past experience. We act on the basis, not of raw, sensory data, but on the basis of the *meaning* data has for us. The perception of self is a configuration of meanings imposed on our person, our sensations, our behavior. The perception of environment is also a configuration of meanings imposed on entities existing in and events occurring in that environment.

> The effective environment in which men live and act is made up of all kinds of meanings—meanings of physical objects, of people, of colors, of emotional reactions, of images of various types of activity. Since meanings are generally believed to depend upon the characteristics of the objects themselves, those who have somewhat different backgrounds of experience often get into arguments over what things "really" are. . . .[19]
>
> . . . What people generally call "reality" is a working orientation over which there is a high degree of consensus.[20]

When consensus is lacking, then emotionally biased opinions, attitudes, and beliefs (OAB's) come into action.

OPINIONS, ATTITUDES, AND BELIEFS (OAB'S). We have opinions and beliefs about ourselves and attitudes towards ourselves. These are, in fact, synonymous with the self-image. When opinions, attitudes and beliefs concern, not our personal self, but our physical and social environment, they spark actions that shape the world. Gandhi and his followers *believed* in nonviolent protest. Voters pass or defeat a law on the basis of their *opinion* about the need or effectiveness of the law. Segregationists fight civil-rights legislation because of their ethnic and political *attitudes.* In actuality and in the sociological and psychological literature, opinions, attitudes, and beliefs are not clearly distinguished from each other. "One man's opinion may be another man's attitude and still another man's belief." [21] However, an *opinion* is generally a judgment regarding a current issue. It involves expectation or prediction and can be verbally expressed. We may, for example, have opinions about the behavior of friends, about the seriousness of a situation, about the wisdom of alternative lines of action. A *belief* involves more central concerns and implies trust or confidence. We are generally more tolerant of different opinions that we are of different beliefs. We hold beliefs about God and patriotism and human rights. An *attitude* may be a basic emotional predisposition or it may be a more transitory emotional set. We may have a generally trusting attitude built into our personality structure. We may also have more specific attitudes—predispositions to like a particular person or place. A firmly held attitude, not open to free and rational discussion and resistant to change, is a prejudice.[22] Prejudice implies negative pre-judgment without just grounds or before sufficient knowledge—an emotionally induced astigmatism which unfavorably distorts reality.

PREJUDICE. We readily perceive our friends as individuals with distinctive traits. We perceive strangers, first, not as individuals, but as members of some group. The meaning we attach to that group as a category affects our reactions to the stranger. *Similarity suggests grouping.* This is a general law of perception independent of individual personality. We all tend to use similarities to categorize persons as well as objects or events. "Once any category is defined in terms of a set of properties, our expectations become fixed. . . ."[23] Human categories include those social and racial stereotypes which help create and perpetuate prejudice: "aggressive Jew," "lazy Negro," "dirty Mexican," "stingy Scot," "superstitious Irishman." Insofar as a derogatory stereotype is accepted by those to whom it is applied, they themselves help perpetuate the stereotype and with it the prejudice.

Racial prejudices are transmitted through the culture neatly encapsuled in stereotypes, infecting most readily those whom fortuitous experience has first sensitized.

> I have personally experienced the subtle irrationality of racial prejudice. In high school I had maintained an unflattering image of Mexicans as a group even though my only experiences with them as individuals had been pleasant. My attitude was inconsistent with my experience, and it troubled me. Was I reacting to real people or to an unrealistic stereotype? Was I prejudiced? As a child I had lived in a town where the Mexicans were on the "wrong side of the tracks." The town slums were Mexican slums. They were located upstream on an irrigation canal which ran near my home, and one of the few taboos imposed on me was that I must never, never under any circumstances, swim in that canal. I insisted on knowing why. Why? Because the water was contaminated, my mother said, polluted by slum privies which lined the canal upstream. She was reporting a fact, not expressing a prejudice, but I did not perceive the distinction then. I made associations supported by community consensus: Mexicans—dirty . . . Mexicans—a personal threat . . . Hot, and I can't swim in the canal—Mexicans. Once, when I was thirteen, I violated the taboo and swam in the canal. I didn't get sick physically, but I did emotionally. For weeks I felt so guilty I could hardly look at my mother; guilt intensified my growing prejudice. *Guilt . . . shame . . . dirty . . . Mexicans.* The Mexicans in that particular community were victims of economic discrimination. The fault was not theirs, but circumstances provided the rationale for prejudice. I was sensitized. The infection took.[24]

Unpleasant childhood experiences are sometimes recalled, not to explain prejudice, but to rationalize it. Most prejudices are acquired gradually over a period of time as part of the total socialization process. Racial attitudes, like other OAB's, tend to reflect the norms to which the individual has been exposed in his family and his community. For this reason, one's own prejudices are often unrecognized.

> Prejudiced people ordinarily underestimate the extent of their own prejudices. . . . In general, the prejudiced person is unaware of the influences affecting him, is not accurate in his self-knowledge, is not given to feelings of shame.

On the contrary, he is disposed to regard his hostilities as natural and as fully justified by virtue of the misbehavior of the minority groups whom he dislikes.[25]

Prejudice is born of emotion, not logic; and "reasoning against a prejudice is like fighting a shadow." *

STABILITY OF OAB'S. Opinions, attitudes, and beliefs—no matter how intense—are all emotionally biased; all tend to be acquired early in life and to persist throughout life. A child normally identifies first with his parents and accepts their OAB's uncritically. He tends to concur with them in areas of religion, education, personal and social relations, and public affairs. By the time he encounters conflicting OAB's, those he has acquired from his parents have become, in effect, his own, and he tends to defend them as such. Children as young as ten years of age, for example, stoutly support political preferences consistent with those of their parents, and in the United States, two-thirds to three-fourths of the adults—in spite of social-economic class or occupational discrepancy—vote for the party usually supported by their fathers.[26] The early incorporation of OAB's tends to make them particularly resistant to change. When OAB's are challenged, emotions are aroused!

OAB's are deeply rooted in personality structure, but they function in a social context and are either strengthened or weakened by group pressures. In Rome we tend to do as the Romans do. But, paradoxically, this tendency towards conformity can lead to change. Although we usually identify with congenial groups, if we do identify with a group having OAB's different from our own, our OAB's tend to shift in the direction of group norms. A liberal businessman locating in a conservative community and belonging to local business associations tends to become more conservative. Even if compliance with group norms is forced, OAB's still tend to shift. A person forced to do or say something discordant with his OAB's tends to change those OAB's to correspond more closely with his required behavior.† [27]

Our own society is so diverse that within it an individual can find group support for almost any OAB he holds. In all complex societies, particularly democratic ones with a large educated middle class, OAB's tend to be highly differentiated.

A wide range of OAB's makes for a flexible total society—with shifting norms and goals—a society more responsive than a dogmatic one to changing conditions. This same diversity, however, is part of the inconsistency and discontinuity of our culture and contributes to the difficulties a maturing individual experiences in perceiving clearly and coherently either himself or his environment.

---

* Charles Mildmay, 1820-?

† This finding is consistent with the general theory of *cognitive dissonance*, which indicates that when one's recognized OAB's or knowledge disagree with each other or with behavior, the individual tends to reduce the dissonance by changing behavior or cognition.[28] *Conscience* is another facet of cognitive dissonance.

Modes of Perception

What we perceive is related to what actually exists. The perceptions of the normal person under normal circumstances * are anchored in reality and dependent on the sensory input system. However, individuals with different personality structures do perceive differently under the same conditions of stimulation. *What* one perceives is in part determined by *how* one perceives. Two characteristic modes of perception have been experimentally determined.

Which way is up? And *how do we know?* We have two ways to orient ourselves in space: first, by physiological responses to gravity; second, by alignment with stable objects in the environment. For any one individual, which mode of perception is the dominant one? Ordinarily, the two means of determining the upright position coincide with and reinforce each other. The only way to tell whether an individual is relatively "field dependent"—acting on perceptual cues in the external environment—or "field independent"—acting on his own innate sensations—is to set up experimental situations in which the two modes of perception give contradictory information. In one of several experiments, each subject in turn sat in a chair—which could be tilted to left or right any degree—and looked into a small "room," which could also be tilted. With the "room" tilted, the experimenter moved the chair at the subject's direction until the subject reported himself upright. Some subjects consistently brought the chair close to the true vertical; others had to be more or less aligned with the room before they felt "straight." Some subjects, tilted as much as 35 degrees—in one extreme case, 52 degrees—answered "Yes!" when asked if that was the position in which they ordinarily sat to eat dinner. The performance of a subject on this test corresponded with his performance on two other tests: ability to determine the verticality of a rod seen against a tilted frame, and ability to see a simple geometric figure in a complex geometric field.

---

* Normal *illusions* are false perceptions of existing stimuli, as in common optical illusions.

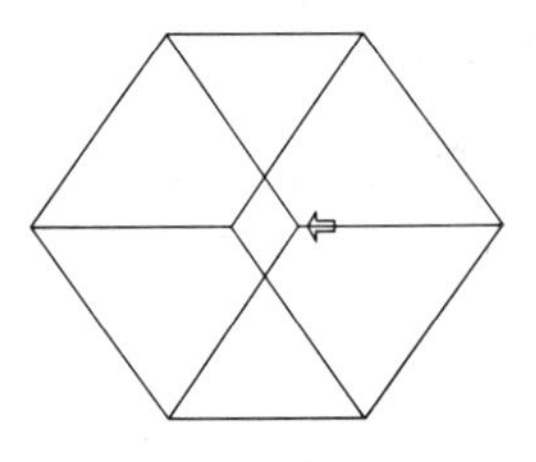

Looked at long enough, the point indicated by the arrow appears as alternately the near and then the far corner of the cube. *Hallucinations* are perceptions in the absence of appropriate stimuli, as in an alcoholic's stampeding pink elephants during *delirium tremens. Delusions* are false beliefs as in delusions of grandeur or persecution. Psychotic persons typically suffer both hallucinations and delusions.

In children, field independence increases with age, but any one child tends to maintain his relative position within his age group. A child testing field independent relative to his peers at ten years of age tests field independent relative to his peers at seventeen years of age. This finding indicates that mode of perception develops early in life and is a stable and central aspect of personality structure.

Relative to a field-dependent child, the personality of the field-independent child is more complex. He shows greater independence in a variety of situations, has a clearer self-image, wider and better developed interests, and shows, more often than his field-dependent peers, a desire and capacity for actively coping with the environment. How an individual perceives the upright is representative of how he perceives himself and his environment.

To what extent field-independent or field-dependent perception is determined by life experience is not determined, but in a preliminary study of mother-child relationships, field-dependent children generally had "growth-constricting" mothers—mothers who restricted activities, limited curiosity, and stressed conformity. Field-independent children, in contrast, generally had "growth-fostering" mothers. How an individual perceives the upright may be related to other variables not yet investigated—constitutional factors such as rate of maturation and health, for example; but it is a characteristic aspect of personality structure determined to a demonstrable degree by socializing agents of whom the mother is a prime representative.[29]

Psychological Homeostasis

Personality structure is a complex of action potentials. Personality itself, as expressed in behavior, is an action system. The habits and understandings which make up the structure of personality and guide perceptions are tenacious and self-perpetuating. Once we have achieved a serviceable set of habits and understandings, we tend to protect and defend them. Consciously and subconsciously we try to keep our action system functioning as smoothly and as effortlessly as possible. When sensory evidence begins to depart from the familiar, we all tend to cling to the familiar. Once we have achieved object perception, for example, we perceive that object as enduring under different circumstances. A door is rectangular, a dinner plate, round—even though from different perspectives the door may be a trapezoid, the plate, an ellipse. We protect our habits and understandings by selecting out of the environment what we want to perceive, and out of what we do perceive, what we want to remember.

SELECTIVE PERCEPTION. We all seek a congenial environment. Our good friends tend to support or at least tolerate our OAB's and share our enthusiasms. The magazines we read tend to be those whose editorial policy we like. We need reassurance and support, but we cannot always select our environment nor control the conditions of it. We can, however, select to some extent what sensory data in that environment we admit to consciousness, and we can impose our own meaning on that data.

> What men are inclined to see in any situation depends upon what they anticipate, and what they anticipate depends upon the meanings with which they have entered the situation. . . . Thus, perceiving is never just receiving; there is always discrimination and selection.[30]

During World War II all persons of Japanese nationality and ancestry living in California were put into concentration camps. Californians were criticized by people in other states, but one spokesman defended the action by saying, "We understand the Japanese. We have lived with them." There was not a single known act of sabotage or espionage committed by any person of Japanese nationality or ancestry prior to, during, or after the attack on Pearl Harbor—either in the Hawaiian Islands or on the Pacific Coast; but war propaganda had created a stereotype which fear could understand. The commanding general of the Western Defense Area, in his official recommendation of evacuation and incarceration, cited the very absence of sabotage "as a disturbing and confirming indication that such action will be taken in the future." Was it yesterday, or more than 2,000 years ago, that Demosthenes said, "Nothing is so easy as to deceive one's self, for what we wish, that we readily believe"?

SELECTIVE MEMORY. If disturbing perceptions do get through our defenses without being denied, rationalized, or otherwise distorted to fit our habits and understandings, we subconsciously make a final stand. We repress memory of the perception.

> . . . pro-Communist and anti-Communist students were asked to memorize paragraphs, some of which were "pro" and some "anti." When tested later, pro-Communists remembered pro-Communist paragraphs and anti-Communists remembered anti-Communist paragraphs better than those paragraphs opposing their prejudices.[31]

If selective memory fails as a line of defense, we can regain equilibrium only by incorporating the new "reality" into our repertoire of concepts.

Physiologists recognize homeostatic mechanisms which maintain physiological equilibrium—mechanisms which insure constant temperature, stable chemical content in body fluids, acid-alkaline balance in the tissues. And psychologists recognize selective perception and selective memory as homeostatic mechanisms which maintain psychological equilibrium and insure a functioning action system. How much psychological stress an individual can tolerate in the form of assault on his habits and understandings without being thrown "off balance" depends on how open he is to experience—how flexible his personality structure. Under laboratory conditions, subjects not open to new experience in the form of changing sensory data tend to stereotype an initial perception and cling to it tenaciously. When a series of pictures making a gradual transition from *dog* to *cat* were shown, subjects differed in the ease with which they made the shift in perception. Those whose original perception of *dog* persisted the longest were intolerant of ambiguous or conflicting perceptions. They stereotyped the original data and continued to force changing data into that stereotype. These same subjects outside the laboratory situation also tended to be closed to new experience. They typically concurred with rigid social stereotypes and were markedly prejudiced in their dealings with minority groups.

Our capacity as individuals or as group members to perceive and adjust to change in sensory data has especially high survival value in the rapidly changing contemporary world. *Can we, through the techniques of socialization we choose, help maturing individuals build a serviceably flexible personality structure?*

CONSENSUS AND CONTROL

When a society has consensus on central norms and goals, the agents of socialization tend to act in accord with each other, and the process of socialization is relatively sure and painless. A maturing individual tends to accept and value whatever those who guide his development consistently accept and value. Consciously and subconsciously he incorporates into his personality structure —as conscience, or (in Freudian terms), a super-ego—controls which motivate him towards the behavior desired or expected of him in his various social roles. When consensus is lacking, as we know, the process of socialization is slower and less certain. The less adequately a society equips its members with inner behavioral controls, the greater the number and variety of external controls it then imposes.

We do not imply that 100 per cent consensus exists or should exist.

> Every age and nation has certain characteristic vices, which prevail almost universally, which scarcely any person scruples to avow, and which even rigid moralists but faintly censure. Succeeding generations change the fashion of their morals with the fashion of the hats and their coaches; take some other kind of wickedness under their patronage, and wonder at the depravity of their ancestors.*

Some societies also impose specific discontinuities in individual learning. For example, we generally expect an individual to be submissive in childhood, to show authority and independence in middle life, and to be submissive again, particularly to married children and in-laws, in old age. What is learned as desirable behavior at one age or under one condition may be undesirable behavior at another. Such contradictory expectations are not universal.

* Thomas Macaulay, 1800-1859.

> Prince Maximilian von Wied, who visited the Crow Indians over a hundred years ago describes a father's boasting about his young son's intractability even when it was the father himself who was flouted; "He will be a man," his father said. He would have been baffled at the idea that a child should show behavior which would obviously make him appear a poor creature in the eyes of his fellows if he used it as an adult. Dr. George Devereux tells . . . of a special case of such an attitude among the Mohave at the present time. The child's mother was white and protested to its father that he must take action when the child disobeyed and struck him. "But why?" the father said, "he is little. He cannot possibly injure me." He did not know of any dichotomy according to which an adult expects obedience and a child must accord it. If his child had been docile, he would simply have judged that it would become a docile adult—an eventuality of which he would not have approved.[32]

Although complete consensus at any one time or over a period of time is unrealistic and probably undesirable, consensus, to the degree that it does exist, facilitates socialization. It makes the process more certain and less painful. With a high degree of consensus, as in a primitive tradition-directed society, parents count on the child's developing conscience and are generally lenient in their child-rearing practices.

> Punishment is very commonly regarded as quite outside the realm of possibility, and natives in many parts of the world have drawn the conclusion from our usual disciplinary methods that white parents do not love their children.[33]

With little consensus, as in our heterogeneous and rapidly changing society, parents and other agents of socialization are often in the difficult position of trying to impose behavior which is not universally expected or desired and towards which the individual is not motivated. Under such conditions the parent or teacher or other agent of socialization tends to set himself up as an authority and insist that his particular norms and goals are "right," and he also tends to force compliance through external and arbitrarily determined controls—rewards (or bribes) and punishments. A parent may give his child ice cream for eating his spinach or a spanking for not eating it. A teacher may give a third-grader a gold star for getting all the words right on a spelling test, or a black mark for getting some wrong. Regardless of the nature of the reward or punishment, such extrinsic behavioral controls have serious shortcomings. The child who gets gold stars for spelling words right may, in the absence of gold stars, be indifferent to how he spells a word. The child who is spanked for doing or not doing something will, if motivation is strong enough, still do what he wants to do—preferably when whoever spanks is not looking!

Extrinsic rewards, although they have limited value, are more effective aids to learning than extrinsic punishment. *Praise does more than spanking can to reinforce the ways of man!* When a response is reinforced by a reward, the response is likely to be repeated. A pigeon learns to peck a circle when his pecking is reinforced by food. A child learns to say "please," when this word brings a smile of approval—or a cookie. When a response is not reinforced, it tends to be eliminated. Ignoring the "please" before it became a learned habit would discourage its use. When a response is followed by punishment, however, the response may be temporarily depressed but it is not eliminated. Punishing a child for not saying "please" or for saying something unprintable will not guarantee that he will say or not say what is demanded. When the punishment or the threat of it is withdrawn, the child will say what he chooses. "When the cat's away, the mice will play." In spite of evidence which disqualifies punishment as an effective way of teaching desirable behavior or eliminating undesirable behavior, we traditionally defend punishment as a technique of socialization. *The Bible rationalizes it:* "He that spareth his rod hateth his son." * *And Mother Goose proclaims its effectiveness:*

> The Queen of Hearts,
> She made some tarts,
> All on a summer's day.
> The Knave of Hearts,
> He stole the tarts,
> And took them clean away.
>
> The King of Hearts
> Called for the tarts,
> And beat the Knave full sore.
> The Knave of Hearts
> Brought back the tarts,
> And vowed he'd steal no more.

Because punishment can force submission and produce at least temporary surface conformity, we do not always perceive the unfortunate by-products.

> The unhappy effects of punishment have run like a dismal thread through our findings. Mothers who punish toilet accidents severely ended up with bed-wetting children. Mothers who punished dependency to get rid of it had more dependent children than mothers who did not punish. Mothers who punished aggressive behavior severely had more aggressive children than mothers who punished lightly. . . . Our evaluation of punishment is that *it is ineffectual over the long term as a technique for eliminating the kind of behavior toward which it is directed.*[34]

In addition to the specific boomerang effect punishment often has, the child who is forced by punishment or threat of punishment to comply with authority may build up resentment against that specific authority, as well as against authority in general. "While undoubtedly it [punishment] often stops a particular form of aggression, at least momentarily, it appears to generate more hostility in the child and lead to further aggressive outbursts at

---

* *Proverbs* 13:24.

some other time or place." [35] "The Knave of Hearts brought back the tarts, and vowed he'd steal no more," but maybe he shot the King's deer or put sand in the royal bed.

Extrinsic punishment does more than affect surface behavior. It influences the development of the total personality structure. In the process of socialization the maturing individual identifies first with his parents, then with other agents of socialization. "The less the parental warmth and identification or the more the parental punishment, the slower the development of conscience." [36] This slow development of conscience starts a self-defeating sequence. Inadequate inner controls call for sterner outer controls, which further inhibit the development of inner controls. Juvenile delinquents, as a group, have experienced more physical punishment from their parents than nondelinquents.[37] The more physical punishment is used in childhood, the greater the probability that the child or adolescent will engage in delinquent behavior.

Punishment not only fails to eliminate the kind of behavior towards which it is directed, it sometimes actually fixates that behavior.

> If an animal from rat to man is faced with a basically unsolvable problem and forced to attempt to solve it, some form of undesirable or maladaptive behavior appears. If punishment follows this undesirable behavior, the maladaptive behavior itself becomes fixated.[38]

Stereotypy—the tendency to blind, repetitive, fixated behavior, has been extensively studied in rats. A rat can be taught to discriminate between a card marked with a white circle on a black background and one with a black circle on a white background by always being rewarded with food when he jumps to the white circle. In one experiment, cards were so set up that when the rat jumped to the card with the white circle, he knocked over the card and gained access to food. When he jumped to the card with the black circle, he bumped against the card and fell into a net. He was forced to jump from a stand one way or another—left or right—by a jet of air. Once the rat learned to discriminate between the two cards, he was frustrated by being arbitrarily rewarded and punished fifty per cent of the time on a random basis. He was faced with an insoluble problem; no matter which way he jumped, he stood an equal chance of being punished or rewarded. Under these conditions his behavior became rigid and nonadaptive. He jumped regularly to one side, regardless of the stimulus card, regardless of how much he was punished. Such fixated behavior is so resistant to change that if a rat jumping repeatedly to the black circle on the right is punished every time, he may jump right as many as 200 trials—even when the other card is removed to make access to food safe.[39] The behavior of a frustrated and punished rat became so rigidly fixed that he could not perceive the alternative—jumping to food available to him through the open window.

The experiments with stereotypy in rats, suggest analogies with human behavior.

> It is quite possible, though not proved, that some forms of persistent behavior, such as thumb sucking in young children or stuttering, have become more firmly fixed (i.e., stereotyped) because punishment and repeated frustration in efforts to get rid of them have intensified the undesirable responses. The persistence of difficulties in arithmetic and reading and spelling among bright children (and some adults) may be explained in part as a consequence of errors similarly stereotyped by early frustration . . .[40]

Other case studies suggest that harsh punishment by parents—in combination with such other severe disciplinary treatment as emphasis on morality and unquestioning obedience—tends to produce the inflexible "black-and-white" thinking and intolerance characteristic of the "authoritarian" personality.[41]

The kind of a population a society needs and wants determines to a considerable degree the techniques it sanctions to effect socialization. A totalitarian society needs the conformity, intolerance, and blind allegiance of authoritarian personalities.[42] A democratic society, in contrast, needs the autonomy, tolerance and farsighted problem-solving approach of creative personalities.

> Ordinary problem solving requires flexibility, striking out in new directions when the original path to the goal is blocked. When repeated frustration baffles a person, especially if the frustration arises through punishment, some of this flexibility appears to be lost, and he stupidly makes the same effort again and again, though experience has shown its futility.[43]

One of the problems of socialization in our heterogeneous society is to spare maturing individuals the kind of punishing frustration which blocks problem solving. This poses a dilemma. The absence of consensus (characteristic of heterogeneity) makes for a slow development of inner controls. Inadequate inner controls tend to bring external social controls in the form of rewards and punishments into action. However, behavior learned in response to external rewards tends to be discontinued in the absence of the reward, and behavior suppressed or coerced in response to punishment is unpredictable. It tends to give way to other behavior when the punishment or threat of punishment is removed, or it may be so fixated that it is maladaptive. Furthermore, the experience of punishment itself inhibits the development of inner controls.

Only anarchists would eliminate all external controls; only sentimentalists would eliminate all frustrations. But agents of socialization, especially parents and teachers, could eliminate much meaningless frustration through farsighted control of the environment, redefinition of individual and group goals, redirection of individual and group behavior, and other tactical maneuvers. And society itself might sanction only those social controls which contributed to the making of autonomous and responsible citizens.

Meaningful frustrations are those with which the individual can cope. We all learn by encountering obstacles we can overcome, deficiencies we can recover, conflicts we can resolve. Intrinsic punishment, too, is meaningful. It is always informative and logically related to action. The hot pot burns the probing finger. The green apple cramps the empty stomach. Intrinsic punishment consistently relates to reality and teaches consideration of reality. Social controls, however, in the form of extrinsic punishment as commonly used by parents and teachers and other agents of socialization, tend to be illogical and therefore uninformative. They impose only meaningless and sometimes crippling frustration. Parents who spank, for example, characteristically spank for a variety of "misdeeds" relative to which the spanking itself has no logical connection. They spank a child for playing in the street, for not coming straight home from school, for "talking back," for hitting little sister, for "borrowing" something without asking. . . . To be informative, extrinsic punishment, if used at all, must bear a logical relationship to the action the punishment is intended to discourage. If, for example, a child is spanked for playing in the street, he learns—not that the danger comes from cars—but that it comes from whoever spanks. The only logical way of handling a child who does not yet understand the danger of playing in the street, or is unable to resist the temptation of running into it, is to provide him with a more confined but safer place to play. Parents and teachers and other agents of socialization who would help maturing individuals develop intelligence, independence, and eventually responsibility as citizens, might well echo the Mikado's resolve:

> My object all sublime
> I shall achieve in time—
> To let the punishment fit the crime—
> The punishment fit the crime.*

Techniques of socialization clearly related, intrinsically or extrinsically, to the requirements of situations, orient to reality and thereby favor the development of an open and flexible personality structure. Such techniques help the individual perceive his own needs and attributes in relationship to his social and physical environment, to consider alternate lines of action, to evaluate probable consequences, and to make logical choices. In short, techniques of socialization which are themselves reasonable teach reason. The four-year-old, the fourteen-year-old, and the forty-year-old members of society all have problems to solve. One cultural continuity a heterogeneous society such as our own could achieve is continuity in the *techniques*, if not the content of socialization. We could, as a society, cultivate those techniques of socialization which encouraged learning, not fixed habits nor blind obedience, but skills and understandings conducive to problem-solving behavior at increasingly mature levels.

---

* Sir William Schwenck Gilbert (1836-1911), *The Mikado,* Act II.

ETHNOCENTRISM

A society maintains and perpetuates itself by building its own norms and goals into the personality structure of its members and by bolstering those inner controls when they are inadequate, by a system of rewards and punishments. Inevitably, a well-socialized individual comes to feel that the society with which he identifies is the best. His own group, his own ethnic community become the standard by which he judges others. Such ethnocentrism is so universal that it could be included in a list of cultural uniformities. Among primitives, the name of the tribe is often the same as the name for all mankind. More knowledgeable peoples are less provincial but not necessarily any less ethnocentric.

When the Russians launched the first artificial satellite in October, 1957, we stood flatfooted on the ground, peering into the night sky trying to get a glimpse of Sputnik I in orbit. Then shock set in. *Why didn't we have a satellite? How did the Russians do it first?* We indulged in soul-searching, excuse-making, blame-fixing. The press of this country tried desperately to explain how the Russians, who had only one automobile for every sixty-four persons compared to our one for every three and four-tenths persons, could possibly have gotten into outer space first. What about "American know-how"? For generations we have been indoctrinated with a superman mythology. We are strong, clever, honest, noble. We are the good guys. "They" are the bad guys. We always win. "God is on our side." When the Russians made a major scientific coup, we were incredulous; but we still never assumed that we couldn't have done it if we had just tried. The trouble was with the Administration's "false economy." Or maybe it was "inter-service rivalry." Perhaps we just failed to recognize the "propaganda value" of such a feat. One news commentator even suggested that the Russians copied our projected satellite from pictures printed in *Life* magazine.

Ethnocentrism can distort not only what is happening, but what has happened. If you read enough history, you realize that there are no impartial facts. History happens, but ethnocentric men record it. "Historians generally illustrate rather than correct the ideas of the communities within which they live and work." [44]

Eastern historians write world history from their point of view. A Mohammedan writer, describing the "medieval siege of Europe," said this:

> In A.D. 712, says Ameer Ali, Musa crossed into France. "Standing on the Pyrenees, the dauntless Viceroy conceived the project of conquering the whole of Europe. . . . The cautious and hesitating policy of the Damascene Court lost the glorious opportunity, with the consequence that Europe remained enveloped in intellectual darkness for the next eight centuries." [45]

During these eight centuries of "intellectual darkness," anonymous medieval scholars made their contributions to history, philosophy, and theology and established Europe's first universities; anonymous medieval builders erected the great cathedrals; men such as Dante, Petrarch, Boccaccio, Savonarola, and Leonardo da Vinci contributed to the Renaissance, and Columbus set sail for the New World!

Russian historians write United States history from their point of view.

> On July 4, 1776, under the pressure of the popular masses, the Congress adopted the "Declaration of Independence" drawn up by Jefferson, an outright opponent of slavery. It proclaimed the secession of the American colonies from England and declared ". . . that all men are created equal; that they are endowed by their Creator with certain unalienable rights; that among these are life, liberty and the pursuit of happiness. . . ." The Declaration affirmed that the people themselves have the right to establish state power and government, and proclaimed the concept that the source of power was the people themselves, i.e., the concept of democracy. But the advanced, progressive concepts of the Declaration were used by the bourgeoisie for the consolidation of the powers of the propertied class, and, besides, of the white people only. The "unalienable rights of man" did not apply either to the Negroes or Indians. The Declaration did not abolish slavery, neither did it stop the dispossession and extermination of Indians; it preserved the exploitation of wage workers. . . .
>
> Before the War of Independence, in the English colonies of North America, the power was in the hands of the landed aristocracy. The War of Independence against the English was accompanied by the struggle of farmers, workers, and the revolutionary bourgeoisie against the big landowner aristocrats.
>
> After the confiscation of the estates of many aristocrats and the banishment of the latter from the U.S.A., the power passed into the hands of the commercial and industrial bourgeoisie of the North and the slave-owning planters of the South.
>
> Thus, during the Revolutionary War, in the course of a bitter class struggle, power in the U.S.A. passed from one class to another, i.e., from the landed aristocracy to the commercial and industrial bourgeoisie which ruled in alliance with the slave-owning planters of the South. A bourgeois revolution took place in the U.S.A., the estates were swept away, a republic was established and slavery was abolished in the Northern States. The capitalists and the slaveholders took advantage of the victory of the people to consolidate their supremacy.
>
> V. I. Lenin wrote that afterwards, as a result of the bourgeoisie consolidating its power in the U.S.A., the U.S.A. became "one of the foremost countries as regards the depth of the abyss which lies between the handful of arrogant billionaires who are wallowing in filth and luxury, and the millions of toilers who are constantly living on the verge of pauperism. . . ."
>
> The American bourgeoisie took advantage of the struggle of the popular masses against the English in order to come to power, and, once in power, like the English bourgeoisie in the 17th century, it instensified its oppression of the popular masses. In North America, under the name of "government by the people" (democracy), a so-called bourgeois democracy was established which, in actual fact, is the power of the bourgeoisie.[46]

Historians, like other mortals, express their perceptions in terms of language, and historians in different cultures speaking different languages do perceive the same events in different ways.

Raw data is given meaning by the perceiver in the only terms he knows—those his culture makes available to him. Furthermore, the process of socialization purposefully prejudices those born into a society in favor of that society.

Among primitive cave men, ethnocentrism undoubtedly had survival value. Individuals survive only in groups, and loyalty to the group and its characteristic ways has become a prime virtue. Moral codes prescribing behavior towards members of one's own group differ and often contradict those prescribing behavior towards members of other groups. Killing someone within one's group, for example, is typically a sin; killing "enemies" from outside, typically a virtue. Throughout history heroes have been those who have killed the largest number of "enemy" outsiders. Such ancient moral codes still prevail today, but modern weapons have put us all in the same "cave."

> The modern world is witnessing a rapid expansion of social horizons. . . . The rapid technological and scientific progress of the current era bids fair to alter our daily lives and even our ways of thinking so profoundly that the new culture patterns will have to be based on universal human needs and social imperatives.[47]

Moderate ethnocentrism, expressed in loyalty and pride, is consistent with a positive self-image. But excessive ethnocentrism, expressed, as it often is, in blind allegiance and intolerance, betrays a closed and rigid personality structure.

Change is rampant. *Are those whose actions spring from excessive ethnocentrism clinging to a stereotype of the fading past? Have they, in the process of socialization, been crippled in their capacity to deal constructively with the realities of our time?*

To the degree that socialization fails the individual, it fails society.

Notes

1. Margaret Mead, "The Modern Study of Mankind," in *An Outline of Man's Knowledge of the Modern World,* Lyman Bryson, ed. (Garden City, New York: Doubleday & Company, Inc., 1960), p. 327.
2. Margaret Mead, *Sex and Temperament in Three Primitive Societies* (New York: A Mentor Book, 1950), p. 191.
3. *Ibid.,* p. 42.
4. *Ibid.,* pp. 135-141.
5. Joseph Church, *Language and the Discovery of Reality* (New York: Random House, 1961), p. 137.
6. From the personal files of Eugene Mead.
7. *San Francisco Chronicle,* November 5, 1957, p. 1.
8. Pearl Binder, *Muffs and Morals* (New York: William Morrow & Company, Inc., n.d.), pp. 37-38.
9. *San Francisco Chronicle,* May 8, 1964, p. 42.
10. Eric Hoffer, *The Passionate State of Mind* (New York: Harper & Row, Publishers, 1955), p. 80.
11. Charles Horton Cooley, *Human Nature and the Social Order* (New York: Charles Scribner's Sons, 1902), pp. 102-103.
12. Hoffer, *The Passionate State of Mind,* p. 149.
13. Sylvia Leff, as narrated to authors.
14. Carl R. Rogers, "Becoming a Person" in James A. Dyal, *Readings in Psychology* (New York: McGraw-Hill Book Co., 1962), p. 360.
15. Ruth Benedict, "Continuities and Discontinuities in Cultural Conditioning" in *Personality in Nature, Society, and Culture,* Clyde Kluckhohn and Henry A. Murray, eds. (New York. Alfred A. Knopf, Inc., 1948), pp. 416-417.
16. *San Francisco Chronicle,* May 8, 1964, p. 42.
17. "Sunrise in California, and the Coming of Day" (from the *Los Angeles Mirror-News*), *The New Yorker,* April 25, 1959, p. 77.
18. Tamotsu Shibutani, *Society and Personality* (Englewood Cliffs, N.J.: Prentice-Hall, Inc., 1961), p. 108.
19. *Ibid.,* p. 98.
20. *Ibid.,* p. 118.
21. Bernard Berelson and Gary A. Steiner, *Human Behavior* (New York: Harcourt, Brace & World, Inc., 1963), p. 558.
22. Ernest R. Hilgard, *Introduction to Psychology* (New York & Burlingame: Harcourt, Brace & World, Inc., 3rd ed., 1962), p. 628.
23. Shibutani, *Society and Personality,* p. 102.
24. From the personal files of Eugene Mead.
25. Gordon W. Allport and Bernard M. Kramer, "Some Roots of Prejudice," *Journal of Psychology,* 22, 1946, p. 39.
26. Berelson and Steiner, *Human Behavior,* p. 562.
27. Leon Festinger and J. M. Carlsmith, "Cognitive Consequences of Forced Compliance," *Journal of Abnormal and Social Psychology,* 58: 1959, pp. 203-210.
28. Leon Festinger, *A Theory of Cognitive Dissonance* (New York: Harper & Row, Publishers, 1957).
29. Herman A. Witkin, "The Perception of the Upright," *Scientific American,* February, 1959, pp. 50-56.
30. Shibutani, *Society and Personality,* p. 109.

31. Clifford T. Morgan, *Introduction to Psychology* (New York: McGraw-Hill, Inc., 1956), p. 359.
32. Ruth Benedict, *op. cit.*, p. 165.
33. *Ibid.*, p. 419.
34. Robert R. Sears, Eleanor E. Maccoby, and Harry Levin, *Patterns of Child Rearing* (New York: Harper & Row, Publishers, 1957), p. 484.
35. Sears, et al., *Patterns of Child Rearing*, p. 266.
36. Berelson and Steiner, *Human Behavior*, p. 77.
37. Sheldon and Eleanor Glueck, *Unraveling Juvenile Delinquency* (Cambridge: Harvard University Press, 1950).
38. Lynde G. Steckle, *Problems of Human Adjustment* (New York: Harper & Row, Publishers, Revised Edition, 1957), p. 31.
39. N. R. F. Maier, N. M. Glaser, and J. B. Klee, "Studies of Abnormal Behavior in the Rat: III. The Development of Behavior Fixation Through Frustration." *Journal of Experimental Psychology*, Vol. 26, 1940.
40. Ernest R. Hilgard, *Introduction to Psychology* (New York & Burlingame: Harcourt, Brace & World, Inc., 3rd ed., 1962), p. 509.
41. Berelson and Steiner, *Human Behavior*, p. 259.
42. *Ibid.*, pp. 258-259.
43. Hilgard, *Introduction to Psychology*, p. 508.
44. Arnold J. Toynbee, *A Study of History*, Abridgment of Volumes I-VI, by D. C. Somervell (New York and London: Oxford University Press, 1946), p. 1.
45. Frederick J. Teggart, *Theory and Processes of History* (Berkeley and Los Angeles: University of California Press, 1941), pp. 46-47.
46. A. V. Efinov, *Modern History* (A Textbook for the Eighth Class of Secondary School), translated from the Russian by B. I. Groudinko (Leningrad: State Textbook Publishing House of the Ministry of Education of the R.S.F.S.R., Leningrad Branch, 1959), pp. 29-35.
47. Ralph Linton, "Universal Ethical Principles," in *Moral Principles in Action*, ed., Ruth Nanda Anshen, Chapter xxxii, Volume VI of the series, *Science of Culture* (New York: Harper & Row, Publishers, 1952).

PANY.

If we had no failings ourselves we should not take so much pleasure in finding out those of others.

FRANÇOIS DE LA ROCHEFOUCAULD (1630-1680)

7

When Socialization Fails

SOCIALIZATION "TAKES" WITH most of us. We gradually learn to be "human." We submit with relative good grace to the mores and taboos and laws which surround us, meeting our needs and pursuing our goals as best we can within the framework of the established social order.

> All our lives long, every day and every hour, we are engaged in the process of accommodating our changed and unchanged selves to changed and unchanged surroundings; living, in fact, is nothing else than this process of accommodation; when we fail in it a little we are stupid; when we fail flagrantly we are mad; when we suspend it temporarily we sleep; when we give up the attempt altogether we die. In quiet, uneventful lives the changes internal and external are so small that there is little or no strain in the process of fusion and accommodation; in other lives there is great strain, but there is also great fusing and accommodating power; in others great strain with little accommodating power. A life will be successful or not, according as the power of accommodation is equal to or unequal to the strain of fusing and adjusting internal and external changes.[1]

Accommodating power resides in personality structure—the by-product of socialization. Rate of socialization, as we know, decreases with age; it is rapid in childhood, slower in later years. The number and severity of strains or stresses to which an individual is exposed, however, tend to increase with maturity. It is, therefore, not surprising that basic variables involved in personality development are most critical in early life, while the symptoms of dysfunction—although often present in childhood—may not be obvious or persistent until adolescence and early adulthood, when greater demands are made on whatever powers of accommodation an individual may have.

The over-all crime rate reaches a peak in the late teens for males and early twenties for females. In the United States certain crimes are associated with certain age groups: car theft with teens; robbery and rape with the twenties; gambling and drug addiction with the thirties; drunkenness, embezzlement, and fraud in later years.[2] Schizophrenic reactions—the most prevalent disorder of hospitalized mental patients—may appear in early infancy or in old age, but symptoms typically become clearly manifest in late adolescence and early adulthood.[3]

Antisocial and asocial behavior—the personality dysfunctioning which we consider as failures of socialization—are, however, always relative to the cultural norms of a particular society. Characteristics or traits valued in one society may be deplored in another. In the United States, for example, economic, political, and educational institutions have typically rewarded competitive behavior, and the agents of socialization tend to encourage such behavior. If an infant son walks, talks, and gets along without diapers before the child next door, his parents are proud to call him a big boy. If in school he learns to read and spell and do two-times-two sooner and better than his classmates, he gets more praise, coupled, perhaps, with A's or gold stars. The child who shrinks from competition with others worries his parents and teachers. What's wrong with him? Is he insecure? Is he inferior? Vigorous competition is the American way. We consider it healthy, but not so all societies. In the Hopi reservation schools, for example, our teachers have been puzzled by the noncompetitive behavior of Indian children. A teacher may say, "Put up your hand when you have finished your arithmetic." A child may finish his arithmetic but not put up his hand. Why? He does not want to be first. He does not want to be better. Would that not shame his friends? And when he plays games, he prefers just to play without keeping score. He doesn't want to win or lose. His behavior is normal for a Hopi; it would not be normal for an up-and-coming All-American. . . . In every society there is an interplay between role requirements of positions integral to the particular social structure and the personality types encouraged and recruited. Furthermore, attitudes differ in different societies towards traits which are dependent less on socialization than on hereditary or constitutional factors. In the United States, for example, the known epileptic is barred from some positions in the social structure. He is often not accepted in public educational institutions; many private schools and colleges refuse him admission; most states deny him a driver's license; few employers will hire him; and in some states he cannot marry. In contrast, the epileptic has had positions of honor and acclaim in some other societies. Mohammed was, or was credited with being an epileptic, and Moslems are characteristically still tolerant of epileptics.

Insofar as the characteristics or traits an individual has or can acquire coincide with those needed and valued by a particular society, he is well socialized, *relative to that society*. Insofar as an individual does not have or cannot acquire such characteristics or traits, he is thereby limited in the number of sanctioned roles he can play in society and is, to that extent, a relative failure of socialization. Success or failure, normality and abnormality are thus deviations from cultural consensus or statistical averages.

> Much madness is divinest sense
> To a discerning eye:
> Much sense the starkest madness.
> 'Tis the majority
> In this, as all prevails.
> Assent, and you are sane:
> Demur—you're straightway dangerous,
> And handled with a chain.*

Most of us, by definition, are adequately socialized. We have our minor successes and our minor failures. We are consistently neither "saints" nor "sinners."

For those who are set apart by the extent or degree of undesirable deviation from cultural norms, deviation may be either specific or general.

Failure of socialization may be specific—in the area of particular institutions. An individual may accept the values of conventional monogamy. He may be a loving father and devoted husband, but he may reject his economic responsibility. Another individual may have learned his school lessons well and be able to cope with the laws of higher mathematics, but he may not be able or willing to cope with marriage laws.

Failure of socialization may be nonspecific—a general inadequacy in all institutional areas. An individual may flunk out of school, be unable to hold a job, desert his wife and children, dodge the draft, and show up at church missions only when he is hungry and needs a free meal.

Since socialization is a process, not an accomplished fact, it is relative to time and circumstance and to each individual's own inherent capacity for learning. For any normally intelligent individual, socialization continues throughout the life span as increased understanding of and capacity to cope with one's own society and its cultural norms. When an individual cannot come to terms with his society and its culture, then society—as judge—proclaims that individual a failure of socialization.

FORMS OF FAILURE

Read the headlines in any metropolitan newspaper:

> "FATHER WHIPS CHILD TO DEATH"
> "BOY KILLS FOUR IN FAMILY"
> "BOY HATES SCHOOL, KILLS SELF"

* Emily Dickinson, 1830-1886.

"BANK BANDIT RING BROKEN"
"DOCTORS ROB HEALTH PLAN OF $2,000,000"
"INSURANCE 'WIZARD' DEFRAUDS $2,459,701"
"LONELY 'GHOST' FOUND IN PARK"
"AN ADDICT AT 18—HOOKED 5 YEARS"

In these and thousands of other instances socialization has failed. Symptoms of failure may be acute or chronic, severe or mild. Some symptoms are predominantly antisocial: delinquent or criminal aggression against society. Other symptoms are predominantly asocial: neurotic or psychotic withdrawal from society. Although antisocial and asocial symptoms are not mutually exclusive, the behavior of any one individual is usually dominated by a tendency to move either *against* or *away from* others.

Antisocial Behavior

A teacher at San Quentin prison wrote of the car thieves, burglars, addicts, safe-crackers and murderers in his class:

> My students, for their part, were not by any means immoralists. They were, on the whole, conventionally moral, but moral in a curiously one-eyed way. The burglars, for instance, could be as intolerant of the use of narcotics as the flintiest elder of the Dutch Reformed Church. Narcotics users usually scorned the immorality of writing bad checks. Check writers saw nothing but corruption in car thievery, while car thieves, forgers, and the rest looked with loathing on sex crimes.
>
> . . . Of the fifty-odd convicts I taught during my first semester, only Garrett was consistently immoral. Moreover, he was immoral deliberately, and not through any accidental lapse of his faculties. He bore his immorality proudly, preached it earnestly, and at times seemed to consider himself a latter-day St. Paul among the Gentiles.
>
> . . . In my American literature class, we began by reading Jack London's "The Sea Wolf." . . . I started a discussion one day of the Weltanschauung of the hero, Wolf Larsen. Garrett promptly described Larsen as a moral weakling. By a train of thought that now eludes me, I was reminded of that old philosophy-class chestnut, the case of the Chinese mandarin. Let us suppose, I told the class, that in the city of Peiping there lives an elderly Chinese gentleman who has outlived his social and biological usefulness. He suffers from galloping senility. Furthermore, he is a victim of cancer, is in such constant pain that he no longer finds any pleasure in life, and can't reasonably be expected to live out the month. He has no family to mourn his passing. If by willing his destruction you could assure yourself of everlasting happiness, would you press the button that would send the old gentleman to his reward? Here I drew a push button on the blackboard.
>
> The response was not much different from that of the philosophy class in New Haven, where I had first been presented with this problem. Some confessed to a repugnance for taking life, which would prevent them from pressing the button. Others were unashamedly prepared to do the mandarin in as long

as they would not be held to account for the murder. Still others had religious scruples. How could they be sure they wouldn't be punished in the hereafter?

Garrett waited until everyone else was through. Then he rendered his opinion. "Teacher, I'd press that button if it meant killing every Chinaman in the world. And I'd do it if it gave me only one hour of happiness."

He had gone too far for the rest of the class. There was a cry of "Stop shucking us, Garrett!"

"Dummy up, everybody," Garrett said. "I want to ask teacher a question. . . . Now, you've been supposing things, teacher. Let me do some supposing for you. Let's suppose your kid is dying from leukemia. Let's suppose your wife has heart disease. Let's suppose that if you don't push that button they're both going to die and you're going to come down with the most painful goddam disease anyone has ever had. What would you do then?"

I stalled by observing that he'd stacked the deck pretty heavily.

Garrett was satisfied. "That's all I'm trying to say, teacher. The deck is always stacked. The only people who are moral are the ones who don't have any real problems."

As I led the class back to a discussion of Wolf Larsen, I had the uncomfortable feeling that Garrett had scored a point.[4]

The point is that most people do have problems. Crime is sometimes a matter of chance or expediency; morality, a matter of definition and interpretation. All "criminals" are not without morality; all "crime" is not committed by "criminals." The average person every day acts in ways which are technically unlawful or to some degree unmoral. Sometimes he is ignorant of the law. Sometimes he is deliberately following an accepted and well-rationalized practice such as loading a business expense account; and sometimes, because of the pressures of a situation, he behaves contrary to his own ideal standards. (Take time out to consider your own behavior!) The antisocial continuum extends from the casual to the calculating, and infiltrates all society from nursery school to grave, and from tenement slum to mansion.

Juvenile Delinquency

Every year more than a million and a half children, some casual, some confirmed delinquents, come to the attention of the police and courts for general incorrigibility, infringement of local ordinances and violation of the penal code—including vandalism, sex offenses, theft, assault, and murder. The incidence of known delinquency is increasing at a rate five times greater than the child population. This increase, perhaps in part a reflection of more conscientious law enforcement, has spurred interest in research on the problem. Most children commit casual delinquent acts, yet most children are not delinquent. We need to know why socialization in the long run succeeds for the majority, fails for the minority.

One thousand Boston boys, 94 per cent of whom came from blighted neighborhoods with criminal sub-cultures including street life, gangs, vice, and crime, were matched by age, intelligence, ethnic identity, and neighborhood. Five hundred of the boys were delinquent; the other five hundred were nondelinquent. Of the delinquents, nearly half manifested antisocial behavior before eight years of age, another two-fifths before eleven years of age, making a total of 87.6 per cent who were unmistakably antisocial before puberty. Persistent antisocial behavior first became manifest at an average age of 8.35 years.[5]

The Ford Foundation has given money to establish youth study centers at Syracuse University and the University of Southern California. The United States Office of Education has given research funds to several universities, and other federal funds have been granted the National Institute of Mental Health. The National Education Association has established a special study project to determine the school's responsibility in prevention and control of delinquency. The Division of Juvenile Delinquency services of the United States Childrens' Bureau assists state and local community agencies to improve their work. However, the present expenditure of time and money is grossly inadequate. Emotional disorganization, a basis for both antisocial and asocial behavior, is apparent in at least ten per cent of public school children. A particularly urgent need is for child guidance clinics to help the vulnerable, pre-delinquent child. Consider, for example, the case of Jimmy. His mother wrote:

> . . . I have an 8-year-old boy who is called "a brat," "smart Alec," "stupid ass" and "impudent, ill-bred moron" by the neighbors; is labeled by his teacher as an "emotionally disturbed child"; is labeled by his boys' club director as a "child you can talk to, but you just can't reach"; is labeled by his den mother as a "child who refuses to conform"; and by his doctor as a "genius mentally, but emotionally easily upset."
>
> . . . Here is a child who is unhappy. His school rejects him, his childhood friends reject him; our neighbors and friends reject him, the teachers, boys' club directors, and playground directors reject him because he is such a misfit. . . .
>
> The child needs help. I need help to lead this child back to a normal life. I have tried every method—love . . . explaining; taking away allowance . . . spanking . . . but nothing has changed his cocky, smart alec attitude, nor his contempt of adult authority.
>
> I applied to Child Guidance 13 months ago and am still waiting. . . .
>
> . . . They cry "delinquency" 7 days a week, but here is my son who needs help and guidance and there is none available. . . .
>
> . . . Is there no help for us until it is too late? Is it up to the juvenile board to try and correct them after they have gone afoul of the law? . . .[6]

At the present we only rarely take "the stitch in time." We spend many billions on the care of criminals but only a few million on research and prevention of crime. If Jimmy were treated in a State Child Guidance Center for one year, the cost would be approximately $575 and he would have a chance of living a good life. If he is not helped, he will probably get involved with the law. A year in a State Juvenile Institution would cost approximately $3,000 for one year, and the prognosis would not be favorable; the first crime is usually not the last one. Kerry, for example, was not helped in time.

> A freckled 10-year-old boy admitted today that he shot and wounded a . . . woman because she refused to surrender her purse.
>
> The boy . . . already has been in juvenile court on charges of malicious mischief, burglary, and arson. . . .
>
> Kerry confronted (the woman) with his father's pistol as she walked home from work. "Drop your purse or I'll kill you," he ordered.
>
> (She) ignored the order and Kerry fired.[7]

Juvenile delinquency has never been an isolated or localized problem, but in this century it is spreading from Western to non-Western cultures, from urban to rural areas, from lower to middle and upper-class society. Furthermore, delinquent acts are increasingly malevolent and violent. Four underlying social circumstances correlate with the changing incidence and nature of delinquency: (1) the discontinuity and ambiguity of the adolescent role; (2) anomie or normlessness which make "right" and "wrong" relative rather than definitive concepts; (3) alienation from self through loss of pride and purpose in work as depersonalized man becomes a replaceable unit in the routines of a mechanized and automated economy; (4) world crises which amplify the uncertainties haunting adolescents and give a rationale for purposeless hedonism.[8] These circumstances impinge to some extent on all adolescents in urban-industrial societies, but they engender greatest stress in those who—by reason of poverty, parental neglect or abuse, poor education, conflict of cultural loyalties, physical or mental defect, or other personal problems—are already insecure or embittered.

Although personality cannot be identified as a *cause* of delinquency any more than can environmental circumstances, certain traits are recognized as among the *correlates* of delinquency. Experimental study of delinquents indicates a relationship between frequency of delinquent behavior and traits associated with somatotype (body build). Mesomorphs (hard, heavy physique with preponderance of muscle and boney tissue) have a greater incidence of delinquency than endomorphs (soft, rounded physiques with preponderance of intestinal and visceral tissue), ectomorphs (linear, fragile physiques with preponderance of skin and nervous tissue) or balanced somatotypes.

> To change a potentiality into an actuality, the influence of various other forces, usually sociocultural factors, must come into play. . . . Examining the traits of mesomorphic nondelinquents, it became evident that mesomorphs are more vigorous than the other body types. They are also less sensitive and have a lesser tendency to phantasy than boys of one or another of the remaining body types. In addition, they are less unstable emotionally, less burdened by emotional conflicts, less inhibited in motor responses to stimuli. They are relatively free, as a group, of such inhibitions to antisocial adventures as feelings of inadequacy or marked submissiveness to authority. Such traits are not in themselves necessarily criminogenic; but, unless they are channeled toward socially acceptable

> goals, they are just the kind of traits that might furnish the strength, daring, enterprise, and dynamic tendency to unrestrained action that spell out a high delinquency potential, and such traits are in fact frequently found among delinquents. . . .[9]

Of 500 delinquent boys studied, 60.1 per cent of them were mesomorphs, but a high level of physical energy leads to delinquency only under certain circumstances. The mesomorphic immigrant boy who turns delinquent in a large city ghetto would not necessarily have become delinquent in the old country. Environmental and personality correlates of delinquency are neither causes nor explanations of delinquency. They are only critical variables known to be associated with delinquency. Any act of delinquency is situational behavior—the product of a particular individual coping with particular circumstances.

If the antisocial course of a pre-adolescent delinquent does not change, he may continue in one of three typical deviant patterns: the "retreatist" pattern, the "conflict" pattern, or the "criminal" pattern.[10]

The *retreatist* pattern becomes clear in late and post-adolescence. It is "a reaction against barriers to successful participation in either the criminal or conflict sub-cultures."[11] The adolescent retreats from this "double failure" with feelings of inadequacy and despair. In his attempts to anesthetize himself against the world and his own awareness of inadequacy through narcotics and alcohol, he shifts from an antisocial to an asocial mode of adjustment.

The *conflict pattern* is characteristic of those unable to achieve success as defined by either organized crime or "respectable" society. "Assuming limited access to success-goals by legitimate means, and . . . incomplete internalization of institutional norms, then delinquency will vary according to the availability of illegitimate channels to success-goals."[12] The institutionalized underworld is not open to all comers. Qualifications for an illegal career may be as formidable as for a legal one. The reject may, with others of his uncertain status, continue the violence, vandalism, stealing, and looting characteristic of irrational rebellion.

The *criminal pattern* is the "success" pattern—a prelude to the profitable and rationally calculated crimes of the professional. In this sub-culture the apprentice criminal finds support and approval for his attitudes and actions. He learns and practices skills acquired in the underworld and begins to make the contacts with protectors, "backers," and other middlemen indispensable to institutionalized crime.

Big cities are plagued by gangs of delinquents, many of whose members graduate into big-time crime. Typically these gangs operate under romantic banners: *Egyptian Dragons, Crusaders, Knights, The Lonely Ones, Enchanters, Comanches, Cobras, Demons, Sand Street Angels.* . . . A gang may have as many as sixty regular members, forty hangers-on, and fifty or more collaborating "debs." In such a gang, about fifteen of the brightest, toughest boys belong to the upper echelon; and, if it is an "S" and "A" gang, they have, in addition to a "rumble" leader, one leader for *Social* and another for *Athletic* activities. In peace time, the boys and girls prowl the streets, hang around their favorite meeting place, get drunk on "sneaky Pete" or other cheap wine, sample narcotics, smoke, gamble, play pool, raid stores, guard their "turf," and dance. The debs are organized, too. One 17-year-old girl described herself as the leader of a 200 member girls' "Auxiliary," and told how some of her gang wrecked a candy store and broke both legs of the proprietor. During gang wars, the girls "swing," the boys "rumble." Trespassing on another gang's turf, stealing another's property or girl, even an insult can start a "rumble." This is a vicious conflict lasting only about five minutes, but in that time, the contestants kill and maim each other with knives, machetes, guns, garrison belts, and skin-slashing automotible radio aerials. Typical gang members are bitterly frustrated boys like the Chimp, Pepito, Chocolate, Seven-Up, and Smokey. The Chimp, eighteen, is a nephew of a "famous Brooklyn gangster." He was expelled from a parochial school for bad conduct, arrested once for larceny, and looks forward to getting to the Brooklyn docks, where big-time crime is rampant. Pepito, fourteen, lives with a grandmother who is on relief. He smokes marijuana and is on probation for shoplifting. Chocolate, sixteen, is illiterate and avoids the subways because he cannot read the station names. He is usualy half-drunk. Seven-Up, sixteen, is an orphan who lives with an elderly aunt. He says no one looks after him and no one except his fellow gang members cares about him. Smokey, seventeen, is a gang leader. "People don't understand. . . . I would much rather not bop. It isn't any fun. You don't know what will happen. You may be killed. Or you may kill someone. Would you think it funny if I said that my real ambition was to become a policeman?" [13]

Police records show that, in general, the youngest criminals—those in their late adolescence and early twenties—commit the most serious crimes, get the most severe penalties, and have the highest recidivist rate. *What chance does Smokey have of ever becoming a policeman?*

Adult Delinquency

Adult delinquency includes three major categories: conventional crime, organized crime, and white collar crime. The categories are not mutually exclusive. They serve mainly to clarify the difficulties of socialization by emphasizing three problem areas: attacks by predatory individuals on other individuals; alliances between the criminal sub-culture and "respectable" society; and finally, conflicts between economic and moral values within "respectable" society itself.

CONVENTIONAL CRIME. Conventional crime, the least important category as judged by cost to society in terms of social demoralization, is the most publicized. Criminal homicide, assault with a weapon or intent to kill, robbery, burglary, auto theft, larceny, and rape are the major crimes listed by the FBI. Some such crime is committed in these United States at least every fifteen seconds—often enough to keep the newspapers supplied with dramatic headlines and the public apprehensive. Considering our total population, however, there is a relatively small number of violent predatory individuals. Furthermore, the percentage is dropping. Since 1930 the homicide rate has declined from 8.9 per 100,000 persons to 5.1 in 1962. In 1930, there were 10,500 homicides in the United States; in 1962, there were 9,500, even though the population since 1930 had increased fifty per cent. In 1932, 609 bank robberies had a grand take of $3,400,000. In 1962, when we had 5,300 more banks than in 1932, 461 holdups grossed only $1,800,000.[14] Newspapers tend to give the impression of a rising crime wave, but the facts do not support such a pessimistic view.* Furthermore, crimes that make up the daily fare of newspaper readers are isolated acts with little effect on the larger society.

ORGANIZED CRIME. When Hollywood glamorizes the gangster, the good guys win, the bad guys lose, and crime doesn't pay. But in real life, organized crime exists because it does pay very well. The suave, calculating professionals who deal in gambling, racketeering, prostitution, narcotics, and other profitable illegal operations are rarely caught and exposed. Occasionally, a career criminal does break into the news, as when Arnold Rothstein was shot in the employees's entrance to New York's Park Central Hotel.

> In New York City there was need for a middleman between the politicians and the racketeers. Rothstein, through a series of circumstances . . . became that middleman, and . . . set up the organization which made the gangs into a loose-knit confederacy for business purposes that has lasted to the present day.
>
> Rothstein was many things—gambler, bookmaker, drug wholesaler, moneylender, insurance company owner, speculator. His finger was in every unsavory enterprise in New York. . . .
>
> Rothstein's career in New York's underworld spanned the time from Big Jake Zelig and the killings by Gyp the Blood to Legs Diamond, Owney Madden, and Dutch Schultz. His story is the story of New York politics and sports (including heavy emphasis on racing) and as an indication of the circles in which he moved . . . Herbert Bayard Swope (Pulitzer Prize journalist, 1882-1958) was best man at Rothstein's wedding.
>
> Rothstein was killed as a result of a card game in the same hotel where Albert Anastasia was murdered in 1957. Neither crime has been solved. . . . In 1938, the Rothstein estate was declared bankrupt, the millions he had made, won, and stolen, gone like the evidence in his murder.

---

* Journalistic "crime waves" are not new. In the December, 1852, issue of *Harper's New Monthly Magazine* appeared the following item: "The increase of crime is becoming one of the most startling notices in our daily newspapers. . . . Three, four, five, and, in one case, eight murders are announced in New York for one week. We are becoming familiar with what, twenty years ago, would have shocked the universal conscience. The burglaries, forgeries, arsons, are in like proportion. If there be any difference, the more enormous and startling crimes are multiplying more rapidly than the minor and less bad offenses. The fact, we say, is beyond all doubt, whatever may be the cause or causes—whether temporary and incidental, or inherent in the very modes of thinking and acting which characterize our remarkable age."[15]

Rothstein's death gave the public a brief glimpse of the corruption that reached from the sewers to New York's City Hall.[16]

Professional criminals have become entrenched in our social system; and, like other areas of our increasingly complex society, crime has become institutionalized over the years. "Big Crime" now shares the stage with "Big Business," "Big Labor," and "Big Government." In 1959, the nation was afforded an indication of the extent of organized crime when New York State Police discovered the so-called "Apalachin Conference" of big-time gangsters, who met presumably to discuss underworld strategy. In the subsequent government action against this "syndicate," it became clear that traditional legal machinery was inadequate for dealing with it. Organized crime is protected not only by its own institutional structure, but by mutually advantageous alliances with "reputable" members of the community—businessmen, politicians, public officials, and just plain "honest" folk who have no scruples about breaking laws which do not violate their own consciences. *If you want to bet on the horses and it is inconvenient to do it legally at the race track, why not do it illegally through a bookie?*

WHITE COLLAR CRIME. The career criminal identifies with the underworld. His supporters and protectors identify with "respectable" society. They meet and do business in a morally neutral zone. The white collar criminal, in contrast, identifies primarily with the dominant culture. His crimes are crimes, not of revenge or despair or passion, but of self-interest.

White collar crime is found in business, industry, commerce, politics, and the professions. It takes the form of such unfair practices as financial fraud, rebates, fee-splitting, infringements against patents, copyrights, and trademarks; misrepresentations in advertising, restraint of trade, and profiteering. In white collar crime, an aura of respectablity masks a basic lack of integrity. The deceit is destructive and antisocial in the fullest sense of the word, yet the white collar criminal may never be called a criminal. He may lose his license or be sued for damages, but he is rarely fined or jailed.

Only one robber in the history of the United States has dared a $1,000,000 job, but embezzlers often try for much higher takes. One financier stole $250,000,000, and one investment trust company, through fraudulent manipulations, stole $580,000,000. Although the loss to society from white collar crime far overshadows the loss from conventional crime, the public knows relatively little about white collar crime. You have to watch the inside columns of newspapers for reports such as these.

> House investigators studying operations of the Agriculture Department's giant Commodity Credit Corporation turned their attention today to cases which may involve "windfall profits" in sales of government surplus non-fat dry milk. . . .
>
> Private firms sold non-fat milk to the CCC under the Government's dairy price support program at the support price, which is 14½ cents a pound. The milk itself remained in storage at the seller's warehouses.

The companies then bought it back at the CCC export price of 9.9 cents a pound.

The milk was then sold for export—at considerably above the CCC export price—to the armed forces and, in some cases, other Government agencies.[17]

Twelve more cases were uncovered today of congressmen charging the government up to $1200 a year for office space owned by themselves or their families. . . .

Congressmen, under the law, are allowed $1200 a year for office rent if they cannot find space in a Federal building in their districts.

If they "rent" the space from themselves, they can bill the government and pocket the payments. . . .[18]

White collar crime is a nebulous field, the line between it and some accepted business practices cannot easily be drawn. The following item appeared in the Business and Finance section of a metropolitan newspaper under the heading: "How to Succeed in Business Without Trusting Anybody."

Does a Jekyll-and-Hyde strain run through the ranks of America's business executives?

Does the roaring lion of the executive suite turn into an amiable lamb when he leaves the office?

Researchers at Michigan State University believe so.

They maintain the typical executive is apt to lead a double life with one set of principles for the office, another for home and church.

The researchers have completed a pilot study in which they interviewed 162 executives in every echelon of the management hierarchy.

"The study indicates ambitious business executives do not regard as success-contributing those practices ordinarily regarded as good human relations," says the study director, Dr. Eugene E. Jennings, of M.S.U.'s Business Administration College.

The professor adds:

"A majority of the men we interviewed admitted they believe self-interest is the basis of all human nature, that it is safer to be suspicious of men and assume their nature is more bad than good."

Here are some majority reactions in four human relations areas covered in the study:

Friendship—Loyal subordinates are the mark of a competent executive, but he risks a loss of flexibility by making close friends in areas crucial to his interests.

Agreement—Agreements should commit the other person; past promises need not stand in the way of success.

Decision making—An executive should not allow free participation in decisions crucial to his own interests; a decision once made should not be open to doubt.

Communication—The executive should not expose his hand; superior information is an advantage; never tell all you know and give out information sparingly; don't take advice you didn't ask for.

The researchers hold the double life practice revealed by the study does not mean the executive is immoral.

"It merely indicates," Jennings maintained, "that the ethics of his business life may be forced to take different forms from the ethics of his personal life in some cases." [19]

White collar crime is not unique. Six hundred years before Christ, the Scythian sage Anacharsis said: "These written laws are just like spiders' webs; the small and feeble may be caught and entangled in them, but the rich and mighty force through and despise them."

Individual conscience is typically prompted by the norms of the groups with which one identifies. There is honor among "honest" men, and there is honor of a sort among thieves. But there are those who identify with no group and feel no responsibility to others. They have no conscience. They know, theoretically, the difference between "right" and "wrong," but they don't care. Such amoral individuals, both juvenile and adult, are classified as *psychopaths.*

Psychopathic Delinquency

Psychopaths do not necessarily intend to harm others; they simply use others in whatever way serves their own needs and desires. They have a seemingly intact personality structure but lack the emotional ties to reality which compel the normal person to consider the consequences of his behavior.

> Psychopathy certainly begins very early in life. . . . The consensus seems now to be that psychopathy represents a failure of the basic identification process in the first five years of life, so that the individual becomes incapable of true feelings for others. This failure can in some cases be traced to a disruption of normal family relationships. . . . He is virtually lacking in conscience or superego, although he professes a recognition of and can speak smoothly in terms of devotion to accepted values. He makes glib promises and resolutions, but meanwhile may be picking the pocket of the person he is talking to. . . . Childhood psychopaths supply the bulk of the adult criminal population, but not all of them end up as criminals. Some simply become unpleasant characters who exploit and betray their friends and families but stay within the law. Some become drifters or marginal personalities. Some settle down to shallow respectability on a low socio-economic level. A few, turning their talents into socially acceptable channels, become financial successes. . . .[20]

Psychopaths learn "by rote" the patterns which others tend to follow, and—until they are found out—they can successfully manipulate others. (We know! One personable and persuasive psychopathic student—posing as the grandson of an Algerian leader of the French resistance—nearly sold us a stolen car and took us off on a summer safari to Africa.)

The psychopath's behavior is inconsistent with what he knows or says, but he is untroubled by the dissonance.

This inherent indifference to ethical or moral values makes them particularly successful "confidence men." Patrick Henry (Packy) Lennon, alias Harry Hoffman, was only twenty-nine years old when the New York Evening Journal honored him with a picture captioned, "Don't Let Him Sell You Any Stock." Packy Lennon was so dapper, so dignified, so well-spoken, so bold, and so crafty that, in spite of having his career interrupted by a few jail sentences, he was still in business when he was fifty years old. This was when he managed to get one of the most respectable and respected citizens of Rochester, New York, to hand over a total of $439,121 to him, ostensibly for helping the good old gentleman recover his share of a purely fictitious $60,000,000 legacy. Confidence men are noted for their unscrupulous fleecing of widows, orphans, the aged, and the infirm.

> . . . Lennon distinguished himself by selling some utterly valueless Fyr-Ex stock for nearly twenty thousand dollars to a woman who not only was a widow with four children but at the time was lying in a hospital in a plaster cast, since her back was broken. After she recovered, Lennon and some of his henchmen took her out to lunch, and during the meal he gave her a hundred-dollar bill—for which he had her sign a receipt—as a token of the splendid increments she might expect from her investment in Fyr-Ex. Before the meal was over she excused herself to go to the ladies' room, leaving her purse behind, and when she returned she noticed that the bill was missing from it. She ventured to ask her host where on earth the hundred dollars could have gone, and he responded by demanding, "Are you questioning the honesty of these friends of mine?" [21]

Every crime has a victim, and the experienced and successful confidence man looks for "likely" victims. He looks for persons willing to gamble spare money on the chance of "getting something for nothing." Old-age or infirmity are a special advantage; the victim is less likely to live long enough to be a prosecuting witness! Legal concern has been with the crime and the criminal. Sociological concern extends to the victim and the conditions of the crime. Even in conventional crime, there are murderers and murderees. *Has the victim attracted the criminal and helped set the stage for the crime?*

Asocial Behavior

Circumstances which predispose one individual to antisocial behavior may predispose another to asocial behavior. Both are basically aggressive. The first is aggressive against society; the second is aggressive against the self, although others may suffer indirectly. Asocial behavior involves withdrawal from the realities of the social environment, but goes beyond the temporary relief we all seek when "the world is too much with us. . . ." * As a pathological state, it includes neuroses and psychoses, complicated, in some cases, by alcoholism or addiction. It may exist independently or as a counterpart of antisocial behavior in the same individual. The murderer may be a paranoid schizophrenic;

* William Wordsworth (1770-1850).

the robber may be compulsive; the embezzler may be alcoholic; the prostitute may be a drug addict.

Each individual has limits to the amount of stress he can stand—a threshold of tolerance beyond his powers of endurance. Within his particular limits, however, he maintains psychological homeostasis through a variety of coping devices. Sometimes in the classroom we illustrate coping devices by announcing a quiz on an unexpected and heavy assignment. After a moment of stunned disbelief, the room typically churns with restlessness—with shifting and shuffling and buzzing. Then some students become hostile. They slam their books (indirect aggression) or angrily object to the unfairness (direct aggression). Some withdraw from the horror of it all by looking thoughtfully out of the window (fantasy)* or slumping in gloomy depression (apathy). Others chew their hands or nails; one girl even began sucking her thumb (regression). These reactions are relatively forthright—direct, observable attempts to either attack or escape the situation. The mechanisms of ego defense which deny or distort reality are more devious and not so easily demonstrated publicly. Have you ever *repressed* feelings of jealousy or resentment and then "leaned over backwards" in a *reaction-formation,* being extra nice and solicitous to keep from feeling guilty? Have you ever *projected* your shortcomings and blamed others for faults you could not admit having yourself? Have you ever gotten vicarious satisfaction from accomplishments of others by *identifying* with them? Have you ever compromised with reality by *sublimating*—finding a socially acceptable outlet for needs which you dared not satisfy directly—or by *compensating*—counter-balancing a weakness by developing a strength or forcing yourself to acomplish in an area of weakness? Have you ever *rationalized,* giving plausible rather than the actual but less commendable reasons for your actions? Have you ever called a "lemon" sweet or, like the fox in the fable, said the grapes you couldn't reach were sour anyway? If you indignantly say "NO!" it is not because you haven't used such devices as temporary buffers against stress; it is because defense mechanisms are subconsciously determined. We have to have an exceptionally high degree of objectivity and insight to "catch ourselves."

Different authorities have different systems of classification for the various coping devices of everyday living. They also have different systems of classification for the various pathological states. Categorizing is an intellectual economy measure; it saves us from having to deal anew with each new perception, but categorizing—especially in dealing with human behavior—is deceiving. Human behavior is too varied and varying. It rarely fits neatly into any pigeonhole, even temporarily. However, behavioral scientists do currently indulge in some name calling. We use terms which are part of the popular conceptualization of asocial behavior, but we continually remind ourselves that any

* Read "The Private Life of Walter Mitty," a short story by James Thurber, for an entertaining exposé of one man's fantasies.

system of classification is arbitrary and that by naming we are not really describing and certainly not explaining.

Psychoneurotics

The difference between the normal individual and the psychoneurotic (often simply neurotic) is a matter of degree. The psychoneurotic's stress tolerance may be lower than normal. His reactions to stress-generating frustrations may be more intense and his use of defense mechanisms so habitual that some aspects of reality are not just temporarily denied or distorted but permanently out of focus. Some facts he never faces. Some conflicts he never resolves. He is typically disorganized and unhappy. He tries to maintain himself in his social roles, but his effectiveness is limited by one or a combination of disabling symptoms.

He may suffer a *conversion reaction* in which conflict is converted into a physical symptom. He may be hysterically paralyzed, deaf, mute, or blind, or suffer heart, stomach, or other disorders. Physical disability necessarily means some withdrawal from society: a soldier in front-line battle may awaken with a paralyzed arm; a devoted wife whose religious convictions prevent her from using contraceptives and who is afraid of having more children may become paralyzed from her waist down. Instead of a conversion reaction, the neurotic may have an *anxiety reaction*. He may be haunted by vague undefined fears, as elusive and as threatening as mosquitoes in the dark. His energy is drained by the tension, and he is chronically tired—a victim of neurasthenia. Or, instead of being diffuse, his anxiety may have a focus. He may develop an intense, irrational fear—a *phobia* of high places or open spaces or closed spaces. He may be morbidly concerned with his health—a *hypochondriac* who really tells you how he is when you innocently greet him with, "Hello, how are you?"

The psychoneurotic may be handicapped by *compulsive actions*, as was an acquaintance of ours who stamped out every cigarette butt he saw, even when to do it he had to flag down traffic in the middle of a busy city street. *Compulsive acts* relate to *obsessive ideas*, irrational acts are rationalized by irrational ideas. Two elderly ladies, residents of a hotel, each day wore a clean pair of white gloves. When they were in the dining room, they kept on their gloves and wrapped cleansing tissue around the glasses and the handles of cups and silverware. They rationalized their behavior as a precaution against germs, but they drank from the glasses and cups and ate with the silverware!

The psychoneurotic may become *amnesic* and severely repress entire episodes of experience or entire aspects of personality. He may be found, sometimes far from home, in a state of psychological flight, unable to give name, address, age, or other personal facts, but otherwise mentally intact and capable of intelligent responses.

Multiple personalities, two or more, each usually representing conflicting motives as in "Dr. Jekyll and Mr. Hyde," may in turn control the neurotic. He may be alternately selfish, then overly generous; submissive, then tyrannical; irascible, then gay and affable. Sometimes dissociation is so complete that the personalities go by different names and may be unaware of each other, as in the case of Eve White, once popularized through a movie, "The Three Faces of Eve."

Any one individual may suffer one or several of the various psychoneurotic symptoms—a phenomenon which further complicates attempts to categorize.

> For many years I felt always nauseated and often got the most painful stomach cramps and other intestinal disorders. I had the feeling that I could never get enough air into my lungs, thinking all the time that I must or I would suffocate. This fear of suffocating was intensified when I got pains in my chest for hours at a time whenever I took a breath. I was just able to get enough air with each breath to stay alive, or so I thought, little gasps, each of which gave me a sharp pain. Whenever I tried to breathe more deeply the pain became so unbearable that I thought it would surely kill me.
>
> Every morning I woke up with my jaws hurting because I had been grinding my teeth all night; my fists were clenched tightly and the muscles in my arms, shoulders and back were so sore that I could hardly move. The muscles were so tightly knotted from the tension that it sometimes took a week to be able to walk straight again. I woke up with muscular pains every morning and when I was lucky it was gone after a few hours of moving about. I had continuous headaches which felt as if a tight iron band was clasped around my forehead and the top of my head was being hammered on. My cheekbones hurt and very often I had toothaches for no reason.
>
> My dreams were unending nightmares. I was always running from somebody who wanted to catch me and when I was finally caught I tried desperately to scream, knowing that only this would save me; but no sound escaped. I trained myself to wake up immediately while trying to scream, otherwise it seemed the attempts would never end. Needless to say that I was up for hours after that.
>
> I longed for sleep as it was my only means of escape from thinking about my unhappy life, but even though I often slept for twelve hours at a time, sleep gave me no rest. I awoke as tired as if I had never slept, feeling hopeless and depressed, unable to do anything, just sitting, or dragging myself from one room to the other to do a few things I had to do. I had no wish to live, no interest in anything.
>
> At other times I was nervous and restless. I got skin rashes which made me itch all over; my skin was prickling as if a thousand needles were stuck into it; I actually felt I had to get out of my skin. I had an overwhelming desire to tear myself apart, to climb up the walls because I wanted to get out somehow, all this time saying over and over to myself: "I can't stand this any more. I can't take it any more."
>
> I did not want to live—what last ounce of strength kept me from killing myself I do not know. I was often thinking of different ways to end my life but I knew I would not make the attempt. Instead I was always hoping that something would kill me; a car would run over me, a bridge I was walking on could collapse, or I could have some terrible illness which would finish me off.

> I felt so unloved and unwanted in this world, so utterly alone, nobody cared. Death seemed like peace, away from all that troubled me. I cried and could not stop.[22]

Psychotics

The *psychoneurotic* excessively denies or distorts reality and suffers severely, but he does not lose contact. He is aware of his limitations, and, in spite of them, maintains to some degree his roles in society. The *psychotic* does lose contact with reality, partially or completely; he is, in sociological terms, incapable of playing acceptable social roles. Usually he is hospitalized. A psychotic may see pink alligators and purple cows, hear music from Mars, or converse with angels. He may believe himself to be the Aga Khan or Prince Phillip. He may think a doctor is an enemy plotting to kill him and take his treasure chest of jewels, gold, and bones. He may laugh at a friend's death, cry over a dead fly, talk chaotically, sit immobile for hours, or stage a destructive tirade. Hallucinations, delusions, and/or distorted emotional reactions severely disable all psychotics. Some psychoses—those involving observable damage to the nervous system through accident, disease, nutritional and glandular deficiency, or degeneration from age, alcohol, or drugs—are classified as *organic*. Other psychoses—those involving no known structural changes in the nervous system—are classified as *functional*. These include (1) schizophrenic reactions characterized by emotional and intellectual dysfunction and withdrawal from reality; (2) paranoid reactions in which the personality is intact except for certain highly systematized and logically defended delusions; and (3) affective reactions involving periods of either extreme depression or agitation, or, as in manic-depressive psychoses, alternating periods of both. As in the case of neuroses, theoretical distinctions made among the various psychoses do not necessarily hold. Any one patient may show a variety of changing symptoms. Furthermore, even the division between functional and organic psychoses may be misleading. ". . . we know that physiological reactions are accompanied in all instances by psychological reactions and that psychological reactions to stress are accompanied in all instances by physical reactions."[23]

Experiments on prolonged stress indicate that, whether the cause of stress is physical, as in a wound, chemical, as in contaminated air, or psychological, as in grief, there are common physiological reactions, including changes in the endocrine system and consequent changes in body chemistry (general adaptation syndrome).[24] The blood chemistry of schizophrenics *is* different from that of nonschizophrenics, but we don't know which came first—the schizoid mental processes or the chemical change. *Taraxein,* a substance found in the blood of schizophrenics, if injected into a normal person, will cause temporary schizophrenic symptoms. Other drugs, including *mescaline* and *lysergic acid diethylamide* (LSD) also cause temporary psychoses. There are, however, individual differences in sensitivity to these drugs dependent on hereditary factors * and on past experience—physical and psychological.

With more knowledge and better diagnosis we may find that all psychoses have an organic concomitant and that somatic and psychic functions are so interrelated that cause cannot be assigned singly to one or the other.

We do not know just how many psychoneurotics and psychotics there are in our population. Estimates on psychoneurotics range from twenty to thirty million. Some doctors estimate that as many as sixty per cent of their patients suffer from psychoneurotic symptoms, and one person out of ten spends some part of his life in a mental hospital. Eighty per cent of persons in a study of mid-town Manhattan had some degree of mental illness.[26] The ordinary difficulties of detection and diagnosis of mental illness are increased when symptoms are intensfied or suppressed by alcohol, narcotics, or tranquilizers. In the United States there are 50,000 to 60,000 drug addicts and at least 5,000,000 problem drinkers. Sixty per cent of the arrests made annually are for causes associated with heavy drinking. Alcoholics jam the jails, clog the courts, and over-burden the police system. In Washington, D.C., alone, chronic alcoholics cost the taxpayers $2,000,000 a year. Both alcoholics and addicts are seriously ill emotionally before they become physiologically ill from complications of drink or drug. There are, in addition, millions of people—some with only minor symptoms—who want a vacation from reality, who are trying (with and without medical advice) to relieve their anxieties and tensions by swallowing tranquilizing pills. The unhappy couple who save their marriage by taking Frenquel, the stenographer who slips into the ladies' room to give herself a "fix," the society matron who periodically shuts herself up in her bedroom for a binge and then emerges with a new hat to join the bridge party, the paranoid schizophrenic who rapes the girl he murdered, and the hypochondriac who enjoys being "deathly sick"—all such people, *as individuals,* primarily represent psychological and medical problems. *As an aggregate,* these same people make up a sizeable part of our total population and critically affect the health and efficiency of society.

In his various degrees of withdrawal, an asocial individual does not, in principal, reject all of society. He rejects only those aspects which are personally frustrating and distressing. The goal of any treatment he may receive is towards resocialization—helping him regain and maintain his position in society. However, asocial individuals may identify not with society, but with each other. There are two groups, mainly asocial but embodying some antisocial activities, which live on the periphery of urban life—Bohemians, currently known as Beatniks, and Skid Row derelicts.

* If one identical twin is schizophrenic, the other twin is also schizophrenic in 66 to 68 per cent of the cases. If one fraternal twin is schizophrenic, the other twin is schizophrenic in only 3 to 16 per cent of the cases.[25] However, psychological identification of identical twins with each other is greater than in fraternal twins, and such identification may be as significant a variable as heredity.

Beatniks

Beatniks lead lives of dissent on the fringe of society. They resist conventional society and conform to their own standards of social nonconformity. They are not a "generation." They range in age from fifteen to fifty-five—averaging approximately thirty for men, twenty-three for women. Some haven't graduated from high school; some have Master's and Doctor's degrees. In every big city they are a tourist attraction. They have written about themselves. Philosophers have written about them. Psychiatrists have studied them. They have been accused of making society "the verbal scapegoat for their own neuroticism," [27] and their headquarters have been called "an open-air, come-and-go mental hospital." [28]

> I'm thirty-four now, and I've been making this Beat scene for about six years—three here and three in New Orleans' French Quarter. I got with it in New York. Went there after graduating from Yale—oh, I'm good family, very Boston; very Back Bay—and got a job doing publicity for the movies. It was very white collar and very square, and they all said I had a very good future.
>
> But then I started thinking. I remembered what the old nine-to-five did to my father; he worked like hell and came home at night so pooped that he couldn't do anything but eat and go to bed. He had no joy, no fun, no life. He'd work this for fifty weeks so he could have maybe two weeks of fun during vacation, but then, maybe, he couldn't take a trip because he had to pay his income taxes.
>
> And, as I say, I was in New York. We were worried about The Bomb. I didn't want to be in New York when it landed. And I wanted to ball a little before it did.
>
> And there was this terrible, dragging conformity. Everyone getting married and moving to the suburbs and tithing their lives to General Motors. Everything in-group. All "we" and no "I." So I cut out.[29]

The Beatnik rejects the Protestant ethic. Work, thrift, marriage, "respectability," and other middle-class values seem to him to have lost their relevance in a world so uncertain of its own future. The committed Beatnik chooses to live in the present, detached from the long-term goals which give social institutions their meaning and strength. As with any movement, large or small, the Beats have attracted hangers-on, people who are either essentially derelict or simply in a state of adolescent revolt. Conventional society tends to focus on this minority and to ignore the honest philosophical convictions of those who question traditional mores.[30]

Derelicts

Beatniks are active nonconformists and proud of it. Derelicts drift apathetically into nonconformity and self-contempt, feeling that society has rejected them. Every city has its Skid Row, a haven of despair, inhabited by hopeless and bitter derelicts. Most of them are young, able-bodied men. Some are men and women in late middle age—still able to work. Some are old and feeble. Others are physically or mentally handicapped: "Blinkies" (blind), "Crips" (crippled), "Halfies" (legs off below the knee), "Wingies" (armless), "Crazies" and "Dummies." Some Skid Rowers are on Skid Row because they drink. Others, not primarily alcoholics, drink because they are on Skid Row. And they drink almost anything: "Pink Lady" (canned heat), "White Elephant" (wine and bay rum), "Smoke" (denatured alcohol), shoe polish, rubbing alcohol, and anti-freeze. Some of them take dope.[31] They manage somehow to anesthetize themselves against society. Temporarily they may get hospitalized or jailed for minor crimes, but their lives are apart from the world and they think of their withdrawal as permanent—a purgatory before the grave.

Those who reject or are rejected by the larger conventional society of "normal" people tend to draw together and build up a society of their own. The criminal underworld, Skid Row, the Beat scene—even the homosexuals—are sub-societies with their own sub-cultures. They have their own social structures and processes, their own goals, their own folkways, mores, taboos—even their own argot. Thus do such groups institutionalize and thereby strengthen and rationalize the given forms of unsanctioned behavior. And insofar as politicians, law-enforcement officers, or businessmen are bribed or otherwise corrupted, insofar as others profit from selling drinks to "winos," drawing rent from "pads," even selling weapons to criminals, the antisocial and asocial members of society are exploited and maintained by the larger society.

Suicides

A man once walked into Griffith Park to die. "I just didn't see any future," . . . . .

He had tried hard to die but gave up and became a hermit. For five years he lived without speaking to a human being.

Police captured him when they answered a prowler call at a home near the park. They took him to the Hollywood Police Station, where, haltingly, he told his story.

He had been an infantryman in World War II—got shot through the lung on Okinawa. . . .

In 1954 he decided to die. Police asked why. "You wouldn't understand," he said. "I tried starving to death. The first time I went without food for three days, then again for eleven days. But each time I gave up fasting. I couldn't stand it any more."

He ate scraps left by picnickers in the park. At night he raided the garbage cans of homes on the park's fringe. In the daytime he lived in caves or shelters he built of lumber scraps in remote parts of the hilly park. . . .

He hadn't broken any laws; the police said he could go. They offered him money to buy clothing and food.

"I can get along by myself," he whispered.

> Officers drove him back to where he had been arrested, and he walked back into Griffith Park.[32]

This man lived only because he couldn't face death. Others die because they can't face life.

The Skid Row alcoholic commits slow suicide and dies of cirrhosis of the liver. The Beatnik, by his own definition, sometimes wants desperately to die, but he says, "I'm here and I wish I weren't, but while I have life, I'm going to really live it." Or he says, "I'm here and I wish I weren't, and to hell with it." [33] And as long as his friends say what he is saying, he goes on living. The suicide is beat *and* alone. He feels utterly forlorn—alienated from the life around him, plagued by guilt or fear or anxiety. Each year at least 100,000 people in the United States attempt suicide—enough succeed to make it the ninth major cause of death. (Approximately 16,000 suicides are reported annually; thousands of others are concealed as accidents.) Neuroses, psychoses, alcoholism, and addiction are asocial symptoms. Suicide is final and complete withdrawal.

REACTIONS TO FAILURE

When socialization fails it is not necessarily unredeemable failure. Rehabilitation of criminals in some prisons exceeds ninety-five per cent. Mental patients, the majority of them in some hospitals, get well, some within weeks or months.* Beatniks may be beat only temporarily. Alcoholics join Alcoholics Anonymous and find their way back to full participation in society. Addicts can be cured. Only the suicides are irretrievable. The percentage of people salvaged is directly related to the attitude others take towards them and the adequacy of the means used to help them. We can continue to abandon, scorn or punish—as we have traditionally done—or, with the help of new knowledge and insights from the behavioral sciences, we can build preventative programs into our primary institutions and try to rehabilitate those cases we do not prevent.

Pre-Scientific: Retribution and Despair

Although failure of socialization is a double failure—a failure of society as well as of the individual—the burden of blame traditionally has been on the individual. Mental patients, once fearfully and despairingly chained, are still left to deteriorate behind locked doors in some "hospitals." Suicide, once

---

* Some mental patients, after they get well, are "weller than well." Abraham Lincoln had several attacks of mental illness and was described by his law partner as a "hopeless victim of melancholy." John Stuart Mill, English philosopher and economist, for a period suffered depression and suicidal tendencies. William James, American psychologist, had psychosomatic symptoms and suicidal thoughts. "He became a great man only after he had been a very sick man." [34]

punishable by denial of Christian burial and confiscation of property, is still considered a sin by some churches, and a crime against society in some areas of the United States. Skid Row is a revolving door: addicts, alcoholics, and vagrants are jailed, released, jailed, released. . . . One fifty-four-year old man, jailed 285 times in thirty-two years for petty crimes and drunkenness, has cost city taxpayers $44,863. Thousands of able-bodied men and women sentenced to prison suffer months and years of demoralizing idleness. In eighteenth-century England, pickpockets used to pick the pockets of people who gathered to witness the public execution of a pickpocket. Today we still try to eliminate crime by eliminating the criminal, and prosecuting attorneys still play the Grand Inquisitor:

> His mouth curled, his eyes cold and his voice deliberate, he retold the circumstances in which he said she had committed the following:
>
> Soliciting for prostitution, adultery, aiding and abetting sexual perverts, incest, soliciting an abortion, defrauding a landlord, obtaining money on false pretenses, perjury, extortion, soliciting mayhem, kidnapping, conspiracy, fraud, bribery, forgery, grand theft, bigamy, fictitious checks, and finally murder. . . .
>
> "What are the purposes of punishment? Its very meaning is to inflict some loss. A fundamental purpose of our law is retribution.
>
> "Shall she get seven-years' imprisonment and then go free again or should her life be taken on a proper, equal basis, a life for a life?
>
> "In this case, death is the only proper measure of retribution. . . ." [35]

Criminal laws in the United States are the most severe in the world, and legislatures are currently working to make them more severe. Typically a criminal here serves several times as long a prison sentence as a comparable criminal in any other country.[36] We are not more vindictive than other peoples, but we are more heterogeneous. We cannot count on the concerted force of consistent norms to steady the aberrant members of our society. The conflicts and discontinuities in our society which make for slow and uncertain socialization also make for slow and uncertain rehabilitation. In 1956, 63.5 per cent of all federal prisoners had previous prison records. We tend to impose stronger extrinsic controls, hoping to compensate for the relative lack of intrinsic controls in the individual and of informal controls in society.

The antisocial and the asocial have traditionally suffered in our self-righteous society. We have despaired of their rehabilitation. We have demanded retribution and punishment on the assumption that the criminal is the only perpetrator of his crime. We have looked with contempt on the derelicts and other marginal members of society, forgetting that America was settled and subdued largely by the misfits of Europe who fled the contempt of their "betters"; our shores were flooded by the "wretched refuse"—the impoverished, the drunks, and the criminals. We have abandoned the mentally ill and excluded them from society on the assumption that they cannot benefit from contact with society. Eighty per cent of state mental institutions in the United States still fail to offer treatment to the patients confined in them.[37]

The dominant attitude towards antisocial and asocial behavior is pre-scientific—dominated by the "Aristotelian" mode, which holds that behavior is determined by characteristics of the individual—"instincts," "heredity," "intelligence," "needs," "habits"—and is relatively independent of circumstances. Knowledge from the behavioral sciences, including sociology, is making it increasingly clear that to speak of behavior without references to the environment in which it occurs is meaningless.

Scientific: Prevention and Rehabilitation

In the eighteenth century, a poet wrote, "Society prepares the crime. The criminal commits it." * More recently behavioral scientists have confirmed and extended the poet's insight.

A sociologist:

> . . . The criminal population in America is as much a natural fruit of this society as is the number of its philosophers or artists or businessmen.[38]

A psychologist:

> There are many indications that our emotional stability depends more on our successful avoidance of emotional provocation than on our essential characteristics; that urbanity depends on an urbane social and physical environment . . . the development of what is called "civilization" is the progressive elimination of sources of acute fear, disgust, and anger.[39]

A psychiatrist:

> . . . It is clear that much of the problem of psychiatric disability is related to the social environment. Research in social psychiatry is illuminating the psychology of patients as members of social units and mental illness as a type of participation in a social process.[40]

As research in behavioral sciences gives further knowledge of the many variables determining personality structure, reactions to antisocial and asocial behavior is shifting away from despair and retribution towards prevention and rehabilitation. A new approach is being built on psychiatric concepts. Deviant behavior can be thought of as symptomatic of psychological dysfunction—as an emergency adaptation made by the individual to maintain "the vital balance" when "threatened disorganization evokes tensions which may exceed the power of the habitual 'normal' coping devices of the organism." [41] Adaptation may be at various and sometimes progressively lower levels of total functioning.[42]

> The *first* level or stage or degree of departure from the normal is that state of external and internal affairs which in common parlance is usually called "nervousness." It is a slight but definite impairment of smooth adaptive control, a slight but definite disturbance of organization, a slight but definite failure in coping. . . .

* Count Vittorio Alfieri, Italian poet, 1749-1803.

The relatively mild disturbances of the First Order of dyscontrol psychiatrists may refer to as "anxiety state," "tension state," "mild neuroticism," or "hypochondriasis."

> A *second* level or stage or degree of departure from the normal to increased disorganization is one which . . . rarely results in resignation or hospitalization; it is that group of syndromes which harness individuals with the necessity for expensive compensatory living devices, tension-reducing devices. These are painful symptoms and sometimes pain the environment almost as much as the patient. In the last half-century they have been called "neuroses" and "neurotic syndromes. . . ."

Clinical symptoms representative of the Second Order of dyscontrol are phobias, intoxication and narcotization, compulsions, obsessional thinking, perverse sexual modalities, and ego deformities including infantile, schizoid, and fraudulent personalities.

A First Order of dyscontrol develops when accumulated stress is too great for the individual to handle through habitual coping devices. If First Order devices fail or threaten to fail, a Second Order of dyscontrol develops which may suffice and continue indefinitely, especially if individuals at this level of functioning sustain each other in a deviant sub-culture. However, if Second Order devices fail, the more severe, destructive and alarming symptoms of Third Order dyscontrol appear.

> Our *third* state of regression or disorganization or disequilibrium or dyscontrol is characterized by the escape of the dangerous, destructive impulses, the control of which has caused the ego so much trouble. These are the outbursts, the attacks, the assaults, and the social offenses which result from a considerable degree of ego failure.

Symptoms of Third Order dyscontrol include chronic, repetitive, although relatively mild, aggressions such as paranoid delusions and explosive outbursts of severe "manic" aggressions such as sadistic beatings and murder. As in the case of Second Order dysfunction, victims frequently get social support by joining other equally disturbed persons in extremist social movements. The savage super-patriot to whom all things foreign are anathema,* the bigot who feels threatened by racial and ethnic differences—such persons perceive the world through a personality structure distorted by pathological hate and fear. When "the enemy" comes too close, paranoids endanger themselves and others by viciously striking out in "self-defense." The contagious spread of their delusions can precipitate lynchings, riots, and wars.

> A *fourth* order of dyscontrol involves still more ego failure. Reality loyalty is abandoned completely or very largely; there is disruption of orderly thought as well as behavior; there are demoralization and confusion. These are the

* In the eighteenth century, Samuel Johnson, English author and lexicographer, said: "Patriotism is the last refuge of the scoundrel."

> classical pictures of medieval psychiatry, the "lunacies" of our great-grandfathers, the "insanities" of our grandfathers, the "psychoses" of our fathers.
>
> A *fifth* penultimate stage is proposed, an extremity beyond "psychosis" in the obsolescent sense, the abandonment of the will to live.

From this psychiatric perspective, socialization fails insofar as it fails to equip the individual with the personality structure he needs for coping in socially acceptable ways with the stresses and strains of his particular social milieu. Acceptance of this concept of failure leads to a special concern for building into social institutions those processes and practices conducive to the development and maintenance in individuals of optimum psychological health.

> A crusading New Yorker who practices both law and medicine is fighting to free a client who has been confined for thirty-three years in a mental hospital—and to chart new rights for the mentally ill.
>
> Yesterday this physician-lawyer described his crusade to the American Medical Association:
>
> He is seeking a simple court ruling that every person committed to a mental hospital and kept there against his will has a basic right to adequate treatment—and that if he doesn't get such treatment he must be released. . . .
>
> Dr. Morton Birnbaum, a practicing physician and a former research fellow at Harvard, has been fighting for his legal client for four years. The client is known in court records merely as "Anonymous." He was once a pharmacist in Queens, and he was sent to a New York mental hospital in 1931 after he pulled a fire alarm signal during an acute psychotic episode. He has been there ever since. . . .
>
> In all that time, Dr. Birnbaum charges, his client has received only the most meager psychiatric care; he has been engulfed in the morass of institutional life. For one full year his hospital record showed only a single instance of medical attention—someone noticed him long enough to give him a typhoid shot.[43]

"Anonymous" is just one of thousands of patients who languish unattended in mental "hospitals" across the country. In contrast, a young doctor at the Topeka State Hospital selected for a special program two wards to which the aged and infirm were consigned. The wards housed a total of eighty-eight patients. Their average age was sixty-eight; their average length of stay in the hospital was more than ten years. Fifty-one were bedfast and had been so for an average of ten years; forty-one were spoon-fed every meal. About a dozen had no control of their excretory functions.

The doctor went into these wards of hopeless, vegetating patients with a therapeutic team of cheerful nurses, aides, social workers, and psychiatric residents. He brought in music and television, cages of canaries and potted plants, new lighting fixtures, gay curtains. He planned birthday parties and other social activities. He introduced finger painting, leather tooling, water-color painting, bingo games. The patients themselves painted a shuffleboard court on the floor. One patient was discharged to cooperative relatives three weeks after the program began. By the end of the year, twelve had gone home to live with their families; six had gone out to live by themselves; four went into nursing homes; four found work and became self-supporting. Only nine of the original fifty-one bed patients were still bedfast.[44]

Although even some psychiatrists are skeptical and joke about the "cult of curability," therapy, sometimes unorthodox therapy, has at least been concurrent with a patient's improvement.

A Swedish doctor flew forty-nine patients from a psychiatric hospital near Stockholm to an Italian seaside resort. Most of them were "schizophrenics" of long standing—half of them restricted for years to the hospital grounds, four of them in need of constant attention.

> Under the shock treatment of bright new skies and vividly strange surroundings, tears came to the eyes of a human statue; one man who had barely said a word for years began to talk; another whose mind had seemed utterly sunless laughed for joy at the sight of Rome. People long sunk within themselves began to notice and help their neighbors. After they returned to Sweden, twenty-nine patients were chalked up as having clearly benefited from the holiday, and of these a dozen were scheduled for discharge.[45]

In the treatment of mental patients, conventional custody with its acceptance of illness, authoritarian discipline, social isolation, lock-and-key seclusion, and medical neglect is giving way to active therapy with an acceptance—not of mental illness as such—but as a quality or level of human functioning subject to change through democratic management, group activities, psychochemicals, and psychotherapy.

A shift from custody towards active therapy is also occurring in the penal institutions of the United States. However, of those patients now confined in jails and penitentiaries instead of mental hospitals, more are being harmed than helped. For the young deviant, particularly, prison defeats its theoretical purpose; it is too often not a corrective course but a graduate seminar in crime. The prisoner is grouped with other and often more desperate prisoners under conditions so repressive and so atypical that they could not logically be assumed conducive to the acquisition or acceptance of conventional norms.

> It is not the successful criminal upon whom we inflict our antiquated penal system. It is the unsuccessful criminal, the criminal who really doesn't know how to commit crimes, and who gets caught. Indeed, until he is caught and convicted a man is technically not even called a criminal. The clumsy, the desperate, the obscure, the friendless, the defective, the diseased—these men who commit crimes that do not come off are bad actors, indeed. But they are not the professional criminals, many of whom occupy high places. In some instances the crime is the merest accident or incident or impulse, expressed under unbearable stress. More often the offender is a persistently perverse, lonely, and resentful individual who joins the only group to which he is eligible—the outcasts and the antisocial.
>
> And what do we do with such offenders? After a solemn public ceremony

> we pronounce them enemies of the people, and consign them for arbitrary periods to institutional confinement on the basis of laws written many years ago. Here they languish until time has ground out so many weary months and years. Then with a planlessness and stupidity only surpassed by that of their original incarceration they are dumped back upon society, regardless of whether any change has taken place in them for the better and with every assurance that changes have taken place in them for the worse. Once more they enter the unequal tussle with society. Proscribed for employment by most concerns, they are expected to invent a new way to make a living and to survive without any help from society. . . .
>
> If we were to follow scientific methods, the convicted offender would be detained indefinitely pending a decision as to whether and how and when to reintroduce him successfully into society. All the skill and knowledge of modern behavioral science would be used to examine his personality assets, his liabilities and potentialities, the environment from which he came, its effect upon him, and his effects upon it.
>
> Having arrived at some diagnostic grasp of the offender's personality, those in charge can decide whether there is a chance that he can be redirected into a mutually satisfactory adaptation to the world. If so, the most suitable techniques in education, industrial training, group administration, and psychotherapy should be selectively applied.[46]

Where therapeutic techniques have become part of penal policy, the results have more than justified the effort. Most penologists consider approximately twenty per cent of all prisoners in need of maximum security, and those prisoners in minimum security institutions—admittedly selected—show a high rate of rehabilitation. Compared with an average 63.5 per cent rate of recidivism for federal prisons, Wallkill prison in New York, which puts heavy stress on education and vocational training, has only a 1.5 per cent rate. Because of such demonstrable successes, jails are gradually becoming less like chambers of torture, more like schools and hospitals.

At San Quentin Prison, California ". . . well into this century refractory prisoners were laced into coffin-shaped canvas jackets and thrown into the dungeon, where they howled in pain as the jacket lacings cut off the circulation in their limbs."[47] By 1957, San Quentin had established the largest educational program of any prison in the world, and the California state penal system was one of the most advanced in the nation.

At the California Institution for Men at Chino, some 1,500 prisoners of various ages live today in a ranch-like setting. The "prison" has neither walls nor gun emplacements. The men—minimum security risks with high rehabilitative potential—are chosen from the entire state. They do not wear uniforms, nor do they march, lock-step, to and from their stations. They get both a liberal education and vocational training, learn to participate democratically in prison management, and have a recreation program which includes family picnics on Saturdays, Sundays, and holidays.

California's Conservation Center holds 1,200 minimum and medium security prisoners who are trained to fight fires, replant burned-over forest, combat forest insects and diseases, clear streams, fight erosion, and do other conservation work. Said Governor Edmund G. Brown at the dedication in 1963, the Center provides "dormitories instead of cells, glass instead of bars, dayrooms instead of gun towers, training and counseling facilities rather than walls." Furthermore, it turns "idle men into useful workers and saves money for the taxpayer." [48]

Some penal institutions go a step beyond the minimum security prison. In Saginaw, Michigan, a three-year experimental probation program involving a wide range of criminal offenders demonstrated that with a well-trained staff and caseloads of no more than fifty men, probation could be a safe and satisfactory procedure in seventy per cent of the cases. In New Hampshire, seventy per cent of the felony offenders were on probation in 1960; fewer than ten percent violated their probation. The rationale for probation is that "real rehabilitation can only be performed in freedom." [49]

Further change in penal policy in the United States may be anticipated by the Swedish system.

> A significant proportion of Swedish criminal offenders are committed to mental hospitals rather than to prisons, for Swedish law permits considerable flexibility in the treatment of these offenders. During the fifteen-year period 1935-1950, ninety-six persons were convicted of murder in Sweden, and eighty per cent of them were committed to mental hospitals, their stays there varying from eight months to fifteen years.[50]

Those prisons which do exist in Sweden are mainly open prisons—without walls, gun towers, or armed guards. Prisoners furnish their rooms with the comforts of home—carpets, curtains, pictures, flowers, radios, and many have home furloughs every four months.

WHO IS TO BLAME?

Delinquents, criminals, neurotics, psychotics, Beatniks, derelicts and other dysfunctional personalities are not alien bodies in an otherwise healthy social system. Our society, far from being consistently moral and rational, is in constant conflict with its own cultural ideals.

Mores of individuals and groups often contradict rather than reinforce each other: family, religious, education, economic, and political values rarely coincide. Groups with legal status may rationalize illegal actions: churches—often accepted as models of morality—regularly raise funds by bingo parties and raffles, even in states where gambling is against the law. Segregation reaches a peak on Sunday mornings when groups professing to acknowledge the fatherhood of God and the brotherhood of man meet to worship. School boards too often dismiss as expensive or irrelevant proposals for better schools, better teachers, better playgrounds and more of them. Conservationists—and psychiatrists—plead for the preservation of wilderness areas which commercial interests would exploit. Incompatible values and goals within and among social institutions are many and varied, but none are as totally contradictory as those within the government itself. In time of war, the military trains individuals to commit acts of violence which are against conscience and which, in time of peace, would be prosecuted as criminal.

Socialization works against itself when pressures exerted on an individual at one time are inconsistent with those exerted at another time. *When socialization fails, is it a failure of the agents of socialization to implant acceptable norms and goals in a sound personality structure or willfully perverse behavior on the part of the individual?* Pre-scientific attitudes and practices relative to antisocial and asocial behavior generally agree with those of the Duchess in *Alice in Wonderland*:

> Speak roughly to your little boy
> And beat him when he sneezes.
> He only does it to annoy,
> Because he knows it teases.

Now we are not certain he only does it to annoy. We are beginning to look for the irritating "allergens." We are asking, *How delinquent, how irrational are the institutions of society? Is Society itself yet socialized? When socialization fails, who can trace the tangled lineage of blame?*

Notes

1. Samuel Butler, *The Way of All Flesh* (New York: Dutton, 1903) in Karl Menninger, *The Vital Balance* (New York: The Viking Press, Inc., 1963), p. 125.
2. Bernard Berelson and Gary A. Steiner, *Human Behavior* (New York: Harcourt, Brace & World, Inc., 1963), p. 627.
3. Ernest R. Hilgard, *Introduction to Psychology* (New York, Burlingame: Harcourt, Brace & World, Inc., 3rd ed., 1962), p. 525.
4. Kenneth Lamott, "Socrates at San Quentin," *The New Yorker,* May 2, 1959, pp. 130-132.
5. Sheldon and Eleanor Glueck, *Unraveling Juvenile Delinquency* (Cambridge: Harvard University Press, 1950).
6. Undated brochure distributed by Mental Health Association of Marin County, California.
7. *San Francisco Chronicle,* October 30, 1958, p. 7.
8. Jane Fator, "Juvenile Delinquency: A Theoretical Overview," in *Juvenile Delinquency, An Analysis of Theory and Research Towards a Program of Action* (United Community Fund of San Francisco, 1961), pp. 42-65.
9. Sheldon and Eleanor Glueck, *Family Environment and Delinquency* (Boston: Houghton Mifflin Company, 1962), pp. 14-15.
10. Richard A. Cloward and Lloyd E. Ohlin, *New Perspectives on Juvenile Delinquency* (New York: School of Social Work, Columbia University, 1959).
11. Cloward and Ohlin, *op. cit.,* p. 127.
12. Cloward and Ohlin, *op. cit.,* p. 89.
13. *Time Magazine,* April 7, 1958, pp. 21-22.
14. James V. Bennett (Director of the Federal Bureau of Prisons), "A Cool Look at 'The Crime Crisis,'" *Harper's Magazine,* April, 1964, p. 125.
15. Reprinted in *Harper's Magazine,* April, 1964, p. 126.
16. Ralph J. Gleason, review of *The Big Bankroll, The Life and Times of Arnold Rothstein,* by Leo Katcher (Harper & Row, Publishers, 1959) in "This World," *San Francisco Chronicle,* March 22, 1959, p. 15.
17. *San Francisco Chronicle,* March 29, 1959, p. 11.
18. *San Francisco Chronicle,* April 1, 1959, p. 8.
19. *San Francisco Chronicle,* April 12, 1959, p. 29.
20. L. Joseph Stone and Joseph Church, *Childhood and Adolescence* (New York: Random House, 1957), pp. 368-369.
21. E. J. Kahn, Jr., "Annals of Crime," *The New Yorker,* April 11, 1959, p. 126.
22. From an anonymous student report.
23. Menninger, *The Vital Balance,* p. 188.
24. Hans Selye, *The Stress of Life* (New York: McGraw-Hill, Inc., 1956), also *The Physiology and Pathology of Exposure to Stress* (Montreal: Acta, 1950).
25. F. J. Kallmann, *Heredity in Health and Mental Disorder* (New York: W. W. Norton & Company, Inc., 1953).
26. Leo Srole, Thomas Langner, Stanley Michael, Marvin Opler, and Thomas Rennie, *Mental Health in the Metropolis: The Midtown Manhattan Study* (New York: McGraw-Hill Book Company, 1962).
27. Francis Rigney, "What Makes Beatniks Tick," *San Francisco Chronicle,* April 2, 1959, p. 6.

28. Allen Brown, "Life and Love Among the Beatniks," in "This World," *San Francisco Chronicle,* June 15, 1958, p. 4.
29. Allen Brown, "Life and Love Among the Beatniks," "This World," *San Francisco Chronicle,* June 22, 1958, pp. 5-6.
30. Gene Feldman and Max Gartenberg, eds., *The Beat Generation and the Angry Young Men* (New York: Dell Publishing Co., Inc., 1958).
31. Sara Harris, *Skid Row, U.S.A.* (Garden City, New York: Doubleday & Company, Inc., 1956).
32. *San Francisco Chronicle,* April 5, 1959, pp. 1-2.
33. Allen Brown, "Life and Love Among the Beatniks," in "This World," *San Francisco Chronicle,* June 15, 1958, p. 5.
34. Menninger, *The Vital Balance,* pp. 406-407.
35. *San Francisco Chronicle,* March 21, 1959, p. 6.
36. Bennett, "A Cool Look at 'The Crime Crisis,'" p. 125.
37. Menninger, *The Vital Balance,* p. 416.
38. Earl Raab and Gertrude Jaeger Selznick, *Major Social Problems* (New York: Harper & Row, Publishers, 1959), p. 148.
39. D. O. Hebb, "The Mammal and His Environment," *American Journal of Psychiatry,* Vol. CXI, 1955, p. 831.
40. Francis J. Braceland, "Modern Trends in Psychiatry," *Therapeutic Notes,* Vol. 65, No. 4, April, 1958, pp. 97-98.
41. Menninger, *The Vital Balance,* p. 153.
42. *Ibid.,* pp. 162-163.
43. David Perlman, "A Battle for Rights of the Mentally Ill," *San Francisco Chronicle,* June 25, 1964, pp. 1 and 13.
44. Menninger, *The Vital Balance,* p. 391.
45. Robert Littel, "Schizophrenics in the Sun," *Harper's Magazine,* September, 1962, p. 62.
46. Menninger, "Verdict Guilty—Now What?," *Harper's Magazine,* August, 1959, pp. 61-62.
47. Lamott, "Socrates at San Quentin," p. 123.
48. *San Francisco Chronicle,* July 14, 1963, p. 1A.
49. Dr. Marcel Frym, President of the American Society of Criminology, as quoted in *Newsweek,* April 25, 1960, p. 116.
50. Marshall B. Clinard, *Sociology of Deviant Behavior* (New York: Holt, Rinehart & Winston, Inc., 1957), p. 517.

Man seeketh in society
comfort, use, and protection.

FRANCIS BACON (1561-1626)

iv

Society—Agent of Man

We are members one of another.

Ephesians 4:25

8

Togetherness

MAN IS THE CREATURE of culture. Culture is the creature of man—man, not alone, but *in society, together* with other men.

Society as the Patient, The Web of Society, The Affluent Society, The Folk Society, The Sane Society, Mass Society, The Multigroup Society—all these are sociological topics. Sociology is the study of man in *society. Society* is the key word. What does it mean?

Society is an enduring, cooperating social system, a patterned system of interaction, functioning to maintain itself and perpetuate the species. Society includes the social structures through which individuals and groups interact as well as the processes which characterize such interaction. *Homo sapiens* is a biological being, but *man* is a social being, and his aspirations and capabilities take on new meaning when seen in the context of society.

Human society is extraordinarly complicated. It is decreed, as are simpler plant and animal societies, by biological necessity, but it is shaped by culture. In *Brave New World*,[1] men and women are bred to fit the categories of a fixed social scheme; but in reality, human destiny is not predetermined and society is not stable. *Homo sapiens* is an unspecialized, adaptable species born into a society of many specializations. By choice or chance, a particular individual belongs to a segment of world society defined by geographical, political, and class boundaries. Were this his only identification, he would still be at sea. "Society" is too impersonally defined, too vast, too diverse.

An individual needs safe harbors wherein he can find others of his kind—secure vantage points from which he can view the larger social panorama. It is within the social harbors we call *groups* that action meaningful to the individual takes place, and through groups that he defines his place in the large, formidable hierarchy of a modern society.

UNITED WE STAND

Every day you, as one individual, interact voluntarily, and sometimes involuntarily, with many different groups, large and small, intimate and impersonal, formal and casual. Each group, in your interaction with it, exerts some degree of pressure on you for conformity to its particular values. You feel the pressure first in childhood: "Aw, Dad, all the other kids . . ." Even as adults we still, consciously or unconsciously, tend to adjust our behavior to the norms of the groups with which we identify.

"The group is a jealous master. It encourages participation, indeed, demands it, but it demands one kind of participation—its own kind—and the better integrated with it a member becomes the less free he is to express himself in other ways."[2] "The price of being independent is to be shut out of the group."[3] How to belong without being submerged is a dilemma which one can solve only by charting an ideological direction between the extremes of compliance and independence. The dilemma is inescapable. We each need individual identity, yet we need each other; we must find our unique selves, yet we must belong or perish.

For perspective on the personal and social problems involved in the complex interactions of individuals and groups, we need some understanding of (1) the nature of groups; (2) groups in action, including intra- and intergroup relationships; and (3) social processes.

Genesis of Groups

Man alone, isolated from others of his kind, is only a biological being. Within and through groups he becomes a human, social being, a person playing a variety of social roles. The *potential* for social interaction is innate, but the *ability* to interact is learned. The long period of infant helplessness in monkeys, apes, and humans makes it imperative that the young be nurtured by others. An adequate nurturing experience is the first crucial step in social development; association with peers is the next. Nurturance and peer group associations combined not only make it possible for an individual to interact with others, but this experience then makes it impossible for him to maintain his physical and psychological equilibrium without continued interaction. The individual is born and bred a group member. Groups are so integral a part of man's history that early behavioral scientists got caught in circular reasoning, trying to explain gregariousness in terms of itself. *Homo sapiens,* they said, had a *gregarious instinct,* which was only saying that we form groups because we have a tendency to form groups. This unfruitful conjecture was based on limited evidence: fossil indications of group life among prehistoric men and deductive reasoning from observing the behavior of primates in zoos and laboratories. Today zoologists, anthropologists, and psychologists—through field studies of simians in their native habitat, of primitive societies, and of the special society of children—are contributing to our understanding of the prehistoric beginnings of human society. We now think we know why our primate cousins form groups. Through groups they protect the individual and perpetuate the species, and within groups they find, as individuals, mutual support and pleasure. Assuming comparable social development among all primates, we have a clue as to why early pre-agricultural man formed groups. Groups are functional; they were first formed to meet specific biological and psychological needs.

The social groupings of simians are comparable to social groupings in primitive societies. "Children" grow away from the family and spend increasingly more time with their peers. Females have "hen parties," and males gang-up with their "pals." Anthropologists once perceived the family as the key group in the development of society, because the family nurtured and protected the young and perpetuated the species. Now, however, they recognize clubs, secret societies, clans, and other friendship or nonkinship groups as also significant. One anti-feminist anthropologist based his case for the importance of nonkinship groups on what he perceived as a basic antagonism between the sexes.*

> Women, conservative and concerned only with the family and the kinship unit, were really selfishly antisocial; they tried to keep men isolated in the little world of marriage. But, men, who did not like women anyway, always tended to escape into hunting and warlike activities. . . . Because their sex love was more profound than men's, women were able to overcome their dislike of the loathsome male creatures. But men, once sexually gratified, were anxious to rid themselves of the stifling bonds flung about them by their sex partners.[4]

Other anthropologists have stressed more positive bases for groups—similarity of age, status, or interests. Some primitive groups are hunting clubs, others provide a social setting for making musical instruments or weapons, for wood-carving and leatherwork, for ancestor worship and other rituals. The important general consensus is that the primitive clubman—as well as the primitive family man—has played an important role in the development of society.

We do not have to follow the anthropologist to the distant retreats of primitive men to see society in the making. Within our own complex, modern

---

* Heinrich Schurtz (1863-1903). Herr Schurtz could have been reacting with less than scientific objectivity to the rampant feminist movement of the late nineteenth century.

society, children have a social life of their own which tends to recapitulate the social experience of the race. Observe children and you observe the genesis of groups and of society.

The society of children is a special sub-culture with traditions and values of its own. "This children's sub-culture shares many of the attributes of primitive cultures. It is handed down by word of mouth, it includes many rituals * whose original meaning has been lost, it is hidebound and resistant to alien—in this case, adult—influences." [5]

> . . . Younger children . . . lurk around the fringes of established neighborhood groups, drinking in the wisdom and manner of the older children, avidly learning and practicing the rituals . . . and occasionally merging with the group. Probably the first real coalition of younger school children consists in the sharing of a secret. Genuine affiliation and membership, and the climax of love for the secret society are found in the middle of this age range (6 to 12). By the time the later middle years are reached, groups and gangs are less likely to exist exclusively for the sake of belongingness or for the formal rites they practice, and are more likely to be organized around particular kinds of activities and functions. The older school child is likely to be involved in and handle easily multiple memberships and affiliations. The fact that he is moving closer to adult society and its cleavages is also evident in the composition of the groups and cliques to which he belongs. In the patterning of social organization during the middle years, as in other aspects of development, we can see at work the general principles of increasing differentiation followed by functional subordination. For instance, the gang spirit at first appears as something valuable in its own right, so that just being with the gang is satisfaction enough; later, the value lies in the things the gang does. . . .
>
> Left to themselves, children are likely to define their affiliations on a geographical base: the home block (except in rural areas). Outside "our block" one has a strong sense of being in alien or even hostile territory.[6]
>
> Toward the middle of the school years, group life is often marked by a change from the loose shifting organization of the gang or neighborhood group to short-lived but tightly and elaborately organized clubs, usually with an overabundance of officers, codified rules, ceremonies, oaths, and vague but portentous secrets. When they band together into clubs, children enunciate ambitious if ill-defined purposes and goals, but the underlying, unspoken motivation seems to be to further formalize and solidify the children's sense of belonging.[7]

Group commonly connotes rapport and fellowship, but sociologically, love and hate are equally binding. Three five-year-old boys may happily play cowboy together. They constitute a group. Ten minutes later they may be fighting over who has the horse. They still constitute a group. "Groups are sociological wholes; the unity of these sociological wholes can be defined

* Children, like primitives, venerate custom. Many contemporary games and chants have come almost unchanged through centuries of cataclysmic changes in adult society. Among the most ancient are hopscotch, marbles, crack-the-whip, hide-and-seek, duck on the rock, blindman's buff, Red Rover, dodge-ball, keep-away, Jacks, and London Bridge.

operationally in the same way as a unity of any other dynamic whole, namely, by the interdependence of its parts." [8] When two or more individuals communicate with each other in any way, they interact and thereby constitute a group. Communication may be by words or gestures, smoke signals or code, across a room or across a continent. It is the interaction, the conscious stimulus-response interdependence which is essential. Even an entertainer and an audience constitute a group. Within a group, meaning is exchanged. The parts are interdependent; the whole is organized. Stimulus evokes response, and response in turn becomes a stimulus and evokes a counter-response. Some lead, others follow; and interaction is guided, tacitly or explicitly, by the structure of the group.

> It happens with actors . . . that every audience is a new audience. A nuance understood and approved is responsible for the power, ease, and success of the very next line we utter. We know our parts; we have played them time and again for many years, but the moment there is a failure of response from the audience, we become mere lifeless puppets. Indeed, it is always wrong to say that an audience follows the actors with interest. It is the actors who follow the audience; the play is in its hands. If it were not ridiculous, it would be for us to applaud the audience and for the audience to acknowledge our applause.[9]

Group is sometimes used in a broad sense, synonymous with *aggregate* and *category*. Aggregate, however, correctly refers to individuals held together only in some physical sense: people in an airport waiting room, residents of a river valley; and category refers to individuals identified by some common characteristic: blondes, bald-headed men, students, school drop-outs. Even age groups such as teen-agers and octogenarians, minority groups, occupational groups or racial groups are, technically, categories. Interaction, not proximity or similarity, is the essential matrix of a group.

Classification of Groups—Objective Criteria

Countless groups make up the hierarchy of modern society, and we can only begin to understand the similarities and differences among them if we find some bases for classification. Is the group intimate or impersonal? Is the organization formal or casual? Is membership a condition of birth or circumstance, a matter of deliberate choice, or as a result of coercion? These questions involve objective criteria which determine whether a group is *Primary* or *Secondary, Psychological* or *Organizational, Optional* or *Non-Optional.*

Primary and Secondary Groups

Human beings form groups, and groups, in turn, form human beings. To ask which is most basic is like asking, "Which came first, the chicken or the egg?"

> . . . human nature is not something existing separately in the individual, but a *group-nature or primary phase of society*, a relatively simple and general condition of the social mind . . . It is the nature which is developed and expressed in those simple, face-to-face groups that are somewhat alike in all societies: groups of the family, the playground, and the neighborhood. In the essential similarity of these is to be found the basis, in experience, for similar ideas and sentiments in the human mind. In these, everywhere, human nature comes into existence. Man does not have it at birth; he cannot acquire it except through fellowship; and it decays in isolation.[10]

The small, intimate, "face-to-face" groups of family, playground and neighborhood are the *primary groups* of society.

> Primary groups are primary in the sense that they give the individual his earliest and completest experience of social unity, and also in the sense that they do not change in the same degree as more elaborate relations, but form a comparatively permanent source out of which the latter are ever springing. . . .[11]
>
> . . . The result of intimate association, psychologically, is a certain fusion of individualities in a common whole, so that one's very self, for many purposes at least, is the common life and purpose of the group. Perhaps the simplest way of describing this wholeness is by saying that it is a "we"; it involves the sort of sympathy and mutual identification for which "we" is the natural expression.[12]

The primary groups of folk societies are of two types: the intimate neighborhood and the extended family. In both cases, the strong "we" feeling is reinforced by cultural homogeneity. The people are typically semi-literate or illiterate and earn livelihoods as hunters, herdsmen, or farmers. The only significant division of labor is the universal one of sex. Everyone is familiar with and participates in the traditions of the society, and strangers come as welcome traders or as enemies—rarely as immigrants. In contrast, urban groups are mainly the alliances of institutional structure, formed, not by kinship or friendship, but by contract or agreement. Strangers come as immigrants, and they may remain strangers, even to their neighbors. In the complex, heterogeneous urban environment, neighborhood intimacy does not come naturally and the geographic and social mobility characteristic of urban life makes it easier to shed relatives than to gather them together in an extended family.

In its beginning, human society was made up exclusively of *primary groups,* but the general course of civilization has been from small folk communities dominated by primary groups to large urban societies dominated by a network of impersonal *secondary groups.*

A shift from folk society to urban society brings a shift from *Gemeinschaft* to *Gessellschaft* community structure.[13] In the *Gemeinschaft,* or "communal society," people feel a strong sense of belonging; they are either kith or kin. People do not voluntarily join a *Gemeinschaft* society. They are born into it or they "grow" into it as into a clique of friends. Social roles arise spontaneously out of one's "natural" position within the community: father, mother, child of a hunter, brother of a chief. . . . In the *Gesellschaft,* or "associational society," on the other hand, most social relations are voluntary and based upon self-interest.

Gemeinschaft relations, which characterize primary groups, are based on sentiment and compassion. Concern is for the welfare of others in the group and mutual obligations are limited only by the resources of each member. Felt obligations in primary groups often lead to self-sacrifice. (One friend said that she never realized her mother liked any part of a chicken except the wings and back until she herself married. Her husband preferred breast; both children wanted drumsticks. As her mother before her, she ate what was left —back and wings.)

Gesellschaft relations, which characterize the secondary groups of urban society, are based on reason and expediency. The concern of each individual is for his own self-interest, and mutual obligations are limited to those informally implied in the relationship or formally specified by contract. The personal needs and problems of others are irrelevant, and the subject of communication is confined to the practical necessities of the situation. If you stop for gas at a service station, you don't really care if the attendant has a headache; you don't expect him to show you a picture of his wife and children or complain about his mother-in-law. You expect and want no more than courteous, efficient service. In an urban society, transactions must be made with impersonal dispatch or the work would never get done. *Gesellschaft* relations are neither better nor worse than *Gemeinschaft* relations. They simply serve a different purpose.

Organizational and Psychological Groups

A group is not merely the sum of its members. As a dynamic whole, it has properties of its own; its stability and goals are different from those of the individuals who comprise it. Some groups, both primary and secondary, exist as *planned organizations,* buttressed by a name or symbol, specific beliefs and behavior, laws and by-laws, and such cultural props as songs, oaths, pins, hats, and dues. *Organizations* typically outlive the members; the groupness is a persisting structure imposed by the organization on varying memberships.

The relative permanence of organizations gives them status, particularly in the thoughts of their own members. We once noticed the conviviality which pervaded a San Francisco hotel lobby and said, "A convention!" To verify the hunch, we approached a man and asked what group he represented. He steadied himself and said, between hiccups, "The National Macaroni and Spaghetti Manufacturers of America!" He was proud. Belonging sustains a man! Many other organizations—occupational, educational, religious, racial, recreational, political, economic and fraternal—also claim loyal memberships. For example:

Antique Automobile Club of America
Amies de la Jeune Fille

Association of Inner Wheel Clubs
Society for the Preservation and Encouragement of Barber Shop Singing in America
Chinchilla Breeders of America
Congrès International pour le Latin Vivant *
Ducks Unlimited
American Feline Society
Friends of the Pleistocene *
Hay Fever Prevention Society
Horseshoe Pitchers Association of America
Laryngological, Rhinological, and Otological Society
Loyal Order of Moose
International Association of Seed Crushers *
International Committee for Silent Games *
International Union for Protecting Public Morality *
International Union for the Study of Social Insects *
Women's National Sabbath Alliance
National Button Society of America
National Association of Watch and Clock Collectors
Permanent International Committee of Underground Town Planning *
Society for the Abolition of Blasphemy Laws *
Symposium on Responsibility *
United Order of True Sisters

These are all relatively small voluntary organizations of limited influence, but civilization brings centralization, and some corporate organizations are so large that their power reaches across continents and through cultures. These include gigantic economic bureaucracies such as duPont, General Motors, Shell Oil Company, National Fruit Company, and international military alliances such as NATO and SEATO.

Other groups, in extreme contrast to bureaucratic organizations, exist only because two or more individuals perceive themselves as a group; the groupness is a tenuous structure imposed by individuals on each other. Such a "psychological group" [14] persists only as long as the particular individuals involved maintain their interdependence, and, commonly, the group members outlive the group.

> The cars of the migrant people crawled out of the side roads onto the great cross-country highway, and they took the migrant way to the West. In the daylight they scuttled like bugs to the westward; and as the dark caught them, they clustered like bugs near to shelter and to water. And because they were lonely and perplexed, because they had all come from a place of sadness and worry and defeat, and because they were all going to a new mysterious place, they huddled together; they talked together; they shared their lives, their

---

* From a partial list of international organizations reporting to the Library of Congress, Washington, D.C.—*The New Yorker,* August 9, 1958, p. 15.
Other organizations listed in *The World Almanac,* Harry Hansen, ed. (New York: New York *World Telegram,* 1960), pp. 502-517.

food, and the things they hoped for in the new country. Thus it might be that one family camped near a spring, and another camped for the spring and for company, and a third because two families had pioneered the place and found it good. And when the sun went down, perhaps twenty families and twenty cars were there.

In the evening a strange thing happened: the twenty families became one family, the children were the children of all. The loss of home became one loss, and the golden time in the West was one dream. And it might be that a sick child threw despair into the hearts of twenty families, of a hundred people; that a birth there in a tent kept a hundred people quiet and awestruck through the night and filled a hundred people with the birth-joy in the morning. A family which the night before had been lost and fearful might search its goods to find a present for a new baby. In the evening, sitting about the fires, the twenty were one. They grew to be units of the camps, units of the evenings and the nights. A guitar unwrapped from a blanket and tuned—and the songs, which were all of the people, were sung in the nights. Men sang the words, and women hummed the tunes.

Every night a world created, complete with furniture—friends made and enemies established; a world complete with braggarts and with cowards, with quiet men, with humble men, with kindly men. Every night relationships that make a world, established; and every morning the world torn down like a circus.[15]

Optional and Non-Optional Groups

Organizations are planned; psychological groups happen spontaneously. Membership in either may be *optional* or *non-optional.* Some groups you choose; others, such as the Army, choose you.* Although the ancient philosophical problem of free will has not been settled, modern scientific thought assumes a limited freedom at best, and we do not always have as much choice as we think. *Optional* and *non-optional* are relative classifications. Aptitude, experience, and the pressures of an immediate situation tilt every decision one way or another. A clique of friends is a relatively optional group. Groups based on race and sex are relatively non-optional. Sometimes, however, racial identity is ambiguous and the individual does have a choice. A light Negro can pass for white. A darker Negro with aquiline features can straighten his hair and pass for Arabian or Indian. Sometimes even sex is ambiguous. An hermaphrodite, born with physiological characteristics of both sexes, may live part of his life as "he," the rest of it as "she." James may undergo surgical operation and emerge as Jane. In other cases, an individual's emotional affiliation may contradict his sex.

The only completely non-optional group is ancestral family. We can choose friends and lovers, but not relatives. Juliet urged Romeo to disclaim his heritage

*The Army is relatively non-optional. Some individuals enlist; others protest the draft and claim exemption on the basis of homosexuality, mental or physical disability, or moral objections to war.

and change his name, but genetically, Romeo would always be Romeo, son of Montague.

> O Romeo, Romeo! wherefore art thou Romeo?
> Deny thy father and refuse thy name;
> Or, if thou wilt not, be but sworn my love,
> And I'll no longer be a Capulet . . .
> 'Tis but thy name that is my enemy;
> Thou art thyself, though not a Montague.
> What's Montague? it is nor hand, nor foot,
> Nor arm, nor face, nor any other part
> Belonging to a man. O, be some other name!
> What's in a name? that which we call a rose,
> By any other name would smell as sweet;
> So Romeo would, were he not Romeo call'd,
> Retain that dear perfection which he owes
> Without that title. Romeo, doff thy name,
> And for that name which is no part of thee
> Take all myself.[16]

Primary and *Secondary, Optional* and *Non-Optional, Psychological* and *Organizational* are neither absolute nor mutually exclusive classifications. Instead, they are theoretical reference points implying *more of this* and *less of that.*

The family, for example, often thought of as *Primary, Optional* and *Psychological,* actually has elements of all of the opposite categories. There is calculated self-interest, characteristic of secondary groups: "Better write Auntie or she might not remember your birthday!" There is the coercion associated with non-optional groups: "If you dare divorce me, I'll sue you for a pretty penny!" And there are organizational aspects in the surname, family crest or coat-of-arms, family rules and rituals.

Classification of Groups—Subjective Criteria

Any objectively defined group—Primary or Secondary, Psychological or Organizational, Optional or Non-Optional—can be further described subjectively as a *Membership* group or a *Reference* group, an *In-group* or an *Out-group,* depending on what the group means to the particular individual. Any one group is variously perceived: one man's in-group may be another man's out-group, and one man's membership group may be another man's reference group.*

* Reference groups are usually thought of in the positive sense, but they also function negatively. "Don't act like a ——————!" Furthermore, any one individual may have a conflict of loyalties. His membership in one group may be incompatible with that in another, yet he may be psychologically committed to both.

Reference Groups and Membership Groups

Implicit in the distinction between *membership* and *reference* groups is the recognition that group membership is not just physical belonging but also psychological belonging. Groups in which we actively participate or in which we have a formally determined place are obviously *membership* groups. They may or may not have any profound effect on behavior. You may, for example, be a registered Republican, yet vote Democratic. However, if you identify strongly with a membership group and depend on the group norms to sustain your own point of view, then the *membership* group also functions as a *reference group*. You are allied with it in spirit as well as in fact. There are other groups to which you do not belong but to which you aspire. You accept the attitudes and behavior of a particular group as your own in the wishful thought that imitating its members will make you accepted by them.

Reference groups are particularly significant to the striving individual in a mobile society where myths and hope abound. They are status symbols, upward steps on the social ladder. Glory as well as guilt is had by association. If a socially ambitious freshman set his sights on a particular fraternity, he should know that:

> . . . Many fraternities make a preliminary investigation of a prospective pledge before he occupies his dormitory room. What was his high school record? Athletics? Politics? Cheer-leading? Scholarship? Debating? Does he come from a respectable family? Would his parents fit in if asked to be chaperons at a fraternity function? Did they go to college? Is his father an alumnus of the fraternity—or of some other good fraternity? Is his family able to give him a substantial allowance? Will he have a car at college? [17]

The really farsighted aspirant even goes through high school systematically playing the right role for the brothers he hopes to have. Similarly, if an ambitious man chooses a particular country club as a reference group, he knows that:

> Country clubs vary greatly in both characteristics and expense. A few, like the Myopia Hunt, the Tuxedo, the Saddle and Cycle, the Burlingame, and several others in this class, are more expensive to belong to than any clubs in London or New York, and are precisely the same in matters of membership and management. It is quite as difficult to be elected to them as to any of the exclusive clubs in the cities—more so if anything—because they are open to the family and friends of every member, whereas in a man's club in a city his membership gives the privilege of the club to no one but himself personally. The test question always put by (club) governors at elections is, "Are the candidate's friends as well as his family likely to be agreeable to the present members of the club?" If not, he is not admitted.[18]

He who wants to belong minds his manners, his politics, his religion, and picks his wife and friends carefully.

Reference groups and membership groups in their relationship to each other make the fact of social stratification a personal experience. We believe the myths of our society. Fame and fortune are not just will-o'-the-wisps. Fame *does* come to the unknown; fortune *is* found by the poor. Few of us live without aspirations. We hope for a better job, higher pay, a new car, a house in a respectable neighborhood. If we are middle class, we hope our children will at least be upper middle class. We all try in one way or another to "keep up with, or excel, the Joneses." Reference groups thus become the most subtle of tyrants. By them we orient our lives.

In-Groups and Out-Groups

In-groups are "we." *Out-groups* are "they." The stronger our identification with a group, the more our status is linked to that of the group and the less objective we are in evaluating it. We tend to perceive the positive aspects of our group, the negative aspects of other groups. From our point of view, "we" are better than "they." When we want to emphasize our superiority, we use labels: "reds," "Commies," "gringos," "kikes," "wops," "egg-heads," "squares," and thus we build ideological as well as physical barriers against "them." The cleavage defined by in-groups and out-groups may be as confined and intense as the traditional enmity between the Montagues and Capulets, or it may be as broad and brooding as the suspicion separating believers from non-believers.

In-groups and out-groups occur at all levels, and the more an in-group approximates the character of a primary group, the greater our loyalty and the stronger our feeling of belonging. In the Air Force, for example, men feel the greatest loyalty to the crew of their own plane with whom they have intimate face-to-face relationships. They have an ever-widening circle of diminishing loyalty as the in-groups become larger. A bomber wing (or fighting unit) evokes more in-group feeling than the Air Force; and the latter more than the total armed forces or the United States itself.

Whether large and generalized or small and specific, in-groups and out-groups have a tenuous identity. The boundaries between them respond with curious facility to social expediency. A threatening outsider can force rivals into an alliance. With changing circumstances or goals, in-groups and out-groups can ignore dissensions and reorient themselves in relation to a common cause.

GREETINGS TO A RUSSIAN STEAMER (1861)

Russia and the United States have always been, are now, and will doubtless ever remain fast friends. San Francisco therefore greeted with delight the arrival last Friday of the Russian war steamer *Calevala,* bearing 173 crewmen and 17 officers.

This sloop of war comes to us from the only nation in the world to cordially sympathize with our Government in crushing the most monstrous treason recorded in history. Prince Gortschakoff recently wrote to President Lincoln that it is the destiny of Russia and America to preserve the balance of power in the world. And we will undoubtedly support that country in the great wars of the future to decide the question of national supremacy in Europe.

At a time when England and France are witnessing our civil war with undisguised satisfaction, we turn with grateful pride to our natural friend and ally, Russia. And the citizens of San Francisco have opened their hearts and homes to the Czar's subjects who will remain in our port for several weeks.[19]

But long-term alliances are the exception rather than the rule. It is for short-term alliances that peoples have suffered and died.

During World War II, Great Britain, Russia, and China were all our allies; we were fighting Fascism together. But Great Britain was once an enemy out-group. We fought them for independence in 1776, and we fought them again in 1812. Today Russia and China are enemies in a cold war because we perceive them as formidable economic and political out-groups challenging *our* way of life. Tomorrow the Russians may align themselves with the United States and other "have" nations in a new in-group against the "have-not" nations of Asia and South America. In-groups of nations and individuals are opportunistic, and expediency can make strange bedfellows. Who knows who "we" will be tomorrow?

In-groups and out-groups are both uniting and disuniting. They act as cradles of ethnocentrism, fostering "group-bound" thinking and prejudice, as well as group tensions.

> . . . What we are pointing to is the danger inherent in the multiplicity of compartmented groups unless some way is found of evoking the primary sense of unity that far transcends them.
>
> For these conditions strengthen the natural tendency to group-bound thinking, the gravest peril in the social orientation of modern man. We tend to view the members of other groups as—members of other groups, rather than as persons. They are workers or they are employers; they are miners or teamsters or elevator operators, not individuals; they are manufacturers or bankers or civil servants, not fellow men. We see them in the light of the alleged attributes of their group, with all the distortions fostered by difference of interest or of station. The tendency itself is as old as human nature. It is as old as the first Cain who was a tiller of the ground and looked askance on the first Abel who was a keeper of sheep. But modern organization has enormously extended its range and intensified its expression. It is the business of every organization to assert its own interests over (and) against the interests of other organizations—this principle has just as much sway whether we live in a socio-capitalist or in a socialist economy. The executive of every organization is an agency trained and specialized for this process of assertion. Practically every organization labors to promote in its membership the sense of the paramountcy of the group interest. Thus there are many forces assiduously at work to propagate group consciousness and indirectly to minimize and to weaken the integrity of the greater community.[20]

Paradoxically, in-groups also cut across formidable barriers. Common human sympathies and interests can unite persons whom cultural differences might otherwise separate.

> We once had the privilege of having a young woman from Lahore, Pakistan, as a guest in our home. She wore sari and sandals; her religion was Islam, she defended the tradition of arranged marriages. Our cultures were half a world apart, yet our rapport was immediate. The reasons? She was a warm-hearted, intelligent human being *first*, a Pakistani *second*. She had a Master's degree in sociology and the ability and willingness to appraise her culture and ours frankly and objectively. We had more essentials in common with her than with the majority of people in our own neighborhood among whom we have lived for years. Attiya stayed with us only three days; yet, when we said goodbye, it was to a dear friend. We had no reservations. She "belonged." [21]

If *society* is the focus of study, as it traditionally has been in sociology, then society is perceived as a composite of variously defined groups: primary and secondary, organizational and psychological, optional and non-optional, membership groups and reference groups, in-groups and out-groups. If, however, the *group* is the focus of study, as it is becoming under the influence of experimental social psychology, then groups are perceived *as* society and attention is directed to group structure and processes.

Group Structure

"You have to go through channels." In large, formal groups—the Navy, for example, or a business organization—"channels" are the structure through which authority and responsibility flow. If an individual has a complaint, a question, a suggestion, he can't deal directly. He has to go through channels.

"Is the lady of the house in?" The door-to-door salesman asks this question in deference to the structure of the intimate family group. He knows from experience that the "lady of the house" is the usual purchasing agent.

"Let's ask George. He'll probably know." Even in the most informal friendship group there is some role differentiation. Some individuals are leaders; others are followers.

Leaders and followers . . . father, mother, big sister, little brother . . . president, vice-president, assistant to the vice-president . . . Fleet Admiral, Admiral, Vice Admiral, Rear Admiral . . . Every group, by definition, is organized—tenuously or tightly. Within every group there is a pattern of relationships. Members assume different positions, have different roles and correspondingly different rights and duties. The person filling a particular position is expected to manifest behavior and attitudes defined by group norms as appropriate to that position. The master is expected to command. The servant is expected to obey.

Awareness of the relationship between group *structure* and individual and group *behavior* first came as a by-product of the study of other social phenomena. For example, a study of juvenile groups in Chicago revealed facts of general significance:

> Every member of a gang tends to have a definite status within the group. Common enterprises require a division of labor. Successful conflict (with other gangs, the police, or the community in general) necessitates a certain amount of leadership, unreflective though it may be, and a consequent subordination and discipline of members. As the gang develops complex activities, the positions of individuals within the group are defined and social roles become more sharply differentiated.[22]

And the gang leader has to play his role to keep his position.

> The leader spends more money on his followers than they on him . . .
>
> The leader is the man who acts when the situation requires action. He is more resourceful than his followers. . . . He is the most independent in judgment. . . .
>
> When he gives his word to one of his boys, he keeps it. The followers look to him for advice and encouragement. . . .
>
> The leader is respected for his fair-mindedness. Whereas there may be hard feelings among some of the followers, the leader cannot bear a grudge against any man in the group. . . .
>
> The leader does not deal with his followers as an undifferentiated group . . . (He) mobilizes the group by dealing first with his lieutenant . . .[23]

Only when the various positions in a group are clearly defined and each member knows and accepts his role can the group function harmoniously and efficiently. However, group structure is more than a practical necessity. It is related to the fundamental human need to achieve psychological homeostasis.

> The actions of other individuals . . . are always relevant to the problems of tension reduction of any given individual. . . . It is to the advantage of every individual in a group to stabilize the potential activity of others toward him, favorably if possible, but in any case in such a way that he can predict it. . . . All of them, even those who may wish to exploit the others, have some interest in bringing about stability. A basic assumption here is that what we call the "social structure" of groups can be understood primarily as a system of solutions to the functional problems of interaction which become institutionalized in order to reduce the tensions growing out of uncertainty and unpredictability in the actions of others.[24]

If an individual would understand a group, certainly if he would influence it, he must be aware of its structure and communicate with those members who "count." If an individual would go further and be a member of the group, he must find a place in the group. Marginal members, "hangers-on," are not tolerated for long—if at all.

> . . . In certain Australian groups, recognized blood relationships are extended to include not only the whole tribe but numerous individuals in other tribes as well. It is said that when a stranger visits such a tribe the old men

investigate his genealogy until they find some point in common with one of the genealogies within their own group. When such a point of contact has been established, they can determine the relationship of statuses which immediately fit him into the social body. If they are unable to find such a common point of relationship they usually kill the stranger simply because they do not know what else to do with him. They have no reference points other than blood relationships by which statuses might be assigned to him.[25]

In our society, rejection of the misfit is not usually so arbitrary and peremptory. We are inclined to give a man a chance—time to find and prove himself. The Greek-letter fraternity pledge, the probationary teacher, the apprentice salesman—these are devices to test the individual. If he doesn't fit, if he can't play a role, then the group rejects him.* He has no place to go but out!

Groups in Action

Individuals interact within groups. Groups interact within society. All social interactions, intra-group and inter-group, are exceedingly complex. Individuals and groups constantly shift into new relationships like pieces of colored glass in a vast and intricate kaleidoscope. Any attempt to describe social processes is like making a still picture of a moving scene: the life is lost, and what is captured is true only for a particular time under particular conditions.

Intra-Group Relationships

Within a group, relationships may be congenial or antagonistic, action productive or nonproductive, morale high or low. What makes the difference? It isn't just the nature of the positions defined by the group, the persons involved in those positions, or the circumstances under which the group is functioning. Group behavior has no single cause; it is the result of dynamic interaction of group personnel through the agency of group structure in a manner indicated not only by that structure but by the total environment. Change the organization of the group, change any of the persons involved,† or change any critical aspect of the physical or psychological environment, and group behavior also tends to change.

> In Stalin's day, shock workers were honored by the Communist party, but were often resented by their fellow employees for giving the government an excuse to raise work quotas. The way to be popular around the plant today, how-

---

* If the individual anticipates rejection, he may try to save face by rejecting the group first: "You can't fire me; I quit!"

† The ideal "organization man" *can* take another's place in a group because he will change himself to fit the stereotyped role he is expected to play rather than cause any disruptive change in the group.

ever, is to exceed your production norm. Team spirit is now part of the industrial system. All workers in a high-output factory receive higher salaries; those in inefficient plants earn less. Thus, a man with a base pay of 900 rubles a month not only takes home 1,300 rubles if he turns out 225 per cent of his norm, he also helps boost his factory's production record. On the other hand, slackers and absentee workers get scolded by a council composed of other employees, and can be disciplined if they don't mend their ways. The new leadership of the Soviet Union has found that group pressure works better than police pressure. . . .[26]

How the attitudes and behavior of any one person in a group affect the behavior of all the others, and how their reactions, in turn, ricochet and impel further reactions, and how group decisions are made and actions taken—these are problems of *Group Dynamics.* This special theoretical and experimental field is part of the new emphasis in social psychology which has gradually shifted from *individuals in groups* to the *groups* themselves.*

Group psychology today is very much a frontier—its variables are not well defined; its findings are not well integrated. Yet, already its results are being applied with vigor. The industrialist is concerned with the production norms of the small, informal group in his factory; he learns how to reduce absenteeism by developing social interdependence in the work team. The teacher of engineering increases the creativity of his class by "brainstorming," a group technique in which the analytic, critical functions of groups are separated from the group processes which enhance ideational fluency. The politician applies the lessons of conformity in creating political-social clubs to replace the vote-getting ward-heeler. The department store personnel director integrates the Negro sales clerk in the cosmetic department through use of the *fait accompli* technique. The marriage counselor obtains insight into the division of functions between husband and wife from findings about role differentiation in small groups. Those concerned with civil defense and administration of relief in natural catastrophes can work more effectively if they understand the power of group loyalties in determining people's behavior in a disaster situation. The social worker increases the cohesiveness of his settlement groups through his deepened knowledge of group leadership and the psychology of group participation. The United Nations official mediates inter-nation conflict more adequately because of his knowledge of discrepancy in group images. The psychiatrist uses discoveries about the social nature of "reality" in group psychotherapy with neurotic patients.

Little wonder that the group psychologist pioneers with diligence. Beyond him a rich area waits to be explored.[27]

Inter-Group Relationships

The interaction of individuals within groups is paralleled by an equally dynamic interaction of groups within society. The identity and status of any

* Prior to 1940 social psychology was mainly concerned with how the individual became socialized and how his attitudes towards society developed.

one group is defined by that of other groups and action by one induces counteraction by others. At every stratum in the social hierarchy, minority groups and majority groups, strong groups and weak groups, jockey for position. At the very top in our particular society are the economic, political, and military institutions—the domain of "the power elite." * Family, religion and education are lesser, decentralized institutions subordinate to the big three. The total is a complex, precarious equilibrium—an equilibrium constantly threatened by inner stresses and outside pressures.

> Many historical forces combine to make the relation of group to group the central issue of modern society. This issue takes different forms in different lands, but it besets them all. And in a special way it challenges the United States of America. Our people are mostly unaware of the nature of the challenge. They are mostly unaware of the threat to the integrity of this nation that lies in the existing relations of its groups. They do not perceive that its units, its well-being, its creed, and its historical tradition are altogether menaced.
>
> Mankind has made great advances toward the solution of many of its ancient problems. But *this* problem is not only unsolved, it has become greatly aggravated. The aggravation has come in the train of technological and social change. The different groups—ethnic groups and culture groups and interest groups—becoming more mobile, coming more into contact with one another and at more points, find far more occasion for clashes than in the simpler, more insulated, and more communized life of earlier days.[29]

Group-bound thinking in a multi-group society does create a multiplicity of clashes: white vs. black, Christian vs. non-Christian, capitalism vs. communism, our gang vs. your gang. The problem is not how to eliminate groups but how to create a larger, all-encompassing in-group to command a common loyalty.

> . . . aggressiveness is not the only motive governing the interaction of members of the same species. In gregarious animals there are equally innate patterns of behavior leading to mutual help and support, and one may assert that altruism is no less deeply rooted than aggressiveness. Man can be as basically good as he can be bad, but he is good primarily toward his family and friends. He has had to learn in the course of history that his family has grown, coming to encompass first his clan, then his tribe and his nation. Perhaps man will eventually be wise enough to learn that his family now includes all mankind.[30]

* The power elite is composed of men whose positions enable them to transcend the ordinary environments of ordinary men and women; they are in positions to make decisions having major consequences. Whether they do or do not make such decisions is less important than the fact that they do occupy such pivotal positions: their failure to act, their failure to make decisions, is itself an act that is often of greater consequence than the decisions they do make. For they are in command of the major hierarchies and organizations of modern society. They rule the big corporations. They run the machinery of the state and claim its prerogatives. They direct the military establishment. They occupy the strategic command posts of the social structure, in which are now centered the effective means of the power and the wealth and the celebrity which they enjoy.[28]

Social Processes

Try now to get the total picture: individuals interacting in groups, groups interacting in society, and all of society, the "greater community," held together in a complex and precarious equilibrium. What, now, are the social processes which maintain or threaten that equilibrium?

The basic forms of social interaction are commonly labeled: *conflict, competition, assimilation, cooperation,* and *accommodation.* These processes can be thought of as social equivalents of biological relationships: conflict and competition are *antagonistic;* assimilation and cooperation are *symbiotic;* and accommodation is *commensal.**

Conflict is a hostile encounter, a clash or divergence of interests or opinions, especially a mental or moral struggle involving incompatible aims. It exists latently as dissatisfaction or tension, overtly as active hostility. As long as both sides in a conflict fight actively, the relationship is *antagonistic.* Should either gain the upper hand and exploit the other as passive prey, then the relationship is *parasitic.* Conflict arises out of a divergence of interests; but even if all individuals and all groups were loyal to an all-encompassing in-group and felt allegiance to a common goal, there still would be differences regarding ways and means of achieving that goal.

Although commonly considered undesirable, conflict is not always without value.

> Conflict increases strength of character in various ways—through victory, through learning how to handle defeat, through the discovery of hidden reserves of strength, or the realization that one has convictions worth fighting for. In conflict, a child learns to withstand the pressure of other personalities and to keep his head in the face of such powerful emotions as anger, fear, and elation. Defeat, if not too drastic, strengthens his capacity for self-discipline or may lead to a beneficial change of attitude. When two children fight over the possession of something that both want and end up deciding to take turns, they are developing the sense of fair play, justice, and keeping one's word that is so basic to the individual's sense of personal security and his ability to inspire this feeling in others.
>
> And finally, it is conflict that teaches the invaluable skills of compromise . . . and develops the quality of empathy—the ability to feel with another person, to put oneself in his shoes even when one disagrees with him.[31]

Conflict, then, is not necessarily a destructive, disuniting process. When experienced by the individual, it can be a constructive socializing force. Further-

* Biological relationships are of four main kinds: *symbiotic:* individuals of different species live together for mutual benefit; *parasitic:* the advantages are all on one side; *commensal:* individuals live in, with, or on another with no apparent advantage or disadvantage; and *antagonistic:* individuals or groups of individuals oppose or resist each other.

more, when experienced by a group, it can be a uniting force. "We are unified both by hating in common and being hated in common."[32] Members of a threatened group tend to rally and work together with heightened morale. We cannot and should not eliminate conflict, but we can and should control the expression of conflict. "Ideas cannot be killed by violence."[33]

Competition is the endeavor to gain what another is also endeavoring to gain. It is a contest for the acquisition of something. Competition may be formally controlled by laws and rules or informally regulated by folkways. Competing television networks are subject to control by the Federal Communications Commission. Competing football teams comply with the rules of the game. Competing suitors follow an unwritten code. Competing individuals or competing groups may or may not know with whom they compete. When they do know each other and are personally and directly involved with each other, the competition is *antagonistic* and specifically known as rivalry. Rivalry is but one step removed from conflict.

Theoretically, competition is a basic process in our capitalist economy. Capitalism, you will recall, has been called the economic equivalent of the biological law of natural selection. The word *competition* comes from the same root as *competent,* and ideally, competition is a trial of ability. However, as a social process, competence does not necessarily determine the outcome of competition. Manufacturers of peanut butter, toothpaste, shirts, refrigerators and all other consumer products compete for customers, but *does the manufacturer who sells the most necessarily have the best product?*

Assimilation is the process of absorbing, incorporating, or converting. A *psychological system assimilates culture.* You, for example, are in the process of assimilating values, attitudes, beliefs, behavior. *An economic system assimilates—and thus eliminates—competitors.* "If you can't beat them, join them." The small-town drug store sells out to a national company. The neighborhood grocery becomes part of a supermarket chain. Big business becomes bigger by assimilating other business, and we enact anti-trust laws to prevent assimilation from becoming monopoly. *A political system assimilates states.* In the course of western expansion, the United States assimilated Texas, New Mexico, Nevada, Utah, Arizona, California, and part of Colorado. All this had been part of Mexico. *A social system assimilates various racial groups.* The immigrant Chinese, Puerto Rican, Italian, German, Irish, Mexican, Pakistani may only *tolerate* American ways, but his children, his grandchildren, his great-grandchildren, will *make* American ways. Eventually, ultimate assimilation through intermarriage will so tangle the racial roots that the concept of race itself may become obsolete. Insofar as the individual or group being assimilated willingly identifies with the expanding system, the process itself can be mutually advantageous or *symbiotic.*

Cooperation is collective action for a common aim. Individuals and/or groups act and interact for mutual benefit in a clearly symbiotic relationship. Plants and animals cooperate in maintaining the chemical equilibrium of the atmosphere: animals utilize oxygen and release carbon dioxide; plants utilize carbon dioxide and release oxygen. Cooperation is recognized as a biological necessity, but it is not yet fully recognized as a social necessity. We think of free enterprise as a competitive system rather than a cooperative one. For example, Buick competes with Chrysler, Mercury with Pontiac, Cadillac with Lincoln, Ford with Chevrolet. They all compete with each other. *Competition* provides the choice, but *cooperation* builds the car. Management cooperates with labor. Designers cooperate with plant men. Mold-makers, assembly workers, machinists, upholsterers, painters, and all the other plant men cooperate with each other.

Cooperation also functions in more subtle ways. Two classic Harvard Business School studies indicate a fallacy in the common concept of "economic man" motivated by self-interest and thriving on competition.[34] For five years industrial psychologists kept records of the work of six girls assembling telephone relays in a Western Electric Company plant. The problem: what conditions or circumstances favorably affected output? The girls were given rest periods. Rest periods were removed. Light was increased. Light was reduced. Piece-work pay was established. Piece-work pay was discontinued. No matter what the change, work output increased. The girls had been told about the experiment and its importance. They felt part of a significant project. They cooperated with the psychologists, with the supervisors, and with each other. Competitive tensions gave way to feelings of security. What affected work output was not any specific working condition, but the experiment itself, which engendered a cooperative *esprit de corps.*

In a second study, fourteen men in the same company were put into a "bank wiring" room. They were not told that they were subjects of an experiment. They were simply put on a pay-incentive system in which the production of the group would be taken as the basis for pay. The men were suspicious of the company. They agreed among themselves to hold their production down to the original level. An informal primary group developed among those men who assumed the role of establishing and enforcing the work norms. They punished the "rate busters" who worked too hard as well as the slackers who didn't work hard enough. By thus cooperating to keep their production at a fixed level, the men worked against their immediate self-interest.

Such research has profoundly affected labor-management relationships. Management has become increasingly alert to the practical advantages of making workers feel like "part of the family."

Accommodation is a neutral adjustment, a commensal relationship. It involves compromise, tolerance, co-existence. It is a putting-up-with rather than acceptance or rejection. Neither individuals nor groups can always agree, but they can agree not to disagree. Accommodation is one aspect of democracy. Racial groups, religious groups, political groups coexist within the borders of the United States. We accept accommodation as a reasonable and honorable process. *Can we apply the same process, with equal honor and reason, beyond our borders in those critical circumstances where cooperation seems impossible and conflict is unthinkable?*

Social processes are mutable. In response to internal stresses or external pressures, the attitudes and actions of both individuals and groups can shift. A hungry man, plagued by the tension of his own internal disequilibrium, is less reasonable, less amiable, than when he is comfortably fed. Similarly, a deprived group, agitated from within by the unfulfilled needs of its members, may be hostile and competitive. The same group, with a satisfied, secure membership may be friendly and cooperative. Also, a man, nagged by his wife and in-laws, may be irascible and boorish. Under less external pressure, he may be amenable and charming. Similarly, a group threatened by external forces may see conflict as the only means of self-preservation. In an environment which is accepting rather than threatening, the same group may willingly cooperate or accommodate. As sociologists learn more about intra- and inter-group interaction, they hope to do more than describe the social processes involved. They hope eventually to predict and direct them.

DIVIDED WE FALL

United we stand. Divided we fall. "No living organism is biologically solitary in its origin and few are solitary in their lives." [35] Shake apart the cells of a frog's egg into water during the early stage of development, and the separated cells will migrate toward each other and reestablish contact. Separate an individual amoeba from other amoebae, and it will make its way back to the group. Remove a caterpillar from other caterpillars, and it actively seeks to rejoin them.[36] Continue up the evolutionary scale and social life becomes increasingly complex and compelling. ". . . there is reason to believe that, with few exceptions, the solitary animal is, in any species, an abnormal creature," [37] and at the human level, isolation is a most devastating weapon, because "ultimately that which sustains humans is their personality organization born out of secure and stable group identifications." [38]

During the Korean War, Chinese communists achieved remarkable control over American POW's by breaking up group structure. Men were together physically but isolated psychologically. They were, in effect, maneuvered into self-imposed solitary confinement.

> The most significant feature of Chinese prisoner camp control was the systematic destruction of the prisoners' formal and informal group structure. Soon after arrival at a camp, the men were segregated by race, nationality, and rank. The Chinese put their own men in charge of the platoons and companies, and made arbitrary selections of POW squad leaders to remind the prisoners that their old rank system no longer had any validity. In addition, the Chinese attempted to undermine *informal* group structure by prohibiting any kind of group meetings, and by systematically fomenting mutual distrust by playing men off against one another. The most effective device to this end was the

practice of obtaining from informers or Chinese spies detailed information about someone's activities, no matter how trivial, then calling him in to interrogate him about it. Such detailed surveillance of the men's activities made them feel that their own ranks were so infiltrated by spies and informers that it was not safe to trust anyone. . . .

Loyalties to home and country were undermined by the systematic manipulation of mail. Usually only mail which carried bad news was delivered. If a man received no mail at all, the Chinese suggested that his loved ones had abandoned him.

Feelings of social isolation were increased by the complete information control maintained in the camps. Only the Communist press, radio, magazines, and movies were allowed.

The weakening of the prisoner group's structure is particularly significant because we depend to such an extent on consensual validation in judging ourselves and others. The prisoners lost their most important sources of information and support concerning standards of behavior and beliefs. Often men who attempted to resist the Chinese by means other than *outright* obstruction or aggression failed to obtain the active support of others, often earning their suspicion instead.[39]

The destruction of group structure weakened already weak men. An unprecedented 38 per cent of them died. Most died of disease, malnutrition and exposure, but the death of some could not be explained by their physical condition. Death seemed to be the result of abnormal apathy—what the prisoners themselves called "give-up-itis." A man would retreat into his self-imposed isolation so deeply that it became a psychological prison as inescapable as a cell of iron bars. He would then refuse to eat, to exercise, or to care for himself; and eventually, in complete regression, he would curl up on his bunk in the fetal position and die.

We must belong or perish. The group sustains, but the group also dominates and can lead the unwary individual into unthinking conformity. The group has both greater inertia and greater impetus than the individual. ". . . Group context . . . is like extra weight."[40] The group is slow to act; and once started on a line of action, it is slow to change. When new conditions invalidate the traditional structure of the group, the processes of intra- or inter-group action, or ideational goals, the group as an entity adapts more slowly than its best informed members, yet by virtue of its strength and authority it can overawe the individual and compel him to abandon his own judgment.*

Conflict between the individual and the group has kept man from ever being completely satisfied with things as they are. It is a source of the "divine discontent" which has impelled his unique development. Now, in this twentieth century, man still "seeketh in society comfort, use, and protection." *Will he find it?*

---

* David Riesman, in *The Lonely Crowd* (1950), C. Wright Mills, in *The Power Elite* (1956), and William H. Whyte, in *The Organization Man* (1956), have pointed with concern to the growing conformity in American society.

Notes

1. Aldous Huxley, *Brave New World* (New York: Harper & Row, Publishers, 1932).
2. William H. Whyte, Jr., *The Organization Man* (New York: Simon and Schuster, Inc., 1956), pp. 359-360.
3. Norman Mailer, as reported by William Hogan, in "Between the Lines," *The San Francisco Chronicle*, October 15, 1961, "This World" sec., p. 34.
4. H. R. Hays, *From Ape to Angel* (New York: Alfred A. Knopf, Inc., 1958), p. 201.
5. L. Joseph Stone and Joseph Church, *Childhood and Adolescence* (New York: Random House, 1957), p. 206.
6. *Ibid.*, p. 217.
7. *Ibid.*, pp. 220-221.
8. Kurt Lewin, "Experiments in Democracy" in *Man and Society*, Jerome G. Manin and Samuel I. Clark, eds. (New York: The Macmillan Company, 1960), p. 278.
9. Madeleine Renaud quoted in *The New Yorker*, February 23, 1957, p. 28.
10. Charles Horton Cooley, "In the Formation of Human Nature," in *Man and Society*, Jerome G. Manis and Samuel I. Clark, eds. (New York: The Macmillan Company, 1960), p. 472. (Reprinted from Cooley, *Social Organization.*)
11. *Ibid.*, p. 471.
12. *Ibid.*, p. 469.
13. Ferdinand Toennies, *Community and Society, Gemeinschaft und Gesellschaft*, translated by C. P. Loomis (East Lansing: Michigan State University Press, 1956).
14. David Krech and Richard S. Crutchfield, *Theory and Problems of Social Psychology* (New York: McGraw-Hill Book Co., 1948), p. 368.
15. John Steinbeck, *The Grapes of Wrath* (New York: The Viking Press, Inc., 1939), p. 264.
16. William Shakespeare, *Romeo and Juliet*, Act II, Scene II.
17. Harry C. Bredemeier and Jackson Toby, *Social Problems in America* (New York: John Wiley and Sons, Inc., 1960), p. 115.
18. Emily Post, *Etiquette* (New York: Funk & Wagnalls Co., 1950), p. 572.
19. "Greetings to a Russian Steamer (1861)," Compiled by Gordon Roadarmel, *The San Francisco Chronicle*, November 1, 1961, *Bonanza* sec., p. 9.
20. Robert M. MacIver, "The Multigroup Society," in *Man and Society*, Jerome G. Manis and Samuel I. Clark, eds. (New York: The Macmillan Company, 1960), p. 460.
21. From the personal files of Eugene and Fanchon Mead.
22. Frederic M. Thrasher, *The Gang* (Chicago: University of Chicago Press, 1927), p. 328.
23. William F. Whyte, *Street Corner Society* (Chicago: University of Chicago Press, 1943), p. 258-261.
24. Robert F. Bales, *Interaction Process Analysis* (Cambridge: Addison-Wesley Press, 1950), pp. 15-16.
25. Ralph Linton, *The Study of Man* (New York: Appleton-Century-Crofts, Inc., 1936), p. 124.
26. "The Big Change in Russia," *Look Magazine*, June 21, 1960, p. 35.
27. Harold Guetzkow, "Group Processes," in Floyd L. Ruch, *Psychology and Life* (Chicago: Scott, Foresman & Company, 1958), p. 550.
28. C. Wright Mills, *The Power Elite* (New York: Oxford University Press, Inc., 1956), p. 3.

29. MacIver, *op. cit.*, p. 459.
30. Irenäus Eibl-Eibesfeldt, "The Fighting Behavior of Animals," *Scientific American*, December, 1961, p. 122.
31. Dr. Jerome D. Frank, M.D., *Harper's Magazine*, April, 1957.
32. Eric Hofer, *The Passionate State of Mind* (New York: Harper & Row, Publishers, 1954), p. 138.
33. Edgar Snow, *Journey to the Beginning* (New York: Random House, 1958), p. 398.
34. George Caspar Homans, "Group Factors in Worker Production," in *Readings in Social Psychology*, Eleanor E. Maccoby, Theodore M. Newcomb, and Eugene L. Hartley, eds. (New York: Holt, Rinehart & Winston, Inc., 1958), pp. 583-595.
35. Ashley Montagu, *On Being Human* (New York: Henry Schuman, 1950), p. 30.
36. *Ibid.*, pp. 31-32.
37. *Ibid.*, p. 31.
38. Edgar H. Schein, "Reactions Patterns to Severe, Chronic Stress in American Army Prisoners of War of the Chinese," *The Journal of Social Issues*, Vol. 13, No. 3, 1957, p. 29.
39. *Ibid.*, pp. 24-25.
40. Michael S. Olmsted, *The Small Group* (New York: Random House, 1959), p. 71.

Distinction of rank is necessary
for the economy of the world.

NICHOLAS ROWE (1674–1718)

9

Stratification—Social, Economic, and Political

SOCIETY IS AN INCLUSIVE, self-perpetuating system. It exists in time as a continuing action and interaction of individuals and groups, and it changes with time. Society is never static; but for the purpose of analysis, we must declare a halt and assume an artificial situation with individuals and groups stopped in their tracks. We can then see the "parts" of this complex relationship we call society. It has surprisingly distinct social, economic, and political strata with ethnic and racial "intrusions." Rising up vertically through the horizontal strata are power pyramids drawing together from all strata those with professional, cultural, or other common compelling interests. The single individual moves within this complex three-dimensional structure, locating himself first in one position, then in another, in accordance with the various roles he plays.

In groups and in society as a whole, some individuals are actually or potentially more important, useful, or powerful than others. We speak of upper class, middle class, lower class; of royalty and commoners, of professionals, white collar, and blue collar workers; of diploma elite and supporting classes; of management and labor; of high brows, low brows, and middle brows. The levels or strata are variously defined, but however defined, they cut across groups and communities, redistributing the individuals within them relative to the total social hierarchy. Sometimes the degree of importance and power bears an inverse relationship to the number of people involved, as in medieval society: relatively few nobility and clergy at the top, bourgeoisie in the middle, and the peasants in the largest number at the bottom. However, in an open society such as ours, the largest number of individuals group about the mean: the power elite at the top, the great middle class in the middle, unskilled laborers, illiterates, casualties, and outcasts at the bottom.

We may not like this picture. Stratification implies inequality, and the Declaration of Independence states that "all men are created equal." We tend to resent the idea of inequality, but *what equalities do we seek?* Moral equivalence as human beings and the "inalienable rights" of "life, liberty, and the pursuit of happiness"? Yes, but what about equality of endowment, equality of performance, equality of possessions? In these men seem inescapably unequal.

UNIVERSALITY OF STRATIFICATION

Stratification is universal. Even animal societies are stratified. A herd of cows has a leader who regularly comes into the barn first at feeding time. Others assume definite places in line behind her. A flock of chickens has a "pecking order." Chicken *A* has pecking privileges over *B*, *B* over *C*, *C* over *D*, and so on. The order, once established, tends to persist. Male rats, shortly after maturity, enter a "round robin of fights" to determine their place in the scheme of things. A dominant male rules a territory and a harem, and tolerates the presence of only those males who respect his position. A subordinate male spends most of his time hidden in a burrow and sneaks out into the open only long enough to get food and water.[1] Among social animals, the position of an individual in the hierarchy is determined by the power he holds through his strength, his aggressiveness and/or his cunning.

Stratification, as accepted inequality, is not confined to sub-human societies.

> Looking at the cultures of the world one finds that no society is "classless," that is, unstratified. There are some primitive communities so small that no class strata appear, the social organization resting almost entirely on age, sex, and kinship; but even here chieftainship, individual prowess, and clan or family property introduce an incipient stratification. As soon as greater size and complexity are attained, stratification unmistakably appears.[2]

As an example, consider the primitive Tahitian society. In Tahiti the basic social unit is an enlarged or extended family, commonly composed of two or three brothers with their wives and children. Tahitians trace descent from the patrilineal line and no distinction is made between siblings and cousins.

> In any large family almost anywhere a hierarchy becomes established among the brothers and sisters in the sense that the older ones have some authority over the younger. But this kind of social ordering among the group of brothers and sisters is elaborate and intricate in Tahiti, and it establishes the

position of the individual for his whole life and in relation to the entire body of related families. Each individual family, and even lines of descent, within a lineage hold a rank with reference to all others depending on its origin and position relative to the main line of descent. Descent through a line of first-borns is a complete recapitulation in each generation of all of the original power and status of the founder of the lineage, with a sort of compounding of status the farther back it can be traced.

In this kind of society, the ability to recount an extensive genealogy is of great importance, and people of high status can trace their ancestors as far back as fifty generations. The main line of descent and each branch are named, and a first-born son takes his name from his father when he succeeds to his father's position. A subsidiary personal name allows individuals in a line of descent to be identified in each generation. This system of names or titles is exactly like that of the European nobility, and the titles are always evocative of specific status privileges, duties, and responsibilities.

The subdivisions of rank are a continuous gradation from top to bottom, but it is conventional to describe the society as composed of essentially three grades of people. The immediate families of the chiefs of the paramount lineages in the larger districts are called the *Ari'i,* the heads of lesser lineages and their families are of an intermediate group called *Ra'atira.* The remainder of the population are classed as *Manahune.*[3]

The position of any individual in the Tahitian hierarchy is not, as in animal hierarchies, a direct result of *actual* power held through strength, aggressiveness, or cunning, but it is correlated with *assumed* power, granted by the society. Tahitians believe that

> A kind of spiritual *power* or force called *Mana* is possessed by all individuals, but in varying degrees, corresponding to rank. An *Ari'i* possesses a great amount of this sacred power, because he is closer to the ancestral gods who are the source of it, and lower ranks have relatively less.[4]

In theory, one can posit a society without stratification, but *in fact,* no such society is known to exist. Some societies, the *kibbutzim* of Israel, for example, have professed but not achieved equality.

> The Israeli *kibbutz* . . . depends for its successful operation upon the few who have the ability, experience, and judgment to manage the collective. The managers, by that very dependence upon them, come to hold a higher status than other *kibbutz* members. Given this "necessary" differential in *power* and status, stratification is the inevitable result.[5]

Notice that in the stratification of societies, animal societies and human societies, the common factor determining the total hierarchy is *power—actual or potential.* In animal societies, power is a direct index of strength, aggressiveness, and/or cunning. In human societies, it is not. Man, as the creature of culture, is not full master of his own fate. His fate is conditioned by social, economic, and political forces outside his control. The positions he commands in society are determined not by his actions directly, but by the value his particular culture puts on them.

BASIS OF STRATIFICATION

Through *mutual dependence* and *consensus of values*, an aggregate of individuals becomes a society. *Mutual dependence* assumes a variety of work necessary to the survival and well-being of society; this work must be defined and assigned. *Consensus of values* implies agreement as to the relative importance of this work and of the *qualities, performances,* and *possessions* associated with the individuals doing it.[6]

Stratification in any particular society is based upon and justified by the values of that society. Qualities, performances, and possessions valued in one may be ignored or discredited in another. The cross-eyed girl next door who underwent an operation to have her eyes straightened would have been proud of her double vision were she an ancient Mayan.* Excessive fat on buttocks and thighs—steatopygia—is a sign of beauty among the Hottentots and Bushmen of South Africa, not a signal for dieting. The worker of black magic, honored in the Trobriand Islands, would be suspect if he set up shop on a city street. A Kalinga head hunter of the Philippines would be jailed, not feted, if he brought home a human head on the end of his stake. An albino deer skin or a woodpecker scalp is of more value to the Yurok Indians of California than a mutation mink coat. *Qualities, performances,* and *possessions*—these are the general categories about which value judgments are made.

Qualities belong to an individual and cannot ordinarily be altered. Race, sex, and kinship, crossed eyes, and steatopygic buttocks are qualities. *Performances* are accomplishments and achievements: black magic, head-hunting, taxi-driving, stamp collecting, having to pay $10,000 income tax, being elected to an honorary society. *Possessions* are acquired, and the term includes material possessions as well as skills and cultivated talents. Read in the newspaper that "Mrs. H. and her daughter had at least a dozen fur coats—minks, ermines, and chinchillas," stolen from their home, and you have a clue to the social position of Mrs. H. and her daughter. Fur coats, diamond rings, a Rolls Royce, Rembrandt etchings, a mountain cabin, Lincoln pennies, comic books, and bottle caps are all possessions. So, too, is a trained singing voice, skill at chess, badminton, or tight-rope walking. Possessions, in the sense of skills or talents, are differentiated from performances when an individual known to have a skill or talent is credited for the mere possession of it; many an individual "rides on his reputation" long after he has ceased to perform. *Qualities, performances* and *possessions* define what we are, what we do, and what we have.

Actions speak for us—louder than words. Actions which reverberate no farther than the family circle are relatively private and relate to the problem of stratification only insofar as they reveal a style of life characteristic of a

---

* Mayan parents even tried to make their children cross-eyed. A ball of resin tied to a lock of the child's hair so that it dangled in front of his eyes would sometimes do the trick.

particular stratum. But *social actions*—those which are directed towards socially desirable goals by socially sanctioned means—are public testimony of our qualities, our performances, and our possessions. Whatever social actions we take are judged not by universal standards, but by the limited scale of values adopted by our particular society. Invent a zipper, organize a crusade, get an A.B. degree, train fleas, compose a concerto, do a rain dance, collect stamps, build a canoe, make bread, paint portraits, find a uranium deposit, type 140 words a minute—which is of most value? Which is most desirable, useful, or important? How could you answer unless you know the society in which the actions take place? "Sparta honored its soldiers, ancient China its wise men, medieval Europe its bishops." [7] When social actions are evaluated, and they always are, stratification is the consequence.

DIMENSIONS OF STRATIFICATION

No matter how you divide it, it is still society. And sociologists, probing the nature of society, do divide it in a number of ways. Although the divisions are theoretical and arbitrary, they do suggest ways of perceiving different aspects of the social mass. To help understand stratification in a complex urban society, we can think of social action as taking place in three interrelated spheres—social, economic, and political—and of giving rise to three corresponding hierarchies.[8] *Status, class,* and *power* refer to rank position within these hierarchies.

Status

Relative position, or rank, in the social hierarchy is commonly called *status.* The term refers to the position, to the incumbent, and to the value placed on the incumbent's performance of his role. Thus the position of bus driver has a recognized status; a man, as a bus driver, has a recognized status; and, within the limits of his role, he can achieve differential status by his performance. A bus driver with a good safety record has higher status than a bus driver with a poor safety record. The rewards of high status, prestige, honor, or symbols of such intangibles, are meaningful only in a community setting.

> To have a thing is nothing, if you've not
> the chance to show it,
> And to know a thing is nothing, unless
> others know you know it.[9]

We define status and acquire status through significant others. The Maoris of New Zealand valued tattoos, and the status-seeking Maori got tattooed. Maoris valued courage, and they ate the hearts of slain enemies to gain it. Hollywood values grooming, and an actor will spend $15.00 on a hair trim, an actress $20,000 in a year for hair tinting and treating, cutting, and curling.

Hollywood values wealth, so stars, to prove they have it, will buy $25,000 cars equipped with telephone, television, hi-fi, and cocktail bar; they will have $100,000 wardrobes, and build $500,000 homes. The Maoris and the stars live half a world apart. Their values are different, but their motivation is the same: to gain or maintain status.

Status seeking is a universal game. It is not only the natives of New Zealand and Hollywood who jockey for social position, ". . . most of us surround ourselves, wittingly or unwittingly, with status symbols we hope will influence the raters appraising us. . . ." [10] The child shows off his new toy. The girl chases the boy with the fancy sports car. The teacher dangles his Phi Beta Kappa key from his belt. The doctor hangs his diploma in his office. The socialite sits in a box seat at the opera. The yachtsman displays his trophies in a glass case. The dying man buys an expensive casket.

Status is ego-sustaining, and we seek to gain or maintain status in one situation after another. Class position and political power are major sources of status, but we have as many sources of status as we have group affiliations. A student, for example, may have high status in his social set, high status in his family, middle status in a French class, low status in a math class, high status in the ski club. Should our various statuses be widely divergent, we are confused and insecure. Consciously or unconsciously, we try to "save face." Our defense may be to withdraw, actually or psychologically, from the group in which our status is disproportionately low; to disparage or otherwise attack the group or the leaders of it; or to excuse or otherwise rationalize our position in it. Because we each have a "looking-glass self," status, as a measure of the esteem of others, is an immediate and personal experience—inseparable from our self-image and functioning personality.

Class

Relative position in the economic hierarchy is commonly called *class.** The rewards of class are more tangible than those of status. The higher the class, the better the individual's chances in life and chances for life. Class position is determined mainly by objective criteria—the possessions in the form of material goods and services which the individual has or can command. The original class position of an individual is a biological and social inheritance. In the real upper classes, *family*—ancestors and relatives—count for as much as or more than the individual and his achievements. The real upper-class family is an extended kin group, an in-group often sharing with other families in the group income from a common inheritance. Some families, by a combination of economic, educational, and political devices, have managed to remain upper class generation after generation. This is true even in the United States.

* Although class and status are sometimes used interchangeably, we find the distinction, originally made by Max Weber, of *class as economic position* and *status as social position,* particularly useful for an understanding of stratification in urban society.

The Scotts, for example, boasted that in seven generations there had never been a non-Protestant marriage.

> The tradition . . . had a severe test in recent years. A son in one family, who had spent four years in the armed services . . . asked a middle-class Catholic girl to marry him. The engagement was announced by the girl's family, to the consternation of the Scotts. The Scotts immediately brought pressure on the boy to "break off the affair." His mother "bristled" at the very idea of her son's marriage; his father "had a talk with him"; his 84-year-old paternal grandmother snorted, "A Scott marry a Flaherty, never!" A great-aunt remarked icily, "No Scott is dissolute enough to *have* to marry a Flaherty." After the first shock of indignation had passed, the young man was told he was welcome in "any Scott home" without that "Flaherty flip." A few weeks later his maternal grandfather told him he would be disinherited if he "demeaned" himself by marrying "that girl."
>
> After several months of family and class pressure against the marriage, the young man "saw his error" and broke the engagement. A year later he married a family-approved "nice" girl from one of the other "old" families in the city. Today he is assistant cashier in his wife's family's bank, and his father is building him a fine suburban home.[11]

Although *class* distinguishes between the "haves" and the "have-nots," mere possessions are not the only consideration in the established upper class. Even where the aristocracy is untitled, *time* is a status factor. *How long* the family has had money is almost as crucial as *how much* they have. Good "old" families, "proper" Bostonians or New Yorkers, for example, have pre-Civil War fortunes. Late nineteenth-century wealth is new. Phenomenal economic success can catapult an unknown family into the established upper-class domain, but the position of its members is marginal and insecure.

> While its head is busy making a "million bucks," the family acquires the purchasable symbols associated with the wealthy American family: a large house, fine furniture, big automobiles, and expensive clothes. . . . The new family is able to meet the *means test,* but not the *lineage test* of the established families. Consequently, it is generally systematically excluded from membership in the most prestigeful cliques and associations in the community.* This is resented, especially by the wife and children; less often by the tycoon.[12]

If one can climb up through one class stratum to another, one can also slip back down; but just as it takes time to achieve the unpretentious, casual acceptance of wealth characteristic of the established upper class, so, too, does it take time to lose it. Even when economic disaster strikes, habitual adherence to class ways will give a lingering aura of wealth and sustain the status of a good old family. However, if financial stability is irrevocably lost, the family

* Henry Ford, self-made billionaire, was never accepted by the established upper class. For a portrait of a self-made man seeking to climb the social ladder as he climbs the financial one, see *The Rise of Silas Lapham* by William Dean Howells.

loses its cohesion, individual members strike out for themselves, and the family, as such, eventually fades into obscurity. Mobility is a two-way road.

Power

Relative position in a political hierarchy—meaning any organizational structure—is called power. The amount of power an individual has, the degree, in other words, to which he can impose his will in communal action even against the resistance of others, is related to both his status and his class. An individual of high class and high status usually has commensurate power, or if he doesn't have it, he is inclined to seek it. The wealthy young engineer, secure in his social and class position, may go in for local politics. The established lawyer may run for governor. Government service is the most obvious political hierarchy, but you can "play politics" right in your own backyard. In the broad sense, *power* includes the systems of administration in social, economic, and governmental organizations, as well as in less formal group structure. The president of a corporation, the trustee of a university, the boss of a labor union, the gangster, the school principal, the team captain, the neighborhood bully—all, within their sphere, have power over others.

Power is not the only means of controlling behavior. *Influence* and *persuasion* may do the same. An individual author, teacher, or radio announcer, or even a man on a soap box, can *influence* others without having any real power over them. A planning commissioner can *persuade* a real estate developer to adopt a good subdivision plan, but unless he can compel him to do so he has no real power. A policeman or a military officer, on the other hand, is an obvious and simple example of a person invested with power. As spokesman for the political state or organization, he can say "Do this—or else." Most often, however, power appears in more subtle garments than khaki and brass; and sometimes it is difficult to distinguish from persuasion. Such hidden power —"the iron hand in the velvet glove"—often operates through the *elimination of choice.* We can act only on those alternatives to action which we can perceive. When, for example, writers, teachers, or radio announcers present "fact" they may be presenting only what appear as facts to those controlling the mass communications media. If so, they are no longer acting completely as individuals, but as agents of "the powers that be," and they are controlling action by presenting less information than necessary for the reader or listener to make a really "free" decision. However, for convenience's sake, we distinguish *influence* and *persuasion,* exerted through the social and economic hierarchies, from *power,* exerted through political hierarchies.

Although power is often held in conjunction with economic or social position, it is also an entity—and an end—in itself. As in animal hierarchies, power may indicate superior strength, aggressiveness, and/or cunning. The political boss, for example, may have neither a high social nor economic position, but he manipulates others from behind the scenes and effects far-reaching decisions. Power, in such a case, is its own reward.

"Rulers and administrators exercise power. We learn which person or organization has power by learning whose version of order prevails."[13] Although some individuals in the United States have great power—the President, for example—most power in our society resides not with individuals but with organizations. Political parties mobilize the power of individual voters. Organized sectors in our complex economy—farmers, industrialists, labor unions, retailers, consumers, and such associations as the American Legion, the National Council of Churches, the National Educational Association, and the American Medical Association—have political power commensurate with the effectiveness of their lobbies.

We cannot readily measure power, but we can observe its implementation. Lawyers make up about one-tenth of one per cent of the population, but they fill the majority of ranking political offices. "For various periods, 70 per cent of all presidents, vice-presidents, and cabinet members have been lawyers, and so have 57 per cent of all senators, 56 per cent of all members of the House of Representatives, and 52 per cent of all state governors."[14] Lawyers, in either a legal or political role, do not *hold* power as much as they *represent* it. They usually speak for interests other than their own and further "versions of order" sought by power blocs.

The various positions of any one individual in a modern urban society are related to the three interrelated dimensions of stratification: status, class and power. Status is the important dimension in everyday personal affairs. It determines acceptability. Whom you invite to dinner, whom you let into your club, whom you consider marrying—these are mainly matters of status, of subjective evaluation of individual qualities, performances and possessions. Class and power, however, are the important dimensions in the affairs of society. They are related to the forces for and against societary change. "Automation May Ruin Capitalism"—this was a front page headline, and the article went on to say:

> Computers and automation threaten to create vast unemployment and social unrest . . . while technology can replace human labor and even do much of the "thinking" for government and business leaders, cybernation * may spell the end of the United States' economic system . . . cybernation will eliminate entire job categories ranging from factory and farm labor to middle-management executives . . . cybernation's economic advantages make cybernation inevitable. . . . The ultimate effects on society . . . would not be conducive to maintaining the spirit of a capitalist society.[15]

Think what this means. If cybernetics were to displace workers sufficiently to threaten capitalism, then the economic and political hierarchies would be disrupted. Old sources of wealth and power would be eliminated. New ones would be created. In a cybernetic revolution, the economic and political positions of some individuals would suffer, those of others would soar; while status,

* The word is derived from cybernetics, the comparative study of the control systems formed by the brain and nervous system in man and mechanical-electrical systems in computing machines.

as measured by the esteem of family, friends and affiliates, could, theoretically, remain constant.

Although status, class, and power are interrelated, they are, obviously, not necessarily commensurate. The political boss may have more power than his status or class would indicate. The high-status professor may live in genteel poverty and have little influence outside his academic circle. The bartender may have a large bank account but low status and little power. Status, class, and power are distinct dimensions of stratification, and all are necessary to define adequately the position of any one individual in the total society. *Where do you stand? How do you know?*

STRATIFICATION, U.S.A.

"Benjamin F. Fairless, son of a coal miner, who became head of the huge United States Steel Corporation at 55, died yesterday. . . ." [16] The birth of Benjamin Fairless was of importance only to his family. His death 71 years later was national news. Who was he? How did he get that way?

Benjamin Fairless was one of four children of a Welsh coal miner. When he was two years old, his uncle, owner of a grocery store in Justus, Ohio, adopted him and gave him the opportunity to go to school. He graduated from high school at seventeen, got a job teaching, and saved money for college. He graduated from college as a civil engineer, became supervisor of a construction gang, and later, engineer for a steel company. With each advance in education and occupation he acquired higher status, higher class, and more power. He became president of the Carnegie-Illinois Steel Corporation, then president of the United States Steel Corporation, and finally, Chairman of the Board and chief executive officer. In the industry, he was "Mr. Steel."

Benjamin Fairless had lived a legend. He was an Horatio Alger hero come to life,* one of the many poor boys who have made good in this land of opportunity. He himself said:

> "In what other country of this world could I have fared as well as I have here in the United States? Had I been born in Wales, there is little doubt that I should now be working proudly, but inevitably, in the coal mines there, as the men of my family have always done for generations past." [17]

Benjamin Fairless had even more illustrious predecessors. Benjamin Franklin, self-taught son of a soap and candle maker, lived to stand before kings. Abraham Lincoln was born in a log cabin. The philanthropist, Andrew

* Horatio Alger (1834-1899) wrote a series of books for boys, including *Jed, the Poorhouse Boy, Luck and Pluck, Ragged Dick,* and *Tattered Tom.* Always his heroes succeeded through hard work and perseverance. Such emphasis on success is a cultural theme. It was born of the Protestant ethic which made economic success a symbol of the "chosen" and failure a symbol of the "damned," and it has been sustained not only through continued indoctrination but by the triumphs of those who actually lived the legend.

Carnegie, who gave away millions of dollars, was the son of a poor Scottish weaver. These men and many more worked their way from the bottom to the top of "Society, U.S.A.," from rags to reputation, riches, and power. In the United States we sanction such mobility. We believe in competition. We like to see the best man win—and sometimes he does. The experience of success brings the expectation of further success. When men were asked, "Do you think the years ahead seem to hold for you personally a good chance for advancement?" 63 per cent of those in the highest income group said, "Yes," compared with 48 per cent of those in the lowest income group. The relatively unsuccessful, however, to compensate for personal frustration, may identify with their sons. When asked, "Do you think your son's opportunities to succeed will be better than those you have had?" 65 per cent of the poor white and 75 per cent of the Negroes said, "Yes." [18] *Mobility* is an insignia of the American Way; it implies the right of each to enjoy whatever social status, economic advantage, and political power he can achieve. *Are mobility and equality contradictory values? Does one tend to negate the other? Is full equality either possible or desirable?* *

Mobility

Mobility implies "openness"—somewhere to go and some way of getting there. Democratic ideals, westward expansion, industrialization, and urbanization set the stage in the United States for individual achievement. Ours is an "open" society—a society of people "on the make." †

In a lifetime span of eighty years, from 1870 to 1950, the United States changed from a rural to an industrial nation. This meant a radical redistribution of jobs: farm workers declined from more than one-half to less than one-eighth of the total. Urban workers—professional, business, and clerical—increased from one-eighth to almost one-half. In just one generation, 1920 to 1950, the number of professional men in the country almost tripled; [21] and, in addition, sons and daughters of farmers moved by the millions to the cities to become proprietors, managers, clerks, and skilled workers. From mid-century tech-

* A common theme of Utopian schemes and social reforms is the reduction or elimination of mobility. In some it would be achieved through the *fixed inequality* of a scientifically stratified society as in Plato's *Republic* or Huxley's *Brave New World*. In others it would be achieved through *equality* in a classless society as foretold in the *Communist Manifesto*. Theory, however, does not always translate into practice. Under the Communists, Russia has at least ten classes ranging from officials, scientists, artists, and writers down through managers, bureaucrats, workers, and peasants.[19]

† Although ours is an open system, it is not necessarily more open than that of other technologically advanced and advancing nations. Sample surveys taken after World War II include the following comparative rates of upward mobility: [20] (Rates are for generational mobility as determined by the percentage of males in elite and nonmanual occupations whose fathers had been manual laborers.) India, 1.4 and 27.13; Great Britain, 2.2 and 24.8; Sweden 3.5 and 25.5; France 3.5 and 30.1; Japan 7.0 and 23.7; Brazil 5.3 and 29.4; United States, 7.8 and 28.8; Russia, 14.5 (manual in this instance = working class) and 34.9.

nological advance has continued, and there is no end in sight. Technicians and administrators will be needed in greater numbers than unskilled workers whom machines more readily replace. Furthermore, shortages exist in the professions, and greater ones are predicted. To implement and interpret the technological changes, scientists, teachers, doctors, and engineers are needed in increasing numbers. There is still some place to go if you are interested, and education is the surest way to get there.

Qualifications for Mobility

A century ago mobility was epitomized in the success of the entrepreneur. Peter Donahue, for example, born in 1822 in Glasgow of poor Irish parents, labored in a factory when he was nine, migrated to the United States with his parents at eleven, skipped school, and became a machinist's apprentice. He went to California in '49 to dig for gold. He stayed to serve the diggers. He opened a blacksmith shop in a tent and made their tools. Fifteen years later, as brother-in-law of the governor, he counted his accomplishments. He had developed his blacksmith shop into California's first cast-iron foundry and machine shop, expanded the foundry and shop into the Union Iron Works, and sold it to Bethlehem Steel for $1,000,000. In his spare time he had formed San Francisco's first gas company, organized the first street-car line, become co-owner of the San Francisco–San Jose Railroad Company, operated the coastal steamer and Sacramento River boat lines, and established the North Pacific Railroad.[22] Today, in contrast, mobility is epitomized not by the self-made, self-educated entrepreneur but by the college-educated *organization man* [23] who climbs the bureaucratic ladder.

Peter Donahue *skipped* school and became a tycoon. Benjamin Fairless, born 69 years later, *went* to school and became a tycoon. The difference is significant. Said one executive:

> Men of my own age group (among the executives), I would say that about fifty-fifty are college or non-college. The men in the age group starting out now are probably ninety per cent college. . . . It's the attitude of top management; they have felt, or perhaps learned over the years, that from a dollars and cents standpoint it is an asset to the company, for the college-trained man is a better risk for promotion and advancement. The mortality is not as high. . . .[24]

Measures of Mobility

We have had the privilege of entertaining in our home a young man from Uganda—the second member of the Ba-Hima tribe ever to be in the United States. He came as a scholarship student in political science, and he expected to return to his country in four years with an A.B. degree. This degree would work magic. With it he could be one of the political leaders of his country. His position in society with the degree would automatically be far higher than he could hope for without it. Education was a measure—and a means—not only of his personal mobility, but of *generational* mobility. His deceased father, a primitive and obscure man, had bought his bride with cows. His mother first heard of the United States when her son told her he was coming here.

Although personal and generational mobility is not so dramatic in our society, Job's sons and daughters—progeny of the poor and the uneducated—do take their place in commencement lines across the nation. In cap and gown, they receive their diplomas—tickets of admission to upper and upper-middle class occupations. College enrollment in the United States increased from 237,592 in 1900 to 3,610,000 in 1960. There are more faculty members now than there were students in 1900. In 1900 only one man in sixty graduated from college. In 1954 the proportion was closer to one in eight.[25] In succeeding generations the proportion will approximate one in four or five.*

The colleges and universities are besieged. Why? Mainly because, in terms of mobility,† education is the "modern freeway." [27] The era of the self-made, self-educated man is past.

> The Second World War . . . gave the fundamental impetus to this situation. American colleges and universities experienced a tremendous expansion immediately after it in terms of students, functions, activities and plants. Further, the demands of the war and the enrollment wave of veterans afterward precipitated radical changes in the organization and ideologies of the university and the academic profession. For the first time in recent history the universities experienced a real demand for the services they had to offer. There was a time in 1942 when it became exigently necessary for many people concerned with the operation of the war to know something about the tides at an insignificant island named Betio in the atoll of Tarawa; later the effect of individual "rotation" upon the combat efficiency of units became of pressing importance; and still later the peculiar and esoteric behaviors of the particles in the subatomic world were of extravagant concern. Knowledge as *knowledge* for the first time in American history became a commodity in general demand. And the only source for thousands of such essential pieces of information lay in the minds and the laboratories of the colleges and universities. . . .[28]

Academic knowledge proved of practical value in war; it has also proved of practical value in peace. Personnel men from business and industry now screen graduates of universities, colleges, and even junior colleges for promising employees. Fifty-five per cent of college graduates get into high-paying professional occupations; 17.9 per cent become proprietors and managers; 15.1 per cent are clerks and salesmen. In contrast, 56.8 per cent of high school graduates are craftsmen, foremen, operatives, service workers, farmers, and

---

* Educators estimate that 20 to 25 per cent of the population have the minimum intelligence necessary to be graduated from college.[26]

† Sociologists distinguish between minor gains which come through performance and seniority and true mobility or major gains which carry the individual across occupational and/or class lines.

laborers. Only 11.3 per cent of the college graduates work in these relatively low-paid blue-collar jobs.[29] In his lifetime, the average college graduate earns approximately two-fifths more than the average high school graduate,[30] and if his degree is from an Ivy League college, he does still better.* Income correlates with occupation, and occupation now correlates with education.

Consequences of Mobility

The United States has the oldest unchanged form of government in the world today. *Can this be, at least in part, because upward mobility is a source of both vitality and stability?* Mobility vitalizes society by letting new blood into old veins; it stabilizes society by substituting personal change for revolutionary social change. Self-made men, as well as aspiring others, tend to be political conservatives—that is, they accept the notion that a man is master of his own fate. If a man has made good or thinks he can, he believes in the system. Despite humble origins, the older and more successful a man becomes, the more conservative he becomes.[32] Self-made men are loyal sons of the status quo. But some of their sons, men of inherited wealth and social position, often turn out to be political liberals—that is, they may know, if only through their own experience, that a man's fate depends not only on himself, but on the social conditions which surround him. If such a man is ambitious to have a power position commensurate with his social and economic position, he can go into politics.† If he is also a man of conscience, he is concerned with the problem of making social conditions as favorable as possible for other men. The conservative father, in loyalty to the status quo which nurtured him, might tolerate conditions of inequality on which revolutionists thrive. The liberal son, perceiving the danger of inflexibility to society as well as to his own position, may seek adaptive change through legislative processes. If so, he acts in the tradition of the British aristocrats who, secure in their own upper-class position, developed a sense of *noblesse oblige* and became socialists or laborites. Conservative fathers balanced by liberal sons (and a liberal intelligentsia) are a counter-revolutionary combination. Mobility is more than an insignia of the American Way; it has been insurance for the American Way.

---

* When mobility, as measured by better work and more pay, is overemphasized, education tends to be perceived only as a means to an end. Twenty-four lower middle-class high school boys with I.Q.'s in the top quartile all thought of school and the possibility of college solely as steps to jobs. Characteristically, they, their parents, and most of their teachers put more value on the diploma than on the learning it represented. They had little or no appreciation of education for its own sake—as a source of subtle pleasures and satisfactions.[31] And, because higher education is the aim of so many, the individual seeking it may be like Alice in *Through the Looking Glass,* who had to run faster and faster just to keep in place. Education does not necessarily put the individual ahead of those around him. It may simply help him keep up with the crowd.

† Politically liberal men of inherited wealth and social position include Franklin D. Roosevelt, Averell Harriman, G. Mennen Williams, Herbert Lehman, Nelson Rockefeller and John F. Kennedy. Without questioning motives, we note that as conservatives such men would have limited support. They could too easily be accused of acting from selfish interests.

Mobility may vitalize and stabilize society, but it also has other less salutary personal consequences. For the capable, aspiring individual, mobility means opportunity for self-realization. It may also mean ulcers or arteriosclerosis, for

> . . . successful mobility places the individual, for some period of time, in a marginal social position. The individual's former friends and associates may find him threatening; his success is a mark of their failure. His newly-created friends and associates, produced by his successful move, may find him too "different," too "raw," and too recent to be accepted as a *bona fide* member. The individual thus finds himself suspended in a "success limbo," socially unattached for the moment to any group.[33]

Family as well as friends and affiliates may become casualties of mobility. If a wife can't keep up with her husband, she automatically becomes a liability. Some corporations even suggest that a man drop the wife who lags behind in the mobility race.[34]

Success may bring financial as well as personal insecurity. An upwardly mobile man may feel compelled to get his wife a mink coat, send his son to an Ivy League college, move to a better home on which he must pay higher taxes, trade in his old car for a new one, get a second car for his wife . . . all of which he can't really afford.

"Climbers . . . appear to move more or less successfully," but show "severe anxiety, depression, sometimes . . . antisocial acting out, and in some extreme cases . . . suicidal attempts. . . ." [35] It takes an especially strong man to stomach success. As measured by insecurities, conflicts, and doctor bills, the price is sometimes more than the average man can stand. But if success is costly, what about failure? *Are there enough high level jobs to accommodate those who want them?*

In theory every boy has a chance to be President, but only one President is elected every four years. Four boys are born every minute—8,480,000 in four years. *What chance has any one of them to be President of the United States or even of U. S. Steel?* If a boy has his heart set on being president of something, anything short of that is frustrating failure. He can fail because he is afraid of trying, or he can fail because he actually tried but without success. Experience of failure influences an individual's ability to adjust his aspirations and efforts to reality. He tends either to grossly overestimate or underestimate what he can do.[36] And failure, like success, takes its toll in mental health. The "climbers" who seem to get ahead by-pass the "strivers." The "strivers" are characteristically "ambitious dreamers," or, "if they do not dream, they constantly plan and scheme, rush from one pursuit to another, or from one 'big deal' to another, hoping to succeed sufficiently to climb upward in the social system, but always disappointed and frustrated, complaining and rationalizing about what they consider bad luck and failure." [37]

Colleges and universities are crowded with students seeking passports to "success" because they have been led to believe that the only meaningful life is a "successful" one. *Is this true, or are our values confused?* Colleges and universities are instruments of a kind of education suited only to some individuals. Others may profit more from vocational training or apprenticeship work or some other learning experience. We doom many to failure so that a few may succeed. *Should human dignity and worth be reassessed "in terms of those qualities of mind and spirit that are within the reach of every human being"?* [38]

The negative consequences of mobility are more than personal. As more and more people compete with each other and try to get ahead, there is a "diffusion of insecurity" and a "fragmentation of the social order." [39] Mobile people tend to be self-centered people—less likely to be concerned with group needs and more apt to sacrifice traditional ethics and work standards to expediency. In an effort to appear successful, the student may cheat to get the grade. The businessman may lie to get the sale. The politician may compromise to get the vote. Opportunism may quiet conscience.

Barriers to Mobility

Half the population of the United States is below the median in intelligence; half is above. By definition, this is necessarily true. If all individuals had equal access to education and occupation, we could then expect intellectual level to coincide with occupational level. High school graduates are approximately 10 points above the median I.Q. of 100, entering college freshmen are 15 points above, and graduating seniors 21 points above.[40] To this extent tested intelligence * does correlate with educational achievement, and thence, theoretically, with occupational level. However, two-thirds of the boys in the top 20 per cent of the population in intelligence never get through college; [41] and although the highest level jobs are held by individuals of high intelligence and the lowest level jobs by those of relatively low intelligence, the intermediate jobs are nonselective. The clerk in the department store might have an I.Q. of 98 or one of 148. Differential status, class, and power, insofar as they do not coincide with genetic differences in individual potential, are socially imposed inequalities. This means that despite our open society barriers to mobility exist. *What are they?*

Social Barriers

Society *ascribes* some statuses; it permits individuals to *achieve* others. Those statuses or positions in society which are independent of performance and are automatically associated with an individual because of biological or social factors are *ascribed* statuses. These include race, sex, age, family relationship, and, in some societies, occupation and affiliation. Some ascribed statuses are acquired at birth, others in the course of a lifetime. Ascribed statuses are

* I.Q. indicates functioning intelligence, not innate potential. It is determined in part by environmental factors, particularly incentives to and opportunities for learning.

the backbone of society, the essential, underlying structure; but some statuses in some societies are *achieved.* Those statuses which a society bestows on an individual as reward * for personal worth or performance in competitive areas such as education and occupation and income are *achieved* statuses. Because we are a competitive society sanctioning upward mobility, an unusual number of statuses *are* open to achievement. Compare, for example, your present status and future possibilities with what you might have were you a Tahitian.

> All individuals . . . occupy a single pigeonhole of status. Consequently a father can pass on his rank and responsibilities to only one son—the position can be occupied by no more than one incumbent. . . . The first-born son at full maturity has the adult responsibility over his brothers and sisters, and is accorded obedience and deference by them. The second son is a sort of deputy and would take the position should his older brother be absent or die, up to the time when the older brother's first-born son was old enough to succeed to it. The youngest son in a large family is a woebegone figure, for he has little chance for distinction in the line of succession; his status will always be lower than that of his older brothers as long as they live.[42]

We would feel stifled in a society with such an elaborate and rigid system of stratification. We could not accept such obvious and inexorable restraints. In the United States ascribed status can be superseded by achieved status. The seventh son of a corporation lawyer, for example, acquires a higher ascribed status at birth than does the first son of a plumber. And most probably, the lawyer's son will attend high-status schools and eventually enter a high-status occupation. However, the plumber's son, given enough education, could be a Nobel prize-winning scientist and, through occupation and income, achieve a status higher than that of the lawyer's son. The possibility is there, but—and this "but" is important—the lower a person's *ascribed* status, the more difficult it is to *achieve* high status. Low ascribed status is a social barrier to mobility.

Economic Barriers

Status is a social safety valve. If a prophet is without honor in his own house, he can go to his neighbor's. Status is a system of stratification congenial to ego-development and consistent with democratic values. Class carries implications of differences beyond individual control. Impersonal possessions—amount and source of income, amount of leisure, place of residence—take precedence over personal possessions: skills and talents, qualities, or perform-

---

* Reinforced behavior is learned, and society, through a system of reinforcements, can direct individual behavior. We exert ourselves most in those areas where achievement is rewarded by social esteem (honor and prestige), or by material tokens of that esteem. For example, a young man has a poor chance of getting a scholarship to a university if he is an outstanding poet. He has an excellent chance if he is an outstanding quarterback. If Russia is ahead of us in any intellectual or aesthetic field—if Russia is producing more or better scientists, engineers, doctors, musicians, dancers—it is because, as a society, Russia is rewarding such achievement more effectively than we are.

ances. Class was the primary filter through which Marx saw society. He assumed that class position "determined a set of all-inclusive life-conditions for the individual," [43] and that the individual was a lifetime captive of his class. We bristle at the implication that we are captive of anything or anyone. We insist not only on freedom of speech and worship and freedom from want and fear,* but on personal freedom. We do not want to identify with a class when such identification implies limitations we are not ready to accept. However unpalatable the class concept may be to us, a walk from slums to suburbs in any urban area leaves no doubt that class is a social fact.

Class structure in the United States is not a "clearly differentiated system of class levels with full consensus and awareness of the criteria and the occupants of the levels." [44] It is not easy to say who belongs to which class and why, but sociological research suggests at least five general classes or "ideal types": [45] *upper class* (1 per cent of the population), *upper-middle* (nine per cent), *lower-middle* (40 per cent), *working class* (40 per cent) and *lower class* (10 per cent).† The upper and upper-middle are sometimes referred to as the *diploma elite* in contrast to the three other *supporting classes.* The related indices of income, education, occupation and attitudes—the syndromes typical of each class—suggest the following dominant types.

Upper Class. The son learns to live graciously. If he belongs to the established aristocracy, he is secure in his past—to the ancestral manor born; if he is progeny of the *nouveau riche,* he is insecure in the present and alert to the nuances in values and ways which distinguish the true gentleman. He will have to learn the rules of upper class living thoroughly, and only when he is completely accepted and completely secure will he dare break them. The son of the *nouveau riche,* to be thoroughly initiated, will need the extra socialization provided by a prestige preparatory school and an Ivy League college. Although he cannot accent his home with heirlooms, he will eventually find in antique shops the status symbols he did not inherit. He may find himself embarrassed by the heartiness of his entrepreneurial father or the tenseness of his socially ambitious mother, and he will try to "marry well" to secure his position. The son of the true upper class, in contrast, has a completely self-assured father who is a most successful business or professional man —a member of the Board of Directors of a bank, a business, or a university. His mother is active in "society" and supports the arts and charities. His home and the homes of his relatives are city or surburban mansions with servants who "live in." He has vacationed abroad and is on intimate terms with aristocrats in other countries. His support comes, as does his family's, mainly from interest, dividends, or rent; and he will probably augment this by choosing a wife from his own exclusive set. He expects to remain rich and become powerful by following his father's footsteps, or perhaps by going into politics. But even if he does nothing in particular he will still be "somebody."

* *The Four Freedoms* set forth by Franklin D. Roosevelt in his message to Congress January 6, 1941, as goals of a new world order.

† These percentages are, of course, approximate.

Upper-middle Class. The capable son, with the encouragement of his parents, sets his sights on a career. He goes to good public or private schools, and expects to keep going until he has an advanced academic degree or a special degree in medicine, law, architecture, or business administration. His father, a business or professional man, is his model. The son knows his parents identify with him and expect him to do well. He also knows that he can attain his goals and theirs only by hard work; and he is inclined to pursue his career obsessively. He is future-oriented. He has been taught from childhood to postpone gratification. He will not be as knowledgeable as the upper-class son; he won't talk as easily of art or music or literature or politics or other fields outside his specialty mainly because it takes more time to be a dilettante than he is willing to spare from his career. He may even begrudge time to his family. He will need a generous, cooperative and capable wife who will entertain his friends, make useful community contacts, rear children of whom he, in turn, can be proud, and generally subordinate herself to help him in his competitive striving. He believes in himself, and will expect no less from his wife and children. He may, as he gets older and tired, find that in passing by the smaller pleasures for greater promises, he has lived an emotionally marginal life.

Lower-middle Class. The son is in limbo, suspended between anonymity and achievement. His parents are modest people. They go to church,* watch T.V., work hard to keep things "nice"—their house painted, the shrubs pruned, the lawn weeded. They have taught him to be a good boy, respectful, and obedient. He will be interested in how much money the fathers of his friends make. His own father's pay, if good, probably reflects not his personal achievement, but rather the strength of the union to which he belongs. An intelligent son who doesn't mind leaving his family and boyhood friends behind in the mobility race can go to college and try for an upper-middle class career. If he gets it, he may be tortured by the question, "Do I really belong?" and to reassure himself, he may put excessive emphasis on status symbols: the right address, the right car, the right clothes. He is likely to appear neurotic and dissatisfied with himself.† If he married the lower-middle class girl who was his boyhood sweetheart, he may be dissatisfied with her, too. Without the intelligence or motivation to pursue a career, he will, like his father, settle for a job. His choice will be broad. He can try for semi-professional or semi-managerial work; he can become a skilled craftsman or a shop foreman; or, if he can manage financially, he might even get his own small business or farm. If he does stay within the confines of his class, as most lower-middle class boys do, his "success" will be limited. He will probably put more emphasis on his role as a consumer than on his role as a producer, and take more pride in material *possessions* than in *performances.* He will marry younger and have more chil-

* Although upper-middle class families may have the largest proportion of formal church members, the lower-middle class families are the most regular churchgoers.[47]

† Sociologically-oriented psychiatrists consider the neurotic personality typical of the competitive middle-class segment of the population.[48]

dren than his career-minded brother; and though his life may be routine, it will be relatively stable, family-centered, and not without personal satisfactions.

Working Class. The son learns to get by, and to take what he can get when he can get it. The relatively poor school he attends* means little to him. He might drop out because he sees no connection between book learning and the life he knows, or he might hang around until a high school diploma is put in his hand. He rarely has enough courage and ambition to go to college. Even if his grades are good enough and his teachers encourage him, his family and his friends wouldn't understand. His mother might be proud and like the idea of college, but she is tired and over-worked and the sensible thing for the boy to do is get a job and help pay his way in the family. After all, his mother has to work waiting on tables because, in spite of union membership, his father is laid off from work by the factory in bad times. His years of seniority have given his father only a modicum of security over fellow workers, but no differential in pay. His work is semiskilled, and experience is worth little when there is little to learn. Being a nobody in society, he tries to be a somebody at home. He says the boy talks like a —— dictionary and has "too much education" already. He enjoys authority over his wife and children and will try to hold that authority, not through superior wisdom but through superior strength. The son got his first lessons in "stern" reality from his father's heavy calloused hand. If the son wants to escape the factory life that trapped his father, he can try running a gas station or a little retail store; but the money he earns is more important to him than the work he does. He will marry a girl who has no more education or ambition than he has—often he "has" to marry her. He will have more than the average number of children,† and, burdened by their needs, he will live from day to day, more as a spectator than as an active participant in the vital life and work of the world.

Lower Class. The son is the apathetic low man on the totem pole. In contrast to the working class son who is "clean poor," the lower class son is "dirty poor." Everybody looks down on him, and he tends to accept the idea that he is "no good." He gets out of school as soon as the law allows or sooner. His father and mother work irregularly at menial jobs and draw on relief to keep him clothed and fed and housed even in a decrepit slum apartment. Although he may have average or even better-than-average intelligence, his general health ‡ and lack of technical and social skills are a great handicap to

---

* Education in the United States is free, but it is not yet equal. In working class and lower class neighborhoods, the schools, like the houses, are often old, poorly equipped, and over-crowded. The teacher's job is a composite of policeman, social worker, and clinical psychologist; and teachers who want to teach seek better schools.

† Almost one-half of the children in the United States are in families who, together, have only one-tenth of our national income.

‡ A lower-class person is eleven times more likely to suffer from schizophrenia than an upper-class person,[49] and, if for no other reason than the fact that doctors and medicine cost money, he is likely to have more than his share of physical ailments.

the development of any native capacity he might possess. In his hopelessness and frustration he may strike out against society and get arrested as a juvenile delinquent. But violence and counter-violence, misdeed and punishment are no novelty to him; they are but an extension into the larger society of the patterns he has learned from family and a deprived if not delinquent sub-culture. If he doesn't lapse into the life of an habitual criminal, become alcoholic or psychotic, he will live a minimal life of baffled resignation, convinced that he has nothing to gain and nothing to lose.

Our society is so large and complex that the average individual has little or no sense of class involvement. In fact, he may not know to what class he belongs. He does not think in terms of class warfare nor of the "masses" versus the "classes." Rather he is a "Status Seeker"—individually trying to improve his own position without necessarily displacing anyone else.

Although most people, whether they know it or not, do meet the criteria of one class or another, a significant number of others do not. Mobile people, for example, may be lower-middle class in income and occupation, upper-middle class in education and value orientation. Such inconsistencies are usually a clue to their aspirations or their failures. In addition, there are variant groups—such as intellectuals, artists, and ethnic minorities—and deviant groups—such as prosperous prostitutes and professional criminals—who are outside the dominant class patterns. They cannot be categorized by class without misrepresentation, but they need to be taken into account.

> That there be individuals and whole groups of individuals who live in accordance with patterns which express variant rather than the dominantly stressed orientation is, it is maintained, essential to the maintenance of the society. *Variant values are, therefore, not only permitted but actually required.* It has been the mistake of many in the social sciences, and of many in the field of practical affairs as well, to treat all behavior and certain aspects of motivation which do not accord with the dominant values as some kind of deviance. It is urged that we cease to confuse the deviant who by his behavior calls down the sanctions of his group with the variant who is accepted and frequently required as far as the total social system is concerned. This is especially true in a society such as ours, where beneath the surface of what has so often been called our compulsive conformity, there lies a wide range of variation. The dynamic interplay of the dominant and the variant is one of the outstanding features of American society, but as yet it has been little analyzed or understood.[50]

The many dimensions of stratification in the United States do not change the fact that class, personally experienced as income, occupation, education, and attitudes, limits or enhances chances for life and chances in life. Poverty is a handicap; wealth an advantage. It takes money to be born alive and to stay alive. Infant mortality bears an inverse relationship to income: the lower the income, the higher the mortality. Life expectancy bears a similar relationship. Those in the upper classes are generally healthier than those in the lower classes, and when they do get sick, physically or mentally,* they get more adequate care. It takes money to get a good education; it takes a good education to get a good job; and it generally takes money to make money. However, such simple measures do not give a full picture of class as a social reality affecting human behavior. It takes a minimum of security to be able to look ahead and plan for tomorrow. Realistic ambition is a luxury which can be afforded by only the more robust of the lower classes. The class values and attitudes incorporated by the child in the formative years of his personality predisposes him toward a way of life. Table 1 compares the percentages of boys at different intellectual and class levels who planned to go to college.[52]

TABLE I *Percentage of Boys Who Expected to Go to College, by I.Q. and Father's Occupation* [a]

	I. Q. QUINTILE					
	Low				*High*	*All Quintiles*
Father's Occupation	1	2	3	4	5	
Major white collar	56%	72%	79%	82%	89%	80%
Middle white collar	28	36	47	53	76	52
Minor white collar	12	20	22	29	55	26
Skilled labor & service	4	15	19	22	40	19
Other labor & service	9	6	10	14	29	12
All Occupations	11%	17%	24%	30%	52%	27%

[a] Boston area, 1950—3,348 boys in their sophomore and junior years in high school. Those of lowest intelligence and motivation had already been eliminated.

Notice that among boys of comparable tested intelligence, the class level of the boy's family as indicated by the father's occupation is a major variable. In the highest I.Q. quintile, only 29 per cent of the sons of unskilled labor and service workers had academic ambitions, as compared with 89 per cent of the sons of major white collar workers. Furthermore, the 1960 Census revealed that one out of three 16-year-old boys whose parents had not completed high school and whose family income was $3,000 per year or less had dropped out of school. Among boys whose parents had graduated from high school and whose family income was $7,000 or more per year, only one in seventeen were dropouts.

There is wasted talent in all groups, but the greatest loss is at the lower levels. An upper-class boy tends to accept going to college as he accepts other upper-class ways; it is simply the thing to do. A lower or working class boy—

* In an out-patient mental clinic where cost was no factor, the higher the social class of the patient, the better his treatment. Characteristically, lower-class patients were treated by students, middle-class patients by residents-in-training, and higher-class patients by senior staff members.[51]

even a lower-middle class one—has different models. If his parents are adjusted to their way of life, they have no reason to try to influence him to want anything different. He is not likely to have or to assert what might seem like pretentious ambitions against the despair, distrust, disapproval, or indifference of his family and friends.

Class erects more than economic barriers to mobility; it erects formidable psychological barriers which only the exceptional can surmount.

Political Barriers

Because the poor and the uneducated are disfranchised by ignorance, apathy, and embarrassment, as well as by poll taxes and intimidation, class, in effect, is also a political barrier to mobility. A national survey which divided the population into three economic groups—an upper quarter, a middle half, and a lower quarter—showed the corresponding proportion of voters in the 1944 presidential election to be 84, 68, and 53 per cent.[53] An upper-middle-class woman will campaign for a candidate. A lower class woman will vote "if I'm awake and have the strength."[54] Not only in the formal political area are the lower classes rendered relatively powerless. They are, in general, non-participators, and power, like status, is meaningful only in group interaction. ". . . economic and educational limitations accompanying low status produce a lack of interest in and a lack of self-confidence in dealing with certain important areas of our culture. . . ."[55] ". . . In every type of group, without exception—church, fraternal, service, recreational, patriotic, political, cultural—membership on the part of the lower income class was markedly lower."[56]

It costs money to belong; it takes time and energy; it also takes self-confidence and competence. A working-class mother, aware of her shabby clothes, her poor grammar, her crude manners, will hesitate to appear even at a P.T.A. meeting. People in the lower classes, in general, tend to keep to themselves. They are too embarrassed or too confused or too tired to take advantage of the group contacts open to them. They forfeit the opportunities they have to better themselves. They have limited participation and, therefore, they have limited political power.* Without political power, what is left? Only the power of protest—the violent, naked, physical power of the back alley jungles.

Thus it is that in a society which is formally "open class," social, economic, and political barriers to mobility create and maintain inequalities.

Equality or Equivalence?

In modern urban societies as in animal and primitive societies, the decisive measure of true equality is power—power to act or not to act, power to give or receive, power to command, power to choose. . . . Power, actual or potential,

* Membership in labor unions is a source of power for some persons who would otherwise be politically helpless.

is the ultimate expression of class and status as well as of political position. Since power, of whatever sort, has scarcity value, the more one person or group or institution or nation has in a particular situation, the less, in relative measure, another has. Any "balance of power" is as tenuous as the balance of a teeter-totter on a fulcrum. The slightest gain or loss affects the relationship.

Power-plays, large and small, are constantly going on within every society. The average individual, however, is most aware of his own shifting power within his immediate milieu. He measures himself, not against the total society, but only against others within his own particular section of society.

> Instead of being divided horizontally into levels and strata, as we are used to thinking of it, our society has increasingly become divided vertically. Instead of broad upper, middle, and lower classes that cut across the society of the nation like the clear but uneven slices on a geological model, we now have a series of almost free-standing pyramids, each with its several levels and each one topped by an aristocracy of its own. It is a far cry from the top of one of these pyramids to that of the next, and communication between the members of the aristocracies is occasionally difficult, for they not only speak different languages, but their minds are on quite different things.* They have different notions of what constitutes success (though they all like money, of course), and their "status symbols" . . . are as unlike as, say, a swimming pool and an academic hood.[57]

Business pyramids, political pyramids, labor pyramids, academic pyramids . . . each pyramid within the larger society has its own hierarchy. "As a functioning mechanism, a society must somehow distribute its members in social positions and induce them to perform the duties of these positions." [59] Power tends to accrue to those who perform well. Equality exists only as a conventional assumption intended to eliminate endless disputes over the many differences on which privilege could be based.

> Age, birth, merit, strength, color of skin, are adventitious details of the person, which can establish no rational ranking; for the strong man may be the wrong age for authority, the old man stupid or born in the wrong place. No scheme of inequality can be defended as corresponding to natural fact. And natural fact itself is elusive. Superior or inferior can be determined only with respect to a single quality for a single purpose. Nor can a man's qualities be added together and averaged to give a final score of merit. In short, men are incommensurable and must be deemed equal.

---

* A story by the president of the Carnegie Corporation indicates the psychological distance which can exist between pyramids.

At a reception following the commencement ceremony at one of our leading universities, a biologist whom I had known for years introduced me to his prospective son-in-law, and confided later that he was disappointed in his daughter's choice. I asked about his objections to the lad (who had impressed me very well). Was he stupid? No. Lazy? No. Ill-tempered? No. Finally my friend grinned wryly and said, "He works in a bank. He even wants to be president of it eventually."

"Is that bad?" I asked.

"Well, no . . . but I had hoped she'd pick a scientist—or at least an academic man. I don't even know how to talk to a banker!" [58]

> . . . Militant democrats might therefore begin to take equality for granted, instead of nervously trying to measure it hourly in self-defense. Identity of function and status is impossible, but equivalence we can have.[60]

Social, economic, and political inequalities define the social system and make mobility possible; equivalence in the sense of moral equality sustains the self and makes a meaningful life possible. "Honor is not a matter of any man's calling, merely, but rather of his own actions in it." *

* John S. Dwight (1813-1893).

Notes

1. John B. Calhoun, "Population Density and Social Pathology," *Scientific American,* February, 1962, p. 142.
2. Kingsley Davis, *Human Society* (New York: The Macmillan Company, 1949), p. 366.
3. Elman R. Service, *A Profile of Primitive Culture* (New York: Harper & Row, Publishers, 1958), pp. 251-252.
4. *Ibid.*, p. 252.
5. Leonard Reissman, *Class in American Society* (New York: Free Press of Glencoe, Inc., 1959), p. 388.
6. Talcott Parsons, "A Revised Analytical Approach to the Theory of Stratification," in *Class, Status and Power,* R. Bendix and S. M. Lipset, eds. (New York: Free Press of Glencoe, Inc., 1953), p. 94.
7. Joseph A. Kahl, *The American Class Structure* (New York: Holt, Rinehart & Winston, Inc., 1957), p. 9.
8. Max Weber, "Class, Status and Party," in H. H. Gerth and C. W. Mills, eds, & trans., from Max Weber, *Essays in Sociology,* Chap. 7 (New York: Oxford University Press, 1946).
9. Lord Nancy (source unknown), John Bartlett, *Familiar Quotations* (Boston: Little, Brown & Co., 1937), p. 942.
10. Vance Packard, *The Status Seekers* (New York: David McKay Company, Inc., 1959).
11. August B. Hollingshead, "Class Differences in Family Stability," in R. Bendix and S. M. Lipset, eds., *Class, Status and Power* (New York: Free Press of Glencoe, Inc., 1953), p. 287.
12. Hollingshead, *op. cit.*, pp. 287-288.
13. Murray Gendell and Hans L. Zetterberg, *A Sociological Almanac for the United States* (New York: Charles Scribner's Sons, 1964), p. 9.
14. *Ibid.*, p. 9.
15. *The San Francisco Chronicle,* January 29, 1962, p. 1.
16. *The San Francisco Chronicle,* January 2, 1962, p. 1.
17. *The San Francisco Chronicle,* January 2, 1962, p. 22.
18. *Public Opinion Quarterly,* XI (1947), p. 167.
19. Alex Inkeles, "Social Stratification and Mobility in the Soviet Union 1940-50," *American Sociological Review,* Vol. 15, August, 1950, pp. 465-479.
20. S. M. Miller, "Comparative Social Mobility," *Current Sociology,* Vol. 9, (1960), p. 40.
21. Kahl, *The American Class Structure,* p. 255.
22. *The San Francisco Chronicle,* February 2, 1962, p. 12.
23. William H. Whyte, Jr., *The Organization Man* (New York: Simon and Schuster, Inc., 1956).
24. Kahl, *op. cit.*, p. 276.
25. Dael Wolfle, *America's Resources of Specialized Talent* (New York: Harper & Row, Publishers, 1954), p. 24.
26. Reissman, *op. cit.*, p. 332.
27. Kahl, *op. cit.*, p. 282.
28. Reece McGee, *Social Disorganization in America* (San Francisco: Chandler Publishing Company, 1962), p. 103.
29. Kahl, *op. cit.*, p. 278.
30. Paul C. Glick, "Educational Attainment and Occupational Advancement," in *Transactions of the Second World Congress of Sociology* (London: International Sociological Association, 1954), Vol. II, pp. 183-194.

31. Kahl, "Educational and Occupational Aspirations of 'Common Man' Boys," *Harvard Educational Review,* XXIII, Summer, 1953, p. 188.
32. Kahl, *op. cit.,* p. 293.
33. Reissman, *op. cit.,* p. 371.
34. "The Wives of Management," *Fortune,* October, 1951, and "The Corporation and the Wife," *Fortune,* November, 1951.
35. August B. Hollingshead and Frederick C. Redlich, *Social Class and Mental Illness* (New York: John Wiley & Sons, Inc., 1958), pp. 367-370.
36. Pauline Snedden Sears, "Levels of Aspiration in Academically Successful and Unsuccessful Children," *Journal of Abnormal Social Psychology,* No. 35, 1940, pp. 498-536.
37. Hollingshead and Redlich, *op. cit.,* p. 371.
38. John W. Gardner, *Excellence* (New York: Harper & Row, Publishers, 1961), p. 81.
39. Melvin M. Tumin, "Some Unapplauded Consequences of Social Mobility in a Mass Society," *Social Forces,* October, 1957, pp. 32-37.
40. Kahl, *op. cit.,* p. 282.
41. *Ibid.,* p. 282.
42. Service, *A Profile of Primitive Culture,* p. 251.
43. Reissman, *op. cit.,* p. 51.
44. *Ibid.,* p. 224.
45. Kahl, *op. cit.,* pp. 187-217.
46. Packard, *op. cit.,* p. 38.
47. Kahl, *op. cit.,* p. 203.
48. Karen Horney, *The Neurotic Personality of Our Time* (New York: W. W. Norton & Company, Inc., 1937).
49. Hollingshead and Redlich, "Social Stratification and Psychiatric Disorders," American Sociological Review, Vol. 18, No. 2, April, 1953.
50. Florence Rockwood Kluckhohn, "Dominant and Variant Value Orientations," in *Personality in Nature, Society and Culture,* second edition, Clyde Kluckhohn and Henry A. Murray, eds. (New York: Alfred A. Knopf, Inc., 1956), p. 352-353.
51. Jerome K. Myers and Leslie Schaffer, "Social Stratification and Psychiatric Practice: A Study of an Out-Patient Clinic," *American Sociological Review,* Vol. 19, No. 3, June, 1954.
52. Kahl, *op. cit.,* p. 283.
53. Genevieve Knupfer, "Portrait of the Underdog," in *Class, Status, and Power,* R. Bendix and S. M. Lipset, eds. (New York: Free Press of Glencoe, Inc., 1953), p. 252.
54. Ben Northrup, *Tape Recorded Interview with Edith, 1956* (unpublished).
55. Knupfer, *op. cit.,* p. 256.
56. W. G. Mather, Jr., "Income and Social Participation," *American Sociological Review,* Vol. 6 (1941), p. 380.
57. Russell Lynes, *A Surfeit of Honey* (New York: Harper & Row, Publishers, 1957), p. 15.
58. John W. Gardner, *Excellence,* p. 10.
59. Kingsley Davis and Wilbert E. Moore, "Some Principles of Stratification," *American Sociological Review,* April, 1945, p. 215.
60. Jacques Barzun, *The House of Intellect* (New York: Harper & Row, Publishers, 1959), p. 260.

Men's natures are alike; it is their habits that carry them far apart.

CONFUCIUS (551–478 B.C.)

10

Stratification— Ethnic and Racial

"GIVE ME YOUR TIRED, your poor, your huddled masses yearning to breathe free, the wretched refuse of your teeming shore. Send these, the homeless, tempest-tost to me." *

By 1960, a total of forty-two million people, "yearning to be free," had immigrated to North America. This most extensive migratory tide in history, a spectrum of ethnic and racial groups, flowed out across the country, inundating and dispossessing the native Indians. Millions came voluntarily in search of freedom; hundreds of thousands more came involuntarily in chains, forcefully denied their freedom.†

The earliest New England settlers were self-conscious Puritans with a built-in sense of superiority. "God hath sifted a whole nation that he might send choice grain into this wilderness." [1] The Puritans were not the aristocrats of England, but they did include some moderately well-to-do and educated people. (Half of the eighty ministers in New England in 1643 were graduates of Oxford or Cambridge.) [2]

* Inscribed on the pedestal of the Statue of Liberty, 1908.

† Statistics on the number of slaves imported into this country are neither accurate nor complete. Traders brought more than 2,000,000 into the total British Colonial area (including the West Indies). Official records show 400,000 sold in the thirteen colonies and the United States between 1619, when the first slave market opened in Jamestown, and 1808, when Congress outlawed the slave trade. Thousands more were sold "off the record" both before and after 1808.

For the most part, however, they were ambitious middle- and lower-class laborers, tradesmen, and artisans intent not only on gaining religious freedom but on bettering their social and economic positions. They came from a clearly stratified society; they remained class-conscious and became race-conscious through contact with Negro slaves and Indians. They imported Negroes as chattel to serve their economic needs. They pushed aside and slaughtered Indians as savage children of the devil, that God-fearing whites might prosper.

These first settlers were white Anglo-Saxon Protestants (WASPs) and Dutch. They were joined by Germans, Swiss, and Scotch-Irish—people enough like themselves to assimilate easily. Together, as "Americans," they established the colonies, fought the War of Independence, and opened the frontier. Until the late nineteenth century, immigrants were mainly from the British Isles, northwest Europe, and Scandinavia. By 1890, however, the pattern changed. Industrial development, particularly in England, France, Belgium, and Germany, reduced emigration by luring people into factories, while unrest and poverty in southern and eastern Europe induced an increasing number of Slavs, Poles, Hungarians, Greeks, Italians, Russians, and Lithuanians to emigrate. In the two decades between 1890 and 1910, 8,000,000 immigrants to the United States (sixty per cent of the total) were southern and eastern Europeans, compared to 250,000 (five per cent of the total) in the two decades between 1860 and 1880.

These new immigrants were "different." They were not fair-skinned Protestants, but darker-complexioned Catholics or Jews, with what seemed strange and often uncouth ways. Furthermore, they came, not by the thousands, but by the millions. From the first census in 1790 until 1825, immigrants had averaged only about 8,000 a year at all ports. Each decade thereafter the number increased, to a high point of 8,795,386 between 1901 and 1910. Many were illiterate peasants with the primary intent—not of founding a new home and helping build a new nation but of accumulating money and returning with it to the "old country." The frontier had closed, and instead of moving westward and dispersing, as had so many immigrants before them, these later immigrants tended to huddle in the growing urban-industrial centers where work in factories and mines was readily available. They voluntarily remained aliens and sought their comfort and security within their own ethnic groups.

> . . . In 1890, forty-one per cent of the people of Chicago were foreign-born, and three-quarters were either foreign-born or the children of immigrants.[3] By the time of World War I, there were five million people in the United States who could not speak, read, or write English. More than half of the adult immigrants had never become citizens.[4]

"Americans" generally disliked and distrusted these aliens. They especially resented their willingness to accept low wages. This, intentionally or not, beat down the native working class. After the first World War, millions more people looked to the United States for asylum. The wage scale was high—we took no chances. Congress enacted immigration laws which ended, perhaps forever, the open-door policy.

The door closed on a heterogeneous, fragmented society. WASPs—with their class-conscious, race-conscious Puritan traditions—dominated the eastern states. The French, following their early explorers, concentrated near the mouth of the St. Lawrence in Canada and along the lower Mississippi in Louisiana. The Scandinavians settled in the Great Lakes area. The Spanish, along with the Mexicans, occupied the Southwest. Orientals were along the Pacific Coast. The emancipated Negroes, still segregated from the former master whites and generally despised by the poor whites, stayed largely in the South. The least successful of the southern and eastern Europeans kept to the racial ghettos in urban centers. Relatively few Indians ventured beyond the reservations. A nation "conceived in Liberty and dedicated to the proposition that all men are created equal" had transposed relatively insignificant biological and cultural traits into significant sociological facts. Stereotyped opinions, attitudes and beliefs held by members of one race or ethnic group regarding those of others established patterns of stratification which cut across the traditional strata of status, class and power. The various ethnic and racial groups had their own power pyramids, but in the larger society WASPs were in control. Minority groups had lesser positions. The greater the felt alienation (social distance) of a group from WASPs, the slower the assimilation, the greater the discrimination, and the more limited the opportunities for upward mobility.

PREJUDICE AND SOCIAL DISCRIMINATION

Ethnic and racial stratification in the United States has been, and still is, a shifting pattern of relationships. Each successive group as it has become established has tended to resent newcomers. WASPs originally resented all southern and eastern European "aliens." Various alien groups, in turn, resented each other and the Negroes who began migrating from the South to northern urban centers after the Civil War. Urban Negroes, particularly in New York, now resent the incoming Puerto Ricans. Prejudice is the common defense among all those of uncertain status who feel their positions threatened.

> There are four basic types of feeling that seem to be always present in race prejudice in the dominant group. They are (1) a feeling of superiority, (2) a feeling that the subordinate race is intrinsically different and alien, (3) a feeling of proprietary claim to certain areas of privilege and advantage, and (4) a fear and suspicion that the subordinate race harbors designs on the prerogatives of the dominant race. . . . It should be clear that these four basic feelings of race prejudice definitely refer to a positional arrangement of the racial groups. The feeling of superiority places the subordinate people *below;* the feeling

of alienation places them *beyond;* the feeling of proprietary claim excludes them from the prerogatives of position; and the fear of encroachment is an emotional recoil from the endangering of group position. As these features suggest, the positional relation of the two racial groups is crucial in race prejudice. The dominant group is not concerned with the subordinate group as such but it is deeply concerned with its position *vis-à-vis* the subordinate group. This is epitomized in the key and universal expression that a given race is all right in "its place." . . . The source of race prejudice lies in a felt challenge to this sense of group position. The challenge, one must recognize, may come in many different ways. It may be in the form of an affront to feelings of group superiority; it may be in the form of attempts at familiarity or transgressing the boundary line of group exclusiveness; it may be in the form of encroachment at countless points of proprietary claim; it may be a challenge to power and privilege; it may take the form of economic competition. Race prejudice is a defensive reaction to such challenging of the sense of group position. It consists of the disturbed feelings, usually of marked hostility, that are thereby aroused. As such, race prejudice is a protective device. It functions, however shortsightedly, to preserve the integrity and the position of the dominant group.[5]

Whether or not an individual or any ethnic or racial group *needs* to feel superior to someone of another ethnic or racial group is a function of personality as well as of social circumstance. Research studies indicate that ethnic attitudes, particularly negative ones, tend to be not a considered response to tested reality but an emotional reaction to an assumed reality.

. . . The investigator used an eight-step social distance test with a list of thirty-five ethnic groups arranged in alphabetical order. Of the thirty-five, thirty-two were bona fide designations of national, racial, and religious groups. Three, however, were fictitious, . . . Danireans, Pireneans, Wallonians. These three groups were listed in their proper alphabetical order without any differentiating marks . . . the results showed a consistent, high correlation between responses to existing groups and to nonexistent groups.[6]

. . . One student . . . made a mark next to each of the nonesuch and as a footnote wrote: "I don't know anything about them, therefore I would exclude them from my country." A classmate of this student also made marks next to each of the nonesuch groups, but he wrote: "I don't know anything about them; therefore I have no prejudices against them." [7]

Both subjects responded to the same verbal stimuli: Danireans, Pireneans and Wallonians. The fact that their responses were at opposite poles of the scale indicates that they responded—not to the stimuli but to their particular perception of the stimuli.* Generally, the more secure and accepted the individual perceives himself to be, the more accepting he is of others. And, conversely, the more tenuous and insecure the individual, the more rejecting he is—as if by belittling others he could aggrandize himself. Super-patriots who cling to a national image for security are typically bigots.[8]

---

* Chapter 6.

Insecure individuals reinforcing each other make up the hard core of prejudice—socially expressed through discriminatory mores, taboos, and laws. In the United States, social discrimination and the accompanying ethnic and racial stratification have particular significance relative to those minority groups within the United States which assimilate most slowly: Jews, Orientals, American Indians, and Negroes.

JEWISH MINORITIES

Jews are victims of a double prejudice—a theological one dating back to the beginning of Christianity, and a pseudo-scientific one dating from the beginning of the nineteenth century. Prejudice is widespread in all countries of Western civilization, and in some it supports more or less clandestine centers of anti-Semitism maintained by sympathizers of or former collaborators with the Nazi regime.

> Theological anti-Semitism dates back to early Christian times, when the first Christian Churches seemed to be nothing more than a dissidence from the Judaism to which they were opposed. The story of the Crucifixion as told in the Gospels, and the cry attributed to the Jews: "May his blood be visited upon us and upon our children" led to the conclusion that the Jews, by causing Jesus to be crucified, had judged and condemned themselves!
>
> And indeed, from that time on, the Fathers of the Church, powerless to convert the Jews, elaborated a doctrine which laid down that, having committed the crime of deicide, the Jews were condemned to eternal punishment and, like Cain, must wander over the world bearing witness by their abasement and servitude to the truth of the dogmas and the triumph of Christianity.
>
> Consequently, the status of the Jews, which was on the whole good in Roman and barbarian Europe, deteriorated as that same Europe became Christianized and learned to read. The great turning point was the period of the earliest Crusades, when first great massacres of Jews took place, against a background of religious exaltation of the masses. It was then that the tales of ritual murders committed by the Jews, profanations of the Host, poisoning of wells, and other similar legends, were spread. From then onwards, when an epidemic, famine or other calamity occurred, the Jews served as scapegoats: from time to time the people rose up and massacred them, whilst the princes alternately extorted wealth from them to fill their own treasuries or sent them into exile. In these circumstances, the Jews in the end became the chief pariahs of Europe.[9]

In the late sixteenth century, Shakespeare stereotyped the Jew as Shylock —the *Merchant of Venice;* then, through him, pleaded the cause of Jews.

> Hath not a Jew eyes? Hath not a Jew hands, organs, dimensions, senses, affections, passions? Fed with the same food, hurt with the same weapons, subject to the same diseases, healed by the same means, warmed and cooled by the same winter and summer, as a Christian is? If you prick us, do we not

bleed? If you tickle us, do we not laugh? If you poison us, do we not die? And if you wrong us, shall we not revenge? *

But no pleas on the part of Jews or their spokesmen changed the prevailing prejudice until the *Age of Enlightenment,* when philosophers succeeded in pointing out that the miserable condition of the Jews was not a divine malediction but a state to which Christian society had relegated them. The idea gained wide enough acceptance in an increasingly secular society to lead to political action; and between 1789 and 1848, Jews in all countries of Western Europe became "full citizens," with rights equal to those of Protestants and Catholics.

Ghettos disappeared and theological anti-Semitism diminished, but the contempt that Christians for centuries had been taught did not magically disappear.† It found a new rationale in the social ascendance of Jews impatient to compensate for their long abasement. Traits Christians identified in themselves as virtues they perceived in Jews as vices. Christians praised themselves as being "thrifty" and "ambitious"; they resented Jews for being "mercenary" and "aggressive." Furthermore, science was a new authority which set up various academic systems of classifying *Homo sapiens* according to physical types with assumed emotional and mental correlates. Hasty hypotheses led to the erroneous assumption that Jews were a "race," rather than an ethnic group.‡ The "scientific anti-Semitism" of the Nazi movement taught, not the Christian *contempt* for Jews, but *hatred* of Jews, and in Germany under Hitler (1933-1945), Nazis tortured and put to death some 6,000,000 men, women, and children. "Nazism made birth a crime punishable by death. Jews, half-Jews, quarter-Jews died for no other reason than their descendancy. . . ."[10]

In the United States, anti-Semitism smolders. Christians retain much of their traditional prejudice, unsupported though it is by either theology or science. They furthermore tend to categorize Jews as a single cohesive ethnic group, unaware that among contemporary Jews are Zionists, anti-Zionists, and a large overlapping group of liberal nonreligious Jews. The philosophical commitments of these different groups affect their readiness for assimilation.

Religious Zionists, for example, emphasize the difference between Jews and non-Jews, insist on Jewish unity and fealty of the individual to the group. They tend to support tradition in religion and customs, to assume the inevitability of anti-Semitism in Christian societies, and to expect refuge and an end to their marginality only within the Jewish homeland. Their in-group response to out-group pressures has tended to make theirs a self-fulfilling prophesy.

---

* William Shakespeare, *Merchant of Venice,* Act III, Scene I.

† Not until 1964 were Jews formally absolved from special guilt in Christ's death by the Roman Catholic Ecumenical Council. "All that happened to Christ in His Passion cannot be attributed to the whole [Jewish] people then alive, much less to that of today."

‡ Arabs are the purest representatives of the Semitic "racial type" in the world, yet, for primarily political reasons, they are violently anti-Jewish.

Religious anti-Zionists, in contrast, assume the essential sameness of Jews and non-Jews and consequently grant the individual more freedom to leave the group and identify with the larger society. They hold that Jews are a religious, not a tribal or even a cultural group, and recognize that rapid changes in contemporary society call for changes in the Jewish religion. Anti-Zionists anticipate integration of Jews into the larger Christian society and an eventual end to anti-Semitism.[11]

Before the persecution of the Jews under Hitler in Germany and the consequent rise of anti-Semitism, Zionists in the United States tended to be predominantly parvenu Jews of generally Orthodox background from the ghettos of eastern Europe. However, the Zionist movement in the United States today has support even among old established families which previously had been anti-Zionist.

"In our rapidly changing society, there is no consensus upon the boundaries of an ethnic group nor upon the criteria of definition of the group upon which the boundaries are based,"[12] yet non-Jews do tend to stereotype Jews as a distinct group. Within the United States, attitudes towards those branded by the stereotype vary, but many persons privately harbor prejudice and many groups publicly reveal prejudice. A discriminatory pattern in education showed clearly in 1949. The admission rate of high-school students to college was 77 per cent for Protestants, 67 per cent for Catholics, and 56 per cent for Jews.[13] Departments within colleges had secondary "quota systems." Said Dr. Albert Sprague Coolidge of Harvard in testimony before a legislative committee, "We know perfectly well that names ending in a '*berg*' or a '*stein*' have to be skipped by the board of selections for scholarships in chemistry." (The restrictive chemical industry in this case provided most of the chemistry scholarships and had a "gentleman's agreement" with the University.)[14] In 1960, 50 per cent of *public* colleges in the South and 20 per cent of those in the North and West asked questions regarding religion on application forms. Answers to such questions, the President's Commission on Higher Education pointed out, can be used for discriminatory purposes.[15] Although academic discrimination seems to be declining,* quota systems in graduate and professional schools—particularly medical ones—still do limit occupational opportunities for some upwardly mobile Jews. Furthermore, approximately 20 per cent of job orders received by commercial employment agencies between 1951 and 1957 for white collar jobs and higher executive positions excluded Jews.[17] However, because Jews have been successfully self-employed in both the professions and small businesses, and have had access to some high-paying jobs, discrimination against Jews has not worked any general economic hardship on them. The Jewish population in the United States is predominantly middle-class. Socially, however, Jews are excluded from or restricted by various social clubs, resort

* In the 1940's, 90 per cent of all colleges and universities required statements regarding religious preference on application forms. Between 1950 and 1960 the average percentage of Jewish students in the private Ivy League colleges rose from 15 to 22 per cent.[16]

hotels, restaurants, and some residential districts. As late as 1955, one-third of 248 cities ranging in population from 10,000 to 500,000 denied Jews entrance to the Junior League, certain high status clubs, and exclusive residential areas.[18] In only 20 per cent of the cities, mainly the smaller ones, were *some* Jews fully accepted. And, in spite of student protests, some national college fraternities either exclude Jews or have quota systems. The relative scarcity of Jews in public office is a reflection of prevailing prejudice against them. Not until 1949 was a Jew elected to the United States Senate.* The one Jew previously in the Senate had been appointed in 1915, thirty-four years earlier.

Attitude surveys designed to uncover prejudice among WASPs reveal an inverse relationship between class position and strength of prejudice. The higher his class, the less prejudiced is the WASP against all non-WASPs, *except Jews.* The higher his class, the more prejudiced he tends to be against Jews. Upper-class WASPs began to discriminate when they felt their own social and economic positions jeopardized by academically and economically successful Jews. The higher the position to which the Jew aspires, the more discrimination he is likely to encounter.

A Caucasian, however, of whatever ethnic group, can Anglicize his name, identify with the ways of the WASPs, intermarry, and, within a generation or two, lose ethnic identity in the "melting pot." Racial identity cannot be shed as easily. Each of the three major races—Caucasoid, Mongoloid, and Negroid—has an "ideal type," with such characteristic biological traits as skin color, hair color and texture, head proportion, shape of eyelid fold. Approximately fifty racially linked traits make up an estimated one per cent of man's total genetic inheritance.[19] "Race" is no more than a convenient designation for the central tendencies of a group relative to such biological traits. More variation in these traits exists among members of any single race than among the average individuals of the several races. However, race-conscious persons tend to look for "tell-tale" signs, and classify individuals accordingly.

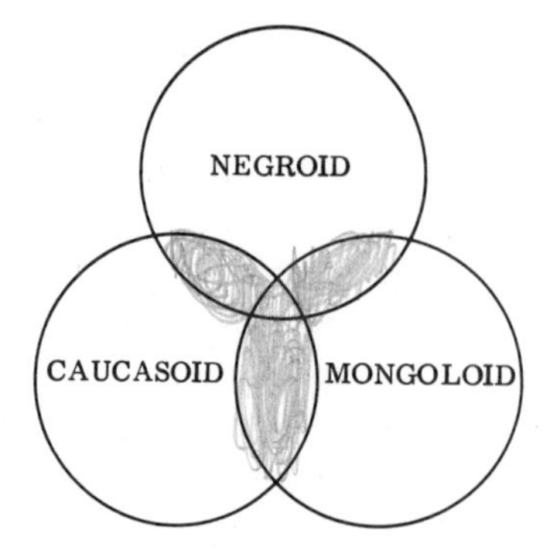

Circles Represent Overlapping of Racial Traits, Measured Either Singly or as a Configuration

* Herbert Lehman, formerly governor of New York.

ORIENTAL MINORITIES

With racial minorities as with ethnic ones, the larger and denser the population, the more likely the majority is to perceive the group as threatening and to set up barriers against its members. The Oriental minorities on the Pacific Coast are a case in point. The Chinese in the nineteenth century first bore the brunt of anti-Oriental feeling.

> In the beginning race prejudice was subordinated to industrial necessity. The Chinese were among "the most worthy of our new adopted citizens," "our most orderly and industrious citizens," "the best immigrants in California"; they were "thrifty," "sober," "tractable," "inoffensive," "law-abiding"; they showed "an all-round ability" and an "adaptability" beyond praise. As laborers on the ranches they were not competitors, as they had been in the mines. But in the cities, as years passed, as the immigration of whites continued and mining became less profitable, the manifold activities of the Chinese brought them again into competition with white labour in an increasingly large number of occupations. . . . The Chinese were now "a distinct people," "unassimilable," "keeping to their own customs and laws." They "did not settle in America"; "they carried back gold to their homes"; they "went back to China." Their mere presence "lowered the plane of living"; they "shut out the white labour." They were "clannish," "dangerous" because of their secret societies, "criminal," "secretive in their actions," "debased and servile," "deceitful and vicious," inferior from a mental and moral point of view, immeasurably lower than the Indians, for instance. . . . They were "filthy and loathsome in their habits," and their "unsanitary quarters made the neighborhood uninhabitable." They were "undesirable as workers and as residents of the country." [20] *

At the turn of the century, the increasing number of Japanese immigrants shifted the focus of anti-Oriental feeling and precipitated the two most severe outbreaks of racism in California history.

A resolution to establish segregated schools for Oriental children in San Francisco—passed May 6, 1905—nearly started a war between the United States and Japan.

> *Resolved,* That the Board of Education is determined in its efforts to effect the establishment of separate schools for Chinese and Japanese pupils, not only for the purpose of relieving congestion at present prevailing in our schools, but also for the higher end that our children should not be placed in any position where their youthful impressions may be affected by association with pupils of the Mongolian race.[21]

This resolution did not go into practical effect until fall, 1906. Meanwhile, in April of that year, the disastrous earthquake and fire had struck San Fran-

* In response to such stereotypes, Congress passed the Chinese Exclusion Act of 1882. During World War II this act was modified to allow 105 Chinese immigrants a year to enter the United States.

cisco. In the subsequent Red Cross relief drive, citizens of Japan contributed more than all the other nations of the world combined. They felt it particularly ungracious of the Board of Education to implement the discriminatory resolution. Many Japanese called for a declaration of war against the United States; some of them, not understanding the nature of our federal system, simply wanted to declare war on California. Only three-way negotiations between President Theodore Roosevelt, the Japanese ambassador, and the San Francisco Board of Education finally resolved the dispute.*

The attack on Pearl Harbor in 1941 brought a second outburst of anti-Japanese sentiment. Under the fear and pressure of war, the Federal Government took 110,000 Japanese—the majority American-born citizens—from their homes on the West Coast to government concentration camps. Officials justified the act as a military necessity; their argument lost weight, however, when Italian prisoners of war released from prison camps on week-end passes wandered through the California cities from which American citizens of Japanese descent—including women and children—had been removed as "security risks."

After the war, anti-Japanese feeling subsided. Those Japanese who fearfully returned to the Coast were surprised to find their reception far less hostile than they had anticipated. By the mid-1950's, Japanese-Americans had generally re-established themselves, although they did suffer—as before the war—both job and housing discrimination. Japanese and Chinese still make up a minority group distinct enough in those cities where they concentrate to be a tourist attraction. Orientals are *in* but not *of* American society.

AMERICAN INDIANS

These original Americans of ancient Mongoloid heritage came to the New World as Stone Age people, crossing from Siberia into Alaska as long as 20,000 years ago. Over the centuries they made their way down the North and South American continents, and when the white men came, they were undergoing processes of change comparable to those which had brought "civilization" to the Old World some 3,000 years earlier. We call their progeny "Indians," but they differ widely in biological features, in stature, head shape, and skin color, as well as in language and other cultural traits. Today, like their Oriental cousins, they are tourist attractions. On their reservations, and at country fairs, they sell their artifacts, put on costumes, perform dances, and otherwise conjure up fragments of their dying cultures.

Until 1870 the United States government dealt with Indian tribes as little foreign nations, making and breaking treaties with them, as expedience indicated. General Sheridan expressed the attitude towards Indians prevalent in the nineteenth century when he said, "The only good Indians I ever saw

---

* Congress outlawed Japanese immigration in 1924. The McCarran-Walter Act of 1952 modified this law to allow 185 Japanese immigrants a year.

were dead." The government supported action which elevated many an Indian to this state of "goodness."

> From 1857 to 1879 the Cheyennes were embroiled in almost continuous fighting with the Americans. The wars were not of their own choosing, but were forced upon them by whites who were little disposed to discriminate among Indians. The Cheyennes were made to suffer for the more aggressive hostility of the Sioux, Kiowas, and Comanches, until they, too, were inextricably involved in the bitter, bloody death struggles from which there was no escape but humiliating surrender and the ignoble lassitude of reservation life. A number of the fights were pitched battles between campaigning troops and sizable bodies of warriors; some, such as those at Ash Hollow (1855) and Sand Creek (1864), were unprovoked assaults on friendly Cheyenne camps in which women and children were slaughtered along with the men who tried to defend them.[22]

After 1880, the government brought shooting wars with Indians to an end, but legal attacks on them have never entirely ended.

Feelings of guilt and attempts at reform now temper the government's traditional antagonism and paternalism. In 1924, in recognition of the service of some 10,000 Indians in World War I, Congress passed a law granting citizenship to all Indians. Although state and federal court decisions have since conclusively supported the citizenship rights of Indians and maintained that the government has no more legal authority over the personal actions of an Indian than over those of any other citizen, Indians frequently "cannot have access to their own funds without the consent of Congress or the Department of the Interior, or both, and withholding of funds can be used to force agreements." [23] In 1934 Congress passed the Indian Reorganization Act, under which Indians modernized their tribal organization and became able to protest wrongs and more effectively defend their rights. Since 1953 the official policy of the Indian Bureau—as stated in the House Concurrent Resolution 108—has encouraged qualified Indians to leave reservations.

> It is the policy of Congress, as rapidly as possible, to make the Indians within the United States subject to the same laws and entitled to the same privileges and responsibilities as are applicable to other citizens of the United States, to end their status as wards of the United States, and to grant them all of the rights and prerogatives pertaining to American citizenship.

Critics of government policy view the resolution cynically.

> From the very beginnings of this nation, the chief issue around which Federal Indian policy has revolved has been, not how to assimilate the Indian nations whose lands we usurped, but how best to transfer Indian lands and resources to non-Indians.[24]

The Indian Bureau is in the difficult position of trying to amend wrongs against a people who have learned "never to trust a white man." However, the Bureau does help Indians leaving reservations to get jobs and housing in urban centers, and the Bureau is furthering its integration policy by contracting for the admission of Indian children to state schools. In 1956 Indian children in seventeen states attended regular public schools instead of special federal Indian schools. However, the Indian, once he has left the reservation, forfeits the rights he had as a resident and competes with those who stereotype him as a "no-good Indian" and ask why he doesn't go back to the reservation "where he belongs."

Indians are not going to "vanish" and thereby eliminate the ethical and sociological problems their presence raises.* Some few Indians—New England Indians, for example—who were neither put on reservations nor segregated, have, in effect, vanished; they exist only as legendary figures in some family genealogies. The English gentleman, John Rolfe, did marry Pocahontas. Other Indians have retained their identity and achieved status as educated and economically successful individuals, but most Indians belong to a deprived minority.

Three-fourths of the 400,000 Indians counted in 1956 had an annual income of $1,500.00 or below; the median was $725, compared with the national median of $2,619.[25] Between fifteen and twenty per cent of the adults had never been to school, and seventeen per cent of school-age children were not enrolled in school. Infant mortality among the Navajos was seven times the national average. The tuberculosis rate was nine times, and death from measles was twenty-nine times that of the general population.

As late as 1959 some Indian tribes along the Atlantic Coast east of the Appalachian Mountains and deep into the South had no federal status. Many are recognized only to the extent of being more or less segregated and, although partly or largely white in ancestry, forbidden by law to marry whites.[26]

Discovery of oil and gas on lands assigned to Indians brought many wealth; but—as in the case of the 2,000 Osage Indians of Oklahoma who received $265,000,000 in oil royalties between 1915 and 1931—lack of experience in a money economy negated much of their gain. ". . . ninety per cent of this total went 'down the wind' of ruined Osages and corrupted and corrupting whites." [27]

White men now cultivate the corn, sweet potatoes, and the "Irish" potatoes domesticated by Indians before the Irish ever reached this continent. The world thanks—or blames—the Indians for tobacco. It is generally conceded, though not proved, that the framers of the United States Constitution took ideas from the League of the Iroquois.

> The pattern of states within a state that we call federalism, the habit of treating chiefs as servants of the people instead of masters, the insistence that the community must respect the diversity of men and their dreams—all these things were part of the American way of life before 1492.[28]

---

* The Indian population did dwindle from approximately 1,000,000 in 1492 to 250,000 at the end of the nineteenth century. In the twentieth century, the population began to increase, and by 1960 it had reached 400,000.

The Dutch paid the Indians $24.00 for Manhattan Island, but most of our cities and towns stand on land less legally acquired. In 1933 only 47,000,000 acres in the entire United States remained in Indian ownership. "Pale faces" stripped the Indian of his land, his culture, his pride. *Who can blame him if becoming "just like a white man" is not his heart's desire?*

AMERICAN NEGROES

Discovery of the New World and the consequent development of the vast North and South American continents demanded cheap labor on an unprecedented scale. From the beginning, slave traders supplied a large part of the demand with Negroes captured in Africa. In 1619, twelve years after the founding of Jamestown and one year before the arrival of the Pilgrims, Virginia settlers bought their first twenty Negro slaves. More than 300 years later, nearly twenty million Negroes in the United States felt themselves still in bondage.

Stratification Through Slavery

The Negro as slave had no human rights. He was to slave trader and slave master alike a possession over which they had property rights. The slave traders handled Negroes in transit as impersonally as any other cargo.

> The passage to the New World took about six weeks in good weather, and every night the slaves were packed "spoon fashion" below the decks, so close together they had to lie on their sides. They were shackled together in two's, and the horrors of the passage became particularly evident in rough weather . . . when the slaves were perforce kept below decks by day as well as by night, and the portholes had to be shut. Negroes were more seriously affected by seasickness than Europeans, and in stormy weather may well have been too ill to think about the buckets provided for their use; but in any event the buckets were almost inaccessible in that mass of human wretchedness, where it was hardly possible to walk without treading on others, and those trodden upon were apt to retaliate by biting the intruding foot. Sooner or later the slaves were obliged to wallow in their own vomiting and filth, and the stench in the confined area became overpoweringly foul. Nor was it made better by the stifling heat and the lack of air. Many a fight and many a death took place when men less prostrate than others struggled and bit and fought to get near the gratings, through which alone came some semblance of fresh air. In such an atmosphere, epidemics were only too likely and dysentery could run through the ship, carrying off numbers not only of the slaves but also of the crew. The misery was intense; it explained and more than justified the efforts at insurrection which were often made and were sometimes successful.[29]

And after masters bought those captives who survived the passage, they still had no human rights. A master could separate a slave from his spouse and his children. A slave could not legally marry, own property, vote, testify in court, or move about without permission; neither was he permitted to learn to read or write. His master, as punishment, might whip him, or, for such a crime as trying to run away, kill him. Elaborate slave codes protected the privileges of the master.

> At the heart of every code was the requirement that slaves submit to their masters and respect all white men. The Louisiana code of 1806 proclaimed this most lucidly: "The condition of the slave being merely a passive one, his subordination to his master and to all who represent him is not susceptible of modification or restriction . . . he owes to his master, and to all his family, a respect without bounds, and an absolute obedience, and he is consequently to execute all the orders which he receives from him, his said master, or from them." A slave was neither to raise his hand against a white man nor to use insulting or abusive language. Any number of acts, said a North Carolina judge, may constitute "insolence"—it may be merely "a look, the pointing of a finger, a refusal or neglect to step out of the way when a white person is seen to approach. But each of such acts violates the rules of propriety, and if tolerated, would destroy that subordination, upon which our social system rests." [30]

The behavior of white masters was calculated to make the Negro slaves feel personally inferior.

> They had "to know and keep their places," to "feel the difference between master and slave," to understand that bondage was their natural status. They had to feel that African ancestry tainted them, that their color was a badge of degradation. In the country they were to show their respect for even their master's non-slaveholding neighbors; in the towns they were to give way on the streets to the most wretched white men. The line between the races must never be crossed, for familiarity caused slaves to forget their lowly station and to become "impudent." [31]

Even "free" Negroes—and some were technically free—were subjected before the Civil War to severe restrictions. Their anomalous status threatened the institution of slavery by seeming to refute the fact "that nature's God intended the African for the status of slavery." [32]

When the British Parliament outlawed slavery in all British dominions in 1834, Northern abolitionists increased their agitation, and Southerners were troubled. They believed, as did Northerners, in the abstract concepts of freedom and equality, but the economy of the South was built on cotton and slaves.

> To stem our guilt, we began to defend the indefensible: we declared that God had made the white race superior to other races—and thereby tried to justify our exploitation of darker men. . . . Perhaps we should not blame our old grandfathers too much. They lived in a time of ignorance, when there were few facts about genetics or cultures or the human body and mind. No one knew the real reasons why pigmentation of the skin differs in different parts of the earth; the effects of thousands of years of climate and food and inbreeding

had not been studied. There were, as yet, no means, no techniques for acquiring such knowledge. And so, in their guilty need to justify what could not be justified, they fell back on superstitions and old wives' tales, on half-truths and whole lies—piling up these verbal defenses until they had walled themselves away from what they could not bear to see.[33]

Slave owners had slavery so successfully rationalized into the Southern way of life that some eighty per cent of *all* Southerners believed in the system.

Woodland Falls, Ala.
October 24, 1865

Dear Uncle Butler:

. . . I do not think with you that slavery, as it existed among us, was an evil. There were evils and abuses connected with it, as there are with the marriage and parental relations. Like them, it is a Divine institution, as the Bible abundantly shows; and God gave the laws for regulating it in both the Old and New Testaments. Placed a guard about it in two commandments, in the first protecting the slave and in the last the owner. In the 24 c of Genesis and 35 v slaves are called a blessing *bestowed by God* on Abraham. He directed the Israelites to go to the heathen and buy them, and said they should be an *inheritance forever* to their children. In the New Testament the Institution is recognized and upheld by the duties of both Master and slave being distinctly laid down. Once I thought as you do and would have rejoiced to have been able to cast off the responsibility of being a slaveholder: but this I could not, let me turn which way I would, for God had made me one, and if I gave them their freedom, or sold them I could not shift the responsibility, for as they were a sacred trust to me it was my duty to watch over them and try to train them for heaven, and if evil befell them in other hands I would be in part accountable. Had I lived North I have no doubt I would have been an abolitionist because I would not have studied the subject as I have. I am now of the opinion that abolitionism has its root in infidelity. It is man setting his notions above the written word of God.[34]

Because slave owners could admit no evil in slavery, they bitterly resented the Civil War and the Emancipation Proclamation. A nephew writes to the same Uncle Butler:

Cannon Burke County, Georgia
October 3, 1865

Dear Uncle Butler:

I had paid my Fathers Estate out of debt at the beginning of the war and we were all in comfortable and easy circumstances. The war has stripped us of everything except our land. Mr. Lincoln's proclamation (whether legal or not it boots not) has deprived us of our Negroes and we are now poor indeed, having land without labor to work it—for we have not the remotest hope that we can make free labor profitable in this country. Cotton is the only crop we can grow to any profit here and that can only be raised by compulsory labor—labor that we can command from January to January. So you need not expect any more

> cotton from the South. In my judgement, the extinction of slavery will prove the ruin of the North as well as the South. Take away the cotton raised by the South and the United States will stand before the world like "Sampson shorn of his locks." What is New England (saintly New England) to do for cotton and what are you Western people to do for a market for your grains, pork, horses, etc.? Do you expect to sell these things to Free Negroes, or as they are politely termed "Freemen"? This utter prostration of every interest—*this upheaving of the very foundations of society and imperiling the peace of our home and the safety of our lives,* is all for what? Simply to accomplish a political idea—that your Northern politicians may get on the stump and say—"*There is not a slave that breathes the air of America.*" What folly—stupendous folly, that the poor Negroes should be ruined—crushed for such an idea. He, poor creature, is to be the *worst sufferer* turned out upon the world without a protector—*landless, homeless, houseless,* and without even wits to make a living. They are to live by "compensated labor" when every intelligent man must know that there was not a slave at the South that did not get more clear money from his Master at the end of the year than he could hope to earn in any other way. There was not a laboring chap upon the earth whose physical wants and conditions were better cared for than the slaves of the South. The highest evidence of which is the *increase of the race.* But enough of this, you will pardon this digression. I have been led into it by the utter prostration and ruin that awaits us. . . .[35]

The Civil War maintained the political Union of the States and ended the institution of slavery, but it left the states still divided on the Negro question, and Negroes are not yet free.

Stratification Through Caste *

For twelve years after the Civil War (1865-1877), federal troops occupied the South trying to enforce some semblance of the equality determined by the Emancipation Proclamation, Congressional enactments, and Constitutional Amendments. The war was ended but not won. Following the Reconstruction period, discriminatory laws gradually replaced slavery with a caste system embodying now-familiar Negro-white differentials in status, class and power.

The first Jim Crow law in the nation—that requiring separate railway coaches—passed the Mississippi legislature in 1888.

> (The presence of Negroes) on trains upon equal terms with white men was once regarded as normal, acceptable, and unobjectionable . . . black man and white man once rode them together and without a partition between them. Later on the stateways apparently changed the folkways—or at any rate the railways—for the partitions and Jim Crow became universal. And the new seating arrangements came to seem as normal, unchangeable, and inevitable as the old ways. And so it was with the soda fountains, eating places, bars, waiting rooms, street cars, and circuses.[36]

* Some sociologists would challenge the use of *caste* in this context. Call the constellation of folkways, mores, taboos, and laws which have defined the Negro position in the United States by any other name, it is still unique and needs some distinctive designation.

Segregation and the doctrine, "separate but equal," got judicial blessing from the Federal Supreme Court in 1896.

> We consider the underlying fallacy of the plaintiff's argument to consist in the assumption that the enforced separation of the two races straps the colored race with a badge of inferiority. If this is so it is not by reason of anything found in the act, but solely because the colored race chooses to put that construction upon it.

Segregationists welcomed these words and passed more Jim Crow laws. Once segregation was "the law of the land," disfranchisement followed—through poll taxes,* discriminatory literacy tests, violence and threats of violence. In Louisiana in 1896, for example, 130,334 Negroes voted; in 1904 only 1,342 voted; and, as late as 1948, after considerable increase in the Negro population, only 1,672 voted.†

> (During) . . . the 'seventies, 'eighties, and 'nineties the Negroes voted in large numbers. White leaders of the opposing parties encouraged them to vote and earnestly solicited their votes. Qualified and acknowledged leaders of Southern white opinion were on record as saying that it was proper, inevitable, and desirable that they should vote. Yet after the disfranchisement measures were passed around 1900, the Negroes ceased to vote. And at that time qualified and acknowledged leaders of white opinion said that it was unthinkable that they should ever be permitted to vote.[37]

By 1913 Jim Crow reached Washington, and the "White House" took on a new meaning. The nation's capital became a city of segregated housing, segregated schools, segregated restaurants, segregated swimming pools, segregated theaters, segregated bowling alleys, and so on and on.

Efforts initiated by the Reconstruction to integrate the Negro into the larger society ended in failure. Caste replaced slavery.

The Nature of Caste

The term "*caste*" has an alien ring. It connotes India, Brahmans, untouchables, fakirs, and sacred cows. However, seven essentials of the Indian caste system [39] are manifest in the position of the Negroes in the United States.

1. *Membership in a caste is hereditary.* In the United States an individual is born either white or nonwhite by social definition. A child inherits the social status of his parents, or of the nonwhite parent, in the case of mixed marriages. Mixed marriages are rare, but illicit miscegenation accounts for the fact that approximately seventy per cent of all Negroes in the United

---

* Poll taxes were an upper-class device which discriminated against the poor white as well as against the Negro. It disfranchised a larger *percentage* of Negroes but a larger *number* of whites.

† The recovery under the Civil Rights movement has been as dramatic as the original loss. The number of Negro voters in Louisiana was 106,724 in 1952; 161,410, in 1956.[38]

States have some Caucasoid ancestry, and some twenty per cent of all Caucasoids have some Negro ancestry.

2. *Membership in a caste is fixed for life.* The only way an American Negro can fully avoid discriminations inherent in caste membership is to "pass" for white. Biologically, a Negro who could "*pass*" for white would *be* white; but we define race as caste. A "Negro" who "passes" over the color line loses his "white" status if he is discovered. *Negro* is variously defined. In Georgia, anyone who has any ascertainable amount of Negro blood is a Negro.

3. *Choice of a marriage partner is endogamous.* Laws prohibit Negro-white marriages in approximately half of the States in the United States; mores prohibit them in all others. Even in Hawaii, where Oriental-white marriages are common, Negro-white marriages are relatively uncommon and not quite fully accepted.

4. *Consciousness of caste membership is emphasized by identification of individuals by caste name.* Negroes are "hyphenated Americans." They are generally called, not simply Americans, but American Negroes. Newspapers, for example, tend to identify those who are actors, entertainers or otherwise newsworthy by race: Negro actor, Negro halfback, Negro doctor. . . . Outside the South, identification of criminals is one recent exception to this general rule.

5. *The caste may be united by a common traditional occupation.* In India, members of a single caste tend to have the same occupation. In the United States, Negroes follow a wide range of occupations; however, the "cotton pickin'" heavy duty jobs are not "white man's work." In San Francisco, summer 1962, we observed six men "working" on a construction job. Five white men stood around a hole in which a Negro was digging with pick and shovel. An hour later the scene had shifted only slightly. The hole was deeper, but the white men were still standing and the Negro was still digging. In general, low-status jobs are Negro jobs. This is true for women as well as for men. The domestics hired to do the cleaning and laundry in homes throughout the country are mostly Negro women.

Whites tend to resist those Negroes who would compete with them for the more desirable jobs. When the first Negro hired by a West Coast municipal transportation system was training for a motorman's job in 1940, he was physically attacked several times—so violently that twice he was knocked unconscious. He "hung tough," however, stayed on the job, and managed to break that particular racial barrier. Some years later he applied for a job requiring security clearance. Investigating agents sought us out and, in reference to his being the first Negro motorman in the city, asked, "Do you think he was trying to advance the cause of his race, or did he just want a job?"

6. *The relative prestige of different castes in a locality is well established and jealously guarded.* We measure prestige by a variety of status symbols—the "right" label in the suit of clothes, the "famous" restaurant, the "exclusive" neighborhood. Relative prestige is a function of availability. Whites use resi-

dential restrictions, for example, to maintain supposed "prestige" of a given neighborhood and rationalize such restrictions in terms of "protecting property values." However, a five-year study by the Fund for the Republic, covering 10,000 real estate transactions in six northern and western cities found that when nonwhites buy houses in white neighborhoods, real estate values are four times more likely to rise or remain constant than to decline.[40] Unscrupulous realtors, however, help keep alive the fear of Negro infiltration by the technique of "block busting." They panic whites into selling their property at a loss to the realtors themselves. The realtors then resell at an inflated price to Negroes who willingly pay more than market value to get desirable housing.

7. *Contact between the castes is limited.* Segregation with all its contact taboos is a version of the *ritual avoidance* typical of caste. Contact between Negroes and whites is socially sanctioned as long as the status difference holds. A white household accepts a Negro as a servant but rarely as a friend or a boarder. Eating and drinking together as equals has been a particularly strict taboo in the South. A Southern white who temporarily darkened his skin and traveled through the South as a Negro wrote:

> On Chartres Street in the French Quarter I walked toward Brennan's, one of New Orleans' famed restaurants. Forgetting myself for a moment, I stopped to study the menu that was elegantly exposed in a show window. I read, realizing that a few days earlier I could have gone in and ordered anything on the menu. But now, though I was the same person with the same appetite, the same appreciation, and even the same wallet, no power on earth could get me inside this place for a meal.[41]

The taboo extended even to ordinary restaurants. During World War II, when a trainload of German prisoners stopped at a Southern station for lunch, the prisoners ate in the station restaurant; the Negro G.I.'s guarding them went hungry. No "colored" restaurant was available. The eating-drinking taboo even inspired a soft-drink vending machine with segregated coin slots marked "Colored" and "White."[42]

Ritual avoidance underlies school segregation. The University of Oklahoma admitted its first Negro student in 1948 under a Federal District Court Order, but assigned him to a separate classroom where he could neither see nor adequately hear his professors. He protested. The District Court ruled against him, but he carried his case to the Federal Supreme Court. Under Federal Court order the university gave him a desk in the regular classroom—with a railing around it. Credit goes to white students for tearing down the railing! Segregation pursues the Negro even into the grave. Many parts of the country have segregated cemeteries, and some have segregated war memorials. At least one community in the United States has a segregated pet cemetery,[43] assignment made by—not the color of the pet—but the color of the pet's owner. And Atlanta courts have even used separate Bibles for swearing in Negro and white witnesses.

SUMTER'S MEMORIAL TO ITS WHITE SOLDIERS

In solemn and thankful remembrance of
the unselfish and patriotic sacrifice on
the part of the white men of Sumter
County who served in the forces of the
United States in the war against Germany
and her allies for the preservation of
the rights of mankind throughout the
world, this park is given and dedicated
in perpetuity for the use of the white
people only of Sumter.

Deed of Gift in trust executed by
thirty-seven citizens, August 1st, 1919.*

Avoidance rituals usually apply only to *American* Negroes. Before the 1953 Superior Court decision declaring segregation unconstitutional, restaurants in Washington, D.C., would serve dark-skinned persons *if* they showed credentials proving they were foreign representatives; and American white girls at one international religious conference would dance with African representatives *only* if they wore native costumes.

Function of Caste

Slavery provided advantages to whites which caste has perpetuated. Some whites find the deference the caste system demands of Negroes psychologically exhilarating. Some predatory white males have taken advantage of the particularly helpless position of the Negro woman. But the greatest advantage to the greatest number of whites has been an economic one.

Negroes in 1964 made up 92.1 per cent of the nonwhite population in the United States. In them whites have had a large pool of unskilled labor which unequal educational opportunities have helped insure. Economic exploitation of Negroes occurs in all parts of the country, but it has been particularly evident in the South.

> When we toured the South in 1955, every white family we visited—both middle and upper-middle class families—had at least part-time Negro help. In one home, for example, a maid arrived at 7:00 a.m., six days a week. She prepared the breakfast, served it, washed the dishes (by hand), and got one school-age child on her way. While baby-sitting two pre-schoolers, she made the beds, cleaned house, prepared and served lunch, washed lunch dishes, laundered and ironed clothes, prepared and served dinner, washed dinner dishes, and then went home. On Saturdays she left after lunch. Sunday was her day off. The family paid her eighty dollars a month. The woman was a widow with two children to support, and we asked how she could possibly live on eighty dollars a month. Our host said, "Oh, she can't. She works nights in a beauty shop." [44]

---

* From a bronze plaque on a war memorial photographed by Ralph Prior.

The median income for nonwhite families in the United States in 1960 was 54 per cent that of the national average. For the Southern Negro it was 43.4 per cent that of the Southern white. The United States Department of Labor lists more than 5,000 skilled and professional occupations. For these more remunerative occupations, relatively few Negroes qualify—not because more couldn't have qualified, but because the caste system has effectively prevented their doing so.

> . . . The haughty American Nation . . . makes the Negro clean its boots and then proves the moral and physical inferiority of the Negro by the fact that he is a shoeblack.[45]

Maintenance of Caste

Both Negroes and whites have contributed to the maintenance of caste—the whites by insistence on their inherent superiority, and the Negroes by their acceptance of inferiority.

Whites, particularly in the South, have characteristically demanded deference from Negroes, deference which they have backed up by custom, law, and, not infrequently, physical force.

> . . . I walked along the hot, dusty road, sweating and leading my bicycle by the handlebars.
>
> A car slowed at my side.
>
> "What's the matter, boy?" a white man called.
>
> I told him my bicycle was broken and I was walking back to town.
>
> "That's too bad," he said, "Hop on the running board."
>
> He stopped the car. I clutched hard at my bicycle with one hand and clung to the side of the car with the other.
>
> "All set?"
>
> "Yes, sir," I answered. The car started.
>
> It was full of young white men. They were drinking. I watched the flask pass from mouth to mouth.
>
> "Wanna drink, boy?" one asked.
>
> I laughed, the wind whipping my face . . . I said:
>
> "Oh, no!"
>
> The words were hardly out of my mouth before I felt something hard and cold smash me between the eyes. It was the empty whisky bottle. I . . . fell backwards from the speeding car into the dust of the road. . . . The white men piled out and stood over me.
>
> "Nigger, ain't yuh learned t' sir t' a white man yet?"
>
> Dazed, I pulled to my feet. My elbows and legs were bleeding. Fists doubled, the white man advanced, kicking my bicycle out of the way.
>
> "Aw, leave the bastard alone. He's got enough," one said.
>
> They stood looking at me as I rubbed my shins, trying to stop the flow of blood. No doubt they felt a sort of contemptuous pity, for one asked:
>
> "Yuh wanna ride t' town now, nigger? Yuh reckon yuh know enough t' ride now?"

"I wanna walk," I said, simply.

Maybe it sounded funny. They laughed.

"Well, walk, yuh black son-of-a-bitch!"

When they left, they comforted me with:

"Nigger, yuh sho better be damn glad it was us yuh talked t' tha' way. Yuh're a lucky bastard, 'cause if yuh'd said tha' t' somebody else, yuh might've been a dead nigger now." [46]

In response to violations of racial etiquette, insubordination or insult, Southern whites have committed crimes of violence with impunity against even free Negroes. Physical assault is largely a lower-class phenomenon; but the Negro has been more defenseless against the acts of extremists in the South than elsewhere. ". . . For over 50 years—1890 to 1945—there was not a single case in any of the Southern states in which a white who committed a crime against a Negro was punished by law in any way." [47]

Gross inequality under the law is a focus of Negro discontent.

In 1955 I had the opportunity to preside over a sociology class in a Negro university in the deep South. I asked the students how many planned to leave the South after they graduated. There were forty students in the room, and thirty-nine hands went up immediately. I pressed them for reasons. One spoke up with a vehemence which the rest acclaimed: "I want to leave, because I want to find freedom from fear. I was in the Navy for several years and spent a lot of time in many states outside the South. For the first time in my life I felt the law was on my side. If I got into trouble, I could turn to the law for help. Here I can be put in jail for demanding my Constitutional rights." I reminded him that the law in the rest of the country was not necessarily color blind, but he insisted the relative difference was enough to be important to him.[48]

Caste is most clearly defined in the South, but it is maintained in other parts of the country by a variety of means.* In 1956, 400,000 college students belonged to fraternities and sororities. "Estimates of the number of Negro students now belonging to once restricted houses on Fraternity Row run as high as forty or fifty." [49] One in ten thousand is not integration. *How integrated are the schools and colleges and social organizations in your community? How integrated is your community? Can Negroes live anywhere, go anywhere—to restaurants, hotels, shops, theaters—without fear of rebuff?*

The Mason-Dixon Line divided white as well as Negro society. Agents of socialization instill regional attitudes in whites and Negroes alike. In all schools, north and south, east and west, the textbooks used are neither too deprecatory of the United States nor of the states in which the books are used. Southern children get a different view of the Old South than do children in other parts of the country: slavery was not an evil thing, but the Reconstruction was.

* In 1962 the police and fire departments of Atlanta, Georgia, were better integrated than those in San Francisco, California. In San Francisco and other cities of the West and North, Negro schoolchildren were effectively segregated, not by law, but by local residential restrictions.

> [Even Negroes] read of the chivalrous deeds of men and women of the Old White South, and now and then an acknowledgment of the perfection in servitude achieved by some devoted black coachman or cook. They swallow without retch the fantastic stories of the iniquities of Reconstruction and the detailed accounts of Negro legislators as scoundrels and ignoramuses. These accounts are supplemented by inspired essays which attempt to be redolent with charm of the Old Plantation, and the perfumed fragrance of the magnolias and cape jasmine evokes for them as readily as for white youths a sublime land of Never-Never, of chaste ladies and brave men with the graces of the perfect gentlewoman and gentleman, of mint-juleps, sugar-cured hams, and gracious manners.[50]

More Negro boys in the South are named for Robert E. Lee than for Abraham Lincoln.[51]

Effects of Caste

From 1896 until 1954, "separate but equal" was the "law of the land," separate and unequal the result. The full gambit of inequalities experienced by the Negro has extended from the relatively superficial inconveniences of limited access to public accommodations to such fundamental concerns as educational opportunities and life expectancy. In no part of the United States have Negroes been able to compete on an equal basis with whites for status, class, or power. Although a few Negroes are millionaires, the status and power usually associated with wealth in the larger society have been denied them. Racial stratification has defined a line across which full mobility has been, for all practical purposes, impossible.

Negroes learn early to identify with the image of the Negro presented to them by society. Theirs has been a "looking-glass self"—a self assumed to be inferior or at least subservient to whites. Among Negro children, as young as four to six years of age, half already feel inferior to white children, and three-fourths prefer to play with white children.[52] Rejection of both themselves and their race has indicated a tacit acceptance of caste which, in itself, has helped maintain caste.

The importance of education in a mobile society makes school segregation a particularly significant area of discrimination. During the school year, 1935-1936, ten Southern states spent an average of three times more money for the education of a white child than for the education of a Negro child. During this same period, those Southern counties where the school population was 75 per cent or more Negro spent approximately thirteen times more money for the education of each white child as for each Negro.[53] In 1930, thirty-four years after the Supreme Court "separate but equal" decision, the salaries of Negro schoolteachers averaged $400 per year, compared to $900 paid to white teachers.[54] By 1940 the gap had begun to narrow, but salaries for Negro teachers were still only 54 per cent those of white teachers.[55] The social consequences of unequal educational opportunities for Negroes include higher illiteracy rate, higher crime rate, lower economic position, and limited upward mobility.

A correlate of low social, economic, and political position—among Negroes as among other groups—is relatively low life expectancy. In 1928 the ratio of hospital beds in the country averaged one to 139 for whites, one to 1,941 for Negroes. Furthermore, the general hospital facilities to which Negroes had access were inferior to those for whites. In 1937 Southern doctors delivered only some 35 per cent of Negro babies, compared to 90 per cent of southern white babies and 96 per cent of Northern babies of both races.[56] The consequences of all these discrepancies were telling. In 1940 the registered infant mortality rate was 69 per cent higher for Negroes than for whites, the rate of stillbirths more than twice as high, and the maternal mortality rate more than two and one-half times as high.[57] In 1940 the life expectancy of Chicago Negroes was 11.3 years less than that of whites. By 1960, the high infant mortality and poor health still prevalent among Negroes made life expectancy at birth 7.5 years less than the national average for whites.

Discrimination varies from region to region and even from community to community, but nowhere in the United States have Negroes entirely escaped its damaging consequences. At the beginning of this century, the "Negro problem"—if thought of only in terms of population—was a Southern problem. In 1900 the percentage of Negroes in the total population was 1.9 in the Northeast, 1.9 in the North central area, 0.7 in the West, and 32.3 in the South. By 1960 migration of Negroes from the South to other parts of the country brought the percentage of Negroes up to 6.8 in the Northeast, 6.7 in the North central area, 3.9 in the West, and down to 20.6 in the South.[58] The "Negro problem" has not remained in any sense a Southern problem; it is now and will continue to be a national problem, with significant effects on the relationship of the United States to all nonwhite nations in the world.

Breaking Caste

"Separate" was not and never had been in any sense "equal," but until the Roosevelt "New Deal" (1933-1945), Negroes made few effective protests. In the 1940's a series of court decisions nibbled at the inequalities of caste structure, but not until the 1950's did the issue of segregation approach the Supreme Court. In an effort to forestall an unfavorable decision on school segregation, Southern states took steps towards equality. Between 1940 and 1952 salaries of Negro teachers in the South increased from 54 per cent to 87 per cent of those for white teachers. In North Carolina, Tennessee, and Virginia, they average more than for white teachers. Capital outlay for Negro school children increased from 23 per cent of that for white children in 1940 to 82 per cent in 1952.

> . . . Implied, and sometimes openly stated, was a plea of guilty to omissions of the past; Governor Byrnes of South Carolina said candidly: "To meet this situation we are forced to do now what we should have been doing for the last fifty years." [59]

But time had run out. The South did too little too late. The mood of the country and the Supreme Court had changed. On May 17, 1954, Chief Justice Warren wrote the unanimous decision.

> Does segregation of children in public schools solely on the basis of race, even though the physical facilities and other "tangible" factors may be equal, deprive the children of the minority group of equal educational opportunities? We believe that it does.
>
> To separate them from others of similar age and qualifications solely because of their race generates a feeling of inferiority as to their status in the community that may affect their hearts and minds in a way unlikely ever to be undone.
>
> We conclude that in the field of public education the doctrine of "separate but equal" has no place. Separate educational facilities are inherently unequal.

One year later the Supreme Court declared that the elimination of enforced segregation in schools must proceed "with all deliberate speed."

Prior to the Supreme Court decision, seventeen states, plus the District of Columbia, maintained segregated schools. The District of Columbia and the border states of Delaware, Maryland, Kentucky, Missouri and Oklahoma began desegregating, and by 1960 had approximately one-sixth of their Negro students in integrated schools. Other states resisted. One Southern Senator in 1955 warned: "Every white man will get out his shotgun to keep the 'Nigras' out of our schools." * And in some cities Negro children could get safely to school only with police escort.

In spite of Southern resistance to school integration, Negroes gained hope from the legal action supporting it. They organized, demonstrated, and otherwise prepared to protest restrictions on their fundamental citizenship rights. This protest movement had a strength forged in part by the frustration and bitterness of World War II Negro servicemen subjected to segregation while fighting against Nazi racists for "freedom and democracy."

> Segregation in the Army is making enemies of the Negro soldiers, demoralizing them. You may wonder why they don't rebel. They do, but individually, and in result are either transferred to Southern parts, placed in the guard house, or given dishonorable discharge from the Army. Thus they accept much that otherwise would cause trouble. Every six months the Articles of War are read to us. It was not until yesterday when they were read to me, that I realized that if I continued to do what I call fighting at home for democracy, I face a dishonorable discharge, life imprisonment or death (if they should find out); however, I am fast reaching a point of not caring even if it costs my life. *Any Negro would rather give his life at home fighting for a cause he can understand, than against an enemy whose principles are the same as those of our so-called democracy.*[60]

---

* Six years later the leading city of his deep-South state integrated its schools without incident.

Another G.I. was even more disgusted.

> Honest to God, I hope Hitler wins the war. If he does and comes over here, he will treat American white people the way they treat us. They'll know then what it feels like to be treated like dogs. They'll understand how we feel. Then we'll all get somewhere.[61]

The protest movement gained further strength as it won issues. When Martin Luther King—borrowing the passive resistance techniques of India's leader Mahatma Gandhi—led a successful Montgomery bus boycott, he set the pattern for the sit-in demonstrations by which Negroes effected integration at lunch counters in eight Southern cities within a four-week period. The Negro self-image began to shift.

> Once plagued with a tragic sense of inferiority resulting from the crippling effects of slavery and segregation, the Negro has been driven to re-evaluate himself. He has come to feel that he is somebody. . . . This growing self-respect has inspired the Negro with a new determination to struggle and sacrifice until first-class citizenship becomes a reality.[62]

Officially the Federal Government supported the protest movement and was willing to help Negroes attain "first-class citizenship."

> We preach freedom around the world, and we mean it. And we cherish our freedom here at home. But are we to say to the world—and much more importantly to each other—that this is the land of the free, except for the Negroes; that we have no second-class citizens, except Negroes; that we have no class or caste system, no ghettos, no master race, except with respect to Negroes?
>
> Now the time has come for this nation to fulfill its promise.
>
> The fires of frustration and discord are burning in every city, North and South. Where legal remedies are not at hand, redress is sought in the streets in demonstrations, parades, and protests, which create tensions and threaten violence—and threaten lives.
>
> We face, therefore, a moral crisis as a country and a people. It cannot be met by repressive police action. It cannot be left to increased demonstrations in the streets. It cannot be quieted by token moves or talk. It is a time to act in the Congress, in your state and local legislative body, and above all, in all of our daily lives.
>
> It is not enough to pin the blame on others, to say this is a problem of one section of the country or another, or deplore the facts that we face. A great change is at hand, and our task, our obligation is to make that revolution, that change peaceful and constructive for all.
>
> Those who do nothing are inviting shame as well as violence. Those who act boldly are recognizing right as well as reality. . . .*

By 1963 the Negro protest movement was no longer confined to the South. Negroes demonstrated in most major cities of the nation. In the summer of 1963, when a quarter of a million Negroes staged the *March on Washington*

---

* John F. Kennedy, Civil Rights Address to the Nation, June, 1963.

and gathered in front of the Lincoln Memorial to present their cause and their claims, television, radio, and the press relayed the message to the nation. The "due date" of the 100-year-old Emancipation Proclamation had come.

In June, 1964, exactly one year to the day after President Kennedy asked for it, the United States Senate enacted the Civil Rights Bill.*

A spokesman for the traditional South, two years before the passage of the Civil Rights Bill, had asserted, *"I draw the line in the dust . . . and say, segregation now, segregation tomorrow, segregation forever."* † But historical and sociological forces favor integration. The rise of the African nations has given American Negroes a historical and racial focus. The achieved status of individual Negroes, particularly in the professions, and the successes of the Negro protest movement have given them courage. Industrialism in the South is improving the economic position of Southern Negroes. (If only to prevent their forming a group of potential strike-breakers, Negroes are now admitted to industrial unions and given jobs in factories with whites.) Urbanization in the South and the contested 1964 Supreme Court ruling that both houses of every State legislature "must be apportioned on a population basis" reduce the weight of rural votes and give meaning to those of an increasing number of urban Negroes.‡ *Currents of change erase lines drawn in dust.*

TOWARDS EQUIVALENCE

Those forces working for the integration of the Negro in the larger society—directly or indirectly—further the integration of other racial and ethnic groups. In addition, anthropological and psychological knowledge make the position of white supremists—based only on "superstitions and old wives' tales, on half-truths and whole lies"—increasingly untenable. There is no inherent superiority of one race over another.

In the international power struggles of this twentieth century, race is a

---

* Opponents of the Bill branded it as "communist," but on March 1, 1875, forty-two years before the Russian Revolution, the United States Congress passed a Civil Rights Act which declared:

> "All persons within the jurisdiction of the United States shall be entitled to the full and equal enjoyment of the accommodations, advantages, facilities, and privileges of inns, public conveyances on land or water, theaters and other places of public amusement; subject only to the conditions and limitations established by law, and applicable alike to citizens of every race and color, regardless of any previous condition of servitude."

In addition to reaffirming the public accommodations clause of the 1875 Civil Rights Act (effectively negated by the "separate but equal" Supreme Court decision in 1896), the 1964 law bans discrimination in schools, hiring, firing, promotions, union membership, and voting. It further forbids the use of federal money to support state or local programs which discriminate on the basis of race.

† Inaugural address of Governor George Wallace of Alabama, 1962.

‡ Because the majority of Negroes originally served plantation owners, they were once predominantly rural residents; today they are predominantly urban.

prime issue. Nonwhites are growing in both numbers and strength. The population differential is increasing in favor of the nonwhites; * the power differential—which has been in favor of the whites—is decreasing. Particularly to the nonwhite nations of Africa and Asia and Communist China, interracial actions within the United States speak louder than sweet words of "freedom" and "democracy." Communist nations compare the racial tensions in the United States with those of the Belgians in the Congo, the Portuguese in Angola, and the Boers in South Africa. They seize upon any publicized act of discrimination as a missile in the struggle for the allegiance of the uncommitted peoples of the world—most of whom are nonwhite. Problems of ethnic and racial stratification in the United States are inextricably involved in larger international issues.

The struggle of increasingly assertive Negroes and other racial minorities for equivalence as human beings is part of a total world picture. Everywhere, as underdeveloped societies gain control of the tools and techniques of modern science and industry, the place of the technologically superior whites is challenged. The ethnic and racial stratification of the world society, as well as that of the United States, is now untenable. Science points to culture, not to race, as the basis of those differences in economic, social, and political power which are the essentials of stratification. Ethnic and racial groups everywhere are on the move, and the members of the dominant white race must be prepared for the fact that movement causes friction. The resistance inevitably offered by entrenched institutions will only increase this friction. *What is the solution?*

---

* Chapter 12.

Notes

1. James Truslow Adams, The Epic of America (Boston: Little, Brown & Company, 1933), p. 45.
2. *Ibid.*, p. 59.
3. Joseph Kahl, *The American Class Structure* (New York: Holt, Rinehart & Winston, Inc., 1957), p. 224.
4. *Ibid.*, p. 224.
5. Herbert Blumer, "Race Prejudice as a Sense of Group Position," *The Pacific Sociological Review,* I, No. 1 (1958), pp. 4-5.
6. Eugene L. and Ruth E. Hartley, *Fundamentals of Social Psychology* (New York: Alfred A. Knopf, Inc., 1959), p. 701.
7. *Ibid.*, p. 701.
8. Gordon W. Allport, *The Nature of Prejudice* (New York: Doubleday Anchor Books, Doubleday & Company, Inc., abridged edition; C. Addison Wesley Publishing Company, Inc., 1954, 1958), p. 380.
9. Léon Poliakow, "A Look at Modern Anti-Semitism," *The Unesco Courier,* October, 1960, p. 14.
10. *Ibid.*, p. 15.
11. Irving Manuel Witt, "Liberalism and Conservatism in Zionist and Anti-Zionist Ideologies" (Ph.D. Dissertation, University of California, 1958).
12. *Ibid.*, p. 4.
13. Elmo Roper, *Factors Affecting the Admission of High School Seniors to College* (Washington, D.C.: American Council on Education, 1949).
14. Cary McWilliams, "Does Social Discrimination Really Matter," *Commentary,* November, 1947, p. 412.
15. Earl Raab and Gertrude Jaeger Selznick, *Major Social Problems,* 2nd ed. (New York: Harper & Row, Publishers, 1964), p. 205.
16. *Ibid.*, p. 205.
17. *Ibid.*, p. 204.
18. *Ibid.*, p. 206.
19. C. M. Kluckhohn, *Mirror for Man* (New York: McGraw-Hill Book Company, Inc., 1949), p. 122.
20. B. Schrieke, *Alien Americans: A Study of Race Relations* (New York: The Viking Press, Inc., 1936), pp. 10-12.
21. Thomas Bailey, *Theodore Roosevelt and the Japanese-American Crisis* (Palo Alto, Cal.: Stanford University Press, 1934), p. 14.
22. E. Adamson Hoebel, *The Cheyennes: Indians of the Great Plains* (New York: Holt, Rinehart & Winston, Inc., 1960), p. 2.
23. Oliver La Farge, *A Pictorial History of the American Indian* (New York: Crown Publishers, Inc., 1959), p. 13.
24. Dorothy Van de Mark, "Raid on the Reservation," *Harper's Magazine,* March, 1956, p. 49.
25. Louisa R. Shotwell, "Who Are the American Indians?" in *American Indians,* Walter M. Daniels, ed. (New York: H. W. Wilson Co., 1957)), pp. 14-16.
26. La Farge, *A Pictorial History of the American Indian,* p. 230.
27. John Collier, *Indians of the Americas* (New York: A Mentor Book, 1947), p. 143.

28. Ralph Nader, "American Indians: People Without a Future," *Harvard Law Record,* April 5, 1956.
29. O. A. Sherrard, *Freedom from Fear* (New York: St. Martin's Press, Inc., 1959), p. 65.
30. Kenneth M. Stampp, *The Peculiar Institution* (New York: Alfred A. Knopf, Inc., 1956), pp. 207-208.
31. *Ibid.,* p. 145.
32. *The Jackson Mississippian,* February 26, 1858, quoted in Stampp, *The Peculiar Institution,* p. 145.
33. Lillian Smith, *Now Is the Time* (New York: Dell Publishing Company, Inc., 1955), pp. 36-37.
34. Letter from the family records of Eugene Mead.
35. Letter from the family records of Eugene Mead.
36. C. Vann Woodward, *The Strange Career of Jim Crow* (New York: Oxford University Press, Inc., 1957), pp. 91-92.
37. *Ibid.,* p. 91.
38. *Ibid.,* p. 127.
39. Kingsley Davis, *Human Society* (New York: The Macmillan Company, 1949), pp. 378-379.
40. Luigi Laurenti, *Property Value and Race* (Berkeley, Cal.: University of California Press, Inc., 1957), p. 87.
41. John Howard Griffin, *Black Like Me* (Boston: Houghton Mifflin Company, 1961), p. 44.
42. Robert Bierstedt, *The Social Order* (New York: McGraw-Hill Book Company, 1957), p. 443.
43. *Ibid.,* p. 443.
44. From the files of Eugene and Fanchon Mead.
45. George Bernard Shaw, *Man and Superman,* quoted in Myrdal, *An American Dilemma,* p. 101.
46. Richard Wright, *"The Ethics of Living Jim Crow,"* in *The Negro Caravan,* Sterling A. Brown, *et. al.,* eds. (New York: The Dryden Press, Inc., 1941), pp. 1056-1057.
47. Arnold M. Rose, "Race and Ethnic Relations," in *Contemporary Social Problems,* Robert K. Merton and Robert A. Nisbet, eds. (New York and Burlingame: Harcourt, Brace & World, Inc., 1961), p. 358.
48. From the files of Eugene Mead.
49. *U.S. News and World Report,* November 9, 1956, p. 9.
50. Horace Mann Bond, "A Negro Looks at His South," in *The Negro Caravan,* p. 1032.
51. *Ibid.,* p. 1032.
52. Mary Ellen Goodman, *Race Awareness in Young Children* (Cambridge: Addison-Wesley Publishing Co., 1952), p. 62.
53. Gunnar Myrdal, *An American Dilemma* (New York: Harper & Row, Publishers, 1944), pp. 339-341.
54. Harry Ashmore, *The Negro and the Schools* (Chapel Hill, N. C.: The University of North Carolina Press, 1954), p. 18.
55. *Ibid.,* p. 159.
56. Myrdal, *An American Dilemma,* p. 172.
57. *Ibid.,* pp. 174-175.
58. *A Sociological Almanac for the United States,* 2nd ed., Murray Gendell and Hans L. Zetterberg, eds. (New York: Charles Scribner's Sons, 1964), p. 43.
59. Ashmore, *The Negro and the Schools,* p. 109.

60. William Y. Bell, Jr., "The Threat to Negro Soldier Morale," an unpublished U.S.O. report, October, 1943.
61. Bell, "The Negro Warrior's Home Front," Phylon: *The Atlanta University Review of Race & Culture,* Third Quarter, 1944, p. 277.
62. Martin Luther King, Jr., *Stride Toward Freedom* (New York: Harper & Row, Publishers, 1958), p. 154.

Men come together in cities in order to live;

they remain together in order to live the good life.

ARISTOTLE (384–322 B.C.)

11

Communities—Decline and Renewal

TOGETHERNESS DESCRIBES SOCIETY as a process—an interaction of individuals in groups and of groups in society. *Stratification* pictures society as an entity in which individuals and groups have rank positions depending on the assumed values of their social actions. Now, in *Communities,* society, as process and entity, has a setting—a geographically and architecturally defined environment. Communities are territorial groups whose members partake of a common social life. They are sub-totals of society, and through them sociologists study such social facts and processes as: urbanization, industrialization, bureaucratization, stratification, and slums. Sociological concern with communities is also ecological; it includes the interplay between place and people. Men shape their physical environment. *Does this environment, in turn, help shape men and their society?*

The city was once a physical and psychological community—a setting for a continuous and exuberant social drama—a place of intensified, diverse activity, of satisfying individual and group interaction. When the physical structure of the city is right, when it has human scale and human purpose, the social drama is facilitated and heightened. But—and this is the concern of those who value both urbanity and humanity—when the setting is not right, when it is made disordered and incoherent by growth that is misdirected or excessive, the drama is depressed, the social action frustrated. When the city can no longer absorb and integrate diversity, when there is no all-

PHIZ MOZESSON

encompassing order, no common concerns, community is weakened and the individual as well as the larger society suffers.

Most of the cities in the United States have grown like Topsy—without design. Their form has been dictated not by the needs of community, but by the enterprise of industry and commerce. Unless we define and implement our goals, we are going to get more of the kind of urbanization we already have. *Do we want it? Do our present cities provide for the purposes of society, or do we have social starvation, as we have physical starvation, in the midst of plenty?*

HISTORICAL PERSPECTIVE

Travel the world today, and you will find communities in every stage of development: villages of a few hundred people as primitive as their prehistoric prototypes; towns as coherent in plan and limited in population as those of medieval Europe or colonial New England; larger cities and vast urban complexes covering hundreds of square miles and counting population in the millions. These widely different physical settings for human habitat document two periods of community development: pre-industrial and post-industrial.

Pre-Industrial Development

When the villages and towns and cities of the world were tenuously linked to each other by relay runners, by horsemen, by patient beasts of overland caravans, by wind-powered or man-powered boats, the development of culture and community was slow. Thousands and thousands of years separated the developmental stages of community from Neolithic village to ancient metropolis.

First Stage: *Eopolis.** A prehistoric village was no more than a cluster of families following a way of life determined by custom and by the restrictions and resources of the geographic locale. There were mining villages, fishing villages, and agricultural villages, but labor was only a part-time activity, inseparable from religion and law, education and play. It was apportioned mainly according to age and sex and strength, and specialization and stratification were at a minimum. The community was the total culture, and participation in the common life was everyone's right and responsibility. A man might venture to a neighboring village for a tool or a wife; but the village as a whole was characteristically self-reliant and self-sufficient. It could hold its own, essentially intact, for generations. "Such villages might reproduce and multiply

---

* *Eo,* from the Greek, means dawn or beginning; *megalo* means great. *Polis* means city; it is commonly used in combination, as in cosmopolis (world-city) and metropolis (mother-city). *Eopolis, Polis, Metropolis,* and *Megalopolis* identify developmental stages defined by Lewis Mumford.[1]

without any impulse to change their pattern of life: as long as nutrition and reproduction, the pleasures of the belly and the genitals, were the chief ends of life, neolithic village culture met every requirement."[2] But the pleasures and needs of men are not limited to the physical. Men come together not only to sustain, reproduce, and protect life; they come together to enhance life.

Opportunity for individual fulfillment is limited in the isolated village. Its ways are too routine; the perspective of its people is too limited; its incestuous culture too stagnant. It takes strangers with strange ways to stimulate self-appraisal and change. The mobilization of wealth and power and vitality in a larger association of neighboring villages was logically and actually the next step.

Second Stage: *Polis.* Like the village, the city has no definite birth date in cultural history, but the most likely time and place was centuries before Christ in the fertile valleys of such rivers as the Nile, the Tigris-Euphrates, the Indus, and the Hwang Ho. Rivers were natural highways that linked the villages along their banks and made association possible; the need for cooperation in long-range planning for irrigation and flood control made it expedient. In the eighth century B.C., for example, Nineveh, capital of the Assyrian Empire, lay by the upper reaches of the Tigris River near what is now Mosul in Northern Iraq. High on a 90-foot plateau were the palaces and temples—homes of kings and gods. Within massive stone walls on the plain below were the lesser buildings and dwellings. Here the streets were thronged with thousands of people: nobles in brilliant gowns, scarred veterans of battle, meditative priests, merchants calling their wares, envoys from client states; traders, mailmen bearing tablets of dried brick with impressed cuneiform characters, sculptors carving bas reliefs for the Palace of Sennacherib or Ashurbanipal, government officials, secretaries and guards, rough clad laborers and slaves.

The ancient city was the setting for social action more complex than ever a village could support. The city widened the scope of human activities, but the city also exacted a sacrifice. The individual played a smaller part in the larger society and could know the whole only vicariously. In the city a man might spend a lifetime as a barber, an embalmer, a carpenter, cobbler, currier, or scribe. The various facets of his public life, worship and work, learning and governing, began to be dominated by specialists. In the cities of ancient Egypt, fifth century B.C., the division and subdivision of labor rivaled our own. Gone, for example, was the omnipotent village medicine man: "some physicians are for the eyes, others for the head, others for the teeth, others for the belly, and others for internal disorders."[3] Then, as now, a man's work, his manner of life, mode of dress, place of dwelling, property or lack of property determined his position in society. Specialization and stratification characterized the urban way of life.

Third Stage: *Metropolis.* The ancient cities were autonomous and vied with each other for power. Those with better resources and more strategic locations were able to attract the most people, concentrate culture, and control economic and political enterprise. The emergence of a big city—a mother city—from a multitude of smaller cities was sporadic through history, but after the fourteenth century when the modern state began to take shape, the development of metropolitan centers was stimulated by the need for centralization of political as well as economic and social power.* By the seventeenth century, London, with a population of 250,000, was the largest city in the western world.

Post-Industrial Development

From the nineteenth century on, industry was the urbanizer. New towns sprang up around factories; old cities expanded to unprecedented size. Techniques for long-distance communication and rapid transportation quickened the pace and extended the scope of colonization.

> Here was a chance to build on a firm foundation and make a fresh start: such a chance as democracy had claimed for itself in political government. Almost everywhere that chance was fumbled. In an age of rapid technical progress the city, as a *social* unit, lay outside the circle of invention. Except for utilities such as gas mains, water pipes, and sanitary equipment, often belatedly introduced, often slipshod and inadequate, the industrial city could claim no important improvements over the seventeenth-century town. Indeed, the most wealthy and "progressive" metropolises often denied themselves elementary necessities of life like light and air that even backward villages still possessed.[5]

The Industrial Revolution brought changes for which no one was prepared. The tempered eighteenth-century society was disrupted; the precarious balance between citizen and city destroyed. New "towns" † sprang up around factories; old cities expanded to unprecedented size. Of all the nations, England industrialized most rapidly; and London, which had a population of 800,000 near the end of the eighteenth century, counted more than 1,000,000 early in the nineteenth.

The Industrial Revolution disrupted Old World communities. It shaped those of the New World. Provincial New England towns had barely established themselves before the pioneers and their covered wagons started West. The railroads followed the pioneers, and population way stations sprang up across the interior plains near sources of materials and power. The pre-industrial New England town had been dominated by the Common and the Church. The new commercial towns were dominated by the railroad station and the hotel. By the latter half of the nineteenth century, railroad building was big

---

* The metropolis also dominated cultural activity. In them religion, philosophy, literature, art, and drama reached the stage of self-conscious criticism and expression. Platonic Athens, Dantean Florence, Shakespearean London, and Emersonian Boston were each, in turn, a model pre-industrial metropolis.[4]

† The factory towns were towns in name only. Neither Manchester nor Birmingham, for example, even functioned politically as incorporated boroughs until 1838. They were "man heaps, machine-warrens, not organs of human association." [6]

business in a rapidly developing economy. To 35,000 miles of railroad in operation in 1865, 122,000 more were added by 1887, including the first transcontinental railroad.[7] Thousands more rail miles, added before the end of the century, made a vast transportation network which supplemented natural waterways and opened a domestic market of unprecedented size to ambitious entrepreneurs. Towns and villages far from navigable waters were nurtured by the new life line. Many of them grew into cities; some became metropolitan centers.

Following the railroads, a second urban life line—a network of highways—developed in the twentieth century. When Henry Ford's first gasoline motor car—two cylinders, four horsepower—emerged from his workshop in 1892, who could foresee what its progeny would do to transportation and urban development? Even the four-cylinder Model T, ready for the market in 1908, was a tentative experiment. By mid-century, the automobile industry in the United States alone sold 6,665,863 passenger cars and 1,337,193 trucks and buses; [8] and federal, state, and local governments maintained 3,094,462 miles of rural roads to accommodate them.* All roads didn't lead to Rome, but they did lead to cities.

> For the metropolis is where, by and large, the big money, the big decisions, and the big reputations are made. It is the nucleus of power. It is the GHQ. It is the place to go for shows, crowds, dazzle, and adventure. And so, decade after decade, it pulls toward it the restless, the ambitious, the energetic, the lovers of excitement, the young men and women who want to be at the center of things, where opportunity may be around the next corner and there is a feeling in the air that anything can happen. "Bam, whang, whang goes the drum, tootle-te-tootle the fife. Oh, for a day in the city square, there is no such pleasure in life!" [10]

A song, popular in the second decade of this century asked, "How ya gonna keep 'em down on the farm?" A generation later, the answer was clear, "You can't!" American society, which was 5.1 per cent urban in 1790 and 39.7 per cent urban in 1900, was 69.9 per cent urban by 1960.[11]

The material benefits which industrialization and urbanization have brought to the United States have stirred the rest of the world, and restless "backward" countries are getting ready to "take-off." †

> Brazil has one of the most rural populations in the world. In 1950, 64 per cent of the population was officially classified as rural and 36 per cent as urban and suburban. This was substantially the reverse of the relative situation in the United States at that time. However, for the decade ending in 1950 the rural population increased by only 18 per cent, whereas the urban population

* Rural roads are those outside the metropolitan areas. Municipal roads total an additional 416,198 miles.[9]

† "Take-off" is the transition from a static, pre-industrial society to a growing industrial one—from penury to affluence, from bondage to biological needs to freedom to discover and satisfy psychological needs.[12]

> increased by almost 50 per cent. The disparate growth of the cities was not due to natural increase but was largely accounted for by migration from rural areas of the country. The essentially rural character of the Brazilian population is a survival of the colonial and imperial periods and reflects the predominantly agricultural economy of the nation. The factors which are responsible for the shift now in process are growing industrialization, with its accompanying urbanization, improved transportation facilities between the rural districts and the cities, and the continuing high death rate of the rural population, which tends to counterbalance the greater fertility of its women.
>
> . . . To correct the traditional maldistribution of the Brazilian population in order to meet the changed requirements of the modern era is a primary concern of those who direct the destinies of the state. The origins of the problem lie in the survival of a pattern of isolated population centers along the coast, like Belém, Salvador, Rio de Janeiro, and Santos-Sao Paulo, separated from one another by large areas of wilderness and depending on a precarious food supply from the efforts of a nomadic and backward peasant population in their respective hinterlands. The principal feature of this massive program of resettlement is centered about the government's policy of a "march to the west," represented by the construction of Brasilia * and by the building of truck roads into the empty spaces of the interior.[13]

Four-fifths of the people of the world still live in villages,[14] but if what happened in England and Europe and the United States and is now happening in Brazil can be taken as typical, urbanization will follow industrialization in China, India, Africa, Mexico, Argentina, and other "underdeveloped" areas. Eventually all the countries which are now bystanders will shift to an urban-industrial economy and become active participants in the developing world culture.[15]

Plato (427-347 B.C.) defined the desirable size of a city as 5,000—the number of people who could hear the voice of an orator and so partake of political life. In the seventeenth century the General Assembly of Massachusetts, to encourage participation in civic affairs, ordered that no one should live more than half a mile from his Common. Now in this industrial era we have tended to equate the growth of cities with "progress," but bigger is not necessarily better for the community, nor for the institutions of the community, including business. There is an optimum size beyond which increment in either population or area brings problems which far outweigh any possible benefits, and in many instances, contemporary as well as historical, this point of diminishing returns has already been passed.

Fourth Stage: *Megalopolis.* The Megalopolis concentrates on bigness and power. Representatives include Alexandria, third century B.C.; Rome, second century A.D.; Byzantium, tenth century; Paris, eighteenth century; and New York, early twentieth century.[16] The Megalopolis seeks aggrandizement.

* This new architect-designed capital is on a central plateau in the interior state of Goías. When the project was initiated in 1956, the only practicable connection with the coastal cities was by air.

It builds high, wide, and extravagantly. It dwarfs its people and overrides their needs. In this stage community ends and chaos begins.

CONTEMPORARY PROBLEMS

In the twentieth century a city is not limited by the range of a speaker's voice, by the distance a man can conveniently walk, by encompassing walls, the location of a factory, or even by public transportation. The end of the trolley line may be 109th Street, but the streets and highways and private automobiles go on and on.* By 1960 Tokyo, the largest city in the world, had a population of 9,311,774. London was next with 8,171,902, then New York with 7,781,984. Shanghai and Moscow both had populations of more than 5,000,000; Bombay and Peiping more than 4,000,000. Ten other cities counted more than 3,000,000 people; fourteen more than 2,000,000.[18]

In the United States, contemporary community problems come to focus in the Megalopolis. New York, for example, had its most phenomenal growth in the nineteenth century when tides of European immigrants settled there.† Between 1900 and 1950 its population approximately doubled as did the population of the country as a whole. By 1950 Greater New York, including Richmond, Manhattan, the Bronx, Brooklyn, and Queens, covered 320 square miles and its population of 7,891,957 was gasping for breath.

> . . . a city can no longer cope with its people, when—through overcrowding, inefficiency, corruption, and greed—it sacrifices for the limitless pursuit of financial profit, those amenities which spell civilized living. It is a point of strangulation, of brutality against the individual, of ferocious tension; and if proof of this condition were wanted, a walk on unfashionable streets or a ride in the subway would provide. This city is full of fragmented people, from those who talk to themselves and move jerkily to those whose faces are set in hostility or negation. The population of New York is not a gay one; it is too busy fighting to survive. . . .[19]

The lights on Broadway may be bright; but, it is true, the people are not gay. The individual is troubled in the abyss of urban anonymity. This you can see and hear for yourself; but what the sensitive individual can perceive, science can further document.

In Manhattan's residential midtown a team of psychiatrists and social scientists have probed behind the façade of apartment houses and slum tenements to study the 175,000 who live there. They are a heterogeneous population: young and old, married and unmarried, immigrants and native-born. They include the major nationality groups, the major religions, the full range of economic strata from rich to poor, and a broad occupational spectrum: from

* The number of motor vehicles, including automobiles, trucks, buses, and motorcycles in the United States in the mid-fifties was 388.9 per 1,000 population compared to a world average of 31.3.[17]

† New York City has more Irish than Dublin, and nearly as many Italians as Rome.

career woman and housewife to domestic, from business executive or professional man to shopkeeper, taxi driver, skilled and unskilled laborer and unemployed. The research team wanted to know what manner of community and what kind of psychological climate prevailed in this densely populated urban area. They wanted, particularly, to assess the mental health of the residents in the most productive age group—20 through 59 years old. They found that just one adult out of five had good mental health. The majority had significant symptoms of sub-clinical tension and distress; the remainder had marked, severe, or incapacitating symptoms clinically known to psychiatrists.[20]

When a city can no longer cope with its people, some people cannot or will not cope with the city. Between 1950 and 1960 New York, along with seven other major cities in the United States, lost population. However, younger cities, heedless of the malaise of the Megalopolis, continued growing.* Los Angeles headed them all. Between 1900 and 1950 the population went from 102,479 to 1,970,358—an increase of 1,822 per cent! From 1950 to 1960 it gained 508,657 more people and became the third largest city in the nation. In another generation, it expects to be first. People have invaded the mountain valleys, the farm lands, the desert, and the seacoast, covering nearly 455 square miles with a metropolitan crazy quilt—"a hundred suburbs in search of a city." [22]

Urbs

Those of you who live in a city, particularly in a pathologically overgrown Megalopolis, are aware of urban problems; some of them are your own. In the United States, as elsewhere in the world, cities suffer *pollution, paralysis,* and *decay*—all of which tend to destroy them as settings congenial not only to community but to life itself.

Pollution

Fresh water, clean air, and open space are natural amenities without which life is insupportable, yet increasingly the city air and water are fouled and open land destroyed or defiled. This is in addition to the general background of contamination.

WATER POLLUTION. Providing drinking water traditionally has been a community function. First, a stream or spring was guarded as the water source. (In villages in India and other under-developed areas of the world, women still walk half a mile or more to a designated stream to get the day's supply of

* New York, down 2.9 per cent; Chicago, down 3.5 per cent; Philadelphia, down 5.4 per cent; Detroit, down 9.6 per cent; Baltimore, down 3.0 per cent; Cleveland, down 4.9 per cent; Washington, D.C., down 6.9 per cent; St. Louis, down 13.6 per cent. Los Angeles and Houston were the only two of the big ten to gain population: Los Angeles, up 24.2 per cent; Houston, up 56.4 per cent.[21]

water.) Second, water was brought to public pumps or fountains. And finally, water was piped into private homes. Urban dwellers in the United States turn on the faucet, water flows out, and we think nothing of it; but we are perhaps the last generation to enjoy this luxury. We are beginning to run out of water. During the summer months the needs of our industrial society exceed annual rainfall, and we are drawing heavily on underground water reserves.[23]

The supply of water is not the only problem. If water comes out of the faucet, we assume it is fit to drink. But public health officials are concerned about chemical waste in the water supplies. Detergent, for example, is now the most widely used cleaning agent, but, unlike soap, it is not broken down by bacteria, filter beds, or other chemicals. It goes through all known controls and is picked up again by cities using rivers or ground water. Detergent is only one of some 499,600 chemicals developed in the past twenty years.[24] Into the nation's waters we dump tons of these compounds plus tons of sewage, some raw, some only partially treated.* "The number of American cities with splendid waterfronts whose citizens drink diluted sewage and have no place to swim is a national disgrace."[26]

The historic Potomac flows through Washington D.C. Originally and potentially it was a recreational asset. Today it is thick with debris and silt and sewage from which only 32 per cent of the solids have been removed, and if it rains too hard, completely untreated sewage overflows directly into the river. In midsummer, the Potomac moves leisurely; tides swish the accumulating filth back and forth, and it takes one polluted drop 40 days to pass through the city.[27]

In California, where population is increasing at the rate of 1500 a day, the reality and danger of water pollution creates increasing concern. San Diego has spent millions of dollars creating an aquatic park out of a notoriously polluted harbor, but parts of the bay shoreline are still unsafe for recreation. Los Angeles has extended its sewage lines to discharge at the edge of a deep underwater canyon, but industries dumping waste into the Los Angeles inner harbor have sterilized the sea life, and with some tides the pollution moves into the outer harbor, endangering the bait industry which supplies half the fishermen in California. In the Central Valley, sewage and industrial waste are dumped into streams and rivers, and in hot weather some of the small streams are so dry that their flow is mostly sewage effluent, unsafe even for irrigation. In South San Francisco Bay, human and industrial waste have destroyed oyster beds and fisheries, and the tons of sewage given only primary treatment continue to pollute the water.[28]

---

* Most cities give sewage "primary" treatment which reduces pollution by 30 to 40 per cent. Garbage is not as readily disposed of as human excreta and industrial waste. The City of New York gave up scavenger pigs as volunteer members of the Board of Health in the nineteenth century, and by 1935 the 5,000,000 tons of refuse being dumped yearly six miles off the coast of New York was changing the color of the water.[25] The current cost of garbage collection and street cleaning in New York is approximately $50,000,000 a year. The 1960 budget for the United Nations was only $15,000,000 more.

AIR POLLUTION. Breathe deeply of the dry pine-scented wind in the mountains, of the tangy salt sea breeze, of the warm sweet air of flowering orchards or new-mown fields of hay. Even take in the lusty odors of a well-kept barnyard. But take short, shallow breaths here in the city, for the air reeks with lethal gasoline exhaust, with factory fumes, with stale subway smells, sour garbage, and burning rubbish.* The average person eats only between two and three pounds of food and drinks about four pounds of water a day, but he breathes thirty pounds of air! He would be loathe to eat or drink the impurities now fouling city air. In 1958 the exhaust products *just from trucks, buses and private automobiles* in the United States totaled 169,600,000,000 pounds of deadly carbon monoxide, 21,200,000,000 pounds of "cancer-bearing" organic vapors, technically known as hydrocarbons, and 3,975,000,000 pounds of smog-producing oxides of nitrogen.[29] This, added to tons of aldehydes, sulphur compounds, organic acids, zinc, lead, and other metallic oxides released by industry, has already created a major menace to health with which communities have not yet effectively dealt.† And increasing use of nuclear energy for industrial purposes poses still another problem—the control and dispersal of radioactive wastes.

It is difficult to measure the physiological and psychological effects suffered by people because of air polution, but the yearly cost as determined by damage to buildings and materials, plants and animals, and loss of potentially valuable chemicals in the smog itself is estimated to be, just in the United States, at least $4,000,000,000 a year.[31] Polluted air defiles everything it touches. *Are cities literally choking themselves to death?*

LAND POLLUTION. The natural environment is ours not to ravage, but to maintain. But we spew our waste into the rivers and belch it into the air.‡ And we bulldoze across hills, valleys, tidelands and the life they naturally support. There was a time when man had reverence for this heritage.

> When man founded a town and commenced the foundations of its walls, or when he cleared a site merely for a single hut, he went with care through elaborate conciliatory rituals—adoration and sacrifice . . . due homage was granted to the spirit of the place.[32]

What happens today? Land developers and surveyors with measuring tapes are followed by crews that level the hills, fill in the swamps, destroy the habitat of bird and beast, of native flowers, shrubs, and trees—all to get so many uniform lots on which can be built the same number of essentially uniform houses. Only the rare subdivider and builder proceeds with any concern for the original qualities of a site. The Megalopolis is spreading with the capricious-

* One summer day we sat next to a man on a bench overlooking the crowded beach of Coney Island. He remarked, "I wouldn't give two cents for the whole damn Coney Island. I just come out here for the air."

† In 1958 at least 10,000 communities in the United States had air pollution problems. Only 250 had any active control program.[30]

‡ Wags have called the United States "the effluent society."

ness and rapidity of wildfire. What is wrong is not growth, but the irrational, unplanned urban sprawl which is defiling the open spaces.*

> The character and quality of such urban sprawl is readily recognized: neon-bright strip cities along main traveled roads; housing tracts in profusion; clogged roads and billboard alleys; a chaotic mixture of supermarkets, used car lots, and pizza parlors; the asphalt plain of parking spaces; instead of parks, gray-looking fields forlornly waiting to be subdivided. These are the qualities of most of our new urban areas—of our *slurbs*—our sloppy, sleazy, slovenly, slipshod semi-cities.[34]

Cities need open spaces around them—space for ranches and farms, for conservation of water and timber, for flood control, for game reserves and bird sanctuaries, for a sense of urban identity, and particularly for personal refreshment and recreation. The expected increase in population, plus higher average income, more leisure, and greater geographic mobility, are expected to multiply the demand for recreational areas ten times in the next fifty years. There should be at least thirty acres of reasonably convenient parks and wilderness per thousand people for active recreational use plus further acreage for other kinds of open space.[35]

Cities need open space around them, and they need space within them—space for parks and playgrounds, space for private gardens, space to buffer noise and give relief to the eye, space to let the sun come through. *But how many cities have enough parks? In how many neighborhoods are streets the only playing field? How many homes have windows with "views" to the colorless concrete and asphalt of sidewalks and streets, to the sterile stand of service poles and wires, to the stark facade of other drab houses?* Many cities of the world have excitingly beautiful natural settings. Look at Rio, Hong Kong, Vancouver, San Francisco. If any of the original beauty of the site remains it is more often in spite of, than because of, man's actions.

Decay

Cities are overcrowded and overbuilt, but while many middle- and upper-class families are moving out, others, particularly low-income poorly educated families, including Negroes, Puerto Ricans, whites from backward rural areas, and other struggling minorities, are moving in, seeking opportunities only the city can offer. They move into the housing they can afford, the substandard housing in decaying neighborhoods. "There is a great deal of seriously substandard housing in American communities, and spreading 'gray areas' in various stages of actual or potential decay, plus commercial and industrial blight." [36] As early as 1931, a Federal committee on home building and ownership reported that our houses constitute "the largest mass of obsolete and dis-

---

* In California an average of 375 acres of open farm land are bulldozed daily to make way for new subdivisions. This amounts to 140,000 acres annually.[33]

credited equipment in the country." [37] Tour Manhattan's upper East Side and see the six-story, cold-water tenements, surrounded by knee-deep garbage. In these tenements as many as twenty people live in a four-room flat. Make a pilgrimage to our national capital. As late as 1955 there were 25,000 outhouses in the small Southwest section, some of them just across the street from the Health, Education, and Welfare building which houses the United States Public Health Service offices. These particular slums are being replaced with town houses and luxury apartments for those who can afford them, but just outside the business zone are acres of other dilapidated and overcrowded dwellings. In the Northwest section more than 25 per cent of the housing is deficient in three or more critical aspects, including inadequate plumbing and water supply.[38] Walk through San Francisco's Chinatown—not along Grant Avenue with the tourists, but through the back alleys. You'll find people in fifteen to twenty apartments sharing two toilets and one bath, and thirty beds in one basement room with only a door opening onto the street for ventilation. Look around Phoenix. There you will find flimsy stables converted into two-room apartments with neither toilets nor running water. Pick your city at random and you will find slums which breed disease, crime, and despair.

Slums are a local problem which cannot be solved by local means. In recognition of the need for Federal help in realizing the national goal of a decent home in a suitable environment for every family, Congress has given Federal aid for low-rent public housing since 1937, for broader slum clearance and private redevelopment programs since 1949, and for comprehensive renewal, including rehabilitation and conservation of marginal property since 1954. More than 400 communities have active renewal programs, but the rate of progress has not yet caught up with the decay. Between 1950 and 1960, approximately 15,000 acres of slums and blight were acquired for redevelopment and public housing, but several hundred thousand acres should be razed. More than a million substandard dwellings were demolished; ten million more should be.[39] But until adequate low-priced housing is available, comprehensive slum clearance is impossible. Displaced families simply crowd into other slums, making conditions worse than before. Even with Federal aid, old slums persist, blight is overtaking marginal areas, and the city is losing its supporting middle-class families to surrounding *slurbs.** *Is the city to be only for the poor who can go nowhere else, for the minority groups who are not accepted anywhere else, for the childless, and for the very rich who can afford the best of the city and shield themselves against the worst?*

---

* When middle-class families leave the city, they take their spending money and their tax money with them. The merchants and the city both suffer financially. A national business census indicates that the central business districts are getting a smaller and smaller percentage of retail sales. Between 1948 and 1954, the loss in Dallas was 38.2 per cent; in Los Angeles 37.8 per cent; in Chicago 25.7 per cent; in Philadelphia 28 per cent; and in New York City, 16 per cent.[40] Furthermore, the middle-class neighborhoods more than support themselves. Blighted areas do not: they yield less in taxes but cost more as measured by the fire, police, health, and welfare services the city provides for them.

Paralysis

In downtown New York at the turn of the century, a one-horse vehicle averaged 11.5 miles an hour. Sixty years later, a 220-horsepower automobile is doing well to average 6.0 miles an hour. After the business day starts in lower Manhattan, a healthy pedestrian can cross town faster than even the most aggressive taxi driver. In fact, taxis will not even venture into some areas during business hours. It costs them too much in time to get out again. However, during off-hours and on the perimeter of the main business district, the cab drivers win the ulcers which are their badge of service.

> A friend rode with a taxi driver whose intense determination to get through just one intersection without having to stop led him to step on the gas when he saw a break in the traffic ahead, even though another driver with similar intent was bearing towards the intersection from the cross street. Just before the taxis crashed, the other driver screeched to a stop. The winner kept grimly on, muttering, "I knew all the time that — was yellow!"

The elevator and structural steel which makes skyscrapers possible and the high land values which seemed to make them necessary set the stage for the paralyzing congestion of the urban core, but all of us who live or work in a city contribute to the painful here-to-there, there-to-here choreography. Why? Mainly because we rarely live within walking distance of work or anyplace else we need to go, and when public transportation is inadequate, as it now is in most cities, we drive a car.* To accommodate the cars we build freeways and parking facilities. Parking space and freeways in turn encourage more people to drive, which creates further demand for more freeways and still more parking space. *Where does this lead?*

Consider the rapidly growing state of California as a specific example. No city in California has a rapid-transit system.† Most people drive their own cars, and in California a car, small or large, carries an average of 1.7 persons. And that .7 of a person, even before he is old enough for a driver's license, wants his own car. The State anticipates 32 million people and 17 million cars by 1980.[42]

To accommodate all the cars, the legislature in 1959 approved a 10.5 billion dollar twenty-year plan for a state freeway system—12,400 miles of controlled access highways. We made an aerial survey of one freeway which was to be extended 3.5 miles south from Los Angeles towards San Diego, to see what effect it had on population distribution and traffic. From the air, the picture was clear: subdividers were following the freeway and houses were

* On a typical business day in 1956, 519,000 vehicles entered downtown Manhattan, 137,000 or 36 per cent more than on a similar day in 1948. However, they carried 10 per cent fewer people. With more people driving their own cars, fewer are using public transportation. The American Transit Association reports that passengers carried by public transit dropped from 17.2 billion in 1950 to 9.7 billion in 1958.[41]

† By 1964 the San Francisco Bay Region was building a rapid-transit system.

packed in solid blocks right to the end of the completed section. For 3.5 miles farther along the intended extension, where road work was just beginning, the orange groves were coming out and a checker board of tract blocks was being put in. By the time the freeway extension was complete, the houses were ready for occupancy. They were offered at relatively low prices and on easy payment plans. They sold fast to people for whom more elbow room and a home of their own was worth the time and money it would cost to commute back into the city.

The Southern California Research Council has concluded that the mass transportation problems of the Los Angeles metropolitan area will not be solved by the completion of the freeways, and that alternative forms of safe, convenient, and fast public transit must be provided. In the absence of adequate public transportation, each new freeway produces a disproportionate increase in traffic which overloads older existing freeways and makes the new ones obsolete even before they are finished.[43]

The Los Angeles example is specific, but the lesson is general. A United States Senate report stated: "In most cities traffic congestion is not improving but worsening. It is becoming clear that progress cannot be made through using private autos for metropolitan mass transportation. . . ." [44] In some cases freeways do what they are supposed to do—take thousands of cars off congested streets and direct them to their destination faster and safer. But there is a growing revolt by cities against freeways because they create their own traffic, direct cars into already congested areas, cut through neighborhoods and historic sites, parks, and recreational areas, and are actually an inefficient and expensive means of transporting people.* Even after a person manages to get his car through the traffic into the city, he has to park it someplace while he does whatever he came to do, and an average car takes up 140 square feet of space. To make room for cars, cities have to give up space that could be used for something else—pedestrian malls or parks or buildings.† Are cities for automobiles or for people? If we want to reclaim cities as a setting for the human intercourse that makes them pleasant and profitable, we have to find a way of diverting or turning back the tide of autos. A Senate committee on national transportation policy contends that free mass transit—express buses and electric trains—for commuters would cost less than providing the highways and parking space commuters need for their autos.[49]

* Freeways transport cars better than they do people. On a typical California freeway, no more than 2,500 people pass a given location in one hour. A good rapid-transit system can move 40,000 to 60,000 people in the same amount of time.[45] In actual carrying capacity, one rapid-transit line equals that of 32,000 cars.[46]

† In Los Angeles, parking areas, streets, and loading facilities take up two-thirds of the land in the central business district.[47] If the auto-dominated system of Los Angeles were followed in Washington, D.C., by 1980 that area would need an 18-lane superhighway leading out of the central business district, and many criss-crossing 10-, 12-, and 14-lane freeways.[48]

Efficient and economical though it may be, public transit takes extra psychological toll.

> I was riding the New York Eighth Avenue subway one evening when I noticed a man dressed in painter's overalls push his way aggressively through the crowd at Columbus Circle. He elbowed his way onto the train muttering curses as he came. He stood cramped in a small space, glowering at the people who had blocked his way. They were talking loudly and paid no attention to him. The painter seemed to become more tense and more angry, and he finally charged back towards me, cursing and knocking people aside. I had become empathically involved watching him, and, as he drew near, I impulsively said, "Easy, boy!" He whirled and glowered at me venomously, then tears filled his eyes and he sobbed, "It isn't easy!" [50]

The distraught painter was right. No matter how you travel in the present overgrown, overpopulated Megalopolis, it isn't easy. Perhaps the congestion and paralysis will someday be relieved by increasing the kinds of transportation available, by a balance between slow and fast, public and private means: pleasant malls for those who want to walk, limited-access highways for those who want to drive, and buses, ferries, subways, electric trains, helicopters, and jet planes for those who want to go farther or faster. But in the meantime, the cities are in trouble. The Megalopolis is no longer a means of community but a barrier to community; no longer a protector and nurturer of life but a threat to life *—an unsafe place to live or work or move around in. The magnetism of the central city has been counteracted. Pollution, decay, and paralysis have set up centrifugal forces which are sending population to the surburban periphery.

Suburbs

When people crowd into cities, they create problems. When they move out, they create more problems. Between 1950 and 1960, population in urban centers increased eight per cent; suburban population increased 47 per cent.[51] Even in the first century A.D. the Roman epigrammatist, Marcus Valerius Martial, said: *"Rus mihi dulce sub urbe est,"*—"To me the country on the outskirts of the city is sweet." "Man has been moving to the suburbs ever since he invented the urbs," [52] but never before has there been such a mass exodus. One-third of the population of the United States now lives in Suburbia.

> The metropolis has repelled a considerable number of those whom it drew to it: repelled them with its noise, soot, fumes, barren pavements, traffic tie-ups, nervous pressures, and inhuman dimensions, and especially with the apparent unsuitability of the life it imposes upon small children. It has not repelled many

* Historically cities have been strongholds to which people could scurry in case of enemy attack. Today, in addition to the routine hazards announced by the wail of ambulance, police, and fire sirens, they are the most vulnerable of military targets.

> of these people all the way back to the countryside, for its magnetic power is too strong for that; what it has done has been to hold them within its sphere of influence like so many planets—or more literally, to drive them part way out of town, to attempt to live *by* the city and yet *in* the country: to enjoy the power and glory of the city and yet at the same time, by daily travel, to enjoy quiet in place of its noise, clean fresh air and uninhibited sunshine in place of its soot and fumes, greenery and gardens in place of its barren pavements, living space in place of its congestion, peace in place of its nervous pressures, a neighborly village life in place of its vast anonymity, and an environment in which children will be able to work and play naturally.[53]

The grass on the suburban side of the fence may look greener, but there are bugs in it. Sociologists in the past decades of this century have pointed to the slums as a symbol of urban disorganization. Now they are pointing to the suburbs for the same reason.* Certainly, many thousands of families live full and contented lives in suburban pastures, but behind the facade of health, happiness, and achievement which the suburbs as a whole present to the casual observer, there is a surprising degree of discontent and social disorganization. There are various types of suburbs, of course: new ones and old ones, better ones and worse ones. Some are working-class suburbs; some cater to particular occupational groups—the families of men, for example, who work in communications, in television and radio networks, or for publishing companies.[54] Others serve as stop-over stations for junior executives who will move to a higher status suburb as soon as their position in "the organization" requires it.[55] Still other suburbs are made up of more expensive, individually designed homes occupied by independent business and professional men.[56] But whatever the age or the type, suburbs are rarely "real" communities in the traditional sense; the population is too homogeneous, the activity too limited.

A "real" community, in the traditional sense, has variety—variety of opinion and action; it is a segment of the whole of society. It is built on lasting human relations, and its people represent the continuity of generations. There are pregnant women, babies, teen-agers, and grandparents celebrating their golden wedding anniversary. It insures a full range of activities through an economic base which provides diverse employment for its citizens and through different political, cultural, religious, recreational, and educational opportunities. Suburbs suffer from too much sameness; they have been characterized as "Child-dominated matriarchies by day and co-ed dormitories by night." [57]

The suburban husband is popularly perceived as career-conscious and upwardly mobile, the wife as frustrated by domestic life, the teen-agers as "fast" and irresponsible, the younger children as over-protected. But all such stereotypes over generalize. Suburban homogeneity is part reality, part facade. Each architecturally homogenous suburb does attract its own relatively homogenous age, ethnic, and economic group. Furthermore, if only because home is comfortable and urban amenities miles away, suburbanites may depend dispro-

* Satellite towns are sometimes considered suburbs, but in our discussion of suburbs, we refer to those mass produced by commercial builders mainly since World War II.

portionately on cultural umbilical cords—the radio and television which, with few exceptions, do little to encourage individuality. However, the residents of even a single suburb differ in interests and values; they are not peas in a pod. And suburbanites *in toto* are an aggregate of groups made up of persons who choose for various reasons to reside outside the city limits. Only one pervading difference holds between suburbs and economically comparable urban neighborhoods. The suburbs are more self-consciously child-oriented. Said one urban friend, "I know it sounds corny, but I want to move to the suburbs so Johnny can play in Little League." *

Super-Urbs

Sprawling slurbs along with tidy suburbs are spanning the space between the Megalopolis and its satellite cities and towns, creating super-urbs,† some of them hundreds of miles long. In 1958 there were fifteen such regions which together claimed approximately half of our population and a disproportionate share of wealth, industry, and trade. By 1975 the super-urbs are expected to have at least sixty per cent of the population and seventy per cent of all retail trade.[59]

The traditional geographical and political boundaries we now take for granted are coming to have less and less meaning.[60] Not only are there new alignments (Southern New England, for example, has more in common with the New York-New Jersey area than it has with New Hampshire, Vermont, or Maine[61]), but the traditional distinctions between country and city are disappearing. The main difference left is that of population density. In manners and morals the city mouse and his country cousin are alike. What has happened is that the urban circles of influence, with the aid of rapid transportation and instantaneous long-distance communication, have spread wider and wider until they have overlapped, creating super-urbs with super problems and super opportunities.

> Let me give you an example of the sort of life we at Yale found when we arbitrarily chose for study a section of Connecticut which included seventy-nine towns, an area comprising several urban cores surrounded by rural-urban fringe. We discovered, first of all, that 24 per cent of the population lived on 86 per cent of the residential land. On this land some people have built their homes with their own hands, others have ordered expensive country estates, and still others have bought houses in subdivisions. There is still some unbuilt-on land around

---

* Although children dominate the suburbs, they are not as privileged as one might assume. They are isolated from the realities of the working world—from farming and manufacturing and commerce. This poverty of experiences places a particular educational burden on the school and the home.[58] Furthermore, suburban children, like their city cousins, are victims of whatever discontent and confusion their parents suffer.

† Also called Strip-cities, regional cities, and urban regions. The largest is the Atlantic Urban Region, stretching from Boston to Washington, D.C. It is dominated by New York City; but Boston, Philadelphia, and Washington, as well as Hartford, New Haven, and other smaller centers have subordinate spheres of influence.

Super Cities

nearly all of the houses, though low-income families are likely to be on small building lots.

This is the kind of district where a housewife's remark that she is just going to take the children over to the neighbor's house means that she is going to drive them five miles down a country road. Or if she says she's just running down to the store, she may drive fifteen miles to a shopping center, or a supermarket, or an upholsterer. . . .

The family that lives in the rural-urban fringe is not beholden to any one central business district either for shopping or for employment. Travel time is the chief factor here, not distance, and it is quite possible that husband and wife may go in opposite directions to get to their jobs. In all of Connecticut only 3 per cent of the population lives on farms—which means that almost everybody commutes to work. They do not necessarily commute to cities but to factories and offices located in small towns about the state, or they may even cross the state border into Massachusetts and New York. These people are urbanized folk, and for all practical purposes, the entire state of Connecticut might properly be considered part of an urban region.[62]

If the Megalopolis is in danger of turning into one big slum, inter-urbia is in danger of becoming even a bigger one. Assuming our population does increase by the estimated 30,000,000 people between 1960 and 1970, where are they going to live? Certainly not down on the farm; most of them will be in urban regions. Without far-sighted regional planning, the highways and low-ways, power lines and gas-line clearings, slurbs and suburbs, shoe-string commercial developments and shopping centers—all needed to accommodate the population—will take paths of least resistance, scarring what is left of landscape, eclipsing what is left of community.

COMMUNITY REGENERATION

Violence and delinquency are not confined to the slums; the striving, neurotic personality is not confined to the suburbs; and mental illness is not confined to midtown Manhattan. Such personal disorders are *concomitants, but not necessarily consequences,* of community disorder and disintegration. They indicate the profound influence which a total culture, with its tension-producing and tension-relieving mechanism, has on the adaptive system of human beings. The community setting, the frustrations and satisfactions it engenders, are aspects of the culture, contributing to or alleviating tensions from other sources.

Disgusting and physically harmful pollution, ugly decay, frustrating paralysis, senseless sprawl, loneliness in the midst of crowds—all the familiar aspects of a chaotic urban environment—contribute to the total stress suffered by an individual. In contrast, an ordered, coherent environment providing such amenities as good air, good water, good earth, and good company tends to alleviate tensions and reduce the total stress load. No one concerned with the health of individuals and of society would argue against the need for the physical regeneration of community, but the form it should take has been variously conceived. Just how should a new community be designed or an old one redesigned? What should be the nature of its architecture, its street plan, its land use? Two contradictory concepts have thus far influenced community planning and urban renewal in the United States: the *decentralized horizontal* "Garden City" and the *centralized vertical* "Radiant City."

The Garden City was originally described as a self-sufficient, self-contained community limited in size by a permanent agricultural and recreational green belt. All land would be public land, held in trust for the community. The Garden City idea, originally conceived by the Englishman, Ebenezer Howard, in addition to influencing the plan of many private subdivisions, inspired the building of four small but complete communities: Radburn, New Jersey *

---

* Radburn was designed as an answer to the enigma, "How to live with the auto," or "How to live in spite of it." Elements of the Radburn plan included: (1) superblocks with houses facing inward to the large parks in the center of the superblocks; (2) specialized roads built for a specific use—service lanes, secondary roads around superblocks, main through-roads, and express highways; (3) as complete separation as possible of pedestrian and automobile by different routing of pedestrian and motor traffic and by the use of under- and overpasses where they crossed.[63]

and the government-owned Greenbelt towns: * Greenbelt, Maryland; Greendale, Wisconsin; and Greenhills, Ohio. In philosophy, they were embodiments of ideas stemming not just from Ebenezer Howard and his fellow civic planner, Patrick Geddes, but also from the economist Thorstein Veblen, the sociologist Charles Horton Cooley, the educational philosopher John Dewey, and the social philosopher Lewis Mumford. In physical design, they were adaptations of the traditional New England town. Ultimate land use was set at 100 acres for community stores and buildings, 1,000 acres for homes, 1,800 acres for parks and 2,100 acres for farms.[65]

Greenbelt, for example, was designed and built as a harmonious whole. The location of the highways and streets and footpaths and buildings was indicated by the natural site—a high curved plateau. The focus for the common life of the town is the community center. Here is the shopping, recreational, and entertainment center, the school, church, bus terminal, post office, and government offices. Superblocks, resembling small parks with dwellings around the borders, form the main residential area. Other houses and apartment buildings are variously located. Footpaths are, in the main, completely separate from motor traffic. The town is as shielded from encroachment by its green belt as the medieval town was by its stone walls and fortifications.

A privately planned version of the government-sponsored Greenbelt towns is the city of Columbia now building in Howard County, Maryland.† [66] The master plan for Columbia was produced by professional planners with the collaboration of a crew of other experts including architects, lawyers, political scientists, economists, psychologists, psychiatrists, social psychologists, sociologists, ecologists, educators, industrialists, and business leaders. The city, when full grown, will accommodate a diverse population of 125,000 people. Garden apartments and homes ranging in cost from $10,000 to $100,000 group in neighborhoods of three to five hundred families. Each neighborhood has a primary school and is set off from adjoining neighborhoods by trees and green space. Neighborhoods, in turn, join together some three thousand families to make a village oriented to upper schools and libraries. At the center of the total complex of villages are the local college, the main library, community auditorium, theatre, businesses, and consumer services. Research and development firms, manufacturers' distributors, and industries promise an economic

* These communities are not Garden Cities in the original sense of rural-industrial self-sufficiency. Greenhills and Greendale do use the surrounding open space for farming, but none of the three has any important industry. Greenbelt is mainly a dormitory town serving Washington, D.C. The Greenbelt towns were built as demonstration suburbs on the outskirts of crowded cities by the Resettlement Administration during the Roosevelt administration (1933 to 1945), in the hope that every growing metropolis would develop a chain of similar communities around its borders to forestall disorderly and inefficient expansion.[64]

† The developer, James W. Rouse, is president of the Community Research and Development Corporation, head of the American Council to Improve our Neighborhoods (ACTION) and co-author with Nathaniel Keith of *No Slums in Ten Years,* a plan for the redevelopment of Washington, D.C.

base and social balance unprecedented in other planned communities in the U.S.*

Behind the physical plan of Columbia is acceptance of the philosophical doctrine that "We think and feel and act differently because of the different conditions under which life goes on." [67] Columbia is an open community, integrated racially and representative of a range of socio-economic levels from lower middle to upper class. The builders of Columbia hope to demonstrate that diversity within a coherent, rationally designed community generates a vitality which can combat the loneliness, irresponsibility, and superficiality too often found in the over-powering urbs and formless slurbs.

In 1964 when the United States was on the threshold of a population boom which experts predicted would double the population by the year 2000, more than 20 new communities, some larger in scope but lesser in concept than Columbia, were in various stages of development. Although some militant individualists may object to such master planning, new towns do represent a shifting architectural emphasis and a hope for community regeneration.

The Radiant City, conceived by the French architect Le Corbusier,† opposes the suburban nature of the Garden City with its "squandering of utilities," "fabulous host of vehicles," "crushing budget" for roads and railways, and "gigantic expense" for equipment and maintenance.[68] The vertical city would be economically concentrated. Each residential unit would be a structure of superimposed dwellings containing a restaurant and the other domestic services, such as cleaning and laundering, usually supplied by a hotel. It would be built above ground on stilts; underneath would be a park which included facilities for sports, maternity home, nursery school, primary school, club house—everything, in fact, necessary for the convenience and pleasure of the inhabitants. Pedestrian and motor traffic would be separated by differences in levels at the approach to each building. Pedestrians would enter on the ground; vehicles would come up ramps to higher level ports. Factories and other industrial buildings would be set in rustic surroundings with a minimum of disturbance to agriculture and the natural terrain. The idea of tall structures raised on stilts above the ground and separated from each other by open space has had widespread influence in the Near East, Russia, and South America. In the United

* Columbia covers some 14,000 acres, 3,500 of which are set aside as permanent open space. Other new towns in the United States include Reston, Virginia (6,810 acres); Clear Lake City, Texas (15,400 acres); Irvine Ranch, a three-town complex centered around the new Irvine campus of the University of California (88,000 acres); Laguna Niguel, California (7,000 acres); Foster City, California (2,600 acres incorporating 13 miles of lagoon waterfront); Sunset, California (12,000 acres); and Marincello, California (2100 acres). Comparable towns are being built in other countries including England, Canada, Scandinavia, and the Soviet Union. In England any new city, in fact, any new development or redevelopment, *must* be built according to a master plan approved by the government. For a discussion of planning in England see Frederick Osborne, *New Towns, The Answer to Megalopolis* (New York: McGraw Hill, 1963).

† Le Corbusier is not a man, but an ideal—a pseudonym for the professional ego of Charles Edouard Jeanneret.

States and Great Britain where people generally prefer living on the ground in separate houses, Le Corbusier's influence has been limited to individual buildings and urban renewal projects.

A third design concept, *Broadacre City,* a vision by Frank Lloyd Wright, has not had specific influence on community planning or urban redevelopment, but in the "City that is Nowhere unless Everywhere" [69] Broadacre City anticipates the total urbanization—or suburbanization—being brought about by the super-urbs. It describes the super-urb, not as it is developing, but as it could develop under the guidance of true democracy and "organic architecture." Under such guidance, geography would set the character of design; no two districts would be alike, but the whole would be unified, just as the deserts and mountains and valleys and plateaus themselves are unified. Spacious landscaped highways would be free of disfiguring signboards and the scaffolding of telegraph and telephone poles and wires. Factories would be noiseless and smokeless. Everyone would live within convenient walking or riding distance of work and pleasure. Roadside markets, small and large industries, tourist camps, hospitals and clinics, churches, museums, schools, parks, design centers, airports, sports centers, little farms, larger ranches, hotels, apartment houses, individual homes—all the desirable elements of our present rural and urban environment would be in convenient, logical, and aesthetic relationship. *Broadacre City* is conceived as a vast new city into which old ones gradually would disappear. The total culture would be a work of art, and the dominant physical expression of the culture would be through organic architecture. If architecture is, as Frank Lloyd Wright contended, "the final proof of quality in any Civilization whatsoever," [70] *what is the quality of our own?*

Look around objectively—our environment is chaotic. Well-designed buildings and groups of buildings are only oases in a desert of visual and functional disorder. Such chaos in the physical environment is a source of stress to the individual and to society. However, it is stress *in toto,* not stress from any particular source, with which we must be concerned if we are to achieve community and individual regeneration. ". . . a feedback mechanism, involving continued relationships between the individual and his culture, is constantly in operation so that inordinate stress, excessive in time, in amount, or in impact upon the person, produces disorder." [71] Stress *in toto* comes not just from the physical environment, but from the culture *in toto,* from all the material means and nonmaterial ways by which our society maintains and perpetuates itself. For this reason community design and redesign tend to fall short of the goal. Architecture, even broadly interpreted as both philosophy and design, is only one approach to the problems of community. We need teams of specialists as in the Columbia project, to direct the full course of community *and* individual growth, for the integrity of one may well depend on the other. "It almost seems as if community in the anthropological sense is necessary before human maturity or individuation can be achieved, while this same maturity is, in turn, a prerequisite for community." [72]

We do know that the interaction and mutual respect which a child experiences in a happy family supports his first steps toward healthy maturity. *Are his later steps comparably dependent upon interaction and mutual respect experienced in the larger community?* If so, community planning is not just a matter of buildings and roads, site plans and zoning; not just solving problems of sewage disposal and pollution, traffic and transportation, slum clearance and suburbs. We are dealing with the fundamental task of democracy: *the definition and realization of those environmental conditions, physical and social, which will give each individual optimum opportunity for the development of his potentials as a private person and as a public citizen.*

The problems of community regeneration, including urban renewal and town, city, and regional planning, are inseparable from the science of society. The solutions are not just technical and economic but sociological and psychological and ethical. *Can we eliminate ghettos before we conquer prejudice? Can we eliminate slums* * *before we conquer poverty of mind and spirit? Can we prevent slurbs without putting social values above economic values? Can we control pollution unless we value public health and natural resources more than private profit? Can we free human potential from the mill of urban-industrial mechanization* † *before we adjust our economic institutions to the realities of automation?*

A community, urban or suburban, needs physical integrity and ethical purpose. And, if it is to fully serve the needs of the individual and of society, it must contribute to the network of social institutions through which individuals and groups can function and with which they can identify. The form and function of our regenerated and emerging communities will reveal the dominant values of American society. *Will they be those of the good life?*

---

* Typical slum clearance programs do not eliminate slums; they simply redistribute them. They are designed, primarily, to protect land values, not human beings. The housing which replaces slums is usually for middle- and sometimes for high-income families.

† Even with partial automation, much of the work still required to maintain a metropolis stultifies the individual.

> The telephone girl who lends her capacities, during the greater part of the living day, to the manipulation of a technical routine that has an eventually high efficiency value but that answers to no spiritual needs of her own is an appalling sacrifice to civilization. As a solution of the problem of culture she is a failure—the more dismal the greater her natural endowment. As with the telephone girls, so, it is to be feared, with the great majority of us, slave-stokers to fires that burn for demons we would destroy, were it not that they appear in the guise of our benefactors.[73]

Notes

1. Lewis Mumford, *The City in History* (New York: Harcourt, Brace & World, Inc., 1961), pp. 285-290.
2. *Ibid.*, p. 19.
3. Mumford, *The Culture of Cities* (New York: Harcourt, Brace & World, Inc., 1938), p. 104.
4. *Ibid.*, p. 288.
5. *Ibid.*, p. 148.
6. *Ibid.*, p. 148.
7. James Truslow Adams, *The Epic of America* (Boston: Little, Brown & Co., 1933), p. 277.
8. U.S. Bureau of the Census, *Statistical Abstract of the United States* (Washington, D.C.: Government Printing Office, 1958), p. 21, Table 15.
9. *The World Almanac*, Harry Hansen, ed. (New York: *New York World-Telegram*, 1962), p. 684.
10. F. L. Allen, "The Big Change in Suburbia, Part I," *Harper's Magazine*, June, 1954, p. 21.
11. *The World Almanac*, Harry Hansen, ed. (New York: *New York World-Telegram*, 1962), p. 255.
12. C. A. Mace, "Human Motivation in an Affluent Society," in *Control of the Mind*, Seymour M. Farber and Roger H. L. Wilson, eds. (New York: McGraw-Hill, Inc., 1961), pp. 144-145.
13. William Lytle Schurz, *Brazil, the Infinite Country* (New York: E. P. Dutton & Co., Inc., 1961), pp. 40-41.
14. Mumford, *The City in History*, p. 54.
15. Stevan Dedeger, "Research: The Motor of Progress," *Bulletin of the Atomic Scientists*, June, 1962, p. 5.
16. Mumford, *The Culture of Cities*, p. 290.
17. Norton Ginsburg, *Atlas of Economic Development* (Chicago: University of Chicago Press, 1961), p. 74.
18. *The World Almanac*, p. 84.
19. Marya Mannes, *The New York I Know* (Philadelphia: J. B. Lippincott Co., 1961), pp. 9-12.
20. Leo Srole, Thomas S. Langner, Stanley T. Michael, Marvin K. Opler, and Thomas A. C. Rennie, *Mental Health in the Metropolis: The Midtown Manhattan Study* (New York: McGraw-Hill, Inc., 1962), Vol. I.
21. "The 'New' U.S., Shown by '60 Census," *U.S. News and World Report*, July 4, 1960, p. 53.
22. William H. Whyte, Jr., introduction to *The Exploding Metropolis*, by the editors of *Fortune* (Garden City, New York: Doubleday Anchor Books, Doubleday & Company, Inc., 1959), p. ix.
23. Robert and Leona Rienow, "The Day the Taps Run Dry," *Harper's Magazine*, October, 1958, pp. 70-78.
24. Catherine Bauer Wurster, "Framework for an Urban Society," in *Goals for Americans*, comprising the Report of the President's Commission on National Goals and Chapters Submitted for the Consideration of the Commission (Englewood Cliffs, N. J.: Prentice-Hall, Inc., 1960), p. 241.
25. Magnus Pyke, "Sludge and Space Travel," *The Listener*, July 2, 1959, p. 18.
26. Dr. Albert Burke, "Dirt, People and History, Part II," Telecast of KRON-TV, San Francisco, November 12, 1961.
27. "Washington: A City in Trouble," *Changing Times*, October, 1958, p. 21.
28. Samuel E. Wood and Alfred E. Heller, *California Going, Going . . .* (Sacramento: *California Tomorrow*, 1962), pp. 16-18.

29. Charles Schaeffer and Art Cosing, "How Much Poison Are You Breathing?," *Harper's Magazine,* October, 1959, p. 62.
30. Dr. Mark D. Hollis, Assistant Surgeon General of the U.S., "Fresh Air Getting Scarce in the U.S.?," *U.S. News and World Report,* October 17, 1958, p. 72.
31. *Ibid.,* p. 72.
32. Richard Neutra, *Mystery and Realities of the Site* (New York: Morgan and Morgan, 1951), p. 12.
33. Wood and Heller, *California, Going, Going* . . ., p. 9.
34. *Ibid.,* p. 10.
35. Wurster, *Goals for Americans,* p. 240.
36. *Ibid.,* p. 229.
37. *Greenbelt Towns, A Demonstration in Suburban Planning* (Washington, D.C.: The Resettlement Administration, 1936), p. 5.
38. "Washington: A City in Trouble," *Changing Times,* October, 1958, p. 20.
39. Wurster, *Goals for Americans,* pp. 229-230.
40. "What's Happening to U.S. Cities," *U.S. News and World Report,* June 20, 1960, p. 84.
41. *Ibid.*
42. Wood and Heller, *California, Going, Going* . . ., p. 20.
43. "Billions for Freeways—But Traffic Gets Worse," *U.S. News and World Report,* March 20, 1961, p. 92.
44. *Ibid.,* p. 90.
45. Wood and Heller, *California, Going, Going* . . ., p. 20.
46. "The Revolt Against Big City Freeways," *U.S. News and World Report,* January 1, 1962, p. 48.
47. *Ibid.,* p. 49.
48. "Billions for Freeways—But Traffic Gets Worse," *U.S. News and World Report,* p. 91.
49. "The Revolt Against Big City Freeways," *U.S. News and World Report,* p. 51.
50. From the records of Eugene Mead.
51. "The 'New' U.S. Shown by '60 Census," *U.S. News and World Report,* p. 52.
52. "Americana," *Time,* June 20, 1960, p. 14.
53. F. L. Allen, "The Big Change in Suburbia, Part I," *Harper's Magazine.* June, 1954, pp. 21-22.
54. A. C. Spectorsky, *The Exurbanites* (New York: Berkley Publishing Corp., 1958), paperback.
55. William H. Whyte, *The Organization Man* (Garden City, New York: Doubleday & Company, Inc., 1957), Part VII.
56. John R. Seeley, R. Alexander, and Elizabeth W. Loosley, *Crestwood Heights* (New York: Basic Books, Inc., 1956).
57. Spectorsky, "Destination Sickness," *What's New* (Chicago, Illinois: Abbott Laboratories, 1958), 204, p. 8.
58. Mumford, *The City in History,* pp. 495-496.
59. "Sprawling 'Strip Cities'—They're All Over U.S.," *U.S. News and World Report,* September 18, 1961, p. 77.
60. Christopher Tunnard, "America's Super Cities," *Harper's Magazine,* August, 1958.
61. *Ibid.,* pp. 60-61.
62. *Ibid.,* pp. 61-62.
63. Clarence B. Stein, *Toward New Towns for America* (The University Press of Liverpool, Agents for the Western Hemisphere Public Administration Service, Chicago, Illinois, 1951), pp. 42-44.
64. *Greenbelt Towns, A Demonstration in Suburban Planning* (Washington, D.C.: The Resettlement Administration, 1936), p. 20.
65. *Ibid.,* p. 20.

66. J. W. Anderson, "A Brand New City for Maryland," *Harper's Magazine,* October, 1964, pp. 100-106.
67. William Heard Kilpatrick, *Education for a Changing Civilization* (New York: The Macmillan Company, 1926), p. 49.
68. Le Corbusier, *Concerning Town Planning* (New Haven: Yale University Press, 1948), p. 68.
69. Frank Lloyd Wright, *When Democracy Builds* (Chicago: University of Chicago Press, 1945), p. 58.
70. *Ibid.,* p. 59.
71. Marvin K. Opley, "The Cultural Backgrounds of Mental Health," in *Culture and Mental Health,* Marvin K. Opler, ed. (New York: The Macmillan Company, 1959), p. 16.
72. Maurice R. Stein, *The Eclipse of Community,* p. 248.
73. Edward Sapir, *Selected Writings of Edward Sapir,* edited by David G. Mendelbaum (Berkeley: University of California Press, 1949), p. 315.

Man perfected by society is the best of all animals;

he is the most terrible of all

when he lives without law, and without justice.

ARISTOTLE (384-322)

V

Social Order in the Making

Fate, Time, Occasion, Chance, and Change.

To these all Things are subject. . . .

PERCY BYSSHE SHELLEY (1792-1822)

12

Change and Anti-Change

IN THE SECOND CENTURY A.D., the Roman emperor Marcus Aurelius observed that "everything is the result of change." Fourteen centuries later the English poet Edmund Spenser wrote of "the ever-whirling wheele of change, the which all mortall things doth sway." * In 1953, the physicist, J. Robert Oppenheimer, said, "Short of rare times of great disasters, civilization has not known such rapid alteration in the conditions of life, such rapid flowing of many varied sciences, such rapid changes in the ideas we have about the world and one another." [1]

Until the beginning of modern science in the seventeenth century, change was perceived as a natural phenomenon which man could neither deter nor advance. The usual pace of change was comfortably slow and catastrophic events were rare. Certainly floods, hurricanes, earthquakes, volcanic eruptions and other short-lived and relatively isolated disasters might disrupt the scene of social action, but when the floods receded, when the hurricane spent itself, when the earth resettled, what life was left tended to reassert itself in traditional ways. Longer lived, more widespread disasters—famine and plague, for example—effected more profound changes clear to historians but not to the people of the time. Barbarian hordes, proud conquistadores, tyrants and traitors have had their day, but most changes which men wrought were not aversive and sudden but

* Edmund Spenser (1533?-1599).

seemingly advantageous and gradual, and the life of individuals and groups within any one society took meaning and direction from the relative stability of the system and its setting.

Today the only social certainty is change and man, himself, is the main innovator.

U. S. MAY CUT DRAFT IN 1970!
JOBS ELIMINATED BY AUTOMATION!
UNITED STATES ESTABLISHES PEACE CORPS!
KENYA GAINS INDEPENDENCE!
POPE APPEALS FOR CHRISTIAN UNITY!

Any society is an active intricate system of action, made up of interdependent and interrelated individuals and groups and existing under conditions imposed by a geographical, biological, and technological environment. In this twentieth century, neither conditions nor social systems remain the same from one day to the next. Change is constant; what varies is the kind, the scope, and the rapidity of change. Some changes occur in the environment —in the scene of social action. Other changes—those we call *societary*—occur in social structures and processes, in group norms, and in individual and group goals. Some changes are minor and local; others have world-wide impact. Some changes occur so slowly they are not apparent in the span of one lifetime; others happen with shocking suddenness. In this twentieth century, change is an overwhelming phenomenon. With knowledge gained from science, men all over the world are instigating and accelerating change. Some changes seem disadvantageous, some advantageous, but the familiar is fading fast. Once solid social edifices seem but sand castles in a turbulent tide.

THEORIES OF CHANGE

World history is a chronicle of change—a narration of significant events in the biographies of social systems. Those who would understand history inevitably speculate about change. *How does it happen? Why does it happen?* Two basic theories of historical change have come to dominate Western thought: cyclical theories and linear theories. Both give perspective to sociology.

Cyclical Theories

The Greeks explained change in terms of historical cycles. Plato, for example, believed the Deity remade the world every 72,000 years. For the first 36,000 years the Deity maintained perfect order; then He relinquished control and let order gradually deteriorate into chaos. After each chaotic collapse, the Deity would establish another Golden Age of perfection. Plato believed himself to be living not in a Golden Age, but in one of tarnished decadence. Plato's pupil Aristotle further thought that all arts, sciences, and institutions had been discovered and lost an infinite number of times. The Romans, in turn, accepted the cyclical theory; and, according to some Pythagoreans, each new cycle *exactly* repeated the preceding ones. Thus an infinite number of Homers would recount an infinite number of Trojan Wars, and an infinite number of Platos would write an infinite number of *Republics.* The cyclical concepts of the ancients were pessimistic. All the miseries of man were to be repeated again and again; progress was impossible.

Some twentieth-century historical philosophers have proposed modified versions of classical cyclical theories. Oswald Spengler, Pitirim Sorokin, and Arnold Toynbee, for example, all stress—not linear change—but the ups and downs of historical cycles.

Oswald Spengler comes close to echoing the pessimism of the Greeks and Romans. *The Decline of the West,* published in 1918, presents the whole history of humanity as without discernible meaning. From Spengler's viewpoint, the conventional division of history into ancient, medieval, and modern is meaningless. Of greater significance are the life histories of separate cultures. Spengler perceived the development of a culture as more a matter of destiny than causation. "There is no question of prudent retreat or wise renunciation. Only dreamers believe there is a way out. Optimism is cowardice." [2] Each culture, like an individual organism, was destined to pass through stages of childhood, youth, maturity, old age, and ultimate death—a life cycle of approximately 1,000 years. Spengler set the beginning of the West circa 900 A.D. and heralded an imminent doomsday. The "civilization" of his time was only an epilogue of *rigor mortis*—an uncreative period of cultural rigidity. Spengler achieved tremendous popularity during the immediate aftermath of World War I, but his reputation, like his model of civilization, has declined in favor of less pessimistic theories, including those of Toynbee and Sorokin.

Arnold Toynbee published his ten-volume work, *Study of History,* between 1934 and 1954. Toynbee does not assume that a culture has a predetermined life span, but he does suggest that every culture passes through stages of origin, growth, and decline—processes determined by the capacity of the culture to respond to challenge. A culture (or civilization) emerges and grows when an intelligent minority responds creatively to the challenge of hardship or adversity—a severe climate, for example, or hostile neighbors. However, conditions which are *too* severe can either prevent the emergence of a civilization or bring about the decline of an existing one.

Pitirim Sorokin published his four-volume *Social and Cultural Dynamics* between 1937 and 1941. Sorokin sees historical change as a straight-line advance up to an *ideational* apex and then a reverse back to a *sensate* nadir. The culture itself never completely dies; parts of a declining sensate materialistic culture are caught up and survive in an advancing ideational one. Each culture carries within itself the dynamics of change; the potentialities of the system unfold and are little influenced by such external factors as biological or geographical forces. Sorokin is more optimistic than either Spengler or Toynbee but less so than contemporary linear theorists.

Linear Theories

Linear theories begin with Medieval Christianity; historical cycles are not consistent with the Christian message. Adam and Eve fell once and for all from a "Golden Age" in the Garden of Eden. According to Christian theory, the Christian era was the old age of humanity, and it would last only enough longer to permit the Deity to gather together the souls of those He had chosen for salvation. A devout Medieval Christian confidently expected the world to end within his own lifetime. The day of ultimate judgment was near, and it would never come again!

During most of the Western Renaissance, the prevailing concept of change was of linear decline from the Golden Age of the Greeks and Romans. Only near the end of this three hundred-year period did "radicals" suggest that Renaissance man was, in fact, building upon the knowledge of the ancients and making "progress." Linear theories of change today emphasize "progress" towards specific goals or evolution towards a better social system.

Best known and most influential of the linear theories is that presented by Karl Marx in *Das Kapital,* published in 1867. Marx perceived a fixed, inevitable pattern of change—an historical sequence destined to culminate in a classless society. He took nineteenth-century industrial Britain as his model and deduced that "the country that is more developed industrially only shows, to the less developed, the image of its own future." [3] He forecast both industrial development and class conflict as inevitable. All value, said Marx, is created by labor, but only a part of it is returned to the laborers. The "surplus value" goes to the capitalists who own the means of production. "Surplus value" reinvested expands the system, further enriching the unproductive capitalists and depriving the productive proletariate. This inherent injustice leads to revolution by the dispossessed proletariate and the setting up by the proletariate of a socialist state. Marx perceived capitalism as a stage in the development of socialism. "Intrinsically, it is not a question of the higher or lower degree of development of the social antagonisms that result from the natural laws of capitalist production. It is a question of these laws themselves, of these tendencies working with iron necessity towards inevitable results." [4] Revolution, Marx stressed, is not manufactured; it is the "midwife" of social change—a relatively minor act of force which makes manifest the already existing trend towards socialism. Belief in the Marxian "laws of history" gives contemporary leaders of the Soviet Union confidence that they will some day "bury" us.*

Sociological theories of change are most commonly linear. Auguste Comte

* By "We will bury you," the Russians mean, "We will surpass you."

(1798-1857), pioneer sociolgist, introduced the concept in his "law of three stages." All knowledge, he insisted, followed a uniform course of progressive development from an initial *theological* stage (causation explained by supernatural beings), through a *metaphysical* stage (causation explained by imaginary entities), to a final *positive* stage (causation explained by natural and invariable laws). Society, too, passed through similar stages. The positive stage of a society would come with the application of sociological knowledge to social phenomena. That Comte considered the positive stage to be morally superior to the others is suggested by the fact that he sent a copy of his *Positive Philosophy* to Emperor Nicholas I of Russia, fully confident that Nicholas, trained as he was in mathematics, would have both enough scientific interest and enough power to impose the reforms needed to make Russia a positive society. Social progress as Comte conceived it had a biological basis, first in man's innate urge to develop his abilities, and second, in his supposed transmission through heredity of such acquired characteristics as improved intellect and morals.[5]

Herbert Spencer (1820-1903) enumerated seven "laws" of change which he combined into one supreme law of evolution. This supreme "law" he believed applicable to all change—physical, biological, and social. See if you can understand it: "Evolution is an integration of matter and concomitant dissipation of motion; during which matter passes from an indefinite, incoherent homogeneity to a definite, coherent heterogeneity; and during which the retained motion undergoes a parallel transformation."[6] Spencer, like Comte, assumed that acquired individual characteristics—both physical and mental—could be inherited and would lead to social betterment. However, while Comte thought in terms of *progress* which could be hastened by rational intervention, Spencer thought in terms of natural *evolution*. "The seeds of civilization existing in the aboriginal man and distributed over the earth were certain in the lapse of time to fall here and there into circumstances fit for their development."[7] In the course of history, "survival of the fittest" would insure cumulative social betterment.

No early sociologist disputed the faith in progress through the operation of natural evolutionary laws, and until recently, concepts of social "progress" and "evolution" have been intermingled in sociological theories of change. As late as 1931 an American sociologist wrote:

> Social evolution is the unfolding and emerging of group life. It is part and parcel of cosmic evolution. From cosmic evolution we come to organic evolution, then to mental evolution, then to social. Social evolution includes as its most important aspect what has been called cultural evolution. Social evolution is illustrated by the development of a powerful nation out of thirteen struggling colonies; by the growth of a transcontinental chain of stores from a shoe-string business without capital; of a religious denomination spreading out over two continents from the preaching of one man. . . .
>
> There is no abysmal conflict between ethics and evolution. The flower of the evolutionary process is the ethical spirit. The rational harmony contem-

> plated here means neither more nor less than the more perfect adjustment and coordination of the permanent forces that make for betterment in the movement in the world, and which, slowly gathering vitality as civilization advances, now mainly require a fuller and more adequate expression to secure them the ultimate control of the movement of social life.[8]

To avoid the presumption that a society *evolves* under organic laws or *progresses* from one stage to another in some desirable direction, sociologists today favor the neutral term *change,* which can be for better or worse! They leave the "grand theories" of change, the *whys* of change, to philosophers of history, and focus instead on the scientific task of determining relationships between kinds of change and analyzing processes of change and mechanisms of anti-change. They assume that the direction change takes is not inherent in society but the result of a particular change on the particular structure, processes, norms, and goals of a particular society in a particular setting.

Some contemporary sociologists distinguish between culture change (change in material and nonmaterial traits) and social change (change in the structures through which men interact and the processes of interaction). Some focus on differential rates of change within culture itself and assume a more frequent and rapid change in the material than in the nonmaterial aspects of culture.* Still other sociologists, recognizing the interdependence of social and culture change, use the terms interchangeably. In our own thinking we cannot clearly disentangle social change from culture change; we cannot use the terms as we define them interchangeably; and we cannot accept a dichotomy which assumes that material change necessarily has either a logical or temporal priority over nonmaterial change. Instead, we find it useful to distinguish between *scene* changes—changes in the geographical, biological, and technological conditions under which society exists—and what we call *societary* changes—changes in the structures and processes of a society and the norms and goals of its culture.† We perceive this total complex as interactive with significant change in any one part causing *stress* and consequent reactive changes in other parts.

SCENE CHANGES

A society survives and maintains itself within a narrow environmental band. Human life is still dependent on the relative stability of such natural

* The *culture lag theory* was formulated by William F. Ogburn and published in *Social Change with Respect to Culture and Original Nature* (New York: B. W. Huebsch, 1922; new edition, New York: The Viking Press, Inc., 1950).

† This distinction is consistent with the four minimal components defined by social action theory: *means, ends, norms,* and *conditions.* Societary change involves the *means* (social structures and processes), *ends* (individual and social goals), and institutional *norms.* Scene changes affect the *conditions*—the setting within which social action takes place.

conditions as fertile soil, rainfall, solar radiation, and atmosphere. Within the confines of this natural setting, man initiates changes; he acts on nature and does not passively wait for nature to act on him. Thus the conditions under which a society exists may be changed by the action of geographical or biological forces or by the action of men.

Geographical Change

Man has built his societies on the crust of the earth, and on the life-sustaining capacity of that relatively thin layer, man's fate ultimately depends. His societies have flourished when rain and sun nurtured seed in fertile soil; his societies have withered or migrated when too much sun and too little rain dessicated the soil or when winds and floods eroded it away.

The Sahara Desert today is a region of dried-up river beds, dead lakes, bleak plateaus, naked mountains, shifting sand dunes, and scattered oases. The entire desert—approximately the size of the United States—barely supports about 2,000,000 people plus camels and a few species of wild animals and birds, spiders, and insects. Primitive rock paintings give mute evidence of the Sahara's once abundant life.

In the United States—before the days of Chambers of Commerce and travel agencies—the region we now call the West was candidly called the Great American Desert. Native Indians had long since abandoned the most arid southwest corner, but in the nineteenth century, eager homesteaders had their hopes alternately encouraged and discouraged by cycles of relative wetness and dryness. Even today settlements which once rimmed the Great Salt Lake in Utah and mountain lakes in Southern California stand deserted on dry flats hundreds of yards from water.

Without water the shells of seed can never soften and the life within can never germinate. Without water, the soil is dust. But deserts are caused by more than lack of rain; the soil itself can be eroded away—stolen by wind or flood.

Consider our own "Dust Bowl," which sent thousands of migrants to California, caused problems of health, housing, and employment—and a prejudice against "Okies." On May 12, 1934, the sky was darkened from the Rocky Mountains to the Atlantic Ocean by particles of topsoil blown from the Great Plains of Kansas, Texas, Oklahoma, New Mexico, and Colorado. The land had been misused, its natural cover destroyed, and when drought came, the exposed earth was caught up in the dry winds. The devastation was great. Congress hastened to establish a Soil Conservation Service, which today has conservation districts encouraging scientific soil management in every state. However, the fact that Lake Mead above Hoover Dam is silting in at an estimated 700,000 tons per day [9] is evidence that our own life-giving land is being lost. Perhaps we can still afford to lose some topsoil; but we cannot afford to lose sight of its importance. The United States now has food surpluses; the Soviet Union has food shortages. Our favorable position is partly due to our farm technology, but it is not independent of the fact that forty per cent of our land is arable, while all but ten per cent of the land in the Soviet Union is too dry, too wet, too cold, or too mountainous to be productive. *How would a reversal of the geographical base of the two countries affect their respective economies?*

Geographical conditions alone do not determine the nature of a society and its culture, but they do limit and modify both. And the survival of any society is related to its capacity to adapt to profound changes in those geographical conditions—changes which we are but slowly beginning to understand.

Biological Change

In the years following the Civil War, the United States tried to destroy the Plains Indians by sanctioning the slaughter of buffalo—the biological base of the Indian economy. When a bill to protect a large herd of buffalo was proposed in the Texas legislature, General Phil Sheridan, then in charge of Indian fighting, went to Austin to protest:

> The buffalo hunters have done more in two years to settle the vexed Indian question than the entire U. S. Army has done in ten years. . . . They are destroying the Indians' commissary. Send them powder and lead if you will, but for the sake of lasting peace let them kill, skin, and sell until the buffalo are exterminated.[10] *

In war men may try to destroy the biological base of each other's economy; in peace they struggle to maintain their own. They compete with each other and with other species for the fruits of the earth, knowing that the health of a society and the wealth of its culture are founded on biological abundance. In *some* parts of the world, men compete for meager fare with each other and with other animals. In India, for example, where people die daily from starvation, sacred monkeys raid the vegetable markets, and some 75,000,000 unproductive cows wander the city streets and the countryside, placidly munching. In drought-stricken areas of Java, rats eat the rice grains as soon as they are planted and strip the fields of sweet potatoes and tapioca. The people, in turn, eat the rats and anything else they can find. In *all* parts of the world, including our own, men also compete with insects, fungi, and other organisms which prey on plants and animals, and with micro-organisms—bacteria and viruses—which prey on man himself. Changing biological conditions in this devouring world have helped shape societies.

The Irish potato famine in the 1840's—the "Great Hunger"—sent a million

---

* At the beginning of the nineteenth century, there were an estimated 50,000,000 buffalo; by 1905 there were fewer than 500.[11] General Sheridan almost got his wish!

and a quarter immigrants across the Atlantic to the United States and Canada and even more across the Irish channel to Great Britain, Liverpool, Glasgow, and ports of South Wales. The Irish took with them a variety of diseases—including typhus, dysentery, and cholera—and an abiding hatred for the English, on whom they blamed their misery. They set up communities, particularly in the United States, "where the name of Britain was accursed and whose descendants continued to be Britain's powerful and bitter enemies, exacting vengeance for the sufferings their forbears endured." [12] The fungus *Phytophthora infestans,* which turned the potato fields of Ireland black almost overnight, is still with us. So, too, is a lingering prejudice against the Irish who, more than one hundred years ago, endangered and burdened the communities into which they crowded.

Locusts are common in arid lands. In the Near East, North Africa, and parts of Asia, plagues of locusts still devastate entire areas. They drift with the wind, can obliterate a grain field in minutes, and have been known to eat even clothing and fence posts. Altogether, men lose to pests of one sort or another approximately one-third of the food planted for human consumption. Even in our own abundant land, the millions of dollars farmers spend on pest control give the impression that we barely manage to keep one bite ahead of the bugs.

Insects and disease attack plants in the field and animals in the barn. Still others attack us directly! They have laid societies waste, as well as inspired such inventions as vaccines, window screens, fly traps, and FLIT!

A female anopheles mosquito takes human blood to nourish her young; she may also inadvertently transmit malaria.* Insects are *vectors* of disease; † micro-organisms—bacteria and virus—are the *cause* of disease. When these minute forms of life attack a large population, we have an *epidemic;* when they attack the majority of the total population, we have a *pandemic.* In the 1918-1919 influenza pandemic, 40 million people in the United States alone sickened, and 300,000 died. Altogether the flu virus infected hundreds of millions of people all over the world and killed nearly 25 million—close to three times the number guns had killed in the World War which was just ending.

The "flu" complicated the recovery of a world weakened by war, but other pandemics in other centuries actually undermined flourishing social institutions. The "Black Death"—now medically identified as bubonic and pneumonic plague—raged from the fourteenth to the seventeeth centuries and killed one-fourth of the entire world population. London, during four terrible months in 1665, lost one-fourth of its population—more than 100,000 people. Brave (or reckless) men drove carts through the darkened streets of the city calling, "Bring out your dead!" Oxford, in 1352, lost two-thirds of its academic popula-

* Three-fourths of the people of the world live in malaria zones and, until the introduction of DDT in 1948, malaria every year struck 300,000,000 people and killed 3,000,000.

† Accrding to the World Health Organization insects as vectors are responsible for half of all human deaths and deformities from disease.

tion. Europe in the Great Dying (1348–1350) lost a full fourth of its population.

In the crowded cities and towns the plague took its greatest toll. Following the Great Dying, serfs deserted their manor lords, and peasants by the thousands abandoned farms and villages to take up the work the dead had left behind. In the towns and cities, serfs and peasants found independence; the lords and ladies lost power; and the declining feudal system broke down—hastened not by deliberate revolt of the men it had so long enslaved, but by a pandemic of micro-organisms.

The economic and political repercussions of the Black Death were accompanied by moral and religious ones. Contemporary chronicles of the London epidemics noted that everywhere there was "drinking, roaring, and surfeiting . . . In one house you might hear them roaring under the pangs of death, in the next tippling, whoring, and belching out blasphemies against God." [13] Were Comte and Spencer or others right in their assumption of progress or moral and intellectual evolution, then we might expect that under stress, human behavior in the fourteenth century would show some superiority to behavior under comparable circumstances 2,000 years earlier. However, in 430 B.C. Thucydides described the "Plague of Athens."

> Men resolved to get out of life the pleasures which could be had speedily and would satisfy their lusts, regarding their bodies and their wealth alike as transitory. . . . No fear of gods or law of men restrained them; for, on the one hand, seeing that all men were perishing alike, they judged that piety or impiety came to the same thing, and, on the other hand, no one expected that he would live to be called to account and pay the penalty for his misdeeds. On the contrary, they believed that the penalty already decreed against them and now hanging over their heads was a far heavier one, and that before it fell it was only reasonable to get some enjoyment out of life." [14]

People living in the days of the Black Death eased their fear and despair, not only by excessive eating, drinking, and making merry, but by excessive scapegoating and praying. They became both extremely superstitious and extremely religious. Distraught Christians persecuted Jews and witches alike. They entreated God and enriched the Church with gifts. But the plague persisted; the faithful as well as the infidels were caught in its purgatory. "A vast and dreadful solitude," said the fourteenth century poet Petrarch, followed the Great Dying; but before the plague spent itself, it had contributed to the decline of feudalism and hastened the Reformation. Many a priest fled his parish in panic, and the inability of the Church to save its members undermined the prestige and power of Catholicism. Reformation leaders stepped in with promises of a more direct and intimate relationship between man and God.

In the past, particularly in pre-industrial societies, changes in the scene of social action have been predominantly wrought by geographical and biological forces. Today, particularly in industrially advanced societies, scene changes are initiated knowingly and deliberately by men.

Technological Change

The technological conditions under which societies maintain themselves have in the course of history been changed by two major revolutions: first, the agricultural revolution which began in the Middle East several thousand years ago and which, over the centuries, shifted societies from a subsistence base of hunting and food-gathering to an agrarian base; and second, the scientific-industrial revolution which in less than two hundred years has brought knowledge of machine techniques and machine-made products to most of mankind. In advanced countries it has put at the command of the average citizen a cortege of energy slaves rivaling in capacity the human slaves who once served kings. It has also put transistor radios into the hands of illiterates and terrible toys into the hands of politicians. Technological change is the dramatic phenomenon of this century.

Since the beginning of the scientific-industrial revolution, one technological innovation has led to another; the rate of increase has been comparable to that of compound interest on money left in the bank. If you put $100.00 in the bank at five per cent interest and let that interest accrue, your principal at the end of the first year would be $105.00; at the end of the second year, $110.25; at the end of the third year, $115.75. The accumulation at first is slow. But that original $100.00 at the end of 100 years of accrued interest would total enough to command almost $1,000.00 interest. The rate of technological change follows the same exponential curve. For thousands of years the speed of man's travel has been limited to the speed of a horse—about 30 miles per hour. In 1830 the "oats barrier" was broken by the "Iron Horse," and later by the "Horseless Carriage." As in the exponential curve for compound interest, early accretions in speed were small. When the Wright Brothers took to the air in 1903, their plane went no faster than a horse, and when Wilbur Wright in 1908 broke all previous records by flying nonstop for 76.5 miles, he averaged only 35.5 miles per hour. Until the invention of jet aircraft and rockets, the speed of "flying machines" increased only eight miles per hour per year. When man took to rockets, he orbited the earth at 18,000 miles per hour, and exactly fifty years and two days after Wilbur Wright's record flight, the Russians hit the moon with an unmanned rocket which left the earth at an approximate speed of 25,000 miles per hour.

Each major technological innovation has, in its time, stimulated other innovations. The automobile, for example, was a technological innovation which called for efficient mass production techniques. (These were first achieved by Henry Ford—as the German word *Fordismus* suggests.) Mass production techniques led to a widening consumer market for automobiles, to new factories, new retail stores, new service facilities, and new skills. It led to the dispersal of population into suburbs, to the building of divided highways and freeways, to a system of licensing drivers, to new kinds of insurance, new laws and new duties for the police force. It changed courtship practices, family living patterns, and leisure-time activities. It increased the accident and death rate. . . . And the automobile is just one technological innovation among thousands which have brought reactive changes in both the social scene and social action.

Technology is the "adopted child" of science, and rapid technological advance reflects rapid scientific advance.* Science, in effect, is a "motor of progress," now increasing its horsepower by 12.5 per cent per year. (Consider the potentialities of accrued interest at that rate!) But science and technology are dependent on research facilities, and these are not evenly distributed. Two-thirds of the world population still live in underdeveloped pre-research cultures.

> Modern science is a key social factor in today's division of the world into developed and underdeveloped countries. Economists have signaled a rapidly growing gap between the rates of growth of the developed and of most of the underdeveloped countries. Research with its continuous creation of new technologies is one of the principal social forces increasing this gap. The developed countries are using research more in a socially planned way as the motor power of their social progress, while the underdeveloped countries still lack this motor.
>
> As one would expect, comparisons of the gross national product percentages show that the less a country is developed, the smaller is its investment in science and the slower its rate of scientific growth. Furthermore, the increase in the research effort in developed countries is being added to an already existing research potential that is incomparably greater than the one in underdeveloped countries.[16]

The division of the world into developed and underdeveloped or newly developing countries has immediate human meaning. In North America in 1950 the average individual had at his command 387 "energy slaves"—units of mechanical or electrical energy equivalent to the work output of one man. The world average in 1950 was 38 energy slaves for every man, woman, and child in the world, but these "slaves," like the technology which fathers them, are unevenly distributed. The average individual in Europe (including Western Russia) had at his command 27 energy slaves; in South America, 28 energy slaves; in Africa and the Mediterranean World, 13; in Asia (including Eastern Russia), two; and in Central America, none.[17]

Since 1950 the postwar recovery of Europe, Russia, and Japan, combined with the rising industrialization of China, has shifted the distribution. The United States, with only six per cent of the world population in 1960, used more than one-third of the world's commercial energy. However, the relative rise in the use of commercial energy by Europe and Asia during the decade from 1950 to 1960 is reflected by shifting political power. Europe has become

* Within the United States, the increase in steel production is a rough index of our total technological growth. Steel output, which averaged only four pounds per person in 1870, rose to 320 pounds per person in 1900, and to 1,700 pounds per person in 1957.[15]

increasingly independent of the United States, and China, increasingly independent of the Soviet Union. This shift in power is but the latest chapter in the history of the scientific-industrial revolution. In the seventeenth century, Europe looked with awe upon the wealth of "the gorgeous East," and Francis Bacon referred to South America as "the money-breeder of Europe." Europeans sought spices in the East, mineral wealth in South America—and slaves in Africa. Today, however, 90 per cent of the world's industrial output—the twentieth-century measure of wealth—is concentrated in areas lived in or settled by Europeans. In relative energy consumption (roughly equivalent to industrial capacity), the "gorgeous East," and "the money-breeder of Europe" are technologically comparable to the United States in the decade before the Civil War.

> . . . science is a unique development limited almost entirely to the western world. . . . A true scientific revolution which could support technology will profoundly affect the cultures of the underdeveloped nations in their deepest traditions. . . . It would be certain to bring about major changes in religious philosophy, ethics, and social structure.[18]

Technological development backed by scientific research tipped the scale of world power in our favor.

Now the already developed industrial nations are in the beginning stages of a third major technological revolution—the *cybernation* revolution.

> A new era of production has begun. Its principles of organization are as different from those of the industrial era as those of the industrial era were different from the agricultural. The cybernation revolution has been brought about by the combination of the computer and the automated self-regulating machine. This results in a system of almost unlimited productive capacity which requires progressively less human labor.[19]

In the little town of Doncaster, England, two machines working twelve hours a day turn out all the light bulbs needed by the entire country. Sand and raw materials go into one end of the automated factory. Packaged light bulbs come out the other. In the United States, automation is already a part of our way of life. Different kinds of computers run entire banks of machines and do in a few minutes what once took many men many hours. The new process makes possible unprecedented mass production of products—including frozen food and automobiles—at a price the average consumer can pay. And without the automated machines now in use by the telephone industry, it would be impossible to handle the growing load of telephone calls without more women than are employed in the entire labor force.[20]

> The fundamental problem posed by the cybernation revolution in the United States is that it invalidates the general mechanism so far employed to undergird people's rights as consumers. Up to this time economic resources have been distributed on the basis of contributions to production, with machines and men competing for employment on somewhat equal terms. In the develop-

> ing cybernated system, potentially unlimited output can be achieved by systems of machines which will require little cooperation from human beings. As machines take over production from men, they absorb an increasing proportion of resources while the men who are displaced become dependent on minimal and unrelated government measures—unemployment insurance, social security, welfare payments. These measures are less and less able to disguise a historic paradox: that a growing proportion of the population is subsisting on minimal incomes, often below the poverty lines, at a time when sufficient productive potential is available to supply the needs of everyone in the United States. . . .[21]
>
> An adequate distribution of the potential abundance of goods and services will be achieved only when it is understood that the major economic problem is not how to increase production but how to distribute the abundance that is the great potential of cybernation. There is an urgent need for a fundamental change in the mechanisms employed to insure consumer rights.[22]

For the present, the major aspects of the cybernation revolution are restricted to the United States. How we cope with its problems and possibilities will influence the course of cybernation everywhere else in the world.

Scene changes—biological, geographical, and technological—may precede or follow societary changes—changes in the structure of society, and in the norms and goals of culture.

SOCIETARY CHANGES

Geographical, biological, and technological change in the conditions under which a society maintains itself inevitably affect the society itself and its culture. Change is no isolated phenomenon; a change of any significance sets up a chain of reactions. Determining the original impetus is always difficult and sometimes impossible. However, some changes are manifest first most clearly in the physical background—the scene of social action; others are manifest most clearly in social action and in the actors themselves.

Men, women, and children make up the cast of actors in the social scene. The changing number, composition, and distribution of this human population are the *demographic* content of a society. The action of the actors, as individuals and as group members, is guided by their relative *positions* in various institutional structures as well as by the cultural norms and goals embodied in those structures.

Demographic Change

The birth of a baby may be a "blessed event" for parents, but it is just one more statistic in a world population growing at a rate which could well lead to "pathological togetherness" and social catastrophe.*

* Chapter 1.

From data supplied by national censuses as well as by historical descriptions, demographers have determined some of the variables which affect major characteristics of population: growth, composition, and distribution.

Growth

A population, like the individuals who comprise it, has both a biological potential (fecundity) and an actual birth rate (fertility). Fecundity depends to some extent on general health and maternal care. Fertility, in turn, depends upon fecundity itself and on a variety of other factors. These include such cultural circumstances as industrialization, urbanization, social stability, prosperity, and such personal circumstances as socio-economic level, education, religion, and marriage.

In some societies, a woman has to produce a baby to prove she is worth marrying, but in most societies marriage is a sanctioned prerequisite to having babies and a determinant of fertility. In India, where the birth rate in 1960 approximated 40.0 (births per 1,000 population), the proportion of never-married women was less than 1.0 per cent. In the United States, where the proportion of never-married women is nearly 10 per cent, the birth rate was 23.6; and in Sweden, where the proportion of never-married women is 21 per cent, the birth rate was 13.7. Marriage, however, is only one of many variables. In the United States, for example, significant shifts have occurred since the late nineteenth century in attitudes towards time of marriage and size of family. Men and women are marrying earlier; fewer marriages are childless, the family size is smaller, and women complete their families earlier. (The median age of a woman at the birth of her last child was 31.9 in 1890, 25.8 in 1960.) The "baby boom" which followed World War II in every Western country except Germany was in part the result of such cultural shifts.

Regarding other cultural and personal conditions favorable to fertility, demographic studies of Western societies support the following generalizations: [23] *

Fertility is higher in technologically underdeveloped countries than in technologically developed ones. (The phenomenal postwar development of Japan brought a drastic reduction in birth rate. The developing society—or ambitious individual—may perceive high fertility as incompatible with "getting ahead" and voluntarily limit fertility.)

Fertility is higher in times of economic prosperity and social stability than in times of depression or rapid change. (In the United States, the birth rate fluctuates with business cycles. Even in the eighteenth-century agrarian societies of northern Europe, years of high birth rates followed years of abundant harvest.)

* These generalizations do not necessarily hold for Eastern cultures. Prior to the Communist regime in China, for example, the relationship between fertility and socio-economic class was direct; the educated and well-to-do had more children than the poor and ignorant.

Fertility is higher in rural than in urban areas and higher in small towns than in metropolitan centers. (City families have more interests outside the family than rural or small-town families. Furthermore, children are a handicap to status-seeking urban parents; they are an economic asset to farm families.)

Fertility is highest in the lowest socio-economic groups. (Ancient Romans called their lowest class *proletarius*—the prolific. They had only their offspring to contribute to the state! In 1957 women in the United States over 45 years of age at the bottom of the socio-economic structure averaged twice as many children as those at the top. However, families at the very top of the socio-economic structure—particularly those with inherited status—have more than the average number of children.)

Fertility is highest among those with the least education. (Education is a necessary prerequisite to the changed attitudes needed to effectively lower fertility. Economic development alone is not sufficient.)

Fertility is higher among Catholics than among Protestants and higher among Protestants than among Jews. (Sub-cultural patterns and religious beliefs affect fertility, but socio-economic status is the more crucial variable. Families of the same socio-economic status but different religion are more alike in fertility than families of the same religion but different socio-economic status.)

Life begins with birth and ends with death, and population growth is obviously not a matter of fertility alone; it is a fertility-mortality ratio. Attitudes towards fertility shift with cultural and personal circumstances, but normal attitudes toward mortality are constant. The healthy individual treasures life; the healthy society supports life, and any innovations which promise to prolong life both individuals and society readily accept.

In the technologically advanced nations, the past 150 years of economic growth and rising standard of living have been accompanied by both a decrease in fertility and a decrease in mortality. Modern medicine and public health practices in these same countries have decreased the mortality rate still further. In the United States, for example, the average life expectancy at birth in 1900 (both sexes—all racial groups) was 47.3 years. In 1959 it was 69.7 years. Because of the simultaneous decline of both fertility and mortality, our population growth and that of other urban industrial nations is relatively slow, and although it poses grave problems,* the total population has not yet reached unmanageable density.

In contrast, modern medicine and public health practices introduced into technologically underdeveloped countries where the fertility rate is still high have made a near-disastrous change in the fertility-morality ratio. In Ceylon, for example, where the percentage of never-married women is only three per cent and fertility is high, malaria control alone reduced mortality 34 per cent in one year. But most of those saved from malaria are condemned to illiteracy and chronic hunger.

---

* Chapter 1.

Societies in the past have dealt with overpopulation in a variety of ways: postponed marriage, enforced celibacy, sexual abstinence, delayed or illegal remarriage, sterilization, contraception, abortion, and infanticide. Increasing population pressure will dictate that contemporary societies also curtail population growth. The effective means may well involve basic societary changes—including changes in cultural norms and goals.

Composition

Growth is only one dimension in which population changes. It also changes in composition—in sex, age, and racial ratios. Both sex and age ratios indirectly affect growth, and, like growth, cause other reactive societary changes.

Sex ratio—the proportion of males to females—is written as the number of males per 100 females. A ratio of 100 means an equal number of both sexes; a number more than 100 means an excess of males; a number less than 100 means a shortage of males. Fecundity and fertility are highest when the sex ratio approximates 100. Any deviation in this ratio has a direct effect on fertility. Some societies have changed the sex ratio deliberately through female infanticide. Other societies have had the sex ratio changed inadvertently through war. Russia, for example, had a catastrophic loss of men in World War II; the 1959 census showed 20,000,000 more women than men. Russian women not only have had to take on some of the traditional work of men,* but, since Russia is a monogamous society, the excess women have been deprived of the essential child-bearing and child-rearing work of women. Were such a disproportionate sex ratio to persist, monogamy could well give way to polygyny.

In the United States, a record immigration of young males in the first decade of this century brought the sex ratio in 1910 to an all-time high of 106. The gradual gain since made by females in longevity has brought the sex ratio by 1960 down to an all-time low of 97. The 1960 census, however, disclosed sharp regional differences. Judy O'Grady in Boston and the Colonel's daughter in Fairbanks may be sisters under the skin, but the Colonel's daughter is more likely to marry—not because of her class position, but because the sex ratio in Alaska is 132; that in Massachusetts, 93. Furthermore, there are urban-rural differences. The 1960 urban sex ratio was 94; the rural ratio, 104. Cities generally attract more women; farms retain more men. And cities which are commercial or administrative centers have a particularly low sex ratio. Washington, D. C., for example, has a ratio of only 88. The surplus unmarried women working in urban centers have an independence unknown to the farm or small-town woman, and they have tended to be more politically active than their married sisters. It was such women who, in the period following the first World War, added their weight to the Suffrage Movement and helped pass the Nineteenth Amendment.

In 1964 a young G. I. was most enthusiastic about the prospects of being

* Some factories are run almost entirely by women, and in 1960, sixty per cent of the collective farm workers and seventy-five per cent of the physicians were women.

sent to Berlin. Why? Because the sex ratio was exceptionally favorable—three females to every male! However, he discovered that Berlin had an aging population. Many of the excess females were old enough to be his mother! The age ratio of a population has implications not just for romantic young G. I.'s, but for all the institutions of society. A population with a high proportion of people in the productive years has a large labor force and a proportionately high economic and military potential. A population with concentrations at either end of the age scale has a high dependency ratio which reduces its economic and military capacity and increases the demands on government—more educational facilities for the young, for example, and more protection for the old. In 1963, Asia, Africa, and Latin America had 80 per cent of the world's children but only 69 per cent of the adults, a demographic fact which currently complicates the economic problems of these newly developing nations.

In contrast, the immigration of adventurous and able-bodied young adults to the United States all through the years of our most rapid growth gave us a favorable age distribution. Now, at an opportune time when mechanization and automation are reducing the need for productive workers, increased life expectancy and a high birth rate are swelling the dependent, nonproductive portions of our population.

The proportion of people living beyond the age of 65 has more than doubled since 1920, and more and more people are enjoying life beyond the Biblical three score and ten. A baby boom followed World War II, and in 1965 half our population was 25 years old or younger. The younger members of society are forcing expansion of educational facilities from nursery schools through college and giving urgency to such programs as the foreign and domestic Peace Corps, the Job Corps, and government-sponsored work-study programs. The older members of society are building "retirement" communities for their own exclusive use and pressuring for more government protection through social security and medical aid.*

Population pyramids graphically present the composition of a population by sex and age. The pyramid for 1900 is typical of an expanding population with high birth and death rates. The 1940 pyramid shows a population low in fertility (as expected during economic depression) and high in the productive middle years—a demographic circumstance which not only contributed to the severity of the depression by providing a surplus labor force, but which handicapped recovery by the relatively small demand for goods and services from those in the dependency years. The 1960 pyramid shows a population low in the productive years and high in the dependency years.

Because factors favoring high fertility are dominant in the colored nations of the world, differential population growth is rapidly changing the racial composition of world population. Between 1950 and 1955, for example, the rate of population increase in southwest Asia was five times the rate in northern

* By 1965 the change in population structure had effectively changed Congressional attitudes towards both Federal aid to education and medical aid to the aged.

MALE AGE FEMALE
70 - 74
65 - 69
60 - 64
55 - 59
50 - 54
45 - 49
40 - 44
35 - 39
30 - 34
25 - 29
20 - 24
15 - 19
10 - 14
5 - 9
0 - 4
7 6 5 4 3 2 1 0 1 2 3 4 5 6 7
PER CENT (U. S., 1900)

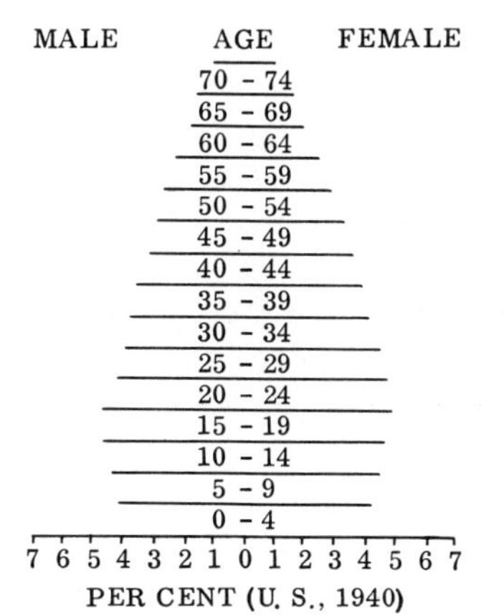

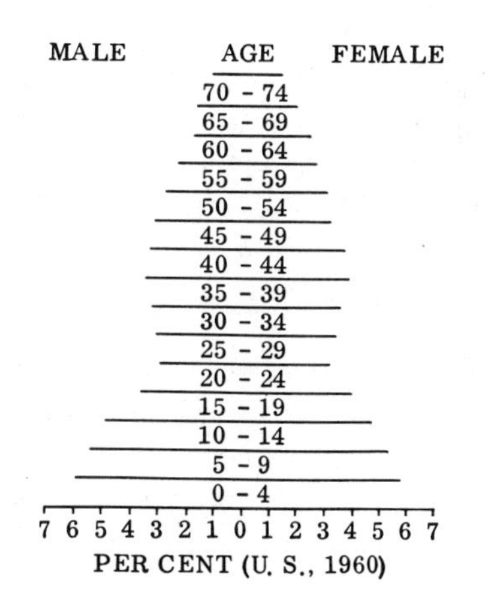

United States Population Pyramids

Europe; in Central America, it was six times as high. At the beginning of this century, the predominantly white nations of Europe, the Soviet Union, and North America had one-third of the world's population; the predominantly yellow, brown, and black nations of Asia, Latin America, Africa, and Oceana had two-thirds. By the year 2000, the ratio is expected to be one-fifth white, four-fifths colored. The white race is a rapidly shrinking minority.

Distribution

Population changes not only in size and composition but also in distribution. Within national boundaries, people move from or to north, south, east, or west, from coastal to interior regions, from rural to urban areas, from urban areas to suburbs, from areas of low density to areas of higher density, and from areas of high density to areas of lower density. And people move from one country to another. They move insofar as they feel free to escape undesirable living conditions or to seek better ones. Migrations within countries, together with immigrations and emigrations, obviously affect the size, composition, and distribution of any given population. The original thirteen United States in 1790 had an average 4.5 persons per square mile; the fifty United States in 1960 had an average 50.5 persons per square mile. Some of this increased density can be accounted for by the progeny of approximately 250,000 original settlers. The progeny of 42,000,000 voluntary immigrants and 1,000,000 conscripts are responsible for the rest.* And any given population is variously distributed; people can concentrate in one small area or disperse over a large one. New Jersey in 1960 had a population density of 806 persons per square mile; Alaska, a density of 0.4. Even if the geographical, biological, and technological conditions were identical, density of population alone would make social structures and cultural norms in Alaska different from those in New Jersey.

The trend of world population is towards larger absolute size, greater density in urban centers and larger metropolitan regions, wider distribution into areas now relatively uninhabited, and a differential growth favoring the colored races. As actors in the social drama change in number, relationship, character and locale, the plot and the action also will change.

Positional Change

Positions structure the institutions of society. Man and wife, priest and laity, manager and clerk, creditor and borrower, king and commoner, master and slave, administrator and teacher, teacher and student—these are all positions in the family, religious, economic, government, and educational institutions of society. But institutions change in structure; positions are eliminated or

* The dispossessed Indians have decreased rather than increased in number (Chapter 10).

added; qualifications necessary for various positions are redefined, and positions shift in status relative to each other.

Major positional changes are brought about by social movements * (either of the reform or revolutionary type) and then formally fixed by law and/or incorporated into the mores. In the United States, for example, the Women's Rights movement, launched in 1848, protested the "prolonged slavery" of women and brought into focus the discontents of one-half the population. In 1905 Grover Cleveland (United States President 1885-1889 and 1893-1897) wrote in the *Ladies' Home Journal*, "Sensible and responsible women do not want to vote. The relative positions to be assumed by man and woman in the working out of our civilization were assigned long ago by a higher intelligence than ours." In 1917 the education of women at the college level was still a debatable issue. A college girl was suspect. ". . . she must be radical, or a bluestocking, or a man hater, or in some way peculiar."[24] In World War I, women began working alongside men in business and industry. In 1920 they won the right to vote. In the years that followed, distinctions once made between "women's work" and "men's work" became increasingly blurred. Old social taboos were relaxed, Victorian codes of propriety disregarded. Wives and mothers openly smoked and drank, and even nice girls ditched their chaperones. By 1965 the most ambitious goals of women had been realized. Their position in the larger society was secure. Not only were women active in politics and the professions, but the United States Congress had written into law their right to equal pay for equal work.

In the United States today, the Civil Rights movement is effecting other significant positional changes. Like the Women's Rights movement, it, too, is an expression of discontents born of awakened hope. *Whenever the position of an individual or group in one area of significant social action is advanced disproportionately beyond that in other areas, the discrepancy kindles discontent.* As Negroes achieved greater economic and educational status, political voice and judicial support, other privileges of citizenship denied them by the larger society loomed ever larger in contrast. As long as the Negro position seemed totally hopeless, Negroes revealed only a surface "contentment" of apathy. But each achievement fired imagination with desire for still greater advances, and the movement grew in breadth and intensity. As in the Women's Rights movement, other seemingly unrelated innovations and events support the Negro cause. The first World War helped bring women into the labor force; the automobile and labor-saving devices for the home helped emancipate them. The integration of the armed forces following the second World War, and the emergence of the African Nations, have favorably changed the Negro's self-image. And television brought the Madison Avenue portrait of middle-class white America into the homes of deprived blacks. Mass communication

---

* Chapter 13.

made the American dream of equal opportunity pandemic, and people previously immune through lack of hope became infected.* The Fourteenth Amendment provides that the rights of citizens are not to be abridged. It describes citizens as *all* persons born or naturalized in the United States. How long will it take Negroes to secure *their* Constitutionally guaranteed rights?

Social revolutions are crisis points in positional change—a culmination of a series of previous positional changes. Successful revolutions bring new groups with different norms and goals into prominence. They occur as do reform movements when previously weak or exploited groups gain strength and hope. A thwarted reform movement can turn into a revolution.

> The emergence of a new economic group with a sense of grievances and a consciousness of its own strength and importance seems to be a necessary condition to the outbreak of any revolution. This class is never composed of miserable dregs of humanity—wretched, starving, and hopeless. On the contrary, its ranks must be permeated by a sense of confidence inspired by previous success and strengthened by the belief that additional effort will bring greater gains in the future. During the years of prosperity preceding the Revolution, the French bourgeoisie had grown to be the dominant economic class . . . its members appear to have been growing richer year by year. . . . But the chief effect of this rising prosperity was to sharpen bourgeois discontent. No matter how much money a merchant, manufacturer, banker, or lawyer might acquire, he was still excluded from political privileges. . . . Besides, he was looked down upon as an inferior by the idle and frivolous nobility. Occasionally some snobbish count or duke would consent to the marriage of his son to the daughter of a wealthy burgher; but one who did often made a practice of referring to the marriage as "manuring [his] land." As the middle class rose in affluence and in consciousness of its own importance, its members were bound to resent such attempts at social discrimination. But above all it was the demand of the commercial, financial, and industrial leaders for political power commensurate with their economic position which made the bourgeoisie a revolutionary class.[25]

A somewhat similar condition underlay the Russian Revolution. The emancipation of the serfs in 1861 destroyed the economic power of the landed nobility, who became, in effect, impotent government pensioners. The autocratic Tzarist regime was unwilling to grant political power to the only group economically strong enough to replace them—the rising industrialists. By refusing the bourgeois industrialists a share in policy making, the autocracy was digging its own grave. The disgruntled bourgeoisie joined with disgruntled Russian intellectuals—"men of no set rank"—who also were denied the opportunity to achieve positions matching their learning and their ideals. Together they effected the overthrow of the Russian monarchy.

---

* For a fuller discussion of the Negro problem see Chapter 10. For a fuller discussion of the Civil Rights movement see Chapter 13.

Positional change—major or minor, reformist or revolutionary—affects the relationship of actors in the social scene and thereby the structures of society. However, back of any change in social structure, demographic as well as positional, are the unconscious and conscious opinions, attitudes, and beliefs held by the actors themselves.

Ideational Change

Geographical, biological, and technological conditions set the scene of social action. A population of men, women, and children are the actors. Positions in the institutional and subsidiary structures of society determine the relationship of actors to each other. But social structures and the role-images associated with positions in social structures are determined by concepts of reality—by the rational and/or emotional judgments of individuals and groups. *The common ideational content of culture is manifest through opinions, attitudes, and beliefs as formed by and expressed through the sanctioned norms and goals of culture.* Change in this symbolic, nonmaterial culture is less obvious than change in either material culture or social structure, but in historical perspective, it is no less potent. The ideas of Jesus affected changes as profound as any made in the wake of a technological innovation. To say "Ideas control the world," may be an exaggeration and oversimplification, yet concepts of reality do move men and the societies of men.

Ideational change comes slowly to some societies, more rapidly to others. Isolated and tradition-bound or rigidly structured societies change slowly. More complex and loosely structured societies in the mainstream of history change more rapidly.

> . . . The total structure of the American system up to now has been relatively favorable to social change. The social structure has been relatively free from rigidly vested status systems. The culture has been marked by strongly rationalistic elements, by an orientation away from traditionalism and toward adaptability and ingenuity in meeting new situations. Internal heterogeneity has made for an extraordinary mingling of cultures in a mobile society undergoing rapid urbanization and industrialization. The cultural focus on business activity and technological development has opened up wide segments of the system to especially rapid change.[26]

Although we have a national self-image congenial to change, we have tended to accept nonsymbolic technological change more readily than symbolic ideational change. We began as a sparse heterogeneous population. The pioneers were practical men, and technology has its own built-in values. A gun is better than a bow and arrow because it shoots farther and straighter. Trains are better than covered wagons because they can carry more people a greater distance in less time. Machines are better than hand tools because they can help men produce more goods, faster. The major ideational elements of our culture the pioneers brought with them in the form of opinions, attitudes, and beliefs, and such emotional learnings are highly resistant to change. It is not easy to demonstrate the superiority of one opinion, attitude, or belief over that of another.

The ideational structure of an individual or a society is pervasive and tenacious, but it can and does change. As individuals we change opinions, attitudes, and beliefs as we find them incompatible with essential new knowledge or new group loyalties. The larger society changes ideologically as the need for change is thrust upon it by a *collision of ideas* or a *challenge of circumstance.*

Ideas in Collision

When the Dutch discovered Australia in the early seventeenth century, the Australoids had an Old Stone Age culture. The people wore no clothes, used no metal or pottery, built no permanent dwellings, had not even invented the wheel. Centuries of isolation had made their primitive tribal structure inflexible and their culture ingrown. Once their social system began to break down under the onslaught of white men, the people seemed to lose the will to survive. Their numbers dwindled from an original 300,000 at the close of the eighteenth century to approximately 40,000 in 1960. These survivors are now protected "wards of the state." They live, as do our American Indians, between two incompatible worlds.[27]

Geographically and biologically, Australia had offered a favorable balance of both nurturing and challenging elements, but the native peoples had not "progressed." * Meanwhile on the Eurasian mainland, during some 20,000 years of commerce, conquest, and migration, ideas as well as men challenged each other and civilization flourished.

Civilizations do not develop in isolation. The genealogy of Western civilization goes back to the ancient cultures of Southwest Asia and North Africa. In this "cradle" of culture, Egyptians, Mesopotamians, Persians, Hebrews, Phrygians, Hittites, Aegeans, Lydians, Phoenicians, Greeks, Etruscans, and Romans had stirring interaction among themselves and with the more distant people of India and China. Ideas as well as techniques familiar to our present culture have an ancient and colorful history.

Egyptian priests and sages preached universal monotheism, forgiveness of sins, and rewards and punishment after death. Egyptian ethics included prohibition of lying, stealing, and murder, and ideals of justice and the equal

* Primitive creatures also survived the ages in Australia and Tasmania. The lungfish has gills and lungs which enable it to live in or out of water. The duckbilled platypus has a broad soft bill, a furry coat, webbed feet, and it lays eggs! Wombats, possums, kangaroos, koalas, and other marsupials give birth to premature young—an evolutionary step between the egg-laying monotremes and true mammals.

rights of men. Egyptians developed architectural principles valid today and they had the concept of "art for art's sake"—of aesthetics as a value independent of practical use. From one or another of the four Mesopotamian peoples (Sumerians, Babylonians, Assyrians, and Persians) come our seven-day week, the division of the day into two twelve-hour periods, belief in horoscopes, the 360-degree circle, and the arithmetical process of multiplication. Through Zoroaster, the ancient Persians bequeathed the assumption that man possesses free will. Christians took from the Hebrews their cosmogony (theory of the origin of the universe), the Ten Commandments, ideals of limited government, the sovereignty of law, regard for individual dignity and worth, and other religious, ethical, and political beliefs. The Hittites and Phrygians were important intermediaries between the East and West, the main connecting links between Mesopotamia, Egypt, and cultures of the Aegean Sea. The Aegeans were among the few ancient peoples to assure substantial equality to all men and a dignified status to women. The Lydians coined money from a mixture of gold and silver. The Phoenicians developed the art of navigation and the completion of an alphabet based on principles first discovered by the Egyptians. The Athenian Greeks were first to build a culture in a spirit of free intellectual inquiry, and to them we trace a majority of the ideals of Western culture. The Hellenistic Greeks made discoveries in mathematics, geography, anatomy, and physics basic to scientific developments made since the seventeenth century. The important legacy from the Romans is their system of law—a system which included the familiar concepts of civil law, common law, and natural law.[28]

The cultural heritage we call Western is not exclusively Western; it is a particular blend of world cultures, just as the dominant culture of the United States is a particular blend from our own bubbling melting pot.

The grafting of one idea upon another—the "hybridization of ideas and experiences" [29]—is in itself an important factor in the development of a culture, but major cultural achievements have been more than mere appropriation and accumulation of ideas.

> . . . it must be insisted that the great advances of mankind have been due, not to the mere aggregation, assemblage, or acquisition of disparate ideas, but to the emergency of a certain type of mental activity which is set up by the opposition of different idea systems . . . civilization is everywhere the result of the stimulus evoked by the friction of one group upon another. The stimulus is mental, and the friction springs from the contact of differing customs and explanations. The simple commingling of ideas undoubtedly takes place, but the important point is that different ideas in regard to the same subject, when maintained in opposition by members of the same group, necessarily evoke comparison and critical discussion. The outcome of this is not always, nor even generally, a choice between two alternatives, for the debate will leave neither of the original positions wholly unchanged, and hence a new idea system will arise which is not a selection of materials drawn from various sources, but a resultant of the juxtaposition of different bodies of thought.[30]

Out of the collision of ancient Eastern and modern Western ideas, a new culture is emerging today in mainland China. In effect, it seems a fearsome dragon—a virile dragon made of more than the traditional gilt paint and colored paper. It was fathered by an *idea* developed by the German Karl Marx through research at the British Museum, nourished by Lenin and Stalin in Russia, and transplanted to China after the turmoil of Japanese invasions during World War II. It is fed now by Chinese leaders who well understand the practical value of Western industrialism. Ideas diffuse in the manner of other innovations, and, like elements of technology, they are likely to strike sparks of change where they land. "Ideas are the factors that lift civilization. They create revolutions. There is more dynamite in an idea than in many bombs." [31]

Ideas are born of men, but the hazards a newborn idea encounters are many. If an idea has validity for enough people, it may in a democratic society become the focus of a public or a social movement. If the idea gradually wins enough devoted supporters and stands the tests of time and tribulation, it may eventually be embodied in the structure or processes of society or the norms and goals of culture.

Although ideational change is often emotionally sparked, it can be deliberately and rationally pursued. Moral indignation, for example, brought the issue of school segregation to the Supreme Court. The Supreme Court ruled that segregation in schools violated the Fourteenth Amendment. This decision was both a response to shifting public opinion regarding civil rights and a recognition of scientific information discounting preconceptions about any innate inferiorities of racial origin. The Supreme Court decision, in turn, forced change in social action and with it further change in OAB's.* In 1942, for example, only two per cent of southern whites favored school integration, compared to fourteen per cent in 1956, and forty-three per cent in 1963. The concurrent change in attitude regarding integration on buses is even greater. In 1942, only four per cent of southern whites favored integration on buses, compared to eighty per cent in 1963.[32] Eventually the ideas of the Negro protest movement (already embodied in the Constitution of the United States) will be fully expressed in the institutions of the United States. Perhaps morality *can* be legislated!

Ideas in Action

Social inventions put ideas into action and make ideational changes clearly manifest. Social inventions are deliberate efforts to create new symbolic meanings, or new social relationships or structures to meet the *challenge of circumstance*. They may range in importance from the casual coining of a campaign slogan, to the invention of writing; or from flash-in-the-pan *ad hoc* committees,

* Because of group pressure, public behavior changes more readily than privately held opinions, attitudes, and beliefs (OAB's), but research in *cognitive dissonance* indicates that attitude change typically follows commitment to action.

to elaborate secondary * institutions. The alphabet, the calendar, systems of weights and measures, the profit system, consumer cooperatives, the Peace Corps—all such means, permanent or transitory, trivial or significant, by which we define and facilitate interpersonal and intergroup action are social inventions. The Constitution of the United States and the Charter of the United Nations are two such inventions of particular significance to our own society.

We tend to take the Constitution for granted, but less than two hundred years ago, the ideas which it embodies had no ordered relationship—theoretical or practical—to each other or to a functioning society. The Constitution was not a wholly new concept, but a new order imposed on existing concepts. For example, the constitutional limitation of the franchise (originally white male property owners) was based on the Athenian practice of "democratic" rule by a privileged class of free citizens; the separation of legislative, judicial, and administrative powers grew out of an eighteenth-century French *misconception* of the structure of English government, presented by Montesquieu in *Spirit of the Laws.* The Bill of Rights is essentially the same as the English Declaration of Rights, made in connection with the "Glorious Revolution" of 1689. Out of the political philosophies of Hobbes, Locke, and Rousseau grew the concept of social contract—government based on the consent of those governed to forfeit some freedom of individual action to establish the state. Experience with the Articles of Confederation plus the successful indigenous League of the Iroquois inspired the federation of states.

The Constitution of the United States was a true social invention—a new departure in government structure. It has proven to be a flexible structure which, through amendments and court interpretations, has been able to incorporate ideational changes originating in the society and, in turn, give added impetus to such changes.

The Constitution was ratified in 1789 by only nine of the existing thirteen colonies. By 1960, one hundred and seventy-one years later, fifty states were united under it. During these years, our society, as a result of modern techniques of communication and travel, had been brought into increasingly intense interaction with other societies around the world. By the end of World War II, isolationism as a policy of any major government had become an untenable position, and when the representatives of fifty nations signed the United Nations Charter in 1945, they conceded that "the concept of absolute sovereignty of a State is unreal." Like the Constitution of the United States, the Charter of the United Nations was a social invention which related existing concepts in a new structure. The text, for example, closely resembles the Covenant of the League of Nations (the pioneer world organization) and the Statute of the World Court, which, in turn, had been built upon the Court of International Justice at The Hague. And the Preamble embodies the

* Deliberately planned institutions are defined as secondary, not because they are less important but because they are usually built on existing primary institutions. The United States Constitution was built on the existing primary institution of government.

familiar hopes and ideals of human rights, equality, justice, social progress, freedom, tolerance, and peace.

> *We the Peoples of the United Nations Determined*
> to save succeeding generations from the scourge of war, which twice in our lifetime has brought untold sorrow to mankind, and to reaffirm faith in fundamental human rights, in the dignity and worth of the human person, in the equal rights of men and women and of nations large and small, and to establish conditions under which justice and respect for the obligations arising from treaties and other sources of international law can be maintained, and to promote social progress and better standards of life in larger freedom,
> *And for These Ends*
> to practice tolerance and live together in peace with one another as good neighbors, and to unite our strength to maintain international peace and security, and to ensure, by the acceptance of principles and the institution of methods, that armed force shall not be used, save in the common interest, and to employ international machinery for the promotion of the economic and social advancement of all peoples,
> *Have Resolved to Combine Our Efforts to Accomplish These Aims.*

The United Nations is an invention in government. Other international organizations, social inventions in their own right, function in other institutional areas such as economics and education, in cooperation with or subordinate to the United Nations. The following are representative: the International Labor Organization (ILO), the Food and Agricultural Organization (FAO), United Nations Education, Scientific and Cultural Organization (UNESCO), the World Health Organization (WHO), and the United Nations Children's Fund (UNICEF). The list is long and continues to grow. In addition, there are other completely independent but supporting organizations: the Peace Corps, for example, and the Experiment in International Living.* These and many other public and private organizations operating in the international area are social inventions made in response to the challenge of contemporary circumstance. They share a commitment: to help individuals and groups in every country perceive the reality and the promise of our common needs.

Scene changes—changes in the geographical, biological, and technological environment—involve sub-human forms of life and things, natural and man-made. *Societary* changes—changes in the structure and processes of society and the norms and goals of the culture—involve people, their characteristics, their positions relative to each other in social systems, and their behavior. People are not merely acted upon by change; they are the actors. Any individual or group

* The Experiment in International Living, less well-known than the Peace Corps, is a private, nonprofit organization devoted to creating mutual respect and understanding among different peoples. One who travels abroad as an "Experimenter" lives as a member of a family in the country he visits.

in a society can initiate change, further change, or oppose change. Sociologists are interested in defining and understanding such action.

PROCESSES OF CHANGE

Change, when it is initiated by men, has predictable processes. It begins when an innovation is recognized as being desirable. It becomes an accomplished fact when the *innovation* is *accepted* and *integrated* into either (or both) the structure or processes of a society and the norms and goals of its culture.

Innovation

An innovation may be a creation, a discovery, or an invention. Although the terms are sometimes used interchangeably, the meanings are not the same. *Creation is a conceptual act,* an insight which brings into being a totally new aspect of reality or reveals new unity in aspects of reality previously perceived as unrelated. Discovery, when it is purposeful and not accidental, may involve an original creative insight, but *discovery itself is an act of verification* demonstrating the existence of a previously unknown or unrecognized fact, principle, or entity. *Invention is a problem-solving act which, for some practical purpose brings known facts, principles, or entities into a new relationship.* Like discovery, invention may involve creative insight, but the invention itself is a tangible instrument of action—technological or social.

Creation

Artists have no monopoly on creativity. Writers, painters, sculptors, architects, composers, and others performing in the visual or temporal arts may or may not be creative in the sense we define the term. On the other hand, scientists and philosophers—in fact, those working with ideas and symbols in any field—may creatively cope with the tasks they set themselves. The significant differences among creative persons are not in *how* they think, but in *what* they think about. Galileo, Da Vinci, Newton, Shakespeare, Einstein, Bartók, for example, were all creative men. Through their own personal action they conceived and imposed new unity on the subject matter with which they dealt. Insofar as thinking is inductive, it is creative. Induction is a conceptual breakthrough which often leaves facts far behind. Formulation of hypotheses and theory building in science are basically creative. Copernicus's theory that the sun, not the earth, is the center of the solar system, and Darwin's theory of evolution once outraged God-fearing man. Physicists didn't recognize the value of Clerk Maxwell's electro-magnetic theories until thirty years after he formulated them. The more creative the theoretical concept, the more difficult it is to communicate, but when creative concepts are finally understood and validated, they shape the ways of men.

Creation is always a personal, individual act. Discovery and invention may involve one or more cooperating individuals.

Discovery

When historians speak of discovery, they refer primarily to geographical discoveries such as those made by the Spanish, Portuguese, British, French, and Dutch in the late fifteenth and early sixteenth centuries. These discoveries, of course, were discoveries only from the egocentric viewpoint of the explorers. The Indians could claim that they discovered Columbus coming out of the sea. Regardless of who discovered whom, geographical discoveries bring profound change. Those of the fifteenth and sixteenth century Age of Discovery caused massive migrations to the New World and hastened the transition from the nonprofit localized economy of the Middle Ages to a far-reaching capitalist system, a system which as it developed and expanded stimulated changes in all the other institutions of Western society.

When scientists speak of discovery, they refer to the discovery of physical phenomena—the properties of lodestone, the existence of hydrogen and oxygen and other chemical elements, the cellular structure of plants, bacteria and viruses, and cosmic rays. They also speak of discoveries of behavioral phenomena—the role of reinforcement in learning, the motivating force of cognitive dissonance in reducing prejudice, the existence of the unconscious.* Scientific discovery supplies the knowledge we need to evaluate and shape ourselves and our environment. Practical discoveries in the physical sciences tend to initiate technological change. Practical discoveries in the behavioral sciences, insofar as they are exploited by political, economic, educational, religious, or military institutions, tend to initiate societary change.

Invention

Inventions grow out of creation, discovery, and other inventions. The invention of the automobile, for example, brought into a new functional relationship a series of patented inventions made over a period of more than fifty years, including the water-jacket cooling system, differential gears, pneumatic tires, gas engine, friction clutch and drive. Leonardo da Vinci designed an airplane on paper (a creative act), but it was more than 400 years before the internal combustion engine and other mechanical parts made possible the

* Bernard Berelson and Gary A. Steiner in *Human Behavior* (New York: Harcourt, Brace & World, Inc., 1964) present an inventory of 5,000 scientific "findings" in the area of behavior.

Wright brothers' airplane. Because inventions build on one another, parallel inventions often occur in the same or comparable cultural settings.

> Who invented the telegraph? Any American who has been through the eighth grade knows that it was Morse and Vail in 1844. But there was an English commercial line seven years earlier, and the Germans credit the telegraph to Sommering, of Munich, in 1809, and in Switzerland there was an electric telegraph in 1774, and one was proposed in Scotland in 1753. The matter becomes rather confused for the eighth grade.[33]

Variations are small changes in existing inventions which, however, over a period of time add up to startling changes. Compare, for example, the "horseless carriage" manufactured at the turn of the century with the contemporary *Thunderbird.*

Inventions are most commonly associated with technology, but, as we already indicated in reference to the Constitution of the United States and the United Nations Charter, inventions can also be instruments of social action.

Diffusion

An innovation of any kind has little impact unless it is recognized, accepted, and integrated into a social system.* An innovation *diffuses* from the point of origin usually first through the mother society and then on to other societies. Like water spreading over rough ground, diffusion from one society to another tends to follow channels of least resistance—channels most often made by social contacts during peaceful communication and commerce, or war.† When Constantinople fell to the Turks in 1453, for example, many of the city's artists, scholars, and artisans fled to the West. The innovations they brought with them are credited by some historians with sparking the European Renaissance. For a more up-to-date example of diffusion, consider the case of Japan. After World War II, Japan made major and minor technological and societary changes consistent with Western patterns, including even the programming on Tokyo television of "Two-Gun Watanabe."

Borrowing

Borrowing, unlike creation, discovery and invention, does not add to the total human achievement. Borrowing is a process, not of innovation but of diffusion. Even though a borrowed trait is an innovation in the receiving culture, an innovation diffuses through borrowing from its point of origin.

---

* The social system is a total interacting complex of social structures and processes, cultural norms, and goals operating in a particular environmental setting. This setting includes natural physical conditions as well as cultural artifacts.

† The relationship between war and change is complex. The demands of war are not stopped by the boundaries of convention. Wars not only increase contact; they disrupt established social structures and cultural norms and often occasion technological "breakthroughs." These variables interact in speeding change.

It is obviously easier to borrow than to innovate, and approximately ninety per cent of the cultural content of any particular industrial society is borrowed. This is true even in the United States, where innovations are deliberately encouraged by billions of dollars spent annually on research and development.*

> Our solid American citizen awakens in a bed built on a pattern which originated in the Near East but which was modified in Northern Europe before it was transmitted to America. He throws back covers made from cotton, domesticated in India, or linen, domesticated in the Near East, or wool from sheep, also domesticated in the Near East, or silk, the use of which was discovered in China. All of these materials have been spun and woven by processes invented in the Near East. He slips into his moccasins, invented by the Indians of the Eastern woodlands, and goes to the bathroom whose fixtures are a mixture of European and American inventions, both of recent date. He takes off his pajamas, a garment invented in India, and washes with soap invented by the ancient Gauls. He then shaves, a masochistic rite which seems to have been derived from either Sumer or ancient Egypt.
>
> Returning to the bedroom, he removes his clothes from a chair of southern European type and proceeds to dress. He puts on garments whose form originally derived from the skin clothing of the nomads of the Asiatic steppes, puts on shoes made from a pattern derived from the classical civilizations of the Mediterranean, and ties around his neck a strip of bright-colored cloth which is a vestigial survival of the shoulder shawls worn by the seventeenth-century Croatians. Before going out for breakfast he glances through the window, made of glass invented in Egypt, and if it is raining puts on overshoes made of rubber discovered by the Central American Indians and takes an umbrella, invented in southeastern Asia. Upon his head he puts a hat made of felt, a material invented in the Asiatic steppes.
>
> On his way to breakfast he stops to buy a paper, paying for it with coins, an ancient Lydian invention. At the restaurant a whole new series of borrowed elements confronts him. His plate is made of a form of pottery invented in China. His knife is of steel, an alloy made in southern India, his fork a medieval Italian invention, and his spoon a derivative of a Roman original. He begins breakfast with an orange, from the eastern Mediterranean, a canteloupe from Persia, or perhaps a piece of African watermelon. With this he has coffee, an Abyssinian plant, with cream and sugar. Both the domestication of cows and the idea of milking them originated in the Near East, while sugar was first made in India. After his fruit and first coffee he goes on to waffles, cakes made by a Scandinavian technique from wheat domesticated in Asia Minor. Over these he pours maple syrup, invented by the Indians of the Eastern woodlands. As a side dish he may have the egg of a species of bird domesticated in Indo-China, or thin strips of the flesh of an animal domesticated in Eastern Asia which have been salted and smoked by a process developed in northern Europe.
>
> When our friend has finished eating he settles back to smoke, an American Indian habit, consuming a plant domesticated in Brazil in either a pipe, derived

---

* During the 1950's more than 60 billion dollars was spent in the United States on research and development. By 1963 the cost was 17 billion dollars per year. The total for the 1960's is expected to be twice that of the 1950's.

> from the Indians of Virginia, or a cigarette, derived from Mexico. If he is hardy enough he may even attempt a cigar, transmitted to us from the Antilles by way of Spain. While smoking he reads the news of the day, imprinted in characters invented by the ancient Semites upon a material invented in China by a process invented in Germany. As he absorbs the accounts of foreign troubles he will, if he is a good conservative citizen, thank a Hebrew deity in an Indo-European language that he is 100 per cent American.[34]

For a borrowed innovation of any kind to function adequately, the borrower must have a culture base into which the innovation can be meaningfully integrated.

Acceptance and Integration

The level of development of a culture functions as a base on which further innovations build. The broader and deeper the base, the more rapid the rate of both innovation and diffusion within a society. The more alike the cultural base of different societies, the more direct and rapid the diffusion of innovations among them. When traits do diffuse to societies with disparate culture bases as from a technologically developed society to underdeveloped ones, culture traits may be so modified or little understood by the borrower that they function in ways quite different from the original intention. A group of Mexican peons, for example, had their own way of using wheelbarrows.

> . . . when furnished with modern wheelbarrows, they removed the wheel and lifted the barrow proper to their backs, supporting it with a forehead tumpline! The Mexican, since the time of the building of great prehistoric pyramids, has moved earth by carrying it in a basket supported on the back in this fashion. Even today the tourist in Mexico City may see earth from the foundations of new skyscrapers being carried out of the ground in this fashion. The knack of handling a wheelbarrow is not something an adult picks up easily, so the willing railway workers, not wishing to displease their masters by rejecting their help, solved the problem by changing the tool to conform to their motor patterns.[35]

Sometimes a borrower appropriates a culture trait without any understanding of its significance.

> Paul Fejos tells how, when working on Soembawa Island, a shaman friend was greatly impressed by the magical power of the letter B, the Bayer trademark appearing on all the products in Dr. Fejos' medicine chest. After several months the native doctor asked permission to use this powerful magic. "Less ethically, and without the permission of the Bayer Company, I released the copyright, and the letter B within the circle was emblazoned on my friend's chest. It gave him a tremendous additional amount of mana, and *de facto* increased his curative powers." [36]

And sometimes the borrower brings into even sharper focus the great cultural gap separating those who would give from those who would receive. On the island of New Guinea native Papuans have watched cargo planes land at Port Moresby and disgorge their freight. The natives have no concept of the world beyond their island, and they have concluded that the airplanes are sent to them by their ancestors in paradise and that the conniving whites lure these heavenly ambassadors into an elaborate trap—the airstrip at Port Moresby. In an effort to thwart the white man and claim what they feel is rightfully theirs, the natives have a Cargo Cult. They have built a runway, a crude dirt track, high in the mountains, complete with a "control" tower of grass and bamboo and a dummy bamboo plane as decoy. The natives light torch runway lights at night and keep vigil around the clock, waiting with patience and confidence for their ship to come in.

A trait borrowed from a technologically advanced culture is not always modified or misinterpreted by or disruptive of an underdeveloped culture. When, for example, the American Indians adopted the European gun, those tribes having a hunting economy became more efficient hunters and more effective warriors. The use of the gun, however, made the Indians more dependent upon trade with the Europeans, increased inter-cultural contact, and thus contributed to the eventual decline of native cultures.

When a society has an adequate culture base for receiving an innovation, acceptance and integration is essentially a process of *internal diffusion.* Internal diffusion *within* a society through acceptance, like diffusion *among* societies through borrowing, tends to have some predictability. In general, the greater prestige accorded the source of the innovation, the more readily the innovation is accepted. Cities, for example, have more prestige than country towns, and innovations are most likely to come via the cities.

> Cities are focal points of change. Most social and economic change begins among the upper classes and then spreads downward to the traditionally inarticulate lower classes and outward to the countryside. The cultural innovations of urban areas have prestige attached to them. This prestige is the motivation which produces the outward and downward diffusion of ideas and behavior forms.[37]

Even in the relatively trivial matter of dress, fashions characteristically start at the top of the urban social hierarchy and move downward through the class levels and, with the help of mail order catalogues, to the rural hinterlands. Cities are the locale of world markets in both ideas and commodities.

Gradual integration of an innovation follows acceptance. Every innovation accepted alters in some way the conditions of behavior. These altered conditions lead, in turn, to other adaptive changes which are, in themselves, innovations. *Integration* is the cumulative result of these reciprocal changes.

MECHANISMS OF ANTI-CHANGE

No matter how open a society may be to innovation, it still contains within itself ever-ready brakes on change.

> Historical experience indicates that no society ever simply abandons its traditional culture. On the contrary, the old culture almost always leaves permanent and significant marks of continuity on the fully modernized society. Nevertheless, the traditional culture must undergo drastic alteration. It is thus of the very nature of the modernizing process that at every step of the way the impulses making for modernization are in active contention with powerful forces tending to retard and to frustrate the transformation of the traditional society into full constructive modernity.[38]

Institutions are made by man for man, and, theoretically, should be changed if inadequate. However the institutions of a society, incorporating as they do folkways, mores, taboos, and laws, buttress and protect not only themselves but the identity and continuity of the total on-going system. Institutions traditionally resist innovation. How effectively even secondary institutions resist, our own calendar demonstrates. The earliest Roman calendar began with March and had ten months. Evidence of this is still frozen into our calendar: September, October, November, and December are derivations from the Roman words for seventh, eighth, ninth and tenth. In the seventh century B.C., the month of January was added to the beginning of the calendar, the month of February to the end, which pushed the four number-named months out of position by one place. In 452 B.C., February was moved to second place, which put September, October, November, and December out of place by two positions. These four months have been technically misnamed for 2,600 years. As children we learn the calendar months by rote. The names take on meaning from holidays and seasons of the year. The familiar is congenial. Who would make the effort to change the calendar now?

Institutions are not impersonal sources of resistance. The mechanisms of anti-change work through people—their individual habits, their group norms, and their vested interests.

Individual Habit

Individuals learn habits—habits of action, habits of thought, habits of feeling. The essential characteristic of a well-learned habit is that an appropriate stimulus tends to elicit the habit. The individual acts or thinks or feels automatically without conscious effort or consideration. We learn sensory motor skills—swimming, driving, typing. We learn intellectual skills—reading, arithmetic, logic. We learn emotional reactions—fear, prejudice, tolerance.

Once learned, habits are an integral part of the individual. They are built into the nervous system and personality structure.

> Conservatives argue against change in institutional structures on the grounds that "you can't change human nature." A truer psychology locates the difficulty elsewhere. It shows that the trouble lies in the inertness of established habit. No matter how accidental and irrational the circumstances of its origin, no matter how different the conditions which now exist to those under which the habit was formed, the latter persists until the environment obstinately rejects it. Habits once formed perpetuate themselves, by acting unremittingly upon the native stock of activities. They stimulate, inhibit, intensify, weaken, select, concentrate and organize the latter into their own likeness. They create out of the formless void of impulses a world made in their own image. Man is a creature of habit, not of reason nor yet of instinct.[39]

The psychologist William James referred to habit as "the enormous flywheel of society." Society is stabilized and regulated by the multitude of habitual responses acquired by its individual members through the long process of socialization. Habits persist because to change them requires conscious thought and effort.

Group Norms

The malleable individual is socialized, more or less successfully, by the society into which he is born. Its ways become his own habitual ways and then he, in turn, supports society. Group norms are those habits shared by a group which guide the individual in his interaction within the group. They are the folkways, mores, and taboos to which he adheres without necessarily questioning either their rationality or their purpose.* An individual incorporates into his own action system a variety of such ready-set responses. They spare him many decisions. He doesn't have to stop to figure out what to do; he *knows* what to do.

Group norms resist change even more strongly than individual habits. An individual habit may be an idiosyncrasy which group pressure can help change. A group norm, in contrast, is shared and has the sanction of the group. But to change a group norm means changing the habits of not one but many individuals, and it requires both a commonly acceptable alternative norm and an acceptable rationale for making the change.

Vested Interests

Vested interests are a logical consequence of individual habit, group norms, and self-interest. Those who have privilege habitually claim privilege and are generally accorded privilege. Stratification is a fact of life in all socie-

---

* Chapter 3.

ties, and individuals and groups in higher social, economic, or political positions hold and try to maintain advantages over those in lower positions.

Vested interests can and do resist innovations of all kinds, technological as well as societary. In England, for example, the development of railroads was resisted first by the landowners.

> The temper of the opposition is to be seen in the remarks of Craven Fitzhardinge Berkeley, a member of Parliament for Cheltenham: "Nothing is more distasteful to me than to hear the echo of our hills reverberating with the noise of hissing railroad engines running through the heart of our hunting country, and destroying that noble sport [fox hunting] to which I have been accustomed from my childhood.[40]

The iron horses won over this genteel opposition, and railroad men, in turn, resisted the upstart horseless carriage. They joined with horse breeders in a new alliance.

> They secured passage of an act of Parliament, in 1861, for the regulation of horseless vehicles which practically made it impossible for them to operate. This act provided that tires must be at least three inches wide, that engines must consume their own smoke, that each vehicle must have at least two drivers, and that no vehicle was to exceed ten miles an hour in the country and five miles an hour in the towns. In 1865 an even more drastic act was passed requiring three drivers for each vehicle, one of whom must precede the carriage at a distance of sixty yards, carrying a red flag by day and a red lantern by night. Speed was reduced to four miles an hour for the country and two miles an hour for the town.[41]

In more recent years the railroads in the United States have fought the growing trucking industry,* each other, organized labor, and the government. In the matter of vested interests, however, the railroads are not unique.

Every group and every individual in society has vested interests and the degrees of support given one by another is in part a reflection of those interests. Consider, for example, the matter of political preference. In countries such as Spain, where the government supports the church, the clergy tend to be politically conservative. In countries with stable governments, the civil servants, who identify closely with the on-going system and are directly dependent on it for their economic security, are typically conservative. In the United States, high-prestige business and religious groups tend to support conservative forces. Professional groups closely allied with business—engineers and lawyers, for example—also tend to be politically conservative (more so than university professors or self-employed professionals such as artists and writers). Al-

* In spite of the fact that the government originally gave railroads valuable land grants for rights of way, the railroads claim that the trucking industry has an unfair advantage because the highways used by trucks are built and maintained by public tax money, while railroads must build and maintain their own roadbeds.

though there are extenuating conditions, it is generally true in the United States, as well as in other Western democracies, that the higher the socio-economic status, the greater the conservative vote.

Social inventions are unlikely to come from individuals or groups traditionally in positions of power. Innovators may have high social status, but, if so, they tend to be well-educated younger members of their group, with a theoretical interest in social problems. The conservatives tend to be those with vested interests in the status quo, who have settled into a social senility of success.

All the mechanisms of anti-change—individual habit, group norms, and vested interests—have come into action during the long history of the tobacco industry. When tobacco first reached Europe in the seventeeth century, the resistance against smoking was bitter. King James I of England condemned smoking as a "foul custom" and "loathsome to the eye, hateful to the nose, harmful to the brain, dangerous to the lungs." Pope Urban VIII excommunicated all who used tobacco. Tzar Michael Feodorovich legislated against it. A first offender was flogged; a second offender had his nose cut off; an incorrigible was beheaded. Even in Vienna late in the eighteenth century police had orders to fire on any smoker.[42] During the nineteenth century and the first half of the twentieth, attitudes changed and smoking became generally acceptable—first for adult males, then for females, and finally for teen-agers. However, in the mid-twentieth century, the intuition of King James I was verified by medical research, and a report by the United States Surgeon General officially condemned smoking as hazardous to health. The announcement called into action individual and group resistance. Habitual smokers rationalized. Young smokers felt they hadn't smoked long enough to do any harm; they could quit when they wanted to, and "Anyway, who wants to live forever?" Middle-aged and older smokers felt the harm was already done. "No use trying to quit now. Besides, you have to die of something!" The tobacco industry did not budge. Its singing commercials sang on. After all, the industry grew a cash crop amounting to more than eight billion dollars a year—the fifth largest in the United States. Tobacco spokesmen belittled the medical findings, saying, "Statistical information is not conclusive evidence." The governor of a large tobacco-producing state defended his tobacco-growing farmers, arguing that the Surgeon General's report was a "review of the previously existing evidence, none of which is conclusive and most of which is based on statistical studies." Congressmen from states with no vested interest in tobacco proposed legislation controlling the sale and advertising of tobacco. Congressmen from tobacco-producing states opposed it.

The sale of cigarettes, against which the Surgeon General's report was mainly directed, declined (at least temporarily) but not markedly, and the sale of pipe tobacco and cigars and snuff went up. An individual can better stand the discomforts of addiction withdrawal if he has group support, and one medical man with sociological insight suggested a concerted effort to shift social attitudes towards smoking. Cuspidors for tobacco chewers disappeared from hotel lobbies when spitting tobacco juice became socially uncouth. Would ash trays disappear if cigarette smoking were thought of as neurotic adult thumb sucking rather than as a social grace?

Any innovation which alters profoundly the conditions of social action or the character, relationship, or ideas of the actors themselves disrupts to some extent the mutuality which exists within the system. The resulting disparity, when cognitively recognized by the society or a significant segment of it, creates *social dissonance. Stress* is the emotionally felt component of such dissonance and, as such, sets the more or less automatic *homeostatic* mechanisms of anti-change into motion.* These mechanisms force a variety of reactions: heel-digging-in resistance and rationalization, counter-proposals, or—if the advantages of the innovation are apparent enough and its proponents insistent enough—eventual capitulation and acceptance. Eventual integration of an acceptable innovation is usually accomplished in a way which least upsets the total system. The system, or that part of the system most affected, makes some gross shifts plus other smaller less obvious ones, like a man on a tightrope who, when he is thrown off balance, makes a few large muscle movements and a myriad of other minor adjustments.

Within all the institutions of society, as within the individual himself, change and anti-change are constantly countervailing forces. Defining and understanding the variables which make an individual open to experience and able to adjust to new circumstances and new knowledge is a concern of psychologists. Defining and understanding the variables which make a society able to accept and integrate useful innovations is a growing concern of sociologists.

SOCIAL DISSONANCE

A society and its culture change and "advance" only through the acceptance and integration of new elements. But neither societies nor all parts of any one society are equally congenial to innovations. Neither are societies equally congenial at all times to all kinds of innovations. In general, a heterogeneous but well-integrated society with an adequate culture base accepts and can successfully integrate innovations useful at its particular level of development. A society accepts most readily innovations in those parts of the system which are least infused with emotional bias—in techniques or tactics, for example, rather than in primary relationships or systems of prestige. Furthermore, a society accepts and integrates most readily those new elements

* Cognitive dissonance is a psychological concept. Homeostasis and stress are physiological ones. We recognize the fallacy of comparing social and organic systems directly, but we find these particular concepts useful in the context of change and anti-change.

which are nonsymbolic and do not threaten the ideology of the society; those which are variations on what is already accepted rather than abrupt departures; those which come from high-prestige sources; and those which are introduced slowly through existing institutions and with adequate educational preparation rather than authoritatively imposed. All societies, regardless of the nature of the innovation, are more congenial to innovations in periods of crisis than in "normal" times.

Because all societies and all parts of any one society are not equally congenial to all kinds of innovations, nor equally capable of those they do accept, there exists within and among the societies of the world disparity in rates of change—technological and societary.

Technological Lag

In April, 1964, President Lyndon Johnson urged the people of the United States to help make the "revolution of rising expectations" in the impoverished countries of the world a "peaceful revolution."

> . . . if we sit here just enjoying our material resources, if we are content to become fat and flabby at 50, and let the rest of the world go by, the time will not be far away when we will be hearing a knock on our door in the middle of the night, and we will be hearing voices clamoring for freedom, independence, food and shelter, just as our revolutionary forefathers clamored for it.[43]

Societary changes, if they are desired by the people involved, can be made with little or no disruption of the total system. "We have learned that changes which people desire, radical or not, can be made swiftly, without great cost, and that a society may nearly redo itself—in a generation—if it wants to."[44] The Japanese village of Suye Mura, for example, experienced a great war, occupation by a foreign power, unsettled economic conditions, a new constitution and a new civil code. Five years after the war, village leaders still followed traditional ways, but the young people had deliberately and more or less successfully changed their ideas and their style of life.[45]

Societary innovations in the form of new social structures and processes and new cultural values and goals are preceding most technological innovations in the underdeveloped and newly developing countries of the world. After World War II, many colonial dependencies and protectorates gained independence, set up new governmental institutions, and established new patterns of economic, political, social, and ethnic stratification. Rapid population increase brought about by the acceptance *without integration* of modern medical techniques is changing the social structure still further. Population growth is explosive in the younger age group where medical success in controlling infectious diseases has saved the most lives. Costa Rica, for example, has 105 persons under the age of fifteen for every 100 adults. Belgium, in comparison, has forty-one persons under fifteen for every 100 adults. Neither private families nor the educational, economic, religious, or governmental institutions in the underdeveloped or newly developing countries are equipped to cope with this growing mass of impatient youth. To support a population growth of three per cent per year (which some countries have) requires an annual capital investment of twenty per cent to increase per capita income by even one per cent. Few of the already impoverished countries can manage to increase their capital investment by even ten per cent per year.

> The magnitude of the problem is staggering.* In Latin America, for example, population growth is already threatening to outpace economic growth—and in some parts of the continent, living standards are actually declining. In 1945 the population of our twenty sister American Republics was 145 million . . . by the year 2000 . . . Latin American population will be 592 million.[46]

Already more than half of the people of Latin America are chronically undernourished and hungry, most children do not go beyond the second grade, and sixty per cent of the population is illiterate. Of the arable land, seventy per cent is owned by two per cent of the population, and in not a single South American country is it a criminal offense to evade income tax. "Corruption is so widespread that much of the U.S. gift of flour for victims of drought in Peru and earthquake in Chile ended on the black market while hundreds of thousands starved." [47]

As cognitive dissonance tests habit patterns and motivates the individual to readjust idea and action, so social dissonance tests traditions and motivates a society to readjust structures and processes, norms and goals. Dissonance between technological lag in impoverished countries relative to both their rich neighbors and their own societary advance is the source of great and potentially dangerous stress. "Those who make peaceful revolution impossible will make violent revolution inevitable." [48]

Societary Lag

Although societary change is preceding most technological change in the "have-not" countries of the world, in the United States and other "have" nations technological change (in the form of tangible products and knowledge and skills associated with such products) is preceding most societary change.

> The world we are living in is totally new. . . . Since the world is totally new, and since it has become so overnight, our ideas are obsolete or obsolescent. In every aspect of our lives, we are living without theory, or what is worse, we are living on the debris of outworn or disproved theory. Our minds are like attics filled with abandoned and useless furniture.
>
> Think of the plight of the economists, whose whole "science" is based on

* In 1964 the Vatican and the U.S. began helping Latin America devise population programs.

> the idea of scarcity. What can they do with a country whose problem is abundance? * Think of the political scientists, who have taught us that the issue in politics is who gets what and how, and who now do not know how to defend democracy when it appears that perhaps other systems may get more cheaper and faster. Think of the scholars in jurisprudence, who have insisted for a hundred years that the law was the command of the sovereign and who do not know what to do with a world in which sovereignty is fading and the cry is for justice. . . .[50]
>
> The present stage of industrialization is totally new. What is new about it is that we have a commitment to the highest possible rate of technological change and the capacity to produce technological change on a scale and with a speed heretofore undreamed of.[51]

The terrifying implications of the disparity between technological and societary change are particularly evident in *CBN*, *contamination*, and *overpopulation*.† Traditional military ideas and practices sanction the making and stockpiling of weapons so grossly out of line with any possible human purpose that no one could sanely conceive of using them.‡ Traditional economic ideas and practices permit private exploitation and contamination of public resources basic to all life. Ignorance as well as traditional religious ideas and practices daily sentence thousands of new-born babies to starvation.

> The present intellectual problem of man is to bring his thought world abreast of his scientific discoveries. Logic, ethics, religion, philosophy, need to be remade into consistency with the situation. Otherwise they fail us in our need.[52]

Once a society has established research facilities in the natural sciences, the rate of technological advance is exponential. Social structures and processes, cultural norms and goals—all with their emotional weight—lag behind. We do not imply that social dissonance is born of competition between rival dichotomies. We perceive the total interaction of societies to each other and to innovations of all kinds as an intricate check and balance system. And the problem, as we see it, is to determine when a particular innovation or a par-

---

* In March, 1964, in a memorandum to President Lyndon Johnson, the Ad Hoc Committee on the Triple Revolution proposed that "society, through its appropriate legal and governmental institutions, undertake an unqualified commitment to provide every individual and every family with an adequate income as a matter of right." The Committee felt this undertaking "to be essential to the emerging economic, social, and political order in this country" and regarded it as "the only policy by which the quarter of our nation now dispossessed and soon-to-be dispossessed by lack of employment can be brought within the abundant society." [49] The Committee's proposal for action intrudes on areas of the society which involve both status rights and strong moral feelings. It threatens traditional ideology and is an abrupt departure from current economic practice. The source has prestige among only certain sophisticated segments of society, and the remedial action is proposed before the average citizen is fully aware that the cybernation crisis exists. For at least these reasons, the proposal will be subjected to the full force of all the mechanisms of anti-change.

† Chapter 1.

‡ Rejection of military tradition, however, is not adequate. We need, for example, selves—not the knowledge of how to make and use them nor the will to use them. Without social inventions to implement alternatives to war, nations would readily rearm.

ticular resistance engenders a dysfunctional or even lethal dissonance and to then find constructive ways of resolving that dissonance.

A dog star'v at his Master's gate
Predicts the ruin of the State.*

Unless resolved, dissonance, in greater degree than Blake portrayed, predicts still wider ruin. *Under emotional stress engendered by dissonance, how do we typically react?*

---

* William Blake (1757-1827), in *Auguries of Innocence.*

Notes

1. J. Robert Oppenheimer, in Thedore H. Von Laue, "Modern Science and the Old Adam," *Bulletin of the Atomic Scientists,* January, 1963, p. 3.
2. Oswald Spengler, *Decline of the West,* quoted in *TIME,* July 1, 1946, p. 58.
3. Karl Marx, *Capital* (New York: The Modern Library, copyright, 1906, by Charles H. Kerr & Company), p. 13.
4. *Ibid.,* p. 13.
5. Roscoe C. Hinkle, Jr. and Gisela J. Hinkle, *The Development of Modern Sociology* (Garden City, New York: Doubleday & Company, Inc., 1954), p. 5.
6. Herbert Spencer, *First Principles,* 1862, p. 407.
7. Spencer, *Social Statics,* revised edition, p. 238.
8. Emory S. Bogardus, *Contemporary Sociology* (Los Angeles: University of Southern California Press, 1931), pp. 386-387.
9. John H. Storer, *The Web of Life* (New York: The Devin-Adair Company, 1954), p. 136.
10. Quoted in Lucius Beebe and Charles Clegg, *The American West* (New York: E. P. Dutton & Co., Inc., 1955), p. 21.
11. Fairfield Osborn, *Our Plundered Planet* (Boston: Little, Brown and Company), p. 64.
12. Cecil Woodham-Smith, *The Great Hunger* (New York: Harper & Row, Publishers, 1962), p. 206.
13. William L. Langer, "The Black Death," *Scientific American,* Vol. 210, No. 2 (February, 1964), p. 117.
14. Quoted in Langer, "The Black Death," *op. cit.,* p. 117.
15. *U.S. News and World Report,* June 7, 1957, pp. 81-82.
16. Stevan Dedijer, "Research; The Motor of Progress," *Bulletin of the Atomic Scientists,* June, 1962, p. 4. © Educational Foundation for Nuclear Science, Inc., 935 E. 60th St., Chicago, Ill., 60637.
17. *World Geographic Atlas,* privately printed for Container Corporation of America, 1953, p. 278.
18. Francis Dart, "The Rub of Cultures," *Foreign Affairs,* January, 1963, pp. 366 and 368.
19. Ad Hoc Committee on the Triple Revolution, *The Triple Revolution: An Appraisal of the Major U.S. Crises and Proposals for Action* (Maurer, Fleischer, Zon and Associates, Inc., 1120 Connecticut Ave. N.W., Washington 36, D.C., 1964), p. 1.
20. Albert Burke, *The Mechanical Mess,* KRON-TV, January 28, 1962.
21. *The Triple Revolution,* pp. 6-7.
22. *Ibid.,* pp. 8-9.
23. Bernard Berelson and Gary A. Steiner, *Human Behavior* (New York: Harcourt, Brace & World, Inc., 1964), pp. 596-600.
24. Agnes Rogers Allen, "The Changing Status of Women," in *The American Story,* Earl Schenck Miers, ed. (New York: Channel Press, 1956), p. 295.
25. Edward McNall Burns and Philip Lee Ralph, *World Civilizations from Ancient to Contemporary* (New York: W. W. Norton & Company, Inc., 1958), Vol. II, pp. 73-74.
26. Robin M. Williams, Jr., *American Society* (New York: Alfred A. Knopf, Inc., 1951), p. 571.
27. Christopher Ralling, "A Vanishing Race," *The Listener,* July 16, 1959, p. 86.

28. Burns and Ralph, *World Civilization,* Vol. I, pp. 62, 82, 92, 115, 117, 130, 132, 233, 247, 282.
29. Henry Balfour, quoted in Frederick J. Teggart, *Theory and Processes of History* (Berkeley: University of California Press, 1941), p. 286.
30. Teggart, *Theory and Processes of History,* pp. 286-287.
31. John H. Vincent (1832-1920), American Methodist Episcopal Bishop.
32. Murray Gendell and Hans L. Zetterberg, *A Sociological Almanac for the United States* (New York: Charles Scribner's Sons, 1964), p. 27.
33. S. C. Gilfillan, "Who Invented It?" *The Scientific Monthly,* XXV, December, 1927, p. 529.
34. Ralph Linton, *The Study of Man* (New York: D. Appleton-Century Company, Inc., 1936), pp. 326-27.
35. George M. Foster, *Traditional Cultures and the Impact of Technological Change* (New York: Harper & Row, Publishers, 1962), p. 164. Information from Wallace Thompson, *The Mexican Mind,* a study of national psychology (Boston: Little, Brown & Co., 1922), p. 52.
36. Foster, *op. cit.,* p. 123, quoting Paul Fejos, "Man, Magic and Medicine," in *Medicine and Anthropology,* Iago Galston, ed. (New York: International University Press, Inc., 1959), pp. 28-29.
37. Foster, *op. cit.,* p. 29.
38. *The Emerging Nations: Their Growth and United States Policy,* Max F. Millikan and Donald L. M. Backmer, eds., Massachusetts Institute of Technology, Center for International Studies (Boston: Little, Brown & Co., 1961), p. 19.
39. John Dewey, *Human Nature and Conduct* (New York: Holt, Rinehart & Winston, Inc., 1922), p. 125.
40. Bernard J. Stern, "Resistances to the Adoption of Technological Change," in Samuel Koenig, et al., *Sociology, A Book of Readings* (Englewood Cliffs, N. J.: Prentice-Hall, Inc., 1953), p. 520.
41. *Ibid.,* p. 524.
42. Georges Herment, *The Pipe* (New York: Simon and Schuster, Inc., 1963).
43. *San Francisco Chronicle,* April 22, 1964, p. 10.
44. Margaret Mead and Manning Hash, in Berelson and Steiner, *Human Behavior* (New York: Harcourt, Brace & World, Inc., 1964), p. 568.
45. *Ibid.,* p. 568.
46. President John F. Kennedy, in a Special Message on Foreign Aid, 1961.
47. Gerald Clark, "Social Dynamite in Latin Poverty," Special Report in the *San Francisco Chronicle,* March 4, 1962, p. 20.
48. President John F. Kennedy, in an address to Latin American diplomats, 1962.
49. *The Triple Revolution: An Appraisal of the Major U.S. Crises and Proposals for Action,* pp. 16-17.
50. Robert M. Hutchins, "The Nurture of Human Life," Center for the Study of Democratic Institutions, *Bulletin,* March, 1961, pp. 4-5.
51. *Ibid.,* p. 5.
52. William Heard Kilpatrick, *Education for a Changing Civilization* (New York: The Macmillan Company, 1926), p. 83.

GD
GA

Those who want change without disturbance
are like those who want the ocean without its roar.

FREDERICK DOUGLAS (1817?-1895)

13

Collective Behavior

BEING A CREATURE OF CULTURE, most of man's social behavior conforms to the expectations of others as defined by folkways, mores, taboos, and laws. This *normative* behavior is the foundation of social institutions and the main focus of sociology. But chance and change do precipitate crises which can render established norms ineffective or inappropriate. When people need to act but have no adequate pattern of behavior to follow, they may act as a *collectivity*. A collectivity, if governed at all, is governed not by formalized norms, but by spontaneous sanctions which arise out of the same situation as the collectivity itself. Society inevitably includes not only the regular, predictable, and traditional behavior of variously organized groups, but the novel, unpredictable behavior of relatively unorganized *collectivities*.

Collective behavior—the behavior of collectivities—is both a product and an instrument of change. As a product of change it characteristically occurs in crisis situations where normative behavior cannot or does not function. When learned norms no longer serve individual or group goals, social homeostasis is disrupted and the social system is under stress. In those individuals and groups whose needs are not being met, tensions mount. Whether tensions exist covertly, concealed beneath the facade of habit, or are overtly expressed, they are ever ready to be mobilized in emotionally charged collective behavior.

WIDE WORLD PHOTOS

> The implications of this simplest form of tension theory for collective behavior are to point toward repeated and aggravated frustrations on a wide scale as accounting for the more vigorous and unconventional forms of collective behavior. When repeated frustrations of important needs affect large numbers of people over an extended period of time, tensions accumulate. These accumulated tensions provide the motive power for behavior which deviates from the conventional. From the standpoint of the social order, the failure of the institutional structure to provide means for the satisfaction of needs generated within it leads to cumulation of tensions, making people susceptible to courses of action not normally indicated or sanctioned in the culture.[1]

As an *instrument of change,* collective behavior is a more or less spontaneous outburst of action aimed, however irrationally, towards the solution of those unique problems which lie beyond common experience. Through trial and error and random experimentation, collective behavior sometimes leads to serviceable solutions, but because it is so emotionally charged, it may get out of bounds. Tension beyond the optimum for effective action tends to limit awareness, interfere with critical facilities, and heighten suggestibility. Emotional contamination can excite collectivities to behavior which individuals alone would never contemplate. The action of collectivities tends to be more extreme than that of normal individuals. However, even when the immediate effect is destructive, collective behavior may contribute to social order in the making.

Collective behavior has various forms: the most spontaneous and elemental are crowds and masses; the most developed and organized are public and social movements. All are infused with emotion. All are products of chance or change, and, in turn, potential instruments of change.

SOCIAL CONTAGION

Find a well-established column of ants intent on their own business and draw a firm finger across their path. This act seems to wipe the path clear of whatever "defined" the situation, and the ants panic. They mill back and forth, run frantically around, and, as if blaming each other for the social breakdown, fight among themselves. The excitement seems contagious, and confusion spreads from the point of crisis for some distance along the column in both directions. *Social contagion*—the diffusion of emotion through a group of individuals—is a common phenomenon among gregarious creatures. Frighten one sheep in a flock, and they all run; frighten one buffalo in a herd, and after a brief period of restless stomping and snorting, they all stampede. Among animals, emotion diffuses with such certain swiftness that social contagion may well have survival value.

The herd, the flock, the covey, the gaggle, the column of ants—the members of these sub-human groups do not surprise us when they react as one, but of humans we hope for less unanimity. "If you can keep your head when all about you are losing theirs. . . . If you can talk with crowds and keep your virtue. . . ." * But the steadiest man cannot always keep his head when those about him are losing theirs. And the most virtuous cannot always keep his virtue in an amoral crowd. Intense emotion *is* contagious. So, too, is the milder sustained emotion we know as mood. Even subtle signs of covert excitement or anger or fear or despair—the pitch of voice, the rate of breathing, the body tension, the moistness or color of skin—one may intercept subconsciously rather than consciously and involuntarily echo. Humans are not immune to social contagion, and insofar as a man succumbs to the primitive purpose of emotion, he forfeits rational self-control.

While emotion can be disruptive, it can also unite. The ties which bind men to each other are not all rational. Compassion is an essential component of the human community.

In Dallas, Texas, on November 22, 1963, two shots from a rifle mortally wounded John Fitzgerald Kennedy, 35th President of the United States. The news was flashed around the world. A Moslem telegraph operator in the Middle East tapped out, "How sorrowful bad!" A Greek-born barber in New York said, "I cry!" The King of Belgium, the President of France, the Prime Minister of Britain, the Chancellor of West Germany, the Deputy Premier of Russia, the Premier of Japan, and other foreign dignitaries flew to Washington. Kennedy had been a policy maker with strong intellectual and ethical commitments. Together with his gracious wife and two young children he had brought a refreshing vigor and clarity of purpose to Capitol Hill. Sorrow and a sense of loss unmatched since the assassination of Abraham Lincoln pervaded the nation. Television, renouncing all commercials, caught and amplified the somber mood. For three days, millions of people at home and abroad empathically watched and listened. They heard the muffled drums, followed the cortege, saw the riderless horse, the flag-draped bier, the mourners, the new grave, the eternal flame. The day after the funeral, routine business began again slowly. When our classes convened, the students still seemed psychologically nauseated—all but two. Two sociology students had lived through the emotional turmoil untouched. *"It all depends on how you felt about Kennedy!" "That's right! What's all the fuss? Just another man shot!"* Prominent Democrats and Republicans alike had responded to the crisis with renewed patriotism—with vows to "crown our good with brotherhood" and purge private and public life of the bitterness and hatred which spur fanatics to violence; but these two students nurtured their venom. Private dislike of Kennedy as a policy maker made them insensitive to grief for Kennedy as a man and national symbol. They are among those unfortunates whose emotional impoverishment alienates them not only from the national community but from the basic mores of humanity.

Only those who identify with humanity can share the common hopes and

---

* Rudyard Kipling, *If* (1865-1936).

passions of humanity. Human emotion is contagious only under certain conditions. Those who perceive themselves and their environment alike have a mutual if unspoken rapport which makes them responsive to each other. Anger then tends to breed more anger; terror, to breed more terror; despair, to breed more despair. Reciprocal stimulation can spiral emotion to a higher and higher pitch; but even as the vortex reaches white heat intensity, some individuals and groups remain coolly aloof. Distance, psychological or actual, immunizes against emotional contagion. The greater the distance from the vortex of excitement, the greater the immunity. Actual distance needs no explanation. We all know that we would be more excited by a riot next door than we would by one fifty miles away. But psychological distance also immunizes. Thus an evangelical, revivalist minister who could stimulate holy rolling and wailing and talking in tongues among a culturally homogeneous rural tent gathering would arouse little more than idle curiosity among a diverse crowd on a city street corner. And never have Negroes become excited enough to join a lynching mob against one of their own. Negroes identify not with the mob but with the victim, and are stimulated less to anger than to fear. Psychological distance imposed by personal limitations or by differences in goals, values, norms, or other cultural traits leads to differences in perception and thus lessens emotional contagion.

Although individuals and groups differ in their susceptibility to social contagion, some unanimity of emotion is prerequisite to collective behavior. *Normative behavior is learned; collective behavior is evoked.*

KINDS OF COLLECTIVE BEHAVIOR

Collective behavior always includes some degree of spontaneous emotional involvement among the members of a relatively unstructured group, but ask of any collectivity, "*How* spontaneous is the action? *How* contagious is the emotion? *How* structured is the group?" There is a difference. Compared with institutionalized normative behavior, all collective behavior is *relatively* spontaneous, unstructured, and unlearned. But because not all collective behavior is equally so, collective behavior can be differentiated as *crowd behavior, mass behavior, contagious mass behavior, publics,* and *social movements.* Each kind of collective behavior has a career—a history of inception and development. Crowds and masses are persistently spontaneous and unstructured. Publics and social movements may become increasingly organized and tutored.

Crowd Behavior

Crowds are visibly spontaneous. Although in popular speech a crowd is any large number of people gathered together in one place, in sociological usage such a collection of individuals must have some interaction and *rapport.*

Pedestrians merely waiting at a busy street corner for a light to change are not sociologically defined as a crowd. The people just happen to be there at the same time. They are intent on their own needs and purposes and are not held together by any interaction—however tenuous. But if the signal failed to change and the people communicated their growing impatience to each other, or if one person ventured to cross the street despite the stalled signal and got hit by a car, then the collection of pedestrians would become a crowd —an interacting group sharing a common emotion and a common interest.

Crowds are not all alike; they vary in character and sociological significance. Of the many classifications of crowd behavior devised to serve sociological thinking, we find most useful that differentiating four types of crowds: *casual, conventionalized, acting,* and *expressive.**

Casual Crowds

The street-corner crowd concerned with the fallen pedestrian would be a *casual* crowd, just as would be the "sidewalk superintendents" who stand watching a building under construction. A casual crowd is most loosely organized; membership readily shifts, and interaction is limited to occasional comments on the focal events.

Conventionalized Crowds

Casual crowds gather to gawk. Conventionalized crowds gather to partake of socially sanctioned emotionality. In conventionalized crowds, individuals can express inhibited emotions and impulses, but the crowd as a whole is ordinarily restrained by being a part of a larger social structure.

> Yet the behavior is not traditional, nor does it follow the ordinary, day-to-day pattern of behavior of the group. Although the situation may be anticipated and even planned, it is still an unusual situation in which unusual norms prevail. The behavior may still properly be termed crowd behavior because the stimulating influence of crowd interaction is necessary in order that the ordinary inhibitions against such behavior may be overcome. There is, furthermore, a permissiveness about the conventionalized crowd which allows and sometimes encourages the emergence of novel and extreme forms of behavior so long as they are consistent with the dominant mood.[3]

Often the conventionalized crowd is manipulated to increase a dominant mood or to incite one. Spectators at a football game, for example, are a conventionalized crowd, free to react to the plays with shouts and wails. However, the rooting section, a segment of the whole, is specifically manipulated by cheerleaders. The intense coordinated emotion expressed by this key group then enhances the excitement of the rest of the crowd. Professional football may

---

* Adapted from Herbert Blumer.[2]

provide better ball playing, but college games, with their spirited rooting sections, win more emotional support.*

The intent of conventionalized crowds is not always that of innocent pleasure and cathartic release of pent-up emotions. In Germany during the Nazi regime, conventionalized crowds were manipulated for more sinister purposes. Hitler, we understand, was greatly impressed by newsreel shots of American college football games and shrewdly used organized cheers to create crowd unity. As witness to the similarity between Nazi and football rallies, we cite one German student refugee who, in spite of the language difference, found the sound effects so alike that during football season he refused to go near a stadium for fear of hearing the clamor of the crowd.

When conventionalized crowds convene, notice that extra police stand by. Excitement is volatile; it readily shifts from one mood to another, and a conventional crowd can transform itself into an acting one. Even though conventionalized crowds tend to be restrained by the larger social structure in which they exist, joyful exuberance can change with startling ease to angry destructiveness. Violence sleeps restlessly beneath the surface of excitement.

Acting Crowds

The conventionalized crowd tends to follow loosely defined expectations within the confines of a larger social structure. An *acting crowd* has no such restraints. It is typically lawless and aggressive. It acts for or against either an image conjured up by the crowd or an actual person or object, and it acts not on the basis of established rules, but on the basis of aroused impulse.

> Just as it is, in this sense, a noncultural group, so likewise is it a nonmoral group. In the light of this fact, it is not difficult to understand that crowd actions may be strange, forbidding, and at times, atrocious. Not having a body of definitions or rules to guide its behavior, and, instead, acting on the basis of impulse, the crowd is fickle, suggestible, and irresponsible.[4]

Acting crowds typically are vehicles through which participants release the tension of built-up frustrations. Poor whites in the South, fearful and resentful of any competition which threatens their vulnerable economic position, lash out at the hapless Negro. Ghetto-ized Negroes in the North, caught in an economic and social trap, impatient and embittered by discrimination, lash out at symbols of white domination.

Popularly, an acting crowd is called a mob—a term connoting disorder, promiscuousness, anger and violence. The revolutionary crowds that stormed the French Bastille in 1789 and the lynching mobs which have stained the

* You have only to imagine yourself alone in a large stadium watching an "exciting game" to realize how much your feelings and behavior are a response to others. To increase the sense of emotional involvement and, theoretically, the pleasure of their audience, television and radio stations often introduce "canned laughter" and "canned applause" at strategic points in studio programs.

history of Negro-white relations in the United States were acting crowds. Because lynching mobs have been the most characteristic kind of acting crowd in the United States, we draw our illustrations from them, distinguishing in the process between "bourbon" and "proletarian" lynchings.[5]

A proletariat lynching, as the name implies, is done by a mob drawn from the lowest social and economic strata. In proletariat lynchings, senseless torture and property damage are the common counterparts of death. In Texas in 1930, a mob burned to the ground the courthouse where a Negro was being tried. The defendant was burned to death, but the mob was not satisfied. They dragged the body through the streets to the Negro section.

> The body was drawn up to the limb of a cottonwood tree in front of a Negro drugstore. The store was forcibly entered and ransacked, the money and valuables pocketed, the confections passed around to the crowd, the furniture and furnishings piled under the Negro's body for fuel. . . . The crowd gave a mighty cheer as flames enveloped the Negro's body. Little boys pointed to the Negro and made suggestive comments as the trousers burned off. Men whispered to each other and laughed aloud. The body was still in its semi-crouched position as it dangled from the chain. The heat caused great blisters and welts to rise upon the flesh as it began to burn. The air was filled with the acrid odor of burning meat.
>
> After the burning of the body, some of the crowd—the onlookers—went home. But the more vicious elements continued ransacking and burning with gasoline the Negro business places, including a hotel, a drug store, two cafés, two barber shops, two dentists' offices, a doctor's office, two undertaking establishments, an Odd Fellows' Hall, a Knights of Pythias building, a theater, a lawyer's office, a life insurance office, a cleaning and pressing shop, and several residences.[6]

The term *mob* can be less aptly applied to the acting crowd involved in bourbon lynchings. In such lynchings, the act is planned, often by leading citizens with the tacit approval of the police or other civil officials. In California in 1935, for example, a mob retaliated with a double lynching for the kidnap-killing of an 18-year-old boy. The governor, far from invoking the law, promised pardon to anyone convicted of taking part and announced, "We show the nation that this state is not going to tolerate kidnappings." United States history is spotted with blood from bourbon lynchings.

In San Francisco, lynchings were part of the vigilante "cleansings" of 1851 and 1856.

> By late in 1849 the criminal populace of San Francisco, largely recruited from the British penal colony at Tasmania, took on aspects of serious menace. Six times in two years the flimsy town was swept by devastating fires, four of them definitely known to have been set so that mobs of thieves could plunder the fugitives. . . . It was a condition of affairs, according to Herbert Asbury, most nearly to approach criminal anarchy in American history. The Sydney Ducks, as the English toughs were known, and the "Hounds," rival gangsters, took pleasure in beating the Chilenos and abusing the prostitutes in their quar-

> ter of town and contributed materially to the formation of the first Vigilance Committee in 1851 . . . a group of armed citizens with military authority determined to take justice out of the impotent courts and put the fear of God in evildoers. Gallows building and other ominous gestures of retribution became visible around the city.[7]

In the twentieth century most bourbon lynchings have been in those particular Southern areas where Negroes are in near or absolute majority and white community leaders feel obligated to maintain white supremacy by rigidly enforcing "racial etiquette." Although rape is the most publicized reason given for lynchings, only a fourth of the lynchings since 1882 have been for sex offenses. The greatest number have been in retaliation to physical assault against a white person and for a variety of miscellaneous misdeeds which super-sensitive whites felt threatened their status:

> "Being a witness," "improper conduct," "insisting on eating in a restaurant," "trying to act like a white man," "being a strike breaker," "discussing a lynching," "making boastful remarks," "slapping a boy," "insisting on voting," "throwing stones," "being a member of Labor's Non-Partisan League," "alleged disrespectful utterance against President Wilson," "giving poor entertainment," "riding in a train with white passengers," "being too prosperous," "not turning out of the road for automobile driven by white person." [8]

When racial tension is high, almost any trivial incident has been seized upon by dominant white supremists as an excuse for lynching a Negro. We are gratified to report, however, that in the United States since World War II, lynchings of all kinds have declined sharply. But how much of this is due to increased morality among the whites, how much to greater strength among the increasingly organized Negroes?

Expressive Crowds

An acting crowd is extrovertive; the focus of attention is outward. The expressive crowd (sometimes called the orgiastic crowd) is introvertive; the focus of each member's attention is inward on his own personal feelings. With no objective but personal gratification and no focus outside itself, the expressive crowd vents emotion in undefined and unrestrained physical activity—activity which tends to become hypnotically rhythmical, as in ritual dancing, spontaneous chanting, and clapping.

> Stated tersely, the crowd has to act, but it has nothing toward which it can act, and so it merely engages in excited movements. The excitement of the crowd stimulates further excitement which does not, however, become organized around some purposive act which the crowd seeks to carry out. In such a situation, the expression of excited feeling becomes an end in itself; the behavior, therefore, may take the form of laughing, weeping, shouting, leaping, and dancing. In its more extreme expression, it may be in the form of uttering gibberish or having violent physical spasms.[9]

Saturnalia provide for off-the-record behavior and typically take expressive form. We have our New Year's Eve parties where we expect a sizable proportion of the population to defy conventional mores in an excess of merrymaking and love-making. The most exuberant large-scale outburst of expressive behavior in our history, however, was no mere New Year's celebration, but VJ night, when World War II ended with victory over Japan. Crowds on the main streets of cities across the nation indulged in emotional orgies—dancing, singing, looting, strip-teasing and seducing in the semi-shelter of doorways.

More typically expressive crowd behavior has religious overtones. The individual forfeits self-control to the tyranny of emotion. He feels possessed by a source divine, for the release of tension is as ecstatic in effect as it is mysterious in origin. And when others are equally pervaded by the glory, the effect seems transcendental.

> When an experience gives complete and full satisfaction, when it is socially stimulated, approved, and sustained, and when it comes in the form of a mysterious possession from the outside, it easily acquires a religious character.[10]

The modern revival meeting brings to the expressive crowd rapturous release from tension and a feeling of spiritual rebirth.

> All the while waves of ecstatic rhythm have been sweeping over the congregation, with the actions of the preacher setting the pace. There are patterns to the rhythmic actions: running around the pulpit, holding trembling hands to the sky, very fast clogging of the feet, swinging the arms in sharp, staccato motions. One girl leaps from her seat as though struck by an electric shock, races four times around the aisles of the church, screaming, "O God . . . do Jesus . . . O God . . . glory, glory, glory . . . give me more . . . more . . . glory, glory, glory"; falling over backward with hands outstretched, her whole body quivering and rhythmically jerking, she collapses at last in a dull heap on the floor, and stays there in comatose condition for several minutes. Others rise and shout at the top of their lungs for five minutes, or bang on something in staccato rhythm. The same persons respond again and again, with perhaps seventy-five individuals represented. Each responds with an individual pattern of motions, but all motions appear to have been culturally conditioned, whether immediately conditioned by the agent or not. One wonders if some form of mass hypnotism is at work.[11]

When expressive crowd behavior is extended in time and the contagion spreads from one collectivity to another, the expressive behavior itself becomes a *craze* or *mania,* compulsively enacted by *crazy crowds.*

A dancing mania possessed the Netherlands late in the fourteenth century. For four months there was almost constant street dancing. Persons of all social classes rushed into the streets and danced compulsively until they fell from exhaustion. Country cousins, hearing of the wild antics in the city, came to observe and taunt, but they, too, got drawn into the dance. Some dancers became so excited they literally beat their brains out by rhythmically banging their heads against walls. The mania spread from the Netherlands throughout Europe. In Germany it was known as St. Vitus Dance,* because of the belief that a visit to a shrine of St. Vitus could cure the compulsion. In Italy it was known as the tarantella, because wild dancing supposedly cured a deep lethargy (tarantism) supposedly caused by a tarantula bite.† Only the sound of music could theoretically arouse a victim from his stupor; he would launch into wild dancing, continue until he collapsed, and awake cured! Because tarantism was considered highly infectious, one victim could trigger compulsive dancing in an entire community.[12]

Crazes are not limited to other times and other places. The "Great American Revival" of the early nineteenth century was a religious craze. Congregations laughed senselessly, danced without restraint, and frequently dropped onto hands and knees, barking, growling, and snapping their teeth. Even the female fans who swooned over Frank Sinatra during World War II and the fans of both sexes who writhed to the songs of Elvis Presley could be thought of as mildly possessed! Fans of the Beatles bought $18,000,000 worth of records (during the world-wide Beatlemania of 1963).[13] Screaming, writhing, swooning, fighting teenagers were the despair of puzzled parents, but the delight of news media. Perhaps even the underworld was pleased when up to half a city's police force was mobilized just to protect the Beatles from their own crazed fans.[14]

Although casual, conventionalized, acting, and expressive crowds differ in character and purpose, they are alike in being emotionally generated, spontaneous in action, and relatively unstructured.

Mass Behavior

The mass, like the crowd, is an elementary collectivity—amorphous, and spontaneous. All those people who hovered by their television sets during the several days following the assassination of President Kennedy were, sociologically speaking, a mass. *They had no common social, economic, political, or religious denominator;* they included citizens and foreigners, Fascists and Communists, Catholics and Protestants, Moslems, Buddhists, non-believers. *They were unknown to each other.* As a total group, the television audience was made up of physically separated anonymous individuals. And *they interacted, not with each other but with an event of common interest*—in this case a personal, national, and world tragedy. What emotional consensus there was came not from direct emotional contagion intrinsic in the mass, but from a common human response to a common perception of experience.

* St. Vitus Dance today is applied to a disorder of the nervous system known medically as chorea.

† Any lethargy must have been psychologically induced, because the bite of a tarantula is only mildly poisonous.

The ideas and events which evoke mass behavior lie outside provincial limits and defy explanation or interpretation by provincial norms.

> The object of mass interest can be thought of as attracting the attention of people away from their local cultures and spheres of life and turning it toward a wider universe, toward areas which are not defined or covered by rules, regulations, or expectations. In this sense the mass can be viewed as constituted by detached and alienated individuals who face objects or areas of life which are interesting, but which are also puzzling and not easy to understand and order. Consequently, before such objects, the members of the mass are likely to be confused and uncertain in their actions. Further, in not being able to communicate with one another, except in limited and imperfect ways, the members of the mass are forced to act separately, as individuals.[15]

In many ways, ours is increasingly a mass society. Urbanization has weakened primary group ties and lessened the authority of primary group norms. Individuals live in partial anomie and depend more and more on mass communication media, not only for recreation, but for information, interpretation, and evaluation. It is sobering to realize that totalitarian societies, both fascist and communist, initially tried to weaken primary groups, particularly that primary, primary group—the family. In such societies, existing organizations are demolished or transformed, thereby creating an unstructured mass which can be manipulated, organized, and mobilized by the leaders.

> The attitude of rising mass movements toward the family is of considerable interest. Almost all of our contemporary movements showed in their early stages a hostile attitude toward the family, and did all they could to discredit and disrupt it. They did it by undermining the authority of the parents; by facilitating divorce; by taking over the responsibility for feeding, educating, and entertaining the children; and by encouraging illegitimacy. Crowded housing, exile, concentration camps, and terror also helped to weaken and break up the family. Still, not one of our contemporary movements was so outspoken in its antagonism toward the family as was early Christianity. Jesus minced no words: "For I am come to set a man at variance against his father, and the daughter against her mother, and the daughter-in-law against her mother-in-law. And a man's foes shall be they of his own household. He that loveth father or mother more than me is not worthy of me." [16]

When primary group affiliations are lost or strained, the individual's security is undermined; his autonomy is weakened. He easily becomes an anonymous member of the mass—easy prey for the benevolent or cynical manipulators of mind and manners. Rabble rousers of national stature can whip a mass society into behavior akin to that of an acting crowd. Such was the fate of Germany under the Nazi regime, where the only item of personal property which could not be repossessed for nonpayment of installments was the radio, so vital was this instrument of communication to the maintenance of the mass.

Contagious Mass Behavior

In crowds, the primary reaction of the individual is to the excitement of others; in the mass, the primary reaction of the individual is to a common stimulus. But crowd and mass are not mutually exclusive; hybrid forms of collective behavior show characteristics of both. In panics, social epidemics, fashions and fads, individuals may begin acting as in a mass, but continue acting in response to crowd-like contagion. Phenomena of this type occur both when individuals are in contact with each other and when they are not.

Panics

In a panic, each individual responds with fear to what he perceives as a personal threat, but the intensity of his fear is heightened by the fear he perceives in others. True panic requires, in addition to a fear stimulus and a fear contagion, the sense of partial entrapment. Then the limited avenues of escape are fiercely competed for. Trampling, crushing, and suffocation are the deadly accompaniments of panic. In the Coconut Grove fire in Boston in 1942, the panicking patrons fought for exit through the revolving door by which they had originally entered.

> Men and women fought their way toward the revolving door; the push of bodies jammed it. Nearby was another door; it was locked tight. There were other exits, but few Coconut Grove patrons knew about them. The lights went out. There was nothing to see now except flames, smoke, and weird moving torches that were men and women with clothing and hair afire.
>
> The eight hundred Coconut Grove patrons pushed and shoved, fell and were trampled . . . most of them were trapped.
>
> Firemen broke down the revolving door, found it blocked by bodies of the dead, six deep. They tried to pull a man out through a side window: his legs were held tight by the mass of struggling people behind him. In an hour the firemen began untangling the piles of bodies. At hospitals and improvised morgues which were turned into charnel houses for the night, four hundred and eighty-four dead were counted.[17]

A panic is a concentrated collectivity—confined in time and space and super-saturated emotionally. It arises in a flash, writhes through a short and frenzied career, and disappears minutes later.

Social Epidemics

A social epidemic is a diffuse panic in which the fear—mild or intense—is usually out of proportion to the threat. In the flying-saucer epidemic of the early 1950's, fear was only a vague apprehension, a sense that "something's up." Although the emotion rampant in a social epidemic may be mild and meandering, it is more likely to be intense and swift and to sweep like a flash fire through a society. In either case, the specific fear stimulus is determined by the cultural context. In the Middle Ages, unidentified flying objects were perceived as angels or the Virgin Mary. Today, when space travel is a possibility, they are perceived as visitors from outer space. During the French Revolution, whole communities in northern France were terrified by the cry, "The Brigands are coming!" even though no one seemed to know quite who the Brigands were or what they might do when they got there. In the United States in 1938 it was Martians, not Brigands, which terrorized. An estimated 1,000,000 persons listening to a radio version of H. G. Wells' *War of the Worlds** mistook fiction for fact. Thousands rushed into the streets to scan the skies. Thousands more, like this usually sensible college senior, tried to escape.

> One of the first things I did was to try to phone my girl in Poughkeepsie, but the lines were all busy, so that just confirmed my impression that the thing was true. We started driving back to Poughkeepsie. We had heard that Princeton was wiped out and gas was spreading over New Jersey and fire, so I figured that there wasn't anything to do—we figured our friends and families were all dead. I made the forty-five miles in thirty-five minutes and didn't even realize it. I drove right through Newburgh and never even knew I went through it. I don't know why we weren't killed. My roommate was crying and praying. He was even more excited than I was—or more noisy about it, anyway; I guess I took it out in pushing the accelerator to the floor. I imagine having to concentrate on the driving held me together somewhat. On Monday, after it was all over, and I started to think of that ride, I was more jittery than when it was happening. The speed was never under 70. I thought I was racing against time. The gas was supposed to be spreading up north. I didn't have any idea exactly what I was fleeing from, and that made me all the more afraid. All I could think of was being burned alive or being gassed. And yet I didn't care somehow whether I hit anything with the car or not. I remember also thinking there wasn't any God. My roommate was really praying and crying all the time. I thought the whole human race was going to be wiped out—that seemed more important than the fact that we were going to die. It seemed awful that everything that had been worked on for years was going to be lost forever.[18]

The *War of the Worlds* was broadcast just a month after the Munich crisis. We had begun to think of the radio as a harbinger of death and destruction. An invasion from Mars seemed a possibility, but not everyone panicked. Many persons kept their wits and checked broadcasts from other radio stations. However, those who did panic crept sheepishly back home, feeling foolish and embarrassed. Not so in Quito, Ecuador, in February, 1949, when the same broadcast evoked the same initial panic response. But instead of creeping sheepishly back to their homes, the Ecuadorians formed a mob and stormed the radio station. They burned the station to the ground, burned the office of the newspaper which owned the station, and killed fifteen people before national

---

* Produced by Mercury Theatre under the direction of Orson Welles.

troops took control. Although collective behavior is not governed by the traditional norms of a culture, it may be modified by those norms.

Social epidemics are not always flash-in-the-pan affairs. Sometimes the fear diffuses through time as well as space. The fear of witchcraft has been with the Western world sporadically since the Middle Ages. In the United States, witch hunts are part of our early history, but the most zealous prosecutions were in the colony of Massachusetts in 1691 and 1692. The epidemic began when ten girls made hysterical accusations against a West Indian slave who had taught them some innocent tricks. The fear spread, and within four months, hundreds of persons had been arrested and charged with witchcraft. Authorities hanged nineteen of the accused and crushed one to death trying to extort a "confession." (Our witches were never burned. That was not the American way!) We have now in this twentieth century found new foci for our terror and other scapegoats for our aggressions, but certain sub-cultural groups in England and Continental Europe still believe in and fear old-fashioned witches.

Epidemics are irrational, and the means used to cope with them tend to be equally irrational. In France in 1601, the following Code applied to sorcerers:

> The judge of the district shall take cognizance of the affair, and try it. The ordinary forms of trials are not to be used in such instances. The suspicion of sorcery is sufficient to authorize the arrest of any individual. If the accused does not confess, he must be placed in close confinement, and trusty persons appointed to draw the truth from him. There are some judges who make promises of pardon, and nevertheless, finally pronounce sentence of execution; but this custom, though authorized by many doctrines, is extremely cruel. If public report accuse the criminal of sorcery, he is a sorcerer. A son is allowed to give evidence against his father. Witnesses of infamous character may be heard, as well as other. Children likewise may be heard. Variations in the answers of the witnesses must not be considered as a presumption favorable to the innocence of the prisoner, if all accuse him of sorcery. The judge may condemn on mere conjecture and presumption; in that case, the criminal must not be burnt, but hanged.[19]

Some of our official reactions to Germans and things German during World War I, and to Japanese and things Japanese during World War II, were as irrational as the seventeenth-century reaction to sorcerers. During World War I, names of German foods were changed: Hamburgers became "liberty sandwiches," hamburger steaks became "Salisbury steaks," sauerkraut became "liberty cabbage." The teaching of the German language was banned in public schools, and German music—Bach, Brahms, and Beethoven included—was not heard in the concert halls. German immigrants were personally persecuted, and even dachshunds, stereotyped in anti-German propaganda posters, were stoned to death on the streets. Then during World War II, fear and hate of the Japanese reached epidemic proportions on the Pacific Coast. Existing economic rivalries and racial prejudice provided the fuel; the bombing of Pearl Harbor was the igniting spark. Japanese homes and businesses were confiscated, and

Japanese men, women, and children were corralled in concentration camps. Said a Hollywood actor in 1943:

> When people in Washington say we must protect American Japanese, they don't know what they're talking about—there's no such thing as an American-Japanese. If we ever permit those termites to stick their filthy fingers into the sacred soil of our state again, we don't deserve to live here ourselves.[20]

And the Governor of Idaho had comparable sentiments:

> The Japs live like rats, breed like rats, and act like rats. I don't want them coming into Idaho.[21]

Now we are engaged in a "cold war" with the communist world, and epidemic hate and fear in the United States have focused on real and imagined Communists. After World War II, when the real challenge of International Communism became apparent, fear brought on a kind of intellectual paralysis. Private citizens and public servants tended to stifle their thoughts, afraid that something they might say could be interpreted as disloyal. Even sociology students, ordinarily outspoken and willing to challenge, were strangely reticent. "Loyalty" boards, in their eagerness to ferret out bonafide Communists, were irrationally prosecuting persons who dared concern themselves with social problems. During this time of reconstruction, when all the human resources a nation could command were needed to deal with postwar disorder, social compassion and tolerance, and even intelligence, were suspect. Witness such questions as these asked by certain loyalty boards.

> Have you ever had Negroes in your home?
>
> There is a suspicion in the record that you are in sympathy with the underprivileged. Is this true?
>
> In your recollection, do you recall ever discussing any topic which might be sympathetic to Communist doctrine?
>
> Are your friends and associates intelligent, clever?
>
> Did you ever hear any political discussions at X's home?
>
> If you are, as you say, a loyal American, why do you persist in denying that you were a member of the Communist Party? [22]

The champion of epidemic anti-Communism was the late Senator Joseph McCarthy. He remained the nation's most prominent Communist hunter for four years without uncovering a single authentic Communist.* Yet the poisonous fear spread until, at its height in 1953, Supreme Court Justice Douglas said:

> A Communist, one with Communist affiliations, one with leftist tendencies, a socialist, a liberal, or just a plain Yankee who does not like this business of the witch hunt and who shouts his protest—these are all put in the same classification.
>
> Anxieties and suspicions are aroused until a community does not know what

* For a full discussion of the whole problem of subversion and civil liberties, see Horton and Leslie, *The Sociology of Social Problems*.[24] Much of our discussion is adapted from this source.

> to believe or whom to trust, until even old neighbors suspect one another. More and more people conclude that the only safe thing to do is to conform: either to stand silent or to join the hunt.[23]

Fear of Communism was epidemic and irrational. Was McCarthyism an equally irrational way of coping with it? A report by Herbert Philbrick, the F.B.I. counter-spy who ranked high in Communist party circles, indicates that it was.

> According to the leaders of the Communist Party, McCarthy has helped them a great deal. The kind of attacks he has made do three things that the comrades like: (1) They add greatly to the confusion, putting up a smoke screen for the party and making it more difficult than ever for people to discern just who is a Communist and who is not; (2) they make the party appear to be a lot stronger than it is; (3) they do considerable damage to some of the "stupid liberals" whom the party hates.[25]

Fear of Communism has not ceased, and now we ask if the methods of our present House of Representatives Un-American Activities Committee are also irrational. Has epidemic fear caused the Committee to react rigidly and shortsightedly rather than with the creative flexibility consistent with long-term goals?

> In one hundred and nine thick volumes of Congressional testimony studied . . . we could find virtually nothing elicited except by accident or inadvertence, to establish the fundamental facts about the types of people who join the party, their family backgrounds, why they leave, the amount and kind of education they received.
>
> The Congressional inquiries often have been called "witch hunts." While it would be dangerous to carry the parallel between these investigations and the Salem witchcraft trials to extremes (e.g., witches were imaginary, while Communists *do* exist), there is a useful analogy. The Salem trials developed as little truth about witches as the Congressional investigations have about Communists. The hysterical courts of Salem seemed to desire only a confession, and immunity was promised to those who confessed. . . . The Congressional committees also have been mainly concerned with confessions.[26]

Apparently, the Communists themselves do not feel threatened by the Un-American Activities Committee. Herbert Philbrick quotes one Communist Party leader:

> "The House Committee? Bah! How much more are we helped than are we harmed? What can they do? They call us before the Committee. So we put on a suitable performance. . . . Going before the House Committee is a chance for winning as many friends as we can to the Party, and creating as many enemies of the American Congress as possible." [27]

No sensible American doubts that Communism is a real threat to our society, yet many sensible Americans doubt the effectiveness and rationality of our anti-Communist techniques. J. Edgar Hoover, head of the F.B.I., cautioned:

> Communism can be defeated by the truth—and only by the truth. Vigilante attacks, irrational tirades, and forceful suppression are instruments which increase and do not decrease the menace.[28]

And President Dwight D. Eisenhower urged:

> . . . guard against those who pretend to defend freedom with weapons from the arsenal of the tyrant, for to defend freedom in ways that destroy freedom is suicide.[29]

Initial individual reaction to a specific fear stimulus—be it fire or flood, Brigands or Martians, witches or Communists—is amplified in panics and epidemics by comparable fear reactions in others. Social contagion then pervades what was originally a mass and stimulates its members to crowd-like behavior.

Fashions and fads are less significant forms of collective behavior than panics and epidemics, but they demonstrate the immediate, everyday impact of social contagion on individuals who otherwise would remain undifferentiated members of the mass. *Fear of something foreign to the group or its environment is the common component in both panics and social epidemics. Anxiety associated with loss of personal status in a group is the common component in fashions and fads.* The anxiety which stimulates fashions and fads is a subtle, haunting, diffuse fear, consciously perceived as merely avoidance of ridicule or censure by a group or exclusion from a group. Those most susceptible to fashions and fads are those most insecure in their group affiliations.

Fashions

Fashions today are deliberately induced, usually by a coalition of designers, manufacturers, merchandisers, and advertisers. The new style itself is the initial stimulus to which the "style-conscious" members of the mass society respond. In the past, the traditional style setters have been the royalty and nobility. Today, particularly in the United States, the style setters are the social elite and movie personalities. The style setters are not compelled by any particular group norms as much as by their own self-image and their own identification with *avant-garde* fashion. As the style spreads through the continued efforts of those who have a financial stake in its success,* more and more people react not

---

* Designers, manufacturers, merchandisers, and advertisers all benefit economically from style changes. Said one manufacturer at a convention in 1950:

> Basic utility cannot be the foundation of a prosperous apparel industry. We in the soft line business have the responsibility to accelerate obsolescence. . . . Money that was not spent for soft lines . . . was not spent on other lines of merchandise, but was saved by the consumer. It is our job to make women unhappy with what they have. You might call us "merchants of unhappiness." We must make these women so unhappy that their husbands can find no happiness or peace in their excessive savings. We have not made our proper contribution to the total economy until we have achieved this result.[30]

only to the style itself and the advertising pressures, but to those high-status others who have already accepted the style. Then common perceptions gradually shift. Comfortable round-toed shoes begin to look clumsy; full-cut pants with cuffs begin to look baggy; jackets with wide-padded shoulders begin to look top-heavy. Eventually the critical point is reached, and the balance changes. The new style is safer than the old. The larger populace in an act of contagious mass behavior embraces the new look, finds it "right," and thereafter loyally resists the next new fashion. Who in the mid-1960's would buy round-toed shoes, padded jackets, wide pants, or bustles, even if they were available?

> In the early nineteenth century, some European nations resisted long pants for men as staunchly as we, in the 1950's, resisted Bermuda shorts for dress wear. In 1812 Cambridge University decreed that students wearing long pants in hall or chapel would be counted absent. And a famous London restaurant refused admittance to the Duke of Wellington, popular hero in Britain's defeat of Napoleon, because the Duke had on long pants. And in 1807, the Tsar of Russia ordered his border guards to bar from entering the country any traveller wearing long pants—unless he would submit to having them cut off at the knee.* [31]

Even today, innovators of new fashions face the risk of arrest. In the summer of 1964, police in Chicago, New York, and other cities led women in topless bathing suits from the beaches. The scene was familiar, though the sex was not. Thirty-five years before, police led males from the beaches of Southern California for the same offense.

When fashion gains religious sanction, it is even more firmly entrenched. Who, if he fears to offend his fellows, would dare to defy his God?

> Mohammedans regard the mouth of a woman as improper, and good Muslim women always cover their mouths in public. In Uzbekistan, this rule was carried to such extremes that all females over the age of ten were obliged to extinguish [sic] themselves out of doors by wearing the *paranchah,* a close-meshed bag of black horsehair which shrouded the head and shoulders and looked like a coal sack. When the penetration of Soviet Russian ideas of female emancipation encouraged some of the more daring among the Uzbek women to discard their *paranchahs,* fanatic mobs, instigated by outraged Mullahs, burned these women alive on public petrol fires for blasphemy. This took place as recently as 1930.[32]

Fashions usually begin near the top of the social order, and the contagion moves downward as "masses follow the classes." In a mobile society such

* Style changes sometimes symbolize political change, and may be resisted as such. The *Sans-Coulottes,* ragged volunteers of the French Revolutionary army, wore long pants instead of the currently fashionable knee breeches. Just as the Russian Revolution (and later the Cuban Revolution) made beards a symbol of radicalism in this century, so the French Revolution made long pants a symbol of radicalism in the early nineteenth century.

as ours, where many strive for prestige, fashion is a convenient status symbol, and fashions change with relative ease. In more rigidly stratified societies, or less affluent ones, upper classes maintain a monopoly on high status symbols, and fashion does not have the same contagious potential.

Those who feel manipulated by fashion designers should recognize, however, that they can fight back. For a number of years in the late 1950's and early 1960's, French dress designers tried to reintroduce the "flat look" of the 1920's. Women simply did not respond favorably, and the effort failed. Deliberate consumer boycotts are difficult to organize, but passive resistance by many individuals can bring financial loss to the fashion innovator.

Fads

Unlike fashions, which are generally introduced by the social elite, fads tend to originate with less privileged groups. Through fashions, the individual identifies with the dominant culture; through fads, he identifies with a self-assertive sub-culture. Following a fashion is an act of conformity. Following a fad is an act of defiance relative to the dominant culture but an act of conformity relative to a sub-cultural group. Should a fad become "fashionable," it ceases to be different enough to serve its purpose, and the original devotees drop it and move on to a new fad.

Fads tend to take the form of ostentatious behavior or dress. The zoot suits during World War II and the black leather jackets and low-hanging jeans of the 1950's were fads. So, too, were such popular dance forms as the Charleston in the 1920's and the Twist in the early 1960's. Even slang—"twenty-three skidoo" in 1910, "swingin'" and "crazy" in 1960—and Beatnik talk—"cool cat," "pad," "man"—qualify as fads. Most sub-cultures have some fad to their credit, or discredit, including the collegiate culture which has been responsible for goldfish-swallowing, john-jamming, and bed-pushing.

Divisive Behavior—Publics

Publics arise as an emotional response to issues of common concern. Issues are more than matters of disagreement. They are those points in debate relative to which persons feel a right and an obligation to take either a negative or a positive stand. By definition, a public is divided against itself and committed to rational discussion as a means of resolving differences and reaching a consensus.

Some major issues arouse a world public. *CBN, contamination,* and *overpopulation* involve people everywhere in discussion and debate. To test bombs or not to test? To spray DDT or not to spray? To give or to withhold contraceptive information? Each decision made on these and the hundreds of other questions growing out of major world issues ultimately affects the maintenance and perpetuation of human society and is rightly the concern of every intelligent person. Other less critical issues arouse only national or local publics. To integrate or not to integrate? To cut or not to cut taxes? To curtail or to extend foreign aid? To shoot for the moon alone or to cooperate with Russia? To build a freeway here, or there? Even such a minor issue as whether or not to install parking meters in a village street can generate a small but vigorous public.

A public, whether large or small, has identity only relative to the particular issue around which it forms. There are, consequently, as many publics as there are issues, and the number of publics to which any single individual belongs is limited only by the number of issues with which he can actively concern himself. One may, for example, be firmly against nuclear bomb testing, accept the Republican national platform, prefer the Democratic position in state affairs, favor a city school bond, oppose a projected increase in sales tax, advocate local option liquor laws, oppose a pending state library, and join with some neighbors in a hot fight to prevent subdividers from destroying a favorite bird-watching area.

Publics have more collective self-awareness and better organization than either crowds or masses, but they are not necessarily more enduring. If the issue around which a public has formed becomes taboo, the public dissolves into the anonymous mass. Or if the issue becomes too hot, emotion displaces rationality, and the public thereby converts itself into an acting crowd.

Prior to the Japanese attack on Pearl Harbor, the public debated the issue of whether or not the United States should enter the war. Debaters expressed a wide spectrum of opinion—often with undisguised emotion. After December 7, 1941, however, the issue no longer existed. The Japanese had answered for the public, and few citizens dared speak out against active involvement. Congress voted in favor of a declaration of war, with but one dissenting vote. Congress was no longer a public, tolerant of dissent, but an angry, acting crowd clamoring for unanimity. The one dissenter, a woman and a lifelong pacifist, had to shut herself up in a telephone booth to escape outraged Congressmen.

Although publics are emotional in origin, they are committed to rational behavior. This rationality, however, is difficult to maintain. Because publics are emotionally involved in issues, those appealing to publics are tempted to appeal emotionally rather than to convince rationally.

Propaganda

Publics are the focus of propaganda. In the pre-scientific world when the final test of truth was authority, propaganda in the hands of authority had a favorable connotation. It meant *to educate in the truth.* However, in a scientifically oriented world, and particularly in a democratic society, predetermined "truth" presented by any "authority" is suspect; and propaganda has taken on unsavory connotations. Webster's New International Dictionary, 1961, notes that propaganda now often refers to "the dissemination of ideas, information, gossip, or the like, for the purpose of helping or injuring a person, an institution, a cause, etc." Propaganda is no longer education in the sense that education, in theory at least, benefits the individual and the total society. Propaganda, as now conceived, benefits only a particular segment of society. *Education creates and maintains publics;* those who are well informed are those most likely to become involved in issues. *Propaganda, in contrast, tends to destroy publics.* The propagandist seeks through various emotional appeals to so weight his side of an issue that he effectively eliminates the issue and thereby eliminates the public which it aroused. Fortunately, a democratic society has two built-in defenses against propagandists: opposing propagandists, and an increasingly sophisticated citizenry.

To aid in identifying propaganda for what it is—an effort to manipulate the public emotionally rather than to educate rationally—we submit a list of commonly used techniques: (1) Name Calling; (2) Glittering Generalities; (3) Transfer; (4) Testimonials; (5) Plain Folks; (6) Card Stacking; (7) Bandwagon; (8) Repetition; (9) Big Lie.*

(1) *Name Calling.* Give a dog a bad name and you ruin his reputation. Call an American a Communist, and he may spend the rest of his life trying to live it down. But because an individual falsely accused can sue for libel, clever propagandists use labels which are devastating but safely vague or elusive: "Fellow traveler," "Fifth Amendment Communist," "Communist sympathizer," "under the influence of a foreign ideology." All such terms are open to various interpretations and only connote, rather than denote, guilt.

(2) *Glittering Generalities.* Toss out a generality such as "the American way," and it can mean all things to all people. To a segregationist, segregation is the American way; to an integrationist, integration is the American way. A propaganda appeal couched in generalities has a general appeal. Who but the most discriminating could object to a politician who stood firmly for motherhood and against sin?

(3) *Transfer.* The transfer arouses uncritical emotions, not through the use of generalities, but through the use of symbols: Old Glory, the Cross, the Bald Eagle.

> Ours must be a moral platform from which there is preached a positive policy based upon the principle of religion and patriotism. For God and country. For Christ and country and the flag—that is our motto as being prepared for action, for Christian American action.†

---

* The first seven techniques were defined by the Institute for Propaganda Analysis, active four years prior to Pearl Harbor, Alfred McClung Lee, Executive Director, 1940-1941.[33]

† Keynote speaker at the Christian Democrat Convention in 1952 in which General Douglas MacArthur was nominated as the candidate for President of the United States.

When a candidate is "wrapped in the flag," he transfers public attention from the substance of his position to the symbols which clothe it.

(4) *Testimonial.* A steel company president testifies, "We get the right steel to the right buyer—faster—by *telephone.*" The chairman of the board for a large shoe company says, "We found *Blue Cross* gives the kind of hospital expense protection our employees need." A socially prominent couple recommends travel on the S.S. *United States.* A world-renowned cellist advertises the joys of a vacation in *Puerto Rico.* All testimonials in both advertising and politics involve a high status person plugging for something or someone. The fallacy, of course, is in assuming that high status automatically confers authoritative judgment.

(5) *Plain Folks.* In the United States, "the common man" is king. He is the democratic symbol, and those who want wide support court his favor. Although our population is predominantly urban, we have a sentimental attachment to the rural; and if a presidential candidate wasn't born in a log cabin—an increasingly difficult feat—his next best recommendation has been to be a country boy of humble background. A successful "plain folk" campaign was waged by Harry Truman in the 1948 presidential race against Thomas Dewey. Dewey too closely fit the "city slicker" stereotype and was no match for the earthy, "give 'em hell" Harry.

(6) *Card Stacking.* Card stacking "rigs the game." It draws conclusions based on unverified premises, tells some, but not all of the truth, implies cause-and-effect relationships which do not exist, or otherwise creates false impressions. A weekly news magazine, for example, gave statistics on the number of young, middle-class white families with children who were moving out of Washington, D.C., to the suburbs, "where the schools are still largely segregated." The implication was that the population shift was a result of school integration in the District of Columbia. A comparable population shift is occurring in metropolitan areas all over the nation, including those where schools have always been integrated.

(7) *Bandwagon.* The bandwagon exploits the desire to belong—especially to the winning team. "This year the big swing is to . . ." The technique is used both in advertising and in political campaigns. Notice that the night before an election, both parties claim ultimate victory. However, in politics, either over-confidence or a sporting root for *der unterhund* can cause the bandwagon approach to backfire. In the 1948 presidential campaign, the Republican wagon was rolling so fast that the day Truman was elected several newspapers carried the headline: DEWEY LANDSLIDE!

(8) *Repetition.* Repeat a lie often enough and someone will eventually believe it. Repeat anything often enough and the engram is surely traced. Singing commercials get their message across even when one consciously dislikes the tune, the words, and the product. The memory is there, and in unguarded moments it comes into consciousness. Haven't you caught yourself humming commercials?

(9) *The Big Lie.* Adolf Hitler was not the first to propagandize with big lies, but he did rationalize the technique in *Mein Kampf.* He who tells a little lie, he noted, is in danger of being refuted by little facts. An outrageous lie knocks the adversary off balance and makes specific facts seem minor, niggling objections. "He wouldn't dare say *that* unless there were some truth to it!" "After all, with so much smoke, there must be some fire!" Like a handful of mud, a hurled lie may fall from its target, but a stain is left where it struck.

Name Calling, Glittering Generalities, Transfer, Testimonial, Plain Folks, Card Stacking, Bandwagon, Repetition, or *Big Lie*—separately or in combination—when used with subtle finesse by knowledgeable propagandists can be formidable manipulative tools. *Let publics beware!* Let publics fortify their rationality with valid information and good will.

Opinion

In the voting booth, one man's vote is as good as another's. However, in the preliminary skirmishes leading up to the voting booth, public issues are not determined by a count of individual opinions equally weighted. Some opinions carry more weight than others.

> Public opinion should be viewed as a collective product. As such, it is not a unanimous opinion with which everyone in the public agrees, nor is it necessarily the opinion of the majority. Being a collective opinion it may be (and usually is) different from the opinion of any of the groups in the public. It can be thought of, perhaps, as a composite opinion formed out of the several opinions that are held in that public; or better, as the central tendency set by the striving among these separate opinions and, consequently, as being shaped by the relative strength and play of opposition among them. In this process, the opinion of some minority group may exert a much greater influence in the shaping of the collective opinion than does the view of the majority group.[34]

Although a public does not have a structured hierarchy as does the larger society, a public is part of the social hierarchy. A Congressman is attuned to those who "count" most. He is not equally responsive to all members of his district. Even a department store manager gives more attention to a complaint if it comes from the mayor's wife than if it comes from the janitor's wife.

Furthermore, opinions, being tinged with emotions, are contagious. When they are exposed in the public arena during debate, those opinions from influential sources are the most virulent, and—even when no propaganda is intended—they tend to break down the defenses of others. One fallacy inherent in public opinion polls is the assumption that such polls measure identical units of opinion equal in number to the individuals polled. But opinion polls cannot measure independent, stable, equally weighted units of public opinion. They can only measure the end product of collective action.

The opinion of a public—even when measured by electric computors—is a volatile product. Its validity is limited to a particular public existing in a particular time and place under particular circumstances. Publics are swayed by both planned propaganda and innocent but influential private opinions. Not without reason have publics been called fickle.

Conative Behavior—Social Movements

The hopes and discontents of a society, in a diffuse, uncoordinated way and through scattered and sporadic individual or group action, can bring about slow shifts in attitudes toward women, war, mental health, smog, birth control, integration, science, and other general images and issues. Out of such cultural drifts or *general* social movements arise movements inspired by definite discontents and definite hopes. Although the early stages are highly emotional, social movements ultimately develop organization, norms, continuity, and considerable stability. Of all forms of collective behavior, social movements are the most highly developed, effect the most profound changes, and contribute most to *social order in the making.*

A successful social movement has a long and complex career characterized by a series of developmental stages which we call *Agitation, Consolidation, Determination, Justification,* and *Tactical Operation.**

Because the Negro protest movement is the most significant social movement in the United States today, we refer to it in illustrating these developmental stages.

Agitation

Discontent muffled by timidity or indecision, oppression suffered through ignorance or inertia—such a social climate invites agitation by men and women bolder, more imaginative, or more righteous than others. Agitators define issues, excite feelings, arouse hopes, and create publics. Where only general misery existed, agitators awaken specific grievances. Where only vague thoughts stirred, agitators kindle specific goals. The term agitator is not necessarily pejorative; our own history provides examples to the contrary: Thomas Paine, Harriet Beecher Stowe, Margaret Fuller, Dorothea Dix, Samuel Gompers. But the agitator is anathema to those his actions threaten, and typically the defenders of the status quo make agitators the scapegoats, blaming them for "rabble rousing" and for creating a problem where none before existed. A leading white citizen of Montgomery, Alabama, asked Martin Luther King: "Over the years we have had such peaceful and harmonious race relations here. Why have you and your associates come in to destroy this long tradition?"[36]

White supremacists insist that the Negro protest movement is the direct product of agitation. Before a Senate Committee in 1963, Governor Ross R. Barnett of Mississippi charged, "The Communists are . . . championing the

* Freely adapted from Herbert Blumer.[35]

cause of the Negroes of America. . . . The Attorney General has been personally responsible for helping to put mobs in the streets. . . . The President and the Attorney General are sowing the seeds of hate and violence." [37]

When the established social order is threatened, those with vested interests in that order tend to blame *agitators* for inciting unrest in a previously contented populace. Agitators have power, but they are not magicians. Any seeds they might sow take root only if they fall on fertile ground. The "peaceful and harmonious race relations" in the South indicated not a true peace but a *Pax Romana*—a fictitious peace born of an enforced and accepted subordination of the Negro. Negroes outside the South have traditionally been more assertive. Southern Negroes have been quiet, not because they were content but because they were without power and without hope.

Consolidation

After agitators have captured the attention and imagination of enough people to start a social movement, leadership shifts to reformers or prophets who consolidate feelings and organize efforts towards positive goals. Out of a growing sense of common purpose and fellowship comes a vitalizing *esprit de corps.*

> Its basis is constituted by a condition of rapport. In developing feelings of intimacy and closeness, people have the sense of sharing a common experience and of forming a select group. In one another's presence they feel at ease and as comrades. Personal reserve breaks down and feelings of strangeness, difference, and alienation disappear. Such conditions of mutual sympathy and responsiveness obviously make for concerted behavior.[38]

With *esprit de corps* comes a strong in-group, out-group feeling: "Those not for us must be against us!" In defiance of perceived "enemies," members "rally 'round the flag." Ceremonials, rituals, parades, demonstrations, and celebrations, as well as more informal meetings with singing and dancing and friendly interaction, sustain the movement and strengthen emotional involvement of the members in it. The song, "We Shall Overcome," developed by the Negro protest movement in the United States, helped many a Negro accept insult, arrest, imprisonment, abuse, and even death.

Determination

"We Shall Overcome"—the title of the song itself symbolizes the next stage of a social movement when growing strength, clearer perspective, and *esprit de corps* makes morale high and purpose determined. History seems to be on "our" side. Liberation of African nations from Colonial domination, for instance, strengthened the Negro protest movement in the United States. ". . . the American Negro can no longer, nor will he ever again, be controlled by white America's image of him. This fact has everything to do with the rise of Africa in world affairs." [39]

Furthermore, God is also on "our" side. Belief in the universal rightness of the cause gives strong religious overtones. In fact, the most successful social movements have greater and lesser "saints" (charismatic leaders),* "sacred" literature, and myths. Nazism † had its Hitler, its bible—*Mein Kampf*—and the myth of the master race. Communism, although anti-religious in its original antagonisms to established churches, has reason to be called "The Gospel according to Saint Marx." The Communist bible is *Das Kapital*, the myth, that of the historic destiny of the proletariat, and in Moscow on public display, the enshrined body of Saint Lenin. All such saints and sacred literature and myths sustain the zealous determination so characteristic of that of the "true believers."

Justification

If a social movement is vital enough to reach this stage of development, it has attracted intellectuals and statesmen who now provide the movement with an ideology. Typically, this ideology is expressed in both erudite and "plain folks" terms. As an abstract logical statement of premises and purposes, the ideology is a weapon of rational defense and attack against intellectual critics of the movement. As a complex of easily comprehended slogans and emotional symbols, it solicits support from the larger less educated populace.

> A rising mass movement attracts and holds a following not by its doctrine and promises but by the refuge it offers from the anxieties, barrenness, and meaninglessness of an individual existence. It cures the poignantly frustrated not by conferring on them an absolute truth or by remedying the difficulties and abuses which made their lives miserable, but by freeing them from their ineffectual selves—and it does this by enfolding and absorbing them into a closely knit and exultant corporate whole.
>
> It is obvious, therefore, that in order to succeed, a mass movement must develop at the earliest possible moment a compact corporate organization and a capacity to absorb and integrate all comers. It is futile to judge the viability of a new movement by the truth of its doctrine and the feasibility of its promises. What has to be judged is its corporate organization for quick and total absorption of the frustrated. [40]

---

* Charisma is a quality of personality which followers identify as nearly magical or superhuman. Charisma was brought into the language by the late nineteenth-century philosopher of religion, Rudolph Otto, who used it to describe the special gift of God's grace claimed by leaders of religious movements and cults: Christ, Mohammed, Martin Luther, John Calvin, Gandhi, Father Divine. When a political leader is thus deified, his power over followers can assume the magnitude of a Hitler; his death can collapse the movement.

† Nazi is an abbreviation of the German term *Na*tionalso*zi*alist.

Ideological justification and popular support for the Negro protest movement comes from Constitutional rights and Judaeo-Christian ideals. Negro ministers are powerful leaders and churches are centers of foment. When Martin Luther King, Baptist minister and head of the Southern Christian Leadership Conference, was jailed in Birmingham (April, 1963), a group of white clergymen publicly criticized him for "unwise and untimely" demonstrations. From his cell King replied. He wrote on borders of newspapers and pieces of toilet paper and smuggled out the scraps. In these words he justified the Negro stand:

> We have waited for more than 340 years for our constitutional and God-given rights. . . . Before the Pilgrims landed at Plymouth, we were here. Before the pen of Jefferson etched across the pages of history the majestic words of the Declaration of Independence, we were here. For more than two centuries, our foreparents labored in this country without wages; they made cotton "king," and they built the homes of their masters in the midst of brutal injustice and shameful humiliation—and yet out of a bottomless vitality, they continued to thrive and develop. If the inexpressible cruelties of slavery could not stop us, the opposition we now face will surely fail. We will win our freedom because the sacred heritage of our nation and the eternal will of God are embodied in our echoing demands.[41]

Only with a guiding ideology expressed in both rational and emotional terms can a social movement justify itself to all comers.

Tactical Operation

Through the stages of *Agitation, Consolidation, Determination, Justification,* and *Tactical Operation,* a social movement gains organized purpose and structural strength. Now comes the time when it must keep faith with believers by making definite gains towards stated objectives. This requires that the leaders of the movement, who would now include administrators, develop tactics appropriate to the particular society and its unique historical and cultural setting. Tactics may be more or less aggressive and include such strategy as propaganda appeals, passive resistance, bribes, lobbies, strikes, boycotts, and even war. The criterion is pragmatic: whatever works is a good tactic. In social movements, ends tend to justify the means.

Because tactics are tested empirically, they are characteristically flexible. However, tactics are occasionally so strictly prescribed by the ideology of a movement that instead of advancing a cause, they actually hinder it. Communist Party tactics developed in Tsarist Russia, a rigidly stratified authoritarian society, have had little success in the United States, a democratic and remarkably mobile society. Appeals to a proletariat which does not solidly identify itself as such have found few listeners. Inflexible tactics doom any social movement to ultimate failure.

Tactics of the Negro movement have been flexible and multi-pronged. The National Association for the Advancement of Colored People (NAACP) has carried the burden of desegregation cases to the Supreme Court. The Southern Christian Leadership Conference has provided fuel and foot soldiers for nonviolent protests. The Urban League has led the fight for equal job opportunities and decent housing. The Congress on Racial Equality (CORE) sponsored the Freedom Rides of 1961 which ended segregated facilities in bus terminals. The Student Nonviolent Coordinating Committee (SNCC or "snick") began with an assault on the economic power structure through restaurant sit-ins and then attacked the political power structure of the deep South with a voter registration drive among Mississippi Negroes. Picketing, protesting, petitioning, boycotting, suing, sitting-in, riding for freedom, marching on mainstreets and on Washington, D.C.—all these measures show how tactics vary with the need.

Some social movements seek reform; some seek revolution. Reform movements would modify the existing social order, often only enough to make practice coincide with preaching. No one in the United States today, for example, is more committed to the ideals of "freedom and justice for all" than the leaders of the Negro movement. Revolutionary movements, in contrast, challenge existing ends, means, and institutional norms, and would create a new social order. Reform movements are "respectable" and typically get support from churches, schools, newspapers, and other social institutions. Revolutionary movements, however, are understandably denied help by the institutions they threaten. A society does not willingly become party to its own destruction. Thus, in the United States we exclude known Communists from the teaching profession, from political offices, and from other positions of influence.

Although initially we can distinguish between reform and revolutionary movements, in practice one may convert to the other. White supremacists, for example, feel so threatened by the Negro movement that they perceive it as a revolution. The inherent danger in such intolerance is obvious: should a reform movement be denied access to the public through institutional channels, it goes underground and becomes, in fact, revolutionary. And its heroes, barred from the public forum, may gain sympathy and support through martyrdom. Conversely, facets of revolutionary ideology may be incorporated in respectable reforms. Communists in Italy, for example, long clamored for land reforms; but after World War II when the de Gasperi government offered a land reform program, the Communists opposed it. "The Communists detest democratic reforms. These changes, they know, will make free government stronger, hence, less likely to be overthrown by revolution." [42] In the United States, Communists committed to revolutionary tactics favor a conservative government; meddling liberals take the teeth out of Communist propaganda by their halfway reforms. But whether reformist or revolutionary in intent, a social movement is a purposeful collectivity "acting with some continuity to promote a change or resist a change * in the society or group of which it is a part." [43]

COLLECTIVE BEHAVIOR AND CHANGE

Collective behavior in all its forms is a reaction to chance and change. An economic depression can precipitate a *panic* run on the banks, angry *crowds* of unemployed, *publics* debating economic issues, reform or even revolutionary *social movements*. In turn, collective behavior is a force for change.

Casual crowds insistently gathering to watch construction workers can lead alert public-relations men to accommodate those crowds by building viewing stands, rather than to frustrate them by putting up board fences. Panics can inspire precautions: new fire regulations, laws against building homes in line with dams, rabies inoculations, quarantines and vaccinations. Fashions, frivolous though they may be, have firm repercussions. When fashionable ladies late in the eigheenth century piled their hair to a height of three feet or more with "bushels of wool, bran, horsehair, and several cushions on a wire foundation," they created coiffures which forced changes in both architecture and transport. "Doors and ceilings of houses had to be heightened to permit their passage, for they were tall enough to brush the chandeliers, and the roofs of sedan chairs had to be hinged." [44] When, during the nineteenth century fashion dictated beaver hats in England and the continent, it sent trappers in the United States searching the wilderness for beavers and brought wealth to those who traded pelts for gold. And, more recently, when undershirts became unfashionable (after Clark Gable removed his shirt and revealed a bare chest in the 1934 Academy Award film, "It Happened One Night"), the underwear industry went into a decline from which it did not fully recover until World War II when the G.I.'s popularized T-shirts.

Change and collective behavior are interactive; they stimulate and intensify each other. As in the familiar conundrum, "Which came first, the chicken or the egg?" we cannot always know whether collective behavior preceded or followed change. But today we know that both are on the increase. Concurrent with the exponential growth of scientific discovery and technological invention have come profound, disruptive changes and vigorous collective behavior. This social ferment is both promising and portentous.

> "Those who are awed by their surroundings do not think of change, no matter how miserable their condition. When our mode of life is so precarious as to make it patent that we cannot control the circumstances of our existence,

* Although *resistance to change* seems inconsistent with *social order in the making*, social movements dedicated to preventing change can cause change by over-reacting. The John Birch Society, representing the extreme political right, would greatly change the check and balance system of our Federal Government in an attempt to prevent change!

> we tend to stick to the proven and the familiar. We counteract a deep feeling of insecurity by making of our existence a fixed routine. We hereby acquire the illusion that we have tamed the unpredictable. Fisherfolk, nomads, and farmers who have to contend with the willful elements, the creative worker who depends on inspiration, the savage awed by his surroundings—they all fear change. They face the world as they would an all-powerful jury. The abjectly poor, too, stand in awe of the world around them and are not hospitable to change. It is a dangerous life we live when hunger and cold are at our heels. There is thus a conservatism of the destitute as profound as the conservatism of the privileged, and the former is as much a factor in the perpetuation of the social order as the latter."[45]

When people clamor for change, it is a sign of growing strength and hope. But it is also a warning.

> When hopes and dreams are loose in the streets, it is well for the timid to lock doors, shutter windows, and lie low until the wrath has passed. For there is often a monstrous incongruity between the hopes, however noble and tender, and the action which follows them. It is as if ivied maidens and garlanded youths were to herald the four horsemen of the apocalypse.[46]

The diffusion of technology from the urban-industrial nations to the newly developing ones is changing the perspective of the oppressed and the impoverished peoples of the world and engendering social movements and "revolutions of rising expectations." Established order within nations and among nations is breaking down.

> The confusion and the disarray, the aimlessness and bewilderment which are more or less prevalent everywhere, are the concomitants of the breakup of the established order. We are living amidst the breakup of the established order of the postwar world, and we are finding that much of our thinking is no longer able to explain the facts.[47]

Much of our thinking no longer explains the facts, and much of our behavior no longer fits the facts.

The old order is failing fast; but a new order is in the making. Out of the stress of change—out of hopes and fears and frustrations—collectivities are arising. Some collective behavior is erratic and inspired by fear and rage. Crowds storm citadels of power, panic seizes sensible populations; social epidemics sweep staid countries. Other collective behavior, although emotionally evoked, is potentially more constructive. Thoughtful publics deliberate new issues which flood the local and world scene, and idealistic social movements develop to define the hopes of awakening people. But all collective behavior is intrinsically pathematic. Even the most thoughtful public, if uneducated, can be swayed from intelligent action by propaganda; and the most idealistic social movement, without well-conceived goals, can be misguided.

Collective behavior, engendered by emotion, is an expedient product of the present. Normative behavior, entrenched in the habit system of the individual and in the institutional system of society, is a product of the past. Neither can competently cope with the cataclysmic changes of this century. *Where do we turn for the knowledge and techniques we need to direct the uncertain future?*

Notes

1. Ralph H. Turner and Lewis M. Killian, *Collective Behavior* (Englewood Cliffs, N.J.: Prentice-Hall, Inc., 1957), p. 18.
2. Herbert Blumer, "Collective Behavior," in *New Outline of the Principles of Sociology*, Alfred M. Lee, ed. (New York: Barnes & Noble, Inc., 1951), pp. 178-185.
3. Turner and Killian, *op. cit.*, p. 153.
4. Blumer, *op. cit.*, p. 180.
5. Arthur Raper, *The Tragedy of Lynching* (Chapel Hill: University of North Carolina Press, 1933), no page.
6. Durward Pruden, "A Sociological Study of a Texas Lynching" in Logan Wilson and William L. Kolb, *Sociological Analysis* (New York: Harcourt, Brace & World, Inc., 1949), p. 337.
7. Lucius Beebe and Charles Clegg, *The American West* (New York: E. P. Dutton & Co., Inc., 1955), pp. 122-23.
8. Hadley Cantril, *The Psychology of Social Movements* (New York: John Wiley & Sons, Inc., 1941), p. 82.
9. Blumer, *op. cit.*, p. 183.
10. Blumer, *op. cit.*, p. 184.
11. Liston Pope, *Millhands and Preachers* (New Haven: Yale University Press, 1942), p. 133.
12. Encyclopaedia Britannica, 11th Edition, Vol. 26, p. 416.
13. *Newsweek*, February 24, 1964, p. 56.
14. *Life*, January 31, 1964, p. 30.
15. Blumer, *op. cit.*, p. 186.
16. Eric Hoffer, *The True Believer* (New York: Harper & Row, Publishers, 1951), pp. 34-35. Biblical quote is *Matthew* 10: 35-37.
17. *Time*, December 7, 1942, p. 26.
18. Cantril, *The Invasion From Mars* (Princeton: Princeton University Press, 1940), pp. 51-52.
19. Henri Boquet, Grand Judge of Sainte Claude, Dole, France, August 19, 1601. *Harper's Magazine*, September, 1956, p. 55.
20. Carey McWilliams, *Prejudice; Japanese-Americans: Symbol of Intolerance* (Boston: Little, Brown & Co., 1944), p. 263.
21. *Ibid.*, p. 164.
22. John C. Wahlke, ed., *Loyalty in a Democratic State* (Boston: D. C. Heath & Company, 1952), p. 55. Quoted from transcripts of loyalty board hearings.
23. *U.S. News and World Report*, December 4, 1953.
24. Paul B. Horton and Gerald R. Leslie, *The Sociology of Social Problems* (New York: Appleton-Century-Crofts, Inc., 1960), pp. 576-614.
25. *The Progressive*, March, 1952, p. 5.
26. Morris Ernst and David Loth, *Report on the American Communist* (New York: Holt, Rinehart & Winston, Inc., 1952), pp. 2, 227-228.
27. Herbert Philbrick, *I Led Three Lives* (New York: McGraw-Hill, Inc., 1952), p. 186.
28. *The Progressive*, January, 1953, p. 5.
29. Speech at Mount Rushmore.
30. An unnamed manufacturer quoted in Leonard W. Doob, *Social Psychology* (New York: Holt, Rinehart & Winston, Inc., 1952), p. 410.
31. Pearl Binder, *Muffs and Morals* (New York: William Morrow & Co., Inc., 1954), p. 48.
32. *Ibid.*, pp. 14-15.

33. Alfred McClung Lee and Elizabeth Briant Lee, *The Fine Art of Propaganda* (New York: Harcourt, Brace and Co. and the Institute for Propaganda Analysis, 1939) and Alfred McClung Lee, *How to Understand Propaganda* (New York: Rinehart & Co. Inc., 1952).
34. Blumer, *op. cit.,* p. 191.
35. Blumer, "Social Movements," in *New Outline of the Principles of Sociology,* Alfred M. Lee, ed. (New York: Barnes & Noble, Inc., 1951), pp. 199-214.
36. Martin Luther King, Sr., *Strides Toward Freedom* (New York: Ballantine Books, Inc., 1958), p. 31.
37. *U.S. News and World Report,* July 22, 1963, p. 6.
38. Blumer, "Social Movements," p. 206.
39. James Baldwin, *Nobody Knows My Name* (New York: Dell Publishing Co., Inc., 1962), p. 79.
40. Hoffer, *op. cit.,* pp. 39-40.
41. *Time,* January 3, 1964, p. 15.
42. J. Edgar Hoover, *Masters of Deceit* (New York: Holt, Rinehart & Winston, Inc., 1958), p. 100.
43. Turner and Killian, *op. cit.,* p. 308.
44. Binder, *op. cit.,* pp. 108-109.
45. Hoffer, *op. cit.,* pp. 7-8.
46. *Ibid.,* p. 11.
47. Walter Lippmann, "Breaking Up of the Established Order," *San Francisco Chronicle,* July 11, 1963, p. 12.

Science and technology are the greatest instruments of change in the modern world. . . . What is needed desperately is a deeper and still deeper synthesis of this scientific competence with the idealism that is also dynamic in the cause of humanity.

ABDUS SALAM, *Chief Scientific Advisor to the President of Pakistan in 1964.*

14

Directive Behavior

NORMATIVE BEHAVIOR IS TRADITIONAL; collective behavior is expedient. Neither is strictly rational, and both may be dysfunctional. Normative behavior makes no claim to rationality. A norm which has arisen in response to a past need may no longer serve that or any other need. Even a law, although deliberately and, we assume, rationally designed, may indiscriminantly enforce behavior which in any given situation may or may not be sensible. Of all collective behavior, only publics and social movements pretend rationality. But naive publics are swayed by propaganda appeals and weighted opinion, and the vitality of social movements is emotionally engendered and liable to emotional deflection. Because normative behavior is the backbone of society and resistant to change, collective behavior has been in the past the only means people have had to deal with unusual and unexpected conditions. Now in this twentieth century, modern science, which has engendered such critical new conditions, has made possible a new way of coping, which, tentatively, we call *directive behavior.*

Directive behavior involves the interaction of scientists, educators, publics, and policy makers within a democratic framework, and it does claim rationality. It respects tradition and emotion but serves the exclusive purposes of neither. *Directive behavior mobilizes science in conjunction with conscience, and imagination, to cope with current and coming issues creatively and in ways consistent with human values and long-term goals.*

Both normative and collective behavior connote inadvertent or deliberate conformity: the individual, convinced or not, acts with the group. Neither implies independent action or leadership; directive behavior implies both. In directive behavior an individual or group of individuals for any problem at any level of society uses as referents not tradition, not private or prevailing opinion, but the facts and theories of science and the common rights of man. Insofar as directive behavior bypasses tradition and emotion to define new behavior patterns or new goals or to build new social structures, it involves creative independence; and insofar as it is understood and accepted by others, it involves democratic leadership.

THE ROLE OF SCIENTISTS

The difficulties involved in implementing directive behavior lie not only in the resistance to change embedded in society and in the deficiencies of our usual modes of behavior, but in lack of articulation between science and social processes.

> We have not yet learned how to apply modern science in a manner which is consistent with its enormous power and its present inadequacies. We have not yet learned to discern in these complex problems the proper roles of scientific knowledge and social judgment.
>
> Until effective means for dealing with these questions are developed, we will be in continuous danger from unanticipated and poorly understood hazards. If we are to live securely with the new inventions of modern science, we shall need as well new inventions to govern the relations between science and society.
>
> Although the task of developing such new procedures is formidable, . . . the scientific community might have done a great deal to mitigate the present conflicts about insecticides, fallout, and smog if it had applied the customary principles of scientific inquiry to these problems at the right time. Clearly, the decisive time to evaluate the risks and benefits of a new technological program is *before* it is put into effect. The longer such an evaluation is delayed, the less its value to society, for once the process has become embedded in a vast economic or political commitment, it may be impossible to alter.
>
> In this task, the scientist's duty is plain, for it is no different from his responsibilities toward the development of all scientific knowledge. The scientist must examine all the evidence and summarize it in a statement of what is known, what is assumed, what is doubtful, and what is possibly erroneous. He must also describe the limits of the relevant knowledge, for these will reveal what new knowledge is needed to avoid the dangers of acting in ignorance.[1]

Scientists in the past, intent on advancing their science and less keenly aware of their directive role, have accepted more casually the implications of the knowledge they made available. After Alfred Nobel invented dynamite and ballistite and was trying to perfect an aerial rocket, he remarked, "Well, you know, it *is* rather fiendish things we are working on." But then he added,

"They are so interesting as purely theoretical problems." [2] Other scientists have expressed specific concerns too late and to an uncomprehending audience.

> . . . A discovery made in 1939 in the most abstruse field of science—nuclear physics—ushered the world into the new era. The atom bomb burst onto unsuspecting mankind in August, 1945, with the destruction of a Japanese city and sudden death of 75,000 people—the work of a single plane, dropping a single bomb! Some scientists, who had worked in secret on the development of this weapon, tried in the last moment to prevent its use by impressing on the government the fateful significance of this step, signalling, as it did, the transformation of wars into mass holocausts. They pointed out the inevitability of other nations acquiring these weapons in a few years, and the danger this would create for the security of the United States. They argued that what to do with the bomb should be considered a major political problem, rather than a routine military decision. The Frank Report, of June, 1945, which presented these views, caused hardly a ripple in Washington. Hiroshima and Nagasaki were wiped out, the war ended, and the nuclear arms race began. Five years later, it became a race in thermonuclear weapons; in still another five years, a race in ballistic missiles able to deliver city-incinerating weapons across the ocean.[3]

The physical scientists have already demonstrated the power of their knowledge. The biological scientists, now in a position to modify transfer of genetic information from one generation to the next, envision eventual control over man's own physical and psychological evolution. And the behavioral scientists, increasing rapidly in their understanding of individual and group processes, predict more or less control over man's behavior. The continued achievements of biological and behavioral scientists pose moral problems astounding in scope and as grave as or graver than any posed by the physical scientists' control of inanimate matter.

As a discipline, science is concerned with what *is*, not with what *ought to be*. *Science* and *conscience* as words have a common root; yet science itself has no conscience. Conscience implies not only the power to judge the moral quality of one's thoughts or acts, but a feeling of obligation to enjoin what is "good." Science, as accumulated knowledge systematized and formulated into propositions about reality, is essentially *amoral*.

> When Franklin D. Roosevelt was President of the United States (1933-1945), he called in a leading economist to advise him how to cope with a financial crisis. "You know the situation we are facing . . . I want you to tell me whether or not to raise the gold content of the dollar."
>
> "I'm very sorry, Mr. President," the professor replied. "I can't answer that question. I can tell you what will happen if you do raise the gold content of the dollar, and I can tell you what will happen if you don't. But whether or not you *ought* to raise it is not a scientific question." [4]

Such neutrality is imperative to the integrity of science and to that of the scientist *in his professional role*.

Science is strictly amoral; it is neither a Frankenstein monster nor a Fairy Godmother, but it has the potentialities of both. The scientist, because he perceives the dual power of science more clearly than anyone else, is now taking the lead in *directive behavior*, which, because it involves citizenship as well as science, and moral principles as well as empirical proofs, can help insure that the experimental frame of mind does not override the public good.

Behavioral Science and the Directive Potential

In 1963, the National Academy of Sciences, originally an obscure honor society, celebrated its 100th anniversary and a new role—that of an influential advisory body for the United States Government. The Academy membership at that time was limited to physical and biological scientists. We tend to assume that these scientists function conscientiously within their professional roles and give only verifiable information and rational unbiased conclusions. We have been slow, however, to accept the services of behavioral scientists in the same spirit. Private interests and partisan issues are so clearly involved in those public issues, such as birth control, mental health, and integration, which concern behavioral scientists, that we have hesitated to credit either the scientists or their data with rational objectivity. The scientists themselves recognize the difficulty. A statement by a psychologist to psychologists applies equally to sociologists and other behavioral scientists.

> The psychologist working on public issues may wear any of three hats, but he should be aware of which hat is appropriate for which occasion. On some occasions, he may legitimately don his "professional" hat—when he speaks as a psychological scientist on the basis of hard facts and generally accepted principles. On other occasions, he should wear his "specialist" hat—when he speaks as an individual psychologist who, by virtue of his special training and experience, may claim a higher probability of correct insights and opinions in certain areas than those not so trained. On yet other occasions, he must explicitly display his "citizen" hat—when he speaks his opinions, expresses his attitudes, and takes his stand on matters where neither his science nor his expertise give him any obvious advantage over other equally intelligent citizens.[5]

The general public does not yet appreciate the rapid advance of the behavioral sciences and the directive potential the behavioral scientists have in their professional and specialist hats, but, officially, the United States Government does.* And so do the behavioral scientists, themselves! In recognition of their directive role, behavioral scientists are increasingly involved in action-oriented research † and in professional organizations through which

* See the President's Science Advisory Committee report, "Strengthening the Behavioral Sciences."[6]

† As distinct from "pure" or "basic" research, which increases understanding but makes no commitment to practical concerns.

they can make their data and their services available to publics and policy makers. Of the many agencies in this country involved in action-oriented research and education, we describe two: the *Behavior Research Council* and the *Institute for the Study of Democratic Institutions.*

The Behavior Research Council

The Council is a private, nonprofit research and educational institution wholly independent of political parties, government agencies, or any special interest group. It was organized in 1963 for the purpose of making available unbiased information and advice on the probable "costs and consequences of alternative possible solutions for the problems of men in society." Because decisions on public issues and policies depend in part on national values and national objectives, the Behavior Research Council proposed that it begin work by *ascertaining* (not advocating) the goals currently cherished and sought by the people of the United States.

Such an undertaking might proceed:

> (1) To discover by suitable research, including the study of constitutions and statutes (State and Federal), court decisions, and public opinion surveys of the citizenry and of responsible leaders in government and in public life what are in fact the *values* and objectives of the nation and of its various subgroups and the hierarchical structure of these values, as well as the relative intensity with which they are held and pursued;
>
> (2) To provide scientific appraisal of the adequacy of *the means* currently invoked in the pursuit of declared values;
>
> (3) To draw scientifically warranted conclusions as to the feasibility, costs, and repercussions of alternative proposed solutions.[7]

Should the Behavioral Research Council find that the nation is following or contemplating programs leading towards ends other than those declared to be cherished, the Council would point out the incongruity. And should the Council find certain institutional forms and activities inconsistent with national values and goals, it would indicate the scientific basis for such a conclusion.

The Behavioral Council does not intend that any scientific priesthood usurp the right and responsibility of publics and policy makers to decide social, economic and political issues.

> The studies and reports of the Behavioral Research Council would simply aim to make available to the people the warranted assertions that can be made regarding the costs and consequences of alternative possible solutions for the problems of men in society. . . . Whether or not, and to what extent, this educational information and advice is used would remain the responsibility of the citizens, *not* of the Behavioral Research Council.[8]

The Council brings talented researchers from all behavioral sciences together to cooperate on long-term, large-scale social problems. As a matter of policy, it gives priority to those inter-disciplinary research projects promising the most enduring benefits to the most people.

Center for the Study of Democratic Institutions *

The scientists and intellectuals at work in this unique "think tank" are attempting something not being done by any university, church, corporation, foundation, government agency, or other organization in the United States. They are examining "the major institutions of the twentieth century in the light of their impact on the possibilities for the continued existence of democracy." [9] The central question is *if* and *how* a free and just society can be maintained under the impact of political, social, economic, and technological change. The theory held by the president of the Board, Robert Maynard Hutchins (former president of the University of Chicago), that people can think better in beautiful surroundings, partially accounts for the fact that headquarters for the Center is a neoclassic mansion near the crest of Eucalyptus Hill in Montecito, California. There a staff of approximately eighteen resident "thinkers"—often joined by itinerant scholars, diplomats, businessmen, politicians, labor leaders and other intellectuals—meets five mornings a week. The study method is dialogue and discussion. Said one visitor, "Eucalyptus Hill is to the bull session what La Scala is to the opera." [10]

The collaborative creative work of the staff thinkers at the Center is not research in the usual laboratory sense, but it is research in ideas, and records of the staff's cognitive explorations are preserved on tapes and in pamphlets. In 1963, only four years after its establishment, the Center had produced a hundred and twenty pamphlets and other publications. Some four and a half million copies of these have been distributed, largely free of charge. The tapes cost too much to give away. They are sold mainly to radio stations, discussion groups, and teachers. Included are such provocative titles as *Freedom from Myths . . . The Warless World . . . Educational Bankruptcy . . . Black and White in America . . . What Can the Individual American Do About Democracy? . . . The Role of Government in the Economy . . . The Society of the Qualified Man.*

> Isolate the problems, measure their magnitude, measure our progress in dealing with them. This, I take it, is what the Center for the Study of Democratic Institutions is all about—the steady effort to discover the common good in democratic fashion, by assembling together persons from varied backgrounds, with diverse specialties and competences, for discussion and debate.
>
> The Center may be a pioneering effort, but its roots are sunk deep in the Academy of ancient Greece, the medieval university, the New England town meetings, and a long list of later devices to make democracy work. Getting good men to think together, though not to think alike; bringing the cumulative wisdom of such persons to bear on present and emerging problems; and,

* Center for the Study of Democratic Institutions, Box 4068, Santa Barbara, California.

through publications, broadcasts, and meetings . . . widening the circles of discussion and debate.[11]

The Center has been accused of being "an egghead monastery," and, at the other extreme, "an assembly of syndicalists plotting to overthrow the established order." "Actually," one of the staff members explained, "the Center is just trying to figure out, in a general way, what the hell is going on." [12]

Sociologists collaborate with psychologists, anthropologists, economists, political scientists, and colleagues from other behavioral sciences in the Behavioral Research Council, the Institute for the Study of Democratic Institutions, and other inter-disciplinary groups. But of all the individual sciences involved, *sociology* is the one most committed to the acquisition of that knowledge needed by society to intelligently direct its own destiny. Already sociologists have an independent body of such knowledge, which, with continuing study and research, grows in certitude and breadth.

Sociology and the Directive Potential

Although sociology is a young science and still has but relatively few rigorously established scientific truths, sociologists even now serve publics and policy makers through research and directive action.

The unique characteristics of the human variables with which all behavioral sciences deal affects both the scope and the methods of sociology. They extend the legitimate limits of the subject beyond the recognized regularities of human interaction to the unique and the unpredicted. They focus sociological thought on *what is* and beyond, to the *what ifs.* Some sociological information is gleaned from observing social behavior under natural or experimentally limited conditions; other information comes through *survey analyses,* particularly those specialized versions known as attitude surveys and public opinion polls. Both attitude surveys and opinion polls rely on subject samples, and both use the interview, techniques which, in spite of all acknowledged shortcomings, serve the purposes of sociological research. To indicate the serviceable nature of sociological research, we cite an *attitude survey,* a *public opinion poll,* and a *controlled experiment.*

Attitude Surveys

Attitudes are predispositions to respond in a favorable or unfavorable manner toward objects, persons, ideas, or situations. Although basically emotional, and often unconscious, attitudes do affect behavior, and they can be scientifically described and measured. During World War II, the Research Branch of the War Department's Information and Education Division, headed by a sociologist and staffed by psychologists and sociologists, conducted one of the largest attitude surveys ever made. Beginning on the day after Pearl Harbor, and continuing through the war, the researchers did more than two hundred different studies on a total sampling of half a million enlisted men and officers.*

> The surveys were applied to hundreds of problems, many of which do not loom large in the perspective of total war, but were important at the time. Why did men in malarial regions fail to use Atabrine as regularly as they should? What attitudes and practices were associated with trench foot? Which of two kinds of huts did men in Alaska prefer? What were the favored types of winter clothing among front-line troops in Belgium, Luxemburg, and Germany? What radio transcriptions did men want? . . . What were the sources of difficulties in soldiers' relations with the French? Such inquiries were routine and were made in increasing numbers.
>
> Some of the larger-scale enterprises were: studies of soldiers' postwar plans, which provided a factual basis for drawing up the GI Bill of Rights; . . . analyses of problems of occupying troops, which led to changes in occupation policy in Germany.
>
> *One of the most useful researches was the one that established the point system for demobilization at the end of the war* (Italics ours). The President and the War Department decided that the order of demobilization should be determined in terms of what the soldiers themselves wanted. The idea of a point system was conceived in the Research Branch. Representative samples of men throughout the world were queried, and from their responses, the variables of length of service, overseas duty, combat duty, and parenthood emerged as most significant. . . . In view of the explosive tensions in the early demobilization period, historians may find that the establishment of an objective system whose justice was accepted by most men saved the country from what could have been a crisis seriously damaging to American prestige.[13]

Some of the studies underscored the significance of informal social controls. Although it is difficult to conceive of an organization with more formal controls than the Army, it was found that even here the most powerful controls were informal. What kept a man going under the stress of combat was not hatred of the enemy, nor patriotism, nor Army rules, but a strong feeling that he must not lose face in the eyes of his fellows.

Another study led to postwar elimination of segregation in the Armed Forces. The Army first placed entire platoons of Negro volunteers in white infantry companies. After several months of combat, the attitudes of whites who had served with Negroes were compared with the attitudes of those who had not. In divisions with no Negro platoons, sixty-two per cent of the infantrymen said they would dislike very much serving in the same company with Negroes. Of the white soldiers who had been in the same division but not the same company, twenty per cent said they would dislike it very much. Among the white infantrymen who had served in the same company, only seven per cent said they disliked it very much.[14]

---

* The results of this undertaking were published in four volumes by the Princeton University Press in 1949. The volumes were: I. *The American Soldier: Adjustment During Army Life;* II. *The American Soldier: Combat and Its Aftermath;* III. *Experiments on Mass Communication;* IV. *Measurement and Prediction.*

Altogether, this extensive attitude survey on the American soldier opened up new channels of communication for the Army and made evidence rather than conjecture the basis for predicting behavior of soldiers under combat. Such results indicated the directive potential in action-oriented research for civilian as well as military affairs. Since the war, other government agencies, especially those involved in social service and mental health, as well as private groups such as business firms, market researchers, and labor unions, employ research sociologists with increasing frequency.

Public Opinion Polls

Attitudes are conscious or unconscious emotional preferences; opinions are conscious verbalized attitudes which involve an element of expectation. Attitude surveys rate personal feelings; opinion polls predict public reactions to current issues. Will a community support school bonds? Will labor union members vote for the Democratic candidate? Do World War II veterans favor the United Nations? Opinion polls give policy makers the information they need to interpret and direct the "will of the people." *

> In 1963, a national poll of American Negroes demonstrated the strength of the protest movement as well as the finesse of the instrument which measured it. Through a random selection process which gave every Negro in the United States over the age of eighteen an equal chance of being chosen, 1,250 Negroes out of the nineteen million in the United States were picked for interviewing. The standard interview lasted two and one half hours and probed deeply into the critical facets of Negro-white relations. An IBM 7094 analyzed in eighteen minutes the data gained in 3,125 hours of interviewing. Said the director of the research, "It is as though we were able to photograph at split-second intervals an earthquake as it was taking place." [15]
>
> . . . The wave of protest is an authentic, deep-seated, broadly based revolution.† . . . The Negro wants no less than an end to discrimination in all its forms. . . . The revolution is anti-Jim Crow, not anti-white . . . The revolt is committed to nonviolence, though one Negro in five thinks some violence is inevitable. . . . The Negro will, nonetheless, do what he feels he must to win.[16]

These findings, plus those of other polls indicating that Negroes want most the social opportunities 80 per cent of the whites in 1963 were willing to give—namely, job equality [17]—establish a sound beginning for directive behavior on a current and explosive issue.

---

* The Iowa City Consensus on International Affairs polls members on current public issues and transmits results to various federal officials. Imagine what an impact *systematic nation-wide* samplings of informed opinion would have on policy making.

† The Negro protest is not against the total social order as such, and therefore does not technically qualify as a revolution. By rejecting racial stratification, Negroes are actually revitalizing Jeffersonian democracy. The intensity of feeling in the United States on the race issue, however, is such that the alternative to integration is social disintegration, not continued segregation.

Controlled Experiment

Although people are understandably concerned about being drafted as "guinea pigs" for scientific experiments, behavioral scientists do use human subjects in studying individual and group processes. One experiment on intergroup conflict with eleven- and twelve-year old boys in a summer camp, for example, gives clues to the efficacy of alternative ways of coping with larger group conflicts. The boys were originally strangers to each other; all were of superior intelligence, healthy, well adjusted, and all were from unbroken homes and similar economic and religious backgrounds.

> The experiment first induced the boys to form groups. Give hungry boys the job of planning and preparing a meal, for example, and they spontaneously organize and work together. Then, after groups were well established, came tournaments of competitive events in which one group could win only at the expense of others. Winning groups got particularly desirable prizes, and hostilities soon developed between winners and losers. There was name calling, physical fighting, and raiding of each other's cabins. Within any one group, the boys were drawn closer together. Intensified hostility increased in-group out-group identifications in this experimental state of war. The final problem was to minimize hostilities. Bringing the antagonistic groups together under pleasant circumstances—watching a movie or eating—did not help. In fact, the boys used such occasions for fighting with the convenient ammunition—mashed potatoes, for example. The "common enemy" approach was successful in getting two or more groups to join against another group, but this technique meant larger conflicts in the long run—a struggle not among many small powers but among a few big powers. Only activities in which all antagonistic groups *had* to cooperate with each other, such as combating a water shortage, securing a movie, or obtaining food, were effective. Friends chosen from originally antagonistic groups then rose from practically zero to twenty-three per cent. Categorical accusations, "All of them are stinkers," dropped from 21.0 per cent to 1.5 per cent in one group and from 36.5 per cent to 6.0 per cent in another.[18]
>
> What our limited experiments have shown is that the possibilities for achieving harmony are greatly enhanced when groups are brought together to work toward common ends. Then favorable information about a disliked group is seen in a new light, and leaders are in a position to take bolder steps toward cooperation. In short, hostility gives way when groups pull together to achieve overriding goals which are real and compelling to all concerned.[19]

The implications of this experiment for directive behavior seem clear. If change in the conditions under which groups interact drastically affects that interaction, is it not possible that deliberately contrived bases for cooperation between mutually antagonistic groups, or even nations, will not only induce cooperation but change stereotypes and reduce tension?

Research in specialized areas of each of the behavioral sciences is an essential basis for directive behavior. No matter how laudable the intentions of individuals or groups are in their dealings with one another, without specific and reliable knowledge, directive effort can be as misguided as the action of the fabled Oriental monkey.

> Once upon a time, a monkey and a fish were caught up in a great flood. The monkey, agile and experienced, had the good fortune to scramble up a tree to safety. As he looked down into the raging waters, he saw a fish struggling against the swift current. Filled with a humanitarian desire to help his less fortunate fellow, he reached down and scooped the fish from the water. To the monkey's surprise, the fish was not very grateful for this aid. . . . "The educational adviser, unless he is a careful student of his own culture and the culture in which he works, will be acting much like the monkey; and, with the most laudable intentions, he may make decisions equally disastrous." [20]

Research in anthropology, for example, helped prevent the United States from making a monkey of itself in the closing days of World War II. President Roosevelt had originally urged that the "Big Three" (United States, Great Britain, and the Soviet Union) demand "unconditional surrender" from the Axis powers. Anthropologists recommended that the terms be modified to allow the Japanese to keep their Emperor. They knew that the Emperor to the Japanese was not only a symbol of the state and ultimate authority, but a symbol of unity and peace.

> He was all things to all men, a key cultural symbol, far more like a Polynesian sacred chief than a western dictator. The scientists urged that his prestige alone could cause all the far-flung unconquered groups of fanatic soldiers to surrender at the same time. Their view prevailed, and they were right. After the Emperor's broadcast, the Japanese army laid down its arms as one man, and the astonished Americans were greeted by a cheerful, cooperative people who cherished no desire for revenge, indulged in no guerilla warfare, and were quite ready to accept the occupation.*
>
> A wrong decision in this case would have sacrified countless lives.[21]

And research in psychology has helped the United States in recent years to avert outbreaks of international hostilities.

> . . . On April 20, 1964, Mr. Johnson (President Lyndon Johnson) announced a further reduction in the production of enriched uranium and plutonium, the explosive material for nuclear weapons. At the same moment Mr. Khrushchev (Premier Nikita Khrushchev) was announcing that the U.S.S.R. would discontinue construction of two new big atomic reactors, reduce the production of fissionable material, and allocate more of it for peaceful purposes.

---

* The mainland army did obediently surrender, but some individuals paid a high price for their compliance. An executive officer on one of the few remaining Japanese destroyers went into a state of shock. He became functionally deaf and blind. Years later an English friend met him standing in a park, blank-faced, white cane in hand—a bleak ghost of a man dressed in a navy uniform from which all insignia had been removed.[22] There were other casualties on some of the Pacific Islands, where fifteen years later men continued to fight a war they refused to believe had ended.

News stories reported that President Johnson had told the Soviet Ambassador the U. S. was about to make this move, and suggested Moscow do likewise. Premier Khrushchev agreed, and the stage was set for parallel and similar announcements.

This is a capsulized example of what Professor Osgood (Charles E. Osgood, former President of the American Psychological Association) calls "graduated reciprocation in tension reduction," (GRIT)* a formula for a series of independent actions calculated to overcome hostility and reassure an adversary.[23]

In countless other situations, scientists, wearing their professional and specialist hats, can provide the facts and principles and informed opinions needed for creative problem solving. In the long history of ocean travel, far more lives have been saved through advances in navigation, based on "pure" research in mathematics and astronomy, than by the design of pumps and lifeboats. And can anyone doubt that in our continuing history, more of the problems of men in society will be solved by advances in sociology and other behavioral sciences than by specific practical action?

Directive Sociology †

The central task of sociology as a scientific profession is "the development of its discipline and the training of its successors in carrying on that function."[24] However, the nature of sociological subject matter does cast the sociologist in directive roles. Sociologists are under increasing pressure from the involvement of sociology in ideational controversy.

> Some will have to serve as mediators between the profession and the public, on occasion entering the forum of discussion on their own initiative. Retreat of the whole profession into technical preoccupations could be dangerous in the long run. . . .[25]

Government agencies, the military, political parties, labor unions, business firms, health and service organizations, and other public and private groups are looking with increasing expectation to sociologists—not only for raw research data, but for help in interpreting and acting on such data. In the directive role, the sociologist puts on his specialist hat and participates in policy making—sometimes at a local, sometimes at a national level.

When the swimming pools of Washington, D. C., were first desegregated, racial violence flared. The pools were closed, and the police commissioner asked the advice of Dr. Joseph Lohman, a sociologist with practical police experi-

---

* The GRIT program is based on the psychological principle that tension beyond a certain optimum level narrows awareness of alternatives and increases the chance of irrational actions.

† We suggest the term *directive sociology* in lieu of applied sociology, because *applied*—although it specifically means using or adopting abstract principles and theories in connection with concrete problems—has the connotation of laying on or administering and does not necessarily imply the understanding, consent, and active involvement of those concerned.

ence. Dr. Lohman did not lecture about the nature of prejudice or what could or should be done about it; he merely told the police that when the pools were reopened, they were to arrest any trouble makers without regard for race. Their own feeling in the matter was not to influence their performance of duty. The pools were reopened, the impartial policy put into effect, and the pools were integrated peacefully.

The sociologist clarified the structure of the immediate situation: the police were to function in strict accord with the role-image; the swimmers were to respect the pool rules. With rights and duties defined and justice assured, the whites and the Negroes were able to accommodate to each other.

Integrating a swimming pool is a relatively minor issue, but it is a prototype of larger issues in which two or more groups come into conflict. The sociological principle involved—that of clarifying the structure of a situation—can be applied even in the world arena.

If the rights and duties of nations were clearly defined by international law, and *if* an international police could impartially enforce that law, even traditionally antagonistic nations could be directed into accommodative if not cooperative interaction. Such *what-ifing* may seem hopelessly optimistic, but it does have official blessing. In 1963, the Chief Justice of the United States Supreme Court (Earl Warren) spoke before a World Peace Through Law conference in Athens. He urged as a step towards peace that lawyers of all nations work together to establish (1) a body of international law, (2) an international court, and (3) an international police force to enforce international law and the court decisions.

Although all behavorial sciences have a directive function, sociology is the most closely involved with the issues around which publics develop and the most likely, therefore, to antagonize established authority. Witness the fate sociology has suffered in totalitarian societies.

Following the Russian Revolution, some specific research projects—those felt by the political authorities to advance Marxist-Leninist theory—continued, but sociology as theory development disappeared. In Italy, Fascism suppressed both sociological research *and* theory. The Hitler regime obliterated scientific sociology in Germany and subsequently suppressed it in the other conquered countries of Europe. Why this widespread sabotage?

> Certainly it is not because sociologists are judged to be useless in practice, enclosed in an "ivory tower," gathering knowledge without answering the question: "knowledge for what?" Rather it is because they are considered dangerous by the adherents of certain ideologies, dangerous not only as theorists whose generalizations may disagree with the dogmas of Communism, fascism, naziism, or some other doctrine, but also as objective investigators of contemporary events. Agents who, under the guidance of some ideology, introduce changes in social reality which from their point of view are absolutely *right* cannot bear to have their activity and its results scientifically investigated or objectively compared with the activities of others whose ideologies conflict with their own.[26]

Sociology has "graduated from being one of the least respectable of the social disciplines to being one of the most controversial." [27] Precisely because sociology is controversial and vulnerable to attack by those whose power it threatens, a sociologist called upon for directive action tries on every occasion to make very clear which of his three hats he is wearing. He feels under special obligation as a professional and a specialist to maintain the highest possible standards of scientific competence and objectivity. To do otherwise would invalidate and jeopardize both research and directive sociology.

Sociology, together with other behavioral sciences and the natural sciences, can strengthen democratic processes by providing the information and insights publics and policy makers need for rational action. "For science is today one of the few common languages of mankind; it can provide a basis for understanding and communication of ideas between people . . . independent of political boundaries and of ideologies." [28] But to build and maintain a bridge across the intellectual marsh which separates scientists and lay citizens, we need the unceasing efforts of *educators*.

THE ROLE OF EDUCATORS

> The intellectual distance between what the knowing people know and what the unknowing people believe and think they know is threatening to finish off western civilization. . . . The cacophony of nonsense and half-sense and misapplied common sense that passes for civic wisdom does not add up to a joyful sound.[29]

When a scientist, especially a behavioral scientist, becomes involved in a public issue or social problem, his first and often most difficult job is to convince others that the knowledge and insights he has to offer are relevant and useful. Directive behavior presumes communication and interaction between scientists and citizens—an impossible achievement unless educators can bridge the "understanding gap" now separating them. Educators, we should note, include not only the professional educators employed by schools and colleges and universities, but the inadvertent nonprofessional educators, particularly those who work through mass-communication media and play up the problems and possibilities of scientific theory and fact as news or human interest stories.

Each of the behavioral sciences has professional representatives in the educational institutions of this country.* Some are recruiting disciples; some are awakening publics; and all, by trying to make science more meaningful, are strengthening the directive potential. Our special concern, however, in this context is with the particular role of the educators in sociology.

* Scientists and professional educators both recognize the inadequacy of the present curricula and are calling for a true integration of the sciences and humanities from kindergarten through college.

In the United States we tend to have a naïve faith in education. We prescribe it routinely as a cure for social ills, forgetting that education is not an agency *outside* society which can be brought in to effect reform, but an institution *of* society which tends to uphold the values prevailing in that society.

> . . . whether education will help to solve our social problems depends upon the validity of what we teach. There is no doubt that much of what we now teach on social subjects is worse than useless, because it consists merely of transmitting the errors, prejudices, and speculations of bygone generations. Unless knowledge is constantly tested and replenished through scientific research, education may be an enemy rather than an aid to social amelioration.[30]

The research and theory making of academic sociology does test, replenish, and vitalize knowledge of social subjects, and that knowledge is increasingly available directly through undergraduate courses in sociology and through the sociological content of related disciplines. At the beginning of this century, sociology was established as an academic subject in only two universities, the University of Chicago and Columbia University. By 1960, sociology had gained academic citizenship in every major university in the United States. Sometimes sociology is included in the economics and political science complex, sometimes in the psychology and anthropology one; it has essential insights to offer both.*

In their educative role within academic institutions, sociologists help form public opinion. In the classroom, the sociologist exposes human behavior and belief to critical scientific intelligence. In doing so, he inevitably supports or assaults certain private values which the students themselves hold. Thus the classroom may become a setting for the unmasking of attitudes and the making and unmaking of opinion. At the undergraduate level, sociology has primarily a "general education function, helping to orient the student to aspects of the world in which he lives." [31]

As the strategic importance of sociology gains recognition, sociologists are being appointed to the faculty in schools of education, public administration, business, law, and divinity. And some medical schools, convinced of the relationship between social phenomena and health (especially mental health and public health), have appointed sociologists to positions comparable to those held by biochemists, bacteriologists, and other natural scientists.

> In a highly differentiated society where applied science is rapidly increasing in importance in the social as well as natural science fields, such schools are the most appropriate point of articulation between a scientific profession and the many urgent practical social needs. In general it is sounder that the primary responsibilities for implementation should be borne by members of applied professions, rather than by scientists as such. The existence of such a mediating

* The ready and wholehearted acceptance of sociology into the academic community in the United States contrasts with the marginal status given it by universities in England and Europe. Oxford and Cambridge have a minimal offering. And fewer than half the universities in Europe include sociology in the curriculum.

> structure provides a highly important protection of the scientific profession's central function against many types of diversionary pressures.[32]

The sociological perspective is penetrating a wider and wider range of academic fields, and simultaneously, the area of enlightened citizenship from which directive behavior can emerge is expanding. The sociological perspective is strengthening the respect for scientific "truth," even when that "truth" proves one's cherished beliefs to be mere delusions.

> Sociology is slowly entering into the broader current of opinion. It is doing so very unequally. As the subject becomes established in the universities, and as larger proportions of the population enter into universities or orient themselves toward the higher culture formed by universities, . . . so sociology will pass beyond the condition of an academic speciality, practiced and thought about only in academic environments. It will become part of educated opinion. It has in fact already begun to become integral to the opinion of the more curious and the more reflective sections of society. This educated opinion even now receives reinforcement from the creation of a body of sociological literature capable of being read and appreciated and even sought out by the educated public outside the universities.[33]

Furthermore, a larger and larger percentage of the general public is seeking higher education.* One effect of this "democratization" of higher education is to draw more and better informed citizens into action as policy makers and as members of publics and social movements. The degree to which one accepts social responsibility is not only a measure of emotional maturity but a function of educational and class level. The higher the educational and class level, the greater the conviction that individual action matters; hence the greater the chance of involvement in public issues.

The political apathy typical of lower-class persons, particularly those in minority groups, expresses a general sense of helplessness and incompetence relative to the affairs of society. In states, for example, where Negroes are free to vote, many lower-class Negroes do not vote even on issues directly affecting them; they simply do not seem to perceive the self-help function of political involvement. In fact, a haunting question for those who cope professionally with the immediate personal and social problems arising within even a relatively circumscribed neighborhood is: "*How can ordinary people be involved in making decisions about such matters as social planning and community development that vitally affect them?*" † If one does not know that individual action makes a difference at the local level, how completely baffled he must feel when confronted with larger national and international issues.

One becomes ego-involved only in those tasks perceived as neither too far beneath nor too far beyond one's capabilities. It is part of the purpose of educators in sociology to help acquaint the next generation of publics and policy

---

* Chapter 5.

† E. P. Stephenson, Director, Richmond Neighborhood Center, Richmond, California.

makers with some of the critical social issues of their time and to give them a sense of individual responsibility and power relative to those issues. It is part of the purpose of educators in sociology to awaken latent publics, to involve persons in the democratic task of self-direction, to make responsible citizenship possible and comprehensible. Sociology provides a framework of social concepts in relationship to which the individual can see himself and his times with relative objectivity. And it offers social facts and theories with which the individual alone or as a member of a public or social movement can bolster his independent thought and rationality. The sociological perspective can stir to social action some who might otherwise stand back, silent and uncomprehending. Education in sociology is long-term insurance against the default of democracy.

THE ROLE OF PUBLICS AND POLICY MAKERS

The survival of democracy as a social system depends in large part on the existence of active publics and responsive policy makers willing and able to make reasonable choices if given relevant and reliable information. Today the most critical and controversial issues involve scientific problems overwhelming in their complexity, yet both publics and policy makers function in relative ignorance.

Scientific attitude and scientific understandings have not yet become integral to either private or public action. This is not surprising. For at least fifty thousand years man has been developing his habit and endocrine systems. For at least six thousand years of recorded history, man has been building his social institutions. Only for the last few hundred years has he made science an organized enterprise, and only in the last few decades—through nuclear explosions, computers that learn, automation, television, satellites, and other tragedies and triumphs of technology—has he been fully aware of the power he has tapped through science. A fraction of a century is a short time for the engrained systems of individuals and societies to adapt to new conditions of life.

> Nonetheless, it is at their increasing peril that men and nations have gone on living the same old life histories. They have yet to grasp the new choices, the new ends of life and action, that the change in their relationship to nature has made not only possible but imperative.[34]

Few scientists have left professional fields of research, practice, or education for that of statesmanship. Legislators and administrators characteristically come from the fields of business and law—not science. This does not necessarily handicap directive behavior. Policy makers do not need to be scientists; they need only to understand and respect the general theories and facts of science.

> . . . We do not need scientists in Congress as much as people capable of asking intelligent questions of scientists. Not being asked the proper question is the main complaint of scientific experts asked to testify in Congress or give advice to the military. One British minister said, "Scientists should be on tap, and not on top; but for this system to operate, those on top must know whom, when, and how to tap!" * [35]

Only out of the ranks of educated citizens can come the scientifically literate publics and policy makers qualified to participate in intellectual controversy on critical public issues and to determine public policy.

> According to the theory of a republic, the citizen is supposed to inform himself on all these issues in order to cast his vote with full appreciation of the probable costs and consequences of his actions. But how can he? Propaganda and alleged "facts" bombard him every waking hour. Lobbies for innumerable factions and special interests invade the legislatures and the halls of Congress to agitate, implore, threaten, and bribe the representatives of the people. These representatives are themselves frequently in no better position than the ordinary citizen. Even the most conscientious public official cannot maintain an adequate research organization to provide him the knowledge and technical advice required for his wise decision on questions that come before him. *Neither the citizen nor his representatives have adequate and effective access to an unbiased source dedicated solely to reporting scientifically on the probable costs and consequences of alternate proposed policies or solutions.*[36]

In ignorance, publics and policy makers alike may apply old rules to new conditions (normative behavior) or try expedient emotionally biased solutions (collective behavior). And the common man, confronted with what seem to be impossible tasks of citizenship may simply take refuge behind the barricade of everyday routines. Average citizens may abdicate; they may stand back and interpret what they cannot avoid and cannot understand as some fable of the past or some fiction of the future. To accept such passivity is to castrate democracy. Emotional and intellectual detachment from significant social issues is the way of the mass society we are in danger of becoming, not the way of the democracy we would like to reaffirm.

To disclaim personal responsibility and let oneself be inundated by the great onrushing stream of history is to be party to the making of a mass society. After World War II when the horrors of the Nazi concentration camps became known and the German public was made to share the guilt and shame, a com-

* Cut-backs in military expenditures in 1964 made clear the need to shift the economy away from dependence on Federal defense and space programs. In California, the Brown administration tapped scientific and engineering talent to take up some of the slack in the aerospace industry and to experiment with the use of computerized analytical techniques in combating stereotyped thinking and reaching creative solutions to social problems. Aerospace research teams and systems engineers began collaboration with social scientists in the development of four major projects: (1) a long-range state-wide transportation system; (2) an analysis of prisons and mental hospitals; (3) a system of waste disposal to reduce air, water, and soil pollution; (4) a method of collecting, storing, and retrieving information regarding state functions to minimize guesswork in policy-making.

mon defense was, "But we didn't know what was going on," and, "Even if we had known, what could we have done?"

A mass society is especially vulnerable to manipulation. Certainly every society, including our own, does manipulate and even coerce its members to some extent, tempering them to fit its institutions; but today, "We (the scientists) can choose to use our growing knowledge to enslave people in ways never dreamed of before, depersonalizing them, controlling them by means so carefully selected that they will perhaps never be aware of their loss of personhood." [37] Science does have awesome power, and we, the people, have reason to remember that "eternal vigilance is the price of liberty." * The directive role of behavioral scientists particularly has been limited, because, in our democratic society, all self-styled "experts" are suspect. We are well aware that Plato's philosopher kings ruled a totalitarian "republic" with an iron hand, that Machiavelli analyzed and recommended techniques of control favorable to *The Prince*—aversive to his subjects. And the rule of Communist societies by intellectual bureaucrats reinforces suspicions that philosophers, scientists, or other intellectuals today would not necessarily govern benevolently.

> In no other social order, past or present, has the intellectual so completely come into his own as in the Communist regimes. Never before has his superior status been so self-evident and his social usefulness so unquestioned. The bureaucracy which manages and controls every field of activity is staffed by people who consider themselves intellectuals. Writers, poets, artists, scientists, professors, journalists, and others engaged in intellectual pursuits are accorded the high social status of superior civil servants. They are the aristocrats, the rich, the prominent, the indispensable, the pampered and petted. It is the wildest dream of the man of words come true.
>
> And what of the masses in this intellectual's paradise? They have found in the intellectual the most formidable taskmaster in history. No other regime has treated the masses so callously as raw material, to be experimented on and manipulated at will.[38]

The dangers inherent in knowledge are real, but so are the benefits. The natural sciences are putting a growing array of energy slaves at man's command and are increasingly freeing him from darkness, cold, disease and other scourges of the past. The behavioral sciences promise equally great gifts.

> . . . We can choose to use the behavioral sciences in ways which will free, not control; which will bring about constructive variability, not conformity; which will develop creativity, not contentment; which will facilitate each person in his self-directed process of becoming, which will aid individuals, groups, and even the concept of science to become self-transcending in freshly adaptive ways of meeting life and its problems. The choice is up to us. . . .[39]

It is the role of publics and policy makers to make that choice—to help rationally determine which means, ends, and goals will serve the common needs of man and the survival needs of society under the unique conditions im-

* John Philpot Curran (1750-1817).

posed by twentieth-century science. Scientifically literate publics and policy makers can choose to use all science in ways which will free man, not control him. "Of all the servants of morality, science is the greatest; for it is the one serious way we have to discover what means are likeliest to lead to the realization of the ends we cherish." [40]

In the past we could afford to let many public issues be decided by relatively uninformed publics, by short-sighted policy makers, by clamoring pressure groups, or by tradition. Today the issues are so great in potential harm or benefit that informed reason—not ignorance, passion, or habit—must determine the outcome. The unreasoned assassination of President John F. Kennedy, champion of reason, underlined in one man's blood a bitter lesson: "that our civilization, our very lives depend on the day-to-day triumph of Reason over Chaos, and that we maintain the razor-thin margin of victory only by unceasing vigilance and labor." [41]

Can we resolve the dilemma of democracy in this scientific age by bringing the task of responsible citizenship within reach of the average man? Can we bridge the gap between the public's limited comprehension of critical issues and the democratic commitment to let publics and policy makers decide those issues? Can we, the people, reclaim responsibility for our own destiny?

THE DIRECTIVE IMPERATIVE

Citizens and scientists alike have a directive imperative—to learn through science to live in the new world science is creating. And sociology can help us do this. By sharing its insights into human interaction with the actors themselves, sociology can strengthen rationality and protect against blind habits and disruptive emotions. We have evidence that when the need for change is clearly understood and when those involved help plan the change, change is accepted rather than resisted.[42] Scientists in their directive role and with the help of educators must make the need for change clear, and citizens must get involved in the plans for change.

> What we do not take part in initiating and developing and producing, what we engage in without our own choosing and aspiring, is not felt as ours. What we do not feel as ours lacks in the experience of inner urgency and in sense of responsibility. The important thing to actualize at the very start is not immediate technical proficiency, but the feeling of participation, the feeling that we have functions in the larger scheme of things, the feeling that we have indispensable roles with others in things that all feel should be done.[43]

Is there any other way within a democratic framework to cope effectively with *CBN, contamination, overpopulation,* and the many other issues which plague twentieth-century man?

Almost twenty centuries ago, Plutarch wrote: "Only those persons who live in obedience to reason are worthy to be accounted free." Man does have a will to live and a capacity for rationality. However, he is endangered by twin anachronisms: a reliance upon outmoded norms whose sole authority is tradition, and a tendency to "shoot from the hip" in short-sighted and emotional response. More than a hundred years ago, Abraham Lincoln wrote as if for today: *"The dogmas of a quiet past are inadequate for the stormy present. As our case is new, so we must act anew and think anew."* In this twentieth century, out of the disparity between the rates of technological and societary change have arisen conditions which no creature on earth has ever before faced—exigencies and issues with which we cannot afford to deal irrationally. Neither can we afford to be discouraged by the difficulties and disagreements which encumber our attempts at rational directive behavior. We are individually and socially equipped to solve the problems we have brought upon ourselves. We have an infinite capacity for learning, and we can transmit our learning through culture to succeeding generations. *Can we now, by synthesizing scientific competence with idealism, revise the traditional means, ends, and norms of the social order to serve the common needs of Man Among Men?*

Notes

1. Barry Commoner, "Scientific Statesmanship," *Bulletin of Atomic Scientists,* October, 1963, p. 9. © Educational Foundation for Nuclear Science, Inc., 935 E. 60th St., Chicago, Ill., 60637.
2. Robert Shapler, "Adventures of a Pacifist," *The New Yorker,* March 22, 1958, p. 70.
3. Eugene Rabinowitch, "Scientific Revolution: The New Content of Politics," *Bulletin of Atomic Scientists,* October, 1963, pp. 13-14. © Educational Foundation for Nuclear Science, Inc., 935 E. 60th St., Chicago, Ill., 60637.
4. Robert Bierstedt, "Social Science and Social Values," *Bulletin of the American Association of University Professors,* XXXIV, No. 2 (Summer 1948), p. 313.
5. Charles E. Osgood, "The Psychologist in International Affairs," in *Taboo Topics,* Norman-Farberow, ed. (New York: Atherton Press, 1963), p. 116.
6. *Behavioral Science,* Vol. 7, No. 3, 1962.
7. Rollo Handy and Paul Kurtz, *A Current Appraisal of the Behavioral Sciences,* Sect. 1 (Great Barrington, Massachusetts: Behavioral Research Council, 1963), p. 5.
8. *Ibid.,* p. iii.
9. John Bainbridge, "Feel Free," *The New Yorker,* November 9, 1963, p. 105.
10. *Ibid.,* p. 105.
11. Adlai Stevenson, "The Prospects for Democracy Around the World," Address at the *Convocation on Challenges to Democracy in the Next Decade,* Center for the Study of Democratic Institutions, 1962.
12. Bainbridge, *op. cit.,* p. 105.
13. Samuel A. Stouffer, "A Study of Attitudes," *Scientific American,* May, 1949, reprint number 455, pp. 3-4.
14. *Ibid.,* p. 6.
15. "The Negro in America," *Newsweek,* July 29, 1963, p. 17.
16. *Ibid.,* pp. 15-16.
17. Gunnar Myrdal, *An American Dilemma* (New York: Harper & Row, Publishers, 1944), pp. 57-67. And Gendell and Zetterberg, *A Sociological Almanac,* p. 26.
18. Muzafer Sherif, "Superordinate Goals in the Reduction of Intergroup Conflict," *The American Journal of Sociology,* LXIII, No. 4, January, 1958.
19. Sherif, "Experiments in Group Conflict," *Scientific American,* November, 1956, reprint number 454, p. 6.
20. Don Adams, "The Monkey and the Fish: Cultural Pitfalls of an Educational Adviser," *International Development Review* (2), 1960, pp. 22-24. Cited in George M. Foster, *Traditional Cultures: and the Impact of Technological Change* (New York: Harper & Row, Publishers, 1962), p. 1.
21. H. R. Hays, *From Ape to Angel* (New York: Alfred A. Knopf, Inc., 1958), 412.
22. Anthony West, "The Stranger," *The New Yorker,* May 16, 1959, p. 112.
23. *Sane World,* June 1, 1964, p. 2. See also Charles E. Osgood, *An Alternative to War or Surrender* (Urbana: University of Illinois Press, 1962).
24. Talcott Parsons, "Some Problems Confronting Sociology as a Profession," in *Sociology, the Progress of a Decade,* Seymour Martin Lipset and Neil J. Smelser, eds. (Englewood Cliffs, New Jersey: Prentice-Hall, Inc., 1961), p. 29.
25. *Ibid.,* p. 29.

26. Florian Znaniecki, "European and American Sociology After Two World Wars," *The American Journal of Sociology,* LVI, No. 3, 1950, p. 218.
27. Parsons, *op. cit.,* p. 22.
28. George B. Kestiakowsky, *Bulletin of the Atomic Scientists,* January, 1962, p. 20.
29. Hallock Hoffman (of the Institute for the Study of Democratic Institutions), "The Understanding Gap," KPFA Commentary, October 13, 1963.
30. George A. Lundberg, *Can Science Save Us?* (New York: Longmans, Green & Co., Inc., 1947), p. 7.
31. Parsons, *op. cit.,* p. 23.
32. *Ibid.,* p. 27.
33. Talcott Parsons, Edward Shils, Kaspar D. Naegele, Jesse R. Pitts, eds., *Theories of Society II* (New York: Free Press of Glencoe, Inc.). From Edward Shils, "The Calling of Sociology," p. 1432.
34. Gerald Piel, *Science in the Cause of Man* (New York: Alfred A. Knopf, Inc., 1962), p. viii.
35. Rabinowitch, *op. cit.,* p. 15.
36. Handy and Kurtz, *A Current Appraisal of the Behavioral Sciences* (Great Barrington, Massachusetts: Behavioral Research Council, 1963), p. i.
37. Carl Rogers, "The Control of Human Behavior," in *Readings on the Psychology of Adjustment,* Leon Gorlow and Walter Katkovsky, eds. (New York: McGraw-Hill, Inc., 1959), p. 518.
38. Eric Hoffer, *The Ordeal of Change* (New York: Harper & Row, Publishers, 1963), pp. 50-51.
39. Rogers, *op. cit.,* p. 518.
40. William R. Dennes, quoted in Joel H. Hildebrand, "How Scientists Work and Think," Office of Naval Research *Research and Reviews,* 1956, p. 34.
41. *The New Yorker,* December 14, 1963, p. 45.
42. L. Coch and J. R. P. French, Jr., "Overcoming Resistance to Change," *Human Relations,* 1, pp. 512-532 (or in Ernest R. Hilgard, *Introduction to Psychology* (New York: Harcourt, Brace & World, Inc., 1962, 3rd ed.).
43. Musafer and Carolyn W. Sherif, *Reference Groups* (New York: Harper & Row, Publishers, 1964), pp. 314-315.

Index